E–Government Services Design, Adoption, and Evaluation

Vishanth Weerakkody
Brunel University, UK

Information Science
REFERENCE

Managing Director:	Lindsay Johnston
Editorial Director:	Joel Gamon
Book Production Manager:	Jennifer Yoder
Publishing Systems Analyst:	Adrienne Freeland
Assistant Acquisitions Editor:	Kayla Wolfe
Typesetter:	Henry Ulrich
Cover Design:	Nick Newcomer

Published in the United States of America by
Information Science Reference (an imprint of IGI Global)
701 E. Chocolate Avenue
Hershey PA 17033
Tel: 717-533-8845
Fax: 717-533-8661
E-mail: cust@igi-global.com
Web site: http://www.igi-global.com

Library of Congress Cataloging-in-Publication Data

E-government services design, adoption, and evaluation / Vishanth Weerakkody, editor.
    p. cm.
  Includes bibliographical references and index.
  Summary: "This book covers the assessment and implementation of electronic/digital government technologies in organizations, providing readers with an understanding of e-government and its applications and impact on organizations around the world"--Provided by publisher.
  ISBN 978-1-4666-2458-0 (hardcover) -- ISBN 978-1-4666-2459-7 (ebook) -- ISBN 978-1-4666-2460-3 (print & perpetual access) 1. Internet in public administration. 2. Electronic government information. 3. Public administration--Technological innovations. I. Weerakkody, Vishanth.
  JF1525.A8E2385 2012
  352.3'802854678--dc23
                                                2012023352

British Cataloguing in Publication Data
A Cataloguing in Publication record for this book is available from the British Library.

The views expressed in this book are those of the authors, but not necessarily of the publisher.

Table of Contents

Detailed Table of Contents

    Kostas Ergazakis, National Technical University of Athens, Greece
    Kostas Metaxiotis, University of Piraeus, Greece
    Tassos Tsitsanis, National Technical University of Athens, Greece

The concept of e-Participation is important for both citizens and decision makers. From the citizen's perspective, e-Participation provides the opportunity to achieve and satisfy the need to be heard by politicians and participate in the decision-making and policy formulation processes through the use of ICT. On the other side, politicians are also able to promote and encourage public participation through communication channels with citizens and act in line with public opinion. During the past years, the e-Participation landscape has been growing and developed. Currently, there are many applied forms and areas of e-Participation. At the same time, there are a growing variety of tools and technologies that are available to enhance e-Participation. In this paper, the authors present a complete overview of the e-Participation landscape, through the state-of-the-art review of these tools, technologies and areas of e-Participation. This overview is of value to researchers and practitioners who want to have a knowledge base for further research and practical implementation in the wider field of e-Participation.

    Teta Stamati, National and Kapodistrian University of Athens, Greece
    Drakoulis Martakos, National and Kapodistrian University of Athens, Greece

The paper examines the critical success factors for employees' adoption of the unified Local Government Access Framework (LGAF), deployed for the Central Union of Municipalities and Communities of Greece. Following an extensive bibliographical survey, an initial conceptual framework (CF1) based on the Technology Acceptance Model (TAM) for LGAF adoption is proposed, which is empirically explored within sixteen Local Governments Organizations. The CF1 is revised using the structured-case approach. New concepts discovered during each research cycle revealed that LGAF adoption is a procedure of experiential judgement. The applicability of the TAM is investigated and the model is enhanced, exploring additional variables that affect perceived ease of use, perceived usefulness and actual use. A final complementary CF2 is presented and the evaluation of this model according to the data received from the case studies is discussed.

Chapter 3

Hanuv Mann, Carleton University, Canada
Gerald Grant, Carleton University, Canada
Inder Jit Singh Mann, Carleton University, Canada

In this paper, the authors identify and explore the optimal scope of a generic city-level e-Government program. In order to corroborate theoretical research, a comprehensive feature comparison of different e-Government elements/services, of select city web sites from various countries in the world is conducted. The research finds that despite the manifest common features, the inherent scope of service provision by the websites studied is unique. This finding gives rise to the understanding that customizing e-Government initiatives is ideally conducive to the local needs of the constituents.

Chapter 4

Bahar Movahedi, Carleton University, Canada
Ren-Xiang (Paul) Tan, University of London, UK
Kayvan Miri Lavassani, Carleton University, Canada

The concept of Electronic Government (EG) has evolved significantly during the past few decades. Several development models have been presented in the literature to illustrate the advancement and adoption of EG practices. Recent developments in EG adoption that emphasize the process view call for a new perspective to EG adoption. Based on the review of most cited stage models of EG adoption, a comprehensive stage model is recommended in this paper. Furthermore, this paper utilizes the recommended stage model and proposes a process based framework for analyzing the EG adoption.

Chapter 5

Rakhi Tripathi, Indian Institute of Technology Delhi, India
M. P. Gupta, Indian Institute of Technology Delhi, India
Jaijit Bhattacharya, Indian Institute of Technology Delhi, India

Interoperability is an important pre-condition for achieving higher stages of e-government and further ensures that a one stop portal will become a reality. Interoperability results from vertical and horizontal integration. The question arises: How can the level of interoperability and degree of integration be ascertained? This paper suggests a framework. It begins by identifying critical factors necessary for the successful adoption of interoperability technology along three dimensions of integration—process integration, communication integration, and data integration. Factors are formed from a literature review and discussions with webmasters and IT professionals working on portal development in various government departments of India. These factors are useful in further evaluation across the three dimensions and locate the position of a government portal in a technology adoption space. It is then possible to ascertain a portal's current level of integration sophistication.

Chapter 6

Ramaraj Palanisamy, St. Francis Xavier University, Canada
Bhasker Mukerji, St. Francis Xavier University, Canada

The emergence of Radio Frequency Identification (RFID) technology has affected the functions and roles of business organizations. RFID technology provides technical solutions across a variety of industries in the public and private sectors. E-government is being increasingly utilized by governments in different countries to increase the efficiency of services provided to citizens. Although the use of e-Government is allowing timely, effective services online, many challenges must still be overcome to maximize the utility e-Government can provide to citizens. RFID is disseminating in a variety of new areas and movement exists toward the adoption of RFID in e-Government, but several issues and challenges must be addressed. This paper examines both e-Government and RFID from an individual perspective and explores the possible issues and challenges associated with RFID technology adoption in e-Government. Based on a review of literature, a conceptual model has been developed illustrating the various issues and challenges and how they would impact the RFID adoption in e-Government.

Chapter 7

Yogesh K. Dwivedi, Swansea University, UK
Mohamad Hisyam Selamat, Universiti Utara Malaysia, Malaysia
Banita Lal, Nottingham Trent University, UK

This study examines the factors affecting the adoption of broadband Internet in a developing country context by focusing on Malaysia. The data relating to these factors was collected using a survey approach. The findings of this paper suggest that constructs such as relative advantage, utilitarian outcomes, service quality, and primary influence are important factors affecting Malaysian accountants' broadband adoption and Internet use behaviour. The paper proceeds to outline the research limitations and implications.

Chapter 8

Amitabh Ojha, Indian Institute of Technology Delhi, India
G. P. Sahu, National Institute of Technology, India
M. P. Gupta, Indian Institute of Technology Delhi, India

Evidence exists that citizens' demand for pay-to-use e-government services is highly price-elastic. But research on citizens' adoption of e-government remains almost entirely pre-occupied with contexts wherein it is implicit that citizens would not face any monetary cost implications. The fact that Technology Acceptance model (TAM) and Perceived Characteristics of Innovating (PCI) do not factor in potential adopters' monetary cost perceptions is a plausible reason for such bias in research efforts. The paper posits a model wherein the value perceived by a citizen in government-to-citizen (G2C) online channel, and traditional public service delivery channel are antecedents of his or her intention to use the online channel. The model was tested in the context of the rail ticketing service of Indian Railways (a Department of India's federal government). Results support the hypothesized paths, and offer useful managerial guidance to encourage citizens' adoption. The paper discusses the prospect of certain adverse consequences for public administration and citizens, which could be linked to e-government and user charges, and ways to mitigate them. Research implications are also discussed.

Chapter 9

Government organizations differ significantly from private sector organizations in terms of their processes, culture, and ways of working. Plagued with phlegmatic and often lackadaisical work systems, government organizations tend to resist dramatic changes usually associated with technology based interventions. This study examines the effect of one dominant factor, organizational culture, on the success of e-government initiatives. To test the research model, survey data was collected from 315 respondents in 13 government organizations in India. The results indicate that a government organization which performs well on e-government projects exhibits specific cultural traits. Results also indicate that bureaucratic dimension, which emerges as the dominant cultural dimension in government organizations, is both positively and negatively related to e-government performance dimensions. The supportive and innovative dimensions of organizational culture are positively related to work process improvement and the job satisfaction of the user associated with e-government projects. Implications for practice and research are provided by interpreting the results in the context of the process paradox. The results show that while government and public sector organizations can use culture to positively impact efficiency dimensions of e-government performance, the dominant bureaucratic culture will tend to hinder systemic and enterprise-wide e-government performance.

This paper presents an empirical study of the risk factors of large governmental information systems (IS) projects. For this purpose the Official Decisions of the Greek Government Information Technology Projects Advisory Committee (ITPAC) concerning 80 large IS projects have been analyzed and interviews with its members have been conducted. From this analysis 21 risk factors have been identified, and further elaborated and associated with inherent particular characteristics of the public sector, extending existing approaches in the literature. A categorization of them with respect to origin revealed that they are associated with the management, the processes, and the content of these projects. Results show that behind the identified risk factors there are political factors, which are associated with intra-organizational and inter-organizational politics and competition, and can be regarded as 'second level' risk sources. The risk factors identified in this study are compared with the ones found by similar studies conducted in Hong Kong, Finland, and the United States, and also with the ones mentioned by OECD reports. Similarities and differences are discussed.

Gisela Gil-Egui, Fairfield University, USA
William F. Vásquez, Fairfield University, USA
Alissa M. Mebus, Symmetry Partners, LLC, USA
Sarah C. Sherrier, Green Room Entertainment, USA

This paper explores national governments' prioritization of environmental matters within their e-government websites, in order to provide empirical evidence related to the way "green" issues are articulated in different countries' policymaking agendas. Through a multi-pronged methodological approach combining frame analysis, factor analysis, inferential statistics, and qualitative interpretation, explicit and visual allusions related to environmental policies, initiatives, challenges, and agencies in the home page or main portal of the national governments for 189 UN members were coded. Results show that only 39.1% of the analyzed e-government sites included environmental references, and no strong pattern characterized the framing of environmental concerns by governments. Correlation and regression analyses revealed that GDP per capita and contribution to global CO_2 emissions have more weight than other variables in a nation's propensity to highlight environmental issues within their e-government websites. Findings are discussed in light of framing theory, as well as in light of implications for governments' public image and for actual environmental advocacy.

Heiko Hornung, University of Campinas, Brazil
M. Cecília C. Baranauskas, University of Campinas, Brazil

The tendency of computer use spreading out into more and more areas of life has the potential to bring benefits to people's lives. Examples are electronic government services in areas such as public health or social assistance. The same phenomenon, however, could leave behind people who face different barriers regarding the access to those services, for example people with disabilities, low literacy or low computer skills. This work sheds light on the question of how to facilitate the interaction with those services considering people with diverse physical and intellectual conditions. This study analyzes design ideas utilized in four prototypes of a registration service and explored by user representatives. The results of this analysis inform a design rationale in order to support designers in making design decisions tailored to the respective application and social usage context.

Vincent Homburg, Erasmus University Rotterdam, The Netherlands
Andres Dijkshoorn, Erasmus University Rotterdam, The Netherlands

This article describes the trend of personalization in electronic service delivery, with a special focus on municipal electronic service delivery in the Netherlands. Personalization of electronic services refers to the one-to-one citizen orientation using authentication, profiling and customization techniques. The percentage of Dutch municipalities offering services through personalized electronic counters has increased from 14% (2006) to 28% (2009). Using binary logistic regression analyses of 2008 survey data, it is concluded that personalization is positively associated with size of municipalities but not with e-government and policy innovation statements, nor with explicit political responsibility with respect to e-government development. Based on these findings, alternative explanations for the adoption and diffusion of personalized e-government services are suggested.

Chapter 14

Nigel Martin, The Australian National University, Australia
John Rice, University of Adelaide, Australia

This paper uses data from a program of customer interviews and focus group research conducted by the Australian government to develop an electronic services evaluation and design framework. A proven theory building approach has been used to develop and confirm the various components of electronic government (e-government) use and satisfaction from original government studies conducted in Australia and to create the new evaluation framework. Building on the extant e-government literature, the reintroduction of the original data into the framework yielded some emergent observations and insights for future e-government design, including the somewhat paradoxical importance of human contacts and interactions in electronic channels, service efficiency and process factors that impinge on customer satisfaction and dissatisfaction, and a potential growth trajectory for telephony based e-government for older segments of the community.

Chapter 15

Craig P. Orgeron, Mississippi Department of Information Technology Services, USA
Doug Goodman, University of Texas at Dallas, USA

Governments at all levels are faced with the challenge of transformation and the need to reinvent government systems in order to deliver efficient and cost effective services. E-government presents a tremendous impetus to move forward in the 21st century with higher quality, cost-effective, government services, and a better relationship between citizens and government. This research considers theoretical foundations from the Technology Acceptance Model (TAM), the Web Trust Model (WTM), and SERVQUAL to form a parsimonious model of citizen adoption and satisfaction for e-government services. The authors find that usefulness, or end-user convenience, to be the principal determinant of e-government adoption and satisfaction, unaffected even when controlling demographic variables such as race, income, and education are introduced.

Chapter 16

Subhajyoti Ray, Xavier Institute of Management, Bhubaneswar, India

Although the use of ICT by government has demonstrated its potential in improving government services, worldwide there are more failures than successes of e-Government projects. In the context of developing countries, including India, authors have observed equally high failure rates. Therefore, it is important to understand the barriers to implementation of e-Government, especially in developing countries. This paper develops a comprehensive understanding of barriers to e-Government services for citizens in developing countries. This study was carried out in India, a developing country with a massive commitment to e-Government at policy and implementation levels. Based on variables identified from research, a survey of the key practitioners in e-Government was conducted to generate evidence on perceptions of barriers to e-Government. Even though a relatively small number of responses were received, the responses could be evaluated using principal component analysis to understand the latent structure of the barriers. Finally, 7 critical factors with 30 items are extracted that describe the latent structure of barriers to e-Government in development.

Chapter 17

In terms of public services, governments do not yet know how to treat users as different and unique individuals. At worst, users are still considered an undifferentiated mass, or at best as segments. However, the benefits of universal personalisation in public services are within reach technologically through e-government developments. Universal personalisation will involve achieving a balance between top-down government- and data-driven services, on the one hand, and bottom-up self-directed and user-driven services on the other. There are at least three main technological, organisational and societal drivers. First, top-down data-driven, often automatic, services based on the huge data resources available in the cloud and the technologies enabling the systematic exploitation of these by governments. Second, increasing opportunities for users themselves or their intermediaries to select or create their own service environments, bottom-up, through 'user-driven' services, drawing directly on the data cloud. Third, a move to 'everyday', location-driven e-government based largely on mobile smart phones using GPS and local data clouds, where public services are offered depending on where people are as well as who they are and what they are doing. This paper examines practitioners and researchers and describes model current trends based on secondary research and literature review.

Chapter 18

Current research tells little about how to assess the public incentive policies designed to persuade local governments to set up partnerships. This first paper of ongoing research illustrates an evaluation method based on the 'realist approach', the tenets of which assign a key role to the context in which the mechanisms of a public programme work (or not). The evaluation framework is intended to be a tool to assist and inform future policymaking and practice. The paper provides a picture of the current scientific debate by exploring the relevant literature; outlines a research path aimed at building an empirically-based model for assessing public policies to promote and support local partnerships in the Italian Region of Sardinia; and indicates a possible context of use for the theory through an illustrative example.

Companies are required by law to report all kinds of information to various public agencies. Since most public agencies are autonomous and define their information demands independent of each other, companies have to report information to various agencies in different ways. Accordingly, governments are initiating programs that aim to transform business-to government information exchange to reduce the administrative burden for companies and improve the accountability at the same time. Yet little research is available on the type of transformations needed and the role of the infrastructure. Drawing on a case study, this paper investigates the interplay between technical infrastructure and transformation. In this case study an information brokerage infrastructure based on the Extensible Business Reporting Language (XBRL) was developed providing a one stop shop for companies and public agencies. The case study shows that the infrastructure should be flexible enough to accommodate changes over time but stable enough to attract a large user-base. The increase in efficiency and effectiveness of information exchange processes requires extensive transformation from both public and private parties.

Chapter 20

Kawal Kapoor, Swansea University, UK
Yogesh K. Dwivedi, Swansea University, UK
Michael D. Williams, Swansea University, UK
Mohini Singh, RMIT University, Australia
Mark J. Hughes, Swansea University, UK

Radio Frequency Identification (RFID) is revolutionizing item identification and tracking. The technology demonstrates complexities in terms of (a) huge initial capital investment, (b) validating the need for RFID followed by its implementation decisions, (c) risks associated with consumer acceptance and consequences of incorrect implementation, and (d) capability to support enhancements and upgrades in cordial agreement with the individual implementer organizations. This paper explores the extent of RFID implementation at the Swansea University Library, examining the Social, Technological, Economic, and Managerial (STEM) aspects directly associated with implementation. A focused interview approach was resorted to, for data collection purposes. The core implementation team for RFID at Swansea University was interviewed to gain insights into the study's areas of interest. It was found that self service is the most sought after benefit. It simplifies stock management and enhances security at the libraries. Although the cost of the system remains a concern, varying on the basis of the scale of implementation, vandalism also continues to exist but to a reduced degree. University libraries are public sector organizations, consequently leading these findings to have an insinuation for RFID implementations in other public sector organizations as well.

Nripendra P. Rana, Swansea University, UK
Michael D. Williams, Swansea University, UK
Yogesh K. Dwivedi, Swansea University, UK
Janet Williams, University of Glamorgan, UK

After more than a decade of research in the field of e-government, it is now timely and appropriate to reflect upon the overall developmental directions in the area. This paper explores research progress to date by systematically analyzing the existing body of knowledge on e-government related issues, and reveal if there is lack of theoretical development and rigor in the area. Usable data relating to e-government research currently available were collected from 779 research articles identified from the ISI Web of Knowledge database, and by manually identifying relevant articles from dedicated journals on electronic government such as Transforming Government: People, Process, and Policy (TGPPP), Electronic Government, an International Journal (EGIJ), and International Journal of Electronic Government Research (IJEGR). Based on the investigation of the various studies, findings reveal that generic e-government applications were explored more than any specific applications, and the technology acceptance model (TAM) was the most utilized theory to explain research models. Although a large number of theories and theoretical constructs were borrowed from the reference disciplines, their utilization by e-government researchers appears largely random in approach. The paper also presents limitations and further research directions for future researchers.

Preface

EXAMINING THE IMPACT OF UTILISING VIDEO TO VIDEO TECHNOLOGY FOR DELIVERING PUBLIC SECTOR SERVICES

1. INTRODUCTION

Since the introduction of electronic government as a mainstream mechanism for delivering public services over a decade ago, a persistent problem that has hindered its adoption and diffusion has been the poor take up by citizens. Although various governments have successfully piloted other channels of service delivery such as mobile applications (or mobile government) or digital TV, the impact of these channels are yet to be proven on a broader scale. Studies have shown that the average citizen often prefers to have face to face contact when dealing with public services and this is particularly true for complex services such as health, education and social or domestic services such as social security, housing or employment. While many public sector agencies have succeeded in transforming these simple customer facing services such as payments for services or fines or renewal of applications through the use of e-government, others have struggled to facilitate the more complex services through e-government. As such, questions have been raised on whether the delivery of public services using e-government has contributed to excluding certain segments of society from access to key services. Certainly, the identification of 'social inclusion in the digital age' as a priority area for research by the European Commission indicates that the use of e-government as a mainstream method for public service delivery has raised some concerns among policy makers. Prior research in the field has indeed suggested that socially and economically disadvantaged communities such as the elderly, poor, and disabled are often less engaged with e-government due numerous issues such as lack of access, trust, awareness, usability, et cetera.

In this preface, the authors propose the use of video technology as an alternative and complementary mechanism to replicate both traditional face to face contact and e-government in the provisioning of public services. Authors posit that citizens who are less comfortable or are not enticed to use electronic services due to influencing factors such as trust in e-services, skills, usability, and usefulness may be motivated to actively engage with public services that are offered electronically, if they are supported through a video to video (V2V) connection where a more personalised service can be offered. Such an approach, while eliminating the inefficiencies and inconvenience of traditional face to face services that are offered in a physical premises, has the potential to offer all the benefits of e-government while maintaining the personal touch that is associated with face to face services. Moreover, the V2V approach can facilitate all existing channels that are used to offer e-government services such as personal computers, tablet devices, mobile phones, and digital TV. This will not only ensure that more personalised services are offered to users, but also that all the features of modern hardware devices used to offer these services are fully exploited by the public sector for benefit of their citizens. Furthermore, in areas such as health and education, the impact and value of using V2V cannot be understated. For instance, in health, V2V can contribute to saving lives as well as offering a platform for learning and teaching. Similarly, in education, V2V has potential for many applications in the virtual learning space.

This preface discusses the potential of using high definition video on the Internet to provide public services and the associated benefits it can offer society. In order to do so, it is structured as follows. The next section offers a brief overview of how V2V will work on the Internet followed by examples of the application of V2V in the public sector. This is followed by highlighting examples of how V2V may work in the provisioning of healthcare, education and city or municipality services and the associated benefits to society. Finally, the preface summarises the key benefits offered in the use of V2V technology for public services and concludes by outlining the future directions for the use V2V services in the public sector.

2. THE USE OF HIGH DEFINITION VIDEO IN PUBLIC INFRASTRUCTURE

The concept of using V2V in public services via various applications such as Skype, Google Chat, and FaceTime is not necessarily new. Yet, although these applications are used by millions of users across the globe for business and social or personal purposes, when they are used in public infrastructure, are often limited by technological constraints and cannot extend beyond certain boundaries. This leads to a low image definition, image stuttering, and delays for the user. Such issues result in poor user experience and users are often not able to assimilate the information contained in the video. The authors propose the concept of high definition V2V transmission on the Internet to overcome such problems by using Right of Way (RoW) (see Figure 1) to guarantee a lack of interference from non-desired traffic. The method of RoW has been previously used in some specific virtual private networks (VPNs) by employing appropriate Quality of Service (QoS) based mechanisms. However, the use of RoW that guarantees no interference from unwanted traffic is not offered presently on the mass market. This preface suggests the use of RoW on the public infrastructure (Internet) to allow video traffic to have a guaranteed bandwidth that can alleviate the problems that appear when delivering video together with other unwanted traffic. As such, the authors posit that their solution not only eliminates some of the QoS related problems faced by applications currently available in the mass market (such as Skype and Google video chat) but also offers mechanism for facilitating better services in a number of domains in both the private and public sector. In a public sector context, as outlined in figure 1, the use of high definition (HD) video on demand has the potential to create a LiveCity environment where citizens can be more closely linked with each other and their governments wherever they are (irrespective of location) during their daily life routines. Such an environment will provide the platform where two users can communicate through video using RoW. RoW will ensure that the video traffic is prioritised over other Internet traffic "best effort" enabling an improved quality that will lead to a more realistic virtual presence among users, hence increasing the acceptance of the service that makes use of V2V transmission (Coudriet & Babich, 2012).

Figure 1. High definition video to video communication using right of way

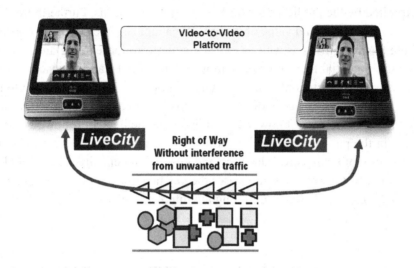

3. APPLICATIONS OF VIDEO-TO-VIDEO IN PUBLIC SERVICES

This research is built on the concept of community and of HD V2V public services that are provided to meet community needs. There are several core public services on which video to video can be delivered such as *Education* (teachers and school children) (Chochliourous et al., 2012), *Public Administration* (municipal administrators in cities) (Weerakkody et al., 2012), *Health* (ambulances, patients, doctors, and nurses) (Stamatelatos et al., 2012), and *City Experience* (museums, tourist, and culture consumers). All these services have different challenges that could be addressed by using HD V2V. Although in some of these services several applications of V2V use already exist, what is proposed here goes beyond these applications and uses RoW in order to get better image quality in V2V. The following examples demonstrates how V2V can be utilised in education, health and city experience.

3.1 Education

Collaborative learning has been shown to have a positive impact on learner experience and achievements (Gokhale, 1995; Johnson & Johnson, 1986; Weerakkody et al., 2012). In this respect, a high definition V2V environment has the potential to facilitate learning and teaching regardless of the learners' and teachers' locations. Using the LiveCity concept, a range of collaborative projects could be implemented in an educational context by connecting schools from different locations. These projects can have different goals such as promoting literacy or improving sports education. Promoting literacy can be achieved where students from different schools can read to each other and discuss a local piece of historical folklore/legend using V2V. This would not only improve literacy but can also improve students' knowledge about each other's heritage. Other scenarios could involve collaborative writing in which students from different schools are paired together to create a story. The pedagogical experience is enhanced this way, by using video-to-video conferences. In these conferences, children could discuss each other's work and improve their critical analysis skills. In sports education, students can showcase a sport that is popular only in their area and during the video conference they will have the opportunity to discuss their experience of this sport with students from other schools located in different areas. V2V can also enhance students' skills where video can be used as a form of assessment through which feedback is given.

3.2 Health

As illnesses often mean a downturn in people's life, health services are probably the most important component of this V2V environment. Today, most health care services offered are either face to face or through voice. When due to various reasons face to face communication is not possible a high definition V2V connection between medical staff and patient can provide richer information and hence a better medical advice/diagnostic. Health services that could benefit by using HD V2V can be classified into: *remote emergency rooms* and preventive *healthcare by tele-consultation and tele-monitoring*. For example, in a city *emergency* case, the baseline is communication by voice. Voice based radio connections and mobile phone connections are available in ambulance and emergency departments in hospitals. Many emergency services have or will be updated with data communications and therefore video can be utilised to provide more information which can help to enhance patient initial diagnostics and decision making regarding treatment options and outcomes. For example, if the emergency personnel need help from the emergency doctor, currently the doctor is able to find information about the patient through the phone, but he cannot see the patient or the results of the analysis performed by the ambulance crew. Having access to this information, a more informed decision can be made about the patient treatment, thus enhancing his chance of recovery. Likewise, usage of HD V2V in *preventive healthcare* can be done through *tele-consultation* and *tele-monitoring*. This would eliminate the need of being physically present in a hospital. This is important especially for patients that need intensive home monitoring by the hospital personnel (GPs, nurses, specialists), as is the case for diabetic patients.

3.3 City Experience

Today, most city administrative services that are available on an over the counter basis are also available online. One constraint that online services have is that the human element is missing. This can be important especially for elderly citizens or in cases where information queries exist or where there is complexity in the nature of the enquiry. Multiple administrative services could be provided by town councils through V2V. These services can be classified into two categories: *Administrative Processes Services* (for example, registration services, statistics, and municipal register of inhabitants, online benefits services, and council tax services) and *Information for Citizens Services* whose objective is to provide general information to citizens and, if appropriate, to transfer the question to another *Administrative Processes Service*. Citizens will be able to access these services in various locations using V2V such as local libraries and dedicated public places in the city. Furthermore, by using V2V, public administrations can create a friendlier alternative to existing e-government services. This can enable a two way communication between citizens and public administration that can facilitate citizens' engagement in decision making, an important aspect of the democratic environment. Moreover, V2V can be used to solve complex queries where a municipality worker can assist a citizen with his service needs by guiding them using a video link, and avoiding the necessity to travel to a physical office to solve his/her queries. In addition, a LiveCity V2V environment can enrich city experiences of citizens or visitors by enabling them to encounter local culture and history through connecting museums and allowing people to interact with exhibits and items of historical or cultural value.

4 BENEFITS OF USING VIDEO TO VIDEO

There are several benefits that using HD V2V will bring to society. First, the RoW approach will enable HD video delivery without interference from other traffic that will alleviate some problems that video delivery currently faces and improve the user experience of video use on the Internet. Second, the LiveCity concept proposed in the article will be using an open set of heterogeneous tools and applications to bridge the gap between existing systems and the requirements of various user communities. Third, usage of HD V2V has various benefits for each of the services outlined above, as described below.

4.1 Education

Usage of HD V2V in education can derive several social and economic benefits. The social impact HD V2V could bring to education are manifold. Schools will have the ability to collaborate on projects regardless of their location, therefore allowing the sharing of resources and teachers facilitating cultural interchanges between schools across the world and therefore increasing awareness of arts, science, and social issues. By doing so, leading teachers will have the opportunity to provide classes to students across the globe facilitating skills transfer offered in better schools towards the less well performing schools between pupils and between teachers, in a cost-efficient way. Furthermore, V2V will allow the easier provisioning of teacher training facilities between schools and training centres resulting in the ability to create richer educational experiences and pupil attainment. In addition, HD V2V will also offer the opportunity for parental involvement in education through the provision of teacher-parent training. All of the above will help improve education standards and, eventually, create a wide universal education system accessible in all sections of society and contribute to generating new a knowledge base, new ideas for learning and teaching through the use of video archives. Finally, the usage of HD V2V will also have economic impacts such as lowering the cost of learning and teaching through sharing of teachers and resources across various locations and the ability to increase the number of teachers and pupils who can undertake training.

4.2 Health

HD V2V in healthcare can be used in *remote emergency rooms* and *preventive healthcare by tele-consultation and tele-monitoring*. For both these services the use of HD V2V can have a significant impact on individual health and quality of life, therefore favourably impacting productivity. Consequently, this will have an impact on longevity (and, in return, in economic terms, on productivity). The value to the economy of improvements in life expectancy is of great importance and can be compared to all other consumption goods and services together. Among the benefits of using HD V2V in *remote emergency rooms* one could highlight: (i) the early availability of expert opinion at the scene when necessary; (ii) ability to optimise the patients' care by deciding which patients can be fast tracked to deliver lifesaving treatment earlier; (iii) earlier recognition of stroke can save lives and improve the chances of independent functioning; (iv) expedite decision making and improve the referral of such patients to the most appropriate centre; (v) earlier delivery of stroke thrombolysis (clot busting medicine) for appropriate patients; (vi) improve outcomes for patients suffering heart attacks by getting the right patient to the right people and the right place; (vii) ensure faster patient recovery, prevent unnecessary loss of life, prevent and minimise trauma in emergency and accident cases; (viii) save tax payers money on medication, hospital, treatment and compensation; (ix) prevent cases of litigation due to mis-diagnosis, improve healthcare services, encourage collaborative work in healthcare, and contribute towards achieving effective management of trauma situations; and (x) the potential learning opportunities for medical staff. For *preventive healthcare by tele-consultation and tele-monitoring,* patients could be provided with faster and more reliable video feeds and medical telemetry tests (tele-diagnosis and tele-monitoring). HD V2V can facilitate and improve the quality of the health service as more often than usual contacts may improve the quality of life and the ambient living conditions for the diabetic patients. Furthermore, the following are examples of potential economic impacts: (i) savings to tax payers' money on medication, hospital, treatment, and compensation (i.e. sick benefits); (ii) preventing the economic impact that the loss of a bread winner may have on families; (iii) reducing the cost of medication due to reduced trauma scores as well as long term costs for patients and governments; (iv) earlier detections and better solutions to health problems via V2V should result in fewer complications and lower medical costs; (v) the availability of medical specialists via V2V will allow for more effective sharing between locations, therefore leading to greater efficiency, therefore lower cost-effectiveness ratio (it refers not only to education but also to tele-diagnosis of disease and tele-monitoring of the health status); (vi) provisioning of services locally so people do not have to travel far out of the community for their needs. For example spending on health care is an especially significant portion of any economy, especially in remote or rural communities and economies.

4.3 City Experience

The usage of HD V2V in municipal services will radically improve the access and range of e-government services available via the Internet. It will also illustrate to the wider community the potential benefits of face-to-face communication for specific services. In doing so, it will provide a number of societal and economic benefits. The social impact is realised by reducing the citizens need to travel to designated buildings in order to conduct local government or municipality services. This could result in a number of concrete benefits for individuals such as lowering travel time and road traffic and pollution, reducing the risk of accidents, or the need for moving into assisted living accommodation for elderly or infirm users by providing complex services via the Internet which would previously have required them to make a visit. Moreover, HD V2V will help improve face-to-face communication resulting in a better user-service provider relationship and improving trust and the uptake of new services as opposed to voice only or web based services. Furthermore, V2V will improve the accessibility and convenience of using e-government services for the less ICT savvy and other offline physical services for the disabled and elderly. For the government, V2V will reduce the cost of physical space needed to provide services to citizens and reduce the cycle time for service delivery and improve service adoption. In relation to arts and culture, they represent to a certain extend a reflection of our history and identity, being able to know more about each other's cultural heritage, and exchange ideas with people regardless of their location and cultural background, has also the potential to integrate us better in an increasingly globalised society. The usage of HD V2V to enhance the city experience can make this possible. For those not willing/having the time to travel, V2V can allow them access to historical and cultural experiences by interacting with its people.

5. SUMMARY

Electronic service delivery in the public sector is aimed at improving efficiency, effectiveness and transparency of governments. With the increasing demand on Internet and its services, public sector organisations have realised the importance of utilizing the relevant applications and technologies in engaging with citizens and other relevant stakeholders in order to ensure a better service delivery. Prior research in the field has indeed suggested that socially and economically disadvantaged communities such as the elderly, poor and disabled are often less engaged with electronic government services due numerous issues such as lack of access, trust, awareness, usability etc. This article offered some insights on how high definition video-to-video communication can be utilised in a number of public sector services in the context of health, education and city experience to overcome some of the current challenges. The article has shown how Right of Way (RoW) can enhance HD V2V delivery and the potential benefits and impacts a LiveCity environment can offer society in various services. The examples examined in the article demonstrated that utilising HD V2V in the public sector can have a valuable economic impact by lowering costs of services through sharing of resources and skills across various service domains and locations enriching citizens' experiences.

Vishanth Weerakkody
Brunel University, UK

Ramzi El-Haddadeh
Brunel University, UK

Andreea Molnar
Brunel University, UK

ACKNOWLEDGMENT

The authors wish to acknowledge the contributions made to this preface by the LiveCity Consortium of partners and the European commission

REFERENCES

Chochliourous, I. P., Spiliopoulou, A. S., Sfakianakis, E., Stephanakis, I., Morris, D., & Kennedy, M. (2012). Enhancing education and learning capabilities via the implementation of video-to-video communications. *First Intelligent Innovative Ways for Video-to-Video Communication in Modern Smart Cities Workshop, Artificial Intelligence Applications and Innovations*, (pp. 268-278).

Coudriet, G. A., & Babich, J. E. (2012). Effective design of audio/video conference rooms. *Sound and Vibration, 46*(7), 8–11.

Gokhale, A. A. (1995). Collaborative learning enhances critical thinking. *Journal of Technology Education, 7*(1). Retrieved October 23, 2012, from http://scholar.lib.vt.edu/ejournals/JTE/v7n1/gokhale. jte-v7n1.html?ref=Sawos.Org

Johnson, R. T., & Johnson, D. W. (1986). Action research: Cooperative learning in the science classroom. *Science and Children, 24*, 31–32.

Stamatelatos, M., Katsikas, G., Makris, P., Alonistioti, N., Antonakis, S., Alonistiotis, D., & Theodossiadis, P. (2012). Video-to-video for e-health: Use case, concepts and pilot plan. *First Intelligent Innovative Ways for Video-to-Video Communication in Modern Smart Cities Workshop, Artificial Intelligence Applications and Innovations*, (pp. 268-278).

Totten, S., Sills, T., Digby, A., & Russ, P. (1991). *Cooperative learning: A guide to research*. New York, NY: Garland.

Weerakkody, V., El-Haddadeh, R., Chochliourous, I. P., & Morris, D. (2012). Utilizing a high definition live video platform to facilitate public service delivery. *First Intelligent Innovative Ways for Video-to-Video Communication in Modern Smart Cities Workshop, Artificial Intelligence Applications and Innovations*, (pp. 290-299).

ADDITIONAL READING

LiveCity Consortium. (n.d.). Retrieved from http://ec.europa.eu/information_society/apps/projects/factsheet/index.cfm?project_ref=297291

Chapter 1
A State-of-the-Art Review of Applied Forms and Areas, Tools and Technologies for E-Participation

Kostas Ergazakis
National Technical University of Athens, Greece

Kostas Metaxiotis
University of Piraeus, Greece

Tassos Tsitsanis
National Technical University of Athens, Greece

ABSTRACT

The concept of e-Participation is important for both citizens and decision makers. From the citizen's perspective, e-Participation provides the opportunity to achieve and satisfy the need to be heard by politicians and participate in the decision-making and policy formulation processes through the use of ICT. On the other side, politicians are also able to promote and encourage public participation through communication channels with citizens and act in line with public opinion. During the past years, the e-Participation landscape has been growing and developed. Currently, there are many applied forms and areas of e-Participation. At the same time, there are a growing variety of tools and technologies that are available to enhance e-Participation. In this paper, the authors present a complete overview of the e-Participation landscape, through the state-of-the-art review of these tools, technologies and areas of e-Participation. This overview is of value to researchers and practitioners who want to have a knowledge base for further research and practical implementation in the wider field of e-Participation.

DOI: 10.4018/978-1-4666-2458-0.ch001

1. INTRODUCTION

Over the past ten years, internet and Information and Communication Technologies (ICT) in general, have made available a massive amount of information that is spread around the net rapidly and is continuously updated. Towards this direction, several communication channels have been developed in order to offer improved and increased access to high quality information (in various forms: text, audio, video, maps, etc), appealing to a wide range of audience of all ages and used in everyday basis by many the citizens. In addition to simple information provision, ICT, offer citizens the opportunity to interact among them, express opinions, participate in communities sharing common interests, etc. In general, ICT is a powerful tool that can help increase social engagement of people, creating in this way a unique opportunity for achieving strong public participation in the decision making processes, through several e-Participation forms (Macintosh, Coleman, & Lalljee, 2005). However, the main raised question is: What e-Participation can really achieve?

e-Participation is very important for both citizens and decision makers (Macintosh, 2004, 2006a; Macintosh & Whyte, 2006). From the citizens' perspective, e-Participation offers people the opportunity to achieve and satisfy a main need, the need to be heard by the politicians and interact with them (Adams, Haston, Gillespie, & Macintosh, 2003; Adams, Macintosh, & Johnston, 2005). The main characteristic of representative democracy is that citizens elect those politicians who share common ideas and interests with them, in order to participate on behalf of them in the decision making process (Tambouris, 2008). However, in real life, even political active citizens, they don't often have the opportunity to discuss with politicians, and the expression of their opinion is limited in the narrow context of a simple political conversation with other citizens (Graber, 2002). Therefore, it is important for politicians to be

involved in such conversations, so as to have access to various and diverse opinions and take them into account during the decision making process, increasing in this way, the involvement and participation of citizens in the overall political context (Malina & Macintosh, 2002).

On the other hand, politicians shall promote and encourage public participation in order to create communication channels with citizens and act in line with the public opinion, to the degree that this is possible. Elected representatives are elected from citizens to act for their common interest and it is important to understand that only if they represent citizens in a way that reflects the opinions expressed by the majority, they are going to retain the power that they were given. Thus, governance shall be humanized and, through e-participation, to represent people in direct and accessible terms (Berman & Mulligan, 2003).

Nowadays, there are many applied forms and areas of e-Participation. At the same time, there is a constantly growing variety of respective tools and technologies that are available in order to enhance e-Participation. The main purpose of this paper is to present in a coherent and comprehensive way a complete picture of the e-Participation landscape, through the state-of-the-art review of these tools, technologies and areas of e-Participation. This overview should be of value to researchers and practitioners who wish to have a knowledge base for further research or for any kind of practical implementation, in the wider field of e-Participation.

In this respect, the next section provides a general context and background of the e-Participation field, presents the associated critical challenges as well as some methods to support and increase public participation through electronic means. Section 3 focuses on specific areas, where e-Participation is applied. Section 4 presents existing tools that are used for the enhancement of e-Participation, while section 5 presents technologies supporting e-Participation systems, in terms of information provision and retrieval. Section 6 presents the correlation between e-Participation areas and tools / technologies, and finally, section 7summarizes the main conclusions and some future research challenges.

2. GENERAL CONTEXT AND BACKGROUND OF E-PARTICIPATION

e-Participation is a term that is closely related to e-Democracy and can be defined as the exploitation of ICT for engaging citizens to participate as much as possible to democratic procedures, interacting among them, as well as, with politicians and decision makers and providing them with the necessary information and appropriate rights in a way that reinforces their role in the decision making process (Masters, Macintosh, & Smith, 2004).

However, there are many other definitions of e-Participation and e-Democracy, that focus on several and different aspects of the two terms. Specifically, the United Nations study defines e-participation as "the use of the digital communications media which allow citizens to participate through a more inclusive, open, responsive and deliberative process, in policy making" (Ahmed, 2006, p. 2.

e-Democracy has as purpose to engage citizens to the decision making processes as well as to strengthen the representative democracy, using various channels of internet access, such as public and private PCs, mobile phones, handheld devices, interactive digital TV, etc. The democratic decision making processes can be distinguished into two main categories: the one is concerned with the electoral process and the other with citizens' e-participation into the decision making (Macintosh, 2007).

A previous definition of the term (Hacker & van Dijk, 2000, p. 1, characterizes e-democracy as "a collection of attempts to practice democracy without the limits of time, space and other physical conditions, using ICT or CMC (Computer Mediated Communication) instead, as an addition, not a replacement for traditional 'analogue' political practices".

A further analysis of the term can lead to three distinctive levels of e-Democracy: e-Democracy begins from a very narrow level, which is called the Local e-Democracy and occurs where citizens interact with each other by using ICT, to create small communities that share the same interests and exchange opinions through fora or other forms of online communication (Beynon-Davies, Owens, & Williams, 2003; Bruschi, Fovino, & Lanzi, 2005; Smith, Macintosh, & Whyte, 2006). However, this kind of e-Democracy does not offer the opportunity to interact with decision makers, since its overall goal is the communication among citizens, in order to pursue a common purpose or goal. A broader level of e-Democracy is the one called Internal e-Democracy and refers to the exploitation of ICT in order to improve internal democratic and decision making processes within a government, a political party or an organization (Dahlberg & Siapera, 2006). The scope of Internal e-Democracy is broadened when these improved democratic and decision making processes include citizens that communicate with elected representatives, thus creating a framework of direct and participative democracy instead of representative democracy. In this way, e-Democracy is extended to the broadest possible level and is called External e-Democracy.

Interpreting the above mentioned definitions of e-Democracy, an abstract definition occurs for e-Participation, which stresses the use of ICT in order to create new communication channels that ensure the participation of citizens to democratic and decision making processes (Moreno-Jimenez & Polasek, 2003; Whyte & Macintosh, 2003).

A study of OECD (OECD, 2001), provides the overall framework of ICT usage for supporting online participation of citizens and stresses the overarching objectives of e-Participation, which are summarized in the following directions:

1. Reach a wider audience, to enable broader participation.
2. Support participation through a range of technologies to cater for the diverse technical and communicative skills of citizens.
3. Provide relevant information in a format that is more accessible and understandable by the target audience, in order to enable more informed contributions.
4. Engage with a wider audience to enable deeper contributions and support deliberative debate.

Towards achieving these objectives, several actions should be undertaken focusing on:

• The encouragement of decision makers and public authorities to consider the ways in which they can use e-participation tools to enhance democracy and to develop strategies for implementing e-participation tools where relevant and necessary.
• The exploitation of already accumulated knowledge and experience in the e-participation field, having as main purpose the citizens' benefit.
• The development of new tools based on Web 2.0 technologies, for the enhancement and effective support of democratic decision making processes.
• The sustainability of citizens' e-participation and the reinforcement of public engagement to democratic processes.

Rating the importance of e-Participation objectives, the important role of information provision for enabling more informed contributions by citizens and other stakeholders, should be stressed. Content provision can be embedded in any form of e-participation, creating a pyramid that correlates the range of public participation to the degree that information is provided through e-participation tools, in terms of repositories or information exchange between users. An indicative pyramid, including a small number of such e-Participation tools is presented in Figure 1.

The need to achieve the overarching e-Participation objectives, as set above, combined with the experience that has been gained over the last

Figure 1. The e-participation pyramid

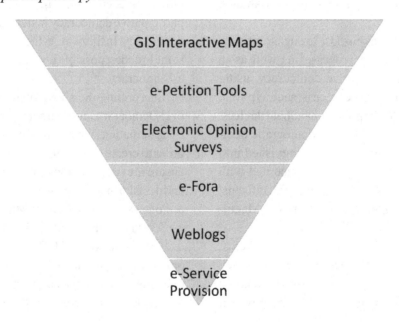

years from the research in the e-Participation field, create a set of challenges and barriers (Smith, & Macintosh, 2007):

1. Social Challenges and Barriers
2. Political Challenges and Barriers
3. Organizational Challenges and Barriers
4. Technological Challenges and Barriers
5. User Engagement

Some methods to support and increase public participation through electronic means, are mentioned by Coleman and Grotze (2001):

- Access to balanced information.
- An open agenda.
- Time to consider issues expansively.
- Freedom from manipulation or coercion.
- A rule-based framework for discussion.
- Participation by an inclusive sample of citizens.
- Scope for free interaction between participants.
- Recognition of differences among participants, but rejection of status-based prejudice.

According to OECD (2001, 2003) there are three key factors for consideration when seeking to use ICT for online citizen engagement, namely: Timing, Tailoring and Integration.

Timing refers to the development of tools that support user engagement to each stage of e-participation processes. Until now, only few countries have developed tools that offer citizens the opportunity to participate in more than one stages of the decision making process. In most cases however, citizens only participate in the first stages of the decision making process and not in the final stages, where the most important decisions regarding the concerned issue are made.

Tailoring, deals with the development of generic e-participation tools that can be easily customized and adapted, in order to meet the expectations and requirements of public bodies

with different agendas and different policy orientation. For example, local governments deal with a considerably smaller audience than national governments, while their agenda includes small scale issues and problems compared to the large scale issues that have to be faced by a national government.

Finally, integration of new online methods with traditional methods, seems to be more effective than e-participation or traditional participation standing alone (Downey & Fenton, 2003). When trying to engage the highest possible number of users, it is important to find ways to combine these two fields, in order to provide information and receive feedback from citizens that have different interests, skills, knowledge and background. This section has provided a general overview, context and background of the e-Participation field (views, definitions, associated terms), by also presenting the associated objectives, critical challenges as well as some methods to support and increase public participation through electronic means. Given that the main purpose of the paper is to present a complete picture of the e-participation landscape, the next section presents the specific areas, where e-participation is applied.

3. APPLIED FORMS AND AREAS OF E-PARTICIPATION

In this section, the focus is on the specific areas that e-Participation is applied, in order to enhance the highest possible engagement and involvement of citizens. The categorization is based on previous research activities conducted by the DEMO-net Excellence Network on e-Participation (available at: www.demo-net.org):

Consultation

Consultation is a two way relationship between citizens and decision makers, the main characteristic of which is that citizens provide feedback to the information made available to them by the decision makers. The overall process of consultation is managed by a public authority, which provides the appropriate information to citizens regarding the issues that are set for consultation, defines a set of questions that need to be answered and, finally, identifies the roles of every stakeholder in the consultation process. The citizens' role in this process is to provide decision makers with their opinions and comments on the issue set for consultation. Citizens can respond interactively, submit online comments and they also have the opportunity to contribute to the consultation with arguments supported by information using online resources like data repositories, RSS feeds and online databases related to the issues of the consultation (Braak, Oostendorp, Prakken, & Vreeswijk, 2006).

Deliberation

Deliberation expands the limits of an online discussion and opinion exchange, regarding important policy issues. ICT offer the opportunity to citizens to be involved, at a high degree, in a deliberation process and actively participate in the decision making, especially in the initial stages of the deliberation procedure (e.g. for the preparation of a law). However, at the latest stages, their role becomes less important, as their participation is usually confined to posting opinions and comments to a discussion that is moderated by domain specialists, legal experts and public officers.

The deliberation process creates a new quality for a modern e-democracy. Electronic deliberation addresses the following important issues:

- It creates a new framework for decision making and legislation formation, based on wide-range public participation.
- It reinforces the trust of people to political institutions, due to the establishment of transparent decision making processes.
- Through deliberation, people are better informed, having access to useful and qualitative information, and they can contribute

with more informed opinions and arguments. In addition, the opinion exchange can bring into light several aspects of an issue, helping to better understand the complete parameters of a problem.

- Through a deliberation process, a common phenomenon is the creation of citizen communities with common interests and ideas, that create a common opinion and support this with very strong and well formulated arguments, empowering in such a way the opinion they express.

Polling

ePolling is the process that uses ICT in order to conduct surveys and measure the public's opinion in a variety of topics. ePolling uses surveys that target a sample of the population that has been chosen in a scientific and statistical way (Bruschi et al., 2005). These surveys are conducted through a series of questions, which end to the extrapolation of generalities in ratio or within confidence intervals. ePolling systems are usually characterized by less stringent security requirements, in relation to eVoting. In particular, they can tolerate errors affecting a small percentage of votes, without compromising the final result. The main actors and characteristics of an e-polling process include: the voters which are the stakeholders that are interested in voting on a specific issue; the polling collector, which usually is a public authority that is responsible for collecting and counting the votes submitted over the process; the party that secures the validity and the transparency of the process; the authentication protocols for the identification of the identity of the voters; and the votes certificates that clarify the eligibility of a voter to participate in the polling process.

Voting

ICT play in important and vital role over the e-voting process as they support the right of citizens to vote and elect their representatives.

e-Voting, however, is a very generic term, as it spreads over a wide range of individual subjects that constitute the voting procedure and extend from the automatic counting of votes, to the use of mobile phones or other forms of technology that give the citizens the ability to authenticate themselves and vote. In any case, e-Voting highly contributes to the participation of citizens, as it offers the opportunity to elderly and disabled persons to participate to the elections procedure by improving accessibility with the use of ICT (Kampitaki, Tambouris, &Tarabanis, 2008; Xenakis, &Macintosh, 2004a, 2004b).

Campaigning

E-Campaigning (or e-Advocacy) deals with the organization of a campaign strategy and the achievement of its goals, by using web tools familiar to most of the internet users. An e-Campaign has clear and measurable goals, targets a specific audience, uses the web and new media in order to approach the targeted audience and aims to create supporters' groups via the development and adoption of a simple and attractive message or quote. A specific form of e-Campaigning used by politicians and political parties in order to gain the support of citizens in the elections procedure, is e-Electioneering (Baringhorst, 2009).

Electioneering

Electioneering is the political campaign including activities directed towards the electorate from the part of the candidates, whose main aim is to be elected. Electioneering uses a wide range of communication tools like posters, flyers, speeches, audio and video for spreading the candidates' messages and persuading the public to vote for them. When ICT are used in the process of electioneering, the term is transformed to e-Electioneering. Candidates tend to use internet and new media in order to establish new communication channels with voters and spread their messages and opinions

to a wider range of citizens. It is considered as the future of the electioneering process, since a strong internet communication strategy and presence may be of critical importance for the final result (Lusoli, 2005).

Petitioning

Petitioning is a way in which citizens can express their opinions and views about issues that concern them. A petition is a formal request to a higher authority, signed by a number of citizens. The right of the subject to petition has been exercised since Saxon times. It was mentioned in the Magna Carta and more explicitly in an Act of 1406. In an era of restricted political rights, the public petition was an important avenue for those who had no parliamentary representation to have their complaints heard. Until recently, the impact of petitions had diminished because public complaints could also be brought to the attention of members through the media. However, with the increasing emphasis on e-Democracy, the impact of petitions is starting to be felt again.

An e-Petition is a petition that has gathered support electronically. E-Petitions allow to petitioners to provide background information on the petition, encourage discussion around the issue so as to help inform those who are interested in signing and those receiving the e-Petition. An e-Petition service forms another channel for the petitioning process and, thus, an online record of e-Petitions can be created and act as an online hub for petitioning information. An e-Petitioning service does not imply any differences in existing constitutional or internal processes. It enables citizens and policy makers to see how petitions are processed in general. e-Petitions have the potential to become an effective tool in creating a constant dialogue between citizens and decision / policy makers and in adding value to the existing democratic, representative structures (Mosca, & Santucci, 2009).

Decision Making

Participation and especially e-Participation is a very critical parameter to a decision making process. Every decision making process produces a final choice among several alternatives, intending this one to be the best solution of a pointed problem. For this reason, all the stakeholders who are being affected by the problem, should participate in the decision-making process by providing useful information, expressing personal opinions and generally contributing with all means. ICT ensure the highest possible participation to this process.

Service Delivery

This area of e-Participation is strongly related with e-Government level 4 and 5 electronic services, which are fully completed via internet, without requiring the citizen's physical presence. It has to do with the transaction stage, where the citizen participates actively in order to achieve his desirable purpose. The strong bond between e-Government and e-Participation is totally understood, since the bigger number of services provided via Internet, the bigger number of citizens will participate (Fraser et al., 2003).

Spatial Planning

ICT is used for the development of systems that can be a strong decision making tool for spatial planning, especially in regions that are of environmental interest. The use of GIS systems, or other technologies like Google Maps or Google Earth, accompanied and connected with useful information, regarding laws, directives and regional authorities' decisions may create a powerful e-participation tool. This tool can aim to the resolution of conflicts between opposing sides, in an automated and fast way as well as to the transparency that can be ensured through spatial planning procedures.

Information Provision

Information provision is a critical parameter of any e-Participation system, as the main scope of an e-Participation process is to create informed participants that can contribute with opinions that are supported by strong arguments, which can be formulated only if a person has deep knowledge of the issue under discussion. That is the reason why information must be well-structured, accurate, legible and immediately related to the corresponding issue. A well informed user should be stimulated in order to actively share his opinion.

Mediation

Mediation, in a broad sense, is consisting of a cognitive process of reconciling mutually interdependent, opposed terms as what one could loosely call "an interpretation" or "an understanding of". Mediation is a form of alternative dispute resolution or "appropriate dispute resolution", aiming to assist two (or more) disputants in reaching an agreement. The parties themselves determine the conditions of any reached settlements - rather than accepting something imposed by a third party. The disputes may involve: states, organizations, communities, individuals or other representatives with a vested interest in the outcome.

In terms of e-Participation, mediators use appropriate techniques - tools and/or skills to initiate and improve dialogue among disputants, aiming to help the parties reach an agreement on the disputed matter. Normally, all parties must view the mediator as impartial. e-Participation systems and tools act usually as mediator among the disputants, in order to achieve a dispute resolution that satisfies all the parties involved in the process.

Community Building

Community building is a field where ICT gives the opportunity to citizens to formulate communities that have a special common characteristic.

These communities either share common interests or stem from specific distinct domains such as regional communities, religious communities, political communities, social communities etc. Community building is the core element of social networking. A representative example is Facebook, where users come together and create groups with the same hobbies, views, likes and dislikes and in such a way they make their voice sound louder. This is a way to recruit more supporters and make citizens more active and much more aware of issues that are of their interest, through interacting with other people and sharing opinions with absolute freedom and without manipulation from power holders.

This section has presented an overview of all the areas of application of e-Participation. However, it is also important to present all the available tools that are commonly used, in order to enhance e-Participation. These tools are thoroughly presented in the next section of the paper.

4. TOOLS FOR ENHANCING E-PARTICIPATION

The development of systems that are used for e-Participation purposes is based on the exploitation of already existing tools that allow users to interact with each other in various ways. Even if these tools cannot be directly characterized as e-Participation tools, however, due to the fact that they concentrate a large number of users within their operation, they can be easily called e-Participation Enhancement Tools.

Chat Rooms

Chat rooms are web applications for virtual communication between users sharing common interests. Chat rooms enable two-way communication in terms of sending and receiving messages in real time. These messages are available to all the users that are connected at the time to the particular chat room. Apart from messages, chat rooms such as Yahoo, use both text and voice simultaneously. The oldest form of true chat rooms is the text-based variety. Nowadays, the most popular of this kind is the Internet Relay Chat (IRC). There are also graphical user interface text-based chat rooms which allow users to select an identifying icon and modify the look of their chat environment. Chats conducted for e-Participation purposes are offered for a limited time-horizon, normally an hour at most.

Blogs

A 'blog' or 'weblog' is a shared online journal where people can post diary entries about their personal experiences, hobbies, and interests. Blogs invite comments from their readership on each post and are very easy to populate. According to Herring et al., blogs are the latest genre of internet communication to attain widespread popularity, yet their characteristics have not been systematically described (Herring, Scheidt, Bonus, & Wright, 2004).

A weblog is often used for communicating personal opinions and widespread information instead of sending a large number of e-mails, or trying to find another way to approach potential supporters of this opinion. Blogs are useful tools for power holders that create a new channel of communication with citizens, in order to share opinions, activities and initiatives.

Blogs could be characterized as interesting management tools, as well, due to the fact that managers can get information about what is going on in their organization. On the other hand, the staff can get information about the management board's activities.

Finally, blogs are excellent dissemination tools, as for example, a committee can post the minutes of a meeting, a manager can post the next steps of a project or the project status and keep in touch with the rest of the project team members.

Blogs are closely connected to information provision and especially this kind of information that sometimes cannot be provided directly by an organization. The provision of such information can create a general feeling to the citizens/recipients, that they can influence opinion or decision making on a specific issue. This, maybe, could be characterized as the most important role of weblogs in the overall democratic and decision making process.

Online Fora

Fora or discussion boards are web applications that allow the online discussion among users that share common interests, views, hobbies or are members of political parties, civic groups and communities of any kind. A forum allows users to exchange messages or comment on messages of other users. Fora are very often moderated, which means that users have to accept the terms of use of a forum and their messages should be compatible to them in order not to be bowdlerized. An online discussion, using a forum, begins with an initial thread in which users reply on messages or post new messages, creating in such a way a rolling dialogue. A specific form of online fora is the structured fora, that offer users the functionality to post for or against an opinion, resulting in a discussion map that provides an overview of the discussion, shows the opinions that gained general acceptance and can be used as a very good decision making tool.

ePetitions

ePetitions are online tools that are mostly used by public administrations or organizations as a mean of pressure towards decision makers. ePetitions are not interactive but collective tools that call people to support for or rally against an issue of their interest by signing the petition so as to collect a significant number of signatures.

ePetitioning tools vary form case to case, giving or not advanced functionalities to users, such as discussion capabilities and information provision in various forms (Beddie, Macintosh, & Malina, 2001; Finnimore, 2008; Iacopini, 2007; Whyte, Renton, & Macintosh, 2005). The most important aspect of an e-petition is its wide dissemination, in order to gather as many as possible voters, since the quantity of votes is the real objective of such a procedure. ePetition tools, as well as, e-voting and e-polling tools, should be characterized by the use of a strict user authentication protocol, in order to avoid multiple voting, which can affect a petition's validity.

ePanels

ePanels make use of other e-participation tools such as discussion forums, deliberative polling tools, expert online chats, e-Petitioning and e-consultation tools, in order to bring participants together in a time-specific debate. Participants are usually recruited, which means that not everybody can participate in a debate, but only persons having expertise in the discussed issue. Participation in e-panels is measured in terms of users attending the debate, which can prove to be a problem-solving process if it is well organized and if it provides easy to understand information. In addition, ePanels can be constituted not only of domain experts but also of a representative sample of citizens and decision makers.

eVoting

eVoting is a term encompassing several different types of voting, embracing both electronic means of casting a vote and electronic means of counting votes. eVoting systems for electorates have been used for over fifty years, debuting with the use of punch cards. Over the years, the evolution in e-Voting brought the use of optical scan voting systems which allow a computer to count a voter's mark on a ballot. Internet based voting systems have gained popularity and have been used for government elections and referendums in several countries. eVoting systems tend to be very popular, as they simplify and speed up a process that used to disengage people to participate in the representative democracy. However, e-voting processes seem to be vulnerable from risks that have to do with user authentication, multiple voting and electoral frauds (Xenakis & Macintosh, 2004c, 2004d).

ePolls

ePolls or quick polls are internet based instant or short time surveys which collect the public opinion via interviewing a random sample of people on a specific question with a simple yes/no answers. They also allow participants to select one answer from a list of alternatives in response to a simple statement of question. ePolls are mostly used as an unofficial tool for gathering initial opinions, that are going to be used as information in an official decision making process. Quick polls, due to their immediate nature and low cost, offer easy to analyze and understand results and are used in a wide range. The only disadvantage of such tools is that there is no way to stop voters from participating more than once, as no authentication mechanisms are used. Finally, polls provide participants the opportunity to view real time results of the survey, just a few moments after they have submitted their vote.

eCommunities

The latest trend in e-Participation systems deals with portals that enhance eParticipation through community building tools and especially social networks. Social networks are very popular among citizens and especially among young people. They find a means to express opinions and communicate to each other, in a way far from the strict and official environment of other e-Participation systems. These eCommunities are created by users that share common interests and opinions. By using new media and several other small scale applications, they try to further advance the dialogue on the issue they participate in. The most famous and widespread tool, referring to the construction of electronic communities, is Facebook, which is a social network that engages a large number of users and deals with several issues, creating in such a way a new culture in public and in e-participation. This culture shows the power of citizens when gathering together and trying to promote participation towards a common objective. Facebook is an illustrative example of tools that aim to create e-Communities and social structures made of nodes, that are tied by one or more specific types of interdependency, such as: values, visions, ideas, financial exchange, friendship, sexual relationships, kinship, dislike, conflict or trade.

Decision Making Tools

The main objective of eParticipation, is the engagement of citizens for contributing and support power holders in the decision making process. Apart from other forms of eParticipation, the development of decision making tools and especially decision making games, seems to be more effective for citizens' engagement, more familiar and pleasant when used by citizens. Decision making games give users the chance to interact with each other through graphic animation environments, that illustrate and simulate relevant aspects of an issue. Decision making games, can make use of other applications that are well known and successful among citizens, such as famous online games or business administration tools, for achieving their purposes. For example, the SimCity game can be a useful tool that can be deployed in a discussion about spatial planning. FEED project, which is funded under the e-Participation 2007 call, is an excellent paradigm of embedding the philosophy of SimCity in the decision making process for issues concerning spatial planning and its consequences for the environment.

Web-Casting Tools

Web-casting tools make use of media technologies in order to distribute media files over the Internet, either live or on-demand. Webcasts use streaming media technology to capture content from a single source and make it available online to the public who are interested in listening or viewing this specific information. Web-casting tools are mostly used, in terms of e-participation, for broadcasting meetings of local, regional or national councils and give citizens the opportunity to be better informed about issues of their interest without requiring their on-site presence in the place that the meeting takes place. However, web-casting tools, do not provide the opportunity to citizens to interact with each other, as they cannot be used for web conferencing purposes.

eConsultation Tools

Several public authorities make use of various eParticipation tools in order to create an e-Consultation environment and simulate the Consultation process through internet. eConsultation tools are fora and blogs that provide information to citizens in multiple ways, to enhance their active participation in a discussion about emerging and public interest issues (Whyte & Macintosh, 2002). Information is provided either in a "traditional way" referring to documents, articles, laws and in general static repositories of data managed by the public authority, or in a "dynamic" way using RSS feeds, webcasts and new media.

In what follows, the most important technologies which support e-Participation systems, in terms of information provision and retrieval, are presented.

5. TECHNOLOGIES APPLIED FOR ENHANCING E-PARTICIPATION

Except for tools that can be directly connected with public participation and can be characterized as e-Participation tools, there is a group of tools and technologies acting in assistance of e-Participation systems in order to support them in terms of information provision and retrieval. These technologies and tools are briefly described in the following sections which summarize the functionality they provide to the users of e-Participation systems and how assist them to be more informed and contribute with well-documented arguments to the overall decision-making process.

Geographic Information Systems

A geographic information system (GIS) integrates hardware, software, and data for capturing, managing, analyzing, and displaying all forms of geographically referenced information.

In a more generic sense, GIS applications are tools that allow users to create interactive queries (user created searches), analyze spatial information, edit data, maps, and present the results of all these operations.

GIS software is distinguished into the following categories:

- Desktop GIS are used to create, edit, manage, analyze and display geographic data. They are sometimes classified into three functionality categories: GIS Viewer, GIS Editor and GIS Analyst.
- Spatial database management systems (Spatial DBMS) are used to store the data, but often also provide analysis and data manipulation functionality.
- WebMap Servers are used to distribute maps over the Internet (see also for the Open Geospatial Consortium standards: WFS and WMS).
- Server GIS provide basically the same functionality as desktop GIS but allow to

access this functionality via networks (so-called geoprocessing).

- WebGIS Clients are used for data display and in order to access analysis and query functionality from Server GIS over the internet or intranet. Usually, there is a distinction between Thin and Thick client. Thin clients (e.g. a web browser used to display Google maps) provide only display and query functionality, while Thick clients (e.g. Google Earth or a Desktop GIS) provide often additional tools for data editing, analysis and display.

- Libraries and Extensions provide additional functionality that is not part of the basic GIS software because it may be not needed by the average user. Such additional functions can cover tools for terrain analysis (e.g. SEXTANTE), tools to read specific data formats (e.g. GDAL and OGR), or tools for the cartographic display of geographic data (e.g. PROJ4).

- Mobile GIS are used for data collection in the field.

In terms of e-participation, GIS tools are often used for spatial planning (Carver et al., 2001) where the interconnection of maps with laws, documents, directives and initiatives can be used for the resolution of conflicts and the support of the decision making process.

Podcasts

A podcast is a series of audio or video digital media files which is distributed over the Internet by syndicated download, through Web feeds, to portable media players and personal computers. Although the same content may also be made available by direct download or streaming, a podcast is distinguished from most other digital media formats by its ability to be syndicated, subscribed to, and downloaded automatically when new content is added. Like the term broadcast, podcast can refer either to the series of content itself or to the method by which it is syndicated. The main purpose of podcasting is information provision. High bandwidth is required if the user wishes to download a number of podcasts and a suitable device capable of replaying the content, such as an iPod.

Online Surveys

An eSurvey is very useful when conducted in parallel with the execution of an e-Consultation procedure. eSurveys are usually short series of questions, that call the user to answer using tick boxes or combo boxes, based on material that has been provided by a public authority during consultation on a specific issue. Surveys are commonly implemented in a number of close-ended questions, with ordered response categories, and some open-ended ones.

Argument Visualization Tools

Argument Visualization Tools are software tools that support the construction and visualization of arguments in various representation formats, for instance, graphs or tables. Typically, these tools produce "box and arrow" diagrams in which premises and conclusions are formulated as statements (Braak et al., 2006). These are represented by nodes that can be joined by lines to display inferences. Arrows are used to indicate their direction.

Newsgroups

A newsgroup is a repository usually within an e-Participation system, for messages posted from many users in different locations. The term may be confusing to some people, because it is usually a discussion group. Newsgroups are technically distinct from - but functionally similar to - discussion forums on the World Wide Web. Newsreader software is used to read newsgroups.

Mailing Lists

A mailing list is a collection of names and addresses used by an individual or an organization to send material to multiple recipients. The term is often extended to include the people subscribed to such a list, so the group of subscribers is referred to as "the mailing list", or simply "the list".

Mailing list is simply a list of e-mail addresses of people that are interested in the same subject, who are members of the same work group, or who are taking class together. When a member of the list sends a note to the group's special address, the e-mail is broadcast to all of the members of the list. The key advantage of a mailing list over approaches such as web-based discussion, is that when a new message becomes available, it is immediately delivered to the participants' mailboxes.

Wikis

Wikis are applications in the web that allow user to view content that has been submitted by other users, edit this content, add more content, or comment on it. Wikis are collaborative platforms where users with common interests are cooperating in order to produce the best possible result. For example, Wikipedia is a workspace (collaborative encyclopaedia, in particular) where users work together in order to offer high quality information to the visitors of the web platform and conserve the validity of the particular web page.

The main characteristic of wikis is that they are extremely user friendly work spaces and do not require important IT background to allow users collaborate. In addition, wikis are step by step applications that, based on the cooperation of the users during a continuous and ongoing process, target to achieve the best possible result.

Most wikis offer at least a title search, and sometimes a full-text search. Alternatively, external search engines such as Google, can sometimes be used on wikis in order to obtain more precise results.

Search Engines

Search engines are online applications that assist users to find and retrieve information from the web, relevant to the keywords they have selected and they are interested in. Search engines differ one from another in terms of the searching functions, searching details, range of search and rating of the findings. There are engines that search all over the web for the desired results, such as Google and Yahoo and engines that are search-specific, finding and retrieving information and content from particular repositories or web sites.

Search engines can be divided into dynamic and static. Static engines offer the user the opportunity to search in repositories, databases and content tanks that contain information that are closely related to a specific issue, for example environmental issues discussed over a deliberation procedure. Dynamic engines use user defined keywords, to retrieve and present information gathered from all over the web. This information is continuously updated, keeping users in touch with the latest news on the issue they are interested in.

The results of the search may be documents, pictures, videos, audio, articles, web sites etc and are presented in a structured way, according to the criteria and the algorithm used by the search engine.

eNewsletters

Newsletters are publications about one main topic that are distributed to a targeted group of recipients, mostly used for dissemination and marketing reasons. Electronic newsletters in particular, are distributed via mailing lists or presented through websites and are considered as one of the most effective solutions for informing people that are interested in a particular topic and have declared their interest by registering in an online newsletter delivery application.

Alerts

Alerts are used in complementary with e-Mails and RSS feeds in order to inform citizens and stakeholders about upcoming events or recently received news. Alerts help people to stay up to date, by participating in events that suit their profile and may be of their interest. In addition, alerts allow to people to receive news that enrich their knowledge on a specific topic, by providing to them the latest information and advancements on it.

Frequently Asked Questions

Frequently Asked Questions, or FAQs are listed questions and answers, all supposed to be frequently asked in some context, and pertaining to a particular topic. Depending on usage, the term may refer specifically to a single frequently asked question, or to an assembled list of many questions and their answers.

Concerning e-participation, FAQs aim to render participation of a system's users easier and help them overcome any difficulties they meet, so as to become active participants.

Natural Language Processing Tools

Natural language processing (NLP) is a field of computer science concerned with the interactions between computers and human (natural) languages. Natural language generation systems convert information from computer databases into readable human language. Natural language understanding systems convert samples of human language into more formal representations, that are easier for computer programs to manipulate.

Other Tools

The aforementioned tools tend to be the most popular in terms of support provided to users of e-Participation systems. However, the development of e-Participation systems is based on and uses a wide range of sub-systems and modules that are described below:

- Ontology Management Tools
- Semantic Annotation Tools
- Workflow Management Tools
- Customer Relationship Management Tools
- Content Management Tools
- Web Portals
- Content Analysis Tools
- Process Management Tools
- Web Service Interface
- Office Automation Tools

6. CORRELATION OF RESULTS

In the previous sections, the majority of e-Participation areas as well as the respective tools that are used to enhance e-Participation, have been presented. However, in practice, it is noticed that some tools are more often used for specific e-participation areas, since they have been proved to be more efficient and effective for these areas. Based on such observations, Table 1 indicates and summarizes the correlation between e-participation areas and e-Participation tools. The sign √ shows a strong correlation between an e-Participation tool or a supporting tool and a specific e-Participation area. It should be mentioned that this table has been elaborated by the authors, based on the combination of existing e-Participation practices' review as well as of authors' practical experience and involvement in e-Participation projects.

7. CONCLUSION

Over the past ten years, several communication channels have been developed, offering to citizens improved and increased access to high quality information, appealing to a wide range of audience of all ages and used in everyday basis by

Table 1. Correlations between e-participation areas and tools

		eParticipation Areas												
		Consultation	Deliberation	Polling	Voting	Campaigning	Electioneering	Petitioning	Decision Making	Service Delivery	Spatial Planning	Information Provision	Mediation	Community Building
e-Participation Tools	Chat Rooms						√		√					√
	Blogs	√	√	√		√	√		√		√	√	√	√
	Fora	√	√				√		√		√		√	√
	e-Petitions					√		√			√			
	e-Panels	√												
	e-Voting				√						√			
	e-Polls	√	√	√		√	√		√		√	√	√	√
	e-Communities							√						√
	Decision Making Tools	√		√	√		√		√		√		√	√
	Webcasting	√		√								√		
	e-Consultation Tools	√												
Supporting Tools	GIS	√	√								√	√		
	Podcasts											√		
	Surveys	√		√		√	√					√	√	√
	Argument Visualization	√	√						√			√		
	Newsgroups													
	Mailing Lists													
	Wikis	√							√			√		
	Search Engines											√		
	Newsletters					√	√					√		
	Alerts											√		
	FAQs											√		
	NLP	√	√											
	Online Surgeries	√										√		
	OMS	√	√									√		
	Semantic Annotation	√	√											
	WFMS											√		
	CRM											√		
	CMS											√		
	Web Portals	√	√	√	√	√	√		√		√	√	√	√
	Content Analysis											√		
	Process Management											√		
	Web Service Interface	√	√	√	√	√	√	√	√	√	√	√	√	√
	Office Automation	√	√	√	√	√	√	√	√	√	√	√	√	√

most of the citizens. In addition to information, ICT, give citizens the opportunity to interact with each other, express opinions and participate in communities with common interests. In general, ICT can be a powerful tool that helps to increase social engagement of citizens, thus creating a unique opportunity for achieving high public participation in the decision making process.

The concept of e-Participation is very important for both citizens and decision makers. From the citizen's perspective, e-Participation provides to people the opportunity to achieve and satisfy the need to be heard by politicians and interact with them as well as to participate in the decision making and policy formulation processes. Politicians, on the other side, shall promote and encourage public participation in order to be capable to create communication channels with citizens. Currently, there is a great variety of applied forms and areas of e-Participation. At the same time, there is also a constantly growing variety of tools and technologies that are available in order to enhance e-Participation.

In this respect, the purpose of this paper has been to present a complete overview of the e-Participation landscape, through the state-of-the-art review of these tools, technologies and areas of e-Participation.

This review covers the majority, if not all, the applied forms and areas of e-Participation and respective tools and technologies. Based on this review, useful conclusions have been also drowned up regarding the correlation between e-Participation areas and e-Participation tools.

REFERENCES

Adams, N., Haston, S., Gillespie, N., & Macintosh, A. (2003, September). *Conventional and Electronic Service Delivery Within Public Authorities: The Issues And Lessons From The Private Sector*. Paper presented at the 2nd International Conference on Electronic Government, Prague, Czech Republic.

Adams, N. J., Macintosh, A., & Johnston, J. (2005). e-Petitioning: Enabling Ground-up Participation. In M. Funabashi & A. Grzech (Eds.), *Challenges of Expanding Internet: E-Commerce, E-Business and E-Government*: *Proceedings of the 5th IFIP Conference on e-Commerce, E-Business and E-Government*, Poznan, Poland.

Ahmed, N. (2006). *An overview of e-participation models*. Retrieved February 6, 2010, from http://unpan1.un.org/intradoc/groups/public/documents/UN/UNPAN023622.pdf

Baringhorst, S. (2009). Political Campaigning in Changing Media Cultures – Typological and Historical Approaches. In Baringhorst, S., Kneip, V., & Niesyto, J. (Eds.), *Political Campaigning on the Web*. London: Transaction Publishers.

Beddie, L., Macintosh, L., & Malina, A. (2001). E-democracy and the Scottish Parliament. In Schmid, B., Stanoevska-Slabeva, K., & Tschammer, V. (Eds.), *Towards the e-society: E-commerce, e-business, and e-government* (pp. 695–706). Dordrecht, The Netherlands: IFIP, Kluwer Academic Publishers.

Berman, J., & Mulligan, D. K. (2003). Digital Grass Roots. Issue Advocacy in the Age of the Internet. In Anderson, D. M., & Cornfield, M. (Eds.), *The Civic Web, Online Politics and Democratic Value* (pp. 77–93). Lanham, MD: Rowman & Littlefield.

Beynon-Davies, D., Owens, I., Williams, M. D., & Hill, R. (2003). *Electronic consultation in the national assembly for Wales*. Paper presented at ECIS, Naples, Italy.

Braak, S. W., Oostendorp, H., Prakken, H., & Vreeswijk, G. A. W. (2006, September). *A critical review of argument visualization tools: do users become better reasoners?* Paper presented at the European Conference on Artificial Intelligence, Trento, Italy.

Bruschi, D., Fovino, I. N., & Lanzi, A. (2005). *A Protocol for Anonymous and Accurate E-Polling, Proceedings of E-Government: Towards Electronic Democracy*. Paper presented at the International Conference TCGOV 2005, Bolzano, Italy.

Carver, S. (2001, December). *The Future of Participatory Approaches Using Geographic Information: developing a research agenda for the 21st Century*. Paper presented at ESF-NSF Meeting on Access and Participatory Approaches in Using Geographical Information, Spoleto, Italy.

Coleman, S., & Grøtze, J. (2001). *Online public engagement in policy deliberation*. Edinburgh, UK: Hansard Society and BT.

Dahlberg, L., & Siapera, S. (2006). *Radical Democracy and the Internet: Interrogating Theory and Practice*. New York: Palgrave Macmillan.

Downey, J., & Fenton, N. (2003). New Media, Counter-Publicity and the Public Sphere. *New Media & Society, 5*, 185–202.

Finnimore, S. (2008). *E-Petitions – the Queensland Experience*. Paper presented at the Anzacatt Seminar.

Fraser, J., Adams, N., Macintosh, A., McKay-Hubbard, A., Lobo, T. P., Pardo, P. F., et al. (2003, May). *Knowledge Management Applied to e-Government Services: the Use of an Ontology*. Paper presented at the 4th Working Conference on Knowledge Management in Electronic Government, Rhodes, Greece.

Graber, D. A. (2002). The Internet and Politics. Emerging Perspectives. In Price, M. E., & Nissenbaum, H. F. (Eds.), *Academy and the Internet. Digital Formations* (*Vol. 12*, pp. 90–119). New York: Peter Lang.

Hacker, K. L., & van Dijk, J. (2000). *Digital Democracy: Issues of Theory and Practice*. Thousand Oaks, CA: Sage.

Herring, S., Scheidt, L. A., Bonus, S., & Wright, E. (2004, January). *Bridging the Gap: A Genre Analysis of Weblogs*. Paper presented at the Hawaii International Conference on Systems Science HICSS-37.

Iacopini, G. (2007). *21st Century Democracy: ePetitioning and local government*. London: New Local Government Network (NLGN).

Kampitaki, D., Tambouris, E., & Tarabanis, K. (2008). e-Electioneering: Current Research Trends. In *Electronic Government* (LNCS 5184, pp. 184-194).

Lusoli, W. (2005). The Internet and the European Parliament Elections: Theoretical perspectives, empirical investigations and proposals for research. *Information Polity, 10*(3-4), 153–163.

Macintosh, A. (2004, January). *Characterizing E-Participation in Policy-Making*. Paper presented at the Thirty-Seventh Annual Hawaii International Conference on System Sciences (HICSS-37), Big Island, Hawaii.

Macintosh, A. (2006). e-Participation in Policy-making: the research and the challenges. In P. Cunningham & M. Cunningham (Eds.) E*xploiting the Knowledge Economy: Issues, Applications and Case Studies* (pp. 364-369). Amsterdam, The Netherlands: IOS Press.

Macintosh, A. (2007). E-democracy and e-participation research in Europe. *Integrated Series in Information Systems, 17*, 85–102. doi:10.1007/978-0-387-71611-4_5

Macintosh, A., Coleman, S., & Lalljee, M. (2005). *e-Methods for public engagement*. Bristol, UK: Bristol City Council.

Macintosh, A., & Whyte, A. (2006). Evaluating how e-Participation changes local democracy. In Z. Irani & A. Ghoneim (Eds.), *Proceedings of the e-Government Workshop 2006*. London: Brunel University.

Malina, A., & Macintosh, A. (2002). e-Democracy: Citizen Engagement and Evaluation. In S. Friedrichs, T. Hart, & O. Schmidt (Eds.), *Balanced E-Government: Von der elektronischen Verwaltung zur digitalen Burgergesellschaft*. Gütersloh, Germany: Bertlesmann Foundation.

Masters, Z., Macintosh, A., & Smith, E. (2004, September). *Young People and E-Democracy: Creating a Culture of Participation*. Paper presented at Third International Conference in E-Government, Zaragoza, Spain.

Moreno-Jimenez, J. M., & Polasek, W. (2003). e-Democracy and Knowledge: A Multi-criteria Framework for the New Democratic Era. *Jouranl of Multi-Criteria Decision Analysis, 12*, 163–176. doi:10.1002/mcda.354

Mosca, L., & Santucci, D. (2009). Petitioning online. The Role of e-Petitions in Web Campaining. In Baringhorst, S., Kneip, V., & Niesyto, J. (Eds.), *Political Campaigning on the Web*. London: Transaction Publishers.

OECD. (2001). *Citizens as Partners: Information, Consultation and Public Participation in Policy-Making*. Paris: Author.

OECD. (2003). *Engaging Citizens Online for Better Policy-making*. Paris: Author.

Smith, E., & Macintosh, A. (2007). *Existing E-Participation Practices with Relevance to WEB. DEP*. Retrieved from http://itc.napier.ac.uk/itc/documents/webdep_e-participation_practices.pdf

Smith, E., Macintosh, A., & Whyte, A. (2006, September). *Organized use of e-democracy tools for young people*. Paper presented at Electronic Government: Communications of the Fifth International EGOV Conference, Krakow, Poland.

Tambouris, E. (2008). *Survey of e-Participation Good Practice Cases*. Paper presented at the European e-Participation Workshop, eDem Conference 2008.

Whyte, A., & Macintosh, A. (2002). Analysis and Evaluation of e-Consultations. *e-Service Journal, 2*(1), 9-34.

Whyte, A., & Macintosh, A. (2003, November). *Evaluating EDEN's Impact on Participation in Local e-Government*. Paper presented at the International Conference on Public Participation and Information Technologies.

Whyte, A., Renton, A., & Macintosh, A. (2005). *e-Petitioning in Kingston and Bristol*. Edinburgh, UK: International Teledemocracy Centre, Napier University.

Xenakis, A., & Macintosh, A. (2004a). Major Issues in Electronic Voting in the context of the UK pilots. *Journal of E-Government, 1*(1), 53–74. doi:10.1300/J399v01n01_06

Xenakis, A., & Macintosh, A. (2004b). E-voting: Who controls the e-electoral process? In Cunningham, P., & Cunningham, M. (Eds.), *E-Adoption and the Knowledge Economy, Issues, Applications, Case Studies* (pp. 739–744). Amsterdam, The Netherlands: IOS Press.

Xenakis, A., & Macintosh, A. (2004c, September). *Trust in public administration e-transactions: e-voting in the UK*. Paper presented at DEXA 2004, Zaragoza, Spain.

Xenakis, A., & Macintosh, A. (2004d, September). *Levels of difficulty in introducing e-voting*. Paper presented at the International Conference in E-Government, EGOV 2004, Zaragoza, Spain.

This work was previously published in the International Journal of Electronic Government Research, Volume 7, Issue 1, edited by Vishanth Weerakkody, pp. 1-19, copyright 2011 by IGI Publishing (an imprint of IGI Global).

Chapter 2
Electronic Transformation of Local Government:
An Exploratory Study

Teta Stamati
National and Kapodistrian University of Athens, Greece

Drakoulis Martakos
National and Kapodistrian University of Athens, Greece

ABSTRACT

The paper examines the critical success factors for employees' adoption of the unified Local Government Access Framework (LGAF), deployed for the Central Union of Municipalities and Communities of Greece. Following an extensive bibliographical survey, an initial conceptual framework (CF1) based on the Technology Acceptance Model (TAM) for LGAF adoption is proposed, which is empirically explored within sixteen Local Governments Organizations. The CF1 is revised using the structured-case approach. New concepts discovered during each research cycle revealed that LGAF adoption is a procedure of experiential judgement. The applicability of the TAM is investigated and the model is enhanced, exploring additional variables that affect perceived ease of use, perceived usefulness and actual use. A final complementary CF2 is presented and the evaluation of this model according to the data received from the case studies is discussed.

INTRODUCTION

Local Government Organizations (LGOs) hold a respectful share in contributing to economic growth and wealth of societies (Irani et al., 2005). Beyond the core administrative and democratic activities, health, education and security are among the service branches adding public value and creating the right environment for prosperous economies. The local government structures are believed to be the essence of participatory democracy. It is through local government that

DOI: 10.4018/978-1-4666-2458-0.ch002

citizens come into direct contact with their elected government, as the power flows from national to local government (Koussouris et al., 2008). Thus, LGOs desks are in many countries an active point of transactions between the government and the citizens.

The Greek National Public Administration System is constituted of a large number of LGOs. Particularly, there are more than one thousand LGOs, mostly municipalities that provide a significant number of governmental services to the citizens, visitors, enterprises based within their geographical limits and other governmental bodies. The exact number of services provided by each LGO varies as they have their own operational framework that depends on parameters related to the distinctiveness of each one. Such parameters can be the financial status, the local population composition, region's cultural characteristics, geopolitical and geographical attributes and other organizational and legal parameters that allow or not the LGO to offer some kinds of services (Koussouris et al., 2008). These services can be split in general categories according to their nature and entity they refer to. Some indicative categories refer to payments, applications, registries, records, certificates and licenses.

LGOs' services were, until recently, provided in a conventional way, which meant that no infrastructure had been developed for electronic services and proved the poor level of Information and Communications Technologies (ICT) adoption. The conventional way of services provision demanded the physical presence of the person that applied for the service in the LGO. Thus the interested person went in a LGO to submit both the application and get the outcome of the requested service (Koussouris et al., 2008). The poor level of ICT adoption by the LGOs was the main reason behind the aforementioned situation and did not allow the electronic provision of services.

Given the importance of services offered by LGOs, it is essential, in the modern technological era, for ICTs to provide solutions in order to transform these traditionally offered services into electronic transactions. These can be initiated over the Internet aiming at the facilitation of the citizen's life, who is the eventual 'customer' of any government. LGOs service branches need to keep pace with innovation and technology developments, thus guaranteeing a lasting quality and provision of public services. The great potential of ICTs to contribute to a competitive and wealthy economy needs to be exploited in LGOs activities. Only through investment in ICT research and effective innovation concepts can the local public administration ensure an innovative, knowledge-enabled, and competitive economy.

The recent trend towards local transformational government has emerged mainly by the expressed aspirations of citizens who are placing new demands on local governments regarding the performance and efficiency, proper accountability and public trust, and a renewed focus on delivering better services and results. Thus, LGOs attempt to re-establish their mission critical operations and this has lead to persistent organizational transformations. Given this fact, currently an important number of the European regions, prefectures, and municipalities have constructed their own presence on the web. In Greece, the situation also seems to be changing recently, as many LGOs are attempting to develop their web presence, by implementing projects mainly funded by the 6th Framework Program and the Greek Information Society. These are aiming to achieve the goal of providing better services, creating new conditions for social activation and improving the communication with the citizens. Through their online presence, many Greek LGOs have also started offering various categories of online services as introduced by Moon (2002) regarding information, interaction and transaction. Modern ICTs heavily impact and shape these activities for cooperating and interacting with stakeholders within country and sometimes across borders. ICTs are changing local government structures and organizational processes producing significant business and technical benefits (Heeks, 1999). Electronic projects are becoming increasingly important for the public administration, and LGOs base their decision to move forward with modern e-platforms expecting benefits such as better services, operational savings and increased program effectiveness (Gil-Garcial et al., 2007).

Although LGOs have travailed to embrace ICTs, these individual attempts resulted frequently in isolated, ad-hoc systems, offering only a part of the services, mainly dissemination of information or at best communication in two ways. Up to now Greek local government structures have not been able to live up to expectations, as they are generally characterized by indolence of service delivery and failure to attract users' participation. The problem is mainly attributed to lack of capacity and technical know-how. Some analysts argue that the local government 'mayhem' has to do with the lack of a secure, privacy-aware, interoperable, scalable, and high-administrative unified framework (Karantjias et al., 2010a). Unambiguously, as the connectivity generated by the Internet is opening new opportunities in service delivery, an integrated local government access framework can be a valid solution in providing value-adding services.

This paper reports on the findings of the use of the structured-case approach to investigate the success factors for a massive Greek e-government initiative that affects the users' adoption and diffusion process. The authors were involved in the whole life cycle development process of the project, including design, implementation and system roll out. A total of sixteen case studies were conducted in Greek LGOs in order to investigate the parameters that ensure the smooth use of the Local Government Access Framework (LGAF). The paper also outlines the contribution of the structured-case approach to build e-government theories according to the interpretivist approach (Walsham, 1995; Yin, 2003; Remenyi, 1998; Denzin & Lincoln, 1998; Hussey & Hussey, 1997; Lee & Baskerville, 2003; Myers, 1997; Orlikowski & Baroudi, 1991; Oates, 2006). To this point, the research shows that the structured-case approach

proves the linkage between the data collected and the conclusions drawn, through the process of knowledge and theory building.

MOTIVATION FOR THE STUDY

Although the engineering world appears today more mature than ever in providing stable technology premises in order to build real interoperable and secure systems (Chetty & Coetzee, 2009) for LGOs, enterprise information architects still struggle to define fundamental principles, strategies and policies in designing large-scale, scalable, extensible and high-administrative local government solutions (Karantjias et al., 2010b).

The adoption of the unified LGAF (LGAF project, 2007) in Greek LGOs has many implications for digital innovations. By establishing a LGO-wide standard, adoption of the LGAF creates incentives to invest in electronic content, and potential to link the LGAF with other ICT applications within local government structures. LGAF reshapes access to information by integrating almost two hundred and fifty electronic government services in many different domains of the public administration such as in *health, social care, education, public transportation, cultural,* and other sectors (LGAF project, 2007). Along with these implications, there are also some organizational and technological constraints on the diffusion of LGAF from the perspective of the social shaping of technology. To this point, some studies emphasize that the evolutionary path of the systems is not predetermined by the systems' technological inner logic or economic imperative, but is rather affected by social, organizational, and cultural factors that surround the systems (Fulk, 1993; Fulk, Schmitz, & Steinfield, 1990; Kling, 2000; Williams & Edge, 1996).

The *LGAF* is a Greek/European co-funded initiative project, deployed for the Central Union of Municipalities and Communities of Greece (www.kedke.gr). It aims to bring together the central government, the local government, the private sector, and the society by providing advanced, secure, privacy-aware, interoperable, and high-administrative national electronic services. The motivation of Greek local administration organizations to reduce administrative costs, as well as to enhance the services they offer, has been the main driving force for the development and implemenetation of the LGAF framework as a mission critical broadband e-government infrastructure within Greece. Thus, LGAF facilitates LGOs to revitalize their operations and make local administration more proactive, efficient, transparent and service oriented. To accomplish this transformation, Greek LGOs are planning to intensively use the LGAF in order to introduce innovations in their organizational structures, practices, capacities, and mobilize, deploy and utilize the human capital and information, technological and financial resources for service delivery to their constituents.

Despite the popularity of web based systems in the local public administration, research on the individual-level factors that influence LGOs and employees' acceptance of e-government initiative has rarely been conducted. Most studies on the adoption of Internet-based technologies in local government administration have largely focused on citizens' use rather than LGOs' employees use, even though employees also play a critical role in the diffusion dynamics of e-government systems. For example, individual employees' perceptions of e-government systems and prior experience may promote or discourage willingness to adopt and may facilitate or restrain use and diffusion of such systems.

Furthermore, few empirical studies have attempted to build a theoretical model that explains the factors that influence technology adoption and use. Given that there is an accumulation of a considerable amount of diffusion research in new technologies, it is surprising that few theoretical models have gone beyond profiling users'

characteristics with regard to the adoption of new technologies.

Thus, the goals of this study are twofold: firstly to understand the factors that affect employees' adoption and on going usage of a local government access framework, and secondly to suggest a conceptual model that explains the dynamics of employees and acceptance of the unified framework. An investigation of employees' perception toward an integrated e-government system for LGOs will help provide a rich background and build a theory of e-government system acceptance, and further enlighten the process of technology adoption and use specifically in the context of local government administration.

TECHNOLOGY ACCEPTANCE THEORY

Examining why people accept or reject new technologies has been one of the most challenging issues in the study of information systems (Swanson, 1988). Among the various efforts to understand the process of user acceptance of a new innovation, the Technology Acceptance Model, introduced by Davis (1986), is one of the most well established theoretical frameworks that describes how users accept and use a technology. The model attempts both to explain the key factors of user acceptance of information systems and to predict the importance of the factors in the diffusion of technological systems (Davis et al., 1989). The model is trying to derive the determinants of computer acceptance that is general, capable of explaining user behaviour across a broad range of end-user computing and systems technologies, while is trying to be parsimonious and theoretically justified (Davis et al., 1989).

The TAM is exploring the factors that affect behavioural intention to use information systems and suggests a linkage between the key variables, namely, perceived usefulness and perceived ease of use and users' attitude, behavioural intention, and actual system adoption and use (Davis, 1986). According to TAM, perceived usefulness (PU) and perceived ease of use (PEOU) influence one's attitude towards system usage, which influences one's behavioural intention to use a system, which in turn, determines actual system usage (Davis et al., 1989).

PU is defined as "the degree to which a person believes that using a particular system would enhance his or her job performance" (Davis, 1989), and PEOU as "the degree to which a person believes that using a particular system would be free of effort" (Davis, 1989). PEOU is predicted to influence PU, because the easier a system is to use, the more useful it can be (Davis, 1989). System acceptance will suffer if users do not perceive a system as useful and easy to use (Davis, 1989).

As Figure 1 illustrates, the TAM is a path model that begins with the impact of external factors. These can be system design characteristics, user characteristics, task characteristics, nature of the development or implementation process, political influences, organizational structure, and so on (Ajzen & Fishbein, 1980; Irani et al., 2005). The TAM suggests that information system usage is determined by behavioural intention, which is viewed as being jointly determined by the user's attitude toward using the system and the PU of the system (Davis et al., 1989).

TAM is based on the Theory of Reasoned Action (TRA), according to which beliefs influence intentions, and intentions influence one's actions (Ajzen & Fishbein, 1972). TRA, introduced by Martin Fishbein and Icek Ajzen (1975, 1980), is derived from previous research that started out as the theory of attitude, which led to the study of attitude and behaviour. TRA stresses that individual behaviour is driven by behavioural intentions, where behavioural intentions are a function of an individual's attitude toward the behaviour and subjective norms (Ajzen & Fishbein, 1972). Attitude toward the behaviour is defined as the individual's feelings about performing the behaviour (Ajzen & Fishbein, 1972). It is designated through an evaluation of one's beliefs regarding the consequences arising from a behaviour and an evaluation of the desirability of these consequences (Ajzen & Fishbein, 1972). Thus, overall attitude can be assessed as the sum of the individual consequence multiplied by the desirability assessments, for all expected consequences of the behaviour. Subjective norm is defined as an individual's perception of whether people important to the individual think the behaviour should be performed (Ajzen & Fishbein, 1972). The contribution of the opinion of any given referent is weighted by the motivation that an individual has to comply with the wishes of that referent. Hence, overall subjective norm can be expressed as the sum of the individual perception multiplied by the motivation assessments, for all relevant referents.

Since Davis' (1986) introduction of the TAM, many studies have been conducted using it in a number of systems usages, testing its appropriateness and modifying it in different contexts. Past research on the model has largely focused on personal computer usage or relatively simple software applications (Chau, 1996; Davis, 1993; Davis et al., 1989; Mathieson, 1991). Recently, in

Figure 1. Technology Acceptance Model (TAM)

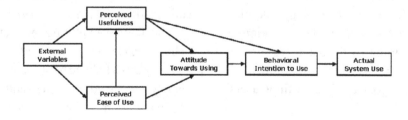

line with the development of web-based technologies, applications of the TAM have been made in the areas of organizational contexts (Hu et al., 1999; Venkatsh, 1999), e-commerce (Jiang et al., 2000) and digital library systems (Davies, 1997).

RESEARCH METHOD AND CASE DESCRIPTION

Although TAM is a well established and documented model for explaining technology acceptance by users, the model has been unable to account comprehensively for the factors that affect users' acceptance of technology systems, due to the original model's intended generality and simplicity. The main TAM's drawback is its lack of explicit inclusion of predecessor variables that influence PEOU and PU (Dishaw & Strong, 1999; Irani et al., 2005). Davis (1989) also claimed that further research should explore other variables that could affect PEOU, PU and actual use. Thus, it is necessary to further investigate the users' acceptance of technology systems with additional constructs considering the specific technology adoption contexts.

One of the most important stages in this research was choosing the appropriate research philosophy, approach and method for the empirical inquiry. The research approach that was followed is an interpretive one (Walsham, 1995; Yin, 2003; Remenyi, 1998; Denzin & Lincoln, 1998; Hussey & Hussey, 1997; Lee & Baskerville, 2003; Myers, 1997; Orlikowski & Baroudi, 1991; Oates, 2006). The research focused on the key issues and challenges that might restrict the adoption of LGAF. In the spirit of the interpretivist school, the approach throughout the study was to understand e-government adoption and to build a new theory, rather than to test established theories. This was achieved by studying a number of existing theories and adoption perspectives as different theoretical lenses through which a complex phenomenon might be viewed.

Considering the aforementioned, the authors adopt a methodological approach based on theory and experience about the adoption process of e-government and proceed to propose an effective holistic model for LGOs e-government that considers technical, human, social, legal and organizational parameters. The research that has been undertaken involves a series of case studies to sixteen LGOs by means of the structured-case research method (Carroll et al., 1998; Carroll & Swatman, 2000), which has been widely used to extend knowledge about the way that government structures evaluate their e-government projects in order to actually use them. The application of the structured-case approach assures scientific rigor that is otherwise inadequate in information systems case study research (Irani et al., 2005).

The structured-case approach provides a focused but flexible methodological approach to the field research process, through the following (Irani et al., 2005).

- Outcomes integration allowing theory, knowledge and practice to emerge from the data collected;
- Researchers guidance to follow and ensure accuracy; and
- Ability to record the processes of knowledge and theory-building.

The structured-case method targets to build theory, which has the form of "a system of interconnected ideas that condense and organise knowledge" (Neuman, 1991). The method attempts to explain, predict and provide understanding (Irani et al., 2005) determining the relationships between concepts in order to build a 'web of meaning' with respect to various issues of users' adoption (Carroll & Swatman, 2000; Irani et al., 2005). The development of conceptual frameworks namely, CF1, CF2. CFn is used to present the process of obtaining knowledge and theory building where CFn is the latest version of the theory built. The theory building process is interrelated with practice (Carroll et al., 1998; Caroll & Swatman, 2000).

Applied research can lead to theory building, which can lead to further field research and theory building (Irani et al., 2005). Thus, each research cycle can lead to changes to the existing CF. As part of the hermeneutic circle each new CF expresses the pre-understanding for the next cycle (Gummerson, 1998) following the natural human action of interpretation and world understanding (Carroll et al., 1998; Irani et al., 2005). Essentially, a spiral towards understanding is enacted as current knowledge and theory foundations for yet another research cycle, which will enhance, revise or evaluate the research understanding. This is particularly appropriate for information systems, as it is an area distinguished by rapid changes, which suggests the need for theory and practice to become closely intertwined (Galliers, 1997). The structured-case will enable theory to be developed that will reflect the concerns, problems and issues facing local government structures (Carroll & Swatman, 2000; Irani et al., 2005).

Conceptual Framework (CF1)

The initial CF1, which is depicted in Figure 2, has been derived from the literature, the practitioners' insights, and the authors' experiences.

As mentioned previously, the limited research undertaken regarding LGOs' employees adoption of e-government systems enforced the authors to use as baseline the TAM in order to develop the initial CF1.

The model integrates constructs from various fields such as information systems, sociology, and public administration. The model is more comprehensive and field specific than the individual theoretical models, and attempts to capture the complex relationships involved in e-government adoption and diffusion. Apart from the main TAM's two constituent, PU and PEOU, as noted in Figure 2, the adoption of e-government in LGOs raises important political, cultural, organizational, technological, human and social issues that must be considered and treated carefully by any LGO contemplating its adoption. The first conceptual model is based on the hypotheses in Table 1.

The theoretical propositions mentioned in the Table 1 are shortly described as follows:

- **Perceived Ease of Use:** Significant field research has taken place the past two decades regarding the effects that the construct PEOU has on both PU and inten-

Figure 2. The Conceptual Framework (CF1) for LGAF adoption

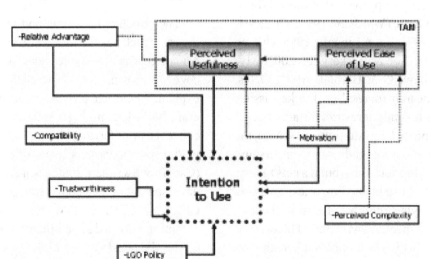

Table 1. Hypotheses

Model Construct	Hypothesis
H1a-Perceived Ease of Use	Higher levels of perceived ease of use will be positively related to higher levels of perceived usefulness of LGAF
H1b-Perceived Ease of Use	Higher levels of perceived ease of use will be positively related to higher levels of intention to use LGAF
H2-Perceived Usefulness	Higher levels of perceived usefulness will be positively related to higher levels of intention to use LGAF
H3a-Perceived Motivation	Higher levels of motivation will be positively related to higher levels of perceived ease of use of LGAF
H3b-Perceived Motivation	Higher levels of motivation will be positively related to higher levels of perceived usefulness of LGAF
H3c-Perceived Motivation	Higher levels of motivation will be positively related to higher levels of intention to use LGAF
H4 - LGO Policy	Higher levels of compliance with LGO's policy will be positively related to higher levels of intention to use LGAF
H5a-Perceived Relative Advantage	Higher levels of perceived relative advantage will be positively related to higher levels of perceived usefulness of LGAF
H5b-Perceived Relative Advantage	Higher levels of perceived relative advantage will be positively related to higher levels of intention to use LGAF
H6-Perceived Compatibility	Higher levels of perceived compatibility will be positively related to higher levels of intention to use LGAF
H7-Perceived Trustworthiness	Higher levels of trustworthiness will be positively related to higher levels of intention to use LGAF
H8-Perceived Complexity	Lower levels of SW complexity will be positively related to higher levels of perceived ease of use of LGAF

tion to use (Davis et al., 1989; Hu et al., 1999; Venkatesh, 1999). Considering this, the authors assume that PEOU will have a positive effect on both PU and behavioral intention to keep using LGAF.

- **Perceived Usefulness:** Considerable theoretical and empirical research work has proved that individual behavioral intention to use an information system is strongly affected by users' PU (Davis et al., 1989; Hu et al., 1999; Jackson et al., 1997; Venkatesh, 1999). The authors consider very likely that high employees' PU will lead them to positive evaluation of the necessity of LGAF.

- **Perceived Motivation:** Additionally to PEOU and PU, potential individual differences in motivation to use a technological innovation were suggested to be one of the most relevant variables in the adoption and use of e-government systems (Hong et al., 2002). Past studies that have investigated the role of motivation in Internet use also confirm that motivation has a positive impact on new technology adoption and diffusion (Stafford & Stern, 2002). Active use of new technology with greater motivation has been found to produce stronger behavioral effects on the use of it (Rubin, 2002).

- **Compliance with LGO's Policy:** Worth mentioned methodological approaches identify the impacts of contextual social factors such as political influences, organizational structure, and social interactions and relationships (Ajzen & Fishbein, 1980; Davis et al., 1989). The authors suggest that LGO's policy can establish communication channels that may either promote employees' adoption and use of the system, or induce resistance from them. However, previous research work highlights that in some cases is hard to impose in a top down manner a technology innovation in an organization (Dutton et al., 2004) and this may lead to a short term use. We should consider employees as the primary users and most critical decision makers about the acceptance and use of a new information system. Whether employees decide to use LGAF from their own will, or due to LGO's policy, this construct can be an important factor in the diffusion process of the e-government system in the local governmental context.

- **Perceived Compatibility:** According to Roger (1995) who introduced the Diffusion of Innovation (DOI) theory, perceived compatibility refers to "the degree to which an innovation is seen to be compatible with existing values, beliefs, experiences, and needs of adopters". Authors consider as an important proposition the fact that higher levels of perceived compatibility are associated with increased intentions to adopt the e-government initiative. Users will be more willing to use online services if these services are congruent with the way they like to interact with others (Carter & Bélanger, 2005).

- **Complexity:** Complexity may be considered to be comparable to TAM's perceived ease of use, and is defined as "the degree to which an innovation is seen by the potential adopter as being relative difficult to use and understand" (Roger, 1995). The initial conceptual approach considers that perceived lower complexity of the proposed e-government system can facilitate indirect users' behavioral intention to keep using the system.

- **Relative Advantage:** In the description of the DOI theory, Roger (1995) defines relative advantage as "the degree to which an innovation is seen as being superior to its predecessor". In addition to PEOU and PU, adopter's perceived relative advantage to use technology systems was found to be one of the most relevant variables in the successful diffusion of information systems (Carter & Bélanger, 2005). Thus, the authors hypothesize that perceived relative advantage can be positively related both to perceived usefulness and intention to use.

- **Trustworthiness:** Perceived trustworthiness is considered as a significant construct in the initial conceptual framework CF1. Trustworthiness can be further divided in two main sub-constructs namely, trust to the initiative and trust to the LGO. Bélanger et al. (2002) define trustworthiness as "the perception of confidence in the electronic marketer's reliability and integrity". Users must have confidence in both the government and the enabling technologies (Carter & Bélanger, 2005). Thus, the hypothesis made by the authors, expresses that higher levels of perceived trustworthiness are positively related to intention to use LGAF. Past studies indicate that trust of the technological innovations is a significant predictor of e-government adoption (Carter & Bélanger, 2005). Considering the perceptions of trustworthiness of the internet technologies, users that perceive the reliability and security of the internet to be low will be less likely to adopt e-government. LGOs' consistency in technological systems can reassure users that e-government is both safe and beneficial. Considering the perceptions of trustworthiness of LGOs, users that perceive the LGO to be more trustworthy will be more likely to adopt e-government (Carter & Bélanger, 2005). Components of trustworthiness identified in previous work on e-commerce, such as integrity and competence (McKnight et al., 2002), can be considered as starting points for LGOs to act on. For instance, LGOs must convey to users that LGOs have both the desire and ability to support e-government information systems designed to meet citizens' needs.

Methodological Approach of the Research Cycle

The first research cycle aimed to validate and further revise the proposed initial conceptual framework CF1. The case studies took place in sixteen LGOs that participated in the project as 'pilots' LGOs. The data collection procedure followed the major prescriptions given by most textbooks in doing fieldwork research (Irani et al., 2005). A variety of secondary data sources, such as internal reports for LGOs operations and requirements and technical reports for standards and specifications, were used to collect data regarding the development of e-government systems,. All in all, a number of data sources, as noted in Figure 3, were used to derive the findings presented herein. These included workshops, interviews, observations, illustrative materials such as newsletters and other publications of the LOGs', and various project documentation. The authors' extensive business experience in

information systems projects, especially for the public sector, along with a predefined interview protocol were used to determine the data needed for the research.

More than seventy in number, regional and national interviews, were conducted with the LGOs Heads, the Chief Technology Officers, the Administrators, the Project Managers, the Consultants, and the general supporting staff at LGO-level. The duration of each interview was approximately forty minutes, and every interview was conducted on a one-to-one basis, so as to stimulate conversation and breakdown any barriers that could otherwise have hindered the knowledge transfer between the interviewer and the interviewee. The authors acted as a neutral medium through which questions and answers were exchanged and therefore endeavoured to eliminate bias. Interviewers' prior extensive experience helped in avoiding any bias in interviews, which mainly occurs when the interviewer tries to adjust the wording of the question to fit the

Figure 3. The process of data collection

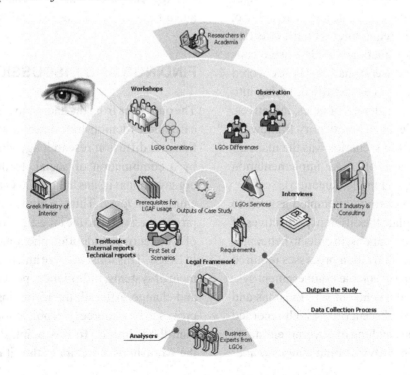

desired answer, or records only selected portions of the respondent's answer. Interviewers did not use follow-up questions in order to elaborate on ambiguous or incomplete answers. In trying to clarify the respondent's answers, the interviewers were really careful not to introduce any ideas that could form part of the respondent's subsequent answer. The interviewers were mindful of the feedback respondents gained from their verbal and non-verbal reactions. As a result, the interviewers avoided giving overt signals, such as smiling and nodding approvingly, when respondents failed to answer a question.

A two-day workshop took place in four different places around Greece with the participation of experts from the LGOs, the Greek Ministry of Interior and the ICT industry. This way, consultants and the academia worked together in collecting all the business and technical information needed. Protocols of procedures were defined beforehand in order to guide the group discussion and to document the LGAF acceptance scenario elements. Based on the workshops and the online consultation inputs, the project consortium and the authors synthesided a set of key factors that LGOs consider as important for the LGAF acceptance and use. Afterwards, a set of requirements for the effective design and implementation of LGAF were consolidated as the first user scenarios. These covered the most important issues identified, taking into account existing inventories, policies, initiatives, and the national legal and regulatory framework in Greece. This set of scenarios was the main input to the next phases of LGAF implementation (analysis, design, and implementation).

The LGAF consortium attempted as well to identify and stimulate the different perpectives of the Greek LGOs' operations, in order to better predict and shape the innovation processes required in the design of an acceptable e-government system. These formed a coherent set of visions and archetypal images of scenarios, which recorded the situation in the handling of government status documents, and identifyied complementary and/or contrasting alternatives and problematic areas. Issues existing between different levels of government (national, regional, and local) were analysed properly, and regional differences that occur due to distinct cultures, diversing local constitutions, and organizational structures were identified.

During this attempt the concept of community of interest was introduced. Organizing e-government services into communities, aimed to reduce the overhead of operating them in small, medium, and big LGOs. Communities are themselves services, created, advertised, discovered, and invoked mostly as web services. In the synthesis of the final scenarios and assessment matrices, each issue that was identified and extracted, was tagged with its origin. Moreover, it gained a topic of interest or a dimension, and it was grouped into a specific category. The gap analysis performed on the conducted categories by adopting accepted methodologies, such as 'Soft Systems Methodology (SSM) (Checkland & Scholes, 1999), 'SWOT analysis' methodology (Harvard Business Press, 2009), and 'ITPOSMO' methodology (Heeks, 1999), allowed us to better identify and validate the differences between the current state of affairs, and a future desired state of LGOs.

FINDINGS AND DISCUSSION

The outcomes from the data analysis of the sixteen case studies demonstrate that e-government adoption and diffusion research agenda is influenced by a combination of social, technological and organizational issues at both LGO and individual employees level. Thus, a multi-disciplinary approach is essential to the investigation and research of e-govenrment adoption phenomeno especially in LGOs. This must involve an effective management of systems, information, policies, processes, and change. Afterall, the technology quite often proves to be a source of problematic issues rather than the solution. To this point, debates during the workshops were about the fit of technology on LGOs' processes and operations rather that developing the right technology.

Some of the variables identified in the CF1 were found to be inter-reliant. The authors followed the classification of e-government terminology described by Irani et al. (2007) and attempted to group the findings as Human and Social Constructs, Organizational Constructs and Technical Constructs, allowing for more specific concepts to emerge within such groupings. In the following paragraphs we use the aforementioned grouping to present our findings –and grounds for future discussions- having as basis the initial proposed framework. Additionally, in the final paragraph a new, revised conseptiual Framework, CF2, is proposed.

Human and Social Constructs of the Conceptual Framework

The construct of compatibility was found to have a significant relationship with use intentions in the context of e-government. During the workshops the participants strongly suggested that LGAF should operate in a manner that "is consistent with individuals' values, beliefs and experiences" and provide information and work support in a manner that is "consistent with what employees are used on within LGO environment". For instance, non-paper forms should be similar to paper forms that employees are familiar with. Compatibility may be achieved by LGOs agreeing to standard interfaces and consistent workflows. Authors enforced employees' involvement in the e-government initiative in order to achieve such standardization. By making interfaces and interactions between the sites similar across LGOs, compatibility was enhanced.

Another significant concern revealed from the data analysis process was the construct of trustworthiness. With respect to perceptions of trustworthiness in technology innovations, employees, who perceived the reliability and security of the internet to be low, presented obstacles in using

LGAF. According to McKnight et al. (2002) in initial relationships, "people use whatever information they have, such as perceptions of a web site, to make trust inferences". Indeed, there was a long debate between participants in the workshops regarding the notion of initial trust to LGAF that refers to "trust in an unfamiliar trustee, a relationship in which the actors do not yet have credible, meaningful information about, or affective bonds with, each other" (McKnight et al., 2002). With respect to the perceptions of trustworthiness in LGOs' mission, employees who perceived Greek government to be trustworthy consider the introduction of LGAF in LGOs as a welcome initiative. The analysis of the data, gathered from interviews, demonstrated that LGO-based trust was mainly associated with an employee's perceptions of the organizational environment, such as the structures, regulations and legislation that make an employee feel safe and trustworthy. Discussions between LGOs representatives revolved around the ensuring privacy through access control mechanisms and work documents security. The decision to engage in e-government transactions required employees to trust the technology through which electronic transactions were to be executed (Lee & Turban, 2001).

Another important construct that authors identified, especially throughout the workshops, was the motivation or the perceived need for working 'over the wire'. In demographic terms, the data analysis revealed that LGAF adopters differed from non-adopters as being younger, ambitious, more educated, and often with higher incomes. Additionally, early LGAF adopters had a more multinational profile with a greater desire to satisfy various communication needs, and were more interested in experimenting with new technologies. This indicated that individual demographic characteristics were also influencing the adoption of e-government services. The cases analysis proved that a group of employees were more likely to keep using LGAF than others. Consequently, we examined two factors namely, the level of prior Internet usage and the employees innovativeness. Individual innovativeness can be defined as 'consumer acceptance' of new ideas (Irani et al., 2005). The findings of the empirical study supported the notion that higher Internet usage led to LGAF adoption. Domain-specific innovativeness, i.e. innovation linked to certain domains rather than as a personality characteristic, was found to influence LGAF adoption.

Finally, there was a group of employees that was persuaded very quickly of the LGAF's significant advantages compared to prior institutional systems. This proved that individual perceived relative advantage enforced the individual intention to use.

Organizational Constructs of the Conceptual Framework

The discussions raised a significant number of organizational issues for local organizational structures. These issues concerned the coordination and ownership between and across LGOs and departments, the political engagement regarding the delivery of technology supported services, the LGO capacity including available resources (human, technical, etc.), change and risk management issues as well as the appropriate legal and legislation framework.

Participants discussed about the nature and mission of LGOs and their relationship with the electronic services provided. There was a clear concern regarding potential future developments and change. As Irani et al (2005) mention in their research agenda "the only constant feature in any e-government-related service is constant change". Clear policies foe LGOs was seen to be critical. Among the key issues, related to the policy-making process, were the following: sense of ownership and the required organisational transformation. There was a main concern about the employees' engagement in the LGOs political processes. There was a long discussion as to how the political processes affect the every day work.

Participants also questioned the fact that local and central government used, up to a point, the e-government agenda as a means to pursue their own political ends. A key concern was about the way to cope with organisational inertia. A particularly important area of risk was identified as the access to e-government services and the associated issue of community inclusion. Learning from e-government experiences in terms of knowledge management and organisational learning was identified as another key theme. Because of the large amount of information at the core of every e-government service, the need for effective and efficient knowledge management arose in one form or another in all of the workshops. Specifically, the issue of transferring knowledge from one context to another was deemed important. Also, in a significant number of interviews and in all the workshops, it emerged that measurement and evaluation techniques were necessary in order to realise the aforementioned learning, organisational and managerial perspectives of e-government. In particular, the need to understand social value, identified within the Human and Social Constructs, was an important prerequisite to establishing appropriate evaluation strategies.

Similarly in order to achieve successful e-government implementations, the necessity of establishing a coherent legitimacy was strongly mentioned. It emerged that the Greek state must carefully consider prerequisites for establishing relationships of trust between government and citizens. The legal aspects must become part of the e-government national roadmap, strategies, and long-term objectives. There was agreement that the legal framework regarding the provision of electronic services 'are still in infancy'. Thus, a cohesive legal framework is definitely required in order to speed the adoption of e-services. During LGAF the main domains of concern identified included the 'Back-Office' re-organization, the inclusive access, the trust and confidence, and the better use of public sector information. Therefore, four main sets of legislation are considered relevant: Personal data protection laws; Privacy and security laws; Information (provision) laws; and Administrative laws in national and international level.

Technical Constructs of the Conceptual Framework

The data retrieving process revealed various issues regarding technical parameters that might affect LGAF adoption and regular use. The general supporting staff in LGOs stressed the need for a framework less complex and more user- friendly regarding i.e. its user interface, the incorporation of forms and templates that employees used previously, etc. The reduction of time it takes to complete a specific work was also considered to be a necessity in the target e-government environment. A worth mentioned percentage of the interviewers and participants in the workshops had a genuine anxiety about the use of innovative technological tools. This attribute was more intense especially with aged employees and the authors decided to call this attribute 'computer anxiety'.

More technical staff of LGOs identified the need for flexible and scalable technology, privacy and security, shared services and common identity management, standards, coordination and integration between LGOs operations and departments, identification and authentication. The notions of scalability and flexibility of e-government systems are often well cited across the literature (Irani et al. 2007). The cases revealed that there is a need to create flexible systems that can adapt and change on demand. The changing nature of e-government also means that accessibility versus information security is an important issue (Irani et al., 2007). There was no definite agreement regarding the issue of what constitutes valid and appropriate access to information within e-government. The issue of how shared operations can be managed was another theme in this area. Multiple facets of this problem were discussed, ranging from purely technical, such as the management of databases,

to organisational such as the implications to LGO's structure. Debates about shared data and appropriate access also demonstrated the issues of privacy and security and identification and authentication. Another technological theme in all LGOs was the issue of interoperability and standardisation. The concerns were revolving around the way that different LGO's departments can be managed, the technical tools needed for integration and the standardisation of certain data and services. The notions of open standards and open source software were also highlighted. In general, interviewees and workshop participants were confused regarding the complexity and the consequences of such developments, and stressed the need for further investigation on their impact. Finally, some important issues were raised regarding the roles and the education needed for working in the new electronic environment.

Conceptual Framework (CF2)

The findings presented in the paragraphs above, resulted in the modification of the initial CF1. The revised framework, CF2, is depicted in Figure 4.

The proposed CF2 is not some kind of magic tool; it can rather be used as the basis for further research. The adoption of LGAF from LGOs is presented as the initial crucial step in the diffusion process in order for LGOs to capture their goals, enable an environment for social and economic growth and contribute to the process of transformation of the Greek local administration towards a leaner and more cost-effective administration. The wide adoption of LGAF facilitates communication and improves the coordination of public authorities at different tiers of government and LGOs up to the departmental level. Further, LGAF enhances the speed and efficiency of operations by streamlining processes, lowering costs, improving research capabilities and improving documentation and record-keeping. The real benefit of LGAF lies not in the use of technological framework per se, but in its application to processes of

Figure 4. The Revised Conceptual Framework (CF2) for LGAF adoption

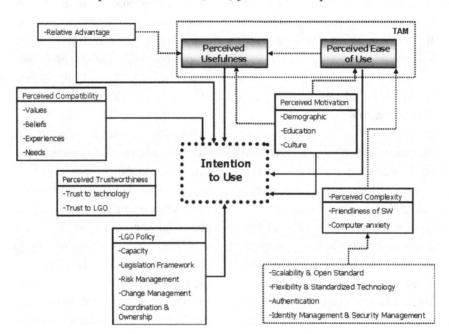

transformation in the Greek bureaucratic public sector.

Both from the perspective of practitioners and from an academic point of view, LGAF represents an essential change in the Greek public sector structure, values, beliefs, culture and the ways of conducting work. In the LGAF initiative, the transformational efforts encompass all the major organizational dimensions including strategy, structure, people, technology and processes as well as the principal external forces such as citizens, suppliers, partners and regulators. As the introduction of LGAF is representing a fundamental change, resistance to change from LGO's employees was anticipated. The main reasons behind resistance to change were the lack of skills to use the new platform; the lack of employees' motivation; employees did not understand the relative advantage of the 'big picture' and the redefinition of the organizational structures and the power distribution. The authors realized that individual employees did not really resist to the change but rather they were resisting to the loss of status, loss of pay, and loss of comfort.

CONCLUSION

Greek government is introducing e-government as a means of reducing costs, improving services and increasing effectiveness and efficiency. Thus, e-government initiatives have been identified as one of the top central government priorities.

The introduction of LGAF results in organizational change, as well as change in the employees' way of work. The employees' acceptance of LGAF raises important political, cultural, organisational, technological and social issues that must be considered carefully by any future e-government initiative in order to achieve a successful acceptance. Beginning with the Greek Local Government case study, findings of the empirical research in sixteen LGOs, demonstrate how an e-government system can be approached and adopted in developing countries, once the identification of advanced practices and conditions for moving towards successful e-government implementations.

Our experience acquired from the LGAF project also accumulate the research findings derived from Intelcities project (Intelcities project, 2004) that brings together twenty European cities and seventy organizations and research groups aiming at pooling advanced knowledge and experience of e-government planning systems and employees and citizen participation from across Europe. The main constructs included in the proposed conceptual model that attempt to analyze the factors that influence Greek LGOs employees' adoption have significant similarities with the factors that affect employees' adoption in local transformational government initiatives in other European countries (Intelcities project, 2004). Specifically, research that took place in local public authorities in European cities, within the scope of the Intelcities project, revealed that almost all the European developing countries are faced with similar issues in the diffusion process of new e-government initiatives as far as the employees' adoption of the new e-government platforms is concerned. Thus, the research undertaken in both projects convince us that core conceptual models such as this presented in the manuscript can explain the dynamics of employees, who most of times behave on a similar way. Thus, both research projects and previous research (Irani & Love, 2001) revealed that LGOs 'e-government failure' is primarily attributable to not meeting organizational expectations that underlines the significance of the human and organisational issues involved in the adoption and diffusion process.

Concluding, the key social, human, organizational and technical issues that affect systems usage and diffusion were investigated. Following an extensive literature review in the field areas of information systems, e-commerce and e-government, a theoretical framework was formulated. The framework was then applied in the case studies to support further data collection and to establish a view of e-government adoption at both LGOs and employees levels. Based on the data collected the initial framework was then revised by using the structured-case approach. As a result, a new conceptual framework which consists of additional concepts and details about the key adoption factors was developed. The framework can be used as a tool to determine the roadmap for adoption of an e-government initiative.

REFERENCES

Ajzen, I., & Fishbein, M. (1972). Attitudes and normative beliefs as factors influencing intentions'. *Journal of Personality and Social Psychology*, *21*, 1–9. doi:10.1037/h0031930

Ajzen, I., & Fishbein, M. (1980). *Understanding Attitudes and Predicting Social Behavior*. Englewood Cliffs, NJ: Prentice Hall.

Bélanger, F., Hiller, J., & Smith, W. (2002). Trustworthiness in electronic commerce: the role of privacy, security, and site attributes. *The Journal of Strategic Information Systems*, *11*, 245–270. doi:10.1016/S0963-8687(02)00018-5

Carroll, J., Dawson, L. L., & Swatman, P. A. (1998). Using Case Studies to Build Theory: Structure and Rigour. In *Proceedings of the 9th Australasian Conference on Information Systems*, Sydney, NSW, Australia.

Carroll, J., & Swatman, P. (2000). Structured-case: a methodological framework for building theory in information systems research. *European Journal of Information Systems*, *9*, 235–242. doi:10.1057/palgrave/ejis/3000374

Carter, L., & Bélanger, F. (2005). The utilization of e-government services: citizen trust, innovation and acceptance factors. *Information Systems Journal*, *15*, 5–25. doi:10.1111/j.1365-2575.2005.00183.x

Chau, P. Y. K. (1996). An empirical assessment of a modified technology acceptance model. *Journal of Management Information Systems*, *13*(2), 185–204.

Checkland, P., & Scholes, J. (1999). *Soft Systems Methodology in Action*. West Sussex, UK: John Wiley & Sons.

Chetty, J., & Coetzee, M. (2009). *Considering Contracts for Governance in Service-Oriented Architectures. Information and Computer Security Architecture (ICSA)*. Retrieved from http://icsa. cs.up.ac.za/issa/2008/Proceedings/Research/6. pdf

Citrin, A. V., Sprott, D. E., Sliverman, S. N., & Stem, D. E. Jr. (2000). Adoption of Internet Shopping: the role of consumer innovativeness. *Industrial Management & Data Systems, 100*(7), 29–300. doi:10.1108/02635570010304806

Davies, C. (1997). Organizational influences on the university electronic library. *Information Processing & Management, 33*(3), 377–392. doi:10.1016/S0306-4573(96)00070-2

Davis, F. D. (1986). *A Technology Acceptance Model for Empirically Testing New End-User Information Systems: Theory and Results*. Unpublished doctoral dissertation, Massachusetts Institute of Technology.

Davis, F. D. (1989). Perceived usefulness, perceived ease of use and user acceptance of information technology. *Management Information Systems Quarterly, 13*, 319–340. doi:10.2307/249008

Davis, F. D. (1993). User acceptance of information technology: System characteristics, user perceptions, and behavior impacts. *International Journal of Man-Machine Studies, 39*, 475–487. doi:10.1006/imms.1993.1022

Davis, F. D., Bagozzi, R. P., & Warshaw, P. R. (1989). User acceptance of computer technology: A comparison of two theoretical models. *Management Science, 35*(8), 982–1003. doi:10.1287/mnsc.35.8.982

Denzin, N. K., & Lincoln, Y. S. (1998). *Collecting and interpreting qualitative materials*. Thousand Oaks, CA: Sage.

Dishaw, M. T., & Strong, D. M. (1999). Extending the technology acceptance model with task-technology fit constructs. *Information & Management, 36*(1), 9–21. doi:10.1016/S0378-7206(98)00101-3

Dutton, W. H., Cheong, P. H., & Park, N. (2004). An ecology of constraints on e-learning in higher education: The case of virtual learning environment. *Prometheus, 22*(2), 131–149. doi:10.1080/0810902042000218337

Fishbein, M., & Ajzen, I. (1975). *Belief, attitude, intention, and behavior: An introduction to theory and research*. Reading, MA: Addison-Wesley.

Fulk, J. (1993). Social construction of communication technology. *Academy of Management Journal, 36*, 921–950. doi:10.2307/256641

Fulk, J., Schmitz, J., & Steinfield, C. W. (1990). A social influence model of technology use. In Fulk, J., & Steinfield, C. W. (Eds.), *Organizations and Communication Technology*. Newbury Park, CA: Sage.

Galliers, R. D. (1997). Reflection on Information Systems: Twelve Points to Debate. In Mingers, J., & Stowell, F. (Eds.), *Information Systems: An Emerging Discipline*. Berkshire, UK: McGraw-Hill.

Gil-Garcia, J. R., Chengalur-Smith, I., & Duchessi, P. (2007). Collaborative e-Government; impediments and benefits of information-sharing projects in the publc sector. *European Journal of Information Systems, 16*, 121–133. doi:10.1057/palgrave.ejis.3000673

Gummerson, E. (1998). *Qualitative Methods in Management Research*. Newbury Park, CA: Sage.

Harvard Business Press. (2009). *SWOT Analysis II: Looking Inside for Strengths and Weaknesses*. Boston: Author.

Heeks, R. (1999). *Reinventing Government in the Information Age*. New York: Routledge. doi:10.4324/9780203204962

Hong, W., Thong, J. Y. L., Wong, W.-M., & Tam, K.-Y. (2002). Determinants of user acceptance of digital libraries: An empirical examination of individual differences and system characteristics. *Journal of Management Information Systems, 18*(3), 97–124.

Hu, P. J., Chau, P. Y. K., Sheng, O. R. L., & Tam, K. Y. (1999). Examining the technology acceptance model using physician acceptance of telemedicine technology. *Journal of Management Information Systems, 16*, 91–112.

Hussey, J., & Hussey, R. (1997). *Business research: a practical guide for undergraduate and postgraduate students*. Basingstoke, UK: Macmillan Business.

Intelcities project. (2004). *Intelligent Cities, 6th Framework Programme*. Retrieved from http://intelcities.iti.gr/intelcities

Irani, Z., Elliman, T., & Jackson, P. (2007). Electronic Transformation of government in the U.K.: a research agenda. *European Journal of Information Systems, 16*, 327–335. doi:10.1057/palgrave.ejis.3000698

Irani, Z., & Love, P. E. D. (2001). The Propagation of Technology Management Taxonomies for Evaluating Investments in Manufacturing Resource Planning (MRPII). *Journal of Management Information Systems, 17*(3), 161–177.

Irani, Z., Love, P. E. D., Elliman, T., Jones, S., & Themistocleous, M. (2005). Evaluationg e-government: learning from the experiences of two UK local authorities. *Information Systems Journal, 15*, 61–82. doi:10.1111/j.1365-2575.2005.00186.x

Jackson, C. M., Chow, S., & Leitch, R. A. (1997). Toward an understanding of the behavioural intentions to use an information system. *Decision Sciences, 28*, 357–389. doi:10.1111/j.1540-5915.1997.tb01315.x

Jiang, J. J., Hsu, M., & Klein, G. (2000). E-commerce user behavior model: An empirical study. *Human Systems Management, 19*, 265–276.

Karantjias, A., Polemi, N., Stamati, T., & Martakos, D. (2010a). Advanced e-Government enterprise Strategies & Solutions. *International Journal of Electronic Governance.*

Karantjias, A., Polemi, N., Stamati, T., & Martakos, D. (2010b). *A user-centric & federated Single-Sign-On IAM system for SOA e/m-frameworks*. International Journal of Electronic Government. doi:10.1504/EG.2010.033589

Kling, R. (2000). Learning about information technologies and social change: The contribution of social informatics. *The Information Society, 16*(3), 217–232. doi:10.1080/01972240050133661

Koussouris, S., Tsitsanis, A., Gionis, G., & Psarras, J. (2008). Designing Generic Municipal Services Process Models towards eGovernment Interoperability Infrastructures. *Electronic Journal for E-Commerce Tools and Applications*. Retrieved from http://www.ejeta.org/specialMay08-issue.php

Lee, A., & Baskerville, R. (2003). Generalizing in information systems research. *Information Systems Research, 14*(3), 221–243. doi:10.1287/isre.14.3.221.16560

Lee, M., & Turban, E. (2001). A trust model for internet shopping. *International Journal of Electronic Commerce, 6*, 75–91.

LGAF project. (2007). *Local Government Access Framework*. Retrieved from http://wiki.kedke.org/wiki/

Mathieson, K. (1991). Predicting user intentions: Comparing the technology acceptance model with the theory of planned behavior. *Information Systems Research, 2*, 173–191. doi:10.1287/isre.2.3.173

McKnight, H., Choudhury, V., & Kacmar, C. (2002). Developing and validating trust measures for e-commerce: an integrative typology. *Information Systems Research, 13*, 334–359. doi:10.1287/isre.13.3.334.81

Myers, M. D. (1997). Qualitative research in information systems. *Management Information Systems Quarterly, 21*(2), 241–242. doi:10.2307/249422

Neuman, W. L. (1991). *Social Research Methods: Qualitative and Quantitative Approaches.* Boston: Allyn and Bacon.

Oates, B. J. (2006). *Researching information systems and computing.* Thousand Oaks, CA: Sage.

Orlikowksi, W. J., & Baroudi, J. (1991). Studying information technology in organizations: research approaches and assumptions. *Information Systems Research, 2*(1), 1–28. doi:10.1287/isre.2.1.1

Remenyi, D. (1998). *Doing research in business and management: an introduction to process and method.* Thousand Oaks, CA: Sage.

Rogers, E. M. (1995). *Diffusion of Innovations* (4th ed.). New York: Free Press.

Rubin, A. M. (2002). The uses-and-gratifications perspective of media effects. In *Media Effects: Advances in Theory and Research* (2nd ed.). Mahwah, NJ: Lawrence Erlbaum Associates.

Shaughnessy, J. J., & Zechmeister, E. B. (1994). *Research Methods in Psychology* (3rd ed.). New York: McGraw Hill.

Stafford, M. R., & Stern, B. (2002). Consumer bidding behavior on Internet auction sites. *International Journal of Electronic Commerce, 7*(1), 135–150.

Swanson, E. B. (1988). *Information System Implementation: Bridging the Gap Between Design and Utilization.* Homewood, IL: Irwin.

Venkatesh, V. (1999). Creation of favourable user perceptions: Exploring the role of intrinsic motivation. *Management Information Systems Quarterly, 23*(2), 239–260. doi:10.2307/249753

Walsham, G. (1995). The emergence of interpretivism in IS research. *Information Systems Research, 6*(4), 376–394. doi:10.1287/isre.6.4.376

Williams, R., & Edge, D. (1996). The social shaping of technology. In *Information and Communication Technologies: Visions and Realities.* New York: Oxford University Press.

Yin, R. K. (2003). *Case study research: design and methods* (3rd ed.). Thousand Oaks, CA: Sage.

This work was previously published in the International Journal of Electronic Government Research, Volume 7, Issue 1, edited by Vishanth Weerakkody, pp. 20-37, copyright 2011 by IGI Publishing (an imprint of IGI Global).

Chapter 3
City E-Government:
Scope and its Realization

Hanuv Mann
Carleton University, Canada

Gerald Grant
Carleton University, Canada

Inder Jit Singh Mann
Carleton University, Canada

ABSTRACT

In this paper, the authors identify and explore the optimal scope of a generic city-level e-Government program. In order to corroborate theoretical research, a comprehensive feature comparison of different e-Government elements/services, of select city web sites from various countries in the world is conducted. The research finds that despite the manifest common features, the inherent scope of service provision by the websites studied is unique. This finding gives rise to the understanding that customizing e-Government initiatives is ideally conducive to the local needs of the constituents.

INTRODUCTION

The allure of "transformation", of making the city government agile, efficient, responsive, and of "potential" cost savings, may seem "irresistible" to a new city government that is committed to change the traditional bureaucratic ways of working as well as to reduce taxation. This trend for electronic government (e-Government) is growing, and 189 countries were online in 2008, as compared to 179 countries in 2005 (United

Nations, 2008). E-government is being increasingly viewed as a vastly available, increasingly acceptable and generally integral aspect of modern government, with potential to enhance efficiency and effectiveness, reduce costs and even transform the government "affecting the management of human, technological, and organizational resources and processes" (Grant & Chau, 2005, p. 1). As far back as in 2001, in an e-Government conference, "New York City's then-mayor, Rudolph Giuliani, presented his city's goals to reduce costs, eliminate

DOI: 10.4018/978-1-4666-2458-0.ch003

bureaucracy and become more open, responsive and accountable" (Ballmer, 2002). Also, it seems that the trend has now shifted from focusing on the "technical issue" of providing a Web site, to having an integrated e-Government solution. The leading consultants' international firm Accenture, in its sixth annual global report of 2005, "Leadership in Customer Service: New Expectations, New Experiences," states that "A look at e-Government programs across the globe shows that continued incremental improvements in this area are unlikely to yield significant boosts to maturity. To advance now, governments must focus on a much broader vision" (Accenture, 2005, p. 1). Such a possibly predicted shift indicates the future provision of customer service to citizens through multiple channels. It is also suggested "that genuine cost savings and quality improvements will occur only if there is a re-engineering of the internal structures and processes of the administration towards a connected form of governance" (United Nations, 2008). These trends are increasingly indicative of the fact that this is the ideal time to rework the basics to bring about the expected efficiency near-future demands will necessitate. We find this as an adequate motivation to study one of the very basic aspects of a city e-government: the scope of a city e-government.

In this paper we attempt to broadly outline the scope of city e-government, essentially to find the area within which the city e-Government is expected to operate. In the absence of any landmark study on the subject it is interesting to look at the scope *ab initio*. After considering the basic paradigms, we look at some studies which have researched the features of city e-Government Web sites and have set up benchmarks grounded in prevailing theory for the same. Then, we study at the city e-Government Web sites of select major cities across the globe and try to ascertain the area within which these e-governments are practically operating at the present. This gives the study checkpoints for the scope that has been actually realized, or achieved in practice, by these city e-governments.

SYNTHESIS OF LITERATURE

E-Government has been defined in various ways, one of the common definitions being: the use of the Internet to deliver services and information to citizens and businesses (Ho & Ni, 2004; Holden, Norris & Fletcher, 2003; Reddick, 2004a). Arguably, this definition needs to encompass other users, other government levels, and also the government employees. A number of studies have looked into the functioning of e-Government at local levels in the U.S. (West, 2001; Kaylor et al., 2001; Edmiston, 2002; Holden, Norris & Fletcher, 2003; Reddick, 2004a; Ho, 2002; Reddick, 2004b; Moon, 2002), in Canada (Charih & Robert, 2004; Kernaghan, 2005; Reddick, 2007), in European Union and in other countries (Torres et al., 2005; Criado & Ramilo, 2003; Archer, 2005). While many studies have focused on the evaluation of features of the city e-Government Web sites, their navigability and content standards; benchmarking studies based on optimal set of functions are relatively less (Stowers, 1999; Johnson & Misic, 1999; West, 2000; Spearman, Welch & Associates, 2000; Norris, Fletcher & Holden, 2001; Kaylor et al., 2001). However, features and functions on a Web site are the manifestations of the extent of the scope of e-Government that has been realized, or achieved, in practice. The realized extent of the scope may actually be only a fraction of the full scope of city e-government. In the public sector, scope is of critical importance, as its lays down a boundary, beyond which any use of public monies or government budget may neither be advisable, nor legally possible. We have not been able to find any literature dealing with the scope of local e-Government in this context; therefore, we start our study from basics.

Defining Scope

For the purpose of this paper we define scope of e-Government as the extent, range or area in which it can act or operate; or has power to control in order to attain its objectives. In this paper we would like to view the "scope" in its twin aspects. Firstly, in its "limiting" aspect, beyond which the city e-Government is constrained to operate, "scope" serves a useful function of clearly defining the main area of operation, or even the "*raison d'etre*" of the e-government. In its second, the "enabling" aspect, "scope" identifies the boundaries, beyond which the city e-Government may "span" to add value, thereby providing its users and/or citizens with an empowering, integrated and seamless e-Government experience.

Implications of Scope

Ab-initio demarcation of the scope of the city e-Government initiative is critical in two ways. Keeping the scope too narrow initially, would lead to a potential waste of an exciting opportunity. On the other hand, focusing on a scope which is too wide to handle, may lead to increased expectations, which may be hard to meet with limited resources. Because of the opening of an additional channel of communication, and possibly because of its 24/7 availability, and its ease of use; a city e-Government initiative may lead to a change in the pattern and/or volume of citizen initiated contacts (CICs) and requests for action (Horrigan, 2004, cited in Reddick, 2007). Whether an increase in CICs, or a lack of increase, is significant is still a subject of debate. Increased CICs maybe the result of enhanced participation of citizens (Thomas & Streib, 2003). This increased participation maybe viewed as benefiting democracy, with increase in service delivery and citizens' confidence in government (Green, 1982); or even as an indicator of functioning of e-Government (Reddick, 2007). Once a new channel becomes available for providing services, increased CICs may arise from awareness about availability of these services and perceived needs for them (Vedlitz, Dyer & Durand, 1980; Hirlinger, 1992; Thomas & Melkers, 1999). These perceived needs maybe for a specific service or its modification (Thomas

& Melkers, 2000; Thomas & Streib, 2003). On the other hand, some researchers argue that CICs may actually decrease because of the clogging of bureaucratic machinery with increased workload (Serra, 1995); while still others argue that CICs will increase because of unhappiness of citizens on any delay in response to requests for action (Moon, Serra, & West, 1993; Thomas & Welkers, 2000).

Since the responsiveness of the city bureaucracy is important for the provision of services, for democracy and for political participation, it is critical to understand the interplay between the scope of e-Government and CIC, and the satisfaction and/or the frustration that unmet needs and expectations can generate. Trying to outline and handle a wider scope than what the city is geared to handle within its limited resources, may lead to an undesirable and maybe unexpected increase in dissatisfaction among the users resulting in negative consequences. Thus understanding scope clearly, in advance, may help in accurate forecasting of the change in workload of city employees that may arise from enhanced service expectations of the citizens because of introduction of the new channel of e-Government. Such a forecast then can be used to suitably mobilize and/or enhance the city resources to cater to increased and/or changing demand for information and service.

Ascertaining the Scope

Issues of Jurisdiction

In a democratic setup, the citizens come together to form a government and generally define its role through a constitution, legislations, acts and subsidiary rules and regulations, which define the area, or scope, within which the government operates. Any action outside this defined area, or scope, is held as *ultra-vires*. In a top down or a totalitarian type of government, the legal jurisdictions and functions are assigned from the top down and thereby these jurisdictions form a boundary for city government, within which it operates. In between these two extremes there exist a number of models of city government jurisdiction.

Scope of e-Government is legally delimited by the legal jurisdiction of the government. Ideally the e-Government solution should integrate the functions of all the levels of government, i.e. the city, state and federal. In this paper we call such a seamless solution an "integrated e-Government solution". The overlap of jurisdictions and the position of the integrated e-Government solution across the jurisdictions, and even outside the jurisdictions, is depicted in Figure 1.

Here it is seen that area covered by an ideal integrated e-Government solution can be quite large; it covers individual jurisdictions of the city, state and federal governments; also, it covers the areas of their overlapping jurisdictions; though not completely. Thus, there may be specific areas, which are not amenable to an optimal e-Government solution, and these specific areas may be more amenable to the traditional ways of governance, and therefore may lie outside the scope of an integrated e-Government solution. Some areas covered by the integrated e-Government solution ellipse can be seen spanning the strict boundaries of legal jurisdiction. These areas may be interpreted as covering the additional services provided by the e-governments in a commercial domain, and/or covering the seamless services provided by the e-Government to the users in collaboration with private players, for example a page with city tourist information may provide seamless links to the reservation portal serving the hotels in the city.

Realization of Scope: Practical Limitations

However, when we try to operationalize this schematic, the scope of an e-Government solution project is further constrained by the shifting

Figure 1. Scope of integrated e-government solution and legal jurisdiction boundaries of federal, state and city governments (Source: Adapted from Mann et al., 2008)

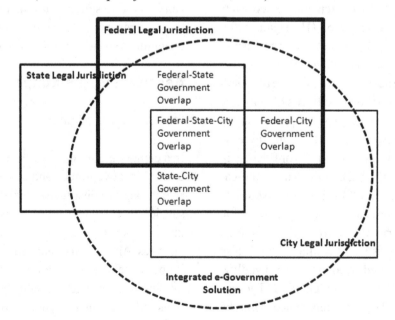

boundaries formed by practical limitations. Some of the practical limitations maybe imposed by vision, strategy, technology and budget at the time of implementation. After first implementation, the legacy systems may, in turn, also have a role to play in imposing practical limitations. When we consider of the theoretically possible extent of integrated e-Government solution as depicted in Figure 1, we find that external environment and other factors impose practical limitations on it, as shown in Figure 2, which in effect make the actual city e-Government project much smaller than the optimal solution.

External environment may have a substantial effect, limiting the scope of integrated city e-Government solutions, as changing political and economic scenarios may force the setting of priorities other than launching of e-Government initiatives. For example, a general meltdown of the dot-com industry may have caused hesitancy among many municipal governments while allocating substantial money to e-Government projects in the ensuing years (Roy, 2003). The scope is, evidently, limited by the vision of the city government, as one can generally achieve only what one can envision. Creation of an effec-

tive and efficient strategy and its implementation is the next limitation; which in turn has to be supported by the available technology. Budget is the next limitation in realization of the full city e-Government scope because not all technology that is available on a given date maybe affordable or cost effective. This is evidenced by a recent survey, which reported that 55% of surveyed municipal (city) governments in Ontario, Canada, planned a budget of CAD $10,000 or less in a fiscal year for e-government; and only 21% budgeted more than CAD $100,000 (Reddick, 2007). One cannot hope to achieve much in less than $1000 per month, even in terms of stand-alone systems, let alone the supporting manpower. Even the budget, once allocated, has to be expended wisely.

Value Creation Process

Once the city e-Government project is budgeted and the implementation phase is rolled out, the scope is affected by the intermediate processes. In any technology project the results may turn out to be different from what is planned initially (Ciborra, 1997). While results in some areas maybe

Figure 2. What limits the scope of e-government: some of the external factors (Source: Adapted from Mann et al., 2008)

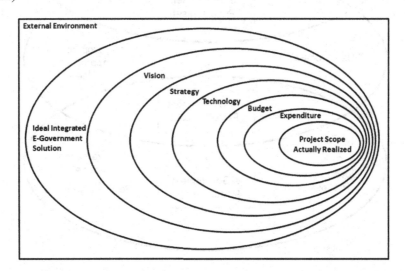

sub-optimal, in the other areas they may surprise even the most optimist proponents of the project. Despite its unpredictable elements, the attainment of the full scope of city e-Government project resulting in a positive e-Government performance, is a goal worth striving for. Thus value creation, in an information technology (IT) project, like e-government, is not a simple process (Ackoff, 1967; Delone, & McLean, 1992; Barua, Kriebel, & Mukhopadhyay, 1995; Hitt & Brynjolfsson, 1996; Delone & McLean, 2003; Melville, Kraemer, & Gurbaxani, 2004). Adapting the model described by Soh & Markus (1995). The multi-step process of value creation in a city e-Government Project is depicted in Figure 3, showing the relationship between the expenditure on e-Government

project (see Figure 1) and creation of value as e-Government performance.

From a city e-Government investment perspective, the value creation process starts from city e-Government investment in IT; which in turn goes through the IT conversion process; which though proper IT management and conversion activities results in city e-Government project assets. Contrary to the seemingly popular belief, the assets themselves do not translate into city e-Government performance (Soh & Markus, 1995). The next step is "IT use process", where the process can succeed or fail, by appropriate or inappropriate use of the e-Government assets. An "appropriate-use process" is likely to lead to positive city e-Government project "impacts". In the next step these "impacts" may lead to city

Figure 3. How e-government project creates value: a process theory (Source: Adapted from Soh & Markus, 1995)

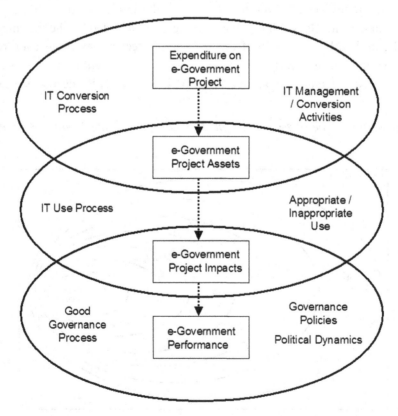

e-Government "performance" through good governance processes that are supported by good governance policies and actual political dynamics, which involves the participation of citizens and other users of city e-government. As is evident, the value creation in city e-Government is a complex process, and depends on many critical intervening processes. Failure to understand the complex process may lead to unrealistic expectations and/or inadequate focus on critical intervening processes. This can result in the potential scope of the initiative not being realized and failure to achieve the desired city e-Government performance end results.

Leadership

Despite the challenges in realization of scope, outstanding leadership may have a substantial influence on any city e-Government initiative (Ho & Ni, 2003) and thereby on its scope. This effect maybe more critical at the time of initial phase and at the implementation of a city e-Government initiative. The influence may start from the stage of creating a long-term and all-encompassing vision; devising and putting into action an effective and efficient strategy and setting up a dynamic independent team or department to implement the same, which is important (Reddick, 2007); effectively harnessing the available technology; being successful in getting adequate budget allocated, again a critical "*sine qua non*" (Reddick, 2007); and ensuring appropriate expenditure on the project. In value creation process (Soh & Markus, 1995) strong leadership may positively catalyze information technology (IT) conversion process, lead the "appropriate use process", ensure implementation of good governance policies and play a crucial role in political dynamic process leading to superior city e-Government performance. Thus a strong leadership may play a critical role in successful realization of scope of city e-Government initiative (Ho & Ni, 2003).

Fuzzy Boundaries Of Scope: Integrated City E-Government and the Governance Junction

When envisaging an integrated e-Government initiative across different levels of government; i.e. the city, state and federal levels; the scope of the city e-Government solution can have fuzzy boundaries. This can translate into a complex integrated structure, forming a "governance junction" at the web-portal, which to an user may look like a simple web-page (Mann et al., 2008). This "governance junction" is a complex integration of functions that needs efficient and effective coordination between different levels of governments, appropriate management of website and functional support at various levels of governance. In addition to the existing governance structures, a suitably empowered coordination cell comprising of members from all concerned government levels, departments and IT experts is a highly useful unit in managing the day to day operations of such a "governance junction". Here, clearly demarcating the roles and responsibilities between the domain experts (belonging to different government levels) and the IT professionals can smoothen the implementation and operation of the "governance junction" functionalities. This can become an effective tool to handle the fuzzy boundaries of scope of the city e-Government.

METHODOLOGY

A Search for Functional Areas in City e-Government

To scope out a new project or an expansion project on city e-government, it would be beneficial to look at the functional areas being covered by comparative city e-governments at other places. This would enable us to understand what scope has been actually realized in practice, by the respective city e-Government initiatives.

In their proposed taxonomy of services/functions offerings by e-governments, Charalabidis et al. (2006) do not incorporate the level, maturity or sophistication of services provided. They, however, provide a basic classification or taxonomy, which can be a good basis when a city wishes to start the e-Government initiative *ab-initio*. The authors discuss the European Union's eEurope+ initiative, which lays down a short-list of "20 Basic Public Services" (Charalabidis et al., 2006, p. 197). The list specifies the service, service-orientation, providing administration, cluster and target level. In listing the 'Basic Public Services', the 'Target Sophistication Level' is based on the work of Layne and Lee (2001), which has been adopted by the European Commission (2002). Briefly, Layne and Lee (2001) describe the stages of sophistication as follows:

Level 1: Information only/static content: This includes contact information.

Level 2: One-way Interaction/dynamic content: Frequent updates, links to other pages, downloadable documents.

Level 3: Two-way Interaction: Submission of request form, a maximum target level for a service where personal presence is required.

Level 4: Full Case Handling.

Torres et al. (2005) analyze the municipal e-Government Web sites measuring two different variables: service maturity (SM) and delivery maturity (DM). Service maturity is handled in two dimensions: SM breadth, i.e. number of services offered; and SM depth, i.e. level of interactivity (whether it is possible to "publish", "interact" and/or "transact"). On the other hand, DM deals with the aspects covering 'sophistication' of Web sites to provide benefits to users, viz. error identification feature, search engine, Web site map, use-promotion, availability of email addresses, public events, online access to plenary sessions, online application filling simplicity, multi-lingual access, user-friendly street map, level of comprehensiveness, seamless navigation, e-democracy features etc.

Kaylor et al. (2001) create a rubric for benchmarking the city e-governments in the United States of America (US) using 51 different functional dimensions, under 12 classes. The authors do not evaluate the aesthetics or ease of use, organization or navigability of the e-Government Web sites. However, if the authors do not find a feature in their search, they do not give points for it. By this method itself, the "ease of use", "organization" and "navigability" may have impacted the study. The authors assign an "e-score" to the Web sites on the basis of following rubric used by Kaylor et al. (2001, p. 306):

1. Information about a given topic exists at the Web site.
2. Link to relevant contact with a phone number or email address exists at the Web site.
3. Downloadable forms available online on a given topic.
4. Transactions or other interaction can take place completely online."

West (2001) studies the features available on city e-Government Web sites in the US to find how urban e-Government can be improved. After studying 1056 Web sites in the largest 70 metropolitan areas of the US, the author lists top ten online services as: payment of parking tickets or traffic violations, filing of complaints, service request, permit application, job applications, request for documents, payment of utility bills, requests for police documents, payment of taxes and reporting of crimes; in the above mentioned order. The author also finds differences, (on the basis of which 25 short-listed features are offered), between the Web sites of city's executive branch, the legislative branch and its portal site.

The realized scope of the city e-Government can be assessed from the functions, features and services available on its Web site. For example,

Reddick (2007) found in his survey that the state of Ontario lags behind in its city e-Government initiatives. As reported, only about 12% of the surveyed municipal governments provided online tax payments as an option; 20% offered option for online registration of recreational facilities; and 68% offered electronic form downloads for manual completion and submission; also implying that the services available on e-Government Web sites are not uniform even within one state. In practice, the features available on a city's e-Government Web site may vary substantially. This is especially so when the Web site is designed, based on the differences in, and the varying perceptions of, the local needs. Therefore, to arrive at a framework to study the "realized scope", we mapped the taxonomy given by Charalabidis et al. (2006); and the features listed in the papers of Torres et al. (2005); Kaylor et al. (2001); and West (2001); arriving at a short-list of 172 features. The services offered, features or the functional areas being addressed by city e-governments, were mapped from the above studies.

Five cities were selected for study and for the comparison of the different services / features available on their e-Government web sites. The city of Ottawa was included because it was the main motivation for this study. It was considered optimal to select one more city from Canada for comparison within the country. Toronto was selected because it is the most populous city in the country, and because Ottawa is also on a growth

path, the comparison might be useful for the future. New York was selected from the US, it being the city with the highest population and with a cosmopolitan makeup, which might be interesting to study from an e-Government perspective. Singapore was selected to represent one of the leading city-states, where all the levels of governments co-exist, and therefore it can potentially be a model of an integrated e-government. Finally, Auckland, New Zealand, was selected to represent a modern developed city from across the globe. Auckland region has a population similar to that of Ottawa, though the city itself had 436,600 residents in 2007 (Auckland City, 2010). The population estimates and Web site addresses of the selected cities are given in Table 1.

We searched for the short listed 172 features and, if offered, assessed the service maturity level by using a rubric based on the one used by Kaylor et al. (2001, p. 306), to calculate an "e-score". Absent features were assigned a score of zero. (The detailed score allocation table is available in the complete paper). However, there were a number of features available in the city e-Government Web-sites, that did not figure in the mapped shortlist, and thus were not taken into account in this study. This fact does not undermine the importance of these features, or their local relevance. This bypassing of "additional" features is a bias intrinsic to this framework. However, since a large set of important features have been covered, the "e-scores" can be seen as a depend-

Table 1. Cities and their populations (Source: Adapted from New York City, 2010; Brinkhoff, 2010; Statistics New Zealand, 2010)

Sr.	City	Country	Estimated Population	Date of Estimate	City Website
1.	New York	United States of America	8,363,710	01/07/2008	www.nyc.gov
2.	Toronto	Canada	5,509,874	01/07/2007	www.toronto.ca
3.	Singapore	Singapore	3,733,900	30/06/2009	www.sg
4.	Auckland	New Zealand	1,436,400	30/06/2009	www.aucklandcity.govt.nz
5.	Ottawa	Canada	1,168,788	01/07/2007	www.ottawa.ca

able measure to find, even if in relative terms, to what extent the scope of the city e-Governments have been realized, at least in providing these services/features. In essence, these services/features, as they exist on a city e-Government Web site, can still be viewed at an "e-Government project asset" stage (Figure 3). How, and to what extent, these available services/features are used; and how, (through an "appropriate use process"), they lead to "e-Government impacts"; and how these impacts, (through a "good governance process") lead to "e-Government performance" (Soh & Markus, 1995); are questions for further research.

FINDINGS AND DISCUSSION

From the comparison of the features it is seen that all the cities have most of the requisite features on their Web sites. The total e-scores of the five cities were as computed, were: New York 305, Toronto 273, Singapore 300, Auckland 258, Ottawa 269. (The comparative table is given at Annexure A of the complete paper). Thus, it is seen that all the five cities have scores that range from 258 to 305, with a mean of 281 and a standard deviation of 20.46. In view of the fact that the Web sites contain a number of features and which are in addition to the target list, this difference in e-scores in these five cities does not seem to be significant. Also, there is substantial variance in the focus of the features and functions, which is probably linked to variations in the local needs. For example, in Singapore, local e-payment system terminals, known as AXS Stations (pronounce as "Access Stations") are widely available on the island 24/7, and can be used for a large number of e-Government payments. As these systems can be used for payment of traffic fines or court fines, only Level 3 functionality is provided on the e-Government Web site for some services.

In view of the local variations, the e-scores may generally be deemed at a similar level. Though it would be hard to infer from this small study that the e-Government e-scores in all the five cities were generally equivalent because they have hit a service "plateau"; but the results seem to tally with the findings in the Accenture's sixth annual global report on government service delivery, "Leadership in Customer Service: New Expectations, New Experiences," which finds that "all countries experienced a drop from previous years' overall e-Government maturity scores, which measured the level to which a government has developed an online presence" (Accenture, 2005, p. 1). This has probably happened because continued incremental improvements in this area do not produce commensurate results. So incremental addition of features may average out the target maturity levels. A United Nations 2008 e-Government Survey, *From e-Government to Connected Governance,* finds that "governments around the world are realizing that continued expansion in e-services is not possible without some kind of integration of back-end government systems... The new approach maintains that genuine cost savings and quality improvements will occur only if there is a re-engineering of the internal structures and processes of the administration towards a connected form of governance" (United Nations, 2008, p. xv). All this indicates the need for a fresh look at the e-Government, starting from the basics, and providing a solution that grows from infrastructure, to integration to transformation. This transformation; "in management of human, technological, and organizational resources and processes"; is the monumental change, which is the objective of e-Government (Grant & Chau, 2005), and not mere technological change. The study of the scope realized in practice by these five cities indicates a high level of advancement, and all the five cities seem to have crossed over from the infrastructure phase into an integrative phase. Even though the Web sites may seem to be similar, they are merely e-Government assets. It cannot be directly inferred whether they will lead to equivalent e-Government impacts and a superior e-Government performance. It would depend on the (process of) proper use of these assets; and a subsequent good governance process, to produce superior e-Government performance (Soh & Markus, 1995), which would be the ultimate realization of scope in practice. Also, even though the five cities studied have most of the target features/functions, the scope of services provided by the e-Government Web site of each of these cities is unique and it underlines the need for customizing the e-Government initiatives to the local needs of the constituents.

CONCLUSION

This paper outlines the scope of a city e-Government initiative. This research contributes by bringing to light limitations posed by city e-Governmental jurisdiction and external factors. Realization of the scope of city e-Government is discussed from the perspective of process theory. The issue of fuzziness of boundaries of scope in an integrated city e-Government initiative is discussed. The authors introduce the construct of "governance junction" to handle the fuzzy boundary issue. Further, to assess the realization of scope; salient services, functions and features are mapped from different studies. A unique study is conducted for services/features offered by five city e-Government initiatives across the globe to compare and contrast the degree to which they realize the scope, by assigning "e-scores" to their Web sites. It is seen that almost all the five cities are at a relatively high level of maturity in service offerings/features. However this may not necessarily correspond to the city "e-Government impacts" and the results leading to superior city "e-Government performance". That would require optimal use and good governance processes to be in place and successful. This paper has contributed to literature by outlining the concept of scope of city e-governments, external factors limiting the realization of scope, the progression from scope

to city e-Government investments, city e-Government assets, city e-Government impacts, and then to city e-Government performance. This paper has mapped the important city e-Government features in web sites and provided a study comparing five city e-Government initiatives. It finds that, though the elements provided on the Web sites have a number of common features, the scope of services provided by Web site of each of the five cities studied is unique, and it emphasizes the need for customizing the initiatives to the local needs of the constituents.

LIMITATIONS AND FUTURE RESEARCH

The study is limited by the fact that it has explored what already exists, and has considered a limited number of representative studies and five important city e-Government Web sites. Study of five city Web sites is limited by the features / functions considered, which in turn are limited by their dependence on a previous model. An actual survey of users/citizens of the target city and its officials would be invaluable to identify their perceived needs and expectations from the city e-government; such a survey may even throw up new features or areas, which have not been hitherto considered for implementation or research.

REFERENCES

Accenture. (2005). *Governments Must Move Beyond e-Government Initiatives to Enhance Customer Service for Citizens, Accenture Study Finds.* Retrieved from http://accenture.tekgroup. com/article_display.cfm? article_id=4205.

Ackoff, R. (1967). Management misinformation systems. *Management Science*, 147–156.

Archer, N. P. (2005). An overview of the change management process in e-government. *International Journal of Electronic Business, 3*(1), 68–87. doi:10.1504/IJEB.2005.006389

Ballmer, S. (2002). The promise of e-government. *Outlook Journal, 1*. Retrieved from http://www.accenture.com/NR/rdonlyres/E4DDAA5B-566F-4CD6-ADA0-E48AD0E1DA1D/0/Ballmer.pdf

Barua, A., Kriebel, C. H., & Mukhopadhyay, T. (1995). Information Technologies and Business Value: An Analytic and Empirical Investigation. *Information Systems Research, 6*(1), 3–23. doi:10.1287/isre.6.1.3

Brinkhoff, T. (2010). *City Population.* Retrieved January 1, 2010, from http://www.citypopulation.de

Charabaldis, Y., Askaounis, D., Gionis, G., Lampathaki, F., & Metaxiotis, K. (2006) Organising Municipal e-Government Systems: A Multifacet Taxonomy of e-Services for Citizens and Businesses. In M. A. Wimmer (Ed.), *Electronic Government: Proceedings of the 5ᵗʰ International Conference, EGOV 2006*, Krakow, Poland. Berlin: Springer-Verlag.

Charih, M., & Robert, J. (2004). Government on-line in the federal government of Canada: The organizational issues. *International Review of Administrative Sciences, 70*(2), 373–384. doi:10.1177/0020852304044262

Ciborra, C. (1997). De profundis? Deconstructing the concept of strategic alignment. *Scandinavian Journal of Information Systems, 9*(1), 67–82.

City, A. (2010). *Auckland city business and economy report 2007.* Retrieved January 1, 2010, from http://www.aucklandcity.govt.nz/auckland/economy/business/2007/population.asp

Criado, J. I., & Ramilo, M. C. (2003). E-government in practice: An analysis of Web site orientation to the citizens in Spanish municipalities. *International Journal of Public Sector Management, 16*(3), 191–218. doi:10.1108/09513550310472320

Delone, W. H., & McLean, E. R. (1992). Information systems success; the quest for the dependent variable. *Information Systems Research, 3*(1), 60–95. doi:10.1287/isre.3.1.60

Delone, W. H., & McLean, E. R. (2003). The DeLone and McLean Model of Information Systems Success: A Ten-Year Update. *Journal of Management Information Systems, 19*(4), 9–30.

Edmiston, K. D. (2002). State and local e-government: Prospects and challenges. *American Review of Public Administration, 33*(1), 20–45. doi:10.1177/0275074002250255

European Commission. (2002). *List of Basic Public Services.* Retrieve from http://ec.europa.eu/information_society/eeurope/2002/action_plan/pdf/basicpublicservices.pdf

Grant, G., & Chau, D. (2005). Developing a Generic Framework for E-Government. *Journal of Global Information Management, 13*(1), 1–31. doi:10.4018/jgim.2005010101

Green, K. R. (1982). Municipal administrators' receptivity to citizens' and elected officials' contacts. *Public Administration Review, 42*(4), 346–353. doi:10.2307/975978

Hirlinger, M. W. (1992). Citizen-initiated contacting of local government officials: A multivariate explanation. *The Journal of Politics, 54*(2), 553–564. doi:10.2307/2132039

Hitt, L. M., & Brynjolfsson, E. (1996). Productivity, Business Profitability, and Consumer Surplus: Three Different Measures of Information Technology Value. *Management Information Systems Quarterly*, 121–142. doi:10.2307/249475

Ho, A. T. K. (2002). Reinventing local governments and the e-government initiative. *Public Administration Review, 62*(4), 434–444. doi:10.1111/0033-3352.00197

Ho, A. T. K., & Ni, A. Y. (2004). Explaining the adoption of e-government features: A case study of Iowa County treasurer's offices. *American Review of Public Administration, 34*(2), 164–180. doi:10.1177/0275074004264355

Holden, S. H., Norris, D. F., & Fletcher, P. D. (2003). Electronic government at the local level: Progress to date and future issues. *Public Performance & Management Review, 26*(4), 325–344. doi:10.1177/1530957603026004002

Horrigan, J. B. (2004). *How Americans get in touch with government*. Washington, DC: Pew Internet & American Life Project.

Johnson, K. L., & Misic, M. M. (1999). Benchmarking: a tool for Web site evaluation and improvement. *Electronic Networking Applications and Policy, 9,* 383–392. doi:10.1108/10662249910297787

Kaylor, C., Deshazo, R., & Van Eck, D. (2001). Gauging e-government: A report on implementing services among American cities. *Government Information Quarterly, 18*(4), 293–307. doi:10.1016/S0740-624X(01)00089-2

Kernaghan, K. (2005). Moving towards the virtual stage: Integrating services and service channels for citizen centered delivery. *International Review of Administrative Sciences, 71*(1), 119–131. doi:10.1177/0020852305051688

Layne, K., & Lee, J. (2001). Developing fully functional e-government: A four-stage model. *Government Information Quarterly, 18,* 122–136. doi:10.1016/S0740-624X(01)00066-1

Mann, I. J. S., Kumar, V., Mann, H., & Kumar, U. (2008). Scope of City E-Government Initiative. In Amitabh, O. (Ed.), *E-Governance in Practice* (pp. 173–184). New Delhi, India: G.I.F.T. Publishing.

Melville, N., Kraemer, K., & Gurbaxani, V. (2004). Review: Information Technology and Organizational Performance: An Integrative Model of IT Business Value. *Management Information Systems Quarterly, 28*(2), 283–322.

Moon, D., Serra, G., & West, J. P. (1993). Citizens' contacts with bureaucratic and legislative officials. *Political Research Quarterly, 46*(4), 931–941.

Moon, M. J. (2002). The evolution of e-government among municipalities: Rhetoric or reality? *Public Administration Review, 62*(4), 424–433. doi:10.1111/0033-3352.00196

New York City. (2010). *The "Current" Population of New York City: Release of Population Estimates by the Census Bureau for July 1, 2008.* Retrieved January 1, 2010, from http://www.nyc.gov/html/dcp/html/census/popcur.shtml

Norris, D. F., Fletcher, P. D., & Holden, S. H. (2001). *Is your local government plugged in? Highlights of the 2000 electronic government survey.* Retrieved from http://www.umbc.edu/mipar/PDFs/e-gov.icma.final-4-25-01.pdf

Reddick, C. G. (2004a). A two-stage model of e-government growth: Theories and empirical evidence for U.S. cities. *Government Information Quarterly, 21*(1), 51–64. doi:10.1016/j.giq.2003.11.004

Reddick, C.G. (2004b). Empirical models of e-government growth in local governments. *e-Service Journal, 3*(2), 59-84.

Reddick, C. G. (2007). E-Government Adoption in Canadian Municipal Governments: A Survey of Ontario Chief Administrative Officers. In Norris, D. F. (Ed.), *Current Issues and Trends in E-Government Research*. Hershey, PA: Cybertech Publishing. doi:10.4018/978-1-59904-283-1.ch014

Roy, J. (2003). The relational dynamics of e-governance: A case study of the city of Ottawa. *Public Performance & Management Review*, *26*(4), 391–403. doi:10.1177/1530957603026004006

Serra, G. (1995). Citizen-initiated contact and satisfaction with bureaucracy: A multivariate analysis. *Journal of Public Administration: Research and Theory*, *5*(2), 175–188.

Soh, C., & Markus, M. L. (1995). *How IT Creates Business Value: A Process Theory Synthesis*. Paper presented at the Sixteenth International Conference on Information System, Amsterdam, The Netherlands.

Spearman, W., & Associates. Inc. (2000). *Use of the Internet for electronic commerce in US cities with populations greater than 500,000*. Retrieved from http://www.prismonline.com

Statistics New Zealand. (2010). *Subnational Population Estimates: At 30 June 2009*. Retrieved January 1, 2010, from http://www.stats.govt.nz/browse_for_stats/population/estimates_and_projections/subnationalpopulationestimates_hotp-30jun09.aspx

Stowers, G. N. L. (1999). Becoming cyberactive: state and local governments on the World Wide Web. *Government Information Quarterly*, *16*(2), 111–127. doi:10.1016/S0740-624X(99)80003-3

Thomas, J. C., & Melkers, J. (1999). Explaining citizen-initiated contacts with municipal bureaucrats: Lessons from the Atlanta experience. *Urban Affairs Review*, *34*(5), 667–690. doi:10.1177/10780879922184130

Thomas, J. C., & Melkers, J. (2000). Citizen contacting of municipal officials: Choosing between appointed administrators and elected leaders. *Journal of Public Administration: Research and Theory*, *11*(1), 51–71. doi:10.1093/oxfordjournals.jpart.a003494

Thomas, J. C., & Streib, G. (2003). The new face of government: Citizen-initiated contacts in the era of e-government. *Journal of Public Administration: Research and Theory*, *13*(1), 83–102. doi:10.1093/jpart/mug010

Torres, L., Pina, V., & Acerete, B. (2005). E-government developments on delivering public services among EU cities. *Government Information Quarterly*, *22*(4), 217–238. doi:10.1016/j.giq.2005.02.004

United Nations. (2008). *e-Government Survey 2008: From e-Government to Connected Governance*. New York: United Nations.

Vedlitz, A., Dyer, J. A., & Durand, R. (1980). Citizen contacts with local governments: A comparative view. *American Journal of Political Science*, *24*(1), 50–67. doi:10.2307/2110924

West, D. M. (2000). *Assessing e-government: the Internet democracy, and service delivery*. Retrieved from http://www.insidepolitics.org/egovtreport00.html

West, D. M. (2001). *Urban E-Government: An Assessment of City Government Websites*. Retrieved from http://www.insidepolitics.org/egovt01city.html

This work was previously published in the International Journal of Electronic Government Research, Volume 7, Issue 1, edited by Vishanth Weerakkody, pp. 38-50, copyright 2011 by IGI Publishing (an imprint of IGI Global).

Chapter 4
Organizational Development in Electronic Government Adoption:
A Process Development Perspective

Bahar Movahedi
Carleton University, Canada

Ren-Xiang (Paul) Tan
University of London, UK

Kayvan Miri Lavassani
Carleton University, Canada

ABSTRACT

The concept of Electronic Government (EG) has evolved significantly during the past few decades. Several development models have been presented in the literature to illustrate the advancement and adoption of EG practices. Recent developments in EG adoption that emphasize the process view call for a new perspective to EG adoption. Based on the review of most cited stage models of EG adoption, a comprehensive stage model is recommended in this paper. Furthermore, this paper utilizes the recommended stage model and proposes a process based framework for analyzing the EG adoption.

1. BACKGROUND

When the military first invented the Internet in the 1960s as a communication network for defense research purposes, it did not envision how the Internet would transform society in just few decades (Ho, 2002). Since the introduction of the Internet, there has been a rapid growth in its use as a communication tool. The exponential growth in internet usage and the application of e-commerce in the private sector, have been mounting pressure on governments to serve its citizens electronically. These applications are recognized in the form of

DOI: 10.4018/978-1-4666-2458-0.ch004

Electronic Government (EG) (Ho, 2002; Holden, Norris & Fletcher, 2003).

The private sector developed the concept of e-commerce, which enables customers to access products and services through a "one stop shop". While customer convenience is a contributory factor for the private sector to utilize Information and Communication Technologies (ICT), the saving cost helps to motivate companies to invest in e-commerce. The Internet not only changed the way people interact and how information is delivered, but it also pressured governments to revisit its service delivery models and methods to their citizens (Cohen & Eimicke, 2002). The private sector share the same stakeholder as the public sector, and it is the stakeholders that contribute the most in terms of increasing the level of pressure for governments to hasten the adaptation of ICT as well as diffusion of technology in provision of public services (Donaldson, 1995; Geroski, 2000). In this context, ICT diffusion refers to the gradual adoption of the technology by different groups of stakeholders.

The Internet is becoming more important not just in economic development, but also in organizational development. The Internet, like other communication technologies, has wide political impact on organizations, their stakeholders, and the relationship among them (Milner, 2006). Several scholars have called for the need to examine and understand the process of adoption of innovative technologies in governments. The importance of understanding the adoption process, becomes more vital when the context is an exceptionally complex environment, like the government. The velocity of adopting technology is reliant on the political setting in the government, and the inclination of those in power (Milner, 2006). Some institutions would allow governments and ruling elites embrace the adoption of new technologies – if they yearn to do so – while other institutions would enable them to delay or disrupt it entirely. Despite these considerations the governments around the world, especially evident in

the developed countries, have already established ambitious goals for the implementation of EG in the public sector (Aichholzer, 2004). The premise for governments to undertake such transformation in the public sector is: governments understand that quality and the cost of public service will ultimately determine the population's overall quality of life, the strength of business activities, and political legitimacy of the government (Aichholzer, 2004). Though this article recognizes the implementation of technology involves complex planning and challenging factors, such as fundamentals in public policy, regulations and financial constraints (Jaeger & Thomson, 2003); the position of this article does not advocate for specific implementation measures, but rather, it will provide an analytical overview of the EG adoption process.

The next section of this paper introduces the concept of EG development, and describes the importance of EG development from the public management perspective. Section three, provides evidences for the shift to the process view of EG adoption. In the following section, a comprehensive stage model of EG adoption is recommended. Furthermore, the recommended model is applied in the process view of EG development framework. In section five, the process view of the EG is described explicitly. Finally, the synthesis of the paper is presented in the last section.

2. DEVELOPMENTS IN ELECTRONIC GOVERNMENT: PUBLIC MANAGEMENT VIEW

EG has developed significantly in the recent decades; governments started to observe the role of EG in improving the service delivery to citizens (United Nations, 2005). EG has also evolved in parallel with technological advancements. The procedures of entrenching EG in the public sector are lessons taken from the private sector. One of the goals of EG is to ensure that government services are to be more citizen-centric and service oriented (Seifert & Chung, 2009). Every concept in usage, either in the public sector or in private sector, requires a change from its predecessors. However the changes do not exclude the existence of its predecessor, but instead the changes are inclusive of the predecessor's foundation and thus, we argue these changes are incremental, and occur within the process development frameworks.

Currently, it is generally established among academies that government departments are beginning to become more collaborative between departments that broke away from its traditional methods of service delivery, where departments have acted independently when directing service delivery (McGuire, 2006). These developments have paved the way toward the implementation of New Public Management (NPM) designs. Within the NPM, departments gradually begin to implement a system of service delivery that are in reaction to the feedbacks provided by citizens, often described as 'citizen centered' service delivery models. NPM is an unintended consequence of the Internet revolution that causes a shift in approach to citizens (Marche & McNiven, 2003). We will argue that this new design is in line, and can be described with the process view of EG adoption.

2.1 Importance of Electronic Government: Developments in the Public Sector

To provide a clear analysis and explanation of the causes for the change in government service delivery mechanisms, which enabled it to incorporate new technologies, this article develops an argument that this incorporation is contributed by paradigm shifts in public administration. Since the late 1990's, government functions and service delivery methods have changed rapidly; Devadoss, Pan and Huang (2002) reasoned the causes for such transformation is due to the impact of technological advances that enable governments to deliver services via the Internet. Arguably, the

advancements of technology also attributed to the adoption of NPM in the public sector. NPM is founded on the themes of desegregation, competition, performance, and a reward system, which promises the move away from traditional practices of public administration toward a transparent and results-oriented form of government (Dunleavy et al., 2005). The implementation of delivery services are directed and supported by efficient and effective public managers (Noordhoek & Saner, 2005). NPM entails the public choice belief that government is too unresponsive, inefficient and a monopoly (O'Flynn, 2007). This is a result of criticisms from the 1970's of the traditional approach, among many, for being functional insularity, inability to measure performances, react to changing circumstances, along with its inability to enable managers to make independent decisions, which further contributes to its inefficiency (Navarra & Cornford, 2005; Marche & McNiven, 2003). However, according to Hernes (2005) NPM is defined as a set of ideas and methods, of which the goal is to combine accountability and efficiency in public administration but also underscore the inherent tensions between logistics of service and accountability from an organizational structure perspective (Hernes, 2005).

While NPM frameworks are being implemented across western nations, it has rarely been the subject of critique and consequent evaluations. One reason may be that public servants may be viewed as agents who do not support the good order and delivery of the services. Members of Parliament, acting as observers on behalf of citizens, do not show interest in this domain since they may be seen not in control in the eye of citizens (Noordhoek & Saner, 2005). Even though not everyone fully conceptualizes NPM principles, it is generally understood that they are the driving force behind the changes in government administration; however, instead of embracing the principles brought forward by NPM, some people greeted them with cynicism and disbelief (Noordhoek & Saner, 2005). Noordhoek and Saner (2005) argue this case through two examples in Switzerland and the Netherlands; both have the knowledge and capital to fully embrace NPM, but instead the principles of NPM evoked a reaction jaded by distaste for a too rational and non-political approach towards people and organizations. In 2004, the region of Zurich voted to halt all NPM related administrative reforms; in the Netherlands, the cabinet and Parliament favored a report that called for the end of the independent status of arms length agencies, which is a pivotal element of NPM (Noordhoek & Saner, 2005). Noordhoek and Saner (2005) argue that these are examples of decline in NPM. However, the authors of this article do not agree or disagree the argument presented since countries such as Australia and New Zealand are exemplars of NPM (O'Flynn, 2007), but rather this article is taking a different road to analyze this paradigm shift.

This new approach highlights the role of governments meeting the demands of citizens, while at the same time positioning themselves to react to changes. As a result, the new term of public administration in the current millennium is one that identifies a horizontal network that composes of private, public and non-profit organizations (Bingham, Nabatchi & O'Leary, 2005). In other words, governance undertakes a stakeholder perspective. According to Freeman (1984), a stakeholder is categorized into four groups: shareholders, employees, customers, and members of the general public (as cited in Clarkson, 1995). The new approach of governance would regard voters as the stakeholders, public administrators as employees, users of governance as customers, and non-voters as members of the general public. EG can be utilized in promoting greater public participation in governance, while concurrently enabling government to better provide services. As Gil-Garcia and Pardo (2005) argue EG focuses on the conceptualization of information technologies for the purpose of public service delivery, to improve effectiveness in public management, as

well as the promotion of democratic values and mechanisms.

In the following sections of the paper, this shift of analysis is described at various aspects of EG development. Specifically we provide evidence of the developments at definition, scope, activity, and organizational development associated with EG. Furthermore, we adopt the process view of organizational development into the context of EG development.

3. ELECTRONIC GOVERNMENT: PROCESS OF INCORPORATING TECHNOLOGY

This article argues toward the evolutionary process development view. This will contribute further to extend our knowledge of the best practices, protocols, and implementation processes of EG in service delivery. To better understand the domain of EG, a review of some of the most cited definitions of EG was conducted. Table 1 displays some of these definitions.

The definitions are sorted by their year of publication. For each definition, the focus of the definition is highlighted. As illustrated in Table 1, there are in fact three trends. The first is technology, as to what technology is and does. The second is the technical aspect of adoption, where it provides description of how technologies are used. The third trend is process adoption, where it gives more focus on analyzing how technologies are incorporated into organizational operations.

There exists a shift in EG literature, from one which focuses on the technology aspect of EG, to the one which is centered around the adoption process of EG. This view is supported in several recent studies including: Dwivedi, Weerakkody and Williams (2009), Azad and Faraj (2009), Janssen, Joha and Zuurmond (2009), Yoon and Chae (2009), Navarra and Cornford (2009) and Kim, Kim and Lee (2009). The focus of this study is mainly on adoption process aspect of EG, how-

Table 1. Definitions of electronic government

Author	Definition	Focus
Heath (2000)	Government becomes e-government when the public sector digitizes its processes and interactions, whether internal or external with business or with the public	Technology
Allen, Juillet, Paquet and Roy (2001)	IT-led reconfiguration of public sector governance –and how, knowledge, power, and purpose are redistributed in light of new technological realities.	Technology
West (2001)	The delivery of government information and services online through the Internet or other digital means	Adoption
Gómez and Ospina (2001); Beaudin (2001)	The use by government agencies of information technologies that have the ability to transform relations with citizens, business, and other arms of the government creating a wealth of new digital connections	Technology
Gronlund (2001); Turban et al. (2002)***	The strategic application of information and communication technology to provide citizens and organizations with more convenient access to government information and services; and to provide delivery of public services to citizens, business partners and suppliers, and those working in the public sector.	Adoption
Fang (2002)	A way for governments to use the most innovative information and communication technologies, particularly web-based Internet applications, to provide citizens and businesses with more convenient access to government information and services, to improve the quality of the services and to provide greater opportunities to participate in democratic institutions and processes	Adoption
Criado, Hughes and Teicher (2002)	Refers to the adoption of information and communication technologies (ICT) by government to improve access to services	Technology
Muir and Oppenheim (2002)*	e-Government refers to the delivery of [government] information and services online through the Internet or other digital means	Adoption
United Nations (2002)**	The use of information and communication technologies to provide public information and services to citizens and businesses.	Adoption
Breu, Hafner, Weber and Novak (2005)	The use of the Internet and other electronic media to improve the collaboration within public agencies and to include citizens and companies in administrative processes	Adoption
West (2005)	Public sector use of the Internet and other digital devices to deliver services, information, and democracy itself.	Adoption
Irani and Elliman (2008)	Process of delivering information and services to customers (citizens, business, and public administration) electronically by Government.	Adoption
Lee, Irani, Osman I, Balci, Ozkan and Medeni (2008)	E-Government is the process of delivering information and services to customers (citizens, business, and public administration) electronically by the government	Adoption (Process View)
Lau, Aboulhoson and Atkin (2008)	The process of connecting citizens digitally to their government in order that they might access information and services offered by government agencies	Adoption (Process View)
Walser, Kuhn and Reidl (2009)	E-government refers to the support of business processes within and across the public administration through the application of IT	Adoption (Process View)

* As cited in Kumar, Mukerji, Butt, Persaud (2007)
** As cited in Dimitrova and Chen (2006)
*** As cited in Phang, Sutanto, Li and Kankanhalli (2005)

ever it is recognized that technology and adoption process are complementary of each other. Bearing in mind these developments, we first explore the stage view of EG development. Following that, the process view is adapted to a multidimensional model of EG development.

4. ELECTRONIC GOVERNMENT ADOPTION

Stages of EG development have been a topic of interest during the past two decades. Several models of EG implementation are presented in the literature, which illustrate the developments in this area. The adoption of EG services can be viewed from different perspectives. The stage view and process view of the EG adoption are the two most common and tightly related views of EG adoption. In this first part of this section, the stage view of EG implementation is described. Later the process view is introduced and described as a more recent and compatible view of EG. The first part of this section identifies eleven, EG adoption stage models based on a comprehensive literature review. The stages in the development models are carefully investigated and subsequently a six-stage EG adoption model, is proposed which presents the comprehensive view of the current EG development models. Figure 1 displays the various models and the proposed six-stage model.

Figure 1. Stages view of electronic government development

Author/s	Stages						Scale
	Cataloging	Interaction	Added services	Transaction	Integration	Org. Transformation	
Hiller and Belanger (2001)	✓	✓	✓	✓		✓	5 Stages
Backus (2001)	✓	✓		✓		✓	4 stage models
Layne and Lee (2001)	✓	✓			✓ [1]		4 stage models
Howard (2001)	✓	✓		✓			3 stage models
United Nations – DPEPA (2002)	✓ [2]	✓		✓	✓		5 stage
Atallab (2001)	✓	✓		✓	✓		4 stage models
Baum and Di Maio, cited in, Seifert and Petersen (2002)	✓	✓		✓		✓	4 stage models
Chandler and Emanuels (2002),	✓	✓		✓	✓		4 stage models
Deloitte research cited in (Al-Sebie, Irani, and Eldabi, 2005)	✓	✓	✓ [3]		✓ [4]		6 stage
Reddick (2004)	✓			✓			Focus on 2 stages
Murphy (2005) as cited in Weerakkody and Dhillon (2008)	✓		✓		✓ [5]		

[1] Includes two stages: Vertical Integration; Horizontal integration
[2] Includes two stages: emerging; enhanced.
[3] Includes three stages: Multi-purpose portals, Portal personalization, clustering of common services.
[4] Consider integration and org. transformation as a single stage.
[5] Includes two stages: Automating & Transformation of business processes; rethinking policy objectives.

According to the proposed six-stage model, EG starts with a unidirectional display of information known as catalogues. In the second stage, the users of the system can interact with the service provider to complete certain tasks. Third stage is categorized with provision of expanded services and personalized solutions for users (Al-Sebie, Irani, & Eldabi, 2005). In the fourth stage of EG development, the services will allow the users to complete certain transactions. Fourth stage is the integration of services and processes in government for enabling the provision of seamless and more diverse services. This fifth integration stage will require vertical and horizontal interaction within and among various functions (Hiller & Belanger, 2001; Backus, 2001). The last stage is organizational transformation, which focuses on automation of organizational processes and transformation of organizational structure as an enabling factor to provide higher level of services to citizens. To achieve this goal, governments will be required to set new "policy objectives" aligned with the new information technology and novel processes. As it is evident from this study, process view of operations, is an integral part of the EG development. The process view of the context of EG is further described on the following section.

4.1 Process View of Electronic Government Adoption

In the previous section, the stage models of EG development were described and a proposed comprehensive model was developed. Process view of the EG, as an integral part of EG development, is identified to be the more recent focus of EG development.

The development of EG can be studied at three levels: technology, internal processes, and external processes (Hiller & Belanger, 2001). Significant changes at the technology level during the past two decades have enabled organizations to move from provision of catalogue information to present dynamic and transactional services to citizen.

Moreover, the attention to internal and external processes has allowed governments to align their information infrastructure with citizens' needs and operational capabilities. The increased maturity of EG operations calls for a shift of attention from management of inter-functional processes to intra-organizational and inter-organizational processes (Gottschalk & Solli-Sæther, 2008). At the early stage of EG adoption, governments are still focused on operation of processes within specific functions. To provide advanced services through EG, organizations start intra-organizational integration to share knowledge. Institutionalization of new processes is a key factor to succeed at this stage. However, to produce further value through EG, the integration of processes, as well as institutionalization of processes needs to be expanded across various organizations involved in EG services. Finally, there is a need to align strategic goals of various government agencies with citizens' requirements and needs (Gottschalk & Solli-Sæther, 2008).

Based on the review of most cited studies in the area of EG development, a framework is proposed to illustrate the process view of EG. This framework is constructed based on the various levels of EG analysis (Hiller & Belanger, 2001), scopes of analysis, core activities in each domain (Gottschalk & Solli-Sæther, 2008), the proposed stage model of EG development and process development in organizations (Melao & Pidd, 2000). EG, in this model is viewed as a tool toward organizational development, where organizations experience a sequential growth, institutionalize new processes and alter their activities and structure (King & Toe, 1997). Figure 2 illustrates the process view of EG development.

According to the proposed EG development model, the current scope of analysis in EG adoption is focused on inter-organizational processes. As a result, the core activity in EG adoption is strategic alignment among various departments (Gottschalk & Solli-Sæther, 2008). Consequently the EG adoption currently is believed to be at

Figure 2. Process view of electronic government development

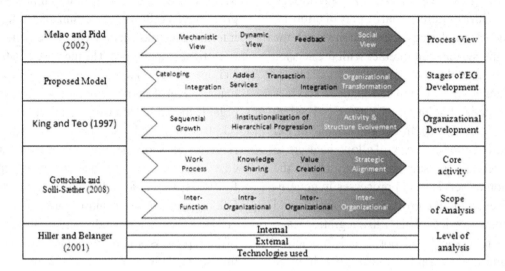

Melao and Pidd (2002)	Mechanistic View	Dynamic View	Feedback	Social View	Process View
Proposed Model	Cataloging Integration	Added Services	Transaction Integration	Organizational Transformation	Stages of EG Development
King and Teo (1997)	Sequential Growth	Institutionalization of Hierarchical Progression		Activity & Structure Evolvement	Organizational Development
Gottschalk and Solli-Sæther (2008)	Work Process	Knowledge Sharing	Value Creation	Strategic Alignment	Core activity
	Inter-Function	Intra-Organizational	Inter-Organizational	Inter-Organizational	Scope of Analysis
Hiller and Belanger (2001)	Internal				Level of analysis
	External				
	Technologies used				

the "activity and structure evolvement" level of organizational development (King & Teo, 1997). This is in line with the latest stage of EG development, which is organizational transformation. In the following section, it is described that the EG development is adaptable to the process view of organizational development. Furthermore, social view is described as the current stage of EG development in public sector.

5. THE PROCESS VIEW OF ELECTRONIC GOVERNMENT DEVELOPMENT

Melao and Pidd (2000), in their seminal study of organizations describe a four-stage model of organizational development. Melao and Pidd, (2000) model is the centerpiece of the EG adoption framework. It is applied to develop the proposed EG adoption framework in this study. According to Melao and Pidd (2000), during the organizational development the execution of processes in organizations is viewed from four perspectives, namely: Mechanistic View, Dynamic View, Interacting feedback loops, and Social Views. In this

section, each view is presented and discussed in the context of EG.

Mechanistic View

In the context of a mechanistic view, the focus is made toward provision of services based on the functional view of service delivery. This view supports an operational perspective that focuses on efficiency and value of defined processes. For example, this view demonstrates that there is a need for governments to reduce transaction costs, while simultaneously increase or maintain efficient service delivery (Berenice & Baron, 2009). According to Finger and Pécoud (2003) the governments (states) has undergone substantial transformation over the past 15 to 20 years, which are caused by series of factors and pressures that have made the governments, to adapt to a new and increasingly global environment. Government's delivery of services to the public incurs a great amount of expenses which are associated with extent of specialized investments have to made to carry out transactions (Ellis, 2004). The underlying incentive for governments to deliver as much as their services in electronic form as possible, is to reduce transaction costs. The governments therefore, rely on improving theirs operational structure, as oppose to its regulation or policy-making functions (Finger & Pécoud, 2003). The government also sought to decrease the financial pressure by passing on the reduced transaction costs to citizens, the primary user of government services; while at the same time increase the government's legitimacy via improving the quality of its services by competitively modernizing its departments (Finger & Pécoud, 2003). However, the barriers that are still prominent in comprehensive implementation of EG include: security, privacy, and financial commitments by governments which are compounded. In addition, administrators and policy makers lack the knowledge and historical expertise in IT management (Norris & Moon, 2008). Moreover, provision of online government services goes beyond enabling user access to information. It also requires interoperability between departments and agencies that are part of the EG system, and a stable IT infrastructure that can handle trading of data between central processors (Norris & Moon, 2005). Where infrastructures are insufficiently established, it can lead to information system downtime that will negatively affect the ability for the system to provide services to its users (Ellis, 2004).

Dynamic View

Government departments have traditionally operated based on the functional design of organizations in the delivery of services, where each individual department has its own culture and operational procedures. Government services have however, evolved toward provision of citizen-centered services. The outcome of government services are delivered in an asymmetrical manner where various service delivering agencies are not just collaborating with each other, but the services that are being delivered fall within the realm of customer service relations. These services are reflective of the needs and wants of its end customers (Patel, 2007). Governments have increasingly begun to offer electronic services that meet the needs of their citizens' life and their business transactions. These services promise enhanced accessibility, and reduced delivery delays and costs (Gouscos, Kalikakis, Legal & Papadopoulou, 2007). These goals require a dynamic view of process.

Prior to EG services, citizens and businesses would often face bureaucratic obstacles when trying to use government services, as procedures were vague and in some cases there was overlapping authority between departments (Gouscos, Kalikakis, Legal & Papadopoulou, 2007). However, given the historical experience of government services delivery, there tends to be a lack of confidence in the government having the ability to provide a resolution that will reduce the lack of trust by its services users (Belanger & Carter, 2008). Trust is defined according to Rotter (1971) in Belanger and Carter (2008) as an expectancy for a delivery of a result that promise toward an individual, group or organization can be relied upon in providing, and are rooted in social learning theory (Belanger & Carter, 2008). This study does not focus on whether users of government services will distrust or trust EG services, the Internet and the government's ability to resolve user's historical concerns about bureaucratic services. Rather, it is argued that there exists a trend where governments are undertaking, as a process, to deliver services that are in reflection of citizen needs and societal changes.

Interacting Feedback Loops

With the developments made in technological aspect of EG infrastructure and the competency of users, the EG systems started to adopt interacting feedback loops in their operation. The early stage of EG had been primarily focused on the need to deliver pure data, where user friendliness and addressing various usage trends were not a priority. However, the rise and mass integration of the digital age from work to daily communication activities have imposed changes in EG.

These changes would require the governments to ensure that users of services are successfully engaged. This called for more attention to the client-adoption aspects of EG services, such as user friendliness and tracking of usage trends. These developments have also paved the way for promotion of higher transparency in government (Bekkers & Moody, 2009).

The emerging trend of using information technology tools by the general populations, along with technological advancements in this area, has not only captured the attention of the businesses, but also government decision-makers, policy institutions and public administrators (Andersen & Henriksen, 2006). Currently, there are wide ranges of research on the best approach on how government delivery services should move forward, where the transformation scope will include external users such as citizens, businesses, and arms-length government agencies (Andersen & Henriksen, 2006). However, the challenge facing public administrators is not only merging IT into government services delivery; another major challenge is the adoption of internal structure that emphasizes citizen-centric and not bureaucratic-centric view (Seifert & Chung, 2009). Prior to undertaking the transformation to EG, administrators and policy-makers must select appropriate services from hierarchical repositories, where the specifically chosen category for each service needs to be a known priori. In doing so, administrator will understand their implicit semantics, which will enable them to design an effective and stable framework where control mechanisms and data flow structures are appropriately designed (Barnickel, Fluegge & Schmidt, 2006). As what Finger and Pécoud (2003) call "operators' modernization", have allowed public services to be delivered increasingly similar way than private and third sector operators. This can provide a potential for the modernized public sector to ultimately be operated partially by private or third sector actors (Finger & Pécoud, 2003).

Social Views

The most recent development in EG services is the need of greater attention to social view of services. The social view of the EG processes is concerned with the way the outcome of the EG services can address the customers' needs and expectations. This social view goes beyond the adoption of technology and enhances the capabilities of users to utilize the EG potentials (Macintosh & Whyte, 2006). Macintosh and Whyte (2006) highlight the importance of social view of EG process, by describing that the success of any EG initiative is pending the participation of citizens. Having a top technical system without the citizens' participation is an example of failed EG initiative. Maad and Coghlan (2008) describe the shift of focus from technical view of EG service to a social perspective. In a recent study, Grundén (2009), expanded this social view of EG services and described the social consequences of services in EG. From her perspective, EG not only includes the end users of the services (the citizens), but also includes the government employees and system operators. During the EG development process, advances along with technical and structural changes should be accompanied with training of the employees about the new ways of doing things. Grundén (2009) views competency development as an integral part and the most social aspect of EG development. Building on the foundation of organizational developments in EG service provision, this study proposed an EG adoption model which includes the social view of EG services.

6. SYNTHESIS

The development of electronic services delivery in governments has evolved substantially within a short period. Departments are becoming more reliant on ICT as the primary channel for citizens and businesses to access their mandated services. Such development of usage is becoming part of the general practices of department strategic planning and will only continue to grow in its importance. The changes that have been made in government service delivery mechanism are not purely in response to shifts in public administration, or shifts in technology advancements and the private sector inclusively; but rather the policy to transform government services are to reflect the emerging citizen expectations, their trends and the need for fiscal conservation. The resulting effects of EG in the new era of public service delivery is the institutionalization of EG into the public domain. The present study contributes to the existing literature by describing the developments in the EG. The current scope of analysis in EG adoption is structured around attention to inter-organizational integration, while the required core activity in this period is identified as strategic alignment among various stakeholders. In regards with the organizational development view of EG, currently governments are concerned with recognizing the required new activity and structure, as well as identifying the best organizational transformation plan. From the process perspective, addressing the social view of EG services is presented as the current major issue, facing public sector. The proposed model is a reflection of the trends that are being implemented in the public sector, and have its share of resentment by public administrator due to the fact that EG is viewed as an external agent that is not part of the traditional framework of public service delivery. However, EG ultimately becomes more utilized and integrated partly due to paradigm shifts in public administration and partly due to the advancement of technology. The proposed EG development model can be employed in future studies for analyzing the current practices and plan of the future EG developments.

REFERENCES

Aichholzer, G. (2004). Scenarios of e-Government in 2010 and implications for strategy design. *Electronic. Journal of E-Government, 2*(1), 1–10.

Al-Sebie, M., Irani, Z., & Eldabi, T. (2005). Issues relating to the transaction stage of the e-government system. *Electronic Government, an International Journal, 2*(4), 446-459.

Allen, B. A., Juillet, L., Paquet, G., & Roy, J. (2001). E-Governance & government on-line in Canada: Partnerships, people & prospects. *Government Information Quarterly, 18*(2), 93–104. doi:10.1016/S0740-624X(01)00063-6

Andersen, K. V., & Henriksen, H. Z. (2006). E-government maturity models: Extension of the Layne and Lee model. *Government Information Quarterly, 23*(2), 236–248. doi:10.1016/j.giq.2005.11.008

Azad, B., & Faraj, S. (2009). E-Government institutionalizing practices of a land registration mapping system. *Government Information Quarterly, 26*(1), 5–14. doi:10.1016/j.giq.2008.08.005

Barnickel, N., Fluegge, M., & Schmidt, K. (2006). Interoperability in eGovernment through Cross-Ontology Semantic Web Service Composition. In *Proceedings of the 3rd European Semantic Web Conference*, Budva, Montenegro.

Beaudin, D. (2001). *A Content Analysis of Disability Access on Government Websites in Australia, the United Kingdom, and the United States*. Retrieved from http://ils.unc.edu/MSpapers/2722.pdf

Bekkers, V., & Moody, R. (2009). Visual Culture and Electronic Government: Exploring a New Generation of E-Government. In M.A. Wimmer et al. (Eds.), *EGOV 2009* (LNCS 5693, pp. 257-269).

Belanger, F., & Carter, L. (2008). Trust and risk in e-government adoption. *The Journal of Strategic Information Systems, 17*, 165–176. doi:10.1016/j.jsis.2007.12.002

Bingham, L. B., Nabatchi, T., & O'Leary, R. (2005). The New Governance: Practices and Processes for Stakeholder and Citizen Participation in the Work of Government. *Public Administration Review, 65*(5), 547–558. doi:10.1111/j.1540-6210.2005.00482.x

Breu, R., Hafner, M., Weber, B., & Novak, A. (2005). Model Driven Security for Inter-organizational Workflows in e-Government. In M. Böhlen et al. (Eds.), *E-Government: Towards Electronic Democracy* (LNCS 3416, pp. 122-133).

Clarkson, M. B. E. (1995). A Stakeholder Framework for Analyzing and Evaluating Corporate Social Performance. *Academy of Management Review, 20*(1), 92–117. doi:10.2307/258888

Cohen, S., & Eimicke, W. (2003). The Future of E-Government: A Project of Potential Trends and Issues. In *Proceedings of the 36th Hawaii International Conference on System Sciences.*

Criado, J. I., Hughes, O., & Teicher, J. (2002, April 8-10). e-Government and managerialism: a second revolution in public management. In *Proceedings of the 6th International Research Symposium on Public Management.*

Devadoss, P. R., Pan, S. L., & Huang, J. C. (2002). Structurational analysis of e-government initiatives: a case study of SCO. *Decision Support Systems, 34*(3), 253–269. doi:10.1016/S0167-9236(02)00120-3

Diego, D. N., & Cornford, T. (2005, May 26-28). ICT, Innovation and Public Management: Governance, Models & Alternatives for e-Government Infrastructures. In *Proceedings of the 13th European Conference on Information Systems, Information Systems in a Rapidly Changing Economy, ECIS 2005,* Regensburg, Germany.

Dimitrova, D. V., & Chen, Y. (2006). Profiling the Adopters of E-Government Information and Services: The Influence of Psychological Characteristics, Civic Mindedness, and Information Channels. *Social Science Computer Review, 24*(2), 172. doi:10.1177/0894439305281517

Donaldson, T., & Preston, L. E. (1995). The Stakeholder Theory of the Corporation: Concepts, Evidence, and Implications. *Academy of Management Review, 20*(1), 65–91. doi:10.2307/258887

Dunleavy, P., Margetts, H., Bastow, S., & Tinkler, J. (2005). New Public Management Is Dead—Long Digital-Era Governance. *Journal of Public Administration: Research and Theory, 16*(3), 467–494. doi:10.1093/jopart/mui057

Dwivedi, Y. K., Weerakkody, V., & Williams, M. D. (2009). Guest editorial: From implementation to adoption: Challenges to successful E-Government diffusion. *Government Information Quarterly, 26*(1), 3–4. doi:10.1016/j.giq.2008.09.001

Ellis, A. (2004). Using the New Institutional Economics in e-Government to deliver transformational change. *Electronic. Journal of E-Government, 2*(2), 126–138.

Fang, Z. (2002). E-government in digital era: concept, practice and development. *International Journal of the Computer, the Internet and Management, 10*(2), 1-22.

Finger, M., & Pécoud, G. (2003). From e-Government to e-Governance? Towards a model of e-Governance. *Electronic. Journal of E-Government, 1*(1), 1–10.

Gil-Garcia, J. R., & Theresa, A. P. (2005). E-government success factors: Mapping practical tools to theoretical foundations. *Government Information Quarterly, 22*(2), 187–216. doi:10.1016/j.giq.2005.02.001

Gomez, R., & Ospina, A. (2001). The Lamp without a Genie: Using Telecentres for Development without expecting Miracles. *The Journal of Development Communication, 12*(2), 26–31.

Gouscos, D., Kalikakis, M., Legal, M., & Papadopoulou, S. (2007). A general model of performance and quality for one-stop e-Government service offerings. *Government Information Quarterly, 24*(4), 860–885. doi:10.1016/j.giq.2006.07.016

Grundén, K. (2009). A Social Perspective on Implementation of e-Government - a Longitudinal Study at the County Administration of Sweden. *Electronic. Journal of E-Government, 7*(1), 65–76.

Heath, W. (2000). *Europe's readiness for e-Government.* Retrieved from http://www.egov.vic.gov.au/pdfs/e-readiness.pdf

Hernes, T. (2005). Four ideal-type organizational responses to New Public Management reforms and some consequences. *International Review of Administrative Sciences, 71*(1), 5–17. doi:10.1177/0020852305051680

Hiller, J., & Belanger, F. (2001). *Privacy Strategies for Electronic Government. E-Government Series.* Arlington, VA: PricewaterhouseCoopers Endowment for the Business of Government.

Ho, A. T. (2002). Reinventing Local Governments and the E-Government Initiative. *Public Administration Review, 62*(4), 434–444. doi:10.1111/0033-3352.00197

Holden, S. H., Norris, D. F., & Fletcher, P. D. (2003). Electronic Government at the Local Level: Progress to Date and Future Issues. *Public Performance & Management Review, 26*(4), 325–344. doi:10.1177/1530957603026004002

Irani, Z., & Elliman, T. (2008). Creating social entrepreneurship in local government. *European Journal of Information Systems, 17*(4), 336–342. doi:10.1057/ejis.2008.35

Jaeger, P. T., & Thompson, K. M. (2003). E-government around the world: Lessons, challenges, and future directions. *Government Information Quarterly, 20,* 389–394. doi:10.1016/j.giq.2003.08.001

Janssen, M., Joha, A., & Zuurmond, A. (2009). Simulation and animation for adopting shared services: Evaluating and comparing alternative arrangements. *Government Information Quarterly, 26*(1), 15–24. doi:10.1016/j.giq.2008.08.004

Kim, S., Kim, H. J., & Lee, H. (2009). An institutional analysis of an e-government system for anti-corruption: The case of OPEN. *Government Information Quarterly, 26*(1), 42–50. doi:10.1016/j.giq.2008.09.002

Kumar, V., Mukerji, B., Butt, I., & Persaud, A. (2007). Factors for Successful e-Government Adoption: a Conceptual Framework. *The Electronic. Journal of E-Government, 5*(1), 63–76.

Lau, T., Aboulhoson, M., Lin, C., & Atkin, D. (2008). Adoption of E-government in three Latin American countries: Argentina, Brazil and Mexico. *Telecommunications Policy, 32*(2), 88–100. doi:10.1016/j.telpol.2007.07.007

Lee, H., Irani, Z., Osman, I. H., Balci, A., Ozkan, S., & Medeni, T. D. (2008). Toward a reference process model for citizen-oriented evaluation of e-Government services. *Transforming Government: People Process and Policy, 2*(4), 297–310. doi:10.1108/17506160810917972

McGuire, M. (2006). Collaborative Public Management: Assessing What We Know and How We Know It. *Public Administration Review, 66*(1), 33–43. doi:10.1111/j.1540-6210.2006.00664.x

Melao, N., & Pidd, M. (2000). A Conceptual Framework for Understanding Business Process and Business Process Modeling. *Information Systems Journal, 10,* 105–129. doi:10.1046/j.1365-2575.2000.00075.x

Milner, H. V. (2006). The Digital Divide: The Role of Political Institutions in Technology Diffusion. *Comparative Political Studies, 39*(2), 176–199. doi:10.1177/0010414005282983

Moon, M. J. (2002). The Evolution of E-Government among Municipalities: Rhetoric or Reality? *Public Administration Review, 62*(4), 424–433. doi:10.1111/0033-3352.00196

Navarra, D. D., & Cornford, T. (2009). Globalization, networks, and governance: Researching global ICT programs. *Government Information Quarterly, 26*(1), 35–41. doi:10.1016/j.giq.2008.08.003

Noordhoek, P., & Saner, R. (2005). Beyond New Public Management: Answering the Claims of Both Politics and Society. *Public Organization Review: A Global Journal, 5*(1), 35-53.

Norris, D. F., & Moon, M. J. (2005). Advancing E-Government at the Grassroots: Tortoise or Hare? *Public Administration Review, 65*(1), 64–75. doi:10.1111/j.1540-6210.2005.00431.x

Patel, N. V. (2007). Deferred Action: Theoretical model of process architecture design for emergent business processes. *International Journal of Business Science and Applied Management, 2*(3), 4–21.

Phang, C. W., Sutanto, J., Li, Y., & Kankanhalli, A. (2005). Senior Citizens' Adoption of E-Government: In Quest of the Antecedents of Perceived Usefulness. In *Proceedings of the 38th Hawaii International Conference on System Sciences.*

Reddick, C. G. (2004). A two-stage model of e-government growth: Theories and empirical evidence for U.S. cities. *Government Information Quarterly, 21*(1), 51–64. doi:10.1016/j.giq.2003.11.004

Seifert, J. W., & Chung, J. (2009). Using E-Government to Reinforce Government–Citizen Relationships: Comparing Government Reform in the United States and China. *Social Science Computer Review, 27*(1), 3–23. doi:10.1177/0894439308316404

Sunny, M., & McNiven, J. D. (2003). E-Government and E-Governance: The Future Isn't What It Used To Be. *Canadian Journal of Administrative Sciences, 20*(1), 74–86.

United Nations. (2005). *United Nations E-Government Survey.* Retrieved from http://unpan1.un.org/intradoc/groups/public/documents/un/unpan021888.pdf

Walser, K., Kuhn, A., & Reidl, R. (2009). Risk management in e-government from the perspective of IT governance. In *Proceedings of the 10th Annual International Conference on Digital Government Research: Social Networks: Making Connections between Citizens, Data and Government* (pp. 315-316).

Weerakkody, V., & Dhillon, G. (2008). Moving from E-Government to T-Government: A Study of Process Reengineering Challenges in a UK Local Authority Context. *International Journal of Electronic Government Research, 4*(4), 1–16.

West, D. M. (2001). *State and Federal E-Government in the United States, 2001 Brown University.* Retrieved from http://www.brown.edu/Departments/Taubman_Center/polreports/egovt01us.html

West, D. M. (2005). *Digital Government: Technology and Public Sector Performance.* Princeton, NJ: Princeton University Press.

Yoon, J., & Chae, M. (2009). Varying criticality of key success factors of national e-Strategy along the status of economic development of nations. *Government Information Quarterly, 26*(1), 25–34. doi:10.1016/j.giq.2008.08.006

This work was previously published in the International Journal of Electronic Government Research, Volume 7, Issue 1, edited by Vishanth Weerakkody, pp. 51-63, copyright 2011 by IGI Publishing (an imprint of IGI Global).

Chapter 5
Identifying Factors of Integration for an Interoperable Government Portal:
A Study in Indian Context

Rakhi Tripathi
Indian Institute of Technology Delhi, India

M. P. Gupta
Indian Institute of Technology Delhi, India

Jaijit Bhattacharya
Indian Institute of Technology Delhi, India

ABSTRACT

Interoperability is an important pre-condition for achieving higher stages of e-government and further ensures that a one stop portal will become a reality. Interoperability results from vertical and horizontal integration. The question arises: How can the level of interoperability and degree of integration be ascertained? This paper suggests a framework. It begins by identifying critical factors necessary for the successful adoption of interoperability technology along three dimensions of integration—process integration, communication integration, and data integration. Factors are formed from a literature review and discussions with webmasters and IT professionals working on portal development in various government departments of India. These factors are useful in further evaluation across the three dimensions and locate the position of a government portal in a technology adoption space. It is then possible to ascertain a portal's current level of integration sophistication.

1. INTRODUCTION

One-stop government portal has emerged worldwide as a trend to offer electronically administrative service packages that meet the needs of citizens' life events and business transactions, with a promise to enhance service accessibility and alleviate service delivery delays and costs. For citizens, it is an important interface that can bring entire government at their doorstep to the extent that it might almost mirror the government itself. One-stop portal becomes a reality if back offices

DOI: 10.4018/978-1-4666-2458-0.ch005

are interoperable (Choudrie & Weerrakody, 2007). Interoperability among Government organizations has been identified as a central issue and a critical prerequisite for the effective functioning of contemporary organizations systems (Klischewski, 2004; Peristeras et al., 2007; Tambouris et al., 2004; Tambouris & Tarabanis, 2005). To achieve an interoperable government, the integration of government information resources and processes, and thus the interoperation of independent information systems, are essential. Economic benefits of interoperability result in lower transaction costs typically utilizing standardized processes. Yet, most integration and interoperation efforts face serious challenges and limitations. Exchanges of information and services are fragmented and complex, plagued by technical and organizational problems (Gouscos et al., 2007).

A distinction should be made between interoperability and integration. Integration is the forming of a larger unit of government entities, temporary or permanent, for the purpose of merging processes and/or sharing information. Interoperation in e-Government occurs whenever independent or heterogeneous information systems or their components controlled by different jurisdictions, administrations, or external partners work together (efficiently and effectively) in a predefined and agreed-upon fashion. E-Government interoperability is the technical capability for e-Government interoperation (Scholl & Klischewski, 2007).

In this paper attempt is made to identify the organizational and technical factors of integration for an interoperable government portal in Indian context. A three dimensional adoption space model proposed by Chen et al. (2005) has been taken up to measure the level of integration. Three dimensions of integration are: Data, Process and Communication. All the dimensions and organizational factors are inter-related. Additionally, the factors of each dimension are in either positive (reinforcing) or negative (balancing) feedback loop. Key inter-relations are demonstrated through causal loop diagrams as they enhance learning processes in

the organisation by evaluating individual's performance based on strategically linked measures (Banker et al., 2004). By identifying the factors along with their relationships, scholars and practitioners have a framework within which they can measure the current position of an organization and focus on improving the factors to achieve interoperability.

The structure of the paper is as follows. In the following section, relevant literature on interoperability is laid out. Section 3, discusses the research methodology used in this research. Next, Section 4 introduces important organizational factors contributing to Integration maturity and influencing the adoption of Interoperability. Section 5 presents integration in three dimensions – data, process and communication and proceeds with their relevant determinants. Section 6 delves into synthesis of affiliation of organizational factors and the technical factors (three dimensions) including discussion. Finally, in section 7 the article offers some conclusions that include limitations of the paper along with future work.

2. LITERATURE REVIEW

The term Interoperability has been defined by different organizations and authors: The European Commission (2003) has defined interoperability as "the means by which the inter-linking of systems, information and ways of working, whether within or between administrations, nationally or across Europe, or with the enterprise sector, occurs". Interoperability is the ability of government organizations to share information and integrate information and business processes by use of common standards and work practices (State Services Commission, 2007). According to the Government Interoperability Framework (Office of the E-Envoy, 2004) and Government CIO (2007), if the coherent exchange of information and services between systems is achieved then the systems can be regarded as truly interoperable.

When information and services are provided to and accepted between systems and organizations, they are said to inter-operate.

Interoperability of systems enables interoperability of organizations. Systems interoperability is concerned with the ability of two or more systems or components to exchange information and to use the information that has been exchanged. Organizational interoperability is concerned with the ability of two or more units to provide services to and accept services from other units, and to use the services so exchanged to enable them to operate effectively together (Legner & Lebreton, 2007). Further interoperability facilitates the re-use of the information (resources) once the levels of integration are achieved. As identified by Traunmüller (2005) and Landsbergen & Wolken (2001), the benefits of interoperability become clear in the following settings: more effectiveness (interconnection instead of isolated solutions), efficiency (reduction of the transaction costs and increase of the involved agents' participation), and responsiveness (better access to more information, making possible the fastest resolution of the problems).

In a narrow sense, the term interoperability is often used to describe technical systems. In a broader sense, social, political, and organizational factors influencing systems and systems performance must also be taken into account (Gottschalk, 2009). Klischewski and Scholl (2006) further stress that systems and applications that interoperate are characterized by the following aspects: independency, heterogeneity, and control by different jurisdictions/administrations or by external actors; yet also cooperation in a predefined and agreed upon fashion. Likewise, Wimmer et al. (2006) stress that interoperation can only be reached by means of open standards, whereby interoperation needs to be addressed on technical, semantic and organizational level alike. The European Interoperability Framework (2003) (EIF) definition identifies three separate aspects: 1. Technical – linking up computer systems by agreeing on standards for presenting, collecting, exchanging, processing, transporting data; 2. Semantic – ensuring that transported data shares the same meaning for link-up systems; 3. Organisational – organising business processes and internal organisation structures for better exchange of data. When dealing with pure technology, the interoperability concept may be defined according to the software discipline, which understands interoperability to be the "ability to exchange functionality and interpretable data between two software entities" (Mowbray & Zahavi, 1995). Issues covered by this concept are usually grouped in two fields: *Application interoperability*, which includes the communications issues, both at the telecommunications network access level and at the network interconnection level; and the distributed applications issues, regarding the remote procedure call/method invocation mechanisms and the public interface exportation/binding; *Semantic interoperability*, which includes both the data interpretation, by means of XML schemas, and the knowledge representation and exploitation, by means of ontologies and agents.

Currently there are several research efforts that try to address interoperability issues in e-government in all three EIF dimensions. Guijarro (2007, 2009) surveyed existing e-government interoperability initiatives and enterprise architectures in the EU and USA. Naiman and Ouksel (1995) classified semantic conflicts in database systems. Park and Ram (2004) also give a description of semantic interoperability conflicts regardless of the application domain, while Ram and Park (2004) propose the resolution of these conflicts using ontology.

There have been initiatives carried out by e-government organizations in the interoperability arena, which have developed the corresponding interoperability frameworks in different countries of the world (Guijarro, 2006). Table 1 summarizes main features of the e-government initiatives. In the United Kingdom, the e-government Unit (eGU), formerly known as Office of the e-Envoy, has based its technical guidance on the e-government Interoperability Framework (e-GIF), which was issued in 2000 (UK Government, 2000). It covers four areas: interconnectivity, data integration, e-services access, and content management. The French ADAE (Agence pour le Développement de l'Administration Électronique) published in January 2002, comprises the recommendations for strengthening public electronic systems coherence and for enabling multi-agency electronic service delivery. Germany's Federal Government Co-ordination and Advisory Agency for IT in the Federal Administration (KBSt), published the Standards and Architectures for e-government Applications (SAGA) in February 2003. SAGA serves as an orientation aid for decision-makers in the e-government teams in German administrations. In Denmark, the National IT and Telecom Agency published the first version of an interoperability framework in 2004 under the name of Danish e-government Interoperability Framework (DIF). DIF is intended as a guideline to public agencies as they develop IT plans and projects. In the United States, the Federal Chief Information Officers Council13 (CIOC) issued the Federal Enterprise Architecture Framework (FEAF) in September 1999. The Asian countries like Hong Kong, Malaysia and Srilanka have also developed their interoperability frameworks. Malaysia has Malaysian Government Interoperability Framework (MyGIF) which was issued in 2003; Hong Kong has Hong Kong Special Administrative Region (HKSARG) framework issued in 2005 and Srilanka's frameworke id LIFe which was issued in 2006. All these frameworks provide Interconnection, data integration, information access, Security and metadata.

In Table 1, majority of the interoperability frameworks are performing data integration. Other focus of the frameworks is: interconnection, content management metadata, telecommunication network access, workflow management, group working, and security.

For interoperability both horizontal and vertical integration forms the basis. Integration can be defined as "the forming of a (temporary or permanent) larger unit of government entities for the purpose of merging processes [and systems] and sharing information" (Klischewski & Scholl, 2006). Integration can be approached in various manners and at various levels (Vernadat, 1996) for example: (i) physical integration (computer networks), ii) application integration (integration of software applications and database systems) and (iii) business integration (co-ordination of functions that manage, control and monitor business processes).

E-Government interoperability has become a crucial issue because recent ICT investments have reinforced the old barriers that made government decision-making, not to mention citizen access to public services, difficult. In a number of governments, agencies are deploying new ICT systems with specifications and solutions relevant to their particular needs but without adequate attention to the need to connect, exchange and re-use data with other agencies' ICT systems. The result is a patchwork of ICT solutions that is not always compatible with each other and an e-government programme that does not meet its goals.

However, there are significant barriers to achieve interoperability in an effective and wide way. These barriers can be classified as politics, organizational, economical and technical (Anderseen & Dawes, 1991): Political - conflicts in the definitions of the levels of privacy in the accesses to the information, predominant organizational culture, etc.; Organizational - lack of experience and absence of the predisposition of sharing, organizational culture, etc.; Economical - lack of resources for disposing the information for other agencies, form of acquisition of the resources, etc.; Technical - incompatibility of adopted hardware and software; property rights. Therefore, interoperability standards setting can be considered as a hard task to achieve, since the

Table 1. Interoperability frameworks developed globally

Country	Interoperability framework	Organization	Year of release	Objective
UK	e-GIF (E-government Interoperability Framework)	eGU (e-government unit)	2000	interconnectivity, data integration, e-services access and content management metadata
France	CCI (Le Cadre Commun d'Inter-operabilite)	ADAE	2002	enabling multi-agency electronic service delivery
Germany	SAGA (Standards and Architectures for e-government Applications)	KDSt	2003	orientation aid for decision-makers in the e-government teams
Denmark	DIF (Danish e- government Interoperability Framework)	ITST	2004	guideline to public agencies as they develop IT plans and projects
USA	EAG (E-government Enterprise Architecture Guidance)	CIOC	1999	guiding the e-government projects across the federal government
Malaysia	MyGIF (Malaysian Government Interoperability Framework)		2003	Interconnection, data integration, information access, Security and metadata
Hong Kong	(HKSARG) Hong Kong Special Administrative Region	IFCG	2005	Data integration, security
Sri Lanka	LIFe	ICTA	2006	Data integration, metadata,

defined specifications have to overcome several barriers to be adopted.

It is often found that Government portals are still far behind the stages of either of their integration steps. The adoption of a new technology such as Interoperability involves a proper assessment of the status of integration (process integration, data integration and technical integration) within the government. Therefore, understanding the factors relevant to the adoption of interoperability will help in achieving integration and further achieving interoperability. Higher the level of integration of an organization, lesser the resources needed to adopt the interoperability technology.

3. RESEARCH METHODOLOGY

Maturity of integration can be understood by the degree of sophistication. "Degree of sophistication" here refers to how an organization applies different technology components, structural factors and human factors for its applications (Gomond & Picavet, 1999; Wollschlaeger, 1998). Further an organization's information technology matu-

rity depends not only on the technological aspect but also on various organizational characteristics (Benbasat et al., 1980; Cheney & Dickson, 1982). Layne and Lee (2001) highlighted the fact that achieving more mature levels of e-government requires higher levels of both technology and organizational complexity.

Evaluating the maturity level of integration requires assessment of integration from multiple dimensions. In our study, integration has been divided into three dimensions: Data Integration, Process Integration and Communication Integration. Given these dimensions, adoption space model proposed by Chen et al. (2003) has been followed to locate the position of an organization's portal for interoperability (Figure 1). Thus it is necessary to specify the factors that contribute to each of the three domains identified. In this study, we focus on determining those organizational and technological factors that are considered explicitly or implicitly critical for measuring integration sophistication in Government departments (Chen et al., 2003) in the context of adopting Interoperability. The organizational factors are inputs and the technical factors are outputs.

Figure 1. Adoption space

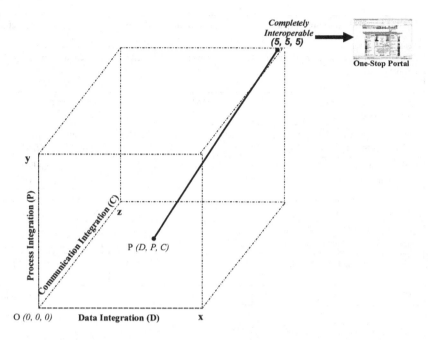

After identifying the dimensions, the position of an organization can be located (point P) through different mechanisms for measurement (Chen et al., 2003). Once the coordinates of an organization in the adoption space are found and the destination is decided, the distance between point P and desirable destination represents the effort that the organization needs to make in order to achieve the desired amount of Interoperability adoption.

The factors were identified from two sources. First, review of current literature in information systems research is used to identify factors found to influence the success of IT initiatives. This review includes the scanning of the top journals in public administration. Articles with a focus on e-government success factors were selected. The literature review also includes selected journal articles and book chapters that specifically address IT success factors in both public and private organizations. Second, interviews and discussions with the high rank Government officials in India were conducted. The officials were selected on the basis of their involvement with e-government

initiatives within departments in central and state governments in India. Few of them are responsible for the national portal of India. Interviews were conducted both personally and over the phone. An in-depth knowledge about portal development and interoperability was attained. This approach provides an opportunity to integrate users in the system design in a feasible manner. Literature review provides a scenario of past that helps in understanding the issues and challenges of the subject. Interviews with experts give clarity on the current situation and helps in finding the key factors. The interview is again a fine method with which to identify incidents that are critical for (dis)satisfaction with the service (Gremler, 2004).

4. ORGANIZATIONAL FACTORS

Besides the technological factors, organizational factors also play a vital role in achieving complete interoperability. In favour of this, organization has to gear up several resources and support which may be a challenge. Studies from the literature reveal that several organizational factors have been identified for successful e-government. Relevant organizational factors that require close attention would be following:

- **Financial Resources:** In a developing country like India, one of the most critical factors is financial resources. Without a proper financial backup even a good plan will fail. To come up with an effective portal a strong financial support is required for manpower, machinery and communication (Chen et al., 2007; Iacouvou et al., 1995; Kannibiran & Banumathi, 2008; Zarei et al., 2008).

- **Top Management Support:** Support of top level management is a key success factor for most new initiatives in an organization, whether they are technology related or not. There are a considerable number of studies that underscore the role of top management support as one of the deciding factors for the success of any IT endeavour (Kambil et al., 2000, Eder & Igbaria, 2001). Many authors suggest that leadership commitment is a key challenge for the success of any knowledge management initiative (Venkatesh et al., 2003; Wang, 2003; Fu et al., 2004; Chang et al., 2005).

- **Technical Expertise:** Chen et al. (2003) put forward that IT skill set is one of the factors affecting adoption and diffusion of innovations for e-business systems. In addition, Anurag Srivastava, IT Director of Madhya Pradesh, India (Personal communication, April 13, 2009) states "A skilled person with an experience in developing portal can easily understand the requirements of the portal and also can help in adopting new technologies". Availability of skilled manpower is a major concern. As a result most government department

in India finds it difficult to successfully implement an e-government project.

- **Strategic Goals:** Development of portal has various stages (Layne & Lee, 2001) and hence, it is essential to have a proper strategic plan to achieve each level of portal. Lack of clarity will lead to an improper infrastructure which will further lead to unsatisfactory results.

- **Promotion Efforts:** People are often unaware of the availability and usefulness of the e-government projects. Adequate training is necessary for the end users to make them understand the benefits of e-government (Brown, 2003; DeLone & Mclea, 2003; Garson, 2003). As stated by Neeta Verma, Senior Technical Director, NIC, India (Personal communication, August 08, 2007), "if the users are unaware of the services provided by the portal then the portal will not be fully utilized". Hence, awareness of the portal's utility among the citizens is requisite.

- **Internal Motivation:** It is essential to have both vertical and horizontal integration within and among different Government departments to achieve one-stop portal. 'At present in some departments of India vertical integration is being achieved. But to achieve horizontal integration a full support from various departments is required' (Janmejay Thakur, Principal System Analyst of Indian Government Tenders, India, Personal Communication, March 3, 2009; Neeta Verma, Senior Technical Director, NIC, India, Personal Communication, August 8, 2007). Thus, every government organization must be encouraged for integration.

- **Collaborative Mindset:** The level of trust that exists between the organization, its sub-units, and its employees greatly influences the amount of knowledge that flows both between individuals and from individuals into the firm's portal (Delong & Fahey, 2000). Many a times the people who are important viz. boss, peers, subordinate do not support the use of e-government (Brown & Brudney, 2003; Edmiston, 2003; Gupta et al., 2005; Heintze & Bretschneider, 2000; Holden et al., 2003; La Porte et al., 2002; Venkatesh et al., 2003). Therefore, attention should be paid to the supporting norms and behavioural practices that manifest trust as an important organizational value.

- **IT Maturity:** If the level of IT maturity is high then fewer efforts are required to achieve a one-stop portal as high IT maturity means higher user awareness, good IT planning, good IT usage history etc. (Benbasat et al, 1980). Furthermore, if the level of IT maturity is low then more efforts are required to achieve one-stop portal. In addition, in firms with a high level of IT management maturity, top management may be expected to have greater knowledge about IT and participation in IS planning (Johnston & Carri, 1988; Lederer & Mendelow, 1987; Sabherwal & King, 1992)

- **Security Apprehensions:** Security is not only a technical issue but also a prime organizational factor. For any portal security is one of the biggest concerns (Layne & Lee, 2001). E-government users are concerned about the security (Petrovic, 2004; Seifert & Relyea, 2004; Suh & Han, 2003) & privacy related issues, which have also been raised by several authors (Andersen & Dawes, 1991; Moon, 2002; Reddick, 2009).

The organizational factors have either positive or negative connection between them and this is described through a Causal loop diagram (Figure 2). The top management support plays an essential role in achieving the level of integration.

Strong top management support will identify and focus on strategic goals which will further raise the demand for technical expertise. Enhanced top management support along with strategic goals and technical expertise will motivate integration of information with other departments. Hence, this will improve the level of integration. Once the level of integration is achieved less support from top level management is required (balancing $-B_1$). There is also a negative feedback of Integration and financial resources (B_4). When the level of integration is low then need for financial resources increase and as the level of integration increases the need for financial resources will decrease. Conversely with high level of integration, the issue of security rises. Therefore, more security measures necessitate as the level of integration increases and vice versa (Reinforcing feedback loop $-R_1$).

In addition there are two loops with top management support. Top management will improve collaborative mindset and have a positive feedback (R_2). Greater IT management maturity can be characterized by top management support and their awareness of the organization's long-term strategic plans (Cash et al., 1992; Earl, 1993; Sabherwal & Kirs, 1994). This will further lead to integration (B_2). Promotion of portal utilities can also help in achieving integration. For this promotion needs to be a part of strategic goals (B_3).

5. DIMENSIONS OF INTEGRATION

With an aim to attain an interoperable Government portal, high degree of Integration is required among back offices. According to Vernadat (1996), integration can be divided into dimensions. In this study integration is divided into three dimensions: Data Integration, Process Integration and Communication Integration. For each dimension different factors have been developed. The factors have been formed from studies in the literature and discus-

Figure 2. Causal loop diagram – organizational factors

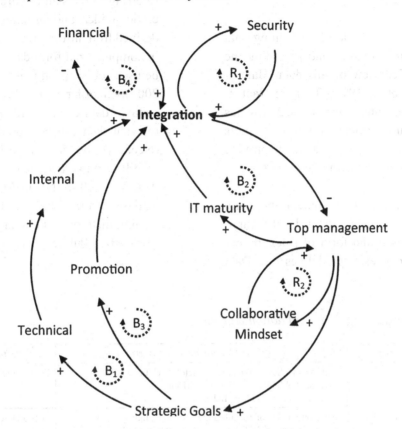

sions with high-ranking government officials, webmasters and IT professionals working on portal development in various government departments of India. Hiller and Bélanger (2001), in particular, stress increasing levels of data integration for true transformational e-government but warn that such data integration raises significant privacy issues when the data involve personally identifiable information. According to Neeta Verma, Senior Technical Director of NIC, India, (Personal Communication, August 8, 2007) in order to achieve any of the three dimensions of integration an appropriate architecture forms the basis. Further she adds that data centres are required for e-governance applications and portals. Ajay K. Singh, Director of Centre for Railway Information Systems, India (Personal Communication, February 28, 2009) states, "For any integration, compatibility

of the existing technologies is the initial step". "Security is the prime concern" pointed by Navin Mittal, Collector, Andhra Pradesh, India (Personal Communication, February 12, 2008). Hardeep S. Hora, Technical Director of NIC, India (Personal Communication, March 7, 2009), concludes that out of the three dimensions the maturity level of process integration is the lowest in India.

E-government interoperability can be achieved through the adoption of standards –"agreement among independent parties about how to go about doing some task" (Bloomberg & Schmelzer, 2006; Furlong, 2008) – or through architecture –"the fundamental organization of a system embodied by its components and their relationships to each other and to the environment, and the principles guiding its design and activity" (IEEE, 2006).

Data Integration

Data integration is an issue of combining data residing at different sources and providing the user with a unified view of this data (Halevy, 2001; Srivastava et al., 1996). There are factors that constitute Data integration. Table 2 provides an overview of studies from literature and experts consulted that have considered factors to provide a better understanding of data integration.

- **Data Centre:** In Government there are multiple diverse data sources: Unstructured data that lies in the form of rules, procedures and concepts, guidelines etc; Data

referring to facts and figures treated as operational idea; and Structured data which is derived from information that can be stored in computerized form database and further be used for decision making (Gupta et al., 2005). In order to handle diverse data a suitable data centre is required where the relevant data can be stored and managed (Neeta Verma, Senior Technical Director of NIC, India, Personal Communication, August 8, 2007; Navin Mittal, Collector, Andhra Pradesh, India, Personal Communication, February 12, 2008; Mirulesh, Public Works Department,

Table 2. Studies examining factors of data integration

Literature Referred	Expert Consulted (2007 – 2009)	Factor Identified
Gupta et al, 2005	Neeta Verma, Senior Technical Director, NIC, India; Mirulesh, Public Works Department (Delhi), India; Navin Mittal, Collector, Andhra Pradesh, India	Data centre
IEEE, 2006	Neeta Verma, Senior Technical Director, NIC, India; Anurag Srivastava, IT Director, Madhya Pradesh India	Data architecture
	K. N. Narayankar, Senior Research Executive, Central Water & Power Research Station, India; Shefali Dash, Deputy Director General, NIC-HQ, India	Data update
Santos & Reinhard, 2007; Rao et al, 2008; Layne & Lee, 2001	Ajay K. Singh, Director, CRIS, India; Ahmed, Software Programmer, Finance Commission of India	Compatible standards
Mach et al, 2006; Hiller & Belanger 2001	Dibakar Ray, Scientist, NIC, India; Huzur Saran, Professor, Department of Computer Science and Engineering, IITD, India; U.C. Nangia, Director, Ministry of Petroleum & Natural Gas, India	Back office integration
Eckerson, 1999	Anurag Srivastava, IT Director, Madhya Pradesh India; Navin Mittal, Collector, Andhra Pradesh, India; Jacob Victor, Joint Director (E-governance), Andhra Pradesh, India	Data security
Weng & Tsai, 2006; Ding et al, 2001,	Dibakar Ray, Scientist, NIC, India; Jacob Victor, Joint Director (E-governance), Andhra Pradesh, India	Ontology
Coyle, 2002; The Open Group 2005,	Anurag Srivastava, IT Director, Madhya Pradesh India; Dibakar Ray, Scientist, NIC, India; Jacob Victor, Joint Director (E-governance), Andhra Pradesh, India	Open standards
IFEG Version 2.4 Report (2005)	Janmejay, Principal System Analyst, Indian Government Tenders, India	Message Formatting Language
"	"	Data Replication
"	"	Data Transformation
"	"	Data Modelling
"	Janmejay, Principal System Analyst, Indian Government Tenders, India; D. C. Mishra, Senior Technical Director, NIC, India,	Data Resource Description

Delhi, India, Personal Communication, March 7, 2009).

- **Data Architecture:** Neeta Verma (Senior Technical Director of NIC, India, Personal Communication, August 08, 2007) and Anurag Srivastava (IT Director, Madhya Pradesh India, Personal Communication, April 13, 2009) testified about their views: with an appropriate data centre the need for integrated data arises to combine all relevant data accessible through data. As proposed by IEEE (2006) architecture for combining all relevant data is necessary where all the databases from different Government departments can be integrated.

- **Data Update:** The data of Government organizations change on a regular basis. For example: Increase and decrease in number of birth rates, death rates, change in addresses etc. Therefore, a regular update of data is crucial (Shefali Dash, Deputy Director General, NIC-HQ, India, Personal Communication, January 28, 2008; K. N. Narayankar, Senior Research Executive, Central Water & Power Research Station, India, Personal Communication, March 17, 2008).

- **Compatible Standards:** In India, incompatible standards are used for maintaining information by every organization separately. This makes data sharing unmanageable. For this reason sharing data with other organizations compatible standards have to be adopted (Ajay K. Singh, Director, Centre for Railway Information Systems, India, Personal Communication, February 28, 2009; Ahmed, a Software Programmer, Finance Commission of India, Telephonic Communication, March 19, 2009). For example, a residential address might be stored in 10 unconnected computer systems. If the technologies are not compatible then there will not be flow of infor-

mation. Adoption of compatible standards will not only save time but also will be cost effective (Layne & Lee, 2001; Rao et al., 2008; Santos & Reinhard, 2007).

- **Back Office Integration:** Discussed with Dibakar Ray (Scientist, National Informatics Centre, India, Personal Communication, October 10, 2007) and U.C. Nangia (Director, Ministry of Petroleum & Natural Gas, India, Personal Communication, May 22, 2009) back office integration is mandatory for a citizen centric portal. For example, citizen enters change of address once and this information is saved by all the other integrated departments. This will improve customer service and provide faster response time (Hiller & Belanger 2001; Mach et al., 2006; Santos, 2008).

- **Data Security:** The organization's portal must adopt mechanisms for data security (Anurag Srivastava, IT Director, Madhya Pradesh, India, Personal Communication, April 13, 2009; Mittal, Collector, Andhra Pradesh, India, Personal Communication, February 12, 2008; Jacob Victor, Joint Director (E-governance), Andhra Pradesh, India, Personal Communication, February 15, 2008) and hence, support cryptography, authentication, firewalls, etc. to safeguard corporate information and prevent unauthorized access. The ability to secure access to diverse range of resources with incompatible security controls is an enormous challenge for portals (Eckerson, 1999).

Specialized technologies for supporting metadata (data of data) are required to accomplish data integration. With literature review and discussions with IT professionals in India (Table 2) the following technologies are found significant for data integration:

- **Ontology:** Ontology is made capable to 'describe metadata' in order to build one complete glossary that will clearly define the data found in the World Wide Web (Weng & Tsai, 2006). The reason ontologies are becoming so popular is largely due to what they promise: a shared and common understanding of some domain that can be communicated between people and application systems (Ding et al., 2002). With colossal government data need for shared domain occurs.

- **Open Standards:** Proprietary standards can sometimes be expensive and it may be cost prohibitive to purchase access to a proprietary standard if it is ever needed (The Open Group, 2005). The use of open standards can help assure interoperability of diverse systems, reduce the risk of vendor lock-in and guarantee data preservation. Three key characteristics of open standards identified by Coyle (2002) are 1) that anyone can use the standards to develop software, 2) anyone can acquire the standards for free or without a significant cost, and 3) the standard has been developed in a way in which anyone can participate.

- **Data Replication:** Data replication is a process of maintaining a defined set of data in more than one location. It involves copying designated changes from one location (a source) to another (a target), and synchronizing the data in both locations (IBM, 2008). Data replication provides support for automated real time data synchronization enabling locality of access for data access regardless of source implementation (E-Governance Standards, n.d.). This technology alleviates back office integration for portal.

- **Data Transformation:** Both structured and unstructured data must often undergo considerable transformation before it can be used by applications. Data transfor- mation enables the translation of data information to support data cleansing and metadata interchange through leveraging industry standards. Some of the open standards that facilitate data transformation are: ANSI SQL, XML (Chen, 2003). EDI standards: UN/EDIFACT, including ANSI X.12 (E-Governance Standards, n.d.).

- **Message Formatting Language:** The Message Formatting Language is used to define the format of data messages and business documents that can be exchanged between applications. This includes defining the standards for the data exchange between the parties. The involved parties can be the internal Government organizations as well as outside agencies (E-Governance Standards, n.d.).

- **Data Modelling:** Data Modelling defines the conventions to be used for representation of system and data models among all the internal government departments. Data modelling is used to provide the conceptual design primarily for human interpretation. UML (Unified Modelling Language) is the most widely used standard for defining and exchanging the data schema and data model. UML has been supported by lots of case tools, designing tools and software testing products (E-Governance Standards, n.d.).

- **Data Resource Description:** Data Resource Description (RDF) defines the language for representing metadata. Metadata commonly defined as data about data, relates to a set of attributes that will capture the semantics of individual data items. Each element contains information related to a particular aspect of the information resource and metadata describes the technical aspects of information resources. (E-Governance Standards, n.d.).

The relation between factors of Data Integration is illustrated through causal loop diagrams

(Figure 3). Loop B_1 is balancing feedback loop which shows that the need for an adequate data centre increases as the level of data integration decreases. With an appropriate data centre the requirement for data security will also increase.

Once the level of integration is achieved the need for data centre will decline – hence, balancing loop. Along with data centre, the technical aspects (Ontology, Data replication, Data modeling, RDF) and updating data becomes necessary (Loop B_2 and B_3). An adequate data centre will lead to adoption of open standards which will further make the software versions compatible (Reinforcing – Loop R_1). Additionally, architecture for combining data will be formed if appropriate data is available in data centre. This architecture will increase Integration of service delivery departments and this will further enhance data

centre (Reinforcing loop – Loop R_2). Same as in loop B_1, an increase in factors will improve the level of integration. Considering the level of data integration is achieved the need for adequate data centre will reduce.

Process Integration

For inter-organizational integration the necessity for process integration increases. Hardeep S. Hora, a Technical director of NIC, Ministry of Tribal Affairs, India (Personal Communication, March 7, 2009) points out that different processes are developed for every level of government organizations. Hence, integration of these processes is essential. The factors of process integration are also derived from reviews and discussions with Indian IT professional that are illustrated in Table 3.

Figure 3. Causal loop diagram for data integration

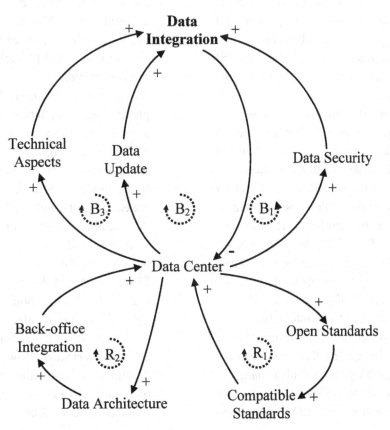

Table 3. Studies and discussions on factors of process integration

Literature Referred	Expert Consulted (2007 – 2009)	Factor Identified
Liu et al, 2005	Ahmed, Software Programmer, Finance Commission of India; Huzur Saran, Professor, Department of Computer Science and Engineering, IITD, India; Ajay K. Singh, Director, CRIS, India,	Process codification
Ghattas & Soffer, 2008; Wittenburg et al, 2007	Anurag Srivastava, IT Director, Madhya Pradesh, India; Hardeep S. Hora, NIC, India; Huzur Saran, Professor, Department of Computer Science and Engineering, IITD, India; Ajay K. Singh, Director, CRIS, India,	Formulation of processes
Ceravolo et al, 2008; Wittenburg et al, 2007	Ahmed, Software Programmer, Finance Commission of India; Navin Mittal, Collector, Andhra Pradesh, India	Process update
DoD, 1996	Shefali Dash, Deputy Director General, NIC-HQ, India; Jacob Victor, Joint Director (E-governance), Andhra Pradesh, India	Reuse
Gugliotta et al, 2005; Liu et al, 2005	Neeta Verma, Senior Technical Director, NIC, India; Janmejay, Principal System Analyst, Indian Government Tenders, India	Middleware
	Hardeep S. Hora, technical director of NIC, India; D. C. Mishra, Senior Technical Director, NIC, India	Open standards

- **Process Codification:** In government organizations every function involves a process. For portal improvement it is important that all the processes are defined and classified. For example applying for passport, a citizen has to undergo a process and further each process has sub processes like verification of personal details etc. Thus all these processes need to be formed and organized (Liu et al., 2005).

- **Formulation of Processes:** Integration of all the processes whether internal or external in a portal is necessary. Internal integration includes all the integration aspects within one organization. External integration covers all the possible integration patterns across multiple organizations (Ghattas & Soffer, 2008; Wittenburg et al., 2007). Continuing with the same example of applying passport, the different processes like verification of personal details, status update etc. need to be integrated.

- **Process Update:** Once the processes are codified and integrated, there is a need for update. Like data, processes also change in Government and so updating of processes is crucial (Ceravolo et al., 2008, Wittenburg et al, 2007). For an example: In a government department, the information is flowing vertically and then later the information flows horizontally. For this either the process is modified or a new process is adopted. Navin Mittal, Collector, Andhra Pradesh, India (Personal Communication, February 12, 2008) concludes that updating is required.

- **Reuse:** Software reuse is the process of implementing or updating software systems using existing software assets (Department of Defense, 1996). A good software reuse process facilitates the increase of productivity, quality, and reliability, and the decrease of costs and implementation time. An initial investment is required to start a software reuse process, but that investment pays for itself in a few reuses.

- **Middleware:** Middleware allows the semantic description, publishing and updating of life events in order to provide citizens with an up-to-date and personalized list of available services; allows the description, identification, instantiation and invocation of services (Gugliotta et al., 2005). It is optional to include middleware in the eGIF as there are other frameworks available that have features of both middleware and back office integration.

- **Open Standards:** Adoption of open standards for combining the processes. As discussed in the last section the use of open standards can help assure interoperability of diverse systems as it avoids the use of vendor lock.

Figure 4 shows the causal loop diagram for the factors which effect Process integration. Loop B_1 is balancing feedback loop which shows for process codification, formulation of all the processes is essential. Further, if the processes are well formulated an architecture with technical aspects has to be formed. This will in return increase the level of Process Integration. Process codification will deteriorate after the achievement of process integration. Loop B_2 is again a balancing loop.

Technical aspects (Middleware) demands open standards. Open standards will acquire process of implementing or updating software systems using existing software assets (reuse) and update. Formation of technical aspects reduces the requirement of open standards – hence balancing loop.

Communication Integration

Communication integration comprises the use of electronic computers, computer software and computer networks to convert, store, protect, process, transmit and securely retrieve information. A set of factors for achieving success inter and intra departmental integration are drawn from the literature and interviewing experts and are presented in Table 4.

- **Networking:** Network architecture is the design of a computer network. It includes the design principles, physical configuration, functional organization, operational procedures, and data formats used as the bases for the design, construction, modification, and operation of a communications network. It outlines the products and services required in data communication networks. For an interoperable portal efficient network architecture is essential.
- **Connectivity:** In government departments' enormous data is stored and shared. With this the requirement for high bandwidth applications, such as live digital ref-

Figure 4. Causal loop diagram for process integration

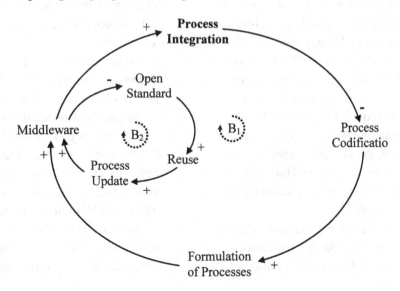

Table 4. Review on factors of communication integration

Literature Referred	Expert Consulted (2007 – 2009)	Factor Identified
	Ronald Noronha, Chief Manager, BPCL, India; Mirulesh, Web Developer, Public Works Department (Delhi), India	Networking
Strover, 2001	R. Vijaya Chakraboraty, Senior Manager (Systems), National Aluminium Corporation Limited, India	Connectivity
Huang et al, 2006; Ardagna & Pernici, 2006; CISCO, 2006	Naveen Agrawal, Technical Director (IT), Department of Land Resources, India; U.C. Nangia, Director, Ministry of Petroleum & Natural Gas, India	Quality of services
Layne & Lee, 2001; Bertot & Jaeger, 2006; Evans & Yen, 2006	Jacob Victor, Joint Director (E-governance), Andhra Pradesh, India; Janmejay, Principal System Analyst, Indian Government Tenders, India	Web and internet technologies
Lin & Lin, 2008	Anurag Srivastava, IT Director, Madhya Pradesh India Shefali Dash, Deputy Director General, NIC-HQ, India Dibakar Ray, Scientist, NIC, India	Interoperability of technologies
Straub & Nance 1990; Rainer et al., 1991	Vinay K. Chaudhary, Engineer, Power Grid Corporation, India; Mittal, Collector, Andhra Pradesh, India	Security
IFEG Version 2.4 Report (2005)	Naveen Agrawal, Technical Director (IT), Department of Land Resources, India; U.C. Nangia, Director, Ministry of Petroleum & Natural Gas, India	Intelligent design
IFEG Version 2.4 Report (2005)	Jacob Victor, Joint Director (E-governance), Andhra Pradesh, India; Janmejay, Principal System Analyst, Indian Government Tenders, India	Network Layer Security

erence continues to increase. For instance if a department sends crucial information to another department and the connectivity is slow then it will consume time (Strover, 2001).

- **Quality of Service:** A communications network transport a multitude of applications and data, including high-quality video and delay-sensitive data such as real-time voice. According to Huang et al., (2006) and Ardagna and Pernici (2006), networks must provide secure, predictable, measurable, and sometimes guaranteed services. Achieving the required Quality of Service (QoS) by managing the delay, delay variation (jitter) and packet loss parameters on a network becomes essential. Thus, QoS is the set of techniques to manage network resources (CISCO).

- **Web and Internet Technologies:** Governments worldwide are increasingly using the Internet to provide public ser-

vices to their constituents (Layne & Lee, 2001). Much of the research has focused on practical and technical dimensions while research on how to improve e-government for users remains scarce (Bertot & Jaeger, 2006). Web-based technologies offer governments more efficient and effective means than traditional physical channels to better serve their citizens (Evans & Yen, 2006).

- **Interoperability of Technologies:** Technical compatibility corresponds to the extent of fit of the new technology with existing data and telecommunications infrastructure (Lin & Lin, 2008). Lin and Lin (2008) concluded that incompatibility of new technologies with existing values and work practices is one of the greatest inhibitors in IT implementation. Thus, when organizations perceive e-government as compatible with existing beliefs and work practices, they are more likely to be positively predisposed to promoting its successful diffusion.

- **Security:** Another concern of the portals is the security of the network. Straub and Nance (1990) remark, "people frequently misuse hardware, programs and computer services". Each of these have specific risks that involves the vulnerability of information system assets to attacks from information system threats, where a "vulnerability" can affect an IS asset negatively (Rainer et al., 1991).

- **Intelligent Design:** The devices and channels that access applications can be of multiple types. Therefore, for an application to be accessed by different access channels, it needs to be intelligent enough so that it can convert the contents to a format that is understandable by the device or the channel medium accessing. Applications that can support all the formats are becoming essential. This will not only make the portal flexible but also reachable to most of the citizens (E-Governance Standards, n.d.). For example, citizens using the portal utilities from mobile phones etc.

- **Network Layer Security:** Network layer security standards deal with the security at the network level. These standards are relevant when for implementing virtual private network (VPN) and secure remote access. The most common standard used for this is Internet Protocol Security (IP sec), which provides a mechanism for securing IP. It is the security standard at the network layer for communication (E-Governance Standards, n.d.).

Figure 5 shows some negative (balancing) and some positive (reinforcing) feedback loops for factors of communication integration. With a decrease in level of communication integration the need for networking increases which require deployment of web and internet technologies. Level of net-

working can be improved by better connectivity and good quality of service. Therefore, there is a positive relation between networking, connectivity and quality of service (Reinforcing – R_1). There is an upward reinforcing feedback loop R_2 between deployment of web and internet technologies and intelligent design for multiple accesses. For example, with an increase with deployment of web and internet technologies there will be an increase in intelligent design for multiple accesses. Further a strong networking and adequate deployment of web and internet technologies will lead to the demand of interoperability of existing technology.

As discussed earlier security remains a concern with every dimension. With an increase in the level of interoperability, the necessity for security measures increases (Balancing feedback loop B_1). Thus all the factors help in achieving communication integration. This will further decrease the need for improved networking.

6. SYNTHESIS AND DISCUSSION

One of the key objectives under the e-government agenda is to achieve a one-stop government portal so that the user is able to access integrated public services through a single point even if these services are actually provided by different departments or authorities. One stop portal requires interoperability and will be achieved after a totally integrated presence stage. Totally integrated presence stage refers to the situation in which government services are fully integrated (vertically and horizontally) (Hiller & Bélanger, 2001; UN & ASPA, 2002). In this stage, governments undertake institutional and administrative reforms that fully employ the potential of information technologies (Grönlund, 2001).

Fully integrated services require complete integration of its dimensions i.e. data, process and communication. To do so different determinants of the dimensions need to be identified. It has been shown that these determinants are not mutually

Figure 5. Causal loop diagram for communication integration

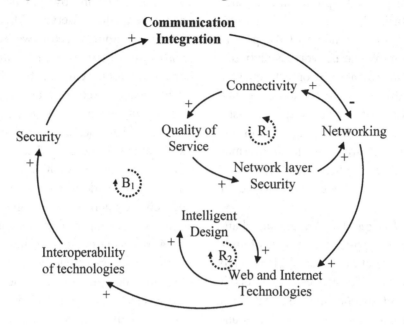

exclusive and thus are related to each other in some way. The three dimensions are also inter-connected and development of one dimension will affect the growth of the other two dimensions.

Information system researchers need to monitor this phenomenon and make contributions where applicable. The estimation of level of integration in three dimensions for electronic government provides a comprehensive structure for organizations to succeed in portal development at all levels. Constant technological change often weakens the value of legacy systems, which have been developed over the years through huge investments. Organizations struggle with the problem of modernizing these systems while keeping their functionality intact. The adoption of interoperability supports the integration of legacy systems for e-government.

For an integrated service, organizational factors play a significant role. Without a strong organizational support no technical aspect can be achieved. Therefore, both organizational as well as the technical factors are mandatory for achieving an interoperable portal. Organizational factors are

the inputs that have an impact on the outputs i.e. technical factors. Likewise all the dimensions are interconnected and major interrelations are shown in Figure 6. Loop R_1 is a reinforcing feedback loop which shows that an improvement in the organizational factors will improve technical factors i.e. the dimensions of integration and the reverse is true as well. For example, an appropriate data centre plan will not be possible without support from top level management. Also if there is a top level management support but there is lack of skilled manpower, the problem of appropriate data centre will still remain.

Within the technical aspects, the three dimensions of integration: data, process and communication are in a reinforcing feedback loop (R_2, R_3 and R_4 loops). An increase in level of integration of any dimension will have a positive feedback on other two dimensions. Hence, increase the level of integration of other two. Similarly the lower level of integration of any dimension will lower the level of integration of the other two dimensions. For example with a weak network backbone, data and process integrations cannot

Figure 6. Causal loop diagram - inputs and outputs

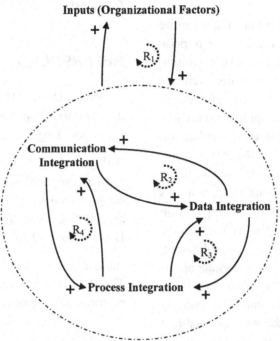

be achieved as the information will not be able to flow. For vertical and horizontal integration an improvement in all the three dimensions is essential along with organizational factors. Lower level of any of the three dimensions will require more efforts in achieving the point of interoperability.

7. CONCLUSION AND FUTURE WORK

The purpose of this paper is to examine interoperability adoption within an organization context. There is an attempt to formalize a way to locate an organization in interoperability adoption space based on an organization's "sophistication levels" of its current level of integration and factors. An interoperability adoption framework proposed by Chen (2003) has been followed. The framework helps organizations to examine their current status in the e-government environment from the per-

spective of three domains, namely data integration, process integration and communication integration. The framework also provides guidelines for government organizations who need to understand the potential benefits of adopting interoperability technology and then assists them in choosing the appropriate path and proper applications. Considering the current status of its IT applications, an organization can utilize this model to measure the efforts/costs that will be incurred by developing its interoperability enabled applications.

The contribution of this paper is two-fold. First, determinants of integration along three dimensions— Data integration, process integration and communication integration have been identified. Studies from literature and discussions with experts exhibit that both technological factors and organizational factors effect the development of government portal. The higher level of integration and organizational factors, the more advanced is the government portal development. Second, all the dimensions along with organizational factors are inter-connected and this has been illustrated by causal loop diagrams.

As future work, the adoption model can be used for other technologies such as enterprise architecture and enterprise architecture integration that being adopted these days. Enterprise architecture (EA) is particularly relevant to organizations that have a large portfolio of applications where problems such as functional overlap, duplication and redundancy are common. EA therefore encompasses the interconnectedness of IS applications, and the degree to which individual IS applications need to be integrated. Enterprise application integration (EAI) refers to 'the plans methods, and tools aimed at modernizing, consolidating, integrating and coordinating the computer applications within an enterprise' (McKeen & Smith, 2002). EAI represents an alternative to "point to point" integration in which the multitude of direct interfaces created between individual IS applications often results in "spaghetti" integration. At technology level, EAI involves the development of messaging middleware, an integration broker that serves as a hub for inter-application communication, and adapters that allow applications to interface to the integration broker. Integration brokers also perform additional functionality such as data translation, messaging logic and transaction management.

While interoperability future looks bright, and several government organizations in India have adopted it, there still exists the question of whether or not it will reach critical mass. It is our opinion that this will happen; however, we cannot speculate when, be it in one year, ten years, or ever. Furthermore, the dimensions in this paper are identified primarily based on studies from literature and discussions with experts and experience with e-government initiatives in Indian government portals. However, the underlying theory of this adoption model shall be applicable to other governments as well. The dimensions and there factors are not constrained and can be further developed according to the requirements for portals.

REFERENCES

Andersen, D. F., & Dawes, S. S. (1991). *Government Information Management. A Primer and Casebook*. Eaglewood Cliffs, NJ: Prentice Hall.

Ardagna, D., & Pernici, B. (2006). Dynamic web service composition with QoS constraints. *International Journal of Business Process Integration and Management, 1*(4), 233–243. doi:10.1504/IJBPIM.2006.012622

Banker, R. D., Chang, H., & Pizzini, M. J. (2004). The Balanced Scorecard: judgmental effects of performance measures linked to strategy. *Accounting Review, 79*(1), 1–23. doi:10.2308/accr.2004.79.1.1

Benbasat, I., Dexter, A. S., & Mantha, R. W. (1980). Impact of Organizational Maturity on Information System Skill Needs. *Management Information Systems Quarterly, 4*(1), 21–34. doi:10.2307/248865

Bertot, J. C., & Jaeger, P. T. (2006). User-centred e-government: Challenges and benefits for government Web sites. *Government Information Quarterly, 23*(2), 163–169. doi:10.1016/j.giq.2006.02.001

Brown, M. M., & Brudney, J. L. (2003). Learning organizations in the public sector: A study of piece agencies employing information and technology to advance knowledge to advance knowledge. *Public Administration Review, 63*(1), 30–43. doi:10.1111/1540-6210.00262

Cash, J. I., McFarlan, F. W., McKenney, J. L., & Applegate, L. M. (1992). *Corporate Information Systems Management: Text and Cases* (3rd ed.). Homewood, IL: Irwin.

Ceravolo, P., Corallo, P., & Elia, G. (2008). Semantic web-based profiled knowledge discovery in community of practice. *International Journal of Business Process Integration and Management, 3*(4), 256–270. doi:10.1504/IJBPIM.2008.024983

Chang, I. C., Li, Y. C., Hung, W. F., & Hwang, H. G. (2005). An empirical study on the impact of quality antecedents on taxpayer's acceptance of internet tax-filing systems. *Government Information Quarterly, 32*(4), 389–410. doi:10.1016/j.giq.2005.05.002

Chen, A., Labrie, R., & Shao, B. (2003). An XML adoption framework for electronic business. *Journal of Electronic Commerce Research, 4*(1), 1–14.

Chen, A. N. K., Sen, S., & Shao, B. B. M. (2005). Strategies for effective Web services adoption for dynamic e-businesses. *Decision Support Systems, 42*(2), 789–809. doi:10.1016/j.dss.2005.05.011

Chen, M. (2003). Factors affecting the adoption and diffusion of XML and Web services standards for e-business systems. *International Journal of Human-Computer Studies, 58*, 259–279. doi:10.1016/S1071-5819(02)00140-4

Chen, M., Chen, A., & Shao, B. (2003). The implications and impacts of Web services to electronic commerce research and practices. *Journal of Electronic Commerce Research, 4*(4), 128–139.

Chen, Y., Chen, H. M., Ching, R. K. H., & Huang, W. W. (2007). Electronic Government Implementation: A Comparison between Developed and Developing Countries. *International Journal of Electronic Government Research, 3*(2), 45–61. doi:10.4018/jegr.2007040103

Cheney, P. H., & Dickson, G. W. (1982). Organizational characteristics and information systems: an exploratory investigation. *Academy of Management Journal, 25*(1), 170–182. doi:10.2307/256032

Choudrie, J., & Weerrakody, V. (2007). Horizontal Process Integration in E-Government: the Perspective of a UK Local Authority. *International Journal of Electronic Government Research, 3*(3), 22–39. doi:10.4018/jegr.2007070102

CISCO. (2006). *Quality of Service*. Retrieved from http://www.cisco.com/en/US/products/ps6558/products_ios_technology_home.html

Coyle, K. (2002). Open source, open standards. *Information Technology and Libraries, 21*(1), 33–36.

DeLone, W., & Mclean, E. (2003). The DeLone and Mclean model for information systems success: A ten year update. *Journal of Management Information Systems, 19*(4), 9–30.

DeLong, D. W., & Fahey, L. (2000). Diagnosing cultural barriers to knowledge management. *The Academy of Management Executive, 14*(4), 113–127.

Department of Defense. (1996). *Software Reuse Executive Primer*. Retrieved from http://sw-eng.falls-church.va.us/ReuseIC/policy/primer/primer.htm

Ding, Y., Fensel, D., Klein, M., & Omelayenko, B. (2002). The semantic web: yet another hip? *Data & Knowledge Engineering, 41*, 205–227. doi:10.1016/S0169-023X(02)00041-1

E-Governance Standards. (n.d.). *IFEG Version 2.4 Report, NIC*. Retrieved from http://egovstandards.gov.in/

Earl, M. J. (1993). Experiences in strategic information systems planning. *Management Information Systems Quarterly, 17*(1), 1–24. doi:10.2307/249507

EC. Commission of the European Communities. (2003). *Linking-up Europe: The importance of interoperability for e-government services*. Brussels, Belgium: Author.

EC. Commission of the European Communities. (2003). *European Interoperability Framework.* Retrieved from http://ec.europa.eu/idabc/servlets/Doc?id=18060

Eckerson, W. (1999). 15 rules for enterprise portals. *Oracle Magazine.* Retrieved from http://www.oracle.com/oramag/oracle/99-Jul/49ind.html

Eder, L. B., & Igbaria, M. (2001). Determinants of intranet diffusion and infusion. *Omega, 29*(3), 233–242. doi:10.1016/S0305-0483(00)00044-X

Edmiston, K. D. (2003). State and local e-government: Prospects and challenges. *American Review of Public Administration, 33*(1), 20–45. doi:10.1177/0275074002250255

EURIM. (2002). *Interoperability - Joined Up Government Needs Joined Up Systems* (EURIM No. 36). Retrieved from http://www.eurim.org.uk/resources/briefings/br36.pdf

Evans, D., & Yen, D. C. (2006). E-Government: Evolving relationship of citizens and government, domestic and international development. *Government Information Quarterly, 23*(2), 207–235. doi:10.1016/j.giq.2005.11.004

Fu, J. R., Chao, W. P., & Farn, C. K. (2004). Determinants of taxpayer's adoption of electronic filing methods in Taiwan: An exploratory study. *Government Information Quarterly, 14*(3), 313–324.

Furlong, S. (2008). Applicability of autonomic computing to e-government problems. *Transforming Government: People. Process and Policy, 2*(1), 8–18.

Garson, G. D. (2003). *Toward an information technology research agenda for public administration.* Hershey, PA: Idea Group Publishing. doi:10.4018/978-1-59140-060-8.ch014

Ghattas, J., & Soffer, P. (2008). Facilitating flexibility in inter-organisational processes: a conceptual model. *International Journal of Business Process Integration and Management, 3*(1), 5–14. doi:10.1504/IJBPIM.2008.019343

Gomond, G., & Picavet, M. (1999). Framework for Managing Intranet-based Applications. In *Proceedings of the 7th International Conference on Emerging Technologies and Factory Automation* (Vol. 2, pp. 1011-1019).

Gottschalk, P. (2009). Maturity levels for interoperability in digital government. *Government Information Quarterly, 26,* 75–81. doi:10.1016/j.giq.2008.03.003

Gouscos, D., Kalikakis, M., Legal, M., & Papadopoulou, S. (2007). A general model of performance and quality for one-stop e-government service offerings. *Government Information Quarterly, 24,* 860–885. doi:10.1016/j.giq.2006.07.016

Government, C. I. O. (2007). *The HKSARG Interoperability Framework, Office of the Government Chief Information Officer, The Government of the Hong Kong Special Administrative Region.* Retrieved from http://www.ogcio.gov.hk

Gremler, D. D. (2004). The critical incident technique in service research. *Journal of Service Research, 7*(1), 65–89. doi:10.1177/1094670504266138

Grönlund, Å. (2001). *Electronic Government: Design, Applications, and Management.* Hershey, PA: Idea Group Publishing. doi:10.4018/978-1-93070-819-8

Gugliotta, A., Cabral, L., Domingue, J., & Roberto, V. Rowlatt, & M., Davies, R. (2005). *A Semantic Web Service-based Architecture for the Interoperability of E-government Services.* Paper presented at the International Conference on E-Government (ICEG2005), Ottawa, ON, Canada.

Guijarro, L. (2006). Interoperability frameworks and enterprise architectures in e-government initiatives in Europe and the United States. *Government Information Quarterly, 24,* 89–101. doi:10.1016/j.giq.2006.05.003

Guijarro, L. (2009). Semantic interoperability in eGovernment initiatives. *Computer Standards & Interfaces, 31*(1), 174–180. doi:10.1016/j.csi.2007.11.011

Gupta, M. P., Kumar, P., & Bhattacharya, J. (2005). *Government Online: Opportunities and Challenges.* New York: Tata McGraw-Hill.

Halevy, A. Y. (2001). Answering queries using views: A survey. *Very Large Database Journal, 10*(4), 270–294. doi:10.1007/s007780100054

Heintze, T., & Bretschneider, S. (2000). Information Technology and restructuring in public organizations: Does adoption of information technology affect organizational structures, communications and decision making. *Journal of Public Administration: Research and Theory, 10*(4), 801–830. doi:10.1093/oxfordjournals.jpart.a024292

Hiller, J. S., & Bélanger, F. (2001). Privacy strategies for electronic government. In Abramson, M. A., & Means, G. E. (Eds.), *E-Government 2001* (pp. 162–198). Lanham, MD: Rowman & Littlefield.

Holden, S. H., Norris, D. F., & Fletcher, P. D. (2003). Electronic government at the local level: Progress to date and future issues. *Public Performance and Management Review, 26*(4), 325–344. doi:10.1177/1530957603026004002

Huang, C., Lo, C., Chao, K., & Younas, M. (2006). Reaching consensus: A moderated fuzzy web services discovery method. *Information and Software Technology, 48*(6), 410–423. doi:10.1016/j.infsof.2005.12.011

Iacouvou, C. L., Benbasat, I., & Dexter, A. S. (1995). Electronic data interchange and small organizations: adoption and impact of technology. *Management Information Systems Quarterly, 19*(4), 465–485. doi:10.2307/249629

IBM. (2008). *Introduction to DB2 for z/OS, version 9.1.* Retrieved from http://publib.boulder.ibm.com/infocenter/dzichelp/v2r2/topic/com.ibm.db29.doc.intro/dsnitk12.pdf?noframes=true

IEEE. (2006). *IEEE Standard Computer Dictionary: A Compilation of IEEE Standard Computer Glossaries.* Retrieved from http://www.sei.cmu.edu/str/indexes/glossary/interoperability.html

Johnston, H. R., & Carrico, S. R. (1988). Developing capabilities to use information strategically. *Management Information Systems Quarterly, 12*(1), 36–48. doi:10.2307/248801

Joia, L. A. (2007). A Heuristic Model to Implement Government-to-Government Projects. *International Journal of Electronic Government Research, 3*(1), 1–18. doi:10.4018/jegr.2007010101

Kambil, A., Kalis, A., Koufaris, M., & Lucas, H. C. (2000). Influences on the corporate adoption of Web technology. *Communications of the ACM, 43*(11), 264–271. doi:10.1145/352515.352528

Kannabiran, G., & Banumathi, T. (2008). E-Governance and ICT Enabled Rural Development in Developing Countries: Critical Lessons from RASI Project in India. *International Journal of Electronic Government Research, 4*(3), 1–19. doi:10.4018/jegr.2008070101

Klischewski, R. (2004). Information Integration or Process Integration? How to Achieve Interoperability in Administration. In R. Traunmüller (Ed.), *EGOV 2004* (LNCS 3183, pp. 57-65).

Klischewski, R., & Scholl, H. J. (2006). Information quality as a common ground for key players in e-government integration and interoperability. In *Proceedings of the Hawaii International Conference on System Sciences (HICSS)*.

Landsbergen, D. J., & Wolken, G. Jr. (2001). Realizing the promise: Government information systems and the fourth generation of information technology. *Public Administration Review, 61*(2), 206–220. doi:10.1111/0033-3352.00023

LaPorte, T. M., & Demchak, C. C., & Anddejong, M. (2002). Democracy and bureaucracy in the age of the Web: Empirical findings and theoretical speculations. *Administration & Society, 34*(4), 411–446. doi:10.1177/0095399702034004004

Layne, K., & Lee, J. (2001). Developing fully functional E-government: A four stage model. *Government Information Quarterly, 18*, 122–136. doi:10.1016/S0740-624X(01)00066-1

Lederer, A. L., & Mendelow, A. L. (1987). Information resource planning: information systems managers' difficulty in determining top management's objectives. *Management Information Systems Quarterly, 13*(3), 388–399.

Lin, H., & Lin, S. (2008). Determinants of e-business diffusion: A test of the technology diffusion perspective. *Technovation, 28*(3), 135–145. doi:10.1016/j.technovation.2007.10.003

Liu, T., Dimpsey, R., Behroozi, A., & Kumaran, S. (2005). Performance modelling of a business process integration middleware. *International Journal of Business Process Integration and Management, 1*(1), 43–52. doi:10.1504/IJB-PIM.2005.006964

Maad, S., & Coghlan, B. (2008). Assessment of the potential use of grid portal features in e-government. *Transforming Government: People. Process and Policy, 2*(2), 128.

Mach, M., Sabol, T., & Paralic, J. (2006). Integration of eGov services: back-office versus front-office integration. In *Proceeding of the Workshop on Semantic Web for e-Government 2006, Workshop at the 3rd European Semantic Web Conference*.

McKeen, J. D., & Smith, H. A. (2002). New developments in practice II: enterprise application integration. *Communications of the Association for Information Systems, 8*, 451–466.

Moon, M. J. (2002). The Evolution of E-government among municipalities: Rhetoric or reality. *Public Administration Review, 62*(4), 424–433. doi:10.1111/0033-3352.00196

Mowbray, T. J., & Zahavi, R. (1995). *The Essential CORBA: Systems Integration Using Distributed Objects*. New York: John Wiley & Sons.

Naiman, C. E., & Ouksel, A. M. (1995). A classification of semantic conflicts in heterogeneous database systems. *Journal of Organizational Computing, 5*(2), 167–193. doi:10.1080/10919399509540248

Office of the E-Envoy. (2004). *E-Government Interoperability Framework, Version 6.0*. Retrieved from http://edina.ac.uk/projects/interoperability/e-gif-v6-0_.pdf

Park, J., & Ram, S. (2004). Information systems interoperability: what lies beneath? *ACM Transactions on Information Systems, 22*(4), 595–632. doi:10.1145/1028099.1028103

Peristeras, V., Loutas, N., Goudos, S. K., & Tarabanis, K. (2007). Semantic interoperability conflicts in pan-European public services. In *Proceedings of the 15th European Conference on Information Systems (ECIS 2007)*, St. Galen, Switzerland (pp. 2173-2184).

Petrovic, O. (2004). New focus in e-government: From security to trust. In Gupta, M. P. (Ed.), *Towards E-government*. New Delhi, India: Tata McGraw-Hill.

Rainer, R. K., Snyder, C. A., & Carr, H. H. (1991). Risk analysis for information technology. *Journal of Management Information Systems, 8*(1), 192–197.

Ram, S., & Park, J. (2004). Semantic Conflict Resolution Ontology (SCROL): an ontology for detecting and resolving data and schema-level semantic conflicts. *IEEE Transactions on Knowledge and Data Engineering, 16*(2), 189–202. doi:10.1109/TKDE.2004.1269597

Rao, R., Tripathi, R., & Gupta, M. P. (2008). Key Issues of Personal Information Integration in Government-Employee E-government. In *Proceedings of the International Conference on E-governance 2008*.

Reddick, C. G. (2009). Factors that Explain the Perceived Effectiveness of E-Government: A Survey of United States City Government Information Technology Directors. *International Journal of Electronic Government Research, 5*(2), 1–15. doi:10.4018/jegr.2009040101

Sabherwal, R., & King, W. R. (1992). Decision processes for developing strategic applications of information systems: a contingency approach. *Decision Sciences, 23*(4), 917–943. doi:10.1111/j.1540-5915.1992.tb00426.x

Sabherwal, R., & Kirs, P. (1994). The alignment between organizational critical success factors and information technology capability in academic institutions. *Decision Sciences, 25*(2), 301–330. doi:10.1111/j.1540-5915.1994.tb01844.x

Santos, E. M. D. (2008). Implementing Interoperability Standards for Electronic Government: An Exploratory Case Study of the E-PING Brazilian Framework. *International Journal of Electronic Government Research, 4*(3), 103–112. doi:10.4018/jegr.2008070106

Santos, E. M. D., & Reinhard, N. (2007). Setting interoperability standards for egovernment: An exploratory case study. *Electronic Government. International Journal (Toronto, Ont.), 4*(4), 379–394.

Scholl, H. J., & Klischewski, R. (2007). E-Government Integration and Interoperability: Framing the Research Agenda. *International Journal of Public Administration, 30*(8), 889–920. doi:10.1080/01900690701402668

Seifert, J. W., & Relyea, H. C. (2004). Do you know where your information is in the homeland security era? *Government Information Quarterly, 21*(4), 399–405. doi:10.1016/j.giq.2004.08.001

Srivastava, D., Dar, S., Jagadish, H. V., & Levy, A. (1996). Answering queries with aggregation using views. In *Proceedings of the 22nd International Conference on Very Large Data Bases (VLDB'96)* (pp. 318-329).

State Services Commission. (2007). *New Zealand E-government Interoperability Framework*. Retrieved from http://www.e.govt.nz

Straub, D. W., & Nance, W. D. (1990). Discovering and disciplining computer abuse in organization: a field study. *Management Information Systems Quarterly, 14*(1), 45–55. doi:10.2307/249307

Strover, S. (2001). Rural internet connectivity. *Telecommunications Policy, 25*(5), 331–347. doi:10.1016/S0308-5961(01)00008-8

Suh, B., & Han, I. (2003). The Impact of Customer Trust and Perception of Security Control on the Acceptance of Electronic Commerce. *International Journal of Electronic Commerce, 7*(3), 135–161.

Tambouris, E., Gorilas, S., Kavadias, G., Apostolou, D., Abecker, A., Stojanovic, L., et al. (2004). Ontology-enabled E-goverment service configuration: an overview of the OntoGov project. In *Knowledge Management in Electronic Government* (LNAI 3035, pp. 106-111).

Tambouris, E., Manouselis, N., & Costopoulou, C. (2007). Metadata for digital collections of e-government resources. *The Electronic Library, 25*(2), 176–192. doi:10.1108/02640470710741313

The Open Group. (2005). *Developer Declaration of Independence.* Retrieved from http://www.opengroup.org/declaration/declaration.htm.

Traunmüller, R. (2005). *Cross-border and Pan-European Services: The Challenges Ahead, Institute for Informatics in Business and Government.* Retrieved from http://www.eisco2005.org/fileadmin/files/eisco2005/

Tripathi, R., Gupta, M. P., & Bhattacharya, J. (2007). Selected Aspects of Interoperability in One-stop Government Portal of India. In *Proceedings of the International Conference on E-Governance* (*ICEG*) *2007.*

UK Government. (2000). *e-Government Interoperability Framework (e-GIF).* Retrieved from http://xml.coverpages.org/egif-UK.html

UN & ASPA. (2002). *Benchmarking E-government: A Global Perspective.* New York: Author.

Venkatesh, V., Morris, M. G., Davis, G. B., & Davis, F. D. (2003). User Acceptance of Information Technology: Toward a Unified View. *Management Information Systems Quarterly, 27*(3), 425–478.

Vernadat, F. B. (1996). *Enterprise Modelling and Integration: Principles and Applications.* London: Chapman & Hall.

Wang, Y. S. (2003). The adoption of electronic tax filing systems: an empirical study. *Government Information Quarterly, 20*(4), 333–352. doi:10.1016/j.giq.2003.08.005

Weng, S., Tsai, H., Liu, S., & Hsu, C. (2006). Ontology construction for information classification. *Expert Systems with Applications, 31*, 1–12. doi:10.1016/j.eswa.2005.09.007

Wimmer, M. (2002). A European perspective towards online one-stop government. *Electronic Commerce Research and Applications, 1*, 92–103. doi:10.1016/S1567-4223(02)00008-X

Wittenburg, A., Matthes, F., Fischer, F., & Hallermeier, T. (2007). Building an integrated IT governance platform at the BMW Group. *International Journal of Business Process Integration and Management, 2*(4), 327–337. doi:10.1504/IJBPIM.2007.017757

Wollschlaeger, M. (1998). Planning, Configuration and Management of Industrial Communication Networks Using Internet Technology. In. *Proceedings of the Global Telecommunications Conference, 2*, 1184–1189.

Zarei, B., Ghapanchi, A., & Sattary, B. (2008). Toward national e-government development models for developing countries: A nine-stage model. *The International Information & Library Review, 40*, 199–207. doi:10.1016/j.iilr.2008.04.001

This work was previously published in the International Journal of Electronic Government Research, Volume 7, Issue 1, edited by Vishanth Weerakkody, pp. 64-88, copyright 2011 by IGI Publishing (an imprint of IGI Global).

Chapter 6
The RFID Technology Adoption in E-Government:
Issues and Challenges

Ramaraj Palanisamy
St. Francis Xavier University, Canada

Bhasker Mukerji
St. Francis Xavier University, Canada

ABSTRACT

The emergence of Radio Frequency Identification (RFID) technology has affected the functions and roles of business organizations. RFID technology provides technical solutions across a variety of industries in the public and private sectors. E-government is being increasingly utilized by governments in different countries to increase the efficiency of services provided to citizens. Although the use of e-Government is allowing timely, effective services online, many challenges must still be overcome to maximize the utility e-Government can provide to citizens. RFID is disseminating in a variety of new areas and movement exists toward the adoption of RFID in e-Government, but several issues and challenges must be addressed. This paper examines both e-Government and RFID from an individual perspective and explores the possible issues and challenges associated with RFID technology adoption in e-Government. Based on a review of literature, a conceptual model has been developed illustrating the various issues and challenges and how they would impact the RFID adoption in e-Government.

INTRODUCTION

Radio frequency Identification (RFID) technology has become a hot topic in the fields of supply chain management and manufacturing. RFID has emerged as part of a new form of inter-organizational system that focuses to improve the efficiency of the processes in the supply chain. Business organizations started taking a hard look at what RFID can do for them and whether they should give further consideration to adopting RFID technology, because it is a technology dramatically changes the capabilities of an organization

DOI: 10.4018/978-1-4666-2458-0.ch006

to acquire vast array of data about the location and properties of any entity that can be physically tagged and wirelessly scanned within certain technical limitations (Coltman et al., 2008). RFID allows any tagged entity to become a mobile, communicating component of the organization's overall information infrastructure. According to the market research analyst IDTechEx (Das, 2005), the cumulative sales of RFID tags for the year 2006 reached over 2.4 billion and RFID smart labels would be needed in a range of areas, such as retailing, logistics, animal and farming, library services, and military equipment. It has become a novel and exciting research area of technological development, and is receiving increasing amounts of attention from the researchers as well as practitioners.

According to experienced early adopters, and academic researchers, RFID facilitates collaboration between organizations (Cantwell, 2006; Lekakos, 2007). In an e-Government context, RFID provides boundless potential in improving effectiveness, efficiency, and tracking e-Government services much more accurately in real-time reducing processing time delays. A number of factors have led to RFID being utilized more in e-Government. The emergence of common practice standards, the rising appearance of information technology infrastructure, technological advances and the importance of real-time intelligence have prompted a surge in the popularity and use of RFID. The different applications of RFID technology have experienced success in various fields, especially in business and many new developments for further RFID use are in the works (Wyld, 2005).

This paper explores the processes in e-Government where RFID technology could be applied and discusses the benefits of this technology in providing value added e-Government services to citizens. The next section begins with a concise overview of e-Government literature, followed by a technical background of RFID. The benefits of RFID are discussed, followed by the findings of how RFID influences the various areas of e-Government services. Following the literature review, a conceptual model for RFID adoption in e-Government is given illustrating the various issues and challenges and how they would impact the RFID adoption in e-Government. Research propositions are evolved from the model and suggested for further research. Finally, the limitations and the areas for further research are discussed followed by concluding remarks.

LITERATURE REVIEW

E-Government

E-governance is the application of electronic means to simplify, and improve the technology-mediated interaction between government and e-governance community comprised of citizens, civil society organizations, private companies, government law makers, and regulators on networks to increase the administrative effectiveness and efficiency in the internal government operations (Marche & McNiven, 2003; Toregas, 2001; Tapscott and Agnew, 1999). E-governance is about moving government services online (Finger & Pecoud, 2003; Waisanen, 2002; West, 2001) by providing easy to navigate and access web portal to all online government services (Lloyd, 2002) in an interactive manner (Alcock & Lenihan, 2001). The potential benefits are: speed, efficiency, convenience, public approval, democratization, and environmental bonuses (Hanson, 2009; Sinrod, 2004). The three main domains of e-governance are (Heeks, 2009; Prattipati, 2003): improving government processes (e-administration), connecting citizens (citizens and e-services), and building external interactions (e-society).

E-governance satisfies the citizen as customer by making use of Information and Communication Technologies (ICT) to exchange information and services with citizens, businesses, and other government agencies (Deakins & Dillon, 2002;

Heeks, 2002; Okot-Uma, n.d.) to bring Simple, Moral, Accountable, Responsive, and Transparent (SMART) governance (e-Governance online). The two key e-governance goals are: good governance of ICTs; and putting ICTs to the service of good governance.

E-governance is also seen as a decisional process. E-government Institute of Rutgers University states: "E-governance involves new channels for accessing government, new styles of leadership, new methods of transacting business, and new systems of organizing and delivering information and services. Its potential for enhancing the government process is immeasurable".

E-governance is a powerful tool in the hands of Government. Commonwealth Center for e-governance says: "E-governance is the commitment to utilize appropriate technologies to enhance governmental relationships, both internal and external, in order to advance democratic expression, human dignity and autonomy, support electronic development and encourage the fair and efficient delivery of services".

Though e-Government gained a significant frequency of use, it has not yet gained widespread acceptance. This is because skeptics of e-Government have laid out potential risks of this new system dramatically outweighing its benefits (Heeks, 2009). Some of the risks are hyper-surveillance, cost implementation, inaccessibility, and false sense of transparency and accountability. The risk behind the hyper-surveillance is that as citizens begin to interact with the government electronically on a large scale it could result in a lack of privacy. The money that has been poured into the development of e-Government, its results have been sub-par (Atkinson, 2008). Inaccessibility risk may be due to a significant portion of the population unable to access the e-Government resource. Since the government controls e-Government, information can be added or removed without public notice and this causes concerns of false sense of transparency and accountability.

RFID Technology

The term RFID is generally used to describe any technology that uses radio signals for identification purposes which, in practice, means any technology that transmits specific identifying numbers using radio (Garfinkel & Rosenberg, 2006). Over the years, RFID has been used in a variety of applications, such as inventory management, anti-theft monitoring of consumer merchandise, and the tagging of livestock. Boeck and Wamba (2007) describe an RFID system as follows: "an electronic tag containing historical, transactional or identifying data are affixed to or embedded in an object". By using an RFID reader, the data are automatically downloaded wirelessly to a computer. Once on the computer, the information can travel anywhere that is accessible by the internet or on a private network. Considered as a wireless technology, RFID not only refers to the tag containing a chip, but also to an antenna for sending and receiving data in order to communicate with an interrogator called reader (Bendavid et al., 2008). The communication is done through radio frequency with the tag and the RFID system has a middleware that manages, filters, aggregates and routes the data captured (Asif & Mandviwalla 2005). Accordingly, RFID is a wireless tracking technology (Karkkainen & Holmstrom, 2002) that allows a reader to activate a transponder on a radio frequency tag attached to, or embedded in, an item, allowing the reader to remotely read and/or write data to the RFID tag (Curtin et al., 2007). RFID is considered advantageous over traditional bar-coding methodologies because it is not considered by "line-of-sight" and multiple tags can be read simultaneously by available readers in the vicinity (Lefebvre et al., 2006; Vlosky & Wilson, 1994). The origin of this technology goes back to its military applications during the Second World War, when British Air Force used this technology to distinguish allied aircrafts from that of enemy aircraft with radar (Asif & Manviwalla, 2005). In the business scenario, the RFID system in integrated with enterprise systems such as warehouse management systems, enterprise resource planning system, and may be combined with other technologies such as global positioning system (GPS).

The structural rudiment of this technology can be broken down into the tag, the reader, and surrounding computing technologies. RFID tags are the chips that are embedded in the product, pallet, or case that store and transmit information about the specific item it is attached to. Tags are made of a hard copper coil consisting of an integrated circuit attached to an antenna then packaged into a housing device appropriate for the application (Delen et al., 2007). Data is stored on the integrated circuit and transmitted through the antenna to the reader by either a passive or active tag. Passive tags are generally more popular, less expensive, with a virtually unlimited lifespan. They use radiated energy from an electromagnetic field that RFID readers generate to transmit information, and will only remain energized while it is within the reader's field of range. Active tags are self powered by a battery and act as a miniature computer and transmitter that receives, stores, and transmits information to the reader about a product. Active tags life span is limited; however the tags do have a longer read range, better accuracy, more complex rewritable information storage, and richer processing capabilities (Bhuptani & Moradpour, 2005). Readers are transmitters and receivers governed by a microprocessor or digital signal processor that communicates with the tags within its field. They use a manufactured antenna to seize data from the tags passing the data to a computer for processing. These readers can have an effective range from anywhere to a few inches to a many meters depending on the frequency and type of tag being used. Data collected from the tags by the reader is then passed through wireless transference to host computing technologies for interpretation, storage, and action by the organization utilizing RFID technology.

A CONCEPTUAL MODEL FOR RFID TECHNOLOGY ADOPTION IN E-GOVERNMENT

As costs of RFID technology come down and use becomes more widespread, RFID technology can be successful in addressing or improving some of the issues faced by the e-Government. As RFID is a useful technology which provides technical solutions across a variety of industries to increase efficiency within each of these sectors, e-Government is attempting to adapt RFID to cater to the requirements of the society and to improve processes. In spite of substantial benefits in proving efficient and effective e-Government services, today's RFID adoption is still limited in e-Government environment due to barriers such as (i) lack of maturity in RFID technology (e.g. read rate, data reliability, high rate of new hardware and software introduction, lack of unified standards for interoperability), (ii) relatively high costs related to hardware, software customization, systems configuration and integration, and training, (iii) RFID Technology Acceptance (iv) security issues (i.e. data access, privacy and legislation), (v) lack of expertise (i.e. specialized skills required for RFID implementation) and (vi) patent challenges (i.e. EPC global's intellectual property (IP) policy and concerns about royalty costs) (Asif & Mandviwalla, 2005; Wu et al., 2006; Li et al., 2006). Despite the growing prevalence of RFID applications, researchers have only recently started to examine these issues, challenges, and factors for RFID technology adoption in e-Government. Building upon the e-Government and RFID literature, this research presents a conceptual model for RFID technology adoption in e-Government, as presented in Figure 1. This model is comprised of issues, challenges, and factors for RFID technology adoption in e-Government.

Figure 1. A conceptual model for RFID technology adoption in e-government

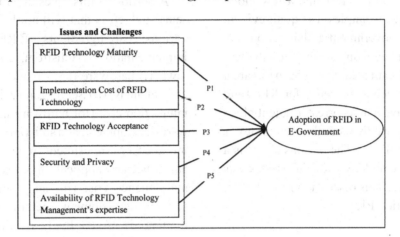

RFID Technology Maturity

RFID is not yet well known technology for the e-Government because at present RFID is still in its infancy and the policy makers and civil servants do not fully understand the potential of it. Some critics may say that the RFID is a new way of doing old things. There is no central body of RFID knowledge and there is no mechanism for sharing the RFID implementation best practices. Another limitation of RFID technology implemented in an inter-organizational/inter-governmental network is conflicting standards that may prohibit the deployment of the technology and abate anticipated effectiveness and efficiency across the network. Accordingly, the interoperability of solutions as well as the RFID technologies is limited. There is a need to align the frequency usage of RFID so that the RFID system can interoperate in different countries (Soon & Gutierrez, 2008) on a global scale. The adoption of divergent RFID technologies undermines the interoperability of tags and readers across a global network, maintaining the perceived benefits of effectiveness and efficiency at the business process level. In summation, mandating the alignment of a global RFID technology standard is essential to perpetuating international interoperability of RFID technology across an inter-governmental network.

Another use of RFID which could be an e-Government application which is in the inception stage is the development of a 'Smart Cane" for helping blind people. Using RFID and being equipped with an ultrasonic sensor, the smart cane works in tandem with a navigational system inside a bag. A speaker on the bag tells the person when there is an obstacle in the way and so the person can navigate their way around with little trouble. If equipment like this becomes more wide-spread it will have ramifications on e-Government as it will help improve social services available to citizens with disabilities. The developers of the smart cane from the University of Central Michigan are optimistic that this technology can be standardized in the future. This would go a long way in the empowering of those with disabilities as well as create cost advantages as these technologies come down in price with further production.

These examples presented above are just a handful of the RFID initiatives being experimented with. Many other applications are being developed to improve processes or address problems in society but most of them are in the inception stage. Initiatives are being taken to address issues such as national identification, vehicle identification, document security, food safety, waste management, infant protection, drug pedigree, medication administration, blood banking and surgical objects tracking, to name a few more. Through the above examples it is quite evident that RFID and e-Government collaborations are in somewhat of a beginning stage. Though there have in fact significant breakthroughs in this area, only the tip of the iceberg is seen so far. RFID and e-Government have a much greater potential for changing the way we live, but the technology is not being put to full use. The reasons are: it is a new innovative technology with high risks, costs and many skeptics. This discussion provides the basis for Proposition P1.

P1: The RFID technology maturity due to its introductory level negatively influences its adoption in e-Government.

Implementation Cost of RFID Technology

Though access to shared information is at the heart of an RFID initiative, in RFID applications where large numbers of tags are used and then disposed of, the running cost of the tags is a central issue. Cost is often mentioned as one of the main barriers of RFID implementation. However, as demonstrated in the field, an initial inherent level of trust and investment that government bodies will not try to bypass the RFID system is necessary if it is to be effective. Implementing the RFID system will initially necessitate a considerable amount of investment in specific areas. There are two types of costs involved – an initial capital cost and an operating cost (Jayaraman et al., 2008). The initial costs would include the cost of setting up the infrastructure for reading the RFID tags. These costs can include RFID readers, the cost of software that handles the interface between RFID readers and the existing system and the cost of training the workers on the use of new system. The operating costs would include (i) the cost of the RFID tag itself (ii) the cost of tagging each item and (iii) the cost of maintaining the RFID readers, and the software upgrades.

A portion of this investment therefore represents sunk costs that will not be recovered. The various cost ingredients of RFID technology implementations (Hellstrom, 2009) are as follows: (i) hardware (tags, readers, process units, and antennas) (ii) Servers and cables (iii) system integration cost (for hardware installation, software development, and software installation) (iv) initial cost of investment (replacing the existing hardware, and application software) (v) system maintenance cost (includes software license, software development, operating the system, and running cost). Accordingly, system integration, the number of readers and the process of applying the tags are issues which in themselves may involve higher costs than the cost of the tags. The cost and benefit of implementing RFID technology in e-Government depend on each specific situation. Consequently, each situation requires its own specific cost–benefit analysis. For example, the US Department of Defense (DOD) has also been using RFID technology to help transform its extremely complicated supply chain (Roberti, 2009). The DOD purchases items such as bullets, airplanes, drugs, tents, food, light bulbs, and laptops on an almost daily basis. On top of that, many of these items are shipped to different locations throughout the world. The DOD's radio-frequency in-transit visibility (ITV) Network is an active RFID-based cargo-tracking system with nodes in about forty countries and over 4000 locations. It tracks an average of 35,000 supply shipments around the world each day. The Department of Defense has increased efficiency and reduced waste by employing active RFID tags in its containers. Between 2010 and 2015 the Department of Defense estimates a budget of about $875 million towards continuing and expanding its use of RFID tags. The above discussion provides the basis for Proposition P2.

P2: The implementation cost of RFID technology negatively influences its adoption in e-Government.

RFID Technology Acceptance

Gaining the e-citizen's acceptance of RFID technology is another important challenge to implementation success as ensuring technological integrity. This suggests that e-Government administration bodies should view RFID application and usage as an 'identification & tracking" issue for detecting human activities (Smith et al., 2005; Smith, 2006, Arellano, 2008) rather than one strictly of technology or economics. Perceived usefulness and perceived ease of use are two widely recognized IT implementation success factors (Davis et al. 1989). Training and communication are two important managerial interventions to influence the acceptance of IT (Amoako-Gyampah & Salam, 2004). For example, the most personal application of RFID technology is the human-implantable RFID chips. These are used for a variety of authentication uses, such as authorizing use of computers, car door and building locks, and even recreational uses such as preferred entrance into nightclubs (Foster & Jaeger, 2007). Especially these chips were required for implantation by some employers who employ people for high-security positions (Verichip, n.d.). Besides, the VeriChip corporation start producing both implantable chips and wrist bracelets for storing health information and tracking patients in hospitals (Verichip, n.d.). In 2007, the company collaborated with a nursing home to implant chips in patients and ended up with the issue of forced implantation (Biever, 2007). Though the RFID bracelets are useful for identification and tracking, when the patients remove them without accepting the technology, the whole purpose of the proposal will be defeated. This discussion provides the basis for Proposition P3.

P3: The e-citizen's acceptance of RFID technology affects its adoption in e-Government.

Security and Privacy Issues

The innovative RFID technology is not without its limitations. It presents some potential security issues to users when the communication between the tags and the reader is exposed to skimming, eavesdropping and tracking (Meingast et al., 2007). When external entities have read access to the tags or related databases with confidential data, data may become compromised during wireless transmission. Skimming occurs when the data on the RF transponder is read without the owner's knowledge or consent using an unauthorized reader. Eavesdropping is the opportunistic interception of information on the chip while the chip is accessed by a legitimate reader. By reading the static information on a transponder, storing it, and following its signal, an unauthorized user can track the transponder and in return, track the individual. The tag security is vulnerable because the data stored is plain text or unencrypted. Besides, encrypting the data requires more space on the tag that results in higher costs, increased processing time, and a larger chip and thereby increasing the requirements for the actual size of the tag (Puffenbarger et al., 2008). Some of the RFID vendors have addressed these security issues by encrypting the actual data transfers.

For instance, a major collaboration between RFID and e-Government that has already begun taking effect in some nations is the issuance of e-passports (Fontana, 2006). These are also known as biometric passports. Currently the United States has a "Passport Card" that uses a simpler form of RFID instead of the contactless smart technology that is used for biometric passports. Fingerprint recognition, facial recognition, and iris recognition are different ways of identification that biometric technology uses for passports and other similar types of ID. This would increase efficiency and speed at the airports, making check-in time and boarding much less of a hassle for people flying. Though various governments have launched the programs to ensure safety and protection for e-passports, there have been a few loopholes in each system. Professional hackers have found ways to bypass these securities and have successfully read passport information, replicated passports (Zetter, 2006), and even changed some passport information (Reid, 2006). The six pieces of information that can be stolen from the RFID chip on a U.S. passport are: passport holder's name, nationality, gender, date of birth, place of birth, and a digitized photograph (Broache, 2006). There have also been several security and privacy concerns that have come to light. Lab demonstrations have shown that a successful eavesdrop on an RFID tag can occur at a distance of one meter (Hancke, 2008). So, many security experts are questioning whether RFID enabled e-passports have enough security built in to survive hackers and protect e-passport users from data theft and other security and privacy intrusions (Fontana, 2006). A threat analysis of RFID passports is given by Ramos et al. (2009) in which authors discuss about the technology and cost requirements for perpetrators attacking the RFID passports.

In case of e-passports, Identity theft is an additional risk. In case of storing unencrypted personally identifiable information on a transponder, such as a name or credit card number, an unauthorized entity can steal this personal data and use it for identity theft (Meingast et al., 2007). Privacy concerns with RFID technology are vast, unauthorized persons can read RFID-tagged items from a safe distance, and most consumers are not aware of the tags or that the items are being tracked. In some cases, cloning may occur when an adversary makes an identical clone of the data on the RFID responder. This clone can be used instead of the original transponder without the user's knowledge. Accordingly tags can potentially be used to identify unique individuals and then be able to automatically locate them in public places. To protect consumer privacy, strategies are being formulated. For instance, EPC (Electronic Product Code) global has developed standard as

a way of addressing public opposition of RFID privacy concerns. Consumer notice, consumer choice, consumer education, record use, retention, and security are included among these standards. Consequently, security and privacy questions have not gone away as many experts are saying that it is not the e-passport is inherently unsecure but that some recently demonstrated hacks and the inevitable advancement of technology such as an increase in RFID antenna power show that the e-passport may not weather its 10-year life span (Fontana, 2006).

Another example is the issuance of RFID enabled licenses (Songini, 2007). The State of Washington is the first U.S. state to partner with the Department of Homeland Security to offer an "Enhanced Driver's License" (EDL) to state residents beginning in January of 2008. The EDL is used to denote identity and citizenship at land and sea border crossings, and incorporate passive ultra high frequency (UHF) RFID technology for remote readability (typically read at ranges up to thirty feet) at ports of entry. After reading the data, the EDL will transmit an identification number to the reader in order to authenticate the license holder in DHS databases. While this eliminates the risk of reading personally identifiable information still presents cloning and tracking risks to the card holder. These EDLs are useful for frequent border crossers and some of these cards are purpose specific and could be carried only when the cardholder anticipates crossing the border, while driver's licenses are used for primary identification. The plan for using RFID technology in the new licenses drew criticism since an RFI-laced ID card can transmit personal information to anyone with the right reader device. Based on the above discussion, this study derives Proposition P4.

P4: Security and privacy concerns related with RFID technology negatively influence its adoption in e-Government.

Availability of Management Expertise on RFID Technology

Drawing on prior research on the RFID benefits realization, one of the most critical barriers is the lack of leadership vision, management vision, and commitment for the role of RFID technology in e-Government. There may be some notable exceptions, as we have discussed in this paper. For example, RFID technology's ability to track the movement of specific assets has great potential for use in response operations during chaotic disasters. Currently geographic information systems (GIS) provides the government with infrastructure and evacuation routes, but the locations are static and do not show the changing locations of objects and people as well as RFID does. This is a new technology that is currently under debate by many governments. It has not yet been fully employed but there are many who believe that it will be highly advanced and beneficial for disaster preparedness and recovery. The overall goal of this implementation is to reduce the threat to the community during a disaster such as tsunami, hurricane, or tornado. RFID has helped and improved businesses in terms of management coordination and efficiency. It is believed that RFID can be applied to an evacuation/disaster response just as it applies to business. The management and coordination will be improved by real-time, location-aware information about people and assets available through the use of RFID (Chatfield et al., 2009). Once the RFID technology is applied in a particular disaster then a similar could be developed and applied to other disasters such as earthquake, wildfire, drought, extreme temperature, storm, flood, and so on. Millions of dollars of damage are being caused by natural disasters. This does not include the social cost of individuals who lose their homes and loved ones. It is believed by experts that these losses can be dramatically reduced by applying RFID to disaster response and relief.

For instance, Texas is the first state government to employ an RFID – enabled emergency evacua-tion system (the Texas Special Needs Evacuation Tracking System, SNETS). SNETS has been tested and was successful in three simulated evacuations but has not yet been fully adopted, nor does it currently have an e-Government link. Here are the two major challenges faced by the Texas Government (Chatfield et al., 2009): (i) the diffusion of the SNETS by regional hospitals and emergency medical professionals and (ii) the integration of the SNETS with e-Government service to share real-time information with concerned families and relatives about evacuation. Though there is evidence supporting the usefulness of RFID for disaster relief, there is currently a lack of leadership, vision and awareness in this field. Texas is an example of RFID's slow emergence in society today.

Besides, RFID has been started using in more sensitive areas such as supply chain security of nuclear materials (Tirschwell, 2009). The United States Department of Energy has been taking steps towards adapting RFID into its current system to monitor nuclear materials. RFID has been used for tracking and monitoring nuclear materials for many years now, but there have recently been significant developments in this technology. The National Laboratory for the Department of Energy has upgraded its current RFID applications. It can now monitor the environmental and physical conditions of containers of nuclear materials in storage and transportation. With nuclear materi-als, health and safety issues have always been a major topic for concern. When nuclear materials are not properly monitored it can lead to both environmental hazards and human casualties. With tens of thousands of different radioactive materials dispersed throughout a country, govern-ment agencies have always had great difficulty in ensuring public safety. With this newly developed system, all data dealing with the history of any nuclear container is readily accessible and can be found with the click of a mouse. The Department of Energy plans on expanding the use of this RFID technology to other hazardous materials, such as containers in chemical plants. This is a perfect example of how government is using RFID to benefit the public sector (through increased safety) and its agents (the Department of energy being able to monitor all aspects of hazardous containers). Developing the RFID technology management expertise becomes so important and military is the first mover on this issue (Tirschwell, 2009). Based on the above discussion, this study derives Proposition P5.

P5: Lack of technology management expertise in RFID technology negatively influences its adoption in e-Government.

ISSUES FOR RESEARCH

There are several research issues that should be addressed to advance both researchers and managers understanding of the concept of RFID adoption in e-Government. The components given in the model may not be an exhaustive list for RFID adoption in e-Government and, as a result, it becomes necessary to identify other components. Research is needed to study the cost of adopting RFID for different stages of its adoption. The organizational readiness is another factor to be considered for RFID adoption. For example, Canada and the United States are among the most ready countries accepting RFID, so there are possibilities for becoming leading innovators of using RFID technologies in e-Government. There are many other areas in the public sector that could benefit from RFID and many others that have already implemented RFID that could further benefit from it. The future research should explore the new areas for RFID applications in e-Government. One such area is using RFID by provincial/ federal governments to assess their citizens' living requirements such as water, power, services, and other basic amenities. For this purpose, the e-citizen must be registered as a "citizen" in a provincial/ federal database. Either

in the SIN card or something similar RFID chip will be installed. In this context RFID technology can be used for both identification and tracking purpose. When the e-citizen registered with a province, the registered information including the service requirements will be transmitted into the personal RFID chip. In a similar database there will be services offered at a particular provincial government. With a cross-referencing of these databases, the provincial government can assess the exact type/ amount of services required by each/ all citizen(s). The usage of RFID technology benefits both the government administration body as well the e-citizens. For the government, there would not be any burden of oversupply of its services that would be lowering the variable cost of e-Government services. The citizens get benefitted because there will be prompt supply of e-Government services (e.g., renewal of driver's license, power, water requirement etc.).

Public safety is a very important issue to both the government and citizens. RFID can be used to improve the public safety. For instance, for the past several years, there have been talks of placing RFID chips in both convicts (that are in jail) and pedophiles. If this does happen there will be extra precautions that can be taken to further protect citizens from the anti-social elements. Both homes and businesses have alarm systems that are either motion censored or detect break-ins; an addition feature would be detecting certain RFID chips, namely the ones of escaped convicts. Collaboration between security companies and government criminal databases would be essential for this to work. For example, if a convict goes to jail, (s)he would have an RFID chip implanted in him/ her; this would be mandatory. If the convict tries to escape (and authorities could not apprehend him/ her quickly enough) and run towards, let us say someone's home that had this additional feature, the alarm would automatically be set off by the escapees RFID chip.

RFID applications in e-Government could benefit the banking sector also. For instance, applying for a loan, whether it is for a house or any type, often can be a lengthy process. Applying, being accepted, and receiving the money can take several days or weeks. If banks, e-Government and RFID work together it could make this lengthy, time consuming process more efficient with quicker results. In databases, the government would keep track of all citizens' purchases, their credit rating, insurance, debt and so on. An RFID chip containing all this information could be placed into a credit card or some sort. If an individual wishes to get a loan, by bringing this card to a banker, the loan application would be immediately approved or rejected for a specific amount, and are given immediate access to the funds. This is another way in which e-Government, RFID could collaborate to benefit both the private and public sectors of a society.

Another issue for future research is the importance of the "people" component for RFID adoption in e-Government. The important actors who have to carry out the tasks of RFID adoption include end-users (e-citizens), planners (e.g. RFID technology providers, vendors etc.), and top management (provincial/ federal governments). Research is therefore needed to develop an integrated perspective of RFID adoption in e-Government by combining the views of all the stakeholders impacted.

IMPLICATIONS AND CONCLUSION

In conclusion, in adopting RFID technology in e-Government, priorities are to be set in order to address the challenges and issues associated with RFID technology. Having said the challenges of adopting RFID technology, what role should government play in dealing with them would be a critical factor for successful adoption of RFID technology. The government organizations need to understand that RFID is not a goal but the means to achieve identification and tracking for efficient and effective services to the citizens. Best practices

in adopting this technology in an e-Government context are to be explored by further research and the knowledge needs to be shared among the governmental bodies. Educating the policy makers of a government regarding the usage and benefits of RFID technology becomes paramount initiative for successful adoption. The education campaign can also include the topics such as why RFID is necessary for the e-Government and what rights and protections are afforded to citizens. For having more confidence on security in RFID adoption, the governments have to obtain and incorporate feedback from security experts and citizens.

REFERENCES

Alcock, R., & Lenihan, D. G. (2001). *Opening the e-government file: governing in the 21st century; results of the crossing boundaries cross-country tour*. Ottawa, ON, Canada: Centre for Collaborative Government.

Amoako-Gyampah, K., & Salam, A. F. (2004). An Extension of the Technology Acceptance Model in an ERP Implementation Environment. *Information & Management, 41*, 731–745. doi:10.1016/j.im.2003.08.010

Arellano, J. (2008). Human RFID Chip Implants. *Rural Telecommunications, 27*(1), 8.

Asif, Z., & Mandviwalla, M. (2005). Integrating the supply chain with RFID. *Communications of the Association for Information Systems, 15*, 393–427.

Atkinson, R. D., & Castro, D. (2008). *Digital Quality of Life: Understanding the Personal and Social Benefits of the Information Technology Revolution*. Retrieved from http://archive.itif.org/index.php?id=179

Bendavid, Y., Lefebvre, E., Lefebvre, E., & Wamba, S. (2008). Exploring the impact of RFID technology and the EPC network on mobile B2B eCommerce: A case study in the retail industry. *International Journal of Production Economics, 112*, 614–629. doi:10.1016/j.ijpe.2007.05.010

Bhuptani, M., & Moradpour, S. (2005). *RFID Field Guide: Deploying Radio Frequency Identifications Systems.*

Biever, C. (2007). Uproar flares over alzheimer's tags. *New Scientist*, 14. doi:10.1016/S0262-4079(07)61223-8

Boeck, H., & Wamba, S. (2007). RFID and buyer-seller relationships in the retail supply chain. *International Journal of Retail & Distribution Management, 36*(6), 433–460. doi:10.1108/09590550810873929

Broache, A. (2006). *RFID passports arrive for Americans.* Retrieved March 2010 from http://news.cnet.com/RFiD-passports-arrive-for-Americans/2100-1028_3-6105534.html

Cantwell, D. (2006). *RFID R&D opportunities and the supply chain.* Paper presented at the RFID Academic Convocation, Cambridge, MA.

Chatfield, A., Hirokazu, T., & Wamba, S. (2009). *E-Government Challenge in Disaster Evacuation Response: The Role of RFID Technology in Building Safe and Secure Local Communities.* Wollongong, NSW, Australia: University of Wollongong.

Coltman, T., Gadh, R., & Michael, K. (2008). RFID and Supply Chain Management. Introduction to the Special Issue. *Journal of Theoretical and Applied Electronic Commerce Research, 3*(1), 3–6.

Curtin, J., Kauffman, R., & Riggins, R. (2007). Making the most out of RFID technology: a research agenda for the study of the adoption, usage and impact of RFID. *Information Technology Management, 8*(2), 87–110. doi:10.1007/s10799-007-0010-1

Das, R. (2005). *RFID tag sales in 2005 - how many and where?* Retrieved from http://www.idtechex.com/products/en/articles/00000398.asp

Davis, F. D. (1989). Perceived usefulness, perceived ease of use, and user acceptance of information technology. *Management Information Systems Quarterly, 13*(3), 319–340. doi:10.2307/249008

Deakins, E., & Dillon, R. (2002). E-government in New Zealand: The local authority perspective. *International Journal of Public Sector Management, 15*(4), 375–399. doi:10.1108/09513550210435728

Delen, D., Hardgrave, B., & Sharda, R. (2007). RFID for Better Supply-Chain Management through Enhanced Information Visibility. *Production and Operations Management, 16*(5), 613–624. doi:10.1111/j.1937-5956.2007.tb00284.x

Finger, M., & Pecoud, G. (2003). *From e-Government to e-Governance? Towards a model of e-governance.* Paper presented at the 3rd European Conference on e-Government, Dublin, Ireland.

Fontana, J. (2006). Here come RFID-enabled passports. *New World (New Orleans, La.), 23*, 18.

Foster, K. R., & Jaeger, J. (2007). RFID inside: The murky ethics of implanted chips. *IEEE Spectrum*, 24–29. doi:10.1109/MSPEC.2007.323430

Garfinkel, S., & Rosenberg, B. (2006). *RFID: Applications, Security, and Privacy.* Upper Saddle River, NJ: Addison- Wesley.

Hancke, G. P. (2008, July). *Eavesdropping Attacks on High-Frequency RFID Tokens. Proceedings of the 4th Workshop on RFID Security (RFIDsec '08).* Retrieved from http://www.rfidblog.org.uk/Hancke-RFIDsec08-Eavesdropping.pdf

Hanson, W. (2009). *Trees talk with Technology.* Retrieved March 2010 from http://www.govtech.com/dc/689715.

Heeks, R. (2002). *E-Government for Development*. Manchester, UK: Institute for Development Policy and Management (IIPM), University of Manchester.

Heeks, R. (2009). Success and Failure in E-Government Projects. In *EGovernment for Development* (pp. 1-3).

Hellstrom, D. (2009). The cost and process of implementing RFID technology to manage and control returnable transport items. *International Journal of Logistics Research and Applications*, *12*(1), 1–21. doi:10.1080/13675560802168526

Jayaramanan, V., Rossb, A. D., & Agarwal, A. (2008). Role of information technology and collaboration in reverse logistics supply chains. *International Journal of Logistics: Research and Applications*, *11*(6), 409–425. doi:10.1080/13675560701694499

Karkkainen, M., & Holmstrom, J. (2002). Wireless product identification: enabler for handling efficiency, customisation and information sharing. *Supply Chain Management: An International Journal*, *7*(4), 242–252. doi:10.1108/13598540210438971

Lefebvre, L. A., Lefebvre, E., Bendavid, Y., Wamba, S. F., & Boeck, H. (2006). *RFID as an enabler of b-to-b e-commerce and its impact on business processes: a pilot study of a supply chain in the retail industry exploiting RFID digital information in enterprise collaboration*. Paper presented at the 39th Annual Hawaii International Conference on System Sciences (HICSS'06).

Lekakos, G. (2007). Exploiting RFID digital information in enterprise collaboration. *Industrial Management & Data Systems*, *107*(8), 110–122. doi:10.1108/02635570710822778

Li, S., Visich, J. K., Khumawala, B. M., & Zhang, C. (2006). Radio Frequency Identification Technology: Applications, Technical Challenges and Strategies. *Sensor Review*, *26*(3), 193–202. doi:10.1108/02602280610675474

Lloyd, R. M. (2002). Electronic Government. *Business and Economic Review*, *48*(4), 15–17.

Marche, S., & McNiven, J. D. (2003). E-government and e-governance: The future isn't what it used to be. *Canadian Journal of Administrative Sciences*, *20*(1), 74–86. doi:10.1111/j.1936-4490.2003.tb00306.x

Meingast, M., King, J., & Mulligan, D. (2007). *Embedded RFID and Everyday Things: A Case Study of the Security and Privacy Risks of the U.S. e-Passport*. Paper presented at the EEE International Conference on RFID.

Okot-Uma, R. W. (n.d.). *Electronic Governance: Reinventing Good Governance*. Retrieved from http://www.electronicgov.net/index.shtml

Prattipati, S. N. (2003). Adoption of e-Governance: Differences between countries in the use of online. *Journal of American Academy of Business*, *3*, 386–391.

Puffenbarger, E., Teer, F., & Kruck, S. (2008). RFID: New Technology on the Horizon for IT Majors. *International Journal of Business Data Communications and Networking*, *4*(1), 64–79.

Ramos, A., Scott, W., Lloyd, D., O'leary, K., & Waldo, J. (2009). A Threat Analysis of RFID Passports. *Communications of the ACM*, *52*(12), 38–42. doi:10.1145/1610252.1610268

Reid, D. (2006). *E-Passports at Risk from Cloning*. Retrieved from http://news.bbc.co.uk/2/hi/programmes/click_online/6182207.stm

Roberti, M. (2009). Saluting the RFID Pioneers in the DOD. *RFID Journal*, 1-2.

Sinrod, E. J. (2004). A look at the pros and cons of e-government. *USA Today.*

Smith, A. (2006). Evolution and Acceptability of Medical Applications of RFID Implants Among Early Users of Technology. *Health Marketing Quarterly, 24,* 121–155. doi:10.1080/07359680802125980

Smith, J., Fishkin, K., Bing, J., Mamishev, A., Hilipose, M., & Rea, A. (2005). RFID-based techniques for human-activity detection. *Communications of the ACM, 48*(9), 39–44. doi:10.1145/1081992.1082018

Songini, M. (2007). Washington State, DHS May Use RFID in Licenses. *Computerworld, 41,* 6.

Soon, C., & Gutiérrez, A. (2008). Effects of the RFID Mandate on Supply Chain Management. *Journal of Theoretical and Applied Electronic Commerce Research, 3*(1), 81–91.

Tapscott, D., & Agnew, D. (1999). Governance in the digital economy. *Finance & Development, 36*(4), 34–37.

Tirschwell, P. (2009). Track and trace, the Army way. *Journal of Commerce, 10*(25), 1.

Toregas, C. (2001). The politics of e-gov: The upcoming struggle for redefining civic engagement. *National Civic Review, 90*(3), 235–240. doi:10.1002/ncr.90304

VeriChip. (n.d.). *Home.* Retrived from http://74.125.113.132/search?q=cache:kfVTExaNxxMJ:www.verichipcorp.com/+VeriChip.com&cd=8&hl=en&ct=clnk&gl=ca

Vlosky, R. P., & Wilson, D. T. (1994). *Interorganizational information system technology adoption effects on buyer-seller relationships in the retailer-supplier channel: an exploratory analysis.* Paper presented at the 10th IMP Annual Conference, Groningen, The Netherlands.

Waisanen, B. (2002). The future of e-government: Technology-fueled management tools. *Public Management, 84*(5), 6–9.

West, D. M. (2001). *State and Federal E-Government in the United States.* Providence, RI: Brown University.

Wu, N. C., Nystrom, M. A., Lin, T. R., & Yu, H. C. (2006). Challenges to global RFID adoption. *Technovation, 26*(12), 1317–1323. doi:10.1016/j.technovation.2005.08.012

Wyld, D. C. (2005). *RFID: The Right Frequency for Government.* Retrieved from http://www.businessofgovernment.org/pdfs/WyldReport4.pdf

Zetter, K. (2006). Clone E-Passports. *Wired,* 1-3.

This work was previously published in the International Journal of Electronic Government Research, Volume 7, Issue 1, edited by Vishanth Weerakkody, pp. 89-101, copyright 2011 by IGI Publishing (an imprint of IGI Global).

Chapter 7
Broadband Adoption and Usage Behavior of Malaysian Accountants

Yogesh K. Dwivedi
Swansea University, UK

Mohamad Hisyam Selamat
Universiti Utara Malaysia, Malaysia

Banita Lal
Nottingham Trent University, UK

ABSTRACT

This study examines the factors affecting the adoption of broadband Internet in a developing country context by focusing on Malaysia. The data relating to these factors was collected using a survey approach. The findings of this paper suggest that constructs such as relative advantage, utilitarian outcomes, service quality, and primary influence are important factors affecting Malaysian accountants' broadband adoption and Internet use behaviour. The paper proceeds to outline the research limitations and implications.

INTRODUCTION

Although broadband diffusion is considered to be an important policy issue in many countries around the globe, there are few studies that have been conducted in order to understand this critical technology management issue within the context of developing countries. The reason for this lack of broadband adoption studies from the developing country perspective could be attributed to the late rollout of broadband services, slow infrastructure development, low tele-density and slow rate of adoption. Since developing countries such as Malaysia are currently lagging in terms broadband adoption -as the current level of adoption is approximately 11% (Keong, 2007) compared to developed countries where adoption rates typically exceed 50%- it is important to undertake research that may help to explain why this is the case, and where an understanding of the determining factors

DOI: 10.4018/978-1-4666-2458-0.ch007

may help to accelerate the process of consumer adoption in developing nations such as Malaysia. Furthermore, a previous study has established relationship between broadband adoption and citizen adoption of emerging electronic government services (Dwivedi, Papazafeiropoulou, Gharavi, & Khoumbati, 2006). This suggests that higher level of broadband penetration is pre-requisite for any effort to promote citizen adoption of electronic government services in Malaysia.

The deployment and adoption of broadband is still in its infancy in Malaysia. A recently published Malaysian broadband market report highlighted the problem of slow broadband adoption amongst the general Malaysian population and the possible barriers inhibiting its widespread diffusion. The report stated that:

Malaysia has been heavily promoting itself as an Information Technology hub in the Asia region. On the back of the Multimedia Super Corridor project, high-tech companies have been at least establishing a presence in Malaysia. But the wider community has not really been embracing technology. There has been surprisingly little interest in broadband Internet, the national broadband penetration being only slightly over 3% at the end of 2006 (Malaysia Broadband Market, 2010).

The problem of slow broadband adoption has been taken seriously by the Malaysian government as they are continuously revising their policy and changing the target growth according to the adoption rate. Recent news from ZDNet Asia further highlights the slow growth of broadband in Malaysia and its consequences:

The slow uptake of broadband services has led the Malaysian government to revise its earlier optimistic penetration targets, prompting industry observers to call for market reform. The government had previously set a target of 75 percent adoption rate by 2010, but only 11.7 percent of

Malaysia's 5.5 million households currently have broadband access, up from 7 percent in 2005. This disappointing state of affairs recently prompted a Cabinet Committee chaired by Deputy Prime Minister Najib Tun Razak to revise the target down to 50 percent by 2010 (Keong, 2007).

Given the situation of Malaysia in terms of the current adoption rate, it was regarded that understanding the effect of the potential factors upon consumers' broadband adoption and usage may help to encourage further diffusion and management of high speed Internet. Therefore, the aim of this study was: *to understand the factors affecting the broadband adoption behavior of Malaysian accountants.* The reasons for selecting accountants sample is provided in methodology section.

Having introduced the topic of interest, the next section provides a brief review of relevant literature followed by a brief discussion on the theoretical basis for examining the adoption of broadband. Then we provide a brief discussion of the research methods utilized for data collection. The findings are presented next. Finally the conclusions, including the limitations and contributions of this research, are provided.

LITERATURE REVIEW

Recently, a few studies on broadband adoption were undertaken to investigate influential factors in developing economies such as Bangladesh, India, Kingdom of Saudi Arabia and Pakistan. The study on broadband adoption in Bangladesh concluded that attitude, primary influence, secondary influence and facilitating conditions resources are important factors for explaining consumers' behavioral intentions to adopt broadband (Dwivedi, Khan, & Papazafeiropoulou, 2007). The key findings of the study on the Kingdom of Saudi Arabia were that the factors with the main influence on attitude towards adoption of broadband were usefulness, service quality, age, usage, type of connection and type of accommodation (Dwivedi & Weerakkody, 2007). Khoumbati et al. (2007) examined the factors affecting consumers' adoption of broadband in Pakistan. This study concluded that primary influence, facilitating conditions resources, cost and perceived ease of use are significant factors for explaining consumers' behavioral intentions to adopt broadband in Pakistan (Khoumbati et al., 2007). Finally, a study on broadband adoption within the Indian context found that the relative advantage, hedonic outcomes and cost are significant factors for explaining consumers' behavioral intentions to adopt broadband in India (Dwivedi, Williams, Lal, Weerakkody, & Bhatt, 2007).

From the above discussion, it can be observed that the factors affecting the individual level of broadband adoption in different countries vary. This argument was further supported by a panel discussion (held in IFIP8.6-2007) on the global diffusion of broadband. Panel members from different countries argued and agreed that the context and factors that affect broadband adoption at both the micro and macro level are diverse and therefore the findings from one study cannot be applied directly to study broadband adoption issues in other countries. Hence, empirical studies should be conducted to examine the influential factors in countries with slow rates of broadband adoption (William et al., 2007). Since the broadband adoption rate in Malaysia is unexpectedly slow, this has provided us with impetus to undertake this exploratory study in order to understand the perception of consumers regarding broadband adoption and its usefulness in Malaysia. Its worthwhile contribution would be to understand the reasons for consumer adoption and non-adoption of subscription-based technologies such as broadband from a developing country perspective. The next section briefly discusses the theoretical basis for examining the factors of consumer adoption and non-adoption of broadband in Malaysia.

THEORETICAL BASIS

The constructs included in this study were adapted and modified from the conceptual model of broadband adoption (Dwivedi, 2005; Dwivedi & Irani, 2009). This model is derived from the model of technology adoption in households (Venkatesh & Brown, 2001). The proposed conceptual model assumed that the dependent variable 'broadband adoption' is influenced by several independent variables that include the attitudinal (relative advantage, utilitarian outcomes, hedonic outcomes and service quality), normative (primary influence and secondary influence), control factors and (knowledge, self-efficacy and facilitating conditions resources). A detailed discussion and justification for including the aforementioned constructs is not possible to include here due to space limitation, however, theoretical information on these constructs can be obtained from original sources (Dwivedi, 2005; Venkatesh & Brown, 2001).

RESEARCH METHODOLOGY

The survey method was utilized for this study (Choudrie & Dwivedi, 2005a). A self-administered questionnaire comprised the primary survey instrument for data collection, since it addresses the issue of reliability of information by reducing and eliminating differences in the way that the questions are asked, and how they are presented (Fowler, 2002). Furthermore, questionnaires facilitate the collection of data within a short period of time from the majority of respondents, which was a significant issue for this research (Fowler, 2002). Keeping the above in mind, multiple and closed questions were mainly included in the questionnaire. The literature review provided an initial understanding of broadband adoption and the basis for the development of a draft questionnaire. The eventual final questionnaire consisted of a total of 13 questions. All 13 questions were close-ended, multiple, Likert scale type in nature. From 13, one question was Likert scale type that consisted of 40 sub questions or items. Total number of items for each construct is presented in Table 2. However, due to space limitations these items are not described within the paper, however, interested readers can find them from original source Dwivedi, Choudrie, and Brink (2006). All 40 Likert scale type questions/items were adapted from Dwivedi, Choudrie, and Brink (2006) and Choudrie and Dwivedi (2006b) and demographic categories were adapted from Choudrie and Dwivedi (2005b). Although the adapted questions were rigorously validated in source studies, we conducted a reliability test to confirm whether the adapted measures were internally consistent. The findings on this are presented in Table 2.

Since a reliable sample frame that represents the whole Malaysian population is not readily available or affordable for researchers, we focused our investigation on a particular segment of the Malaysian population: people who are employed as a 'Chartered Accountant'. Further reasons for such selection were that individuals in such a profession were more likely to have broadband at home or in their office due to professional and business needs, which was the issue for investigation. Thus, the sample of this study consisted of Malaysians employed as Chartered Accountants. The population consisted of Malaysian audit firms registered with the Malaysian Institute of Accountants. There are 1373 audit firms in Malaysia (Malaysian Institute of Accountants, 2007). Using the systematic sampling technique, we selected a sample of 302 Accountancy firms by considering every fourth firm from the sample frame. The questionnaire was sent to the Chartered Accountant of each of the selected audit firms. The questionnaire was administered either as an email attachment or via postal service between August and November 2007. 124 usable questionnaires were returned within the specified time, resulting in a 41% response rate.

The initial stage of data analysis involved checking the responses and providing a unique identification number to each response. Using SPSS (version 14), the research generated the descriptive statistics (i.e. frequencies, percentage and tables) and reliability tests, factor analysis and regression analysis were conducted to analyze and present the research findings.

FINDINGS

Demographic and Internet Access Profile of Survey Respondents

Table 1 presents the demographic and Internet access profile of the survey respondents. Of the 124 responses received, 54% were in the 25-34 year-old age group, which formed the largest response category. The 35-44 year-old age group was the next largest (23.4%). In terms of gender, more male than female respondents (m=58.1%, f=41.9%) participated in the survey (Table 1). All respondents possessed educational qualifications, with 36.3% having an undergraduate degree and 4.8% educated to master/postgraduate level. 8.9% of respondents reported other educational qualifications (Table 1). Responses for household annual income varied between 7.3% for the RM60,000-RM69,000 category and 26.6% for the above RM70,000 category (Table 1). Of the 124 respondents, only 60.5 percent represented the adopters of Internet at home and the remaining 39.5 percent were non-adopters (Table 1). Of the 60.5 percent Internet adopters, 25.3 percent possessed a narrowband connection and 74.7 percent stated that they had a broadband connection at home (Table 1).

Reliability Test

Table 2 illustrates the Cronbach's coefficient alpha values that were estimated to examine the internal consistency .80 for behavioral intention

Table 1. Demographic information of the survey respondents

	Freq.	%		Freq.	%
Age			Gender		
25-34 YEARS	67	54.0	MALE	72	58.1
35-44 YEARS	29	23.4	FEMALE	52	41.9
45-54 YEARS	21	16.9	Total	124	100.0
55-64 YEARS	3	2.4	Home Internet Access		
65-74 YEARS	4	3.2	YES	75	60.5
Total	124	100.0	NO	49	39.5
Income			Total	124	100.0
RM20,000-RM29,000	20	16.1	Type of Internet Access		
RM30,000-RM39,000	12	9.7	DIAL-UP METERED	18	14.5
RM40,000-RM49,000	24	19.4	DIAL-UP UN-METERED	1	.8
RM50,000-RM59,000	26	21.0	BROADBAND WITH DSL/ADSL	31	25.0
RM60,000-RM69,000	9	7.3	BROADBAND WITH CABLE MODEM	12	9.7
ABOVE RM70,000	33	26.6	WIRELESS	13	10.5
Total	124	100.0	N/A	49	39.5
Education			Total	124	100.0
DEGREE	107	86.3	Narrowband vs. Broadband		
MASTER	6	4.8	Narrowband	19	25.3
OTHERS	11	8.9	Broadband & Wireless	56	74.7
Total	124	100.0	Total	75	100.0
Alternative Internet Access Places			Duration of Internet Connection at Home		
WORK PLACE	87	70.2	LESS 12 MONTH	9	7.3
PUBLIC ACCESS POINTS	9	7.3	12-24 MONTH	4	3.2
LOCAL LIBRARY	2	1.6	25-36 MONTH	9	7.3
INTERNET CAFE	26	21.0	ABOVE 36 MONTH	53	42.7
Total	124	100.0	Total	75	100.0

construct. Both utilitarian outcomes and primary influence possessed a reliability value of 0.95. The Cronbach's coefficient alpha values for remaining constructs illustrated in the Table 2. Hinton et al (2004) have suggested four cut-off points for reliability, which includes excellent reliability (0.90 and above), high reliability (0.70-0.90), moderate reliability (0.50-0.70) and low reliability (0.50 and below) (Hinton et al., 2004). The aforementioned values suggest that of the ten constructs, six possess excellent reliability and the remaining four illustrate high reliability. None of the constructs demonstrated a moderate or low reliability (Table 2). The high Cronbach's α values for all constructs imply that they are internally consistent. That means all items of each constructs are measuring the same content universe (i.e. construct). For example, both the items of BI are measuring the same content universe of behavioral intention. Similarly, all ten items of UO are measuring the content universe of utilitarian outcomes construct. In brief, the higher the Cronbach's α value of a construct, the higher the reliability is of measuring the same construct.

Table 2. Reliability of measurements

Constructs	N	Number of Items	Cronbach's Alpha (α)	Type
Behavioural Intention	124	2	0.80	High Reliability
Relative Advantage	124	4	0.89	High Reliability
Utilitarian Outcomes	124	10	0.95	Excellent Reliability
Hedonic Outcomes	124	4	0.85	High Reliability
Service Quality	124	4	0.97	Excellent Reliability
Primary Influence	124	3	0.95	Excellent Reliability
Secondary Influence	124	2	0.92	Excellent Reliability
Facilitating Conditions Resources	124	4	0.87	High Reliability
Knowledge	124	3	0.91	Excellent Reliability
Self-efficacy	124	3	0.94	Excellent Reliability
LEGEND: N= Sample Size				

Descriptive Statistics

Table 3 presents the means and standard deviations of the items related to all 11 constructs included in the study to measure the perceptions regarding broadband adoption. The means and standard deviations of aggregated measures for all the 11 constructs are also illustrated in Table 4.

The respondents showed strong agreement for both of the items of the behavioral intentions (BI1 and BI3), as the mean score varies between 5.69 (SD=1.46) and 5.98 (SD=1.25) (Table 3) with an average score of 5.84 (SD=1.24) (Table 4). Item BI2 of the behavioral intention to change service provider (BISP) construct was also agreed strongly by survey respondents (M = 6.02, SD = 2.17) (Table 3). Amongst the attitudinal constructs the respondents agreed strongly for all of the items of the relative advantage constructs, where item RA1 scored the maximum (M = 6.06, SD = 1.22) and minimum (M = 5.66, SD = 1.62) for item RA3 (Table 3) with the high average score of aggregate measure (M = 5.92, SD = 1.17) (Table 4). A strong agreement was also made for the utilitarian outcomes (M = 5.50, SD = 1.15) and service quality (M = 5.63, SD = 2.19) constructs by survey respondents (Table 4). The importance of hedonic outcomes was relatively less agreed with an average mean score of 4.16 and standard

deviations of 1.57 (Table 4). Amongst the normative constructs, primary influence rated above average (M = 4.97, SD = 1.39) and was agreed more strongly than the secondary influence which was rated slightly above than average (M = 4.28, SD = 1.67) on a 7 point likert scale (Table 4). Self-efficacy was rated stronger (M = 5.64, SD = 1.19) than the other control constructs, namely knowledge (M = 5.29, SD = 1.28) and facilitating conditions resources (M = 5.09, SD = 1.33) (Table 5).

The aforementioned descriptive statistics are the cumulative scores obtained from both broadband and narrowband consumers, and it is expected that the mean score may differ for the two groups. Hence, the findings that illustrate the cross sectional view are presented in the next subsection, which demonstrates broadband consumers' perception of having broadband significantly higher than its narrowband counterpart.

Differences Between Broadband Adopters and Non-Adopters: *t*-Test

Table 5 presents the means and standard deviations of the all the ten aggregate measures included in the study for both narrowband and broadband consumers. Table 5 also provides the results of the *t*-test, which tested the differences between

Table 3. Descriptive statistics

SN	Items	N	Mean	SD	SN	Items	N	Mean	SD
1	BI1	124	5.69	1.46	21	HO4	124	2.58	2.08
2	BI2	124	6.02	2.17	22	SQ1	124	5.57	2.39
3	BI3	124	5.98	1.24	23	SQ2	124	5.66	2.22
4	RA1	124	6.06	1.22	24	SQ3	124	5.60	2.31
5	RA2	124	5.98	1.27	25	SQ4	124	5.66	2.24
6	RA3	124	5.66	1.62	26	PI1	124	4.99	1.46
7	RA4	124	5.97	1.22	27	PI2	124	4.97	1.51
8	UO1	124	5.93	1.20	28	PI3	124	4.93	1.43
9	UO2	124	5.86	1.16	29	SI1	124	4.27	1.76
10	UO3	124	5.72	1.31	30	SI2	124	4.29	1.70
11	UO4	124	5.85	1.25	31	K1	124	5.28	1.28
12	UO5	124	5.13	1.58	32	K2	124	5.33	1.42
13	UO6	124	5.37	1.49	33	K3	124	5.26	1.44
14	UO7	124	5.65	1.25	34	S1	124	5.70	1.31
15	UO8	124	4.92	1.59	35	S2	124	5.62	1.25
16	UO9	124	5.14	1.43	36	S3	124	5.58	1.19
17	UO10	124	5.44	1.46	37	FCR1	124	5.38	1.43
18	HO1	124	4.95	1.78	38	FCR2	124	4.90	1.68
19	HO2	124	4.82	1.84	39	FCR3	124	4.85	1.67
20	HO3	124	4.28	1.86	40	FCR4	124	5.24	1.48
N: Total number of responses. SD: Standard Deviation									

Table 4. Summary of descriptive statistics

SN	Construct	NI	N	Descriptive			
				Mean	**Min**	**Max**	*SD*
1	Behavioural Intention	2	124	5.84	2.00	7.00	1.24
2	BISP	1	124	6.02	1.00	8.00	2.17
3	Relative Advantage	4	124	5.92	3.00	7.00	1.17
4	Utilitarian Outcomes	10	124	5.51	3.00	7.00	1.15
5	Hedonic Outcomes	4	124	4.16	1.00	7.00	1.57
6	Service Quality	4	124	5.63	1.00	8.00	2.19
7	Primary Influence	3	124	4.97	2.00	7.00	1.39
8	Secondary Influence	2	124	4.28	1.00	7.00	1.68
9	Facilitating Conditions Resources	4	124	5.09	1.75	7.00	1.33
10	Knowledge	3	124	5.29	1.67	7.00	1.28
11	Self-efficacy	3	124	5.64	1.00	7.00	1.19
NI: Total number of variables or items. *N*: Total number of responses. *SD*: Standard Deviation							

Table 5. t-Tests to examine equality of group means

Construct	Non-Adop. vs. Adop.	N	M	M Difference	SD	t	df	P (2-tailed)
BI	Non-Adopter	68	5.41	0.88	1.37	4.34	113	.000
	Adopter	56	6.32		.84			
RA	Non-Adopter	68	5.68	0.52	1.25	2.56	121	.012
	Adopter	56	6.20		.99			
UO	Non-Adopter	68	5.33	0.40	1.21	1.96	121	.052
	Adopter	56	5.72		1.05			
HO	Non-Adopter	68	3.95	0.47	1.59	1.69	119	.093
	Adopter	56	4.42		1.53			
SQ	Non-Adopter	68	6.88	-2.76	1.91	-9.21	120	.000
	Adopter	56	4.11		1.43			
PI	Non-Adopter	68	4.73	0.54	1.46	2.19	121	.030
	Adopter	56	5.26		1.27			
SI	Non-Adopter	68	4.36	-0.17	1.54	-0.56	107	.576
	Adopter	56	4.19		1.84			
K	Non-Adopter	68	4.90	0.87	1.27	4.01	121	.000
	Adopter	56	5.77		1.13			
SE	Non-Adopter	68	5.29	0.75	1.34	3.84	111	.000
	Adopter	56	6.05		.80			
FCR	Non-Adopter	68	5.01	0.19	1.41	0.80	121	.427
	Adopter	56	5.20		1.24			

the narrowband and broadband consumers on these constructs. The findings indicate that with the exception of hedonic outcomes, secondary influence and facilitating conditions resources, the non-adopters and adopters of broadband differ significantly on the mean score for the remaining seven constructs. Even though overall both groups (i.e. non-adopters and adopters) view the adoption of broadband positively, the mean scores indicate that adopters have significantly more positive perceptions on the various constructs (except service quality) than non-adopters.

Discriminant Analysis

To confirm the effectiveness of various factors for discriminating adopters from non-adopters, a discriminant analysis was performed using broadband adoption as the dependent variable and behavioral intention, relative advantage,

utilitarian outcomes, hedonic outcomes, service quality, primary influence, secondary influence, facilitating conditions resources, knowledge and self-efficacy as the predictor variables. A total of 124 cases were analyzed. The findings are presented in Tables 6 and 7. A single determinant function was calculated. The value of this function was significantly different for the non-adopters and adopters ($\chi2$ (10, N = 124) = 82.927, p < .001). The correlations between the predictor variables and the discriminant function suggested that service quality was the best predictor of the future adoption of broadband whilst secondary influence was found to be least useful (Table 7).

Overall, the discriminant function successfully predicted the outcome for 85.5% of the cases, with accurate predictions being made for 82.4% of the non-adopters consumers and 89.3% of the adopters (Table 7).

Table 6. Structure matrix

Variable	Function
SQ	.779
BI	-.364
K	-.345
SK	-.319
RA	-.218
PI	-.188
UO	-.168
HO	-.146
FCR	-.069
SI	.050

Frequency of Internet Use

Table 8 illustrates the difference between broadband and narrowband consumers in terms of the frequency of usage or accessibility to the internet. The results indicate clear differences and suggest that the majority of broadband consumers (41.3%) access or use the internet several times a day in comparison to 2.7% of the narrowband consumers. However, the numbers of broadband consumers decrease as the frequency of Internet access decreases. Generally, broadband consumers' online habits in terms of their frequency of Internet access differ from narrowband consumers. Broadband consumers belong to the more frequent categories whilst narrowband consumers belong to the less frequent categories (Table 8). The chi-square test confirmed a significant difference ($\chi 2$ (5, N =

75) = 16.75, p = .005) between narrowband and broadband consumers in terms of the frequency of Internet access (Table 8).

A binary correlation test was also conducted to examine if there was an association between frequency of Internet access and broadband adoption. The results obtained from this test suggest that there was a significant correlation between frequency of Internet access and broadband adoption (Table 9).

Duration of Internet Use

Table 10 illustrates the difference between broadband and narrowband consumers in terms of total time spent on the Internet on a daily basis. Similar to the frequency of internet access, the results indicate that clear differences occur between narrowband and broadband consumers. Generally broadband consumers increase as the number of hours increase. Contrastingly, the number of narrowband consumers increase as the hours decrease. 5.3% of narrowband consumers spend less than half an hour in contrast to no broadband consumers. However, in the 3-4 hours category, broadband consumers (14.7%) exceeded the narrowband consumers (4%). 12.1% of broadband consumers spent more than four hours on the Internet on a daily basis, in comparison to 0% of narrowband users (Table 10). The chi-square test confirmed a significant difference ($\chi 2$ (5, N = 75) = 20.85, p = .008) between the narrowband and

Table 7. Classification results

	Adopter vs. Non-Adopters	Predicted Group Membership		Total
		Non-Adopter	Adopter	
Count	Non-adopter	56	12	68
	Adopter	6	50	56
%	Non-adopter	82.4	17.6	100.0
	Adopter	10.7	89.3	100.0
a. 85.5% of original grouped cases correctly classified.				

Table 8. Frequency of home Internet access

Frequency of Internet Access	Narrowband		Broadband	
	Frequency	Percent	Frequency	Percent
Several times a day	2	2.7	31	41.3
About once a day	6	8.0	13	17.3
3-5 days a week	4	5.3	6	8.0
1-2 days a week	2	2.7	4	5.3
Once every few weeks	1	1.3	1	1.3
Less often	4	5.3	1	1.3
Total	19		56	
χ^2 Test (N=75) Type of connection X Frequency of Internet Access				
	Value	df	p (2-sided)	
Pearson χ^2	16.75	5	.005	

broadband consumers in terms of the total time spent on the Internet on a daily basis (Table 10).

A binary correlation test was also conducted to examine if there was any association between duration of Internet access and broadband adoption. The results obtained from this test suggest that there was a significant correlation between duration of Internet access and broadband adoption (Table 11).

CONCLUSION

This study examined the factors affecting the adoption of broadband Internet in Malaysia. The following main conclusions are drawn from this research. Findings from the descriptive statistics suggested that all the constructs included in this study rated strongly. This suggested that the respondents showed strong agreement in factors included in the study for examining the adoption of broadband. There was then an examination of the differences between the adopters and non-adopters of broadband, employing the t-test and discriminant analysis techniques. The results from the *t*-test and discriminant analysis suggested that significant differences occur between

the responses obtained from the narrowband and broadband consumers with regards to attitudinal, normative and control constructs. The findings related to the usage of the Internet suggested that broadband consumers significantly differ to narrowband users in terms of the online habits and variety of Internet use.

As broadband technologies enable a range of communication and Internet services, studying individuals from Malaysia add one more perspective for understanding the adoption of broadband in developing countries. Thus, this research presents one of the initial efforts towards understanding the broadband adoption behavior of consumers outside of the context of developed countries. The findings are specifically useful for ISPs and

Table 9. Spearman's rho correlations to show association between duration of Internet access and broadband adoption

		Broadband Adoption
Frequency of internet access	Correlation Coefficient	-.442(**)
**Correlation is significant at the 0.01 level (2-tailed).	Sig. (2-tailed)	.000
	N	75

Table 10. Duration of Internet access on a daily basis

Duration of Internet Access	Narrowband		Broadband	
	Frequency	Percent	Frequency	Percent
<1/2 hour	4	5.3	0	0
1/2-1 hour	4	5.3	3	4.0
>1-2 hour	8	10.7	27	36.0
>2-3 hour	0	0	6	8.0
>3-4 hour	3	4.0	11	14.7
=>4 hour	0	0	9	12.1
Total	19		56	
χ^2Test (N=75) Type of connection X Duration of Internet Access				
	Value	df	p (2-sided)	
Pearson χ^2	20.85	5	.008	

Table 11. Spearman's rho correlations to show association between duration of Internet access and broadband adoption

		Broadband Adoption
Duration of internet access	Correlation Coefficient	.350(**)
**Correlation is significant at the 0.01 level (2-tailed).	Sig. (2-tailed)	.002
	N	75

policy makers of Malaysia, as specified above. Factors that are reported as being significant are important and require attention in order to encourage the further adoption and usage of Internet in the country. Additionally, the cost of using the traditional telephone network is very high so broadband Internet can be used as a replacement for offering communication services such as instant messaging or Internet Protocol (IP) telephony.

Governments of many developed and developing countries, including Malaysia, are transforming public sector services by utilizing information and communication technologies to deliver government services to citizens on an 'anywhere anytime basis'. However, full realization of such efforts and investments are only possible if there is wide availability and diffusion of broadband in the respective countries. Therefore, the findings of this study while having direct implications for encouraging broadband diffusion also has indirect implications for encouraging diffusion of emerging electronic government services in a developing country such as Malaysia.

This study has its limitations, such as the generalization of these findings to the whole of Malaysia and the inability to supplement the questionnaire data with interviews or adopt a longitudinal approach to data collection. However, due to time and resource constraints, such limitations could not be overcome. For instance, future research of a similar nature may entail a longer data collection period, which will subsequently eliminate any variables that may have produced anomalies in the result.

REFERENCES

Anonymous. (2007). *Malaysia broadband market.* Retrieved from http://www.budde.com.au/Research/Malaysia-Broadband-Market.html

Choudrie, J., & Dwivedi, Y. K. (2005a). Investigating the research approaches for examining the technology adoption in the household. *Journal of Research Practice, 1*(1), 1–12.

Choudrie, J., & Dwivedi, Y. K. (2005b). The demographics of broadband residential consumers of a British local community: The London Borough of Hillingdon. *Journal of Computer Information Systems, 45*(4), 93–101.

Choudrie, J., & Dwivedi, Y. K. (2006a). A comparative study to examine the socio-economic characteristics of broadband adopters and non-adopters. *Electronic Government: An International Journal, 3*(3), 272–288.

Choudrie, J., & Dwivedi, Y. K. (2006b). Investigating factors influencing adoption of broadband in the household. *Journal of Computer Information Systems, 46*(4), 25–34.

Dwivedi, Y. K. (2005). *Investigating adoption, usage, and impact of broadband: UK households.* Unpublished doctoral dissertation, Brunel University, London, UK.

Dwivedi, Y. K., Choudrie, J., & Brinkman, W. P. (2006). Development of a survey instrument to examine consumer adoption of broadband. *Industrial Management & Data Systems, 106*(5), 700–718. doi:10.1108/02635570610666458

Dwivedi, Y. K., & Irani, Z. (2009). Understanding the adopters and non-adopters of broadband. *Communications of the ACM, 52*(1), 122–125. doi:10.1145/1435417.1435445

Dwivedi, Y. K., Khan, N., & Papazafeiropoulou, A. (2007). Consumer adoption and usage of broadband in Bangladesh. *Electronic Government: An International Journal, 4*(3), 299–313. doi:10.1504/EG.2007.014164

Dwivedi, Y. K., Papazafeiropoulou, A., Gharavi, H., & Khoumbati, K. (2006). Examining the socio-economic determinants of adoption of an e-government initiative 'Government Gateway'. *The Electronic Government: An International Journal, 3*(4), 404–419. doi:10.1504/EG.2006.010801

Dwivedi, Y. K., & Weerakkody, V. (2007). Examining the factors affecting the adoption of broadband in the Kingdom of Saudi Arabia. *Electronic Government: An International Journal, 4*(1), 43–58. doi:10.1504/EG.2007.012178

Dwivedi, Y. K., Williams, M. D., Lal, B., Weerakkody, V., & Bhatt, S. (2007, December 28-30). Understanding factors affecting consumer adoption of broadband in India: A pilot study. In *Proceedings of the 5th International Conference on E-Governance*, Hyderabad, India.

Fowler, F. J. Jr. (2002). *Survey research methods.* London, UK: Sage.

Hinton, P. R., Brownlow, C., McMurray, I., & Cozens, B. (2004). *SPSS explained.* London, UK: Routledge.

Keong, L. M. (2007). *Malaysia lowers broadband target.* Retrieved from http://www.zdnetasia.com/malaysia-lowers-broadband-targets-62032069.htm

Khoumbati, K., Dwivedi, Y. K., Lal, B., & Chen, H. (2007). Broadband adoption in Pakistan. *Electronic Government: An International Journal, 4*(4), 451–465. doi:10.1504/EG.2007.015038

Malaysia broadband market. (2007). Retrieved from http://www.budde.com.au/Research/Malaysia-Broadband-Market.html

Malaysian Institute of Accountants. (2007). *Malaysian Institute of Accountants Directory.* Retrieved from http://www.mia.org.my/new/members_memberfirms_directory.asp

Rogers, E. M. (1995). *Diffusion of innovations.* New York, NY: Free Press.

Venkatesh, V., & Brown, S. (2001). A longitudinal investigation of personal computers in homes: Adoption determinants and emerging challenges. *Management Information Systems Quarterly*, *25*(1), 71–102. doi:10.2307/3250959

Williams, M. D., & Dwivedi, Y. K., Middleton, C., Wilson, D., Falch, M., Schultz, A. et al. (2007). Global diffusion of broadband: Current state and future directions for investigations. In T. McMaster, D. Wastell, E. Ferneley, & J. DeGross (Eds.), *Organizational dynamics of technology-based innovation: Diversifying the research agenda: IFIP TC8 WG 8.6 International Working Conference in Information and Communication Technology* (Vol. 235, pp. 529-532). New York, NY: Springer.

Chapter 8
Citizens' Adoption of Pay-to-Use E-Government Services:
An Empirical Study

Amitabh Ojha
Indian Institute of Technology Delhi, India

G. P. Sahu
National Institute of Technology, India

M. P. Gupta
Indian Institute of Technology Delhi, India

ABSTRACT

Evidence exists that citizens' demand for pay-to-use e-government services is highly price-elastic. But research on citizens' adoption of e-government remains almost entirely pre-occupied with contexts wherein it is implicit that citizens would not face any monetary cost implications. The fact that Technology Acceptance model (TAM) and Perceived Characteristics of Innovating (PCI) do not factor in potential adopters' monetary cost perceptions is a plausible reason for such bias in research efforts. The paper posits a model wherein the value perceived by a citizen in government-to-citizen (G2C) online channel, and traditional public service delivery channel are antecedents of his or her intention to use the online channel. The model was tested in the context of the rail ticketing service of Indian Railways (a Department of India's federal government). Results support the hypothesized paths, and offer useful managerial guidance to encourage citizens' adoption. The paper discusses the prospect of certain adverse consequences for public administration and citizens, which could be linked to e-government and user charges, and ways to mitigate them. Research implications are also discussed.

INTRODUCTION

Today, as governments are increasingly turning to e-government led administrative reform, citizens' slow uptake of governments' online services poses a challenge for reform managers who are respon-sible for the twin targets of improving the quality of public service delivery, and cutting down on operating expenses. On the other hand, citizens who do not embrace these online services, end up wasting precious time in government offices, time which they could have spent in an economically

DOI: 10.4018/978-1-4666-2458-0.ch008

productive activity or at leisure. Therefore, a less used government-to-citizen (G2C) e-government service represents a loss for the government and also the citizens. In addition, under-utilization of e-government services results in a low rate of return on funds invested to develop those services. That is a serious concern, considering that it takes substantial funds to create new e-government services, and it costs even higher to create citizen-centered e-government services (Bertot & Jaeger, 2008). In fact it might be difficult to sustain a severely under-utilized e-government service, particularly if the receipt of certain minimum user charges were essential for its financial viability. The problem can prove particularly acute in case of e-government services which are based on the public-private partnership (PPP) model. But in spite of the stated adverse consequences of low adoption of G2C e-government services, governments can't mandate the use of these services in the way they have been able to mandate the use of many government-to-business (G2B) e-government services. Adoption of e-government in the face of user charges cannot be taken for granted, because citizens' desire for more services from their governments does not necessarily imply their willingness to pay (Winter & Mouritzen, 2001). Therefore the demand for G2C online services is expected to be price-elastic, and there is anecdotal evidence that the adoption rate of G2C online motor vehicle registration renewal skyrocketed in Arizona, after the elimination of $6.95 online user charge (Johnson, 2007). The aforesaid discussion points at the importance of studying citizens' adoption of pay-to-use G2C e-government services, an area which has remained largely ignored so far.

Central to the low adoption of G2C e-government services is the problem of digital divide, the complexity of which can be gauged from its multiple dimensions i.e. technology, telecommunication, economic, information access, and information literacy (Bertot, 2003). Needless to say, that e-government led administrative reform programs need to be matched with concerted efforts at dealing with the digital divide problem. While digital divide keeps a large section of citizenry away from e-government services, it is important however, that citizens who already possess the requisite skills and resources, adopt the G2C online services in big numbers. Focus of the paper is on e-government adoption by the latter category of citizens.

This study proposes a research model to explain the aforesaid category of citizens' intention to adopt a pay-to-use G2C e-government service (which involves user charges), in preference to traditional service delivery (where user charges are not involved). The model is tested in the context of e-ticket service of Indian Railways (IR; a Department of India's federal government). For the sake of clarity on the study context, a brief introduction of IR, its e-ticketing service, and an explanation on the appropriateness of this context for the present study, has been included in the paper. The study's appeal however is not limited to the IR ticketing context, its central purpose being to: (1) demonstrate how the influence of user charges on citizens' adoption of G2C online services could be investigated; and (2) examine the broad implications of e-government user charges for public administration, and citizens.

LITERATURE REVIEW

Focus of the review presented here is on the role of potential (individual) adopter's monetary cost implications in technology acceptance. The review is organized along the following three information systems usage contexts: (a) information systems usage in organizational or institutional settings; (b) citizens' usage of e-government; and (c) business-to-consumer e-commerce. Technology adoption literature per-se is voluminous and has been the topic of several reviews and critiques, sources for which are provided in the sub-sections that follow.

Information Systems Usage in Organizations

Although the term information system (IS) has a much wider connotation, we limit the present discussion under IS adoption to usage in organizational settings. Indeed, prior to the advent of internet and online services, technology adoption literature has almost entirely addressed technology usage in organizational or work-place or institutional settings, wherein individuals are not required to incur any monetary cost for using an information system. IS adoption in organizational contexts is an important research area, and it has seen prolific contribution from researchers for almost two decades now. The theoretical frameworks guiding those IS adoption studies predominantly are Technology Acceptance Model (TAM) (Davis, Bagozzi, & Warshaw, 1989) and Theory of Planned Behavior (TPB) (Ajzen, 1991), while the Diffusion of Innovation/Perceived Characteristics of Innovating (DOI/PCI) (Moore & Benbasat, 1991) was also used, though in fewer instances. Of these theories, TAM has been the most influential (King, & He 2006; Ma & Liu, 2004). For critiques, please see Benbasat and Barki (2007), Lee, Kozar, and Larsen (2003), and Legris, Ingham, and Collerette (2003).

E-Government Usage by Citizens

E-government adoption is emerging as an important research topic, a fact which can be gauged from the steadily increasing number of publications in this area (for reviews, please see Ojha, Sahu, and Gupta (2009) and Titah and Barki (2006)). The focus of discussion here will be on some of the key trends that are apparent from studies of citizens' adoption of e-government services, and as are relevant to this study. First, in most cases those studies are based on TAM and TPB, mirroring a trend similar to IS adoption literature. Second, it is implicit in nearly all those studies, that the

citizen would not face any monetary costs in her decision to adopt an e-government service. The one study in which cost has been considered a factor in e-government adoption is Gilbert, Balestrini, and Littleboy (2004). In that study, 'cost' includes savings to both the individual and the organization. But a citizen can be expected to make a fair judgment only in respect of the cost/saving that she faces, a factor which would among other things shape her e-government usage intentions. Further, those authors have treated 'cost' as a saving i.e a benefit, whereas in our present study context, G2C e-government user charges constitute a barrier. The reason G2C e-government adoption studies dealing with user charges or other monetary implications are almost non-existent, could be due to a sub-set of the following plausible factors: (1) the dominant paradigm i.e. TAM, and even DOI/PCI do not include monetary cost as an antecedent of individuals' usage intentions; (2) while monetary cost perceptions can be included in TPB models as a salient belief, the traditional predominance of organizational or institutional IS usage contexts has meant that monetary costs generally do not figure even in the TPB models of IS adoption; and (3) in the initial phase, few G2C e-government services attracted user charges. And the third trend is, that citizen level e-government adoption studies are beset by adopter-bias i.e. the respondents surveyed were entirely, or predominantly those who were already users of the e-government service in question. Adopter-biased studies can only be of limited help in terms of their ability to guide managerial action to promote the use of a G2C online service by citizens.

Business-to-Consumer E-Commerce

E-commerce adoption is already a substantial area of research, wherein literature continues to grow at a fast rate (Cheung, Chan, & Limayem, 2005; Monsuwé, Dellaert, & de Ruyter, 2004). In keeping with the objectives of this study, discussion here would address the theoretical bases of business-to-consumer (B2C) e-commerce adoption research, and the inclusion of monetary cost perceptions in models explaining individuals' adoption of B2C e-commerce and closely related services e.g. telecommunications services.

The theories underlying the empirical studies on adoption of e-commerce predominantly have been TAM, TPB, and Theory of Reasoned Action (TRA), while DOI/PCI has been used in a few cases. Of these studies, some have also included the consumers' monetary cost perceptions through either of the following two approaches: (1) inclusion of perceived monetary cost as an additional salient belief in the TPB model (Hung, Ku, & Chang, 2003); or (2) extension of the TAM model to include perceived monetary cost as an additional salient belief (Cheong & Park, 2005; Wu & Wang, 2005). A recent TAM critique (Benbasat & Barki, 2007) recommends that additional salient beliefs are appropriately introduced in a TRA or TPB model, and but has criticized the myriad extensions of TAM with additional salient beliefs, an approach that has led to theoretical chaos. Reason for the latter criticism is that unlike TRA or TPB, TAM per-se offers no scope or mechanism for introducing any salient belief beyond perceived usefulness and perceived ease of use.

More recently however, a few studies on adoption of e-commerce and telecom services have introduced perceived value or similar constructs in their research models, and have found empirical support for a direct effect of perceived value on consumers' behavioral intentions (Table 1). While perceived value has been defined in multiple ways (for an extensive review on perceived value, please see Woodall (2003)), for the present discussion, the following definition by Zeithaml (1988) is generally adequate: *Perceived value is the consumer's overall assessment of the utility of a product based on perceptions of what is received and what is given* (p. 14). The models incorporating perceived value are able to explain from 24%

to 82% of the variance in individuals' behavioral intention with respect to the electronic channel (Table 1). These perceived value – behavioral intention models offer the natural advantage that perceived value subsumes the consumers' monetary cost implications through a trade-off between what is received and what is given.

More recently however, a few studies on adoption of e-commerce and telecom services have introduced perceived value or similar constructs in their research models, and have found empirical support for a direct effect of perceived value on consumers' behavioral intentions (Table 1). While perceived value has been defined in multiple ways (Woodall, 2003). For the present discussion, the following definition by Zeithaml (1988) is generally adequate: *Perceived value is the consumer's overall assessment of the utility of a product based on perceptions of what is received and what is given* (p. 14). The models incorporating perceived value are able to explain from 24% to 82% of the variance in individuals' behavioral intention with respect to the electronic channel (Table 1). These perceived value – behavioral intention models offer the natural advantage that perceived value subsumes the consumers' monetary cost implications through a trade-off between what is received and what is given.

INDIAN RAILWAYS AND ITS E-TICKET SERVICE

Indian Railways (IR) is a Department of India's federal government and is headed by the Chairman Railway Board, who is also the Permanent Secretary in the Ministry of Railways, and is answerable to the Railway Minister. In terms of size and scale, IR is among the top five national railway systems of the world. During the year 2006-07, IR transported 17 million passengers and 2 million tones of freight daily across its network comprising of 63,327 route kilometers. During

Table 1. Perceived value (PV) and e-commerce adoption

Reference	Study Context and Key Findings
Chu & Lu (2007)	302 respondents completed an online survey regarding online music purchase in Taiwan. Perceived customer value was posited as the sole direct antecedent of purchase intention (PI). R^2 for PI was 82%.
Kim, Chan, & Gupta (2007)	161 respondents completed an online survey pertaining to mobile internet adoption. PV was posited as the sole direct antecedent of adoption intention (BI). R^2 for BI was 35.9%.
Kleijnen, de Ruyter, & Wetzels (2007)	375 usable responses were collected in Netherlands through personal interviews, the study context being mobile brokerage service. Perceived value of mobile channel usage was the sole direct antecedent of intention to use (BI). R^2 for BI was 39%.
Turel, Serenko, & Bontis (2007)	222 usable responses were received in a survey pertaining to SMS usage. PV was posited as the sole direct antecedent of intention to use (BI). R^2 for BI was 41%.
Overby & Lee (2006)	466 and 361 usable responses were received from high and low frequency shoppers respectively, through an online survey on internet shopping. Utilitarian and Hedonic values were posited as the antecedents of consumer preference for an internet retailer. Utilitarian value showed a higher effect on preference, than did Hedonic value. R^2 for preference was 47%.
Shun & Yunjie (2006)	86 respondents completed an online survey to test a model, which explains customer satisfaction and loyalty in e-commerce settings. Process value and satisfaction explained 58% of the variance in loyalty.
Chiou (2004)	209 usable responses were received through an internet-based survey. Trust, PV, and overall satisfaction showed direct effect on household users' loyalty towards internet service provider.
Wang, Lo, & Yang (2004)	Through face-to-face customer surveys, 348 valid responses were obtained from users of the two mobile service providers of China. Customer satisfaction, and customer value explained 67.8% of the variance in intention to re-purchase the mobile service.
Yang & Peterson (2004)	235 usable responses were received through a web based survey. Customer value and satisfaction explained 75% of the variance in customer loyalty, in e-commerce setting.
Chen & Dubinsky (2003)	99 undergraduate students enrolled at a large state university completed a questionnaire related to internet shopping. PV explained 24% of the variance in purchase intention. Valence of Experience, Perceived product quality, and Product Price had direct significant effect on PV.

the period, IR's revenues and dividend payment to the federal government were INR 627 billion and INR 42 billion respectively. During the same period, the social service obligations borne by IR were valued at INR 37 billion. Main elements of this social service obligation were the losses incurred on: essential commodities carried below cost; passenger and other related services; operation of uneconomic branch lines; and new lines opened for traffic during the last 15 years. IR is the sole provider of cross-country rail transport in India, and it employs 1.4 million personnel. The railway budget is separately presented to, and voted by the Parliament.

In India, the demand for rail travel is generally high vis-à-vis the supply, and hence the need to buy a prior seating/sleeping reservation ticket, which can be purchased up to 90 days in advance of the date of travel. Since 1985, train reservation tickets have been sold by IR through its computerized country-wide passenger reservation system (PRS) counters. At the PRS counters tickets are sold by railway staff mainly on cash payment, the service hours being 8.00 to 20.00 hrs Monday to Saturday, and 8.00 to 14.00 hrs on Sundays. Although purchase of rail reservation tickets at IR's PRS counters does not entail the payment of extra charges, it does involve standing and waiting in queues which could be long and slow moving. Moreover, in geographical regions which experience extreme summers or winters, the time spent standing and waiting in queues can be taxing, if the queuing space is non air-conditioned. In addition to the PRS outlets, tickets can also be purchased online (e-ticket) from the website of Indian Railways Catering and

Figure 1. Research model

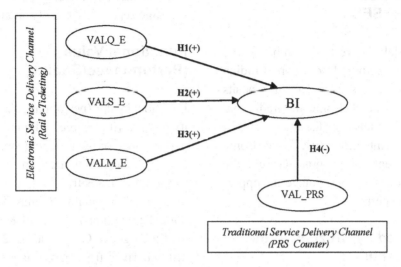

Key:
Passenger Reservation System (PRS)
Functional Value (performance/quality) perceived in electronic channel (VALQ_E)
Social Value perceived in electronic channel (VALS_E)
Functional Value (price/value for money) perceived in electronic channel (VALM_E)
Value perceived in traditional service delivery channel (VAL_PRS)
Behavioral Intention to use the electronic channel (BI)

Tourism Corporation Ltd. (IRCTC), a public sector undertaking under the Ministry of Railways, the online service hours being 5.00 to 23.30 hrs. The rail e-ticketing service was formally introduced in February, 2006. After having booked and paid online for the rail e-ticket, the rail traveler directly prints her ticket from the rail e-ticketing website; an individual can complete this entire process sitting in her office/home. However, purchase of an e-ticket attracts the payment of a service charge (INR 20 for air-conditioned, and INR 10 for non air-conditioned passenger cars) to IRCTC, and in addition, a prescribed transaction fee to the participant credit (debit) card provider or the bank. The rail e-ticketing service offered by IRCTC has been the recipient of Government of India's National Award for e-Governance, 2007-08 for outstanding performance in citizen centric service delivery. As of this writing, 8% of the rail reservation tickets are sold through the online channel, their revenue share being 18%. Hereafter, the terms 'PRS counter' and 'traditional service delivery channel' would mean the same, and will be used interchangeably. In similar vein, the terms 'rail e-ticketing', 'online rail ticketing', and 'electronic (service delivery) channel' will be used interchangeably and they would mean the same i.e online purchase of rail ticket (self-service).

In contrast to India (and a few other countries) where railways are a department of the federal government, elsewhere railways are either private sector entities (e.g. private sector train operating companies in U.K), or are public sector entities at arm's length relationship with the government (e.g. AMTRAK in the U.S). So, while online rail ticketing fits the definition of a G2C e-government service in the Indian context, the same would not apply to say U.K. Recognizing that an online rail ticketing service might not be understood as a G2C e-government service in all country contexts, we therefore take IR's online rail ticketing to be merely a surrogate or proxy of a G2C e-government service which attracts user charges.

RESEARCH MODEL AND HYPOTHESES

The research model (Figure 1) should be viewed in context of the preceding description of Indian Railways and its ticketing system. This study posits the value perceived in electronic and traditional service delivery channels to be the antecedents of citizens' behavioral intention to use the electronic channel. Subsequent sub-sections present the literature support and other rationale in support of the proposed hypothesis.

Value Perceived by Citizens in the Electronic Channel

In view of the theoretical and empirical support for a perceived value – behavioral intention framework in the online context (Table 1), values perceived in electronic channel are posited as antecedents of citizens' behavioral intention to use the electronic channel. Here, the perceived value of electronic channel is treated as multi-dimensional, by adapting the consumer perceived values scale (PERVAL) of Sweeney and Soutar (2001) to the present study context. Founded on Sheth, Newman, and Gross' (1991) theory of consumption values which is applicable to both goods and services, Sweeney and Soutar (2001) identified four values in respect of consumer durable goods i.e functional value (performance/quality), social value, functional value (price/value for money), and emotional value, and showed that these values are direct antecedents of consumers' behavioral intentions. These values, being applicable to the pre-purchase as well as post-purchase stages, are well suited to technology adoption studies where a sample could comprise entirely of non-users/users, or a mix of users and non-users. Of the aforesaid four values, emotional value was not considered relevant to the e-government context. The consumer perceived values proposed by Sweeney and Soutar (2001) have also been used in a previous

study which pertained to adoption of switched message service (SMS) (Turel et al., 2007).

Functional Value (Performance/Quality)

Functional Value (performance/quality) is the utility derived from perceived quality and expected performance of the product (Sweeney & Soutar, 2001). Studies pertaining to online context provide support for a positive influence of: (1) performance/service quality (Dabholkar & Bagozzi, 2002; Parasuraman, Zeithaml, & Malhotra, 2005; Wolfinbarger & Gilly, 2003), (2) as well as the utility derived from performance/service quality (Eastin, 2002; Overby & Lee, 2006; Shun & Yunjie, 2006; To, Liao, & Lin, 2007) on consumers' adoption of the online channel. In similar vein, it is expected that citizens will want to use an e-government service if it is well designed, functions efficiently, and is convenient to use.

H1: Functional Value (performance/quality) perceived in electronic channel positively affects behavioral intention to use the electronic channel (VALQ_E → BI)

Social Value

Social Value refers to the utility derived from a product's ability to enhance social self-concept (Sweeney & Soutar, 2001). Social self-concept is the image that one believes others hold, while the ideal social self-concept denotes the image that one would like others to hold (Sirgy, 1982). In IS adoption literature however, the effect of *image* on behavioral intention has been generally non-significant. But it is plausible, that when an e-government service is still new to people, and is only used by a small minority of citizens, the consequence of using it might be social self-concept enhancing.

H2: Social Value perceived in electronic channel positively affects behavioral intention to use the electronic channel (VALS_E → BI)

Functional Value (Price/Value for Money)

Functional Value (price/value for money) is the utility derived from the product due to the reduction of its perceived short term and longer term costs (Sweeney & Soutar, 2001). Value for money and related constructs have been found to be predictors of individuals' behavioral intentions in the online context (Chen & Dubinsky, 2003; Chiou, 2004; Eastin, 2002; Yang & Peterson, 2004). A citizen's decision to use an e-government service might imply monetary costs implications for her e.g. e-government user charges, charges for internet usage and print-outs, and/or other associated charges. In such an event, a citizen's value for money perception would shape her behavioral intention to use the e-government service.

H3: Functional Value (price/value for money) perceived in electronic channel positively affects behavioral intention to use the electronic channel (VALM_E → BI).

Value Perceived by Citizens in Traditional Service Delivery Channel

Previously, two studies have included the competing channel/store perceptions in their research models, and have found that the former has a significant (negative) effect on individuals' usage/behavioral intention in respect of the focal channel/store (Montoya-Weiss, Voss, & Grewal, 2003; Sirohi, McLaughlin, & Wittink, 1998). In similar vein, Broekhuizen (2006) tried to examine the effect of competing channel perception, but could not do so for lack of discriminant validity. In view of the support available from the aforesaid two studies, it is speculated that inclusion of

citizens' perception of traditional channel should add to the predictive ability of the model.

In the present study setting, respondents incur considerable time and effort costs in the event of buying a rail ticket from Indian Railways' passenger reservation service (PRS) counter, even though this offers them relief from the service charges attracted in e-ticketing. The other benefits at PRS counter could be a sub-set of: relief from internet usage and printing charges; direct service delivery by railway staff; relief from having to visit the rail e-ticketing Indian Railway Catering and Tourism Corporation's website and operate in a self-service mode; and (due to cash payment facility) relief from online payment and hence no worry of cyber-fraud. In the case of PRS counter, we treated value as a trade-off between respondents' time and effort costs, and the benefits perceived by them. Reason for not applying PERVAL (Sweeney & Soutar, 2001) in case of PRS counter is explained. Since purchasing a rail ticket at PRS counter has no novelty and it is a tiresome affair, therefore social value and functional value (performance/quality) are not relevant to the PRS counter. Further, the PERVAL scale for functional value (price/value for money) treats money as the sacrifice, whereas the sacrifice involved at PRS counter is time and effort.

H4: Value perceived in traditional service delivery channel negatively affects behavioral intention to use the electronic channel (VAL_PRS → BI)

RESEARCH METHODOLOGY

Survey Procedure

For this rail e-ticket study context, individuals relevant to the sample are those who have: (1) not yet purchased a rail e-ticket, but have internet skills, and a basic familiarity with the rail e-ticketing

Table 2. Profile of respondents (N = 146)

Attribute	Count	Percentage
Age (years)		
17-23	94	64.4%
24-30	31	21.2%
≥ 31	21	14.4%
Gender		
Male	129	88.4%
Female	17	11.6%
Type of Student (bachelors/ masters)		
Bachelors	81	55.5%
Masters	65	44.5%
Type of Student (full/ part-time)		
Full time	112	76.7%
Part-time (full-time working professional)	34	23.3%
Years of experience with Internet		
1-3	44	30.1%
≥ 4	102	69.9%
Average daily Internet usage (in hrs)		
1-2	67	45.9%
≥ 3	79	54.1%
Previously purchased a rail ticket online ?		
Yes	53	36.3%
No	93	63.7%

classes in the evening, as part-time students. Ahead of the actual survey administration, one of the authors held several contact sessions with the students to brief them about the study, and to request that those who had never purchased a rail e-ticket should visit the relevant website and familiarize themselves with the entire process. During these contact sessions, it had emerged that most first and second year bachelors engineering students buy their rail ticket from the PRS counter, and that they were also examining the option of rail e-ticket. Administration of this survey in university settings facilitated the collection of responses even from those who had never bought a rail ticket online, a task which was difficult otherwise. A total of 350 questionnaires were hand delivered to those willing and fulfilling the aforesaid twin criteria for inclusion in the sample. The number of usable responses collected was 146. Profile of the respondents is summarized in Table 2.

Measures Used in the Survey

The five constructs involved in this study are: Value perceived in traditional service delivery channel (VAL_PRS); Functional Value (performance/quality) perceived in electronic channel (VALQ_E); Social Value perceived in electronic channel (VALS_E); Functional Value (price/ value for money) perceived in electronic channel (VALM_E); and Behavioral Intention to use the electronic channel (BI). Items for measuring the constructs have been adapted from scales used in previous studies and customized to suit the rail ticketing context (Table 3). All items were measured using a seven-point Likert-type scale with anchors from "strongly agree" to "strongly disagree". The survey instrument was refined in two stages: separate consultation with and feedback from five colleagues; followed by a pre-test with 35 students.

process; and (2) those who have purchased a rail e-ticket previously. In view of the adopter bias which has plagued past IS adoption research, and the need to reverse that trend (Jeyaraj, Rottman, & Lacity, 2006) the sample has a larger proportion of individuals who have not yet purchased a rail e-ticket online. Sample for this study comprises entirely of students at two technical universities of North India. These were first year and second year engineering students at bachelors level, and second year masters students from science, engineering, and management disciplines; this also includes full-time working professionals who attend their

Table 3. Items and outer model loadings

Constructs and Items		Loading	Adapted From
Value perceived in traditional service delivery channel (VAL_PRS)			
VAL_PRS1	For the time and effort that I have to put in, purchase of rail ticket from Railway's computer reservation office gives me value	0.89	Parasuraman et al. (2005)
VAL_PRS2	Compared to the benefit in purchasing my rail ticket from Railway's computer reservation office, the time and effort that I have to put in is reasonable	0.81	Kim et al. (2007)
VAL_PRS3	Overall, purchasing a rail ticket from Railway's computer reservation office gives me good value	0.90	Brady, & Robertson (1999)
Functional Value (performance/quality) perceived in electronic channel (VALQ_E)			
VALQ_E1	The online rail reservation website has been well designed	0.80	Sweeney, & Soutar (2001)
VALQ_E2	The online rail reservation website has an acceptable level of quality	0.87	
VALQ_E3	Overall, the online rail reservation website is convenient to use	0.85	Parasuraman et al. (2005)
VALQ_E4	The online rail reservation website gives me a feeling of being in control	0.87	
Social Value perceived in electronic channel (VALS_E)			
VALS_E1	If I use the online rail reservation service, it would help me to feel acceptable among my friends/contacts	0.86	Sweeney, & Soutar (2001)
VALS_E2	The use of online rail reservation service will improve the way I am perceived	0.90	
VALS_E3	If I use the online rail reservation service, it will make a good impression on my friends	0.91	
VALS_E4	When my co-travelers (on train) will see that I use an e-ticket, they will feel impressed with me	0.82	
Functional Value (price/value for money) perceived in electronic channel (VALM_E)			
VALM_E1	The extra charges (service charges) payable on an e-ticket are reasonable	0.86	Sweeney, & Soutar (2001)
VALM_E2	The online rail reservation service offers value for money (service charges)	0.85	
VALM_E3	The quality of online rail reservation service is good, relative to the service charges required to be paid	0.87	
VALM_E4	The online rail reservation service charges are economical	0.86	
Behavioral Intention to use the electronic channel (BI)			
BI1	In the future, I intend to book my rail reservation mostly through internet (e-ticket)	0.95	Venkatesh, & Davis (2000)
BI2	For booking any rail reservations, in future the internet option (e-ticket) will generally be my first choice	0.97	Agarwal, & Prasad (1998)
BI3	It is likely that I'll use the internet to book my rail reservation (e-ticket) on most occasions	0.95	Venkatesh, & Davis (2000)

RESULTS AND DISCUSSION

The data-analytic technique used in this study to assess the psychometric properties of measures and to test the hypothesis is Partial Least Squares (PLS), a latent structural equation modeling technique which takes a variance-based (or components-based) approach. PLS places minimal demands on sample size and data distributions, and it is recommended for situations where the research objective is exploration and theory or model building (Chin, 1998, p. xii). The re-sampling procedure

Table 4. Inter-construct correlations

	Composite Reliability	VAL_PRS	VALQ_E	VALS_E	VALM_E	BI
VAL_PRS	0.90	0.745				
VALQ_E	0.91	-0.100	0.720			
VALS_E	0.93	-0.001	0.306	0.769		
VALM_E	0.92	-0.245	0.245	0.240	0.741	
BI	0.97	-0.520	0.294	0.255	0.439	0.914

Note: The off diagonal elements are the correlations among constructs.
Average Variance Extracted (AVE) has been shown on the leading diagonal.

used to assess the significance of PLS parameter estimates is bootstrapping (200 re-samples). The software implementation of PLS used for data-analysis, is PLS-Graph Version 03.00.

Results

Measurement Model (Outer Model)

Reliability of the measures was assessed through Composite Reliability (CR). In respect of the five constructs involved in the research model, CR ranged from 0.90 to 0.97 (Table 4). The outer model loadings of the items ranged from 0.80 to 0.97 (Table 3). Thus, reliability and loadings are well above the minimum 0.70 level (Fornell & Larcker, 1981). A Principal Component Analysis (PCA) with Varimax rotation showed an expected five factor structure in the data. This was followed up with PLS Factor Analysis, for which the loadings were computed in accordance with the procedure illustrated in Gefen and Straub (2005). To conserve space, only the details of PLS Factor Analysis results are reported here (Table 5). As can be seen, all items pertaining to any one construct, load strongly on to that factor. The Average Variance Extracted (AVE) in respect of each construct is well above the prescribed minimum limit of 0.5 (Fornell & Larcker, 1981), and is higher than the correlation of that construct with other constructs (Table 4). Since AVE would always be lower than its square root, the preceding comparison of inter-construct correlations with AVE rather than the square-root of AVE (the formal procedure), is a more stringent test. Thus, the aforesaid outer model results support the convergent and discriminant validity of measures used in the study.

Structural Model (Inner Model)

The correlation between the explanatory variables (Table 4) indicates that multicollinearity might be a concern. Although PLS is robust against multi-collinearity (Cassel, Hackl, & Westlund, 1999), nevertheless Variance Inflation Factor (VIF) were ascertained before interpreting the the structural model estimates. The VIFs ranged from 1.065 to 1.155, which shows that multicollinearity is not an issue here. PLS analysis results (Figure 2) show that the hypothesized model explains 42% of the variance in BI i.e citizens' behavioral intention to use the electronic channel. The value perceived in traditional service delivery channel had the largest (albeit negative) influence on BI ($\beta = -0.44$, t = 6.63). The functional value (price/value for money) perceived in electronic channel also showed a strong influence on BI ($\beta = 0.26$, t = 3.74). Social value perceived in electronic channel had a relatively smaller effect on BI ($\beta = 0.15$, t = 2.57). Functional value (performance/ quality) had the smallest effect on BI ($\beta = 0.14$, t = 2.25). Thus, the empirical results provide support for all the hypothesized relationships. The various

Table 5. PLS factor analysis results

	VAL_PRS	**VALQ_E**	**VALS_E**	**VALM_E**	**BI**
VAL_PRS1	.885	-.110	.002	-.267	-.492
VAL_PRS2	.805	-.137	-.070	-.202	-.371
VAL_PRS3	.895	-.023	.049	-.163	-.471
VALQ_E1	.013	.802	.308	.251	.149
VALQ_E2	-.120	.866	.256	.239	.219
VALQ_E3	-.042	.854	.204	.155	.244
VALQ_E4	-.141	.870	.287	.210	.325
VALS_E1	-.037	.383	.865	.222	.257
VALS_E2	.012	.341	.905	.205	.193
VALS_E3	-.010	.185	.912	.195	.256
VALS_E4	.053	.136	.823	.228	.160
VALM_E1	-.208	.151	.172	.865	.279
VALM_E2	-.126	.109	.181	.849	.298
VALM_E3	-.209	.323	.259	.866	.429
VALM_E4	-.270	.208	.195	.862	.445
BI1	-.449	.276	.256	.434	.954
BI2	-.541	.281	.220	.415	.966
BI3	-.498	.286	.256	.411	.947

Key:
Functional Value (performance/quality) perceived in electronic channel (VALQ_E)
Social Value perceived in electronic channel (VALS_E)
Functional Value (price/value for money) perceived in electronic channel (VALM_E)
Value perceived in traditional service delivery channel (VAL_PRS)
Behavioral Intention to use the electronic channel (BI)

Figure 2. PLS analysis results

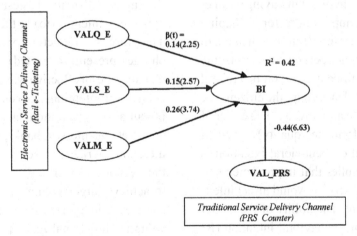

Key:
Passenger Reservation System (PRS)
Functional Value (performance/quality) perceived in electronic channel (VALQ_E)
Social Value perceived in electronic channel (VALS_E)
Functional Value (price/value for money) perceived in electronic channel (VALM_E)
Value perceived in traditional service delivery channel (VAL_PRS)
Behavioral Intention to use the electronic channel (BI)

Table 6. Hypothesis test results

Hypothesis	Hypothesized Path	Result
H1 (+):	Functional Value (performance/quality) perceived in electronic channel → Behavioral Intention to use the electronic channel	Supported
H2 (+):	Social Value perceived in electronic channel → Behavioral Intention to use the electronic channel	Supported
H3 (+):	Functional Value (price/value for money) perceived in electronic channel → Behavioral Intention to use the electronic channel	Supported
H4 (-):	Value perceived in traditional service delivery channel → Behavioral Intention to use the electronic channel	Supported

Note: The '+' and '-' signs within parentheses denote a positive and negative effect respectively.

hypothesized paths and empirical support for the same, are also summarized in Table 6.

Discussion

The value perceived by citizens in traditional service delivery channel shows an attenuating effect on their behavioral intention to use the electronic channel, which is as expected. But it is interesting that value perceived in traditional service delivery channel has the largest effect on behavioral intentions. This might be a reflection of citizens' unwillingness to stand and wait in long and slow moving queues at Indian Railways' passenger reservation service counters. The strong effect of functional value (price/value for money) perceived in electronic channel indicates that the extra service charges involved in buying a rail e-ticket, are indeed an important factor in shaping citizens' intention to use the electronic channel. In this study, the social value perceived in electronic channel shows a significant effect on behavioral intention. This shows that perhaps the citizens see rail e-ticketing service as a novelty. The effect of functional value (performance/quality) perceived in electronic channel on behavioral intention is the smallest. This implies that improvements to quality of e-ticketing service would affect intentions to a lesser extent. The ability of the model to explain the citizens' behavioral intention (R^2 = 0.42) is fair, given its parsimonious nature, and the exploratory nature of this study.

IMPLICATIONS OF THE STUDY

Managerial Implications

If an increasing number of rail travelers in India take to rail e-ticketing service, it will help IR to economize on costs involved in the sale of rail reservation tickets. Empirical results of this study show that the key to attracting more rail travelers to rail e-ticketing service lies in managerial interventions as would cause: (1) citizens' value perceptions in respect of electronic service delivery channel to increase; and (2) citizens' value perceptions in respect of traditional service delivery channel to decrease.

Of the value perceptions in respect of electronic channel, the functional value (price/value for money) had the largest effect on citizens' behavioral intention to use the electronic channel. Therefore any reduction or abolition of service charges, presently attracted in buying a rail e-ticket, would be an effective way to increase citizens' behavioral intentions. Given the need to reduce potential adopters' monetary costs, government agencies, businesses, banks, credit card companies, and internet service providers could explore the avenues of working synergetically in order to achieve larger volumes, economies of scale, and cost reduction. Besides, an increase in social value and functional value (performance/quality) perceptions of the electronic channel would also result in increased behavioral intentions. To enhance citizens' social value perceptions, IR could consider suitable advertising campaigns. For an increase in functional value (performance/quality), improvements along the following sub-set of e-service quality and e-recovery service quality dimensions of Parasuraman et al. (2005) are likely to prove helpful: *Efficiency*, *System Availability*, *Privacy*, *Responsiveness*, and *Contact*. But at the same time, it is important not to lose sight of the fact that the room for encouraging citizens' adoption of electronic channel through enhancement of functional value (performance/quality), is rather limited.

Citizens' value perception in respect of traditional service delivery channel i.e. passenger reservation service (PRS) counter would decrease if the 'give' element increases, and the 'receive' element decreases. Accordingly, the value perception in respect of traditional service delivery channel should decrease, if: (1) the queuing and waiting period at PRS counters increases; (2) service quality at PRS counter deteriorates; (3) comfort level in the queuing area decreases; or (4) service charge on rail e-ticket is reduced or withdrawn.

Implications for Public Administration

Following from the managerial implications discussed in the preceding sub-section, it might appear that a blanket reduction or abolition of user charges will be a good step for G2C online services generally. While such a step encourages citizens' adoption of G2C online services, it however ignores the difficulty presently faced in financing the development and operation of e-government services. So, it is evident that a more nuanced approach is required in the pricing of e-government services, one that supports e-government adoption by citizens and also helps to alleviate the e-government funding problem. In this regard, Chen and Thurmaier (2008) suggest that G2B user charges should be used to fund G2C

services. In similar vein, Johnson (2007) recommends that for reasons of low price-elasticity G2B online services be priced higher, and that governments could consider offering certain G2C online services for free or at a discount (the converse of user charge). These researchers have also suggested that user charge for an e-government service should be determined by the externalities linked to its use. Here, externalities imply the effect of citizens' use of a G2C online service on others and on society at large. To illustrate the point, we re-visit our study context i.e. rail ticketing. In India, rail travel enjoys wide patronage and the positive externalities in citizens' use of rail e-ticketing service are: (1) saving in IR's costs on sale of rail tickets; (2) saving of man-hours lost to the economy by citizens standing in queues; (3) proliferation of e-government usage skills in the social system; and (4) increased prospect of citizens' adoption and use of prospective G2C services. Taking these positive externalities into account, it can be argued that there is a justification for considering the abolition of service charges, and even offering discounts to those, who book rail tickets online. The aforesaid positive externalities being important to government and society at large, the federal government could consider reimbursing appropriate amounts to IRCTC, to neutralize the revenue loss resulting from the suggested service charge elimination and any discounts offered to users of the electronic channel. In India, the federal government has levied cess (e.g. education cess) and surcharge on income tax to fund specific developmental activities. In that light, the federal government could consider levying an e-government development cess on income tax. Another policy initiative to be considered in this regard is a 'tax holiday' scheme for private sector organizations who in collaboration with government agencies, provide e-government services to the citizens. However, should the levy of user charges be considered necessary in case of certain G2C online services, public administrators should ascertain citizens' willingness to pay, through the Contingent valuation method (Carson, 2000). In summarizing, certainly there is a need to consider a reduction or elimination of G2C online user charges and preferably a discount to users of G2C online services. But the final decision in this regard should be criterion-based, and should factor in the following: citizens' ability and willingness to pay; externalities; availability of surpluses from G2B user charge revenues for financing the G2C services; and availability of funding from government for G2C e-government services.

The study results also point at the potential for an adverse outcome in the realm of public administration. Given the pressures to improve the delivery of public services and reduce operating costs, public administrators should find it attractive to promote e-government. Besides, private sector firms offering e-government services under the PPP model will want that an increasing number of citizens use the electronic channel. So, it is plausible that public administrators and other interest groups would prefer that the traditional service delivery channels get worse, or they don't improve. This thesis draws support from our empirical results which show, that increase in citizens' value perception of traditional channel would attenuate their intention to use the electronic channel. In such a scenario, citizens visiting the traditional channels (due to digital divide) would suffer, if there are no laws or administrative procedures which obligate government agencies to: (1) subject their services to citizen satisfaction surveys through a third-party; and (2) adhere to certain minimum standard of service.

Implications for the Citizen

If one compares the scenarios before and after the introduction of e-ticketing by IR, the former period signifies a sense of equality i.e. nearly all individuals queued up at PRS counters, whereas the latter period reflects inequality and differentiation i.e individuals who are internet capable and are able to pay extra service charges, take the quick and easy e-ticket route, while the rest join the long queues at PRS counters. Here, it is pertinent to refer Aberbach and Christensen (2005) who have noted, that while citizens are supposed to be equal in a democratic society, customers however are not equal, the amount they (customers) pay being the determinant of the level of service they get. So, in the first scenario the individual appears a citizen, but in the second scenario she more resembles a customer. Thus, it is apparent that e-government and user charges can have the consequence of metamorphosing the citizen to a customer. The shift in emphasis from 'citizen' to 'customer' is likely to result in increased political inequality due to marginalization of the weaker sections (who might lack the ability to voice their protest/concern effectively), even though it might result in increased operational performance of government agencies (Fountain, 2001). In similar vein, Ryan (2001) suggests that: treating citizens as customers would negatively impact the public confidence in government; over-emphasis on individual satisfaction would be in conflict with the social capital building role of public services; and the language of service producer and consumer helps project the picture of an elitist government.

It is necessary to clarify here, that even though the foregoing line of argument and discussion on *citizen*, *customer*, and *inequality* were anchored in the study's rail ticketing context, in reality they are targeted at public goods and services delivery contexts, where citizens expect to be treated equally by the government. As for the rail ticketing context, it is plausible that citizens have greater tolerance, or even an unquestioning acceptance for the inequality induced by the parallel existence of rail e-ticketing and the PRS counters, which are diametrically opposite in terms of the service quality and convenience they offer.

In developed countries, it is possible that reasonably good service quality awaits a digitally disadvantaged citizen, when she turns up at a traditional public service delivery counter. But in developing countries, it is more likely that such a citizen will either face a pathetic quality of service and/or be compelled to pay bribes even for a legitimate request or service. Although the preceding scenario is largely speculative, it does help to appreciate that the inequality implications of e-government and user charges can be particularly serious in developing country contexts. In this regard, the two suggestions made in the preceding sub-section i.e. a legally or administratively mandated mechanism to verify the upkeep of minimum standards in traditional public service delivery, a criterion-based reduction or abolition of G2C online user charges, and preferably a discount to users of G2C online services, should help alleviate concerns on the aforesaid inequality inducing effect of e-government and user charges. Whether or not public administrators will voluntarily act in those directions, would in part depend on whether they think in terms of the 'equal citizen', or the 'unequal customer'.

Implications for Research

E-government adoption studies have hardly addressed citizens' monetary cost implications such as user charges, etc. This study extends the perceived value - behavioral intention framework, used more recently in e-commerce adoption research, to the e-government domain. It is hoped that this should stimulate further research on citizens' adoption of G2C e-government services in the face of user charges or other financial implications, research which cannot be appropriately pursued through the dominant paradigm i.e. TAM, or DOI/PCI. Also, our results suggest the appropriateness of treating the value perceived in e-government as multi-dimensional. Prior to this study, only two other studies (Ebbers, Pieterson, & Noordman, 2008; Frey & Holden, 2005) had taken a channel perspective of e-government. The unique insights resulting from our treatment of e-government as a service delivery channel alongside the traditional channel, shows that research approaches which tend to view the electronic channel in isolation,

are perhaps less useful in terms of their ability to inform practice. Also, the results indicate that inclusion of citizens' perception of the traditional service delivery channel can improve the predictive ability of the e-government adoption model. Yet another message which should emerge from this study is that e-government adoption research should try and reach out to those citizens who have the internet usage skills, but have not yet adopted the e-government service(s); such research will be more helpful in country contexts where current level of e-government adoption is abysmally low.

LIMITATIONS AND FUTURE WORK

In interpreting the study's results, it is necessary to take into account its limitations, which are listed here. First, this study has used a sample which comprises of bachelors and masters students at two technical universities, nearly a quarter of whom are full-time professionals. Future research on IR e-ticketing adoption should attempt a larger and more diverse sample. Second, the model explains 42% of the variance in citizens' electronic channel usage intentions, even as it is implicit in the model that factors which might have an influence on citizens' usage intentions, are subsumed or fully mediated by the perceived value constructs. Future studies could pursue research efforts to improve the perceived value – usage intention model's explanatory power. Third, due to the cross-sectional design of this study, it is not possible to formally establish causal relationships from the data.

There are some additional avenues for future work, which are not necessarily arising out the limitations of this present research. On the basis of literature support, antecedents of the various perceived value constructs could be included in future studies and their effect empirically verified in the e-government context. It is also suggested that future studies should include the perceived value in respect of competing/alternate service delivery channel in their research models. This will help to improve our understanding of whether the inclusion of citizens' value perceptions of the traditional channel would consistently improve the predictive ability of the e-government adoption model in diverse settings. In respect of those public services, where a self-service e-government channel comes to exist alongside the traditional channel, it would be useful to conduct a longitudinal study to ascertain if traditional service delivery has worsened, remained static, or has improved. Such a study could also factor in the following: whether senior civil servants think that government should offer price and quality differentiated public services, similar to markets; and perception of senior civil servants on investing in improvements to traditional service delivery. Further, research which throws light on G2B and G2C e-government pricing mechanisms of various governments and their impact, would also be valuable. Yet another important question, though peripheral to this study, is that of re-thinking and widening the definition of e-government. The blurring public-private distinction (Musolf & Seidman, 1980; Sellers, 2003; Simon, 1998) and the prospect of many present day functions of governments moving to the private sector (Shleifer, 1998), perhaps justify the case for re-visiting the definition of e-government.

CONCLUSION

G2C e-government adoption researches have almost entirely focused on contexts wherein it is implicit that the citizen would not face any monetary costs in her decision to adopt an online service. As a result, studies on citizens' adoption of pay-to-use G2C online services are non-existent. The study makes an important contribution by addressing this gap in e-government literature. Basic premise of the study is, that the value perceived by a citizen in government-to-citizen (G2C) online channel, and traditional public service delivery channel,

determine her intention to use the online channel. Results support the hypothesized paths, and offer useful managerial guidance for attracting more rail travelers to e-ticketing. Implications of the study have relevance and potential utility for many other pay-to-use G2C online services. Although it might appear from the study results, that a blanket reduction/elimination of user charges or extension of discounts to users of G2C online services will be a good step, connection to recent literature on e-government pricing shows that while this step has merit, it should be criterion-based. The study sounds a warning that public administrators' and other interest groups' e-government promotion agenda might create incentives for neglect and deterioration of traditional channels. In such event, users of traditional channels (weaker sections) would stand to suffer, unless there is a law or administrative procedure to mandate a minimum standard of service delivery. It has been argued in the study, that e-government and user charges could metamorphose the citizen to a customer, and perpetrate inequalities. Upkeep of minimum standards in traditional channel and criterion-based reduction or abolition of user charge and preferably discounts to G2C online users should mitigate the aforesaid inequality concerns.

ACKNOWLEDGMENT

The views expressed here are those of the authors only and not those of Government of India, Ministry of Railways.

REFERENCES

Aberbach, J. D., & Christensen, T. (2005). Citizens and consumers: an NPM dilemma. *Public Management Review*, 7(2), 225–245. doi:10.1080/14719030500091319

Agarwal, R., & Prasad, J. (1998). The antecedents and consequents of user perceptions in information technology adoption. *Decision Support Systems*, *22*(1), 15–29. doi:10.1016/S0167-9236(97)00006-7

Ajzen, I. (1991). The theory of planned behavior. *Organizational Behavior and Human Decision Processes*, *50*(2), 179–211. doi:10.1016/0749-5978(91)90020-T

Benbasat, I., & Barki, H. (2007). Quo Vadis, TAM? *Journal of the Association for Information Systems*, *8*(4), 211–218.

Bertot, J. C. (2003). The multiple dimensions of the digital divide: More than the technology 'haves' and 'have nots'. *Government Information Quarterly*, *20*(2), 185–191. doi:10.1016/S0740-624X(03)00036-4

Bertot, J. C., & Jaeger, P. T. (2008). The e-Government paradox: Better customer service doesn't necessarily cost less. *Government Information Quarterly*, *25*(2), 149–154. doi:10.1016/j.giq.2007.10.002

Brady, M. K., & Robertson, C. J. (1999). An exploratory study of service value in the USA and Ecuador. *International Journal of Service Industry Management*, *10*(5), 469–486. doi:10.1108/09564239910289003

Broekhuizen, T. (2006). *Understanding channel purchase intentions: Measuring online and offline shopping value perceptions*. Ridderkerk, The Netherlands: Labyrinth Publications.

Carson, R. T. (2000). Contingent valuation: A user's guide. *Environmental Science & Technology*, *34*(8), 1413–1418. doi:10.1021/es990728j

Cassel, C., Hackl, P., & Westlund, A. H. (1999). Robustness of partial least-squares method for estimating latent variable quality structures. *Journal of Applied Statistics*, *26*(4), 435–446. doi:10.1080/02664769922322

Chen, Y.-C., & Thurmaier, K. (2008). Advancing e-government: Financing challenges and opportunities. *Public Administration Review*, *68*(3), 537–548. doi:10.1111/j.1540-6210.2008.00889.x

Chen, Z., & Dubinsky, A. J. (2003). A conceptual model of perceived customer value in e-commerce: A preliminary investigation. *Psychology and Marketing*, *20*(4), 323–347. doi:10.1002/mar.10076

Cheong, J. H., & Park, M.-C. (2005). Mobile internet acceptance in Korea. *Internet Research*, *15*(2), 125–140. doi:10.1108/10662240510590324

Cheung, C. M. K., Chan, G. W. W., & Limayem, M. (2005). A critical review of online consumer behavior: Empirical research. *Journal of Electronic Commerce in Organizations*, *3*(4), 1–19. doi:10.4018/jeco.2005100101

Chin, W. W. (1998). Commentary: Issues and opinion on structural equation modeling. *Management Information Systems Quarterly*, *22*(1), vii–xvi.

Chiou, J.-S. (2004). The antecedents of consumers' loyalty toward internet service providers. *Information & Management*, *41*(6), 685–695. doi:10.1016/j.im.2003.08.006

Chu, C.-W., & Lu, H.-P. (2007). Factors influencing online music purchase intention in Taiwan. *Internet Research*, *17*(2), 139–155. doi:10.1108/10662240710737004

Dabholkar, P. A., & Bagozzi, R. P. (2002). An attitudinal model of technology-based self-service: Moderating effects of consumer traits and situational factors. *Journal of the Academy of Marketing Science*, *30*(3), 184–201.

Davis, F. D., Bagozzi, R. P., & Warshaw, P. R. (1989). User acceptance of computer technology: A comparison of two theoretical models. *Management Science*, *35*(8), 982–1003. doi:10.1287/mnsc.35.8.982

Eastin, M. S. (2002). Diffusion of e-commerce: An analysis of the adoption of four e-commerce activities. *Telematics and Informatics, 19*(3), 251–267. doi:10.1016/S0736-5853(01)00005-3

Ebbers, W. E., Pieterson, W. J., & Noordman, H. N. (2008). Electronic government: Rethinking channel management strategies. *Government Information Quarterly, 25*(2), 181–201. doi:10.1016/j.giq.2006.11.003

Fornell, C., & Larcker, D. (1981). Evaluating structural equation models with unobservable variables and measurement error. *JMR, Journal of Marketing Research, 18*(1), 39–50. doi:10.2307/3151312

Fountain, J. E. (2001). Paradoxes of public sector customer service. *Governance: An International Journal of Policy and Administration, 14*(1), 55–73.

Frey, K. N., & Holden, S. H. (2005). Distribution channel management in e-government: Addressing federal information policy issues. *Government Information Quarterly, 22*(4), 685–701. doi:10.1016/j.giq.2006.01.001

Gefen, D., & Straub, D. (2005). A practical guide to factorial validity using PLS-Graph: Tutorial and annotated example. *Communications of the Association for Information Systems, 16*, 91–109.

Gilbert, D., Balestrini, P., & Littleboy, D. (2004). Barriers and benefits in the adoption of e-government. *International Journal of Public Sector Management, 17*(4), 286–301. doi:10.1108/09513550410539794

Hung, S.-Y., Ku, C.-Y., & Chang, C.-M. (2003). Critical factors of WAP services adoption: An empirical study. *Electronic Commerce Research and Applications, 2*(1), 42–60. doi:10.1016/S1567-4223(03)00008-5

Jeyaraj, A., Rottman, J. W., & Lacity, M. C. (2006). A review of the predictors, linkages, and biases in IT innovation adoption research. *Journal of Information Technology, 21*(1), 1–23. doi:10.1057/palgrave.jit.2000056

Johnson, C. L. (2007). A framework for pricing government e-services. *Electronic Commerce Research and Applications, 6*(4), 484–489. doi:10.1016/j.elerap.2007.02.005

Kim, H.-W., Chan, H. C., & Gupta, S. (2007). Value-based adoption of mobile internet: An empirical investigation. *Decision Support Systems, 43*(1), 111–126. doi:10.1016/j.dss.2005.05.009

King, W. R., & He, J. (2006). A meta-analysis of the technology acceptance model. *Information & Management, 43*(6), 740–755. doi:10.1016/j.im.2006.05.003

Kleijnen, M., de Ruyter, K., & Wetzels, M. (2007). An assessment of value creation in mobile service delivery and the moderating role of time consciousness. *Journal of Retailing, 83*(1), 33–46. doi:10.1016/j.jretai.2006.10.004

Lee, Y., Kozar, K. A., & Larsen, K. R. T. (2003). The technology acceptance model: Past, present, and future. *Communications of the Association for Information Systems, 12*, 752–780.

Legris, P., Ingham, J., & Collerette, P. (2003). Why do people use information technology? A critical review of the technology acceptance model. *Information & Management, 40*(3), 191–204. doi:10.1016/S0378-7206(01)00143-4

Ma, Q., & Liu, L. (2004). The technology acceptance model: A meta-analysis of empirical findings. *Journal of Organizational and End User Computing, 16*(1), 59–72. doi:10.4018/joeuc.2004010104

Monsuwé, T. P., Dellaert, B. G. C., & de Ruyter, K. (2004). What drives consumers to shop online? A literature review. *International Journal of Service Industry Management, 15*(1), 102–121. doi:10.1108/09564230410523358

Montoya-Weiss, M. M., Voss, G. B., & Grewal, D. (2003). Determinants of online channel use and overall satisfaction with a relational, multichannel service provider. *Journal of the Academy of Marketing Science, 31*(4), 448–458. doi:10.1177/0092070303254408

Moore, G. C., & Benbasat, I. (1991). Development of an instrument to measure the perceptions of adopting an information technology innovation. *Information Systems Research, 2*(3), 192–222. doi:10.1287/isre.2.3.192

Musolf, L. D., & Seidman, H. (1980). The blurred boundaries of public administration. *Public Administration Review, 40*(2), 124–130. doi:10.2307/975622

Ojha, A., Sahu, G. P., & Gupta, M. P. (2009). Antecedents of paperless income tax filing by young professionals in India: An exploratory study. *Transforming Government: People. Process and Policy, 3*(1), 65–90.

Overby, J. W., & Lee, E.-J. (2006). The effects of utilitarian and hedonic online shopping value on consumer preference and intentions. *Journal of Business Research, 59*(10-11), 1160–1166. doi:10.1016/j.jbusres.2006.03.008

Parasuraman, A., Zeithaml, V. A., & Malhotra, A. (2005). E-S-QUAL - a multiple-item scale for assessing electronic service quality. *Journal of Service Research, 7*(3), 213–233. doi:10.1177/1094670504271156

Ryan, N. (2001). Reconstructing citizens as consumers: Implications for new modes of governance. *Australian Journal of Public Administration, 60*(3), 104–109. doi:10.1111/1467-8500.00229

Sellers, M. P. (2003). Privatization morphs into 'publicization': Businesses look a lot like government. *Public Administration, 81*(3), 607–620. doi:10.1111/1467-9299.00363

Sheth, J. N., Newman, B. I., & Gross, B. L. (1991). Why we buy what we buy: A theory of consumption values. *Journal of Business Research, 22*(2), 159–170. doi:10.1016/0148-2963(91)90050-8

Shleifer, A. (1998). State versus private ownership. *The Journal of Economic Perspectives, 12*(4), 133–150.

Shun, C., & Yunjie, X. (2006). Effects of outcome, process and shopping enjoyment on online consumer behaviour. *Electronic Commerce Research and Applications, 5*(4), 272–281. doi:10.1016/j.elerap.2006.04.004

Simon, H. A. (1998). Why public administration? *Journal of Public Administration: Research and Theory, 8*(1), 1–11.

Sirgy, M. J. (1982). Self-concept in consumer behavior: A critical review. *The Journal of Consumer Research, 9*(3), 287–300. doi:10.1086/208924

Sirohi, N., McLaughlin, E. W., & Wittink, D. R. (1998). A model of consumer perceptions and store loyalty intentions for a supermarket retailer. *Journal of Retailing, 74*(2), 223–245. doi:10.1016/S0022-4359(99)80094-3

Sweeney, J. C., & Soutar, G. N. (2001). Consumer perceived value: The development of a multiple item scale. *Journal of Retailing, 77*(2), 203–220. doi:10.1016/S0022-4359(01)00041-0

Titah, R., & Barki, H. (2006). e-Government adoption and acceptance: A literature review. *International Journal of Electronic Government Research, 2*(3), 23–57. doi:10.4018/jegr.2006070102

To, P.-L., Liao, C., & Lin, T.-H. (2007). Shopping motivations on Internet: A study based on utilitarian and hedonic value. *Technovation, 27*(12), 774–787. doi:10.1016/j.technovation.2007.01.001

Turel, O., Serenko, A., & Bontis, N. (2007). User acceptance of wireless short messaging services: Deconstructing perceived value. *Information & Management, 44*(1), 63–73. doi:10.1016/j.im.2006.10.005

Venkatesh, V., & Davis, F. D. (2000). A theoretical extension of the technology acceptance model: Four longitudinal field studies. *Management Science, 46*(2), 186–204. doi:10.1287/mnsc.46.2.186.11926

Wang, Y., Lo, H.-P., & Yang, Y. (2004). An integrated framework for service quality, customer value, satisfaction: Evidence from China's telecommunication industry. *Information Systems Frontiers, 6*(4), 325–340. doi:10.1023/B:ISFI.0000046375.72726.67

Winter, S., & Mouritzen, P. E. (2001). Why people want something for nothing: The role of asymmetrical illusions. *European Journal of Political Research, 39*(1), 109–143. doi:10.1111/1475-6765.00572

Wolfinbarger, M., & Gilly, M. C. (2003). eTailQ: Dimensionalizing, measuring and predicting etail quality. *Journal of Retailing, 79*(3), 183–198. doi:10.1016/S0022-4359(03)00034-4

Woodall, T. (2003). Conceptualising 'value for the customer': An attributional, structural and dispositional perspective. *Academy of Marketing Science Review*, (12): 1–42.

Wu, J.-H., & Wang, S.-C. (2005). What drives mobile commerce? An empirical evaluation of the revised technology acceptance model. *Information & Management, 42*(5), 719–729. doi:10.1016/j.im.2004.07.001

Yang, Z., & Peterson, R. T. (2004). Customer perceived value, satisfaction, and loyalty: The role of switching costs. *Psychology and Marketing, 21*(10), 799–822. doi:10.1002/mar.20030

Zeithaml, V. A. (1988). Consumer perceptions of price, quality, and value: A means-end model and synthesis of evidence. *Journal of Marketing, 52*(3), 2–22. doi:10.2307/1251446

This work was previously published in the International Journal of Electronic Government Research, Volume 7, Issue 2, edited by Vishanth Weerakkody, pp. 15-35, copyright 2011 by IGI Publishing (an imprint of IGI Global).

Chapter 9
Organizational Culture and E-Government Performance:
An Empirical Study

Shivraj Kanungo
The George Washington University, USA

Vikas Jain
The University of Tampa, USA

ABSTRACT

Government organizations differ significantly from private sector organizations in terms of their processes, culture, and ways of working. Plagued with phlegmatic and often lackadaisical work systems, government organizations tend to resist dramatic changes usually associated with technology based interventions. This study examines the effect of one dominant factor, organizational culture, on the success of e-government initiatives. To test the research model, survey data was collected from 315 respondents in 13 government organizations in India. The results indicate that a government organization which performs well on e-government projects exhibits specific cultural traits. Results also indicate that bureaucratic dimension, which emerges as the dominant cultural dimension in government organizations, is both positively and negatively related to e-government performance dimensions. The supportive and innovative dimensions of organizational culture are positively related to work process improvement and the job satisfaction of the user associated with e-government projects. Implications for practice and research are provided by interpreting the results in the context of the process paradox. The results show that while government and public sector organizations can use culture to positively impact efficiency dimensions of e-government performance, the dominant bureaucratic culture will tend to hinder systemic and enterprise-wide e-government performance.

DOI: 10.4018/978-1-4666-2458-0.ch009

1. INTRODUCTION

The term e-government refers to the use of information and communication technology (ICT) to improve and better the functioning of government systems, improve the delivery of government services to citizens, facilitate better interactions with other agencies or empower citizens through access to information. For instance, the World Bank defines "E-Government" as "the use by government agencies of information technologies (such as Wide Area Networks, the Internet, and mobile computing) that have the ability to transform relations with citizens, businesses, and other arms of government" (World Bank, n.d.). Over the last decade, many government agencies and departments across the world have strengthened their IT-enabled internal operations (Layne & Lee, 2001) and have moved to on-line services to citizens (Ho, 2002).

It is generally hoped that these initiatives will result in improved operations and services. However, the success of such initiatives has tended to be small-scale and gradual. Any initiative at the government level in general and technology initiative such as e-government in particular faces a plethora of issues such as budget scarcity, group conflict, cultural norms, and prevailing patterns of social and political behavior (West, 2008). Usually, government organizations are plagued with phlegmatic and often lackadaisical work systems (Light, 1997) compared to private sector companies which tend to exhibit more organized work systems (Boyne, 2002). Typically, technology initiatives in government organizations are caught between competing requirements among various government agencies which make it difficult to promote technological innovation associated with e-government initiatives. Government organizations are also characterized by strong political processes (Heftez & Warner, 2004) which tend to encourage conflict over resources. Therefore, the success of any e-government initiative is likely to be impacted by the way the government organization collectively reacts to the IT intervention and the way individuals in the organization respond to the initiative. Clearly, the transition to a "genuinely integrated, agile, and holistic government" (Dunleavy et al., 2005, p. 489) is tempered by ground realities – those that include political processes, cultural assumptions and structural constraints. Our study is motivated by the need to address one of these influencers of e-government – culture. Organizational culture is an important aspect that can potentially affect the success of IT initiatives in organizations.

Past studies confirm that a key piece of organizational infrastructure for e-government lies in changing internal government employee culture or the way that things are done in an organization (Peters & Waterman, 1982). Culture, within an organization, can be thought of as a way of life and could have significant impact on organizational performance (Wilkins & Ouchi, 1983). Peters and Waterman (1982) were possibly among the first authors to popularize the notion that having a strong culture is a key to organizational success. In case of government organizations, culture can resist dramatic changes, usually associated with technology based interventions, within a short period of time (Seifert & McLoughlin, 2007). Government organizations typically tend to exhibit strong cultures (Rainey & Steinbauer, 1999) that can inhibit or facilitate the success of various initiatives including the e-government initiatives. The rapid changes in the technology can create additional challenges for government organizations in terms of keeping pace with innovations. This can further accentuate willingness of government organizations to change course and alter the way they work. In such a situation, any e-government initiative instead of bringing positive change in government performance may actually lead to decline in performance.

Culture has been reported to form a key challenge towards the implementation of e-government in the public sector (Maniatopoulos, 2005). The impact of organizational culture on technology based initiatives has been demonstrated through the reflexive relationship between organization culture and information technology use (Olson, 1982). The interest in relating organizational culture and technology based initiatives has remained high as evidenced by similar theorization made by Claver et al. (2006). While aspects of culture have been studied in context of e-government earlier (Kovadid, 2005), its impact on success of e-government initiatives or performance of e-government has not been studied adequately. The current understanding about which cultural traits tend to enhance the performance of e-government and which tend to inhibit the performance is limited. The findings reported in the literature have continued to remain diffused but intriguing enough for researchers to remain interested.

Considering that culture is an important variable in context of government organizations, in this paper, we focus on organizational culture in government organizations as a determinant of e-government performance. Our motivation to study culture as a determinant of e-government performance is driven by the evidence that culture forms a compelling explanatory variable when it comes to explaining organizational failures in general (Leidner & Kayworth, 2006). Therefore, our objective in this paper is to respond to the following questions:

1. What dimensions of organizational culture are related to e-government performance?
2. How are different dimensions of organizational culture related to different aspects of e-government performance?

To address these questions, we develop the theoretical basis for the conceptual model in the subsequent sections. We also describe the dimensions of organizational culture and e-government performance. This is followed by the research methodology, results and analysis, and conclusion.

2. LITERATURE REVIEW

While organizational culture and performance of information systems (IS) in general have been studied in the past, many issues remain open. Some of these issues have to do with how organizational culture and IS performance are defined and operationalized. In context of e-government, the importance of the link between organizational culture and the performance of e-government is captured by the following prescription by Beaumaster (2002) whose study was based on a sample of 138 local government executives in Virginia, "the bottom line for local government administrators must be the creation of an organizational culture where information technology (IT) is valued as a necessary and integral part of the operations and success of the organization. In other words, local governments must create an environment for IT success by developing an organizational culture that deals with IT well."

With that in view, in the next sections, we present the conceptual bases of e-government performance and organizational culture. Following that, we provide the theoretical integration and the relationship between these concepts.

2.1. E-Government Performance

The introduction of digital initiatives by governments across the world has the potential to improve external and internal relationships among the various stakeholders involved in the government services delivery process (including citizens, government employees, external businesses etc) and facilitate sharing of knowledge among these stakeholders (Choudrie et al., 2004). Therefore, performance of digitally enabled government (referred to as e-government) is determined by how well the IT initiative supporting e-government is able to improve government operations and services. From this standpoint, the performance of e-government is somewhat reflective of the value added by IT initiatives in government organizations. Therefore, to understand and identify the metrics for e-government performance, we first review the IT value literature. In the IT value literature, the most common question that researchers focusing on value of information technology initiatives have attempted to answer pertains to the nature of organizational value that is created as a result of investments in information technology. One common theme for assessing information technology value has been "efficiency" in terms of getting things done cheaper (cost efficiency) or faster (productivity) or both. There is plethora of studies that assess IT value using tangible metrics such as financial performance or cost savings. For example, Lee and Menon (2000) use productivity improvement and technical and production efficiency as measures of IT value. Barua et al. (1995) have shown that IT value can be measured as reduction in inventory costs, transportation costs and information handling cost savings and that IT does help in reducing the operating costs. Firm value also appears to be an enduring measure for IT value as evidenced by past research (Bresnahan et al., 2002; Brynjolfsson & Hitt, 1996, 2000; Dehning et al., 2003; Dos Santos et al., 1993). Melville et al. (2004), who employ competitive advantage and operational efficiency as distinct measures of IT value, provide another approach for assessing IT value.

Elsewhere, faced with the complexity of the nature of value information technology provides, researchers have responded by assessing the IT value in achieving effectiveness – essentially a measure of the extent to which IT and related organizational processes produce the desired organizational objectives. In essence, efficiency oriented IT value measures include measures such as cost reduction or productivity improvements while effectiveness oriented measures include those used to assess product or service enhancements or customer satisfaction.

While the metrics used in earlier studies discussed above seem to be appropriate when the organization under consideration has profit motive, these measures are inadequate to assess the performance of e-government for two reasons. First, government organizations do not necessarily have a profit motive (Prager, 1994). These organizations are driven more by their responsibility toward citizens and other internal stake holders. From this standpoint, measuring performance of e-government purely based on financial performance metrics or those that focus on competitive advantage is not appropriate. Second, government organizations are unique in the sense that their operations are influenced, to a great extent, by political forces both within and outside the organization. The organizational culture, beliefs, values, administrative and bureaucratic processes along with political and regulatory constraints tend to determine the direction of any initiative in the organization including e-government initiative. In such a situation, e-government performance needs to be assessed using metrics that address such challenges.

The types of performance measures that seem more appropriate for government organizations relate to inputs (resources needed to produce services), outputs (products and services actually produced), process measures (measuring activities used to produce outputs), efficiency or productivity measures, and service quality measures (Stowers, 2004). In the current literature, a majority of reported government performance measures tend to focus more on the front end services offered by government organizations, as opposed to those that relate to business processes and back end information systems (Peters et al., 2004). For example, some of the front end measures to assess e-government performance include measures such as email response time from the government websites (West, 2008), or user satisfaction with e-government websites (Horan & Abhichandani, 2006). Chircu and Lee (2003) posit that evaluation of IT in government and public sector organizations should serve the dual economic and political objectives instead of merely serving the productivity objective used as the performance measure for IT initiatives in majority of studies (Brynjoffson & Yang, 1996; Lee & Menon, 2000). Delone and McLean (1992) identify six major dimensions of IT performance that include system quality, information quality, use, user satisfaction, individual impact, and organizational impact. These dimensions can be appropriately applied by choosing the appropriate metric under each of the dimensions to assess e-government performance.

From an e-government performance perspective, it seems that a mix of metrics appropriate to the context of government organizations may be suitable to assess e-government performance. E-government performance can also be conceptualized in terms of a continuum based on external and internal focus identified by Melville et al. (2004). Classifying the different conceptualizations of IT value across two dimensions, namely, efficiency-oriented versus effectiveness-oriented, and endogenously versus exogenously determined (Table 1) adapted from Kwon et al. (2002), the relevant measures for e-government performance seem to be those in the shaded quadrants. The shaded quadrants are relevant because government organizations do not operate in a competitive framework and do not have the profit motive.

Table 1. Dimensions of value associated with IS

	Efficiency-oriented	**Effectiveness-oriented**
Endogenously determined	Technical efficiency, Service efficiency Cost savings, Inventory turnover	Skill enhancement, User information satisfaction
Exogenously determined	Service enhancement, Interaction with other government agencies	Firm Value, Market Value

2.2. Organizational Culture

In this section, we cover the general notion of organizational culture and proceed to examine the notion of organizational culture in the context of IT.

Organizational culture connotes and denotes different things to different researchers. Some believe organizational culture has to do with core beliefs and written and unwritten assumptions – thereby implying shared values and assumptions. Therefore culture, within an organization, can be thought of as a way of organizational life. Culture of an organization often goes deeper than written or spoken words and actions of individuals. Hence, culture of an organization is like an iceberg - both seen and unseen (Schein, 1986). In many organizations, the "official" tip of the iceberg conflicts with, or is not representative of, the huge body of underlying assumptions.

Since culture has to do with making meanings, no two authors have adopted a common definition of culture. For instance, Deal and Kennedy (1982) describe culture as a stable collection of values, symbols, rituals, heroes, and stories that operate beneath the surface executing powerful influence in the behavior in the workplace. According to Peters and Waterman (1982), "stories, myths, and legends appear to be very important because they convey the organization's shared values or culture" (p. 75). Taking a clinical approach, Schein (1985) conceptualizes culture as patterns of basic assumptions "invented, discovered, or developed by a given group as it learns to cope with its problems of external adaptation and internal integration - that has worked well enough to be considered valid and, therefore, to be taught to new members as the correct way to perceive, think and feel in relation to those problems" (Schein, 1985, p. 9). Different people are drawn to studying culture for different reasons. Some see culture as managerial key-tools to improve economic output and to socialize organizational members to management-defined values. Others consider culture as a cognitive sense-making tool for organizational members in turbulent environments.

We will consider organizational culture to be the set of meanings and common values that determine how individuals behave and how the organization collectively reacts to organizational interventions like technology. In other words, culture accords the high level rules that guide individual actions of organizational participants, It is, therefore, reasonable to expect that when faced with a complex undertaking like e-government, the existing rules at work will have a significant impact on determining the course of the e-government initiative.

2.3. Organizational Culture in the Context of IT

At the organizational level, there are multiple ways in which relationship between organizational culture and IT has been analyzed. For instance, Bradley et al. (2006) studied two cultural types – entrepreneurial and formal – and found evidence to suggest that variations in IT success (impacts of IT at the strategic, tactical and operational levels) could be explained by differences in corporate culture. Alavi et al. (2005) used a case study to uncover shared values (aspects of culture) like expertise, innovativeness, formalization, collaboration and autonomy and link them to knowledge management outcomes (assessed in terms of making connections with others, developing and accumulating intellectual capital, and collaboration and learning).

In the context of advanced manufacturing technology organizations, McDermott and Stock (1999) have found that group-oriented cultures were associated with higher managerial satisfaction whereas rational-oriented cultures were associated with competitive success. Kanungo (1998) reported a cultural difference (measured by task-orientation and people-orientation) to account for the difference in user satisfaction in the context of networked computer application use.

Romm et al. (1995) argued that most forms of IT have cultural assumptions embedded in them that may conflict with a given firm's values, beliefs and norms. They claimed that such embedded assumptions render technologies as culture bound and that it is necessary to perform a cultural analysis to anticipate the likelihood of fit or misfit between a prospective IT and an organization's culture. Where such misfit occurs, the likely outcome will be user resistance, rejection, or outright sabotage. The interaction perspective assumes that both the IT and the organizational culture are fixed in the short run. Researchers have cautioned managers to consider organizational culture as a binding constraint when implementing IT (Robey & Azevedo, 1994). The binding constraint view is illustrated by advice offered by Pliskin et al. (1993) who warned managers against trying to change a firm's culture

It is important to remember that the culture and IT relationship works both ways. Clearly, technology has redefined the value of communicative and coordination-related aspects in organizations. In addition, IT-enabled processes have institutionalized accountability through built-in formats and reporting procedures; and to a large extent, disciplined the daily routines of operational activities. Although the cultural dominance of old-style workings and resentment towards the demands of management and external agencies remains, there is increasing evidence that information technology is also gradually changing the deeply embedded assumptions of organizational work (Chan, 2001). On the other hand, Lakhani et al. (2009) report that not only do organizations shift the internal culture to engage staff in planning the newly introduced systems and developing meaningful data, but organizations also extend the technology to other parts of the organization to support an integrated model of organizational performance.

In an organization, if some shared beliefs or norms are regarded as being incongruent with technology, then such a lack of fit tends to become a lasting problem; instead of remaining a temporary hurdle that many believe can be easily changed through technological diffusion or through appropriating technology selectively. In the organizational culture tradition of research, such changes to the technology or social system have been referred to as mutual adoption, reinvention, improvisation or drift. For example, when there is a lack of fit between IT and a given culture, the options available to managers include rejecting the IT in question and seek one that is more compatible with the culture, or to redesign the technology (and often compromise on the effectiveness) before implementing it or to proceed with adoption while acknowledging the fact that problems will occur (Gallivan & Srite, 2005). The assumption in such cases is that IT will not only have a pre-determined effect on people and organizations adopting it, but will largely remain independent of the context in which it is adopted, how it is used, or the specific intentions and actions of its users. Given this generic background pertaining to the study of organizational culture and IT, we now move to the theoretical integration to organizational culture and e-government performance.

2.4. Theoretical Integration

The relationship between organizational culture and e-government performance is a complex one. In the case of government organizations, these formulations of relationships may tend to be a little less defined because of the absence of either a profit motive or competitive necessity. Since government organizations continue to emphasize values of a bureaucratic or hierarchical culture (Parker & Bradley, 2000), there is reason to believe that this particular emphasis would results in some aspects of organizational culture that could act as enablers of e-government performance (Hackney & McBride, 1995), while other aspects of organizational culture that could behave as inhibitors to e-government performance (Tolsby,

1998). We therefore discuss the inhibitive role of culture as well as the facilitative role. In doing so, we theorize how culture can play both roles and also, in turn, be impacted by technology.

In the context of e-governance, a key piece of organizational infrastructure for e-government lies in changing internal government employee culture or the "way that things are done around here." Therefore, culture in government organizations is expected to be a determinant of e-government performance. Over the last decade "reinventing government" has been in the forefront of governments in the US, Canada, tens of European nations, and many developing countries (Juthla et al., 2002).

More often than not, the culture of an organization has been considered to inhibit e-government performance. Culture has been reported to form a key challenge towards the implementation of e-government systems in the public sector (Maniatopolous, 2005). The administrative culture appears to be one of the biggest obstacles for an optimized e-government. "This new organizational form entails an augmented openness towards stakeholders, which is not (yet) common to all administrative units" (Schedler & Scharf, 2001. p. 7). The organizational culture comprises position and actions of individuals within the organization that make it work, including the performance of leaders individually and as a team, the agency's commitment to achieve common objectives, and the agency's commitment to training and support.

Since culture describes informal processes, it cannot be controlled directly through deliberate intervention, but is influenced by environmental changes (Schedler & Scharf, 2001). For instance Seifert and McLoughlin (2007) report that state politics and culture can impede or support e-government development. Specifically, the report states that the "organizational culture of a public agency often can resist dramatic change within a short amount of time" (Seifert & McLoughlin, 2007, p. 12). Along the same lines, the strategy document for the Department of Interior states that to "implement e-government, Interior will require change. This change goes beyond the migration, development, and integration of information technology systems to creating an organizational culture that collaborates, trains, and shares information to achieve common goals" (Department of Interior, 2003, p. 15). The implicit statement is that, in general, government department possess a culture that is not necessarily strong when it comes to collaboration and information sharing.

There are also aspects of culture that positively influence the development of e-government. For instance, Pandey et al. (2006) argue that "the degree to which the organization is inclined towards a culture of change to keep innovating and improving itself" (p. 13) influences the performance of e-government. In the UNGC report by Kim (2008), one of the organizational capabilities identified for e-government performance is the culture of inclusion. Specifically, it refers to a "culture with shared norms of integrity, beliefs in honesty, openness, and fairness, and community involvement" (Kim, 2008, p. 62). A clear recommendation is that an organizational culture focusing on managing for results and learning should be considered in order to effectively build the management capacity to enhance transparency. Innovation orientation of an organization's culture is positively linked with the effectiveness of e-government (Moon & Norris, 2005). Peters et al. (2004) argue that delivering effective e-government service requires a move toward a more customer-minded culture.

The social dimension of organizational culture (specifically, the social networking dimension) has been shown to be positively related to knowledge sharing capabilities in the context of e-government (Kim & Lee, 2004). There are very specific cultural traits that are associated with the larger prevailing culture that seep into the government workings to support e-government. Specifically, the culture of high collectivism and the presence of loyal civil servants is the reason pointed out to make it easier for Singapore "to call on agencies to comply with the e-Government blueprint and carry out policies set out by the top leadership" (Ke & Wei, 2004, p. 99). This is perhaps the reason why Singapore has remained an exemplar for e-government. Berce et al. (2008) emphasize that for an organization, a culture of learning is a significant positive determinant of e-government effectiveness.

Gupta and Jana (2003) identify both the facilitative and inhibitive associations of culture with e-government performance when they argue that efficient performance of the organization and accountability might be blocked by an administrative culture that may not be able to cope with the demands of a digital world. At the same time, successful organizations develop a culture of measurement, educating employees on performance measures and uses as they manage their organizations through the processes which e-government delivers. As confirmation of the relationship between culture and e-government performance, Zakareya and Irani (2005) aver forcefully that organizational culture needs to be changed to maximize the potential offered by e-government. Clearly, e-government requires a change in the order of things in the government organization and, to that end, culture emerges to be a critical variable. Any culture will have to change to accommodate the techno-managerial changes heralded by e-government.

Sometimes, the role of culture is relegated from being an antecedent of e-government initiatives to being directly influenced by e-government initiatives. According to the Information Society Commission (2003), "e-government is not about supporting business as usual. Instead, it must focus on using ICTs to transform the structures, operations and perhaps most importantly the culture of government" (p. 12). When framed as such, the directionality of expected influence is clearly from the technological change to culture change – the assumption being that regardless of the culture in place, a new culture needs to be normatively defined and actualized to support e-government.

It can thus be argued that there is a reflexive relationship between organizational culture and e-government performance. In other words, organizational culture can influence e-government performance as much as e-government performance may end up playing a role in modifying or altering aspects of an organization's culture. Assessing the directionality of such causality is beyond the scope of this paper and will require a longitudinal approach. However, the present cross-sectional study can establish the relationship between organizational culture and e-government performance and inform future research to assess causality. In this study, we expect to find that some aspects of organizational culture are not significantly related with e-government performance. We, therefore, state the formal research hypothesis in the null form. Given the preponderance of evidence based on past research that goes both ways, we leave the direction of relationships between aspects of organizational culture and e-government performance undeclared.

- **Hypothesis:** There is no association between dimensions of organizational culture and dimensions of e-government performance.

3. METHODOLOGY

The data used to test the hypotheses came from a survey that was administered to respondents in 13 government agencies and departments in India. These organizations represented a wide cross-section of the government. The sampling plan was designed to ensure that organizations from different functional areas would be included. The sample of organizations included Ministries of Finance, Water Resources, Human Resource Development, Power, Labor, Income Tax, Railways, Information Technology, Education, Home Affairs, Public Utilities and Planning. These organizations are government/public sector organizations which

extensively use information technology to support internal business operations as well as to serve other stakeholders including citizens. The questions were designed such that multiple respondents answered all perceptual questions. This increased the probability of receiving accurate information on various aspects of organizational culture and e-government performance. An initial pilot survey was carried out to test the validity of the survey instrument for e-government performance measures. We developed a questionnaire based on the operationalization of constructs described below. An initial pilot survey was carried out to test the validity of the survey instrument even though the instrument used for the survey was a validated instrument adopted from the literature. We surveyed respondents both at the operational as well as the managerial level in the respondent organizations. A total of 315 responses were received from 13 different government ministries and agencies. The respondent sample included equal representation from males and females with mean age about 36 years. In terms of education, nearly 47% of the respondents had education up-to master level and about 43% had education up-to undergraduate level. The respondents were equally represented from different government agencies.

3.1. Operationalization of Constructs

Two sets of variables are used in this study – one to assess organizational culture and the other to assess e-government performance.

3.2. Operationalizing Organizational Culture

In this study, culture has been used as a set of values and beliefs. Since culture has many dimensions and multiple attributes, different authors have chosen to study culture in their own specific ways. The large number of culture models upon which this investigation could be based mandated the identification and use of an established instrument that could be easily understood, operationalized and applied in such a setting. Zammuto and Krakower (1991) provide an instrument based on the competing values framework (Quinn & Rohrbaugh, 1981) has only four dimensions. The organizational culture inventory (OCI) developed by Cooke and Lafferty (1987) is validated and has twelve dimensions; however, since we were not in a position to use commercially priced instruments, we selected the culture instrument based on the work of Wallach (1983). Wallach (1983) suggests that there are three main types of organizational cultures (i.e. bureaucratic, supportive and innovative). While bureaucratic cultures are indicated by clear lines of authority and regulated/ systematic work flows, innovative cultures are more creative that encourage risk taking. However, supportive cultures, in contrast to bureaucratic and innovative cultures, promote friendly, open, and honest working environment in an organization. Wallach's (1983) cultural dimensions represent a synthesis of the major organizational cultural indices, and are therefore, more comprehensive than other organizational culture operationalizations. Moreover, Wallach's (1983) cultural instrument has been used in public sector environments before (Odom et al., 1990).

The following cultural dimensions based on Wallach (1983) were included to measure culture: Risk taking (OCRISK), Collaborative (OCCOLL), Hierarchical (OCHIER), Procedural (OCPROC), Relationship-oriented (OCRELA), Results-oriented (OCRESU), Creative (OCCREA), Encouraging (OCENCO), Sociable (OCSOCI), Structured (OCSTRU), Pressurized (OCPRES), Ordered (OCORDR), Stimulating (OCSTIM), Regulated (OCREGU), Personal freedom (OCPEFR), Equitable (OCEQUI), Safe (OCSAFE), Challenging (OCCHAL), Enterprising (OCENTR), Established (OCESTA), Cautious (OCCAUT), Trusting (OCTRUS), Driving (OCDRIV), and Power-oriented (OCPOWR). Based on the procedure outlined in Wallach (1983), these scales are used to provide three cultural dimensions named as "bureaucratic," "innovative," and "supportive."

Bureaucratic culture is reflected in cultural traits such as hierarchical, procedural, structured, ordered, regulated, established, solid, cautious, and power oriented. Innovative culture is indicated by aspects such as risk-taking, result-oriented, creative, pressurized, stimulating, challenging, enterprising and driving. Supportive culture is indicated by cultural traits such as supportive, trusting, equitable, safe, social, encouraging, relationships-oriented and collaborative.

3.3. Operationalizing E-Government Performance

Public sector organizations differ from private sector organizations in terms of their focus on accountability, expenditure control and taking a long term perspective (Elpez & Fink, 2006). The usage of information systems that support e-government tends to be emergent and as a result the performance of such systems varies since benefits tend to be apportioned across multiple departments (Heeks, 1998; Kelly, 1995). Based on the literature review, we decided to study e-government performance across four dimensions, including metrics for both front-end and back-end internal operations. These dimensions are internal operations effectiveness, service quality improvement, process improvement, and end user satisfaction/ skill enhancement. These four dimensions are consistent with the three quadrants of IS value that were identified in Table 1.

The dimension of internal operations effectiveness was measured using three items of improved task effectiveness (TE), improved communications (CO), and improved decision making at the task level (DM). The service quality improvement dimension was measured using two items of organizational responsiveness to citizens' requirements (OR) and effectiveness of e-government in delivering quality services to citizens (WH). The process improvement dimension was measured using two items of work process improvement (WP) and development of new processes as a result of e-government (NP). The fourth dimension of end user satisfaction/skill enhancement was measured using two items of job satisfaction of end users (JS) and users' skill enhancement at the individual level (UC). The items for end user satisfaction/skill enhancement dimension were adapted from Elpez and Fink (2006).

3.4. E-Government Performance Scale

Since we had developed the e-government performance questions for this study, we validated the stability of the constructs using confirmatory factor analysis as shown in Table 2.

All of the items should load highly on their own latent variables. Hair et al. (1998) suggest that loadings of 0.5 and greater are practically significant. Tabachnick and Fidell (2001) suggest that the loading of an item on its corresponding construct should be at least 0.32, and that loadings over 0.71 are excellent. The factor analysis results in this study (Table 2) well surpass these criteria in all cases except one.

4. RESULTS

We analyzed the data using two approaches: one following the work of Kanungo et al. (2001) that

uses simple correlation analysis and the other using canonical correlation analysis based on Chatman and Jehn (1994) and Trivellas et al. (2006). We adopted this analytical approach in order to address both the normative as well as emergent notions of culture in the analysis. Correlation analysis helped answer the question of which broad dimensions of culture influence e-government performance. Canonical correlation allowed us to drill down into the individual cultural dimensions that make up the three broad cultural dimensions and helped analyze how culture influences specific aspects of e-government performance.

4.1. Results from Correlating Normative Dimensions of Culture

The first approach provides the basis for the normative approach to organizational culture whereby we calculate three dimensions of culture as suggested by Wallach (1983). The three dimensions are bureaucratic, innovative and supportive. Table 3 shows the correlations between the three dimensions of organizational culture and the nine items used to assess e-government performance. Significant correlations are highlighted.

Correlations in Table 3 show that two items – "work process improvement" and "job satisfaction of the end user" – are sensitive to all three

Table 2. Factor loadings for dimensions of e-government performance

Variable	Factor 1	Factor 2	Factor 3	Factor 4	Variable description
TE	-0.802	0.049	0.005	0.034	Improved task effectiveness
CO	-0.697	0.241	0.089	0.017	Improved communications
DM	-0.738	0.030	-0.085	-0.020	Improved decision making
OR	-0.193	0.769	-0.103	0.103	Organizational responsiveness to citizens' requirements
WH	-0.068	0.833	-0.032	0.038	Overall e-government effectiveness in service delivery
WP	-0.162	-0.236	0.777	-0.040	Work process improvement
NP	0.147	0.070	0.858	-0.060	New processes as result of e-government
JS	-0.047	-0.120	-0.125	-0.842	Job satisfaction of end user
UC	0.072	-0.017	0.252	-0.784	Users' skill enhancement as a result of e-government implementation

Table 3. Correlation coefficients of cultural dimensions

	TE	CO	DM	OR	WH	WP	NP	JS	UC
Bureaucratic	0.01	0.02	0.00	**-0.17****	**-0.13***	**0.14***	0.09	**0.28****	**0.14***
Innovative	0.08	-0.03	-0.02	-0.05	0.04	**0.19****	**0.15***	**0.13***	0.11
Supportive	**0.13***	0.02	-0.01	0.02	0.03	**0.14***	0.09	**0.13***	0.09

* - significant at the 5% level; ** - significant at the 1% level

cultural dimensions. These results also show that the bureaucratic dimension is associated with five e-government performance items, while the innovative and supportive dimensions are each associated with three items of e-government performance. The communication and decision making items are not related to any of the three cultural dimensions.

4.2. Results from Canonical Correlation Analysis

Canonical correlation, the most general form of the linear model (Baggaley, 1981), maximizes the correlation between linear combinations of two sets of variables. It is suitable for research where the complex interaction of many different variables is believed to describe a phenomenon, and / or where new relationships are being explored. We believe that these conditions describe the existing state of research, making canonical correlation an appropriate method.

Canonical correlation was performed between the set of organizational culture variables and the set of IS performance variables using SAS CANCORR. We followed the analytical procedure outlined by Tabachnick and Fidell (2001). The first canonical correlation was .55 (31% overlapping variance); the second was .44 (20% overlapping variance); the third was .43 (19% overlapping variance). The remaining canonical correlations were not relevant. With all canonical correlations included, the F value was computed as $F (207, 2072.9) = 1.71$, $p < 0.0001$; with the first canonical correlation removed, F value was computed

as $F (176, 1865.3) = 1.44$, $p = 0.0003$; with the second canonical correlation removed, F value was computed as $F (147, 1652.8) = 1.32$, $p = 0.0085$. Subsequent F values were not significant. The first three pairs of canonical covariates, therefore, accounted for the significant relationships between the two sets of variables.

Data on the first three pairs of canonical variates are summarized in Table 4. We have shown correlations between variables and canonical correlates, standardized canonical variate coefficients, within set variance accounted for by the canonical variates (percent of variance), redundancies, and canonical correlations in Table 4. Total percent of variance and total redundancy indicate that the first pair of canonical variates was moderately related, but the second and third pair were only minimally related; interpretation of the second and, especially the third, pairs needs to be done with care.

With a cutoff correlation of 0.3, the variables in the organizational culture set that were correlated with the first canonical variate were OCORDR, OCPOWR, OCPROC, and OCDRIV. Among the e-government performance items, job satisfaction of end user, and the negative of task effectiveness, overall e-government effectiveness in service delivery, and organizational responsiveness to citizens' requirements correlated with the first canonical variate. The first pair of canonical variates indicates that organizations with ordered, power-oriented, procedural, and driving as dominant cultural dimensions are associated with high performance on the end user job satisfaction item and low performance on the task effective-

Table 4. Correlations, standardized canonical coefficients, canonical correlations, percents of variance and redundancies between culture and e-government performance variables and their corresponding canonical variates

Culture set	First Canonical Variate		Second Canonical variate		Third Canonical variate	
	Correlation	Coefficient	Correlation	Coefficient	Correlation	Coefficient
OCORDR	0.4941	0.2625	0.0709	0.2088	0.3226	0.3849
OCPOWR	0.4643	0.3779	-0.0542	0.0521	0.2711	0.2024
OCPROC	0.4586	0.4238	0.0689	0.2179	-0.1445	-0.047
OCDRIV	0.4373	0.2505	-0.154	-0.1289	0.2152	0.016
OCHIER	0.2711	-0.1033	-0.1062	-0.2044	-0.2425	-0.3173
OCREGU	0.2178	0.1529	-0.1592	-0.036	0.2628	0.055
OCCAUT	0.2125	0.3166	0.2395	0.4629	-0.0911	-0.3793
OCTRUS	0.2082	0.206	-0.1848	-0.3407	0.0803	0.0444
OCPRES	0.172	0.1303	-0.129	-0.0109	0.3133	0.1486
OCRELA	0.1699	0.0292	-0.013	0.1313	0.1290	-0.0911
OCRISK	0.1468	0.0199	-0.279	-0.1591	0.1530	0.1114
OCSTRU	0.0573	0.0938	-0.1389	-0.2741	0.1307	-0.1297
OCCOLL	0.0501	-0.0231	-0.2073	-0.0387	-0.0499	-0.157
OCSTIM	0.0144	0.0575	0.0638	-0.0829	0.2810	-0.2893
OCSAFE	-0.0334	-0.3077	-0.3001	-0.4539	0.0196	-0.2394
OCEQUI	-0.0745	-0.149	-0.0748	-0.0004	0.4847	0.5227
OCESTA	-0.0787	-0.1889	0.2856	0.5227	0.2757	0.0635
OCRESU	-0.11	-0.1116	-0.1252	-0.0272	0.2251	-0.0686
OCENTR	-0.1133	0.0019	-0.0484	-0.302	0.5575	0.4636
OCCREA	-0.1456	0.1171	-0.3401	-0.833	0.2927	0.0950
OCCHAL	-0.2045	-0.1326	0.1609	0.5164	0.4900	0.4510
OCSOCI	-0.2603	-0.2646	-0.0406	-0.0867	0.1594	-0.089
OCENCO	-0.2636	-0.4284	-0.0066	0.6181	0.1930	-0.1241
Percent of variance	0.06		0.03		0.07	Total = .16
Redundancy	0.02		0.02		0.04	Total = .08
E-government performance set						
JS	0.4627	0.3503	-0.0414	-0.0591	-0.0834	-0.1561
WP	0.1071	-0.0298	0.1534	0.0881	0.7071	0.6945
UC	0.0552	-0.1608	-0.0346	-0.0325	0.1259	0.0795
NP	0.0015	-0.0137	0.1535	0.1365	0.5204	0.2052
CO	-0.1533	0.1899	0.2849	0.2514	-0.3873	-0.5327
DM	-0.3292	-0.1684	0.8009	0.9650	-0.0016	0.1476
TE	-0.4950	-0.308	-0.0566	-0.5198	-0.1433	0.0018
WH	-0.5366	-0.3072	-0.2311	-0.3871	0.206	0.4825
OR	-0.8300	-0.6102	-0.013	0.1076	-0.2787	-0.2648
Percent of variance	0.1800		0.09		0.12	Total = .39
Redundancy	0.05		0.07		0.09	Total = .21
Canonical Correlation	0.55		0.45		0.44	

ness, overall e-government effectiveness in service delivery, and organizational responsiveness to citizens' requirements.

The second canonical variate in the organizational culture set was composed of the negative of creative and safe items, and the corresponding canonical variate from the e-government performance set was improved decision making. Taken as a pair, these variates suggest that organizations that show conservatism in a combination of creative and safe cultural dimensions are associated with lower performance on the decision making aspect of e-government performance.

The third canonical variate in the organizational culture set was composed of ordered, pressurized, equitable, enterprising, and challenging, and the corresponding canonical variates from the e-government performance set were work process improvement, new processes as result of e-government, and the negative of improved communication. This pair of variates indicates that organizations in which ordered, pressurized, equitable, enterprising, and challenging are prominent cultural dimensions tend to be associated with high performance on work process improvement and new processes as a result of e-government but low on the improved communication aspect.

5. DISCUSSION

Our overall results are consistent with what we had hypothesized. All three cultural dimensions are associated with different aspects of e-government performance. We will now scrutinize in detail the relationship between organizational culture and e-government performance.

5.1. Aggregated View of Organizational Culture and E-Government Performance

When the aggregated view of culture is taken as in the correlation analysis, the bureaucratic

dimension of culture shows a negative relationship with "organizational responsiveness to citizens' requirements" and "overall e-government effectiveness in service delivery" and a positive relationship with "work process improvement," "job satisfaction of end user," and "users' skill enhancement as a result of e-government implementation."

The innovative dimension of organizational culture is positively related to "work process improvement," "new processes as result of e-government" and "job satisfaction of end user." Lastly, the supportive dimension of organizational culture is positively related to "improved task effectiveness," "work process improvement," and "job satisfaction of end user."

Two patterns stand out. The first is the combination of negative and positive relationships and the second which is related to the specific items of e-government performance that are particularly sensitive to organizational culture.

The combination of negative and positive correlations can be understood in terms of the process paradox (Keen, 1997). This is defined as the phenomenon wherein organizations (at the enterprise level) may experience a measurable decline while making significant improvements to their individual or functional processes. Clearly, "organizational responsiveness to citizens' requirements" and "overall e-government effectiveness in service delivery" are enterprise-level constructs while "work process improvement," is a process-level construct and "job satisfaction of end user," and "users' skill enhancement as a result of e-government implementation" are individual level constructs. The bureaucratic dimension can be considered the structural dimension of culture. Given that structure determines behavior (Sterman, 2000), our results point out that a bureaucracy will tend to perform sub-optimally at the enterprise level when it comes to e-government performance. However, it is also important to note that bureaucracies will facilitate process improvement and individual performance improvement in the context of information systems. This is not surprising since bureaucracies provide the much needed structure to support standard processes that are so crucial to ensuring that investments in information systems result in organizational payoffs. While it is difficult to change bureaucratic processes, once changed (for the better), bureaucratic processes will be far better poised to leverage information systems than less defined or less structured organizational frameworks.

Two aspects of e-government performance stand out as being consistently positively associated with all three dimensions of organizational culture. They are "work process improvement" and "job satisfaction of end user." This finding is significant because these two e-government performance aspects represent the quantitative and qualitative benefits of information systems in public sector organizations. These two aspects may, in fact, encapsulate the essence of e-government performance in public sector organizations. Clearly, government bureaucracies will benefit by strengthening their innovative and supportive dimensions. These results point to the complex and complementary nature of the intertwined strands of cultural dimensions and how they are related to e-government performance.

5.2. The Disaggregated View of Organizational Culture and E-Government Performance

Given that our results have shown that there is indeed a relationship between organizational culture and e-government performance, results from the canonical correlation analysis can shed more light on the nature of that relationship.

Let us consider the first canonical covariates. The first canonical variate in the culture set identifies an organization that is ordered, power-oriented, procedural and driving. These cultural attributes denote a bureaucratic setup typical of government bureaucracies. The first canonical variate in the e-government performance set char-

acterizes an organization where job satisfaction of end users is high but the organization scores low on organizational responsiveness to citizens' requirements, overall e-government effectiveness in service delivery, and task effectiveness. This result is consistent with that of the aggregated view of culture presented above. It informs us that in government bureaucracies, individual satisfaction tends to be high with e-government performance. However, systemic e-government performance or effectiveness (as opposed to efficiency) due to information systems may be hard to experience.

The second canonical variate in the culture set identifies an organization that is safe and not creative. The second canonical variate in the e-government performance set characterizes an organization where decision making is satisfactory. This scenario typifies a government decision making framework where processes and procedures are followed to the hilt and decisions are made by the book. The implication for e-government performance is that when an information system enables structured decisions, the bureaucratic dimensions of culture act as a facilitator.

The last canonical covariate informs us that organizations with ordered, pressurized, equitable, enterprising and challenging cultural traits tend to be associated with e-government performances characterized by work process improvement and new processes as a result of e-government. However, such organizations may show hindered IS enabled communication. While the finding on IS enabled communication is not clear, the result clearly points out that public sector organizations that need to benefit from information systems need to infuse high performing cultural traits.

6. IMPLICATIONS FOR RESEARCH AND PRACTICE

The findings from this research are important in that they can be said to form what may be considered the initial basis for formalizing the links organizational culture and e-government performance. While these links are non-directional, multiple research avenues have been opened up as a result of these findings. For instance, given that organizational culture is an important contextual variable, the next step could be to consider the role of culture in the context of other individual and group variables in determining their joint influence on e-government performance.

Our study shows that the link between organizational culture and e-government performance is significant. This is an important finding for managers because culture forms an important leveraging variable. While the role of culture as an inhibitive agent in organizational change is better understood, effective leaders also understand that organizational culture can form an effective lever for change. Given that the bureaucratic dimension is most closely intertwined with e-government performance, public managers should realize that the ordered nature of the government and the well-defined processes – that so often tend to be criticized are some of the very reasons that e-government initiatives will be successful. An important strategic option that public managers have is to leverage the bureaucratic dimension during the initial phases of e-government implementation and then attempt to develop policies and measures to help the innovative and supportive dimensions become dominant.

Lastly, an important contribution of this paper lies in the form of a response to research in e-government as what Heeks and Bailur (2007) rightly refer to as "confused positivism ... dominated by over-optimistic, a-theoretical work" (pp. 243). Since most work in e-government tends to highlight the opportunities and success stories, our approach has been to identify factors that would tend to moderate researchers' views and practitioners' expectations. Clearly "culture" has a role to play in determining the success or failure of IT interventions. However, we are well aware of the reflexive nature of the relationship between culture and technology (Olson, 1982)

and therefore, have been circumspect in framing the relationship as based on "correlation" and not a causal one.

7. LIMITATIONS AND FURTHER RESEARCH

There are many ways in which this study can be improved and carried forward. While this study provides evidence of relationship between organizational culture and e-government performance, there need to be multiple follow-up attempts using different conceptualizations of organizational culture.

Correlation-based studies, such as this one, are clearly first steps. We feel that studies that employ multi-level models will be able to glean out a clearer picture of the relationship between culture and e-governance. This approach could also benefit from concentrating on selected culture dimensions. Concentrating on one or two dimensions of culture in future studies will allow researchers to theorize in sufficient detail to design more effective studies. The value of these studies lie in the *ex ante* value of predicting the success of information systems in government settings based on cultural readings just as Irani et al. (2005) have suggested using structured cases.

Furthermore, in addition to quantitative approaches, future studies need to incorporate qualitative as well as longitudinal research methods. This is because both culture and e-governance are dynamic constructs that can display reciprocal influences. Such research approaches are required to better understand the nuances associated with the directionality and the timing of the influences that link organizational culture and e-government performance. Clearly, it will be useful, both theoretically and managerially, to obtain a better idea of the directionality of the influences when it comes to relating organizational culture and e-government performance. While longitudinal studies will help, we believe that methodological options like system dynamics will be able to capture the essence of the reflexive relationship between organizational culture and e-government performance effectively.

8. CONCLUSION

In this study, our objective was to analyze the relationship between organizational culture and e-government performance. This study represents an initial attempt at addressing the dynamic and complex linkages of organizational culture to individual and organizational measures of e-government effectiveness that are fraught with the existence of multiple ambiguities and interactions. Traditionally, culture in government organizations has been viewed as inhibitor of successful IT initiatives. However, results of this study are contrary to this traditional thinking because the results indicate that the bureaucratic dimension, which emerges as the dominant cultural dimension in government organizations, is both positively and negatively related to e-government performance dimensions. Such findings should lead managers in government organizations to carefully focus on the cultural aspects that are not conducive to e-government performance as opposed to those which are supportive of e-government initiatives.

REFERENCES

Alavi, M., Kayworth, T. R., & Leidner, D. E. (2005). An empirical examination of the influence of organizational culture on knowledge management practices. *Journal of Management Information Systems*, *22*(3), 191–224. doi:10.2753/MIS0742-1222220307

Baggaley, A. R. (1981). Multivariate analysis: An introduction for consumers of behavioral research. *Evaluation Review*, *5*, 123–131. doi:10.1177/0193841X8100500106

Barua, A., Kriebel, C. H., & Mukhopadhyay, T. (1995). Information technologies and business value: An analytical and empirical investigation. *Information Systems Research*, *6*(1), 3–23. doi:10.1287/isre.6.1.3

Beaumaster, S. (2002). Local government IT implementation issues: A challenge for public administration. In *Proceedings of the 35th Hawaii International Conference on System Sciences* (Vol. 5, p. 128).

Berce, J., Lanfranco, S., & Vehovar, V. (2008). eGovernance: Information and communication technology, knowledge management and learning culture. *Informatica*, *32*, 189–205.

Boyne, G. A. (2002). Public and private management: What's the difference. *Journal of Management Studies*, *39*(1), 97–122. doi:10.1111/1467-6486.00284

Bradley, R. V., Pridmore, J. L., & Byrd, T. A. (2006). Information systems success in the context of different corporate cultural types: An empirical investigation. *Journal of Management Information Systems*, *23*(2), 267–294. doi:10.2753/MIS0742-1222230211

Bresnahan, T., Brynjolfsson, E., & Hitt, L. M. (2002). Information technology, workplace organization, and the demand for skilled labor: Firm-level evidence. *The Quarterly Journal of Economics*, *117*(1), 339–376. doi:10.1162/003355302753399526

Brynjolfsson, E., & Hitt, L. (1996). Paradox lost? Firm-level evidence on the returns to information systems. *Management Science*, *42*(4), 541–558. doi:10.1287/mnsc.42.4.541

Brynjolfsson, E., & Hitt, L. (2000). Beyond computation: Information technology, organizational transformation and business performance. *The Journal of Economic Perspectives*, *14*(4), 23–48. doi:10.1257/jep.14.4.23

Brynjolfsson, E., & Yang, S. (1996). Information technology and productivity: A review of the literature. *Advances in Computers, 43*, 179–214. doi:10.1016/S0065-2458(08)60644-0

Chan, J. B. L. (2001). The technological game: How information technology is transforming police practice. *Criminology & Criminal Justice, 1*(2), 139–159. doi:10.1177/1466802501001002001

Chatman, J. A., & Jehn, K. A. (1994). Assessing the relationship between industry characteristics and organizational culture: How different can you be? *Academy of Management Journal, 37*(3), 522–553. doi:10.2307/256699

Chircu, A. M., & Lee, D. H. (2003). Understanding IT investments in the public sector: The case of e-government. In *Proceedings of the Ninth Americas Conference on Information Systems* (p. 99).

Choudrie, J., Ghinea, G., & Weerakkody, V. (2004). Evaluating global e-government sites: A view using web diagnostic tools. *Electronic Journal of E-Government, 2*(2), 105–114.

Claver, E., Llopis, J., Gonzalez, M. R., & Gasco, J. L. (2006). The performance of information systems through organizational culture. *Information Technology & People, 14*(3), 247–260. doi:10.1108/09593840110402149

Cooke, R., & Lafferty, J. (1987). *Organizational culture inventory (OCI)*. Plymouth, MI: Human Synergistics.

Deal, T. E., & Kennedy, A. A. (1982). *Corporate culture: The rites and rituals of corporate lives*. Reading, MA: Addison-Wesley.

Dehning, B., Richardson, V. J., & Zmud, R. W. (2003). The value relevance of announcements of transformational information technology investments. *Management Information Systems Quarterly, 27*, 637–656.

Delone, W. H., & McLean, E. R. (1992). Information systems success: The quest for the dependent variable. *Information Systems Research, 3*, 60–95. doi:10.1287/isre.3.1.60

Department of Interior. (2003). e-Government strategy. Retrieved from http://www.doi.gov/e-government/

Dos Santos, B. L., Peffers, K., & Mauer, D. C. (1993). The impact of information technology investment announcements on the market value of the firm. *Information Systems Research, 4*(1), 1–23. doi:10.1287/isre.4.1.1

Dunleavy, P., Margetts, H., Bastow, S., & Tinkler, J. (2005). *New public management is dead – long live digital-era governance*. Oxford, UK: Oxford University Press.

Elpez, I., & Fink, D. (2006, June 25-28). Information systems success in the public sector: Stakeholders' perspectives and emerging alignment model. In *Proceedings of Informing Science + Information Technology Education Joint Conference*, Greater Manchester, UK.

Gallivan, M., & Srite, M. (2005). Information technology and culture: Identifying fragmentary and holistic perspectives of culture. *Information and Organization, 15*(4), 295–338. doi:10.1016/j.infoandorg.2005.02.005

Gupta, M. P., & Jana, D. (2003). E-government evaluation: A framework and case study. *Government Information Quarterly, 20*(4), 365–387. doi:10.1016/j.giq.2003.08.002

Hackney, R. A., & McBride, N. K. (1995). The efficacy of information systems in the public sector: Issues of context and culture. *International Journal of Public Sector Management, 8*(6), 17–29. doi:10.1108/09513559510099991

Hair, J., Anderson, R., Tatham, R., & Black, W. (1998). *Multivariate data analysis* (5th ed.). Upper Saddle River, NJ: Prentice Hall.

Heeks, R. (1998). *Information systems for public sector management*. Manchester, UK: Institute for Development Policy and Management.

Heeks, R., & Bailur, S. (2007). Analyzing e-government research: Perspectives, philosophies, theories, methods, and practice. *Government Information Quarterly, 24*, 243–265. doi:10.1016/j.giq.2006.06.005

Hefetz, A., & Warner, M. (2004). Privatization and its reverse: Explaining the dynamics of the government contracting process. *Journal of Public Administration: Research and Theory, 14*(2), 171–190. doi:10.1093/jopart/muh012

Ho, A. T. (2002). Reinventing local governments and the e-government initiative. *Public Administration Review, 62*(4), 434–444. doi:10.1111/0033-3352.00197

Horan, T., & Abhichandani, T. (2006). Evaluating user satisfaction in an e-government initiative: Results of structural equation modeling and focus group discussions. *Journal of Information Technology Management, 16*, 33–44.

Information Society Commission. (2003). *eGovernment: More than an automation of government services*. Retrieved from http://www.isc.ie/downloads/egovernment.pdf

Irani, Z., Love, P. E. D., Elliman, T., Jones, S., & Themistocleous, M. (2005). Evaluating e-government: Learning from the experiences of two UK local authorities. *Information Systems Journal, 15*(1), 61–82. doi:10.1111/j.1365-2575.2005.00186.x

Juthla, D. N., Bodorik, P., Weatherbee, T., & Hudson, B. (2002). e-Government in execution: Building organizational infrastructure. In *Proceedings of the European Conference on Information Systems*, Gdansk, Poland.

Kanungo, S. (1998). An empirical study of organizational culture and network-based computer use. *Computers in Human Behavior, 14*(1), 79–91. doi:10.1016/S0747-5632(97)00033-2

Kanungo, S., Sadavarti, S., & Srinivas, Y. (2001). Relating IT strategy and organizational culture: An empirical study of public sector units in India. *The Journal of Strategic Information Systems, 10*(1), 29–57. doi:10.1016/S0963-8687(01)00038-5

Ke, W., & Wei, K. K. (2004). Successful e-government in Singapore. *Communications of the ACM, 47*(6), 95–99. doi:10.1145/990680.990687

Keen, P. G. W. (1997). *The process edge: Creating value where it counts*. Boston, MA: Harvard Business School Press.

Kelly, K. L. (1995). *A framework for evaluating public sector geographic information systems (Tech. Rep. No. CTG.GIS-005)*. Albany, NY: University at Albany SUNY.

Kim, S. (2008). *A management capacity framework for local governments to strengthen transparency in local governance in Asia*. Retrieved from from http://www.ungc.org/pds/UNPOG_Local_Governance_Project_Report_SoonheeKim.pdf

Kim, S., & Lee, H. (2004). Organizational factors affecting knowledge sharing capabilities in e-government: An empirical study. In *Proceedings of the Annual National Conference on Digital Government Research*, Seattle, WA (pp. 1-11).

Kovadid, Z. J. (2005). The impact of national culture on worldwide egovernment readiness. *Informing Science: International Journal of an Emerging Transdiscipline, 8*, 143–158.

Kwon, D., Watts-Sussman, S., & Collopy, F. (2002). Value frame, paradox and change: The constructive nature of information technology business value. *Systems and Organizations, 2*(4), 196–220.

Lakhani, H., Guerriero, L., Hatton, L., & Lau, C. (2009). Transforming organizational culture through decision support at Bloorview Kids Rehab. *Electronic Healthcare, 7*(3), 1–8.

Layne, K., & Lee, J. (2001). Developing fully functional e-government: A four stage model. *Government Information Quarterly, 18*, 122–136. doi:10.1016/S0740-624X(01)00066-1

Lee, B., & Menon, N. M. (2000). Information technology value through different normative lenses. *Journal of Management Information Systems, 16*(4), 99–119.

Leidner, D. E., & Kayworth, T. (2006). A review of culture in information systems research: Toward a theory of information technology culture conflict. *Management Information Systems Quarterly, 30*(2), 357–399.

Light, P. (1997). *The tides of reform: Making government work 1945-1995*. New Haven, CT: Yale University Press.

Maniatopoulos, G. (2005, July 4-6). e-Government movements of organizational change: A social shaping approach. In *Proceedings of the 4th International Critical Management Studies Conference*, Cambridge, UK.

McDermott, C. M., & Stock, G. N. (1999). Organizational culture and advanced manufacturing technology implementation. *Journal of Operations Management, 17*, 521–533. doi:10.1016/S0272-6963(99)00008-X

Melville, N., Kraemer, K., & Gurbaxani, V. (2004). Review: Information technology and organizational performance: An integrative model of IT business value. *Management Information Systems Quarterly, 28*(2), 283–222.

Moon, M. J., & Norris, D. F. (2005). Does managerial orientation matter? The adoption of reinventing government and e-government at the municipal level. *Information Systems Journal, 15*(1), 43–60. doi:10.1111/j.1365-2575.2005.00185.x

Odom, R. Y., Boxx, W. R., & Dunn, M. G. (1990). Organizational cultures, commitment, satisfaction, and cohesion. *Public Productivity & Management Review, 14*(2), 157–169. doi:10.2307/3380963

Olson, M. H. (1982). New information technology and organizational culture. *Management Information Systems Quarterly, 6*(5), 71–92. doi:10.2307/248992

Pandey, S., Welch, E., & Wong, W. (2006, December 7-10). Beyond pure efficiency and technological features: Developing a model of measuring e-governance and exploring its performance. In *Proceedings of the Conference on the Determinants of Performance in Public Organizations*, Pok Fu Lam, Hong Kong.

Parker, R., & Bradley, L. (2000). Organizational culture in the public sector: Evidence from six organizations. *International Journal of Public Sector Management, 13*(2), 125–141. doi:10.1108/09513550010338773

Peters, R. M., Janssen, M., & van Engers, T. (2004). Measuring e-government impact: Existing practices and shortcomings. In *Proceedings of the 6th International Conference on Electronic Commerce*, Delft, The Netherlands (pp. 480-489).

Peters, T. J., & Waterman, R. H. (1982). *In search of excellence*. New York, NY: Harper & Row.

Pliskin, N., Romm, T., & Lee, A. S. (1993). Presumed versus actual organizational culture. *The Computer Journal, 36*(3), 143–152. doi:10.1093/comjnl/36.2.143

Prager, J. (1994). Contracting out government services: Lessons from the private sector. *Public Administration Review, 54*(2), 176–184. doi:10.2307/976527

Quinn, R. E., & Rohrbaugh, J. (1981). A competing values approach to organizational effectiveness. *Public Productivity Review, 5*(2), 122–140. doi:10.2307/3380029

Rainey, H. G., & Steinbauer, P. (1999). Galloping elephants: Developing elements of a theory of effective government organizations. *Journal of Public Administration: Research and Theory, 9*(1), 1–32. doi:10.1093/oxfordjournals.jpart.a024401

Robey, D., & Azervedo, A. (1994). Culture analysis of organizational consequences of information technology. *Accounting, Management, and Information Technology, 4*(1), 23–34. doi:10.1016/0959-8022(94)90011-6

Romm, T., Pliskin, N., & Weber, Y. (1995). The relevance of organizational culture to the implementation of human resources information systems. *Asia Pacific Journal of Human Resources, 33*(2), 51–63. doi:10.1177/103841119503300206

Schedler, K., & Scharf, M. C. (2001, October 3-5). *Exploring the interrelations between e-government and the new public management.* Paper presented at the First IFIP Conference on E-Commerce, E-Business, and E-Government, Zurich, Switzerland.

Schein, E. H. (1985). *Organizational culture and leadership.* San Francisco, CA: Jossey- Bass.

Schein, E. H. (1986). What you need to know about organizational culture. *Training and Development Journal, 8*(1), 30–33.

Seifert, J., & McLoughlin, G. (2007). *State e-government strategies: Identifying best practices and applications.* Retrieved from http://www.fas.org/sgp/crs/secrecy/RL34104.pdf

Sterman, J. D. (2000). *Business dynamics: Systems thinking and modeling for a complex world.* New York, NY: McGraw-Hill.

Stowers, G. N. L. (2004). Measuring the performance of e-government. *E-Government Series,* 1-52.

Tabachnick, B. G., & Fidell, L. S. (2001). *Using Multivariate Statistics* (4th ed.). Boston, MA: Allyn and Bacon.

Tolsby, J. (1998). Effects of organizational culture on a large scale IT introduction effort: A case study of the Norwegian army's EDBLF project. *European Journal of Information Systems, 7*(2), 108–114. doi:10.1057/palgrave.ejis.3000295

Trivellas, P., Reklitis, P., & Santouridis, I. (2006). Culture and MIS effectiveness patterns in a quality context: A case study in Greece. *International Journal of Knowledge. Culture and Change Management, 6*(3), 129–144.

Wallach, E. J. (1983). Individuals and organizations: The cultural match. *Training and Development Journal, 37,* 29–36.

West, D. M. (2008). *Improving technology utilization in electronic government around the world.* Retrieved from http://www.brookings.edu/~/media/Files/rc/reports/2008/0817_egovernment_west/0817_egovernment_west.pdf

Wilkins, A. L., & Ouchi, W. G. (1983). Efficient cultures: Exploring the relationship between culture and organizational performance. *Administrative Science Quarterly, 28,* 468–481. doi:10.2307/2392253

World Bank. (n. d.). *Definition of e-government.* Retrieved from http://web.worldbank.org/wbsite/external/topics/extinformationandcommunicationandtechnologies/extegovernment/0,content MDK:20507153~menuPK:702592~pagePK:148956~piPK:216618~theSitePK:702586,00.html

Zakareya, E., & Irani, Z. (2005). E-government adoption: Architecture and barrier. *Business Process Management Journal, 11*(5), 589–611. doi:10.1108/14637150510619902

Zammuto, R. F., & Krakower, J. Y. (1991). Quantitative and qualitative studies of organizational culture. In Woodman, R. W., & Pasmore, W. A. (Eds.), *Research in organizational change and development (Vol. 5).* Greenwich, CT: JAI Press.

APPENDIX

Table 5. Survey instrument table

E-government performance variables	To what extent has the e-government impacted the following areas (1= Not at all; 5: Exceeded expectations)				
	1	2	3	4	5
TASK LEVEL IMPACT					
Task effectiveness					
Inter-office communications					
Official decision making					
ORGANIZATIONAL LEVEL IMPACT					
Organizational responsiveness					
your information system on the whole					
PROCESS LEVEL IMPACT					
new products/ processes as a result of IT					
effect on organizational efficiency					
INDIVIDUAL LEVEL IMPACT					
job scope & job satisfaction of IS personnel					
user capability					

Organizational attribute	To what extent do the organizational attributes describe **your organization**? (1= Not at all; 5: Almost perfectly)				
	1	**2**	**3**	**4**	**5**
a. Risk taking					
b. Collaborative					
c. Hierarchical					
d. Procedural					
e. Relationship-oriented					
f. Results-oriented					
g. Creative					
h. Encouraging					
i. Sociable					
j. Structured					
k. Pressurized					
l. Ordered					
m. Stimulating					
n. Regulated					
o. Personal freedom					
p. Equitable					
q. Safe					
r. Challenging					
s. Enterprising					

continued on following page

Table 5. Continued

t. Established, solid					
u. Cautious					
v. Trusting					
w. Driving					
x. Power-oriented					

This work was previously published in the International Journal of Electronic Government Research, Volume 7, Issue 2, edited by Vishanth Weerakkody, pp. 36-58, copyright 2011 by IGI Publishing (an imprint of IGI Global).

Chapter 10
Why do E–Government Projects Fail? Risk Factors of Large Information Systems Projects in the Greek Public Sector:
An International Comparison

Euripidis Loukis
University of Aegean, Greece

Yannis Charalabidis
University of Aegean, Greece

ABSTRACT

This paper presents an empirical study of the risk factors of large governmental information systems (IS) projects. For this purpose the Official Decisions of the Greek Government Information Technology Projects Advisory Committee (ITPAC) concerning 80 large IS projects have been analyzed and interviews with its members have been conducted. From this analysis 21 risk factors have been identified, and further elaborated and associated with inherent particular characteristics of the public sector, extending existing approaches in the literature. A categorization of them with respect to origin revealed that they are associated with the management, the processes, and the content of these projects. Results show that behind the identified risk factors there are political factors, which are associated with intra-organizational and inter-organizational politics and competition, and can be regarded as 'second level' risk sources. The risk factors identified in this study are compared with the ones found by similar studies conducted in Hong Kong, Finland, and the United States, and also with the ones mentioned by OECD reports. Similarities and differences are discussed.

DOI: 10.4018/978-1-4666-2458-0.ch010

1. INTRODUCTION

Organizations of both private and public sector are making big investments for the development of various kinds of information systems (IS), in order to support and enhance their internal functions and also their communication and transaction with their external environment. However, they experience huge problems in their IS development projects: many of them fail to deliver the expected technical performance, functionality and business benefits within budget and schedule (partial failure), or even are abandoned (complete failure) (McFarlan, 1981; Boem, 1991; Standish Group, 1995, 2001, 2004; Dalcher & Genus, 2003; Gauld, 2007). For this reason there has been considerable literature about IS projects failure, which is reviewed in the next section. However, this previous literature is focused mainly on the private sector, though government organizations experience such problems as well, of similar or even higher magnitude (Poulymenakou & Holmes, 1996; Cabinet Office, 2000; Heeks, 2003; OECD, 2001, 2003; Gauld, 2007) emphasize that in its member states governments have big problems when implementing large IT projects. These problems are regarded by OECD (2001, 2003) as 'the Hidden Threat to E-Government' and it is concluded that 'Unless governments learn to manage the risks connected with large public IT projects, these e-dreams will turn into global nightmares'. Also, previous literature is focused mainly on private sector enterprises of a few highly developed and technologically advanced countries (e.g. USA, Great Britain, etc.), and recently mainly on software development projects.

Therefore the scope of this research should be broadened. Additional research is required concerning the risk factors of government IS projects as well, in multiple cultural and socioeconomic contexts, covering the whole range of activities of the IS projects and not only software development. Also, taking into account that the limited research conducted on the risk factors of government IS

projects has mainly the form of case studies, it is necessary to conduct further research on this topic based on bigger samples of projects in order to draw more generalizable conclusions.

In this direction the research objectives of the present study are:

- To investigate empirically the risk factors of the large government IS projects, based on a big sample of such projects implemented in the Greek public sector,
- To understand the main sources of risk in the large government IS projects,
- To compare with risk factors identified by similar studies conducted in other national contexts, and to identify and analyze similarities and differences.

The results of the present study are generally interesting and useful to researchers, practitioners, professional societies, educational institutions and consulting companies in the areas of public administration and information systems. It is of critical importance to reduce drastically the abovementioned high failure rates of IS projects, by systematically studying and understanding their risk factors, and by developing appropriate strategies for managing them, so that the high and ambitious IS investments made by governments of many countries (Commission of the European Communities, 2005 and 2006; United Nations, 2008) can offer the expected high levels of benefits.

This paper is organized as follows: initially in section 2 the main streams and conclusions of the previous literature on the risk factors of IS projects are briefly reviewed. Next in section 3 the research method and data are described, while in section 4 the results are presented, concerning the risk factors of large Greek Government IS projects. In section 5 these risk factors are analyzed and categorized in order to understand the basic origins of risk. In section 6 the above results are compared with the results of other similar studies conducted in other national contexts, and similarities and differences are identified and analyzed. Finally in section 7 the conclusions, implications and directions for future research are presented.

2. LITERATURE REVIEW

Understanding and reducing the unacceptably high failure rates of IS projects has been a major research topic for more than 30 years, due to the very high financial and non-financial costs of these failures. The main objectives of this research have been the identification of the main risk factors, defined as conditions that can present serious threats to the successful completion of an IS project within budget and schedule (Schmidt et al., 2001), the assessment of the risks they create and the development of strategies for managing these risks. We have made an extensive review of this literature, and in this section in 2.1 its main three research streams are outlined (for each stream some representative studies are cited and the most important of them are discussed in more detail), followed by the main conclusions drawn from this literature review in 2.2.

2.1. Main Research Streams

The first stream investigates the risk factors of IS projects in general in various levels of detail: there are some studies at a higher level of abstraction attempting to identify the main groups or sources of risk factors, while some others go into more detail attempting to identify the particular risk factors aiming to provide direct assistance to IS project managers (Zmud, 1979; Lucas, 1981; McFarlan, 1981; Lyytinen & Hirschheim, 1987; Willcocks & Margetts, 1993; Saarinen & Vepsalainen, 1993; Lai & Mahapatra, 1997; OECD, 2001, 2003; Heeks, 2003; Royal Academy of Engineering and the British Computer Society, 2004; Gauld, 2007). From this stream it is worth mentioning the work of Willcocks and Margetts (1993), who developed an interesting

framework for risk analysis of IS projects, based on the conclusions of previous relevant studies. According to this framework the IS projects face four categories of risk factors as to their source. The first category of risk factors are associated with the 'Outer Context' of the organization, e.g. with the economy, the political environment, the government policies, the market, the competition, etc., and in the public sector with the legal framework (e.g. laws, decrees, guidelines), the funding allocations, etc. The second category of risk factors are associated with the 'Inner Context' of the organization, e.g. with its strategy, structure, management, rewards system, human resources and industrial relations arrangements, culture, IS infrastructure and management, etc. The third category is associated with the 'Content' of the specific IS project, e.g. with its size, technology, impact, etc. Finally the fourth category of risk factors are associated with the 'Process' of the project, e.g. with the implementation plan, the experience of the project team, the participation and training of the users, etc.

With respect to public sector OECD in its relevant Policy Brief (OECD, 2001) state that governments face big problems and failures when implementing large IS projects, and identify a set of basic risk factors of these projects: large size, limited involvement of end-users, inappropriate governance structures, limited attention to business process change, use of emerging and immature technologies, weaknesses in managing relationships with external vendors, lack of specialized and knowledgeable human resources, weaknesses in project management and risk management and lack of accountability of business management. Also, some interesting case studies have been conducted of partially or totally failed IS projects in the public sector, which offer insight into the main risk factors that caused failure. For instance, Gauld (2007) analyzes the failure and abandonment of a large IS project in a public New Zealand hospital. He concluded that, in addition to the risk factors found in private sector IS projects, the public sector organizations face some additional unique political and organizational risk factors, which increase failure rates. In particular, he identified critical political risk factors associated with central policies, directions and 'messages' from Ministries and political leaders (e.g. acquire 'off the self' software used by other hospitals in New Zealand), which put pressure towards selecting solutions being totally inappropriate for the particular public organization; he concludes that in the public sector there is a stronger influence of political factors as opposed to economic factors in the decision making process. Furthermore, he identified critical organizational risk factors associated with the much higher resistance to process reengineering in IS projects, the lower organizational capacity for successful IS projects implementation and the higher complexity of processes that characterizes the public sector in comparison with the private.

However, the IS practitioners' and researchers' community gradually realized that the most risky part of an IS project (i.e. the one with the highest probability of complete or partial failure) is the software development, so a second research stream emerged focusing on the investigation of the risk factors of the software development (sub) projects (Boehm, 1991; Keil et al., 1998; Schmidt et al., 2001; Barki et al., 2001; Walace et al., 2004a, 2004b; Han & Huang, 2007). While the first research stream identified the most important factors that give rise to threats to the successful completion of an IS project as a whole, it was an imperative to examine how important these 'generic' risk factors are for the software development part of the project in particular, and whether there are additional risk factors 'specific' to software development that give rise to significant threats to its successful completion. From this research stream it is worth mentioning an international study of software development projects risk factors presented by Keil et al. (1998) and Schmidt et al. (2001). It is based on three simultaneous 'ranking - type' Delphi surveys conducted in

three different cultural settings: in USA, Finland and Hong Kong. It is concluded that risk factors change with time and also depend highly on the cultural, socioeconomic and organizational context. However, eleven risk factors were found, which were common to all three countries, and are shown in Table 1, in the order of their average rankings (for each of these risk factors the average of its rankings over these three countries was calculated and then used for sorting them).

Recently, after 2000, there is also a trend to investigate not only the generic risk factors that characterize IS projects in general, but also the risk factors that characterize particular types of IS projects, which are considered as highly risky, such as ERP systems projects or e-business projects, giving rise to an interesting new research stream (Sumner, 2000; Addison, 2003; Botta-Genoulaz et al., 2005; Moon, 2007).

2.4. Conclusions from Literature Review

The main conclusion from this literature review is that extensive research has been conducted for identifying and understanding the risk factors and

Table 1. Software projects risk factors common to USA, Finland and Hong Kong

No	Risk Factors
1	Lack of top management commitment to the project
2	Failure to gain user commitment
3	Misunderstanding the requirements
4	Lack of adequate user involvement
5	Lack of required knowledge/skills in the project personnel
6	Lack of frozen requirements
7	Changing scope/objectives
8	Introduction of new technology
9	Failure to manage end-user expectations
10	Insufficient/inappropriate staffing
11	Conflict between user departments

sources of IS projects, in order to reduce the high rates of failures (complete or partial) of these projects for more than 30 years. This research has produced a useful body of knowledge, however, most of the studies that have been conducted in this area are focused on private sector enterprises, even though government organizations experience such problems and failures as well (OECD, 2001; Gauld, 2007); their conclusions cannot be directly and automatically transferred to the government organizations, due to the significant differences of public organizations in comparison with the private ones, which have been extensively analyzed and emphasized in the relevant literature (Caudle et al., 1991; Lane, 1995; Flynn, 2002) and concern their external environment, the scope and nature of their activities, their strict legal constraints, their size, internal structure and processes, etc. Furthermore, the limited research that has been conducted concerning the risk factors of government IS projects has the form of case studies; there is a lack of empirical research based on larger samples of projects which could provide more generalizable conclusions.

Also, most of the studies that have been conducted on IS projects risk factors 'have been limited by the lack of a cross-cultural perspective' (Schmidt et al., 2001), based mainly on data from USA, Great Britain and a few other highly developed and technologically advanced countries. Their conclusions reflect to some extent the cultural, business and technological context of these countries, which is quite different from the context of most other countries (e.g. developing ones); therefore further research is required on IS projects risk factors in other types of national contexts.

Another conclusion drawn from this literature review is that the most recent research on IS projects risk factors is focused mainly on software development projects; it does not investigate sufficiently the risk factors associated with the whole lifecycle of an IS project, which usually includes not only software development activities, but also many other types of activities as well, e.g. request for proposals documents preparation, contracts preparation, negotiation and management activities, hardware procurement activities, networks development activities, etc. So further research is required investigating the risk factors in the whole lifecycle of an IS project.

Based on these conclusions and aiming to contribute to closing the abovementioned research gaps, this study investigates the risk factors of the large public sector IS projects in the Greek public sector. This is a very interesting national context, since Greece does not belong to the few highly developed and technologically advanced countries, has a smaller size of internal market, smaller average firm size and lower intensity of competition; also, it is characterized by lower level of ICT penetration and Internet usage in comparison with the highly developed countries, and in general limited tradition in adopting and using sophisticated technologies in both the public and the private sector.

From the numerous papers on IS projects risk factors we reviewed we selected the most relevant and appropriate ones in order to use their conclusions/findings in our study for addressing our basic research questions which have been stated in the Introduction. In particular, since one of our basic research objectives is to understand the main sources of risk in the large government IS projects, we selected to use in this study the conclusions/findings of two papers that provide frameworks for the classification of the identified risk factors as to their origin: the ones of Willcocks and Margetts (1993) and Wallace et al. (2004a). Also, since another basic research objective of this study is to compare the identified risk factors with the ones found by similar studies in other national contexts, we selected to use for this purpose the studies of Schmidt et al. (2001), OECD (2001) and Gauld (2007).

3. RESEARCH METHOD AND DATA

The research method we followed for identifying the risk factors of the large IS projects was based on the study and analysis of the Official Decisions of the Greek Information Technology Projects Advisory Committee (ITPAC) and also on interviews with all its members. In Greece, all large government IS projects with a budget exceeding 1 million Euro have to be approved by the Minister of Interior, Public Administration and Decentralization. For this purpose the ITPAC has been established, which is a high-level scientific committee, consisting of highly respectable and experienced IS professionals, usually IS Directors of Ministries and University Professors in the area of IS or other relevant areas. For each large IS project the competent Ministry submits to ITPAC a predefined set of documents about it, which includes description of its current IS infrastructure and personnel, detailed functional and technical description of the project, detailed budget, implementation plan and analysis of all project activities, description of project team, request for proposals (RFP) document(s), proposed contract(s), etc. The ITPAC examines these documents, discusses them and finally prepares an proposal to the Minister of Interior, Public Administration and Decentralization concerning the approval or not of the project, and also a number of 'recommendations' concerning necessary modifications, corrective actions, etc.; each recommendation is a 'diplomatic' expression of a highly important risk factor in this project, which can have an extremely negative impact on it if not properly managed.

The research approach we adopted in the present study, based on the analysis of the Official Decisions of ITPAC, is similar to the typical 'Delphi surveys' frequently used by other studies (Schmidt et al., 2001), but offers significant advantages over it: the members of ITPAC have a much more serious, professional and responsible involvement in the identification of the risk factors of IS projects (they have to produce official documents on them) than the participants in a typical Delphi survey, who usually regard it as a 'research exercise' of minor importance for them. Also, the interaction among the members of ITPAC is much higher than the interaction among the participants in a typical Delphi survey. Furthermore, the 'open' research approach we adopted in this study offers significant advantages in comparison to the alternative approach of combining risk factors identified by previous relevant research, creating a consolidated list of risk factors, and then presenting it to experienced experts and asking them to rate the importance of each risk factor of this list (e.g. on a 10 point scale), which has been used by several similar studies. Such a research approach can result in missing significant risk factors, which are specific to the context under examination (i.e. the Greek public sector), but do not exist in the other contexts, from which the above 'consolidated risk factors list' has been derived. Additionally, the above approach is combined with qualitative research (Ragin, 1994; Maylor & Blackmon, 2005) based on in-depth semi-structured interviews with the ITPAC members.

In particular, the research method we followed in this study included the following seven steps, which are shown in Table 2:

1. Initially, the 80 ITPAC Official Decisions between 2000 and 2005 were studied and analyzed.
2. Then, in-depth semi-structured interviews were conducted with all members of the ITPAC, in which they were asked to explain to us in detail the recommendations included in the above Official Decisions and the reasons and justifications behind each of them. All these interviews were conducted in two or three parts of 1-2 hours duration each, tape-recorded and transcribed; finally, in each of these official decisions were attached the explanations of its recommenda-

Table 2. The steps of the research method followed in this study

No	Research Method Steps
1	Study of ITPAC Official Decisions
2	Interviews with all members of ITPAC
3	Consolidation of recommendations
4	Determination of corresponding risk factors
5	Analysis of risk factors and association with public sector characteristics
6	Categorization of risk factors
7	Comparison with the risk factors identified in other studies

tions provided by the ITPAC members in the above interviews.

3. A generalization and consolidation of the recommendations included in the above ITPAC Official Decisions followed, which was necessary because each of them was specialized for a particular project. Each author working separately grouped similar specialized recommendations into one consolidated recommendation and in this way finally produced a list of consolidated recommendations; then the results of the two authors were compared and differences were resolved.

4. For each of these consolidated recommendations each author working separately determined the corresponding risk factor, taking also into account the explanations given by the members of the ITPAC in the interviews of the second step; the results of the two authors were compared and differences were resolved. In this way the list of consolidated recommendations and corresponding risk factors was finalized; then for each of them its relative frequency was calculated (indicating in what percentage of the 80 examined large IS projects this risk factor appears).

5. These risk factors were further analyzed and associated by both authors in cooperation

with the particular characteristics of the public sector, based on the explanations given by the members of the ITPAC in the interviews of the second step.

6. The above risk factors were categorized by both authors, using the framework of Wallace et al. (2004a), and also the framework of Willcocks and Margetts (1993), in order to identify the main sources of risk in the large government IS projects.

7. Finally, these risk factors were compared by both authors in cooperation with the ones identified in the abovementioned relevant study conducted by Schmidt et al. (2001), which has based on three different cultural and socioeconomic contexts (Hong Kong, Finland and USA), and also with the ones mentioned in the relevant Policy Brief of OECD (2001).

4. RESULTS: RISK FACTORS

The consolidated recommendations and the corresponding risk factors identified in the above-mentioned steps (3) and (4) are shown in Table 3 (in the second and third column respectively), in order of relative frequency (shown in the fourth column), which shows in what percentage of the 80 examined large IS projects each of them appears. Also in the last two columns of this table we can see the two categorizations of these risk factor (using the frameworks of Wallace et al. (2004a) and also Willcocks and Margetts (1993) respectively) made in the abovementioned steps (6).

In the following paragraphs the risk factors with the highest relative frequencies are discussed and associated with the particular characteristics of the public sector, taking into account the explanations given by the members of the ITPAC during the interviews. From Table 3 we can see that there are three 'high frequency' risk factors, with relative frequencies higher than or equal to 50%. The first of them is 'Incomplete - problem-

Table 3. Consolidated recommendations and risk factors

No	Recommendation	Risk Factor	Relfr. (%)	Cat_1 (Wal)	Cat_2 (M&W)
1	Clarification-improvement of RFP - Contract	Incomplete - problematic -vague RFP - Contract	64	PRMAN	PRO
2	More IS personnel required	Insufficient IS personnel	52.5	SOC	IC
3	Clarification improvement of project implementation plan	Incomplete - problematic - vague project implementation plan	50	PRMAN	PRO
4	Modification - update of technical specifications	Problematic – obsolete technical specifications	44	TECHN	CO
5	Clarification - modification of project scope	Problematic - vague project scope	37.5	PRMAN	CO
6	Improve project team - more users participation is required	Inappropriate project team - insufficient users involvement	36	PRMAN	PRO
7	Interoperability with existing or under development IS infrastructure	Lack of interoperability with existing or under development IS infrastructure	34	TECHN	CO
8	More emphasis on processes and organizational structures redesign - change management	Lack of processes & organizational structures redesign - lack of proper change management	32.5	PRMAN	CO
9	Ensure maintenance and support of the IS during its whole lifecycle	Inadequate maintenance and support of the IS after the end of the project	29	PRMAN	PRO
10	Exploitation of the IS that will be developed in the project by other public organizations	No exploitation of the IS that will be developed in the project by other public organizations	24	TECHN	CO
11	Ensure rights on the source code of the software	Having no rights on the source code of the software	21	PRMAN	PRO
12	Exploit IS and data of other public organizations	No exploitation of IS and data of other public organizations	16	TECHN	CO
13	More emphasis on the training of users - IS personnel	Insufficient training of users - IS personnel	15	PRMAN	PRO
14	Ensure the protection & exclusive use of critical - personal data entered by private enterprises	Lack of critical - personal data protection	14	PRMAN	PRO
15	Detailed technical-economic study of the networks to be developed in the project	Networks with low performance and/or very high operating cost	11	TECHN	CO
16	Clarification of the general and the IS strategy of the organization, so that the project can be aligned with them	Lack of clear general and IS strategy of the organization, creating problems as to the orientation of the project	10	SOC	IC
17	Project cost reduction	Very high cost of the project	9	PRMAN	CO
18	More emphasis on IS security	Low emphasis on the security of the IS to be developed	7.5	TECHN	CO
19	Avoid heterogeneous technologies in the project	Many heterogeneous techno-logies in the project (e.g. more than one DBMS)	6	TECHN	CO
20	Ensure sufficient space for the installation of the IS	Insufficient space for the installation of the IS	6	PRMAN	IC
21	Prepare plans and capabilities to cope with likely future legal and/or organizational changes that will affect the IS	Legal - organizational changes are expected, that will affect the IS	5	SOC	OC

atic - vague Request for Proposals (RFP) and/or Contract' with relative frequency 64%. In most of the examined large projects the RFP and/or the contract needed extensive improvements and clarifications. Because of the big size and the high complexity of many public organizations and their IS projects it is of critical importance their RFPs and contracts to be clear and complete, describing in detail all the tasks and obligations of both parties (the contractor and the public organization). If the RFP and/or the contract are incomplete, problematic or vague, then serious confusion and conflict might arise during the implementation of the project with negative consequences, e.g. conflicts, legal actions, delays, etc. It should also be taken into account that in Greece, and probably in many other countries, for these large IS projects there is extremely strong competition among the big companies of the ICT industry, which usually belong to big groups and corporations with high political power, good connections with the press and the other media, etc. So if the RFP and/or the contract have even a small flaw, serious problems and conflicts might arise, resulting in legal actions, interpellations in the Parliament, negative publicity in the media, big delays, etc. These characteristics of the external environment of public organizations have been highlighted by the relevant literature (Lane, 1995; Flynn, 2002; Gauld, 2007). However, most public organizations in Greece do not have the required capacity and experience for writing such complex, demanding and sensitive RFPs and contracts.

The second risk factor is 'Insufficient IS personnel', with relative frequency 52.5%. The ITPAC members emphasized to us that the shortage of qualified IS personnel has been a very important problem since the first introduction of ICTs in the Greek Public Administration, and has been repeatedly mentioned in numerous relevant reports and official documents (Ministry to the Presidency of the Government, 1993, 1994; Ministry of National Economy, 1994, 2001). However, in most public organizations it has not

been solved, and has caused many problems and failures in the implementation and the productive operation of many important IS projects, which were financed from various programs of the European Union and the Greek Government. This problem is associated with the difficulty of public organizations to attract highly skilled personnel, due to their salaries structures and bureaucratic mentality. The shortage of qualified IS personnel results in a reduced organizational capacity of public organizations with respect to the implementation of large IS projects, which has been highlighted by the relevant literature (Dawes et al., 1999; Gauld, 2007).

The third risk factor 'Incomplete - problematic - vague project implementation plan', with relative frequency 50% is associated with implementation plans needing further elaboration, analysis into more detail, clarifications and modifications. According to the ITPAC members in many projects the scheduled durations of some important activities were too short, probably due to pressures from the politically appointed upper management to finish the project and show results as quickly as possible; much more time would be required, or else quite negative consequences might arise, e.g. due to incomplete users requirements analysis, limited involvement and training of the users, etc. In some very large, complex and ambitious projects, which would lead to big changes in the daily work practices of numerous public servants, a 'monolithic' implementation approach had been adopted, which would be too risky for such projects. In order to reduce this high risk, the ITPAC recommended that the implementation plans of these projects should be modified, and that modular and incremental approaches should be adopted. This risk factor is associated with the abovementioned lack of organizational capacity of public organizations for managing so large IS projects, in combination with the political environment, which is characterized by pressure for 'quick results'.

Also, there are five 'medium frequency' risk factors, as we can see from Table 3, with relative frequencies between 30% and 50%. The fourth risk factor is 'Problematic - obsolete technical specifications', with relative frequency 44%. In many projects, due to the very long times required for conducting the initial feasibility studies, for the allocation of the necessary financial resources, for writing the RFP(s) and the proposed contract(s), for getting all the necessary approvals, etc., the initial technical specifications had already become obsolete at the time the project was examined by the ITPAC, because of rapid technological changes. Therefore these technical specifications should be modified and updated. The ITPAC members mentioned that in some projects the technical specifications were very narrow and restricted the competition; for this reason they recommended that they should become broader and less restrictive, or else quite negative consequences might arise, e.g. small number of good alternative solutions, higher costs, or even complaints or legal actions by some IS companies excluded due to these specifications, interpellations in the Parliament, negative publicity in the media, big delays, etc. This risk factor is associated with the quite lengthy procurement processes of public organizations and their political environment, which is often characterized by extremely strong competition among companies for winning contracts with the government.

The fifth risk factor is 'Problematic - vague project scope', with relative frequency 37.5%. In many projects the scope was vague and should be elaborated and clarified; important decisions had to be made concerning what should be included in the project and what should not. Also, from the scope of some projects were missing important activities and/or subsystems, so that a redefinition of project scope was necessary. This risk factor is also associated with the abovementioned lack of organizational capacity of public organizations for implementing so large IS projects. The sixth

risk factor is 'Inappropriate project team - insufficient users involvement', with relative frequency 36%. Many project teams consisted mainly of IS personnel and only few representatives of the users; this under-representation of the users in the project team could result in insufficient understanding of users requirements, low level of users commitment to the project, etc., with quite negative consequences. Some of the ITPAC members remarked that in most of the projects having this risk factor the problems in project team composition were associated with 'silo mentalities' and intra-organizational politics and competition, which, as the relevant literature has highlighted (Flynn, 2002; Gauld, 2007), characterize public organizations to a much higher extent than the private ones.

The seventh risk factor is 'Lack of interoperability with existing or under development IS infrastructure' with relative frequency 34%. According to ITPAC members in many projects the project teams had poor communication and coordination with the units responsible for managing the existing IS infrastructure, and also with the project teams of other IS projects being implemented in the same public organization, so proper care had not been taken for achieving interoperability among all these IS. It should be noted that there are also two similar risk factors concerning the interoperability with IS of other public organizations: 'No exploitation of the IS that will be developed in the project by other public organizations' (10th, with relative frequency 24%), and 'No exploitation of IS and data of other public organizations' (12th, with relative frequency 16%). These risk factors are associated on one hand with the high complexity of the internal processes of public organizations and the strong interactions and dependencies among them, which make the interoperability among their IS necessary but at the same time difficult (Traunmuller & Wimmer, 2004; Guijarro, 2004); on the other hand they are associated with the 'silo mentalities' and intra-organizational and inter-organizational politics and competition that characterize public organizations, as mentioned above.

The eighth risk factor is 'Lack of processes and organizational structures redesign – lack of proper change management' with relative frequency 32.5%. It should be noted that this risk factor exists mainly in the largest of the examined government IS projects; the total budget of all the projects having this risk factor is 62.5% of the total budget of all the 80 examined projects. In these very large projects it was necessary to combine the development of an IS with extensive redesign of business processes and organizational structures, accompanied with a change management strategy, or else the business benefits from the IS would be very low. However, as ITPAC members noted, they did not have concrete plans for redesigning business processes and organizational structures, and for managing effectively these big changes. This risk factor is associated with the lower exposure of public organizations to markets and competition, which results in fewer incentives for change and innovation in their internal processes and structures. This trend of public organizations to avoid the redesign of their processes and structures when new IS are developed, so that finally new IS automate and reinforce existing processes and structures, has been highlighted and discussed by the relevant literature (Heintze & Bretschneider, 2000; Kraemer & King, 2006; Gauld, 2007).

Finally, as we can see from Table 3, there are thirteen more risk factors with lower relative frequencies below 30%. We remark that the risk factor 'Insufficient training of users - IS personnel' has a low relative frequency of 15%, which shows that public organizations have realized to a large extent how important the training of users and IS personnel is for the success of their IS projects.

5. ANALYSIS OF ORIGIN OF RISK FACTORS

After analyzing and explaining each of the above 21 identified risk factors separately, we proceeded to a categorization of them in order to understand better their origin. Initially we categorized them using the framework proposed by Wallace et al. (2004) into three classes: risk factors related to the 'social subsystem' (SOC), the 'technical subsystem' (TECHN) and the 'project management' (PRMAN) (see fifth column of Table 3). In order to assess quantitatively how important each of these three risk factor classes/origins is, we calculated for each of them two indices: the number of the risk factors categorized in the particular class and the sum of their relative frequencies; the results are shown in Table 4.

From this table we can see that most of these risk factors are associated with the project management (11 risk factors in total with sum of relative frequencies 3.140), while a smaller number of them are of technical origin (7 risk factors with sum of relative frequencies 1.425) and only a few are of social origin (3 risk factors with sum of relative frequencies 0.625). This result indicates that the large size of these projects makes quite difficult several aspects of their management (such as the appropriate definition of project scope and implementation plan, the formulation of RFP(s) and contract(s), the formation of a multi-participative project team with representatives of all the stakeholder groups e.g. various groups of users and IS personnel, etc., as mentioned in the previous section); these management difficulties, in combination with the low organizational capacity of public organizations for implementing such projects, are significant sources of project risks. It should be noted that the acquisition of knowledge and experience in this area is quite difficult because a public organization usually implements only a very small number of so large IS projects (usually not more than 1 – 2 in a decade).

Table 4. Number and sum of relative frequencies of risk factors for each of the classes/origins proposed by Wallace et al. (2004a)

Origin	Number of Risk Factors	Sum of Rel. Freq. of Risk Factors
Project management	11	3.140
Technical subsystem	7	1.425
Social subsystem	3	0.625

Table 5. Number and sum of relative frequencies of risk factors for each of the classes/origins proposed by Willcocks and Margetts (1993)

Origin	Number of Risk Factors	Sum of Rel. Freq. of Risk Factors
Outer Context (OC)	1	0.050
Inner Context (IC)	3	0.685
Content (CO)	10	2.215
Process (PRO)	7	2.290

Also, we categorized the above 21 identified risk factors using the IS projects risk analysis framework of Willcocks & Margetts (1993) into four classes-origins: 'Process' (PRO), 'Content' (CO) 'Outer Context' (OC) and 'Inner Context' (IC) risk factors (see sixth column of the Table 3). Again, for each of these four risk factors classes/origins we calculated the number of the risk factors categorized in it and the sum of their relative frequencies; the results are shown in Table 5.

From this Table we can see that the most important source of risk are the 'Content' of the project (10 risk factors with sum of relative frequencies 2.215) and the 'Process' followed for the management and implementation of the project (7 risk factors with sum of relative frequencies 2.290). The former risk source (Content) is associated with the big size and the high complexity of the public organizations and their IS projects, the high complexity of the interactions among them, their complex legal frameworks and the strict requirements for security and data protec-

tion. It is also associated with the need to combine the development of IS with extensive redesign of business processes and organizational structures in order to maximize benefits, while there is limited motivation for changes and innovations due to lower exposure of public organizations to markets and competition. The latter risk source (Process) is associated with the inherent difficulties and problems that the management of such large project poses, as mentioned above. Much lower seems to be the importance of the 'Inner Context' (3 risk factors having sum of relative frequencies equal to 0.685) and the 'Outer Context' (1 risk factor, with relative frequencies 0.050) as sources of risk.

Also from the interviews with the ITPAC members some additional inner and outer context risk factors were identified, which did not appear directly in the ITPAC Official Decisions. In particular, behind several of the identified content and process related risk factors in many projects there were some 'political factors', which were mainly associated with intra-organizational and inter-organizational politics and competition. For instance, behind risk factors 6 ('Inappropriate project team - insufficient users involvement') and 7 ('Lack of interoperability with existing or under development IS infrastructure') in many projects there were inner context factors associated with intra-organizational politics and competitions among departments and groups of the public organization developing the new IS. Also, behind factors 3 ('Incomplete - problematic - vague project implementation plan'), 10 ('No exploitation of the IS that will be developed in the project by other public organizations') and 12 ('No exploitation of IS and data of other public organizations') in many projects there were outer context factors associated with inter-organizational politics and competitions among Ministries and Ministers. Therefore these political factors, which are of a different nature than the ones identified by Gauld (2007) (external interventions through central policies, directions and 'messages' from

Ministries and political leaders), can be regarded as a 'second level' risk source that influences to a considerable extent the above 'first-level' risk sources. It should be noted that such political factors exist in the private sector as well, but in the public sector they are much stronger.

Also, from the explanations given by the ITPAC members it was concluded that the importance of the inner and outer context as risk sources was in general much higher than what we had initially assessed from the analysis of the ITPAC Official Decisions. In particular, most of the identified content and process related risk factors in many projects have been generated or intensified by inner and/or outer context factors; some of them had been identified from the analysis of the ITPAC official decisions (e.g. 'Insufficient IS personnel', 'Lack of clear general and IS strategy of the organization', creating problems as to the orientation of the project), while some others were identified from the analysis of the content of our interviews with the ITPAC members (e.g. the factors associated with intra-organizational and inter-organizational politics and competition mentioned in the previous paragraph). For instance, the first risk factor 'Incomplete - problematic - vague RFP - Contract' has been generated, or at least intensified, by the

lack of sufficient experienced personnel (inner context factor) and also the extremely strong competition among the big companies of the IS industry for winning government contracts (outer context factor). Similar hold for the third risk factor 'Incomplete - problematic - vague project implementation plan', which has been generated, or at least intensified, by the lack of sufficient experienced personnel (inner context factor) and the external pressure for 'quick results (outer context factor). Therefore it can be concluded that factors of the inner and the outer context of public organizations have both direct effect and indirect effect (through their effect on content and process related risk factors) on IS project failure probability, as illustrated in Figure 1. This finding is in agreement with the ones of Wallace et al. (2004a) who found statistically significant relations between the basic risk sources of the software projects.

6. COMPARISON WITH RESULTS OF OTHER STUDIES

The top eleven risk factors identified in the present study were compared with the eleven risk factors

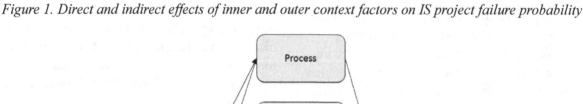

Figure 1. Direct and indirect effects of inner and outer context factors on IS project failure probability

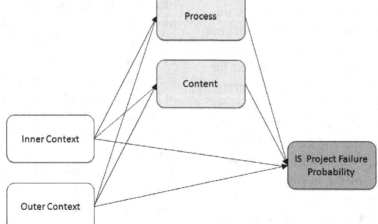

identified by Schmidt et al. (2001) to be common in the relevant 'ranking - type' Delphi surveys they conducted in three countries with different cultural and socioeconomic contexts: Hong Kong, Finland and USA. It should be noted this study is not focused on the public sector of these countries, and is based on the overall experience that the participants in the Delphi surveys had from both the private and the public sector. For each of the top eleven risk factors of the present study, we examined whether it can be matched with any of the eleven common risk factors identified in the above study. The results are shown in the second column of Table 6.

We can see that two out of the top eleven risk factors ('Insufficient IS personnel' and 'Inappropriate project team-insufficient users involvement') can be matched with one or more of the above eleven common risk factors identified by Schmidt et al. (2001). Also three more of the risk factors ('Incomplete - problematic - vague project implementation plan', 'Problematic - vague project scope', 'Lack of processes & organizational structures redesign - lack of proper change management') of the present study can be matched (at least to some extent) with one or more of the risk factors identified by Schmidt et al. (2001) only in one or two of the above three countries. The remaining six risk factors of the present study

Table 6. Comparison between the risk factors identified in the present study and the risk factors identified by Schmidt et al. (2001) and by OECD (2001)

No	Risk factors of the present study	Similar risk factors identified by Schmidt et al (2001)	Similar risk factors identified by OECD (2001)
1	Incomplete - problematic - vague RFP - Contract	N/A	Weaknesses in managing relationships with external vendors
2	Insufficient IS personnel	Insufficient/inappropriate staffing (10) Lack of required knowledge/skills in the project personnel (5)	Lack of specialized and knowledgeable human resources
3	Incomplete - problematic - vague project implementation plan	No Planning or inadequate planning (Finland - 10)	N/A
4	Problematic – obsolete technical specifications	N/A	Use of emerging and still immature technologies
5	Problematic - vague project scope	Unclear/misunderstood cope/objectives (USA - 9)	N/A
6	Inappropriate project team - insufficient users involvement	Lack of required knowledge/skills in the project personnel (5) Insufficient/inappropriate staffing (10) Lack of adequate user involvement (4)	Limited involvement of end-users and inappropriate governance structures
7	Lack of interoperability with existing or under development IS infrastucture	N/A	N/A
8	Lack of processes & organizational structures redesign - lack of proper change management	Not managing change properly (USA - 3, Finland - 4)	Focus on business process change
9	Inadequate maintenance and support of the IS after the end of the project	N/A	N/A
10	No exploitation of the IS that will be developed in the project by other public organizations	N/A	N/A
11	Having no rights on the source code of the software	N/A	N/A

cannot be matched with any of the risk factors identified by Schmidt et al. (2001).

Therefore between the risk factors identified in the present study and the ones identified by Schmidt et al. (2001) there some similarities, but also there are significant differences as well. In particular the first of the risk factors identified in the present study ('Incomplete - problematic - vague RFP - Contract') does not appear in any of the lists of Schmidt et al. (2001). This difference is associated with the big size and the high complexity of the large government IS projects, and also with the complex legal frameworks and legalistic mentality of public organizations (which in Greece is quite strong). It is also associated with the political environment of public organizations, which is characterized by extremely strong competition among big companies of the ICTs industry (most of them having high political power, good connections with the press and the other media, etc.) for winning contracts with the government, high level of public scrutiny of government contracts and projects, etc.

Also the fourth of the risk factors identified in the present study ('Problematic - obsolete technical specifications') does not appear in any of the lists of Schmidt et al. (2001). This difference is associated with the highly complicated and long procurement processes of the public sector, which make the initial technical specifications obsolete by the time the project is examined by the ITPAC. It also reflects the obligation of public organizations to avoid very narrow technical specifications that result in the exclusion of most ICT vendors and restrict the competition. Furthermore, two of the most important risk factors identified in the present study, which both concern interoperability with other IS in the same public organization or in other public organizations ('Lack of interoperability with existing or under development IS infrastructure' and 'No exploitation of the IS that will be developed in the project by other public organizations') do not appear in any of the lists of Schmidt et al. (2001). This difference is as-

sociated with the high complexity of both the internal processes of public organizations and the interactions and interdependencies among them, and also with the 'silos' structure and mentality that characterize public organizations.

The risk factors identified in the present study were also compared with the ones mentioned in the relevant OECD Policy Brief (OECD, 2001). This Policy Brief is dealing with the failures and the risk factors of public sector IS projects and is based on OECD's long experience. Again, for each of the top eleven risk factors of the present study, we examined whether it can be matched with any of risk factors mentioned by OECD; the results are shown in the third column of Table 6. We can see that five out of the top eleven risk factors of the present study can be matched (at least to some extent) with one or more of the risk factors mentioned by OECD. One of them is the first of the risk factors identified in the present study with the highest relative frequency concerning 'Incomplete - problematic - vague RFP – Contract', which can be matched to some extent with the risk factor concerning 'weaknesses in managing relationships with external vendors' mentioned by the OECD; this confirms that the complete and detailed definition of the relationships with external IT vendors in both the RFPs and the contracts is quite important for the success of large government IS projects, much more than in the private sector. Also the risk factor 'Problematic – obsolete technical specifications' can be matched to some extent with the 'Use of emerging and still immature technologies' risk factor mentioned by the OECD; this confirms the importance of appropriate technical specifications for the large government IS projects. Finally, the risk factors 'Insufficient IS personnel', 'Inappropriate project team - insufficient users involvement' and 'Lack of processes & organizational structures redesign - lack of proper change management' can also be matched by similar risk factors from the above OECD Policy Brief; taking into account that the above risk factors had also been matched with one or more of the ones of the study of Schmidt et al. (2001) indicates that these risk factors are highly important for the success of IS projects both in the public and the private sector.

Summarizing, based on the above comparisons we can divide the above top eleven IS projects risk factors identified in the present study into three groups:

- Risk factors which are highly important in both the public and the private sector (factors 2, 3, 5, 6 and 8)
- Risk factors which are highly important only in the public sector (factors 1 and 4)
- Risk factors which are specific to the context of the public sector of Greece and possibly other countries with a similar level of economic and technological development (factors 7, 9, 10 and 11).

7. CONCLUSION, IMPLICATIONS, AND FUTURE RESEARCH DIRECTIONS

7.1. Summary of Conclusions

In this study we investigated the risk factors of the large government IS projects, based on a big sample of such projects from the Greek public sector. We analyzed 80 Official Decisions of the Information Technology Projects Advisory Committee (ITPAC) concerning large IS projects of the Greek Government and conducted extensive interviews with its members. From this analysis 21 highly important risk factors were identified. The most frequently appearing are 'Incomplete - problematic - vague RFP/Contract', 'Insufficient IS personnel', 'Incomplete - problematic - vague project implementation plan', 'Problematic - obsolete technical specifications' and 'Problematic - vague project scope'. The identified risk factors have been associated with the particular characteristics of the public sector, based on the details and explanations given by the members of the ITPAC

in the interviews. The above analysis shows that there are significant risk factors not only in the software development activities of the IS projects, but also in the other activities as well (e.g. in the RFPs and contracts preparation, in hardware procurement, in networks development, etc.), which have been neglected by previous literature.

In order to understand better the risk generation sources and mechanisms in the large government IS projects, the above 21 identified risk factors were classified as to their origin using the frameworks of Wallace et al. (2004a) and Willcocks and Margetts (1993). It was found that most of these risk factors are associated with the project management, while a smaller number of them are of technical origin and only a few are of social origin. Their main risk origins/sources are the 'Content' of the projects and the 'Process' of managing and implementing them, while of lower importance as risk sources are the 'Inner Context' and the 'Outer Context'. However, behind several of the identified content and process related risk factors there are some 'political factors', which are mainly associated with intra-organizational and inter-organizational politics and competition, and can be regarded as a 'second level' risk source that influences the above 'first-level' risk sources. Another interesting conclusion was that factors of the inner and the outer context have not only direct effect but also indirect effect as well (through their effect on content and process related risk factors) on IS project failure probability. Finally, the risk factors identified in the present study were compared with the ones identified in a similar study conducted by Schmidt et al. (2001) in Hong Kong, Finland and USA, and also with the ones mentioned in the relevant Policy Brief of OECD (2001). From this comparison it was concluded that some of the identified IS projects risk factors are specific to the public sector, while some others appear in the private sector as well, as discussed at the end of the previous section.

7.2. Implications for Politicians and Managers

The findings of this study have several implications for politicians and public sector managers:

- A critical risk factor of the large government IS projects is the lack of highly skilled IS personnel in public organizations; therefore in order to overcome this problem public organizations should develop appropriate policies, reward systems, continuous education systems, motives, etc. for attracting and retaining highly skilled IS personnel.

- Another critical risk factor is the lack of the required knowledge and organizational capacity for implementing large and ambitious IS projects in the public organizations. Taking into account that a public organization usually implements only a very small number of such large IS projects (usually not more than 1 – 2 in a decade) the acquisition of knowledge in this area is quite difficult. For this reason only a central public organization, which is competent for the monitoring, supervision and guidance of ICTs development in the whole public sector, such as the Ministry of Interior, Public Administration and Decentralization in Greece, would be appropriate for collecting knowledge from all large government IS projects and then disseminating it to the public organizations who need it. The use of consultants' services should be regarded only as a secondary and complementary mechanism for the acquisition of knowledge in this area, taking into account that the over-reliance on consultants in combination with low organizational capacity for monitoring their services and evaluating their suggestions can have quite negative impacts (Gauld, 2007).

- The 'silo mentality' and the lack of cooperation within and between public organizations very often constitute an important risk factor of the large government IS projects. So it is necessary in such projects to create multi-participative project teams with representatives of all the groups that will be affected by the new IS (e.g. various groups of users and IS personnel); also, the members of these project teams should be appropriately motivated to cooperate, e.g. through bonuses based on the achievement of predefined objectives and in general on team performance, etc.

7.3. Future Research Directions

Further research is required in order to identify and understand better the risk factors of government IS projects in multiple national contexts, their origins, and also the risks resulting from them. Also, the relations between the identified risk factors and their impact on various project success measures should be investigated using advanced quantitative research methods (e.g. structural equation modeling) (Kline, 2005); the model of Figure 1 could be used as basis for future research in this direction. The next step could be the development and statistical validation of multi-dimensional instruments for measuring reliably government IS projects risk, consisting of multi-item constructs measuring various risk dimensions; such instruments would enable the empirical investigation of the dependence of this risk and its dimensions on various factors and of the risk patterns of various types of government IS projects. Another interesting and useful research direction is the development, pilot application and evaluation of appropriate techniques and methodologies for managing the identified risk factors and finally reducing the high failure rates of government IS projects.

REFERENCES

Addison, T. (2003). E-commerce project development risks: Evidence from a Delphi survey. *International Journal of Information Management, 23*, 25–40. doi:10.1016/S0268-4012(02)00066-X

Barki, H., Rivard, S., & Talbot, J. (2001). An integrative contingency model of software project risk management. *Journal of Management Information Systems, 17*(4), 37–69.

Boehm, B. (1991). Software risk management: Principles and Practices. *IEEE Software, 8*, 32–41. doi:10.1109/52.62930

Botta-Genoulaz, V., Millet, P. A., & Grabot, B. (2005). A survey of the recent literature on ERP systems. *Computers in Industry, 56*, 510–522. doi:10.1016/j.compind.2005.02.004

Cabinet Office of UK. (2000). *Review of major government IT projects – successful IT: Modernizing government in action.* Retrieved from http://www.ogc.gov.uk

Caudle, S., Gorr, W., & Newcomer, K. (1991). Key information systems management issues for the public sector. *Management Information Systems Quarterly, 15*(2), 170–188. doi:10.2307/249378

Commission of the European Communities. (2005). *i2010 – a European information society for growth and employment.* Retrieved from http://www.eluxembourg.public.lu/eLuxembourg/i2010.pdf

Commission of the European Communities. (2006). *i2010-eGovernment Action Plan: accelerating egovernment in Europe for the benefit of all.* Retrieved from http://ec.europa.eu/information_society/activities/egovernment/docs/action_plan/comm_pdf_com_2006_0173_f_en_acte.pdf

Dalcher, D., & Genus, A. (2003). Avoiding IS/IT implementation failure. *Technology Analysis and Strategic Management, 15*(4), 403–407. doi:10.1080/095373203000136006

Dawes, S., Bloniarz, P., Connelly, D., Kelly, K., & Pardo, T. (1999). Four realities of IT innovation in government. *Public Management, 28*(1), 1–5.

Flynn, N. (2002). *Public sector management* (4th ed.). London, UK: Pearson Education.

Gauld, R. (2007). Public sector information systems failures: Lessons from a New Zealand hospital organization. *Government Information Quarterly, 24*, 102–114. doi:10.1016/j.giq.2006.02.010

Guijarro, L. (2004, August 30-September 3). Analysis of the interoperability frameworks in e-government initiatives. In *Proceedings of the Third International Conference EGOV,* Zaragoza, Spain.

Han, W., & Huang, S. (2007). An empirical analysis of risk components and performance on software projects. *Journal of Systems and Software, 80*, 42–50. doi:10.1016/j.jss.2006.04.030

Heeks, R. (2003). *Success and failure rates of egovernment in developing/transitional countries: Overview.* Retrieved from http://www.egov4dev.org/success/sfrates.shtml

Heintze, T., & Bretschneider, S. (2000). Information technology and restructuring in public organizations: Does adoption of information technology affect organizational structures, communications and decision making? *Journal of Public Administration: Research and Theory, 10*(4), 801–830. doi:10.1093/oxfordjournals.jpart.a024292

Jiang, J., & Klein, G. (1999). Risks to different access of system success. *Information & Management, 36*, 263–272. doi:10.1016/S0378-7206(99)00024-5

Keil, M., Cule, P., Lyytinen, K., & Schmidt, R. (1998). A framework for identifying software project risks. *Communications of the ACM, 41*, 76–83. doi:10.1145/287831.287843

Kline, R. B. (2005). *Principles and practice of structural equation modeling.* New York, NY: Guilford Press.

Kraemer, K., & King, J. L. (2006). Information technology and administrative reform: Will e-government be different? *International Journal of Electronic Government Research, 2*(1), 1–20. doi:10.4018/jegr.2006010101

Lai, V., & Mahapatra, R. (1997). Exploring the research in information technology implementation. *Information & Management, 32,* 187–201. doi:10.1016/S0378-7206(97)00022-0

Lane, J. E. (1995). *The public sector: Concepts, models and approaches.* London, UK: Sage.

Lucas, H. (1981). *Implementation: The key to successful information systems.* New York, NY: Columbia University Press.

Lyytinen, K., & Hirschheim, R. (1987). Information systems failures – a survey and classification of the empirical literature. In Zorkoczy, P. (Ed.), *Oxford surveys of information technology (Vol. 4,* pp. 257–309). Oxford, UK: Oxford University Press.

Maylor, H., & Blackmon, K. (2005). *Researching business and management.* New York, NY: Macmillan.

McFarlan, F. W. (1981). Portfolio approach to information systems. *Harvard Business Review, 59,* 142–150.

Ministry of National Economy. (1994). *Final report of integrated Mediterranean programs on information technology.*

Ministry of National Economy. (2001). *Operational programme 'information society': European union support framework III.*

Ministry to the Presidency of the Government. (1993). *Programme of administrative modernization 1993-1995.*

Ministry to the Presidency of the Government. (1994). *Operational programme 'Klisthenis' for the modernization of the Greek public administration: European community support framework II.*

Moon, Y. B. (2007). Enterprise resource planning: A review of the literature. *International Journal of Management and Enterprise Development, 4*(3), 235–264. doi:10.1504/IJMED.2007.012679

Organization for Economic Cooperation & Development (OECD). (2001). *The hidden threat to e-government - avoiding large government it failures.* Paris, France: OECD.

Organization for Economic Cooperation & Development (OECD). (2003). *The e-government imperative.* Paris, France: OECD.

Poulymenakou, A., & Holmes, A. (1996). A contingency framework for the investigation of information systems failure. *European Journal of Information Systems, 5,* 34–46. doi:10.1057/ejis.1996.10

Ragin, C. (1994). *Constructing social research.* Thousand Oaks, CA: Sage.

Royal Academy of Engineering and British Computer Society. (2004). *The challenges of complex IT projects.* London, UK: The Royal Academy of Engineering.

Saarinen, T., & Vepsalainen, A. (1993). Managing the risks of information systems implementation. *European Journal of Information Systems, 4,* 283–295. doi:10.1057/ejis.1993.39

Schmidt, R., Lyytinen, K., Keil, M., & Cule, P. (2001). Identifying software project risks: An international Delphi study. *Journal of Management Information Systems, 17,* 5–36.

Standish Group. (1995). *The CHAOS report.* Retrieved from http://www.standishgroup.com

Standish Group. (2001). *Extreme chaos.* Retrieved from http://www.standishgroup.com

Standish Group. (2004). *Third quarter research report*. Retrieved from http://www.standishgroup.com

Sumner, M. (2000). Risk factors in enterprise-wide ERP projects. *Journal of Information Technology, 15*, 317–327. doi:10.1080/02683960010009079

Traunmuller, R., & Wimmer, M. (2004, August 30-September 3). e-Government: The challenges ahead. In *Proceedings of the Third International Conference EGOV*, Zaragoza, Spain.

United Nations. (2008). *UN e-Government survey 2008: From e-Government to connected governance*. New York, NY: United Nations.

Wallace, L., Keil, M., & Arun, R. (2004a). How software project risk affects project performance: An investigation of the dimensions of risk and an exploratory model. *Decision Sciences, 35*(2), 289–321. doi:10.1111/j.00117315.2004.02059.x

Wallace, L., Keil, M., & Arun, R. (2004b). Understanding software project risk: A cluster analysis. *Information & Management, 42*, 115–125. doi:10.1016/j.im.2003.12.007

Willcocks, L., & Margetts, H. (1994). Risk assessment and information systems. *European Journal of Information Systems, 3*(2), 127–138. doi:10.1057/ejis.1994.13

Zmud, R. (1979). Individual differences and MIS success: A review of the empirical literature. *Management Science, 25*(10), 966–979. doi:10.1287/mnsc.25.10.966

This work was previously published in the International Journal of Electronic Government Research, Volume 7, Issue 2, edited by Vishanth Weerakkody, pp. 59-77, copyright 2011 by IGI Publishing (an imprint of IGI Global).

Chapter 11

The Environment as Part of the E-Government Agenda:
Framing Issues and Policies at the Nation-State Level

Gisela Gil-Egui
Fairfield University, USA

Alissa M. Mebus
Symmetry Partners, LLC, USA

William F. Vásquez
Fairfield University, USA

Sarah C. Sherrier
Green Room Entertainment, USA

ABSTRACT

This paper explores national governments' prioritization of environmental matters within their e-government websites, in order to provide empirical evidence related to the way "green" issues are articulated in different countries' policymaking agendas. Through a multi-pronged methodological approach combining frame analysis, factor analysis, inferential statistics, and qualitative interpretation, explicit and visual allusions related to environmental policies, initiatives, challenges, and agencies in the home page or main portal of the national governments for 189 UN members were coded. Results show that only 39.1% of the analyzed e-government sites included environmental references, and no strong pattern characterized the framing of environmental concerns by governments. Correlation and regression analyses revealed that GDP per capita and contribution to global CO_2 emissions have more weight than other variables in a nation's propensity to highlight environmental issues within their e-government websites. Findings are discussed in light of framing theory, as well as in light of implications for governments' public image and for actual environmental advocacy.

INTRODUCTION

Initiatives related to the development of e-government and online public services are underway in almost every nation in the world (United Nations, 2008). As a movement towards digital governance gradually becomes a global reality, it is necessary to gauge ways in which national policy agendas are effectively reflected by categories included in different nations' e-government sites and portals. It is the objective of this project to explore environmental references in such spaces, in order

DOI: 10.4018/978-1-4666-2458-0.ch011

to assess whether and how ecological matters are addressed, as well as how external determinants and broader structural factors generate differences in national approaches to the subject.

The relevance of this study is highlighted by a mainstreaming of concerns related to climate change, and by the increasing number of nations that are adopting measures aimed at promoting environmentally sustainable development (European Commission, 2008; United Nations Department of Economic and Social Affairs, 2009; United Nations Development Programme, 2007; United Nations Environment Programme, 2009). In that sense, the inclusion of "green" references in national e-government portals could provide an indicator of the extent to which environmental matters are prioritized within governments' programmatic decision-making (Navarra & Cornford, 2003; Qureshi, 2005). Moreover, while the scholarly literature on e-government has experienced significant growth in the last decade, this production remains focused on a limited range of topics, mostly related to e-government's infrastructure, dissemination, functionality, and/or its social or administrative context (Anderson & Henriksen, 2005; Chen & Dimitrova, 2006; Chen et al., 2007; Heeks & Bailur, 2007; Yildiz, 2007; West, 2008; Zambrano, 2008). We deem important shedding light on the virtually unexplored connections between e-government and national environmental initiatives (Lim & Tang, 2007; Zavetoski & Shulman, 2002), since the protection of intergenerational rights to clean and abundant natural resources passes through both the inclusion of the matter in the "main menu" of governmental strategies, and its framing as an issue of crucial public interest.

In order to assess national governments' prioritization of environmental issues, our project addressed three specific questions: 1) the extent to which environmental references are included in the home page of each of the 189 UN members reported as having an online governmental presence by 2008 (United Nations, 2008); 2) the

way in which environmental references, when present, are articulated; and 3) the extent to which broader national characteristics in terms of income, development, environmental track record, stage of deployment of e-government structures, and contribution of tourism to gross domestic product (GDP) affect the inclusion and nature of environmental references in e-government portals. In answering these questions, our project combines methodological approaches from frame analysis, factor analysis, descriptive and inferential statistics, and qualitative interpretation, to explain factors affecting inclusion/exclusion, placement, and adoption of particular rhetorical strategies by national government in their dealings with environmental issues within e-government sites.

LITERATURE REVIEW

E-Government, the Internet, and Environmental Issues

Although scholarly production on the separate subjects of e-government and environmental policymaking is extensive and continues to grow, few works have inquired into the intersections of these two areas of research. A study by Lim and Tang (2007) explores the impact of e-government on local governance and "examines how e-government initiatives influence the perceived performance of environmental decision making in an urban context and what organizational and contextual factors affect Web-aided decision performance" (p. 109). The study, which relied on data collected from city government websites and a nationwide survey of city officials in Korea, found that differences in the level of e-government implementation across cities impact environmental decision performance. Additionally, pressure from environmental activists was found related to the extent to which environmental decision-making takes place within e-governance activities.

Expanding the scope of analysis beyond e-government sites, Zavestoski and Shulman (2002) draw upon reflexive modernization, deliberative democracy, and resource mobilization to identify the issues that may prevent Internet's use as a tool for enhanced environmental decision-making. According to these authors, Internet-based *interaction* and *networking* between stakeholders holds great promise for environmental advocacy where more direct interaction is improbable. However, Internet's ability to enhance democratic *participation* in environmental decision-making, or its ability to enhance plurality in the decision-making process itself is still to be corroborated (Zavetoski & Shulman, 2002). In general, observers of the role that information and communication technologies (ICTs) play in citizens' overall engagement with political processes disagree as to whether the Internet and related tools for online interfacing and interaction, such as e-government, promote or deter democracy[1].

As new ICTs increase access to governmental agencies by different interest groups, e-government websites have potential to become not only tools for the provision of information and public services, but also spaces for deliberation and public administration's responsiveness towards other social actors (Dawes, 2008; Zambrano, 2008). Yet the possibilities and limitations of e-government as an enhancer of governmental transparency have been researched mostly from the point of view of efficiency and effectiveness in the implementation of policies (Bekkers & Homburg, 2007; Pina et al., 2007), rather than from the point of view of political legitimacy.

In this regard, and considering the essential role that communication play in building public trust (Terwel et al., 2009), we wonder about the extent to which e-government websites are being used as key propaganda and public image resources for nations' executive power, in ways that replicate the corporate sectors' use of their web pages as public relations (PR) and promotional artifacts. For example, according to Patten (1991), Roberts

(1992) and Snider et al. (2003), "social responsibility" statements within many corporations' web sites reflect the influence of public pressures on those organizations. Revealingly, studies that assess the content of corporate social responsibility statements and reports available online have found ecological/environmental references to be amongst the most recurrent themes (Esrock & Leichty, 1998; Mebus et al., 2008). Corporations engaged in activities that pose a greater threat to the environment are also more likely to disclose formal written codes of ethics and social responsibility statements dealing with environmental issues (Mebus et al., 2008; Reichert et al., 2000). Furthermore, evidence in favor of legitimacy theory[2] exists: companies are more likely to release "socially responsible" information if they believe that their public image is in jeopardy (Campbell, 2003; Patten, 1992; Snider, 2003; Wilmshurst & Frost, 2000). Alternatively, Deegan and Gordon's (1996) analysis of a sample of annual reports for the 1991 financial year revealed environmental disclosure practices to also be self-laudatory, with corporations striving to promote positive aspects of their environmental performances.

Whether national governments include environmental references in their websites with the same self-promotional goals as private corporations or with purely informative purposes, is a question that can be tackled with the help of frame analysis.

Framing Theory

Framing and frames in discursive practices have been conceptualized in various ways. Some conceptualizations focus on the selection and presentation process (Nelson, Clawson, & Oxley, 1997), others on "a central organizing idea for news content" (Tankard et al., 1991), some others as a symbolic and interactive perspective (Gitlin, 1980) or as organizing principles that are socially shared and persistent. For example, framing is described as "the process by which a source defines the essential problem underlying a particular social or political issue and outlines a set of considerations purportedly relevant to that issue" (Nelson, Clawson, & Oxley, 1997, p. 222). Similarly, Tankard et al. (1991, p. 3) conceptualize frames as "a central organizing idea for news content that supplies a context and suggests what the issue is through the use of selection, emphasis, and elaboration." Other researchers, however, conceptualize framing from a more symbolic and interactive perspective, defining frames as the "persistent patterns of cognition, interpretation, and presentation, of selection, emphasis, and exclusion, by which symbol-handlers routinely organize discourse" (Gitlin, 1980, p.7), or the "organizing principles that are socially shared and persistent over time, that work symbolically to meaningfully structure the social world" (Reese, 2003, p. 11).

Frame analysis is an important approach to studying media content, including websites. By identifying the frames in a message, frame analysis provides insights on how message producers structure the message as well as audiences' perception of the message, since the composition of frames that get echoed in official documents and the media frequently have an important impact in shaping public opinion's consideration of the issues addressed by and through such frames (McCombs & Ghanem, 2001; Miller & Riechert, 2001).

In the context of this study, where the environmental references within e-government websites are mostly formulated by national governments without intermediation by other content gatekeepers (i.e., the press or private mass media), we decided to apply Schön and Rein's (1994) definition of frames. These authors propose that frames are "underlying structures of belief, perception and appreciation" upon which policy positions rest (p. 23). They arise from generative metaphors that help define a complex reality in regards to a limited, specific set of features and, subsequently, identify concrete courses of action. Thus, through the process of naming and constructing a reality in

a certain way, stakeholders to an issue gradually "make the 'normative leap' from data to recommendations, from fact to values, from *is* to *ought*" (Schön & Rein, 1994, p.26).

Policy practice, according to Schön and Rein (1994), is informed by different levels of framing, from metacultural ones (e.g., deeply-rooted beliefs about the appropriate role of government in society) to case-specific ones pertaining to particular decisions. Amidst these different levels of framing, however, the authors highlight "institutional action frames," which refer to the way that historically and geographically located expectations about different institutional actors (from the state and governmental agencies to advocacy organizations) shape most of the positions and responses those actors adopt in the face of different situations and challenges (Schön & Rein, 1994). This argument builds upon James March and Johan Olsen's well-known *new institutionalism* theory (1989), whose main tenet is that political actors are frequently determined by a *logic of appropriateness* (as opposed to rational calculations of costs and benefits) which shape their behavior in accordance to patterns and expectations defined by the institutions within which they have been socialized.

Yet institutional frames, themselves, "tend to be complex and hybrid in nature. They do not usually consist in a single, coherent, overarching frame, but in families of related frames" (Schön & Rein, 1994, p. 34). More importantly, they are affected by competing institutional frames and external contingencies. Policy issues are formulated by different stakeholders in ways that try to balance their particular objectives and agendas, while also considering the limitations and possibilities generated by the broader context (including institutional expectations) in which specific frames are to be proposed –a process that Schön and Rein (1994) they call "design rationality":

The designer makes his representation of the object within a field of constraints, acting from intentions implicit in his values and purposes. However, the designer's intentions, constraints, and objectives are not fully given at the outset, and they are not fixed. They emerge in the course of making the object, through a process of seeing, making design moves, and seeing again [...] As the representation of the object takes shape and new qualities are recognized in it, new meanings are apprehended and new intentions are formed (p. 85).

This latent, historically located, and evolving nature of discourse design is highlighted by Schön and Rein (1994) in their explanation of frame construction: "The frames that shape policy are usually tacit, which means that we tend to argue *from* our tacit frames *to* our explicit policy positions" (p. 34).

If this proposition is true, then exploring national governments' prioritization of environmental issues through e-government websites requires ascertaining environment-related frames beyond a mere count of explicit allusions to "green" initiatives, by also inquiring into structural (i.e. institutional) and circumstantial factors affecting national governments' policy-making. Such factors are likely to act as mediators between governments' tacit framing of environmental matters and their explicit policies or stances on the subject as expressed by their e-government portals. The following section of this article describes the way in which we operationalize this process of frame building.

METHODS

Data and Variables

Our primary data was gathered by collecting and exploring the URLs of the main governmental web sites for each of the United Nations' members, which comprised 192 states as of June 2009, following the admission of Montenegro as a new member in 2006. However, as reported in the latest United Nations' E-Government Survey available at the time of writing this report, three nations out of the 192 UN members did not have any form of governmental presence on the World Wide Web by 2008: Central African Republic, Somalia, and Zambia (United Nations, 2008). Once we identified the main governmental page for those nations that possess some form of official online presence, we looked for any kind of environmental reference (i.e. allusions to environmental issues, policies, initiatives, agencies, etc.), for the construction of an index of the nations' propensity to mark the environment as a governmental priority. Details about this index are explained later in this section. Similarly to the 2008 E-Government Readiness report, we focused on each country's self-proclaimed official government home page, online public services' gateway, or national portal. In those cases where none of these existed, we looked at the web site of the Office of the President, the Ministry of Interior Affairs, any ministry/department in charge of information, commerce or tourism or, in the case of a few countries, the only web site using the ".gov" extension within the nation's own domain name.

Conversely, in those cases where there existed both an official government's site and a national portal or a centralized public services portal, we focused on the latter, as they are more likely to include diverse content catered to a plural audience (constituents, interest groups, different stakeholders to an issue).

Despite the fact that many of e-government sites currently offer multilingual versions of their content, we made every effort to read each country's site(s) in its native or official language. In order to do this, we applied our knowledge of different languages, thus covering English, Spanish, French, Italian, and Portuguese. In the case of those sites in languages that we do not dominate, we resorted to Google's Language Tools (http://www.google.com/language_tools?hl=en), which includes an option for translation of web pages.

Determining whether national e-government portals included environmental references or not, and if they did, what kind of references, was accomplished through the design of a coding system that considered only permanent content, tabs, links, cursor-activated flash windows, and/ or prominent visual elements within those sites (i.e. we ignored temporary or contingent content, such as that posted under "News" sections).

While all the authors of this study participated in the design and refining of the coding system, only one author was in charge of the actual coding process, to avoid problems related to inter-coder reliability.

In order to explore factors that can potentially affect nations' inclusion of environmental references within their e-government home pages, we collected the most recent available data on countries' income level (World Bank, n.d.), Gross Domestic Product per capita (in U.S. dollars, current prices, as reported by the International Monetary Fund, 2009 [estimates for 2008]), Human Development Index (United Nations Development Program, 2008), level of development of e-government services in general (as measured by the United Nations' E-Government Survey, 2008), overall environmental performance (as estimated by Yale and Columbia universities' Environmental Performance Index Project, 2008), percentage of Gross Domestic Product generated by tourism and travel activities (World Travel & Tourism Council, n.d.), and CO_2 emissions measured in thousands of metric tons (as reported in 2004 by the U.S. Department of Energy's Carbon Dioxide Information Analysis Center, CDIAC, in data researched for the United Nations' Millennium Development Goals Indicators). Once we coded each nation's e-government website for environmental references, we constructed an index measuring national governments' prioritization of environmental matters in their e-government home pages, and then ran correlation and regression analyses to determine the extent to which the external variables listed above affect countries' performance in our environmental references index.

Operationalizing Environmental Concern

We proposed six indicators for the construction of an index measuring nations' concern with environmental issues as manifested through their e-government websites. Indicator i (EC_i) takes the value of one if a country's e-government home page shows any allusion to environmental matters i, and zero otherwise. Our coding categories included:

1. **Prominence:** Any kind of environmental allusions that are located at a highly visible point of the homepage, or whose dimensions make them hard to miss. This includes prominent non-verbal images showcasing a country's natural resources or landscapes.
2. **"What we do":** Verbal allusions to concrete policies, initiatives, or actions adopted in the country (either by the government or citizens) to protect the environment or address environmental problems.
3. **"What we have":** Verbal allusions to the country's natural resources, whether as sources of energy, trade, or touristy attractions.
4. **"What we face":** Verbal allusions to environmental problems or challenges, whether domestic or global.
5. **"Our commitment":** Verbal allusions to multilateral treaties, agreements or benchmarks related to the environment, such as the Kyoto Protocol or the European Union's Principles for the Environment.
6. **Agencies:** Verbal allusions or direct links to environmental ministries, offices, organizations, or agencies.

Factor analysis was implemented to estimate the relationship between these indicators and the latent national government's propensity to prioritize environmental matters in their agenda, as well as to estimate such latent propensity. This relationship is assumed to follow a linear form:

$$EC_i = \lambda_i \text{ ENVINDEX} + e_i$$

Coefficients λ_i represents the factor loading relating indicators EC_i to the latent factor *ENVINDEX*. The term e_i represents the variance that is unique to the indicators EC_i, and is independent of the corresponding factor and all other e_j.

Factor analysis provides a stronger analytical framework to estimate a national government's environmental prioritization index than traditional methods such as binary variables representing environmental references and the total amount of reported references. First, factors can be used as proxies for latent variables which are unobservable and inestimable using traditional methods. Therefore, *ENVINDEX* can be interpreted as the latent national government's propensity to prioritize environmental matters in their agenda. Second, *ENVINDEX* does not assume different kind of environmental references in e-government websites to equally impact national governments' prioritization of a "green" agenda, given that factor loadings are allowed to vary across indicators of environmental allusions. Finally, factor analysis provides estimates that are adjusted for measurement error, which is a consideration ignored by traditional methods (Brown, 2006).

After conducting our factor analysis, we performed both correlation and regression analyses to determine the extent to which the environmental prioritization index is affected by country's economic and environmental characteristics (X), as follows:

$$\text{ENVINDEX} = X\beta + u$$

where β is a set of coefficients to be estimated, and u is an error term. The set of characteristics X included country's Gross Domestic Product per capita (GDPPC), human development index (HDINDEX), level of development of e-government services in general (EREADYINDEX), environmental performance index (EPI), percentage of Gross Domestic Product generated by tourism and travel activities (TOURISM), and CO_2 emissions measured in thousands of metric tons (CO2).

RESULTS

Our analyses indicate that the different indicators of environmental references we coded within e-government sites and portals relate to only one common factor (eigen value of 2.20228), as shown in Table 1. We assume this factor to represent national governments' prioritization of environmental issues in their agenda, as reflected by their digital portals[3]. Out of the six indicators related to the *ENVINDEX* factor, explicit allusions to environmental policies ("what we do") and relevant governmental agencies present the highest factor loadings (0.798 and 0.744, respectively), followed by references to environmental problems ("what we face") (0.585), prominent placement of environmental references (0.552), touting of domestic natural resources ("what we have") (0.449), and allusion to regional or international treaties or mandates in connection with the environment ("our commitment") (0.401).

After estimating *ENVINDEX* based on the results of the factor analysis, this index was standardized to have a mean of zero and standard deviation of one. The standardized index allowed us to rank countries according to their latent environmental prioritization and measure the separation of their environmental prioritization with respect to the average environmental references in standard deviations. It must be noted that only 74 out of 189 nations considered in our sample showed at least one of the six indicators mentioned above. This fact, by itself, reveals that environmental issues are deemed important enough for inclusion in the home page of national e-government sites only by a minority of countries (39.1%). Contrasting a growing tendency in the private

Table 1. Factor analysis of environmental references

Indicators	Factor Loadings	KMO
Prominence	0.552	0.88
"What we do"	0.798	0.71
"What we have"	0.449	0.77
"What we face"	0.585	0.69
"Our commitment"	0.401	0.76
Agencies	0.744	0.69

sector to highlight the environment as a major concern in their social responsibility statements on the web (Esrock & Leichty, 1998; Mebus et al., 2008), most national governments with an online presence either underplay or ignore the matter in their home pages.

Figure 1 shows the percentage of nations that included each of the indicators constituting our index of environment references within e-government websites. Over a quarter (28.6%) of countries that included any form of environmental reference did it prominently within their e-government pages. Consistent with the factor loadings described before, explicit allusions to environmental policies/initiatives ("what we do") and relevant agencies were the most frequent type of reference, being included 17.7 and 17.1 percent of the times, respectively. Next come allusions to natural resources ("what we have"), included 10.9 percent of the times there was any environmental reference in e-government portals. A small group of countries (7.8%) alluded to environmental problems or challenges ("what we face"). The least recurrent of the different types of environmental references we coded was that alluding to international or regional treaties or mandates in connection with the environment ("our commitment").

Nations with the highest scores within our index of environmental references (i.e. those including more than one of the six different factors we coded) comprise a diverse mix of nations that

seem to challenge simplistic explanations based on connections between a nation's size or developmental level and its government's apparent concern for the environment. Table 2 lists, in descending order, the 48 countries that scored above the average value within our standardized index. Surprisingly, the top 15 nations in this group include actors that are dissimilar in many senses, from well regarded environmental performers (New Zealand, Spain) to big polluters (China, USA), from nations with high human development indices (Sweden, Canada) to nations with low ones (Bangladesh, Burundi), from traditional destinations for people seeking contact with nature (Philippines, Australia, Belize) to places that are not famous for that kind of tourism (Malta, Bulgaria, Pakistan).

In order to uncover and understand underlying elements affecting nations' ranking within our index of environmental references, we ran a series of correlation analyses that made it possible for us to explore possible relations between countries' individual *ENVINDEX* scores and the broader national characteristics described in the methods section of this report as external variables. In general, we found relatively modest correlation coefficients for nations' *ENVINDEX* individual scores and each of the external variables we explored, yet all of them were statistically significant at a P value of <0.1 or less, except for contribution of tourism to individual countries' GDP ($P>0.10$). Table 3 shows that the strongest correlation occurs between each nation's *ENVINDEX* score and the e-government readiness index score (.31, $P<0.01$), followed by the correlation between countries' *ENVINDEX* score and their respective GDP per capita (.30, $P<0.01$), and the correlation between countries' *ENVINDEX* score and their annual contribution to global CO_2 emissions (.24, $P<0.01$).

These coefficients suggest that all the variables described in our methods, except tourism, are related to national governments' propensity to include environmental references in their online

Figure 1. Frequency (%) of indicators comprising ENVINDEX shown by countries

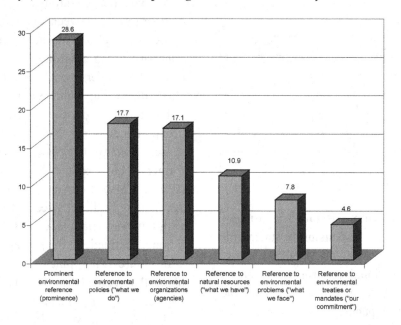

portals. However, the strongest correlation between *ENVIDEX* scores and variables related to wealth, technological sophistication, and/or contribution to global green house gasses can be visually corroborated by the fact that 10 nations within the top 48 ones in our index (that is, 20.8% of them), possess all three of these characteristics.

The relationship between nations' *ENVINDEX* scores and the aspects mentioned in Table 3 was also explored through a regression analysis that allowed us to determine possible relations between any pair of variables while controlling for others. This time, however, nations' contribution in metric tons to global CO_2 emissions, and the percent tourism contributes to their GDP emerged as the most important determinants of countries' scores within our index of national governments' environmental prioritization (see Table 4). Again, the regression coefficients for these two aspects were statistically significant: 3.16e-07 (P<0.05), and .0315936 (P<0.10), respectively

Our regression analysis suggests that, while countries including environmental references in their e-government websites do not follow a clear

pattern in the construction of "green" agendas, there is a higher propensity among their governments to publicize environmental concerns if such nations have bad records in terms of air pollution and/or if tourism contributes substantial portion of their GDP. Not surprisingly, the top 15 nations in our *ENVINDEX* were together responsible for 53% of the global carbon dioxide emissions in 2006 (15 out of 28.4 billion of CO_2 metric tons[4]), and the average contribution of tourism to their GDPs is 10.3%[5].

The emergence of two different explanations for national governments' propensity to include "green matters" in their home web pages (one related to public image, and another to economic interests) underscores the complexities surrounding policy-makers' framing of controversial issues (Miller & Riechert, 2001; Schön & Rein, 1994), including approaches to the protection of the environment, as discussed in the next section of this article.

Table 2. Rank of nations within the environmental references index (ENVINDEX) - top 28 Cases (48 nations)

Country	ENVINDEX	Country	ENVINDEX
3 and above standard deviations		13. United Arab Emirates	1.757812
1. Philippines	3.050477	13. United States of America	1.757812
1. Sweden	3.050477	14. Chad	1.664011
Between 2 and 2.9 standard deviations		15. Belgium	1.48682
2. Malta	2.933074	16. Madagascar	1.37975
2. New Zealand	2.933074	16. Tunisia	1.37975
2. People's Republic of China	2.933074	17. Kiribati	1.278386
3. Singapore	2.555012	18. Bosnia Herzagovina	1.185803
4. Norway	2.538256	18. Oman	1.185803
5. Switzerland	2.538256	19. Mauritius	1.0684
6. Iceland	2.270033	**Between 0 and 0.9 standard deviations**	
7. Spain	2.176233	20. Gambia	.9745991
8. Bulgaria	2.160194	21. Denmark	.9003236
9. Australia	2.15263	22. Bhutan	.8835678
9. Germany	2.15263	22. Equatorial Guinea	.8835678
9. Nigeria	2.15263	22. United Kingdom	.8835678
10. Burundi	2.05883	23. Tanzania	.6903378
Between 1 and 1.9 standard deviations		24. Liechtenstein	.6735819
11. Canada	1.891971	24. Zimbabwe	.6735819
11. Egypt	1.891971	25. Cyprus	.5797812
12. Bangladesh	1.774568	26. France	.5055057
12. Belize	1.774568	27. Bahamas	.2955199
13. Czech Republic	1.757812	27. Cambodia	.2955199
13. Lesotho	1.757812	28. Argentina	.1941553
13. Myanmar	1.757812	28. Indonesia	.1941553
13. Pakistan	1.757812	28. Seychelles	.1941553

DISCUSSION AND CONCLUSION

Our study shows that, overall, prioritization of environmental issues, as measured by the inclusion and recurrence of allusions to the matter within national e-government websites, is still far from being a critical issue for most UN member states. As of 2009, not only nations that include at least one form of environmental reference in their main e-government portal or page constitute a minority in the world community, but the few that do it approach the subject from a diversity of conceptualizations, strategies and degrees of emphases, thus posing potential obstacles to the harmonization of global environmental initiatives.

In this sense, the governmental sector worldwide is lagging behind the corporate one in terms of highlighting environmental concerns as one of the major considerations in the articulation of its public agenda. As demonstrated by several studies, corporations are quickly adopting "green" discourses as part of a public image strategy

Table 3. Correlation between nations' individual scores within the nvironmental References Index (ENVINDEX) and selected variables

Variables	Correlation with ENVINDEX	P Value
GDP Per Capita (GDPPC)	0.30	0.000
Human Development Rank (HDRANK)	-0.23	0.002
E-government readiness index (EREADYINDEX)	0.31	0.000
Environmental Performance Index (EPI)	0.16	0.055
Contribution of Tourism to GDP (TOURISM)	0.002	0.974
Annual contribution, in metric tons, to global CO_2 emissions (CO2)	0.24	0.001

Table 4. Regression Analysis of the Environmental References Index (ENVINDEX)

	Coefficients	P Value
GDPPC	0.00002	0.136
TOURISM	0.03159	0.053
EPI	-0.01659	0.118
CO2 (metric tons)	3.16e-07	0.031
EREADYIND	0.79632	0.506
Constant	0.31382	0.560
Observations	135	
R^2	0.1951	

manifested in corporate responsibility statements posted on major private companies' websites (Esrock & Leichty, 1998; Mebus et al., 2008; Roberts, 1992). If such discourses do not always translate into concrete pro-environment actions, they at least fulfill the purpose of shedding a positive light over their articulators' image in a time of increasingly generalized recognition to

climate change problems and the negative impact of human action on the planet. Still, based on our results, it could be argued that a majority of national governments have not yet understood the potential PR benefits (not to mention many other concrete, positive externalities) of strategically framing environmental issues within the "radar screen" of policy and service priorities defined by their e-portals and sites.

Those nations including environmental reference in their e-government pages constitute a diverse mix of countries with diverging characteristics in terms of wealth, development, environmental track record, and degree of sophistication in government automation. Consequently, the relationship between these aspects and nations' propensity to publicly prioritize environmental concerns and initiatives in their e-government websites is not completely clear or straightforward. On the one hand, findings emerging from our correlation analyses suggest that a number of variables are positively associated with a country's nation's propensity to include environmental references in its e-government portal, but especially GDP per capita, stage of development of e-government systems (UN's e-government readiness index), and annual contribution to carbon emissions. On the other hand, results from our regression analyses reveal that, controlling for other variables, CO_2 emissions and impact of tourism on GDP are the only actual determinants of nations' inclusion of environmental references in their e-government websites.

Despite the different outcomes yielded by the correlation and regression analyses conducted for this study, we can draw some overarching inferences. Given the fact that CO_2 emissions emerged as an important variable in both analyses, it is possible to argue that many national governments, especially in countries with high production of global greenhouse gases, are beginning to include environmental allusions within their e-government websites as a way to "clean" their image, by framing environmental issues as top concerns in their agendas. In other words, while a only minority of nations put the environment at the foreground within their e-government pages, those who do it seem largely motivated by reasons that are similar to those behind many corporations' online statements on the matter (Mebus et al., 2008; Reichert et al., 2000). This could also explain the fact that allusion to specific policies and relevant agencies are the most frequent types of environmental references found in national e-government sites.

Moreover, the fact that GDP per capita and tourism contribution to GDP arose, respectively, as the strongest intervening variables in the correlation and regression analyses, lends additional credence to the pragmatic considerations that seem to underlie the prioritization of environmental concerns within national e-government home pages. First, some observers have proposed that wealthier countries are more able than poorer ones to dedicate resources and administrative capabilities to the protection of the environment (World Bank, 2006). Those capabilities include efficient automation of processes and development of effective information and knowledge systems, which would explain why e-government readiness index emerged as a statistically variable in the correlation analysis. Second, and regardless of wealth, the more reliant a nation's economy is on tourism, the more important it becomes for its government to adopt strategies and discourses aimed at the preservation and promotion of its physical and natural resources.

Implications for Framing Theory

In this sense, the results of our correlation and regression analyses corroborates Schön and Rein's (1994) conceptualization of framing as discursive practices that follow "design rationality," that is, a process of formulating representations of issues in ways that tries to combine the articulator's objectives and agenda, while also taking into account broader contextual elements. First, it is possible to argue that an institutional *logic of appropri-*

ateness (i.e., historically/geographically located expectations as to the role that different political agents, including the state, are to play in the face of public problems such as increasing air pollution), may be pushing some of the nations in our *ENVINDEX* ranking to at least show an explicit concern for the environment in their e-government sites. This seems plausible explanation for countries that: a) have reached a level of economic growth and development which places them in position of leadership regarding confrontation of global problems; b) make such a substantial contribution to global CO_2 emissions and thus are especially pressed to show disposition to also be "part of the solution;" c) are so dependent on their natural resources as sources of wealth that are especially pressured to preserve them; or d) any combination of the above.

Second, the different forms of environmental references found within the e-government sites analyzed in this study, signal the diversity of circumstances and contexts within which national governments initially formulate and then adjust their policy frames. Consequently, the absence of clear patterns in the profile of countries that include "green" references in their e-government portals may reflect different stages in governments' transitions from initial, tacit frames on the environment to explicit policy positions. Our findings in this regard seem consistent with Schön and Rein's (1994) "design rationality" proposed steps for settling policies on controversial issues such as environmentally sustainable development.

Initially presented as a normative exploration of frames, Schön and Rein's (1994) theory posses, in our view, explanatory value when it comes to understanding underlying cognitive and discursive constructions preceding the formulation of governmental positions and their explicit manifestation in policies, whether they are intended to improve a nation's public image or to improve its environmental track record. Thus, the apparently incoherent picture emerging from our analysis gets decoded through the lenses of framing theory as a collection of different junctures in nations' articulation of policy-making concerning the environment.

Limitations and Suggested Paths for Future Research

Beyond these initial readings, our findings should be assumed as exploratory ones. Among our study's limitations we can mention the fact that our assessment of environmental references was restricted to the home page of a highly diverse universe of national e-government websites. As the equivalent of a store's display window, we deem websites' home pages crucial in signaling the most important categories, functions, and issues among all the possible contents and paths to be found in deeper pages. However, different governments' communicational strategies and levels of expertise with digital technologies may determine that extensive or prominent environmental references get located in secondary pages within national e-governments' sites. Investigating those secondary pages may be a logic extension to this study.

Additionally, external variables not considered in this study (e.g. number of multilateral environmental treatises signed by each country, access to clean water, contribution to GDP by polluting and clean industries) might affect national governments' propensity to include environmental references in their electronic portals. Even the variables we took into account for this project posed certain challenges regarding uniformity, as different sources for data cover different universes (some include nations that are non-UN members, while others do not have data for all countries).

Finally, the dynamic nature of the World Wide Web and the growing involvement of countries in initiatives leading to electronic governance underscore the need for multiyear analyses on the subject explored by this study. Longitudinal studies on the matter have the potential of identifying both trends in the evolution of environmental issues in the agenda of national governments and underlying broader factors affecting their inclusion in e-government websites.

Although these questions and limitations insinuate new research paths related to the subject of this report, the preliminary inquiry we attempted on the intersection of e-government and environmental concerns contributes empirical evidence to claims about the alarming lack of attention to which the latter is still subjected at a global level. If, as corroborated by the United Nations through its annual e-government readiness reports, national priorities, governmental openness, and political will are reflected by e-government websites, our results reveal that environmental advocacy has a long road to cover before becoming part of the main agenda of nation-states' policymakers.

REFERENCES

Anderson, K. V., & Henriksen, H. Z. (2005). The first leg of e-government research: Domains and application areas 1998-2003. *International Journal of Electronic Government Research*, *1*(4), 26–44. doi:10.4018/jegr.2005100102

Bekkers, V., & Homburg, V. (2007). The myths of e-government: Looking beyond the assumptions of a new and better government. *The Information Society*, *23*(5), 373–382. doi:10.1080/01972240701572913

Brown, T. A. (2006). *Confirmatory factor analysis for applied research*. New York, NY: Guilford Press.

Campbell, D. (2003). Intra-and intersectoral effects in environmental disclosures: Evidence for legitimacy theory? *Business Strategy and the Environment*, *12*(6), 357–371. doi:10.1002/bse.375

Chen, Y. C., Chen, H. M., Ching, R. K. H., & Huang, W. W. (2007). Electronic government implementation: A comparison between develop and developing countries. *International Journal of Electronic Government Research, 3*(2), 45–61. doi:10.4018/jegr.2007040103

Chen, Y. C., & Dimitrova, D. V. (2006). Electronic government and online engagement: Citizen interaction with government via web portals. *International Journal of Electronic Government Research, 2*(1), 54–76. doi:10.4018/jegr.2006010104

Dawes, S. S. (2008). The evolution and continuing challenges of e-government. *Public Administration Review, 68,* 86–102. doi:10.1111/j.1540-6210.2008.00981.x

Deegan, C., & Gordon, B. (1996). A study of the environmental disclosure policies of Australian corporations. *Accounting and Business Review, 26*(3), 187–199. doi:10.1080/00014788.1996.9729510

Downing, J. D., & Brooten, L. (2007). ICTs and political movements. In Mansell, R., Avgerou, C., Quah, D., & Silverstone, R. (Eds.), *The Oxford handbook of information and communication technologies* (pp. 537–560). Oxford, UK: Oxford University Press.

Esrock, S. L., & Leichty, G. (1998). Social responsibility and corporate Web pages: Self-presentation or agenda-setting? *Public Relations Review, 24*(3). doi:10.1016/S0363-8111(99)80142-8

European Commission. (2008). *Progress on EU sustainable development strategy: Final report.* Retrieved from http://ec.europa.eu/sustainable/docs/sds_progress_report.pdf

Fountain, J. E. (2007). *Bureaucratic reform and e-government in the United States: An institutional perspective.* Retrieved from http://www.inst-informatica.pt/servicos/informacao-e-documentacao/biblioteca-digital/gestao-e-organizacao/EUA_07_006FountainBureauReform.pdf

Gitlin, T. (1980). *The whole world is watching: Mass media in the making and unmaking of the new left.* Berkeley, CA: University of California Press.

Heeks, R., & Bailur, S. (2007). Analyzing e-government research: Perspectives, philosophies, theories, methods, and practice. *Government Information Quarterly, 24*(2), 243–265. doi:10.1016/j.giq.2006.06.005

International Monetary Fund. (2009). *World economic outlook database.* Retrieved from http://www.imf.org/external/pubs/ft/weo/2009/01/weodata/index.aspx

Khor, A. K. H. (2009). *Social contract theory, legitimacy theory and corporate social and environmental disclosure policies: Constructing and theoretical framework.* Retrieved from http://www.docstoc.com/docs/3446392/Social-Contract-Theory-Legitimacy-Theory-and-Corporate-Social-and-Environmental

Lim, J. H., & Tang, S.-Y. (2007). Urban e-government initiatives and environmental decision performance in Korea. *Journal of Public Administration: Research and Theory, 18*(1), 109–138. doi:10.1093/jopart/mum005

Mahrer, H. (2005). Politicians as patrons for e-democracy? Closing the gap between ideals and realities. *International Journal of Electronic Government Research, 1*(3), 51–68. doi:10.4018/jegr.2005070104

McCombs, M., & Ghanem, S. I. (2001). The convergence of agenda setting and framing. In Reese, S. D., Gandy, O. H. Jr, & Grant, A. E. (Eds.), *Framing public life: Perspectives on media and our understanding of the social world* (pp. 67–81). Mahwah, NJ: Lawrence Erlbaum.

Mebus, A., Wiener, S., Buckheit, K., & Symmonds, J. (2008). *Corporate social responsibility and the fortune 100: Evidence for environmental themes.* Paper presented at the 2009 Conference of the National Communication Association, Chicago, IL.

Miller, M. M., & Riechert, B. P. (2001). The spiral of opportunity and frame resonance: Mapping the issue cycle in news and public discourse. In S. D. Reese O. H. Gandy Jr., & A. E. Grant, (Eds.), *Framing public life: Perspectives on media and our understanding of the social world* (pp. 107-122). Mahwah, NJ: Lawrence Erlbaum.

Monnoyer-Smith, L. (2006). Citizen's deliberation on the Internet: An exploratory study. *International Journal of Electronic Government Research, 2*(3), 58–74. doi:10.4018/jegr.2006070103

Navarra, D., & Cornford, T. (2003). A policy making view of e-government innovations in public government. In *Proceedings of the Americas Conference on Information Systems.*

Nelson, T. E., Clawson, R. A., & Oxley, Z. M. (1997). Toward a psychology of framing effects. *Political Behavior, 19*(3), 221–246. doi:10.1023/A:1024834831093

Norris, P., & Curtice, J. (2006). If you build a political web site, will they come? *International Journal of Electronic Government Research, 2*(2), 1–21. doi:10.4018/jegr.2006040101

Patten, D. (1991). Exposure, legitimacy and social disclosure. *Accounting, Organizations and Society, 10*(4), 297–308.

Patten, D. (1992). Intra-industry environmental disclosures in response to the Alaskan oil spill: a note on legitimacy theory. *Accounting, Organizations and Society, 17*(5), 471–475. doi:10.1016/0361-3682(92)90042-Q

Pina, V., Torres, L., & Royo, S. (2007). Are ICTs improving transparency and accountability in the EU regional and local governments? An empirical study. *Public Administration, 85*(2), 449–472. doi:10.1111/j.1467-9299.2007.00654.x

Qureshi, S. (2005). e-Government and IT policy: Choices for government outreach and policy making. *Information Technology for Development, 11*(2), 101–103. doi:10.1002/itdj.20006

Reese, S. D. (2003). Framing public life: A bridging model for media research. In Reese, S. D., Gandy, O. H. Jr, & Grant, A. E. (Eds.), *Framing public life: Perspectives on media and our understanding of the social world* (pp. 7–32). Mahwah, NJ: Lawrence Erlbaum.

Reichert, A. K., Webb, M. S., & Thomas, E. G. (2000). Corporate support for ethical and environmental policies: a financial management perspective. *Journal of Business Ethics, 25*(1), 53–65. doi:10.1023/A:1006078827535

Roberts, R. W. (1992). Determinants of corporate social responsibility disclosures: An application of stakeholder theory. *Accounting, Organizations and Society, 17*(6), 595–612. doi:10.1016/0361-3682(92)90015-K

Schön, D., & Rein, M. (1994). *Frame reflection: Toward the resolution of intractable policy controversies.* New York, NY: BasicBooks.

Snider, J., Hill, P. H., & Martin, D. (2003). Corporate social responsibility in the 21st century: A view from the world's most successful firms. *Journal of Business Ethics, 48*(2), 175–187. doi:10.1023/B:BUSI.0000004606.29523.db

Tankard, J. W., Hendrickson, L., Jr., Silberman, J., Bliss, K. A., & Ghanem, S. (1991, August). *Media frames: Approaches to conceptualization and measurement.* Paper presented at the Annual Conference of the Association for Education in Journalism and Mass Communication, Boston, MA.

Terwel, B. W., Harinck, F., Ellemers, N., & Daamen, D. D. L. (2009). How organizational motives and communications affect public trust in organizations: The case of carbon dioxide capture and storage. *Journal of Environmental Psychology, 29*(2), 290–299. doi:10.1016/j.jenvp.2008.11.004

United Nations. (2008). *UN e-government survey 2008: From e-government to connected governance.* Retrieved from http://unpan1.un.org/intradoc/groups/public/documents/un/unpan028607.pdf

United Nations. (n.d.). *Millennium development goals indicators (Countries' Contribution to CO_2 Global Emissions, in Metric Tons).* Retrieved from http://millenniumindicators.un.org/unsd/mdg/Data.aspx

United Nations Department for Economic and Social Affairs (UN-DESA). (2009). *Member states participating in the 17th session of the commission for sustainable development.* Retrieved from http://www.un.org/esa/dsd/csd/csd_csd17_membstat.shtml

United Nations Development Programme. (2007). *Human development report 2007/2008. Fighting climate change: Human solidarity in a divided world.* Retrieved from http://hdr.undp.org/en/media/HDR_20072008_EN_Complete.pdf

United Nations Development Programme. (2008). *Human development indices.* Retrieved from http://hdr.undp.org/en/media/HDI_2008_EN_Tables.pdf

United Nations Environment Program (UNEP). (2007). *Annual report.* Retrieved from http://unpan1.un.org/intradoc/groups/public/documents/un/unpan028607.pdf

West, D. M. (2008). *Improving technology utilization in electronic government around the world.* Retrieved from http://www.brookings.edu/~/media/Files/rc/reports/2008/0817_egovernment_west/0817_egovernment_west.pdf

Wilmshurtst, D. W., & Frost, G. R. (2000). Corporate environmental reporting: A test of legitimacy theory. *Accounting, Auditing & Accountability Journal, 13*(5), 667–681.

World Bank. (2006). *Where is the wealth of nations? Measuring capital for the 21st century.* Retrieved from http://siteresources.worldbank.org/INTEEI/214578-1110886258964/20748034/All.pdf

World Bank. (n.d.). *Data & statistics – country classification.* Retrieved from http://web.worldbank.org/wbsite/external/datastatistics/0,contentMDK:20420458~menuPK:64133156~pagePK:64133150~piPK:64133175~theSitePK:239419,00.html

World Travel & Tourism Council. (n.d.). *Tourism research – country reports.* Retrieved from http://www.wttc.org/eng/Tourism_Research/Tourism_Economic_Research/Country_Reports/

Yale and Columbia Universities. (2008). *Environmental performance index – country scores.* Retrieved from http://epi.yale.edu/CountryScores

Yildiz, M. (2007). E-government research: Reviewing the literature, limitations and ways forward. *Government Information Quarterly, 24*(3), 43–665. doi:10.1016/j.giq.2007.01.002

Zambrano, R. (2008). E-governance and development: Service delivery to empower the poor. *International Journal of Electronic Government Research, 4*(2), 1–11. doi:10.4018/jegr.2008040101

Zavetoski, S., & Shulman, S. W. (2002). The Internet and environmental decision-making: An introduction. *Organization & Environment, 15*(3), 323–327. doi:10.1177/1086026602153009

ENDNOTES

[1] On the one hand, critics have noted that, in most cases, the Internet operates merely as a traditional mass medium that facilitates summoning and one-to-many dissemination of information (Granjon, 2001, cited by Downing & Brooten, 2007). On the other hand, supporters of a more optimist perspective on the matter argue that evaluation of the role of the Internet in promoting political participation has been based on traditional normative models of an ideal public sphere that do not take into account new relational dynamics fostered by electronic ICTs (Mahrer, 2005; Monnoyer-Smith, 2006; Norris & Curtice, 2006). Authors in this camp suggest that the Internet and the spaces for interaction that it creates have opened new opportunities for cause-oriented activism, facilitated enrichment of social capital for political organizations, and expanded options available to citizens to articulate and communicate their views to governmental representatives (Monnoyer-Smith, 2006; Norris & Curtice, 2006). Beyond their broader impact on governance and democracy, it is clear that information and communication technologies leveraged by government officials and policymakers generate new, more complex relationships across agencies and with nongovernmental organizations that may lead to enhanced public accountability (Fountain, 2007).

[2] According to this theory, "...businesses are bound by the social contract in which the firms agree to perform various socially desired actions in return for approval of their objectives and other rewards, and this ultimately guarantee their continued existence..." (Khor, 2009, p. 2).

[3] The overall Kayser-Meyer-Olkin (KMO) statistic for the *ENVINDEX* factor is 0.7, with none of the factor's components showing a KMO below 0.6.

[4] According to data reported in 2007 by the U.S. Department of Energy's Carbon Dioxide Information Analysis Center (CDIAC).

[5] Based on estimates for 2009 by the World Travel & Tourism Council.

This work was previously published in the International Journal of Electronic Government Research, Volume 7, Issue 2, edited by Vishanth Weerakkody, pp. 78-95, copyright 2011 by IGI Publishing (an imprint of IGI Global).

Chapter 12
Towards a Design Rationale for Inclusive E-Government Services

Heiko Hornung
University of Campinas, Brazil

M. Cecília C. Baranauskas
University of Campinas, Brazil

ABSTRACT

The tendency of computer use spreading out into more and more areas of life has the potential to bring benefits to people's lives. Examples are electronic government services in areas such as public health or social assistance. The same phenomenon, however, could leave behind people who face different barriers regarding the access to those services, for example people with disabilities, low literacy or low computer skills. This work sheds light on the question of how to facilitate the interaction with those services considering people with diverse physical and intellectual conditions. This study analyzes design ideas utilized in four prototypes of a registration service and explored by user representatives. The results of this analysis inform a design rationale in order to support designers in making design decisions tailored to the respective application and social usage context.

1. INTRODUCTION

Information technology is becoming ubiquitous and is being diffused into more and more areas of life. Consequently, its audience is more diverse than ever, demanding special considerations re-garding the user interface and interaction design issues. Bødker (2006) used the term "the third wave of HCI (Human-Computer Interaction)" to discuss some of the related phenomena: whereas second wave HCI focused on work settings and users interacting in well-established communities

DOI: 10.4018/978-1-4666-2458-0.ch012

of practice, the focus of third-wave HCI shifts to computer use in private and public spaces, from workplaces to everyday life. A problem that arises with this third wave is that it might not reach all people, a problem that is also known as the digital divide. In order to cope with the digital divide, many initiatives are underway, often driven by government agencies (e.g. European Commission, 2006).

In developing countries, the gap between those who have access to information and those who have not is the widest. Two of the reasons are the high illiteracy rates and the limited access to information technology in these countries. In Brazil, for example, approximately 14% of the Brazilian people have some kind of impairment (auditory, visual, physical, etc. (IBGE, 2000)), 38% of the population have only basic literacy skills (i.e. are only capable of extracting information from short texts), 37% have no or rudimentary literacy skills (i.e. do not read at all or are only able to extract explicit information from very short texts, e.g. newspaper headlines (IPM, 2005)). In 2008, according to a survey of the Center of Studies about Information and Communication Technology, an agency responsible for producing indicators and statistics for the Brazilian Institute of Geography and Statistics, only 25% of Brazilian households possessed a computer. 61% of all Brazilians aged 10 or older had never accessed the Internet (CE-TIC, 2008). The high illiteracy rate and the large number of people with limited access to computers make the situation in Brazil significantly different from that in developed countries. Nevertheless, aligned with principles of Universal Design or Universal Accessibility (Stephanidis et al., 1998), the findings presented in this paper should also be useful for the context of developed countries.

In 2006, the Brazilian Computer Society (Sociedade Brasileira de Computação, SBC) addressed the problem of the digital divide defining one of the five Grand Challenges for the Brazilian Computer Science Research as: "Participative and Universal Access to Knowledge for the Brazilian Citizen" (SBC, 2006). One important facet of this challenge is related to HCI specific topics. In response to this challenge, this paper elaborates the question of how to design user interfaces that are accessible to our target audience, i.e. users with all kinds of competencies and needs, including low or no literacy skills and low or no computer skills. Even within the community of HCI practitioners, this question is still challenging.

Whereas one can find a substantial amount of literature about accessibility addressing the necessities of visually or physically impaired users, literature addressing the difficulties of users with low literacy skills hardly exists. Hornung et al. (2008) present some examples of relevant literature and point out the fact that existing solutions usually require a considerable amount of prior knowledge from the user, for example training in the use of a screen reader.

Electronic Government (eGovernment) services could make a difference in terms of promoting access to the digital world for those who are not yet connected. Consider the following scenario: today, a user of the Brazilian public health system has to go to one of the public health centers to schedule an appointment with a physician. Normally he or she has to wait in line for a couple of hours (or might even have to return the next day because the numbers have already run out) and gets his or her appointment marked for some days or weeks thereafter. In regions with a low population density, the trip to the health center alone requires considerable time and effort. The benefits of electronically scheduling an appointment on a public access terminal are obvious.

To reach this goal of promoting the access to digital information, an inclusive approach to web design is a necessary aspect to be considered, as these services must be made available to the entire community, including the elderly, those with disabilities, and individuals with a low level of education.

In this paper, we present and discuss results of observing people in the Brazilian scenario interacting with four disposable computer-based prototypes, which were designed for exploring user interface ideas considering access to technology by the less favored. We have also considered lessons already learned from other previous research on societal interfaces (Baranauskas et al., 2008; Neris et al., 2008). As a result, we constructed a design rationale to inform further interaction design of eGovernment applications.

The paper is organized as follows: the next section presents a synthesis of related work; it is followed by an overview of the scenario we are working with and a presentation of four user interface prototypes addressing different solutions for the interaction design; section 4 presents the results of our analysis of the users' interaction with the prototypes; section 5 discusses and summarizes the results in a design rationale; the last section concludes.

2. LITERATURE BACKGROUND

The multidisciplinary nature of eGovernment research involves various issues, ranging from technical to organizational, economical and social (Grönlund, 2005). Literature frequently uses the term "inclusive design" as synonymous of "universal design", having a focus on people with disabilities and the elderly, thus being concerned with creating accessible artifacts (e.g. Petrie & Edwards, 2006; Holzinger et al., 2008). Thus, accessibility is crucial for eGovernment systems in order to be effective, and various guidelines and specific techniques have been proposed as tools to guarantee accessibility (Thatcher et al., 2006). Articles and papers on accessibility in its classical sense abound with solutions to specific interaction difficulties of people; we thus refer to Hornung et al. (2008) for more examples.

The development and deployment of suitable Information Systems (IS) in the eGovernment context requires consideration of legal, cultural and social issues throughout the construction of these systems. Various countries have established national guidelines for the promotion of web accessibility. These are often based on the recommendations of the World Wide Web Consortium (W3C) (W3C, 2009). The United States, for example, developed Section 508 Standards (http://www.section508.gov/), whereas Brazil has developed a similar model (e-MAG – electronic government accessibility model; www.governoeletronico.gov.br/emag/). Moreover, a collection of usability principles and practices, laws and regulations for the US context, as well as case studies with lessons learned can be found at www.usability.gov.

These models provide recommendations for making information technologies accessible to people with disabilities, as well as encouraging the development and adaptation of information about the government for access on Internet. The recommendations suggest that web site developers should use semi-automatic accessibility tools to create and evaluate sites (e.g., daSilva (http://www.dasilva.org.br/), Cynthia Says (http://www.cynthiasays.com/), Lift (http://www.usablenet.com/usablenet_liftmachine.html), and Taw (http://www.tawdis.net/)), as well as assistive technologies to facilitate access by users with disabilities, such as the use of screen readers (e.g., Dosvox/Webvox (http://intervox.nce.ufrj.br/), JAWS (http://www.freedomscientific.com/), and Virtual Vision (http://www.micropower.com.br/v3/en/acessibilidade/index.asp)) to facilitate access by the blind.

Other recommendations are results of individual research efforts. Regarding the adequacy of the format of the visual representation (drawing vs. graphic art vs. photo-realistic or photographic images; black and white vs. grayscale vs. color; animation vs. video) Medhi et al. (2007) present some recommendations, but clearly there is no best solution or recipe for this question. The best characteristics of the visual representation seem to depend on the problem domain as well as on cultural aspects. Regardless of the format of the visual representation, not all information can be represented by static imagery or animations without spoken or signed content. Thus, videos or animations are crucial for users with low or no literacy skills as well as for the deaf and hard of hearing, especially if contents are presented in sign language.

When creating texts for the user interface, the designer can rely on guidelines from the literature. Examples include those for making interfaces accessible to users with low literacy skills (Huenerfauth, 2002) or to users with cognitive impairments (Sevilla et al., 2007). For some languages, "simple speech" guidelines exist (ILSMH European Association, 1998) that recommend not using subjunctive tense, only covering one main idea per sentence, or using practical examples, among others.

Leahy et al. (2003) investigated the effects of redundancy of textual, visual, and auditory information on short time memory and found that in certain configurations, more redundancy can actually lead to poorer performance. This effect depends on the complexity of the information, i.e. more complex information should be presented using complementary rather than redundant textual, visual, and auditory information.

In Hornung and Baranauskas (2007) we provide some pointers to discussions about recommendations like the Web Content Accessibility Guidelines or national regulations. Although those norms undoubtedly are necessary requirements, they are not sufficient. Goldkuhl (2007) gives an example where the design of a web-based service failed because local civil servants had a different understanding of the service in question than the citizens.

Concepts and methods have been adopted from Human-Computer Interaction (HCI) to provide better interfaces, and from Web Engineering to support design, development, evolution, and evaluation (Hitz et al., 2006; David & Henderson-Sellers, 2001). However, special efforts are still necessary if web application systems are to be designed to promote social inclusion and universal

accessibility for the population. Within the context of this paper, we therefore go beyond the classical view of accessibility towards an inclusive scenario that considers people with low literacy skills as well as people with low computer skills. Furthermore, our vision of inclusive design includes the whole cultural and social diversity of a society (Bonacin et al., 2009). Consequently, the term "accessibility" implies understandability or legibility, too. In order to cope with this extended view, it is necessary to widen the mere technical view to a socio-technical view as described by Hornung et al. (2008).

The Design Rationale based argument presented in this work uses the notation of Conklin's gIBIS (graphical Issue-Based Information System) which is in turn based on Kunz's and Rittel's IBIS (Issue-Based Information System; Conklin & Begeman, 1988). A discussion about a particular design problem starts with an issue (or question). For each issue, positions (or ideas) can be articulated that would resolve the issue.

Carroll and Rosson (2003) show how reflective HCI design practices such as the Design Rationale documentation and analysis increase the cohesion between theoretical concepts and the designed artifacts.

3. THE RESEARCH SCENARIO AND METHODOLOGY

Against the background of the Brazilian scenario, this study investigated how to enable and facilitate access to web based services. Potential users of those services included users with impairments as well as low or no literacy or computer skills. The focus on web-based services was a pragmatic choice: web or browser based services (accessible via computer/laptop or mobile devices with http and browser support) were the dominating type of services in Brazil and neither cell phone (via SMS/MMS or WAP) nor TV based services, nor kiosk based or other standalone applications had shown a significant market penetration.

The approach we took was to propose a design rationale based on the analysis of four prototypes of a simple registration service and the observations made during the interaction of end user representatives with those prototypes. The motivation for this approach came from the fact that due to different service types, usage scenarios and users' needs, different answers may have been valid to the questions we posed depending on the contextual situation. Thus, we proposed that a design rationale might provide a better support to the designer in making informed decisions.

The four prototypes were used during an activity with end user representatives recruited from Vila União, a low-income neighborhood in Campinas (a city in São Paulo State, Brazil). The activity was conducted in a telecenter as part of a research project called *e-Cidadania* (engl. e-Citizenship). The goal of this project was to propose solutions to the challenge of designing interaction and user interfaces in systems related to the exercise of citizenship (e-Cidadania, 2007). The project's methodology was based on the principles of Universal Design (Universal Design, 2009) and used methods and techniques from Organizational Semiotics (Liu, 2000), e.g. for the clarification of the problem and for system requirements elicitation. Since many characteristics of the target audience were unknown, it was considered crucial to embed all activities into the approach of Participatory Design (Schuler & Namioka, 1993; Muller et al., 1997). That way the problem statement for example was the result of a shared understanding of the problem considering concerns of all stakeholders. For a brief overview of the project and the methodology we refer to Baranauskas (2009). More details can be found in Hayashi and Baranauskas (2008).

Within the project, the research team worked together with a group of 15 end user representatives, eleven of whom participated in the activity of interacting with the prototypes. Considering the methodology inspired by Participatory Design, the project members found that 15 end user participants plus the team of five to ten researchers was about the maximum viable group size. The constitution of the group of users, as well as a preliminary description of requirements and design guidelines derived from the analysis of abilities of these users, have been described in Baranauskas et al. (2008) and Neris et al. (2008).

The eleven users who interacted with the four prototypes were given the task of registering themselves as new users of a fictitious telecenter using the four prototypes. After the interaction with each prototype, they were asked to fill in a simple form (did you register yourself successfully? was it easy? what did you like most? what did you like least?). A facilitator assisted users who were not comfortable writing on their own. The interactions took place in four different stations each of which was equipped with laptop, mouse, speaker boxes, web cam, microphone and the additional hardware necessary for the execution of the prototypes. At each station, a facilitator and observers were present taking notes. The users were asked to think aloud during the interaction with the prototypes. Additional comments could be made during a collective discussion round.

The interactions were recorded using a screen capture tool that also recorded web cam and microphone input. After each interaction with a prototype, the observers filled in a form registering quantitative (duration of interaction, successful registration) as well as qualitative data (which characteristics made the registration difficult/easy, did the user comment on anything, which strategy did the user employ, did any technical problems occur).

There was no time limit for the interactions and the users were instructed that they could quit at any time. The interaction times ranged from few seconds to 40 minutes, and not all users interacted with all prototypes.

The four prototypes presented in this paper were developed by four groups of three to four post-graduate students of a "Human Factors in Computer Science" discipline at the University of Campinas during the second semester of 2007, in order to experiment with design ideas suitable for the diversity we find in the Brazilian population. Before the activity of prototype creation, the students were appointed three tasks on the topics "Citizens' access to knowledge via technology: developing and developed countries", "Auditory memory: implications on the interaction model", and "Users with low literacy skills, visual or hearing impairments: solutions to access Information and Communication Technology". Each of the three tasks included a review of the relevant literature (refereed journals and conference papers of the past five years), the selection of one to three articles, and a presentation and discussion of the synthesized findings.

The design task was formulated as: "Consider the development of a web application for a telecenter in Brazil. The target users include illiterates, functional illiterates, digitally excluded, the elderly, and people with visual and hearing impairments. Propose a solution for the registration of the target users in the system". The creation of the prototypes was accompanied by in-class activities exercising methods of Participatory Design such as BrainWriting and BrainDrawing (Muller et al., 1997).

The service "telecenter registration" was chosen because of its relative simplicity, which allowed the students to focus on design ideas. According to the methodological frame of reference described above, the objective of the activity was, hence, not to do a comparative usability test of four telecenter registration prototypes, but to understand which design ideas utilized in the four prototypes actually made sense to the end user representatives. The four prototypes were chosen from a total of 16 prototypes, each prototype presenting some unique ideas regarding interaction styles and metaphors.

In the following sections we present the four prototypes and our analysis based on observations of the interaction of the end user representatives with the prototypes.

This prototype (cf. Figure 1) had a minimalist layout, similar in style to general web forms found in various sites throughout the Internet. It was composed of two areas: a header area with the logo of the fictitious telecenter and the title of the service ("Online Registration"), and a central area with a four column form. The first column of the form contained an image in each row, displaying a question mark within a speech bubble. A click on this image would open a pop-up window with context sensitive help, i.e. an explanation of the related form field. The second column contained the field labels, the third column the fields themselves. The last column of the form contained the stylized image of a loudspeaker in each row. A click on this image would "read out loud" the label of the associated form field.

The form had five rows for the fields "name", "date of birth", "ID", "CPF" (Brazilian tax identification number), and "address". The date of birth was split up into three form fields with the labels "day", "month" and "year". The last row of the form contained two image buttons, one with the image of an upright thumb and the label "send" in uppercase letters and one with a twisted arrow pointing to the left (similar to the undo button in many desktop applications) and the label "cancel", also in uppercase letters. The "thumbs up" gesture is widely used in Brazil as a sign of approval or "everything is fine, OK".

The pop-up window (cf. Figure 2) with context sensitive help contained a short text of no more than 15 words explaining which data has to be filled in, an image of a document where this data can be found (e.g. the Brazilian ID card with a highlighted date of birth or an electricity bill with a box highlighting the address field). On opening the pop-up window, an audio file would play, reading the explanatory short text. The audio file could be replayed by clicking on the loudspeaker image.

A click on the "send" button would display a message asking for confirmation and a non-edit-

Figure 1. Prototype 1: Minimalist web form (translated from Portuguese)

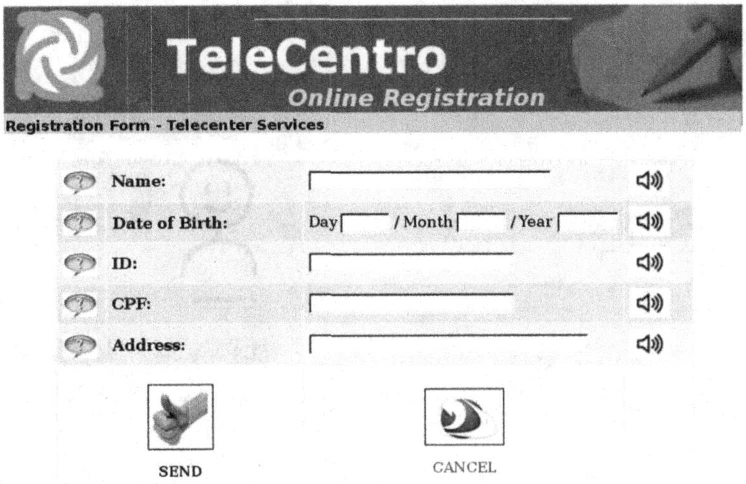

able form displaying the data entered by the user. This form did not contain the help or loudspeaker column. It contained two image buttons, one with the image of an upright thumb and the label "confirm" and the other with the cancel button identical to the previous form. A click on the "confirm" button would open an OK dialog box with the message "data registered with success". A click on the "cancel" button would return to the previous form.

Navigation was possible via both mouse and keyboard ("tab" and "enter"). The prototype did not feature video in sign language but tried to assist deaf people through images with the context sensitive help.

The layout of the second prototype (cf. Figure 3) was similar in style to that of content management systems. The header area contained the logo of the fictitious telecenter, a horizontal navigation bar, and an accessibility bar with breadcrumb links and buttons to increase or decrease the font size. A footer contained copyright information. The central area was made up of two parts, the left part – the service content area – where the actual

Figure 2. Prototype 1: Context-sensitive help in pop-up window (translated from Portuguese)

Figure 3. Prototype 2: Registration wizard (translated from Portuguese)

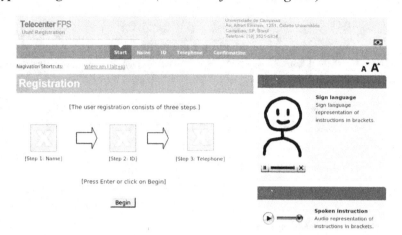

service execution (the registration) would take place and the right part – the media area – that contained redundant audio or video presentations of content in the service content area along with controls to pause/continue video and audio files. The navigation bar contained one item for each step of the registration process: start, name, ID, phone, and confirmation. The initial page (step "start") showed a graphic representation of the main steps of this process. The current step would be highlighted in the navigation bar; non-mandatory fields could be skipped via a "skip" button, although navigation between steps was not possible.

On loading a page, a corresponding video in sign language and an audio message were played back automatically. The video explained the current step (e.g. "type your name and hit 'enter' or click on 'continue'"), i.e. each step had exactly one associated video in sign language. With exception of the final confirmation step, each step also had exactly one associated audio file that would be played back upon loading the page and could be replayed by clicking on the play button of the audio control in the media area.

During each step, only one token of information was requested. An exception was the confirmation page, where all values could be edited "inline": the page contained a table of all previously filled-in fields in rows of three columns (field label, field content, "alter" button). Initially, the field contents were read-only. On clicking the "alter" button, the field content would change into an editable text box and the "alter" button would become a "confirm" button. Navigation in the prototype was possible via mouse or keyboard ("tab", "enter", and some keyboard shortcuts like "alt" + "o" to change the focus to the breadcrumb links).

The basic layout of the third prototype (Figure 4) consisted of a header with the service title, image representations of the registration steps, and buttons to increase or decrease the font size and toggle the screen colors between the regular and a high contrast version. The central content area was composed of 3 lines. The first line contained a short instruction for the user (e.g. "type your name"), the second line contained the "interaction area" with text fields, click buttons, etc. and the third line contained images or animations with hints regarding the execution of the current step. Below the central content area, a one-line footer contained copyright information. Each sentence on the screen had an associated image of a loudspeaker, which would "read" the respective sentence on a click.

On loading a page, the audio file corresponding to the sentence in the first line of the central content area would play back automatically. The

Figure 4. Prototype 3: Assistive registration with additional hardware (translated from Portuguese)

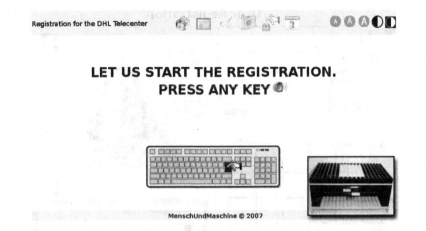

interface did not contain audio controls, i.e. for (re-)playing an audio file, the user had to click on the respective loudspeaker. The prototype used additional hardware and software to facilitate the registration process, namely a scanner with OCR software to read information from an ID card or utility bill, a web cam to take a picture of the registrant, and a fingerprint reader to substitute a text based password. Furthermore, colored stickers were affixed to the main function keys of the keyboard: a green sticker to the "S" key (port. "sim", engl. "yes" to confirm), a red one to "N" (port. "não", engl. "no" to negate), and a blue one on "Enter". The colors of the stickers on the keyboard matched the colors used on the screen.

As in the second prototype, only one token of information was requested during each step. In contrast to prototype 2, the user had to confirm each piece of information before continuing to the next step. Alternatively, the user could return exactly one step to correct the single still unconfirmed piece of information. During the last step, a summary of all registered information was displayed.

Navigation was possible via mouse and keyboard ("enter", "s" and "n"), whereas the valid keys were always made explicit in the user interface via a graphical animation of a hand pressing the respective keys on a keyboard. The prototype did not feature videos in sign language. Instead, it tried to use graphical animations whenever possible (e.g. the message "put your right thumb on the reader" was represented by the animation of a thumb being put onto the fingerprint reader where a photo of the "real" reader was used).

The last prototype had a tiled layout of four areas in two rows and two columns (cf. Figure 5). The uppermost left area – the content area – contained the fields to be filled in by the user. The uppermost right area contained the video area, the lower two areas contained an on-screen keyboard and video caption respectively. All areas except the content area could be collapsed and would show a miniature view of their contents in the collapsed state.

To register on this prototype, only the fields "name" and "personal ID" were required. These were presented in the content area in two rows and a "<field label>: <text field>" format. The fields could be filled-in using the regular or the on-screen keyboard. Below the input fields, a "delete" button could be used to delete the character before the cursor, and a "confirm" button could be used to conclude the registration. A click on this button would result in the confirmation page that displayed the registered information with a big image of a check mark along with a video that played a confirmation message. As an alternative to typing his or her name and per-

Figure 5. Prototype 4: Registration kiosk (translated from Portuguese)

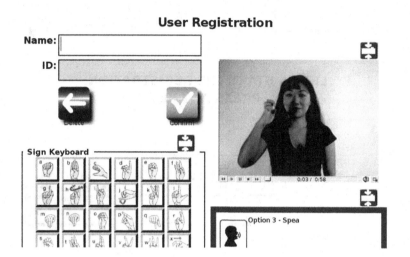

sonal ID, the user could also register his or her fingerprint on a fingerprint reader or speak his or her name out loud.

The videos of the prototype were in signed Portuguese with synchronized spoken language. Signed Portuguese differs from the Brazilian Sign Language insofar as it is an almost one-to-one translation of uttered words into signs and therefore generally does not follow the grammar of the Brazilian Sign Language. The video could be replayed using the video controls of the browser plug-in. The caption was synchronized to the video, i.e. written on the screen as the voice in the video would "speak". Since the caption area was restricted, only the caption associated with the current sentence of the video voice would be displayed.

The on-screen keyboard had an ABCDE layout instead of QWERT. The reasoning behind this was to facilitate typing for users without computer (or typewriter) experience but who had at least a basic notion of the alphabet. On the other hand, people used to the QWERT layout might have shown a decrease in performance. Each key contained a lowercase letter or digit and the corresponding sign of the Brazilian manual alphabet. The keyboard could only be used with the mouse. On clicking a key of the on-screen keyboard, the same image

of the key (letter with sign) would appear in the currently active text field of the content area. On hitting a key on the regular keyboard, the display would switch to character-only and vice versa. Navigation was possible using the regular keyboard ("tab" and "enter") or the mouse.

4. RESULTS OF ANALYZING THE INTERACTION WITH THE PROTOTYPES

Since we did not intend to conduct a quantitative analysis nor a comparable evaluation of the prototypes, we will present the results in a summarized and commented form and only refer to a specific prototype if a particular feature that is not present in other prototypes had a significant effect on the interaction. Our analysis considers all collected data: the questionnaires filled in by each user for each prototype, the observation forms from each observer for each user and prototype, as well as the recorded videos, screen casts and comments during the final discussion round. We will not discuss aspects already covered by our analysis in the previous section or by common accessibility or usability guidelines (Nielsen, 1993; W3C, 2009).

As expected, some of the difficulties we observed are related to the users' lack of skills with computers. We could observe this with peripheral devices (keyboard, mouse), as well as with user interface elements considered as basic knowledge (e.g. scroll bars, OK dialog boxes). Regarding mouse pointing, some users required great efforts to move the mouse pointer to a desired area on the screen. As to clicking, some users clicked the left button firmly which resulted in a mouse movement, which in turn resulted in marking texts or images on the screen, or clicked the right button, which caused confusion when the context menu opened. The latter effect could be avoided disabling the right mouse button for the respective service.

Besides the mouse, users also had difficulties in using the keyboard. Some users pressed keys forcefully, and would hold down the key, which resulted in repetitions of the associated character, an effect that could be avoided turning off keyboard repeat. Other users got confused after accidentally pressing the CAPSLOCK key or did not know the backspace key or the space bar functions.

Another observation in this context is that many of the users with no computer experience did not look at the screen when typing. Thus, they did not perceive key repetition, typos, or the fact that the cursor was not positioned in the form field they wanted to fill.

Regarding interface elements, users with no computer experience had difficulty using scroll bars, e.g. they did not perceive the scroll bar on the right side of the screen and thus did not access content outside the visible area of the screen. Other problems occurred with dialog boxes, even if they only had one button, and with pop-up windows. Scroll bar and dialog box problems were directly related to mouse handling problems. The pop-up window problem, however, occurred because the users did not perceive that they could return by closing this window. Thus, we do not recommend the use of pop-ups. Finally some users got confused because the browser's form input history was not cleared between the interactions of two different users.

Some of the problems we just mentioned could be prevented by disabling or reconfiguring certain keyboard or mouse features. However, this could have a negative effect on users who already have some familiarity with computers and expect a certain behavior from peripheral devices or user interface elements.

Another example where simplifications intended to support users with no experience might negatively affect the interaction of users with more experience is related to filling in form fields. Users with some experience expected an input validation or a hint regarding the input format (e.g. personal ID with or without dots and dashes). When presenting fields with the labels "name" or "address", these users were uncertain if they were supposed to fill in first name and last name and or which components of the address they should provide. Furthermore they were uncertain if they were allowed to use upper and lower case letters and accents. However, we could not determine whether this behavior occurred because they recalled a web application that only accepted input without accents or because they remembered filling in a paper form. This observation is an indication that it is important for designers to be aware of real life experiences of users and the effect on the interaction with computer based services.

A similar immediate phenomenon was observed regarding the mutual effects of previous experience and interaction with the prototypes. Users who interacted with a prototype after having experimented prototype 3 (the one with color stickers on the keyboard), tried to use the "enter" key to proceed to the next step. Furthermore, possibly because prototype 3 established a strong mapping between colors and buttons in the interface and keys on the keyboard, users who interacted with other prototypes were looking for "start" and "confirm" keys on the keyboard. Thus, establishing strong conventions in one interface will have effects on the interaction with other interfaces. On the other hand, this shows that users with no computer experience can quickly adapt to conventions. Thus, on the background of the digital divide, we recommend following some already established conventions regarding the current state of the art in interface design.

With regard to assistive techniques, we observed that many users did not perceive the context sensitive help of prototype 1. Thus, we recommend using inline help within the interface or strongly emphasize interface elements that provide help. In general, the users liked to have different possibilities to conclude the registration. However, one user expressed his dislike of the fingerprint reader. Since user acceptance and trust are very important in electronic Government services, this issue should be further investigated. Some users were uncertain if their registration really had been successful, even when the interface presented a confirmation message. Therefore, regarding electronic government services, we recommend the possibility of printing out important messages (confirmation messages, order/process status, etc.).

An observation that may not seem very significant at first is that the users enjoyed having their photo taken in prototype 3. In the spirit of Bødker's (2006) third wave of HCI and the research on the digital divide, it is important to promote affective relations that motivate the user to interact with the interface and, more importantly, to come back again.

Strategies that the users adopted to execute the task of registering themselves at the fictitious telecenter included: asking the facilitator, using the embedded audio files and searching for icons related to the desired task. The strategy of asking the facilitator emphasizes the importance of trained personnel at the telecenters to assist the end users. These telecenter personnel need to have the required skills regarding the offered electronic services, and need to be aware of the users' different special needs. Finally, regarding the other two mentioned strategies – using embed-

ded audio and searching for related icons – the users expressed their preference for prototypes that enabled interaction without the need to write and that offered embedded audio or visual representations that minimized the need to read. Although the users would perhaps be able to use these interfaces, successfully using the (electronic) government services, we do not recommend text-free interfaces or interfaces without any text input. From the point of view of digital inclusion not much would have been achieved, as they would be restricted to these types of interfaces.

5. DISCUSSION

Regarding multimedia content, all prototypes made use of different media in an attempt to make content accessible or legible to users with different special needs. Visual media used in the prototypes were images, animations and videos, while some animations and videos were featured in sign language. Since none of these media were created by professional graphic designers or video artists, we do not evaluate the created artwork, but analyze the underlying ideas.

Determining which non-textual elements are best-suited for certain kinds of users, which textual elements should be represented by other types of media, as well as the phrasing of textual elements, are additional design activities that are outside the scope of this paper. Since the four prototypes differ significantly from each other and since the intersection of interface elements that can be mapped to identical functions (e.g. "cancel", "submit") is very small, the simplification of not evaluating artwork does not limit the validity of our results.

Kennaway et al. (2007) compare signing avatars with videos in sign language and reach the conclusion that signing avatars have significant advantages over videos in sign language. Yet, cultural aspects also have to be considered: our own activities with end user representatives have shown that they prefer videos with "real" people. However, further investigations will have to be undertaken to examine if this preference would impose a barrier to the interaction with an animated avatar. As to the question of providing synchronized videos with signed Portuguese or a video in spoken Portuguese for the hearing and a video in Brazilian Sign Language for the deaf and hard of hearing, the latter version is more adequate. The syntax of spoken Portuguese and LIBRAS differ significantly, and facial expression, which differs from the lip movement of a spoken word, is an integral component of LIBRAS. Regarding the visual design, both videos can be displayed side-by-side or one within the other, if the screen size permits.

Regarding the representation of audio information, we can choose between concrete sounds, abstract sounds, natural speech and synthesized speech. In the context of eGovernment services, concrete sounds will be inapplicable most of the time (what sound does a tax declaration make?). Regarding abstract sounds, Brewster proposed "earcons" – "auditory icons" – as a technique to, for example, facilitate navigation in menus (Brewster, 1998). While this is certainly a very interesting technique, the benefits for eGovernment services would be limited, since many eGovernment services will only be executed occasionally and abstract sounds are hard to remember if not constantly used.

The use of natural vs. synthesized language finally depends on similar criteria as in the choice of the video format. Considering the user representatives preference towards videos with real people, our practice with the prototypes has surprisingly shown a high acceptance of synthesized speech. Since many of the user representatives had not been exposed to the idea of a computer actually "speaking to them" before; this acceptance rate may be biased by the novelty and further investigations are recommended.

All the prototypes tried to minimize the quantity of text on the screen. Prototypes 1 and 4 used only short field labels in the content area and longer texts in the context sensitive help or in the caption area respectively. Prototypes 2 and 3 tried to use relatively simple sentences with few pieces of information per sentence. Nevertheless, the simplification of the vocabulary may be treated cautiously as it could negatively affect credibility and trust, two important requirements for eGovernment services.

Regarding the display of video captions, it has to be evaluated if these should be used in the same way as television captions or if all text should stay visible all the time in a separate area of the interface. The latter option has two advantages. Users with low literacy skills could try to read the captions but fail because of their slow reading. If the text stays visible until the user chooses another video, users will be able to read the text without haste. The other advantage is that users with better literacy skills will be able to consult the text on the screen instead of being forced to replay the corresponding video in order to look up information that already slipped their auditory memory. A possibility to make the caption more useful to users with low literacy skills is to highlight the text in a karaoke-like manner synchronized to the spoken text.

There are important questions that should be answered before editing texts, videos, or recorded or synchronized audio files, for example: Does the vocabulary have to be localized for users from different regions? Does spoken text have to be adapted in order to reflect regional dialects? Should texts be spoken or synthesized by female or male speakers or using female or male synthesizer voices? Should all texts be spoken by the same speaker? Are different sets of texts required in order to reflect differences between spoken and written language?

Regarding the redundancy of textual, visual and auditory information found in the prototypes, it is not yet clear how the method to measure information complexity presented by Leahy et al. (2003) can be generalized to web based electronic government services, nor if the threshold at which complementary information outperforms redundant information depends on the user profile. We believe however, that redundancy of textual, visual and auditory information could increase the accessibility or intelligibility of a given written text for users with low literacy skills, as well as for the deaf and hard of hearing. Thus, the complexity of information has to be kept sufficiently low.

Beyond common accessibility features like breadcrumb links, font size and contrast changing, the following assistive techniques were offered in the four prototypes: images, photos, animations, videos in Portuguese, videos in Brazilian Sign Language, audio files, simplified vocabulary, cursor focus on first form field, keyboard navigation, request one chunk per screen, on-screen keyboard, inline help, biometric identification or authentication (voice recognition, fingerprint reading), scanner with optical character recognition (OCR) software, character deletion with mouse, visible process.

"Cursor focus on first form field" means that, on loading a new page, the focus of the cursor is automatically set on the first form field on the screen. Regarding the amount of information the user needs to provide, prototypes 2 and 3 request only one chunk per screen whereas prototypes 1 and 4 request multiple chunks, where one chunk can be composed of multiple form fields (e.g. date of birth). "Inline help" means the display of context sensitive help within the same page (e.g. prototype 4) as opposed to the display in a separate window (e.g. prototype 1). "Scanner with OCR software" does not simply mean the existence of the respective hardware device, but emphasizes that it is employed to assist the user in filling in the different form fields. "Visible process" in this case means that the different steps of the registration process are visualized on the screen, for example by a sequence of step labels or images in prototypes 2 or 3 respectively. Since it is difficult, if not impossible, to select images that carry the same meaning to all users, the approach of using additional text labels as in prototype 2 is preferable over the image-only approach of prototype 3.

It should be noted that some techniques that address certain special needs could have a negative effect on other special needs. Automatically starting audio or video playback will interfere with the use of a screen reader. The technique of only requiring one chunk of information per screen could have a negative impact on the performance of more experienced users with sufficient literacy skills, although those users would still be able to execute the respective service. This type of interest conflict could be resolved by user interface tailoring; further analysis of this topic is out of the scope of this paper.

Some techniques are also highly application dependent. For a registration service which will only be executed once by every user, requiring one chunk of information per screen may be adequate; however, this technique is perhaps not applicable to services that are executed repeatedly (e.g. searching articles that meet a set of criteria (topic, date, author, etc.) in an online library).

Many of the aspects discussed above require trade-off decisions that depend on the concrete service or application and the scenario into which this service has to be deployed. The format of a design rationale may support the designer in taking these decisions. In contrast to a design rationale about a concrete product, the design rationale presented here discusses abstract and invariant aspects of design issues present in eGovernment services.

In order to increase the reusability and the understandability of our rationale, we opted for using only the basic constructs of Conklin's and Begeman's (1988) gIBIS: issues, positions, and arguments. The positions do not have to be mutually exclusive, and each position may have one or more arguments that support (+) or refute (-) that position.

Because of the spatial limits of this paper, we chose a tabular instead of a graphical presentation (cf. Table 1). Moreover, we do not repeat recommendations made in the previous sections, but only mention issues that require further reflection.

Table 1. The Design Rationale

Issue	Position	Argument
Service identifica-tion and authenticity	Use official logos and ser-vice names/descriptions	+ users will recognize that they are in a government site + increase users' trust − service descriptions are often written in a language that is not well understood by the users − not all government agencies/services have logos that are known to the user − the knowledge about off-line services that use the same logo might have a negative effect, if on-line and off-line processes differ or if the off-line process has a low user acceptance
	Create logos and service descriptions using methods of participatory design	+ logos for not-so-well-known services will make more sense + develop a vocabulary of terms that can be understood by the users + simplified descriptions may yield a better understanding − oversimplified descriptions can have a negative impact on trust − replacing well established logos may confuse users
	Use SSL certificates	+ increase trust − users with no computer experience could get confused by browser messages (e.g. "this page contains unsafe objects", "certificate expired", etc.)
Process	Display the location within a process in a format simi-lar to a progress bar	+ easy identification of the current location within the process − a progress bar (e.g. "40%" or "step 2 of 5") could be meaningless for users with low computer experience
	Use images to represent steps of a process	+ users with low literacy skills will be able to identify their location within the process − for eGovernment processes, significant images could be hard to find − users with visual impairments will not be able to identify their location just by listening to image descriptions
Images, video and audio files	Use different media redundantly to textual information	+ users, especially those with low literacy skills, can rely on multiple sources to comprehend information − depending on the task complexity, redundancy can have a negative impact on the performance of users with sufficient literacy skills − users of screen readers could be annoyed by redundant information (i.e. when the screen reader reads text and image descriptions that contain the same informa-tion)
	Use media as complemen-tary information to textual information	+ achieve better performance for services with higher task complexity − users cannot construct their understanding anymore easily using redundant representations, because they have to interpret all pieces of complementary information correctly
	Use media to substitute texts	− not always possible to find meaningful images − loss of trust by users with sufficient reading skills because of apparent oversim-plification − manifest exclusion of people with low literacy skills and computer experience, because they will not be able to "grow" and use other text-based services
	On loading a new page, automatically play default audio or video file	+ good assistive technique for users with low literacy skills − experienced users with sufficient reading skills could be annoyed
Login/User authen-tication	Use user name/password or similar data and standard login mechanisms	+ users with low computer experience can get used to standard login mechanisms widely found in the internet − user name and password might not make sense to users with low computer experience − password recovery mechanisms (e.g. send new password to e-mail address) could not work (e.g. user does not have e-mail address, nor does s/he know how to use an e-mail client) − if services are not used on a frequent basis, the user might forget the password

continued on following page

Table 1. Continued

Issue	Position	Argument
	Use physical access tokens (e.g. smart card)	± enable service use by a proxy (e.g. child or other relative) − danger of abuse if these tokens are the only means of authentication − if services are not used on a frequent basis, higher probability of loss of access token − necessary hardware might not be available at all access points
	Use biometric methods	+ lower probability of abuse ± no use by proxies − negative effect on acceptance because of privacy concerns (e.g. fingerprint scanned by government agency; stigmata of using fingerprint in some subcultures) − necessary hardware might not be available at all access points
Data entry	Use scanner/OCR software, barcode readers	+ users with low literacy skills will be able to enter data − scanning data from private documents can conflict with the user's privacy − the necessary hardware might not be available at the user's home, nor in all telecenters
	Instead of using scanners, etc., offer visual hints, e.g. an image of a utility bill with a highlighted address area	+ users with low literacy skills could be able to copy simple data like name, telephone or address + users with low computer skills can familiarize themselves with the keyboard which will help them using other applications − users with no computer skills could not know keys like backspace, space, shift, etc.
	Request one chunk of information per screen	+ supports users with low literacy or computer skills, who could be intimidated by big forms − negative effect on performance of experienced and frequent users
	Request multiple chunks per screen, but try to not exceed the size of the visible screen, avoiding scroll bars	+ good compromise between "one chunk per screen" and "one screen only" − users could get confused if unrelated chunks of data are requested on the same screen − considering users with low literacy skills, it is not clear how to determine the optimal number of chunks per screen
	Display chunks on the same screen as they are requested (e.g. with AJAX)	+ users will have an overview of what they have already entered + the current chunk can be clearly highlighted − unclear how to ensure accessibility for users with visual or cognitive impairments

"Service identification and authenticity" in Table 1 addresses the question of how users can identify that they actually are executing the eGovernment service that they want. Many eGovernment services are procedurally organized. "Process" deals with the question of how to communicate the information of what steps are required to execute the process, which steps have already been done, etc. The issue "Images, video and audio files" deals with the use of different media on a web page, "Login/User authentication" relates to the different possibilities to authenticate the user. Finally, "Data entry" deals with possi-

bilities of how to facilitate the entry of data by users.

Considering the issue "Service identification and authenticity", the question of trust has been discussed by Garcia et al. (2005); for the use of logos, some lessons learned can be found at www.usability.gov. The arguments regarding redundancy of images, videos and audio files follow the results of Leahy et al. (2003). The use of biometric identification devices, for example, has been discussed in eGovernment related literature (Hornung et al., 2008) and was commented by some of the end user representatives. The other issues and arguments in Table 1 can be traced back to the prototype analysis.

Some of the issues presented in Table 1 can be answered differently depending on the particular context we are designing for. Regarding data entry, the scanning of an income declaration issued by the employer would certainly facilitate the income tax declaration, whereas the scanning of a phone or utility bill in order to complete a registration process would unnecessarily capture private data that could lower user acceptance. In some cases, the evaluation, whether an argument is in favor or against a certain position, depends on the policies or norms within the context of the application (e.g. enabling applications to be used by proxies; arguments marked with "±").

One challenge is to determine the context and the set of policies or norms. Regarding the arguments marked with "±", from the point of view of a government agency, enabling a service for use by proxies is generally undesirable because authenticity is compromised. From the end user perspective, it could be desirable to authorize another person to execute a certain service, e.g. a person with low mobility and no computer access at home might want to ask a neighbor to get a status update of a process. While this scenario might uncover and result in a redesign of an overly complicated authorization process, it might also result in the decision to allow the execution of certain services by proxies and thus increase user acceptance.

Design decisions usually require compromises to be made. Issues that have contradicting positions (e.g. "Data entry"), several of which would favor certain user competencies, impose challenges on interface flexibility (e.g. how to present data entry forms for users with different special needs considering the principles of Universal Design). The example of service use by proxies shows that design decisions should be informed by socio-technical approaches like the one previously outlined.

6. CONCLUSION

Whereas there exists a substantial amount of literature addressing accessibility for visually and physically impaired users, there is hardly any literature about interface solutions for users with low literacy skills. This issue is especially relevant for the context of eGovernment applications in countries with a huge diversity in users' capacities and skills regarding the access to information through technology. While this is a fundamental problem in developing countries, it is also a relevant problem in developed societies which, for example, have to provide eGovernment access for immigrants.

This paper has analyzed the problem using the Brazilian scenario of diversity of users as a way of facing the challenge proposed by the Brazilian Computer Society regarding the "participatory and universal access to knowledge for the Brazilian citizen". We looked at the problem and investigated potential solutions under the interaction design and interface features perspective. The study investigated different types of interaction styles and user interface features necessary for access by the target audience of people with low digital and functional literacy, to very basic information services. Our intent was to shed light on the user interface issues the designer must cope with when designing eGovernment systems. The additional challenge comes from the fact that an eGovernment application must be for everyone, including those already living in the digital world.

We have shown how the design of a registration service, informed by literature findings related to issues on societal interfaces, can be used by representative users in the research scenario. Based on the analysis of the interaction of end user representatives with four low-fidelity but executable prototypes, this paper presented an abstract Design Rationale for inclusive eGovernment services. We chose to represent our findings through a Design Rationale, instead of a set of design guidelines, as it supports and more directly expresses context-dependent design decisions. Moreover, our goal was not to communicate concrete design decisions, but to support designers in their process of reflecting about alternatives and deciding which alternatives are the most suitable in their respective social contexts and problem domains. The Design Rationale showed useful as it leads to considerations about solutions to the interaction design that make sense to the target audience within a given service domain, while a set of fixed guidelines cannot always sufficiently consider the concrete societal and cultural contexts.

The Design Rationale presented was applied to the design of eGovernment services currently in use, and is now informing the design of *Vila na Rede* - an inclusive social network system (Hayashi et al., 2009) for citizenship in our country.

ACKNOWLEDGMENT

We thank the authors of the prototypes – Diego Samir Melo Solarte, Eduardo Machado Gonçalves, Elaine Hayashi, Fabio Ivasse, Igor José F. Freitas, Leonardo Cunha, Leonello Dell Anhol Almeida, Paulo Gurgel, Pedro Almeida, Ricardo Caceffo, Samer Eberlin, Vagner Santana – and our colleagues from NIED, InterHAD and IC/ Unicamp. This work has been funded by Microsoft Research – FAPESP Institute for IT research (grant #2007/54564-1) and CAPES (process #01-P-08503/2008).

REFERENCES

W3C. (2009). *Web accessibility initiative (WAI)*. Retrieved from http://www.w3.org/WAI/

Baranauskas, M. C. C. (2009). Socially aware computing. In *Proceedings of the 6th International Conference on Engineering and Computer Education*, Buenos Aires, Argentina.

Baranauskas, M. C. C., Hornung, H., & Martins, M. C. (2008). Design Socialmente Responsável: Desafios de Interface de Usuário no Contexto Brasileiro. In *Proceedings of the 35th Seminário Integrado de Software e Hardware*, Porto Alegre, Brazil (pp. 91-105).

Bødker, S. (2006). When second wave HCI meets third wave challenges. In *Proceedings of the 4th Nordic Conference on Human-Computer Interaction* (pp. 1-8). New York, NY: ACM Press.

Bonacin, R., Melo, A. M., Simoni, C. A. C., & Baranauskas, M. C. C. (2009). Accessibility and interoperability in e-gov systems: Outlining an inclusive development process. *Universal Access in the Information Society*, *9*(1), 17–33. doi:10.1007/s10209-009-0157-0

Brewster, S. A. (1998). Using non-speech sounds to provide navigation cues. *ACM Transactions on Computer-Human Interaction*, *5*(3), 224–259. doi:10.1145/292834.292839

Carrol, J. M., & Rosson, M. B. (2003). Design rationale as theory. In Carrol, J. M. (Ed.), *HCI models, theories and frameworks: Toward a multidisciplinary science* (pp. 431–461). San Francisco, CA: Morgan Kaufmann. doi:10.1016/B978-155860808-5/50015-0

CETIC. (2008). *Centro de Estudos sobre as tecnologias da informação e da comunicação: TIC Domicílios e Usuários 2008*. Retrieved from http://www.cetic.br/usuarios/tic/2008-total-brasil/index.htm

Conklin, J., & Begeman, M. L. (1988). gIBIS: A hypertext tool for exploratory policy discussion. *ACM Transactions on Information Systems*, *6*(4), 303–331. doi:10.1145/58566.59297

David, L., & Henderson-Sellers, B. (2001). Characteristics of web development processes. In *Proceedings of the International Conference on Advances in Infrastructure for Electronic Business, Science and Education on the Internet* (p. 21).

e-Cidadania. (2007). *Systems and methods for the constitution of a culture mediated by information and communication technology.* Retrieved from http://www.nied.unicamp.br/ecidadania

European Commission. (2006). *i2010 eGovernment action plan: Accelerating eGovernment in Europe for the benefit of all.* Retrieved from http://ec.europa.eu/information_society/newsroom/cf/itemshortdetail.cfm?item_id=3140

Garcia, A. C. B., Maciel, C., & Pinto, F. B. (2005). A quality inspection method to evaluate e-government sites. In M. A. Wimmer, R. Traunmüller, A. Grönlund, & K. V. Andersen (Eds.), *Proceedings of the 4th International Conference on Electronic Government* (LNCS 3591, pp. 198-209).

Goldkuhl, G. (2007). What does it mean to serve the citizen in e-services? – Towards a practical theory founded in socio-instrumental pragmatism. *International Journal of Public Information Systems, 3*(3), 135–159.

Grönlund, Å. (2005). State of the art in e-gov research: Surveying conference publications. *International Journal of Electronic Government Research, 1*(4), 1–25. doi:10.4018/jegr.2005100101

Hayashi, E. C. S., & Baranauskas, M. C. C. (2008). Facing the digital divide in a participatory way – an exploratory study. In *Proceedings of the 20th IFIP World Computer Congress on Human-Computer Interaction Symposium* (Vol. 272, pp. 143-154).

Hayashi, E. C. S., Neris, V. P. A., Rodriguez, C., Miranda, L. C., Hornung, H., Santana, V. F., et al. (2009). *Preliminary evaluation of VilanaRede - An inclusive social network system* (Tech. Rep. No. IC-09-40). Campinas, Brazil: University of Campinas.

Hitz, M., Leitner, G., & Melcher, R. (2006). Usability of web applications. In Kappel, G., Pröll, B., Reich, S., & Retschitzegger, W. (Eds.), *Web engineering: The discipline of systematic development of web applications* (pp. 219–246). Chichester, UK: John Wiley & Sons.

Holzinger, A., Searle, G., Kleinberger, T., Seffah, A., & Javahery, H. (2008). Investigating usability metrics for the design and development of applications for the elderly. In K. Miesenberger, J. Klaus, W. Zagler, & A. Karshmer (Eds.), *Proceedings of the 11th International Conference on Computers Helping People with Special Needs* (LNCS 5105, pp. 98-105).

Hornung, H., & Baranauskas, M. C. C. (2007), Interaction design in eGov systems: Challenges for a developing country. In *Proceedings of the 34th Seminário Integrado de Software e Hardware*, Porto Alegre, Brazil (pp. 2217-2231).

Hornung, H., Baranauskas, M. C. C., & de Andrade Tambascia, C. (2008). Assistive technologies and techniques for web based eGov in developing countries. In *Proceedings of the 10th International Conference on Enterprise Information Systems*, Setúbal, Portugal (pp. 248-255).

Huenerfauth, M. P. (2002). *Developing design recommendations for computer interfaces accessible to illiterate users.* Unpublished master's thesis, University College Dublin, Dublin City, Ireland.

IBGE. (2000). *Instituto Brasileiro de Geografia e Estatística: Demographic censuses.* Retrieved from http://www.ibge.gov.br/english/estatistica/populacao/default_censo_2000.shtm

ILSMH European Association. (1998). *Make it simple - European easy-to-read guidelines.* Retrieved from http://www.inclusion-europe.org/publications.htm

IPM. (2005). *Instituto Paulo Montenegro: Indicador de Alfabetismo Funcional.* Retrieved from http://www.ipm.org.br/ipmb_pagina.php?mpg=4.02.00.00.00&ver=por

Kennaway, J. R., Glauert, J. R. W., & Zwitserlood, I. (2007). Providing signed content on the Internet by synthesized animation. *ACM Transactions on Computer-Human Interaction, 14*(3), 15. doi:10.1145/1279700.1279705

Leahy, W., Chandler, P., & Sweller, J. (2003). When auditory presentations should and should not be a component of multimedia instruction. *Applied Cognitive Psychology*, *17*(4), 401–418. doi:10.1002/acp.877

Liu, K. (2000). *Semiotics in information systems engineering*. Cambridge, UK: Cambridge University Press. doi:10.1017/CBO9780511543364

Medhi, I., Prasad, A., & Toyama, K. (2007). Optimal audio-visual representations for illiterate users of computers. In *Proceedings of the 16th International Conference on World Wide Web* (pp. 873-882). New York, NY: ACM Press.

Muller, M. J., Hallewell Haslwanter, J. D., & Dayton, T. (1997). Participatory practices in the software lifecycle. In Helander, M., Landauer, T., & Prabhu, P. (Eds.), *Handbook of human-computer interaction* (pp. 255–297). Amsterdam, The Netherlands: Elsevier.

Neris, V. P. A., Martins, M. C., Prado, M. E. B. B., Hayashi, E. C. S., & Baranauskas, M. C. C. (2008). Design de interfaces para todos – Demandas da diversidade cultural e social. In *Proceedings of the 35ᵗʰ Seminário Integrado de Software e Hardware*, Porto Alegre, Brazil (pp. 76-90).

Nielsen, J. (1993). *Usability engineering*. San Francisco, CA: Morgan Kauffman.

Petrie, H., & Edwards, A. (2006). *Inclusive design and assistive technology as part of the HCI curriculum*. Paper presented at the First Joint BCS/IFIP WG13.1/ICS/EU CONVIVIO HCI Educators' Workshop, Limerick, Ireland.

SBC. (2006). *Grand challenges in computer science research in Brazil – 2006 – 2016*. Retrieved from http://www.sbc.org.br/

Schuler, D., & Namioka, A. (Eds.). (1993). *Participatory design: Principles and practices*. Mahwah, NJ: Lawrence Erlbaum.

Sevilla, J., Herrera, G., Martínez, B., & Alcantud, F. (2007). Web accessibility for individuals with cognitive deficits: A comparative study between an existing commercial Web and its cognitively accessible equivalent. *ACM Transactions on Computer-Human Interaction*, *14*(3), 12. doi:10.1145/1279700.1279702

Stephanidis, C., Akoumianakis, D., Sfyrakis, M., & Paramythis, A. (1998). Universal accessibility in HCI: Process-oriented design guidelines and tool requirements. In *Proceedings of the 4th ERCIM Workshop on User Interfaces for All*.

Thatcher, J., Burkes, M., Heilmann, C., Henry, S., Kirkpatrick, A., & Lauke, P. (2006). *Web accessibility: Web standards and regulatory compliance*. Berkeley, CA: Friends of ED.

Universal Design. (2009). *The Center for Universal Design: Environments and products for all people*. Retrieved from http://www.design.ncsu.edu/cud/

This work was previously published in the International Journal of Electronic Government Research, Volume 7, Issue 3, edited by Vishanth Weerakkody, pp. 1-20, copyright 2011 by IGI Publishing (an imprint of IGI Global).

Chapter 13

Diffusion of Personalized E–Government Services among Dutch Municipalities:
An Empirical Investigation and Explanation

Vincent Homburg
Erasmus University Rotterdam, The Netherlands

Andres Dijkshoorn
Erasmus University Rotterdam, The Netherlands

ABSTRACT

This article describes the trend of personalization in electronic service delivery, with a special focus on municipal electronic service delivery in the Netherlands. Personalization of electronic services refers to the one-to-one citizen orientation using authentication, profiling and customization techniques. The percentage of Dutch municipalities offering services through personalized electronic counters has increased from 14% (2006) to 28% (2009). Using binary logistic regression analyses of 2008 survey data, it is concluded that personalization is positively associated with size of municipalities but not with e-government and policy innovation statements, nor with explicit political responsibility with respect to e-government development. Based on these findings, alternative explanations for the adoption and diffusion of personalized e-government services are suggested.

INTRODUCTION

Various studies have shown that there has been a steady growth in the presence of electronic government services. The increase has been observed in developed countries (defined as members of the Organization for Economic Cooperation and Development OECD) (OECD, 2009), European countries (Horst, Kuttschreuter, & Gutteling, 2007; Janssen & Rotthier, 2005), the Arab world (Al-Nuaim, 2009) and, to a lesser extent, sub-Saharan African countries (Heeks, 2002; Schuppan, 2009). In the literature, specific attention has

DOI: 10.4018/978-1-4666-2458-0.ch013

been given to electronic government in US (Moon, 2002; Reddick, 2009) and UK (Gilbert, Balestrini, & Littleboy, 2004) municipalities.

Apart from this increase in number of services, in the past decades there have been various 'qualitative jumps' (Bekkers & Homburg, 2005). For instance, Layne and Lee identify various stages of electronic service delivery. They suggest that public sector organizations tend to begin with offering cataloguing information, then shift to isolated transactions, and eventually to enabling horizontally and vertically integrated transactions to citizens (Layne & Lee, 2001).

In this article, we focus on a recent qualitative jump: the move to so-called personalized electronic public services. Personalized services (called 'customized services' by Watson and Mundy) are services with which through authorization, profiling and customization, one-to-one relationships between service providers and users are established (Guo & Lu, 2007; Watson & Mundy, 2001). Delivering personalized electronic government services can be understood as fitting the idea of truly citizen-centric government, an idea that has been at the heart of the New Public Management ideology that has, over the past two decades or so, swept over the American and European public sector and beyond (Pollitt, van Thiel, & Homburg, 2007). Furthermore, citizen-centric government was forcefully put forward in a 2009 OECD study (OECD, 2009). The European Commission stipulated in 2007 that the highest level of sophistication of services is the level of 'personalization'.

The core of this article presents a description of the diffusion of technology-enabled personalization of e-government services among all Dutch municipalities between 2006 and 2009, combined with a more detailed analysis of municipal e-government personalization in the Netherlands in 2008. We explicitly focus on the provider's perspective (e.g., municipalities) as opposed to a citizen-centric perspective on service delivery (Butt & Persuad, 2005). The eventual aim is to explain why some municipalities provide per-

sonalized services whereas others do not. In the analysis we seek to explain specific patterns with a binary logistic regression analysis. The focus on municipalities was chosen because municipalities are viewed in many Western countries as the frontrunners in the modernization of interaction between government, on the one hand, and citizens and corporations on the other (Paskaleva, 2008). The focus on a single country, the Netherlands, enables us to demarcate an empirical setting and exclude influences that emerge from national policy initiatives.

The research question of this article is: How can the diffusion of personalization in municipal electronic service delivery in the Netherlands be explained? It is important to theoretically analyze the factors that contribute to and facilitate e-government developments and thereby contribute to the literature on the adoption and diffusion of information technology in the public sector. Until now, few empirical studies have attempted to analyze e-government innovation, and from an analysis of national e-government policy document of various countries, Bekkers and Homburg (2007) have demonstrated that many policy initiatives are inspired by so-called 'myths'. By explicitly confronting one of these 'myths' (the myth of rational planning) with population (as opposed to sample) data of e-government adoption in Dutch municipalities, the phenomenon of personalized e-government is better understood and this might enable local politicians, public managers and e-government project managers to cope with e-government myths in their e-strategy formation efforts and implementation puzzles.

This article is structured as follows. Personalization and personalized e-government services are defined and theoretical and political backgrounds of personalization are identified. Next we discuss data sources and methods used in the analysis. The results of the analyses are presented and conclusions and an assessment of the relevant attributes of e-government personalization are provided.

ORIGINS AND EMPIRICAL MANIFESTATION OF PERSONALIZED E-GOVERNMENT

For the purpose of this study, we define e-government as the redesign of the information relations of a public sector organization with its environment – be it citizens, corporations or other governmental organizations (Bekkers & Homburg, 2005). Although the general definition encompasses information delivery and transactions as well as participatory services, including electronic voting, both in the e-government literature as well as in policy practice, e-government is often narrowed down to electronic service delivery. In this article we also focus on the electronic service delivery component of the e-government phenomenon.

Until recently, electronic services were predominantly presented in a 'one size fits all' manner, presumably reflecting the idea that because many public services are universalistic – meaning that services should be available to each and every citizen – they should be presented in a universalistic way. This mode of public service delivery has been severely criticized. As Leadbeater puts it, "many people's experience is that they are put on hold, kept at arm's length, not told the whole story, tricked by the fine print, redirected to a web site and treated like a number" (Leadbeater, 2004, p. 80). A first attempt to change the situation has been to set up one-stop shops: electronic counters with which horizontally and/or vertically integrated services are delivered to the general public (Layne & Lee, 2001). By borrowing ideas and insights from the marketing literature, especially the concept of personalization, a more radical innovation was considered in order to foster an actual citizen-centric approach to service delivery (Ho, 2002). One of the aspects of such an approach is that contacts are not automatically treated as if they were first time contacts (Peppers, Rogers, & Dorf, 1999), requiring again and again the submission of individual data supporting a request (Allen, Kania, & Yaeckel, 2001). By re-using data,

traditional personal relationships between public service providers and citizens can be restored.

Key in this line of thinking is the notion of personalization and personalized services (Hanson, 1999; Imhoff, Loftis, & Geiger, 2001). Since about 1870, personalization has been studied in the marketing literature. Especially in the 1970s, concepts like segmentation and profiling were given a lot of attention in the context of commercial service delivery (Searby, 2003; Oulasvirta & Blom, 2008). In general, personalization as seen from the lens of marketing concerns itself with learning from customer preferences and past interactions in order to deliver a targeted product or service (Bonett, 2001; Guo & Lu, 2007). In this context, three stages are identified (Vesanen & Raulas, 2006):

- The identification of a target population and recording of interactions between service provider and customer through database integration, list management and data updating – in many cases using customer relationship management applications – in order to assess client behavior and interests;
- The segmentation and differentiation of the target population and profiling of individual customers; and
- The customization (Vankalo, 2004) and delivery of services or products.

These ideas can be applied in part to public service delivery as well. Pieterson, Ebbers, and Van Dijk (2007) describe personalized e-government as an adaptation of an electronic government service to a single citizen, based on user-related information of that particular citizen. Pieterson, Ebbers, and Van Dijk (2007) claim that personalization could reduce administrative burden and, because personalized, one-to-one communication is generally more persuasive than broadcasted public service announcements, thus increasing citizens' compliance to legal principles and duties implied by law.

A practical example of personalized service delivery is a notification sent by e-mail to a citizen when a passport or driver's license is about to expire. Citizens can also be notified of building permits that have been issued to specific companies or other changes in the built environment in the direct vicinity of their homes. These examples are stated here to demonstrate that there are avenues for personalization in public service delivery, not to argue that all public services should be delivered in personalized ways or that public service providers should necessarily mimic developments in the private sector. In fact, there are striking similarities as well as significant differences between commercial services personalization and public services personalization.

First, in many examples of personalization in market relations between commercial service providers and customers, the provided service itself is customized and tailored to the preferences and needs of the customer (Bonett, 2001; Miceli et al., 2007; Oulasvirta & Blom, 2008; Karat, Blom, & Karat, 2004). Think, for instance, of the way the commercial service of a 'holiday' can be tailored to accommodate a specific preference for type of travel, car rental, lodging, etcetera. In public service delivery, because of sound legal principles, many services possess attributes of universalistic services, even if they are presented to citizens in personalized ways. In practice, personalization of public services implies that services are presented in an order and context that is relevant given the history of interactions and/or follows the logic of 'life events' such as birth and death. The services themselves (birth certificates, for instance) remain universalistic.

Second, more than in the case of commercial service delivery, there are important normative questions with respect to the nature and extent of public authority's 'intelligence' of citizen behavior. In political systems that are at least partly founded on principles of liberal democracy, the

recording of needs and assessment of citizens' interests and behavior is highly problematic. Wang, Lee, and Wang (1998) identify four ways in which misuse of information intrudes into people's lives: improper acquisition of information (i.e., tracking people's usage of municipal web sites), improper distribution of data, spamming and improper storage and control of personal information (no opting out, no means of editing incorrect data). This results in a dilemma between achieving customer orientation, on the one hand, and maintaining a proper distance between government and citizen on the other hand. This dilemma is resolved in practice by putting the citizen in the driver's seat and having the citizen choose the level of accuracy and completeness of the information they provide. In this scenario, citizens themselves have more influence and control over their personal information, and they themselves mark the balance between privacy and citizen orientation in personalized services. But even if citizens are willing to sacrifice privacy in exchange for improved orientation towards needs (Chellappa, 2005), privacy ethics state that information is not to be used for purposes that have not been approved by citizens (Pieterson et al., 2007).

Third, an important, more or less operational aim of personalization of commercial and public services alike is to ameliorate problems of information overload for users of services (customers and citizens, respectively). In practice, one can think of techniques like adaptive presentation of content as means to reduce information overload. More than in commercial service delivery, however, there is an ideological flavor to personalization in public service delivery (Leadbeater, 2004). Leadbeater, for instance, decries bureaucratic mass production and over-centralization for creating information asymmetry between service providers and citizens, irresponsiveness and poor public sector performance. Since the advent of the New Public Management, privatization and liberalization have been introduced so as to ameliorate poor performance of public bureaucracies. Through privatization and liberalization, public services are produced and delivered by placing public assets under private ownership and using market-type mechanisms, such as 'the invisible hand', to produce those services that meet citizens' expectations and needs. Leadbeater dismisses consumerism and privatization in the same way that he criticizes bureaucratic modes of production and argues that personalization of public services can be used to offset both bureaucratic failure as well as the failure of markets to deliver equitable access to public goods. He argues that personalization can be used to take personal needs, preferences and interests into account within universal, equitable public service delivery, enabling citizens to have a voice directly in the service as it is delivered. That voice, according to Leadbeater, is unlocked only if citizens have a say over when, where, how, and to what end a service is delivered. Leadbeater's line of reasoning makes clear that personalization is not only an operational solution to problems of information overload, but also a political choice for a specific mode of production and delivery of public services with which specific rights are attributed and with which the relation between government and citizens may be affected: "(…) we need an approach that gives people a direct voice through the way in which everyday services are actually developed and delivered", concludes Leadbeater (2004, p. 56).

Taking into account the three issues mentioned above, we define personalized electronic services as services with which through authorization, profiling and customization, one-to-one relationships between service providers and users are established (Guo & Lu, 2007; Watson & Mundi, 2001). Authorization here means that citizens have to identify themselves, but also that e-government services should allow citizens to unlock needs, preferences and aspirations. Further, it implies that citizens should be allowed greater opportunities to exercise choice over the mix of ways in which their needs might be met electronically, as well

as having a voice in the sense of eventually being enabled to further articulate their preferences.

Personalized e-government service delivery, however, is more than simply an idea that has originated in theoretic analogy (private-sector personalization) and normative debate (a rival to liberalized markets). In practice, many initiatives exist in which personalization plays a role. In Belgium, for instance, the Ministry of Finance has initiated MyMinFin, a personalized e-government service provided by the Tax Authority that enable citizens to not only submit their tax filings electronically, but also to check information and to indicate how they would like to be informed of current and upcoming changes in legislation. Furthermore, in various European countries there are national portals that route citizens' requests to decentralized, personalized websites. Examples of these kinds of portals are the Danish borger. dk, the Estonian eesti.ee initiative, the French mon.service-public.fr website, the Norwegian Norway.no portal, the British www.direct.gov.uk site and the Dutch mijnoverheid.nl site. All the mentioned sites offer more or less customized information from a limited but growing number of sources to citizens.

The anecdotal evidence presented above does not serve to prove that personalization is a necessary next step, nor that personalization of e-government is a problem-free transition. In fact, various obstacles to personalization have been identified in the literature.

First of all, personalization requires cooperation and partnership across various levels of government, as well as the exchange and sharing of information across traditional organizational boundaries. These requirements have proven to be difficult, from a governance (Homburg, 2008) as well as from a technological point of view – e.g. the existence of legacy systems (Pieterson et al., 2007). In practice, various obstacles have been identified. Second, personalization requires large financial investments (West, 2004), and third, public service providers in various countries are still struggling with questions of, for instance, how to deal with legal issues such as digital signatures and Privacy Acts. For a review of these legal questions see Lips, Van der Hof, Prins, and Schudelaro (2004).

DESCRIPTION OF PERSONALIZATION IN DUTCH LOCAL E-GOVERNMENT

In an attempt to move beyond the predominantly case-based or anecdotal empirical evidence of personalization in e-government initiatives, we present here the prevalence of attributes of personalization in a specific jurisdiction, that is, in Dutch municipalities. As many other surveys in the field of e-government research, we use existing survey data. Note that as Reddick (2009) has observed, existing survey research on municipal e-government concentrates mainly on International City/County Management Association datasets. The data that are presented here have been extracted from a larger data set (the national Dutch e-government monitor, http://monitor.overheid.nl) that was commissioned by the Dutch Ministry of the Interior and composed by the 'Government has an answer' program committee. The data set consists of all sorts of e-government characteristics of national and regional authorities (Ministries, water boards, provinces, municipalities), and the data are eventually processed and presented as a benchmark, ranking the performance of authorities in terms of presence, quality of e-services, etcetera (for comparable US initiatives and methodology, refer to McClure & Sprehe, 2000). For the purpose of this study, the items on municipal electronic personalization were extracted from the data set and processed so as to describe the diffusion of personalization in the population of municipalities. The data set covers all Dutch municipalities in the time frame 2006-2009.1 The time frame marks an interval that spans two elections (local elections were held in 2006 and 2010).

In the original data set, various attributes of personalization are recorded.2 The first attribute concerns the use of the national Dutch authorization mechanism for e-government services (digital identity, abbreviated as DigiD). Second, there is the feature of sending personalized (customized) e-mail newsletters. Third, the tracking and tracing attribute records whether it is possible for customers to keep track of the processing of a request by the relevant municipal service providers. Payment, being fourth, refers to the possibility of paying on-line for specific services. Fifth, pre-completed forms refer to forms that are presented to citizens and that can be pre-completed using either data from information profiles that have been created by citizens or data from previous visits. Personalized counters, sixth, refer to electronic websites with adaptive presentation of content (based on previous visits by citizens). The seventh attribute, 'personalized policy consequences', refers to a service that allows citizens to check whether they are eligible for specific benefits, need to pay particular taxes or require particular permits given their circumstances.

Table 1 lists the prevalence of the seven above-mentioned attributes of personalized electronic service delivery by Dutch municipalities in the years 2006, 2007, 2008 and 2009. Overall, in the time frame covered, there is a sharp increase in the offered possibility to use DigiD authentification (from 20.7% in 2006 to 88.2% in 2009) and on-line payment (from 15.9% in 2006 to 80% in 2009). Absolute levels lag somewhat behind, as do growth of possibilities for receiving personalized newsletters, using pre-completed forms, assessing personalized policy consequences and using personalized counters.

EXPLAINING THE DIFFUSION OF PERSONALIZATION

Following the research objective of this paper, the description of the diffusion pattern is an initial but not sufficient means to explain the diffusion of

Table 1. Prevalence of personalization attributes in Dutch municipal e-government services

	2006 (n=458)	2007 (n=443)	2008 (n=443)	2009 (n=441)
DigiD	20.7%	56.7%	76.3%	88.2%
Personalized newsletter	16.4%	21.2%	21.2%	N/A
Tracking & tracing	10.0%	16.0%	28.2%	26.5%
Payment	15.9%	42.4%	61.4%	80.0%
Pre-completed forms	N/A	N/A	17.8%	19.1%
- profiles generated by users			2.3%	5.2%
- automated links			10.8%	12.5%
- automated, user-editable links			4.7%	1.4%
Personalized counters (MyGov.nl)	5.2%	14.2%	23.7%	28.8%
Personalized policy consequences	N/A	N/A	19.4%	18.7%
- internal module			7.0%	N/A
- links to existing websites			12.4%	N/A

personalization. The question remains as to how to explain why some municipalities offer fully personalized electronic services, whereas other do not. The answer to this question is particularly difficult to attain since a specific theory on e-government personalization is not available (Pieterson et al., 2007). E-government in general has been studied extensively in the literature (Holden, Norris, & Fletcher, 2003; Moon, 2002; Reddick, 2009), and there are ample theoretical insights that can be used to draft hypotheses. Existing theoretical models, however, are not necessarily capable of capturing and robustly explaining the diffusion of personalization in the target population of Dutch municipalities. In the literature, two candidate explanations are presented:

- The first is Rogers' model of diffusion of innovations (Rogers, 1995). This model explains how innovations diffuse in societies as a whole as a function of characteristics of the innovation itself, types of communication channels, rate of adoption and characteristics of the social system in which the innovation takes place. For the purposes of this paper, the model is less

likely to be useful, as it makes use of very general, global characteristics that are often beyond the control of municipal stakeholders (public managers, experts, local administrators and politicians).

- The second is Davis' Technology Acceptance Model (TAM) (Venkatesh, Morris, Davis, & Davis, 2003), an exploratory model of the acceptance of technologies across populations of end-users. In this model, the chance of end-users adopting a technology (in the case of personalized e-government, end-users would be citizens using personalized services) is dependent on the end-user's attitude towards technology (i.e., the technology's perceived usefulness and perceived ease of use). For the purposes of this paper this model is less useful, as individual citizens' attitude to personalized services is, in the short term, not likely to result in political decisions about whether or not to adopt specific technologies.

In this paper, we seek a mid-level (meso) explanation of why specific local authorities choose to adopt personalized electronic service desks, whereas others choose not to do so. By 'mid-level' we refer to organizational constructs and variables that refer to organizational practices but also to the political intentions and ambitions that are immanent to organizational behavior in public authorities. Such an approach has been proposed by Bekkers and Homburg (2005) but has to date been little studied empirically. The Information Ecology approach acknowledges technological opportunity as an important driving force behind the diffusion of technologies; however, it also stresses that diffusion takes place in specific cultural, political, intellectual and economic environments, in which specific rules, intentions and practices guide (1) the behavior and interactions of human actors and (2) the development, deployment and use of technologies. In the current paper, we focus on a relatively unsophisticated yet robust variable size and three variables that assess political drive behind the deployment of technology in a specific local government context. In order to explain the adoption of personalized e-government services, we identify the following explanatory constructs:

1. **City Size:** In various studies of technological innovation in municipalities, the size of the city or other municipal unit is considered to be one of the main determinants. City size can be regarded as a proxy for organizational size and will eventually be seen as a proxy for organizational resources (members of staff, budget, size of IT department). Various studies have demonstrated that larger governments are more likely to adopt innovations than are their smaller counterparts. For an overview, refer to Moon and Norris (2005), Norris and Moon, (2005), and West (2004). With regard to American municipalities, Reddick has hypothesized that populations greater than 250,000 have a positive impact on a municipality's e-government maturation, whereas smaller local governments (with populations under 25,000) are expected

to display less developed e-government initiatives (Reddick, 2004). In this study, we identify city size as one of the explanatory variables and identify Hypothesis I: Larger municipalities are more likely to adopt personalization than are smaller municipalities.

2. **Political Motivation of Adoption and Rational Planning Orientation:** Another set of explanatory variables is associated with the construct of the 'technological orientation' of municipal government or, inversely, the degree of political driving force behind technological innovation. It has been observed that e-government in general is to be achieved through corporate information planning and project management techniques. Information planning and project management is presented as a question of *setting goals, formulating action plans, allocating budgets and identifying clear roles and responsibilities* (Bekkers & Homburg, 2007). Bekkers and Homburg refer to the idea that planning and management techniques correlate with successful adoption as 'the myth of rational information management'. They present it as a myth because the use of explicit planning and management techniques is proclaimed in the design literature and echoed in various action programs and implementation plans. Existing survey studies tend to explain e-government development in terms of roles of chief information officers (Reddick, 2009), managerial orientation (Moon & Norris, 2005) or other managerial or organizational variables, thus de-emphasizing the inherent political disposition of municipal organizations. The relevance of politics for municipal e-government development, including personalization, stems from aldermen's responsibility towards their City Councils, but also from the normative aspects of a choice for personalization. Furthermore, in the IS literature, one of the dominant predic-

tors for the success of information systems in general is strategic alignment (Preston & Karahanna, 2009). Strategic alignment can broadly be defined as a shared understanding among salient technology- and policy actors about plans, objectives and vision of ways in which technology is put to use (Reich & Benbasat, 2000). The casual interpretation here is that technological innovations have a chance of success only if their value is acknowledged and supported not only by ICT staff (representatives from the technological domain) but also by aldermen and general public managers (representatives from the policy domain). In this study, we focus on general innovation and e-government ambitions formalized in four-year program plans, and on aldermen having explicit responsibility for e-government deployment as proxy indicators for strategic alignment in municipal government organizations. We therefore identify a number of hypotheses. Hypothesis II states that municipalities with explicit e-government ambitions in their four-year program plans are more likely to adopt personalization than are municipalities without these explicit ambitions. Hypothesis III states that municipalities with explicit innovation ambitions in their program plans are more likely to adopt personalization than are municipalities without these explicit ambitions. Finally, Hypothesis IV states that municipalities in which aldermen have explicit authority over e-government development are more likely to adopt personalization than are municipalities where the aldermen do not have this type of authority.

METHODOLOGY

In order to explain whether a municipality offers services through a personalized electronic service desk, the extracted data set described above was supplemented with data on size (number of in-

habitants, based on Netherlands Statistics data). Furthermore, four-year municipal programs that followed the 2006 elections of all 458 municipalities were first scanned for explicit statements on (1) e-government and (2) innovation. As a next step, in a process of induction and deduction, statements on e-government ambitions, innovation ambitions and authority over e-government development were systematically coded using axial coding techniques (Strauss & Corbin, 1998). We used the 2008 data because at the time of writing, this was the most recent data set available to us that satisfied the conditions for the regression technique we used.

In order to explain the dichotomous dependent variable (presence of personalized electronic service desk), we used binary logistic regression analysis. In general, logistic regression models predict the probability of an event Y_i (in this case, the probability of a municipality having a personalized electronic service desk) with independent variables that are binary, categorical or continuous (Pampel, 2000). The literature on binary logistic regression presents a number of rules of thumb with respect to the allowed number of independent variables to be used in the model in relation to the number of cases. The rule of thumb with respect to sample size is that there should be no more than one independent variable for each ten cases in the sample, the sample being the number of cases of the smaller category (Garson, 2009). In the 2008 data, there are 105 personalized service desks versus 338 municipalities without personalized service desks, enabling the use of maximum 10 (105/10) independent variables. The data set used thus satisfies this condition.

More importantly, logistic regression requires the absence of multicollinearity. Multicollinearity was inspected using collinearity diagnostics, and since all tolerance statistics are above 0.1 and all VIF values are smaller than 10 − even smaller than 4, a threshold value used by Garson (2009) − multicollinearity is a non-issue in the data set (Field, 2009) (see Table A1 and Table A2 in the Appendix).

ANALYSIS

To evaluate the hypotheses described in the previous section, the dependent variable 'personalized electronic counter' was regressed against three binary independent variables (explicit attention to e-government, explicit attention to innovation and explicit alderman responsibility) and one categorical variable (size). Size was coded as (1) 0 – 50,000; (2) 50,000 – 100,000; (3) 100,000-150,000; (4) 150,000 – 200,000; and (5) 200,000 inhabitants and above. The results of the analyses are summarized in Table 2.

The Hosmer and Lemeshow test of significance of the whole model resulted in a non significant value of 1.52 (df=4, p=0.82), indicating that the model adequately fits the data (which is consistent with the overall chi-square of 32.19, p<0.01).

Looking at the hypotheses, we conclude that Hypothesis I is supported by the data. The Wald statistic, which is used to test individual contribution of independent variables (whether the B coefficient is significantly different from zero, in which case the variable does make a contribution to the prediction of the outcome) is 19.46 (df=5,

p<0.01). Obviously, there is an overall positive relation between city size and likelihood of adoption of personalized e-government service desks. The odds ratio Exp(B) and 95% confidence intervals for the size categories (using the smallest size category as reference) are reported in Table 3.

The second, third and fourth hypotheses, however, are not supported by the data (see Table 4 for respective Wald statistics and significance levels).

With the summarized reflections on the hypotheses, the final section of this paper re-examines the hypotheses and underlying theoretical considerations, and comments on alternative explanations and novel directions for research and policy recommendations.

CONCLUSION, DISCUSSION, AND FURTHER RESEARCH

This study examined a recent 'qualitative jump' in the way municipal governments offer electronic services to citizens. The 'qualitative jump' refers to a transition from municipalities offering on-line universalistic services to municipal electronic services that are presented in such a way that they reflect prior visits, histories and known citizens' preferences. Think tanks and expert groups have argued in favor of adopting these so-called personalized e-government services (OECD, 2009), but the topic has already moved from being an abstract idea to a real phenomenon in public ser-

Table 2. Determinants of adoption of personalized e-government counters

Variables	B(SE)	Significance
Constant	-1.28 (0.20)	0.00
Size3		0.00
50 k-100 k	0.73 (0.40)	0.06
100 k-150 k	2.52 (0.71)	0.00
150 k-200 k	3.19 (1.31)	0.00
>200 k	3.28 (1.22)	0.15
Innovation in budget plan	-0.62 (0.79)	0.43
E-Government in budget plan	0.03 (0.28)	0.89
Responsibility for aldermen	-0.08 (0.34)	0.80

Note: $R^2 = 0.10$ (Cox & Snel), $R^2 = 0.14$ (Nagelkerke), chi-square = 32.19 (p<0.01).

Table 3. Odds ratio and their 95% confidence intervals

Size Category	Exp(B)	95% CI (lower)	95% CI (upper)
50 k-100 k	2.08	0.94	4.58
100 k-150 k	12.48	3.07	50.3
150 k-200 k	24.51	1.84	322.45
>200 k	26.62	2.4	295.28

Table 4. Conclusions with respect to hypotheses

Hypothesis (independent variable)	Wald Statistic	Conclusion
1. Larger municipalities are more likely to adopt personalized counters than are smaller municipalities. (Size)	19.46 (p<0.01)	Supported
2. Municipalities with explicit e-government ambitions in their four-year program plans are more likely to adopt personalization than are municipalities that do not have these explicit ambitions. (E-government in budget plan)	0.19 (p=0.89)	Not supported
3. Municipalities with explicit innovation ambitions in their budget plans are more likely to adopt personalization than are municipalities that do not have these explicit ambitions. (Innovation in budget plan)	0.61 (p=0.43)	Not supported
4. Municipalities that give aldermen explicit authority over e-government development are more likely to adopt personalization than are municipalities where aldermen do not have this kind of authority. (Responsibility of aldermen)	0.64 (p=0.80)	Not supported

vice delivery. In this study we described how, in the 2006-2009 time period, Dutch municipalities increasingly featured personalized e-government services.

The theory behind personalized e-government diffusion predicted that city size as well as rational planning and political drive in the form of explicit e-government ambitions, general innovation ambitions and express political responsibility over e-government deployment by aldermen (following the logic of rational planning) are positively associated with personalization. We used binary logistic regression and concluded that size is a predictor of personalization in municipalities but that policy ambitions and aldermen having explicit attention towards e-government do not predict personalized e-government. Below we will look at how these findings should be interpreted.

The fact that size (interpreted as a proxy for a municipality's resources and capacities) is positively associated with adoption is consistent with studies by Moon and Norris (2005) and in general supports the so-called resource-push perspective, a positive association between technical and financial resources and technological innovation (Moon & DeLeon, 2001). Perhaps the more interesting finding of this study is the lack of support for the hypotheses relating ambitions about political e-government and innovation (as expressed in municipal four-year program plans) with the actual

adoption of personalized e-government services. Especially in the information systems literature, emphasis has been placed on the alignment of technological initiatives and general policy (or strategic) plans as a predictor of information system success (Henderson & Venkatraman, 1999). The results of this study show that in fact, this top-level policy support does not make a difference in realizing personalized e-government services. Obviously, personalization as an idea is more of an organizational phenomenon driven by managerial logic, capacities and availability of resources than a political phenomenon boosted by political ambitions and drive.

As for practical implications, a number of recommendations come to mind. The first one that stems from the theoretic framework is that personalization is not a solely operational transition to a 'next phase' in public service delivery. There are important normative considerations that must be taken into account. These considerations refer to the view on citizens in general and their assumed 'voice' capacities in particular. The second one is that if one decides to boost personalized e-government services, it should be taken into account that increasing organizational resources and capacities are more likely to promote personalization than are formulating political ambitions and responsibilities. Overall, this implies that the myth of rational e-government can be 'debunked'.

The pattern that emerges from the innovation of Dutch municipal personalized e-government is that ICT adoption does not always reflect the realm of method, procedure and systematic reasoning. Alternatively, innovations like personalization are likely the result of the bubbling up of new ideas (tinkering and 'bricolage' (Ciborra, 2002; Bekkers & Homburg, 2007; Homburg, 1999).

Future research could possibly examine the exact relation between organizational capacities and resources, on the one hand, and adoption of personalized e-government services on the other hand. This type of research could focus on ways in which 'ideas' (Czarniawska & Sevon, 2005; Homburg & Georgiadou, 2009) such as personalization travel from the sphere of think tanks and experts (for example, OECD reports that promote personalization in e-government initiatives) to that of real-world organizations. Using the results of this study, one can hypothesize that these ideas do not simply institutionalize through (1) political ambitions of local politicians and (2) subsequent implementation at the shop floor of municipal service providers. Rather, they might diffuse through organizational 'contact infection' (Homburg & Georgiadou, 2009) and mimicking, for example because of de-facto regulative pressures of benchmarks, normative pressures of professional associations of information managers, or simply because of organizations copying the developments of neighboring or otherwise associated organizations (DiMaggio & Powell, 1983; Havermans & Woudenberg, 2007). Related to these isomorphic notions is the role of partnerships and networks in the propagation of innovations among similar organizations (Cotterill & King, 2007; Gulati & Gargiulo, 1999). Partnerships and networks, it is found, contribute to the adoption and implementation of e-government initiatives through the sharing of knowledge and expertise among organizations. Closely related to this research is the work from Considine et al., in which they looked at processes of change within municipalities in Australia. They also focused on the importance of networks in the processes of change within these municipalities (Hu, Saunders, & Gebelt, 1997). Here, the importance of networks and contacts between key innovators is found to play an important role in the processes of change and innovation within municipalities. These results give all the more reason to focus on the way these new innovations and ideas travel among and within municipalities and how this travelling is influenced.

Furthermore, this article explicitly takes a provider's perspective on personalization and explains adoption of personalization in terms of characteristics of the provider. Alternatively, an alternative explanation of the diffusion and adoption of personalized e-government could take a citizen's perspective (Butt & Persuad, 2005) by proposing explanatory variables from the side of the citizen, like citizen's express need, expectations, privacy concerns (Chellappa, 2005) and so forth. It must be noted, though, that representative democracies in combination with public hierarchies show longer feedback loops than spot market transactions in e-commerce applications, so that there are ample methodological problems in actually adopting a citizen-centric perspective in explanatory studies.

Another avenue of research activities is to focus on the effects of personalization rather than on the adoption of personalization itself. Especially in the public administration literature there is an implicit hypothesis that personalized e-government services – even more than 'general' e-government services – result in better contacts between government and citizens (more trust in government, improved compliance) (Chellappa, 2005; Montgomery & Smith, 2009; Oulasvirta & Blom, 2008; Wind & Rangaswamy, 2001). The degree to which this actually takes place is an empirical question that needs to be addressed in future research initiatives.

ACKNOWLEDGMENT

The authors thank the Dutch 'Government Has an Answer' program committee for their assistance in disclosing e-government monitoring data, as well as the anonymous referees for their constructive feedback.

REFERENCES

Al-Nuaim, H. (2009). How "E" are Arab municipalities? An evaluation of Arab capital municipal web sites. *International Journal of E-Government Research*, *5*(1), 50–63. doi:10.4018/jegr.2009010104

Allen, C., Kania, D., & Yaeckel, B. (2001). *One-to-one web marketing: Build a relationship marketing strategy one customer at a time*. New York, NY: John Wiley & Sons.

Bekkers, V. J. J. M., & Homburg, V. M. F. (Eds.). (2005). *The information ecology of e-government (E-government as institutional and technological innovation in public administration)* (2nd ed.). Amsterdam, The Netherlands: IOS Press.

Bekkers, V. J. J. M., & Homburg, V. M. F. (2007). The myths of e-government: Looking beyond the assumptions of a new and better government. *The Information Society*, *23*(5), 373–382. doi:10.1080/01972240701572913

Bonett, M. (2001). Personalization of web services: Opportunities and challenges. *Ariadne*, *28*.

Butt, I., & Persuad, A. (2005). Towards a citizen centric model of e-government adoption. In *Proceedings of the 3rd International Conference of E-Governance* (pp. 6-15).

Chellappa, R. (2005). Personalization versus privacy: An empirical examination of the online consumer's dilemma. *Information Technology Management*, *6*(2-3), 181. doi:10.1007/s10799-005-5879-y

Ciborra, C. (2002). *The labyrinths of information*. Oxford, UK: Oxford University Press.

Cotterill, S., & King, S. (2007). Public sector partnerships to deliver local E-government: A social network study. In M. A. Wimmer, H. J. Scholl, & A. Grölund (Eds.), *Proceedings of the 6th International Conference on Electronic Government* (LNCS 4656, pp. 240-251).

Czarniawska, B., & Sevon, B. (2005). *Global ideas: How ideas, objects and practices travel in the global economy*. Copenhagen, Denmark: Copenhagen Business School Press.

DiMaggio, P. J., & Powell, W. W. (1983). The iron cage revisited: Institutional isomorphism and collective rationality in organizational fields. *American Sociological Review*, *48*(2), 147–160. doi:10.2307/2095101

Field, A. (2009). *Discovering statistics using SPSS* (3rd ed.). London, UK: Sage.

Garson, D. (2009). *Quantitative research in public administration*. Retrieved from http://faculty.chass.ncsu.edu/garson/PA765/pa765syl.htm

Gilbert, D., Balestrini, P., & Littleboy, D. (2004). Barriers and benefits in the adoption of e-government. *International Journal of Public Sector Management*, *17*(4), 286–301. doi:10.1108/09513550410539794

Gulati, R., & Gargiulo, M. (1999). Where do interorganizational networks come from? *American Journal of Sociology*, *104*(5), 1439–1493. doi:10.1086/210179

Guo, X., & Lu, J. (2007). Intelligent e-government services with personalized recommendation techniques. *International Journal of Intelligent Systems*, *22*, 401–417. doi:10.1002/int.20206

Hanson, W. (1999). *Principals of internet marketing*. Cincinnati, OH: South Western.

Havermans, D., & Woudenberg, B. M. (2007). *Vermenigvuldigen door delen (11 stappen om te komen tot intergemeentelijke ICT samenwerking).* Den Haag, The Netherlands: ZENC.

Heeks, R. (2002). E-government in Africa: Promise and practice. *Information Polity: The International Journal of Government & Democracy in the Information Age, 7*(2), 97.

Henderson, J. C., & Venkatraman, N. (1999). Strategic alignment: Leveraging information technology for transforming organizations. *IBM Systems Journal, 38*(2), 472. doi:10.1147/SJ.1999.5387096

Ho, A. T. (2002). Reinventing local governments and the e-government initiative. *Public Administration Review, 62*(4), 434–444. doi:10.1111/0033-3352.00197

Holden, S. H., Norris, D. F., & Fletcher, P. D. (2003). Electronic government at the local level. *Public Performance & Management Review, 26*(4), 325–344. doi:10.1177/15309576030260004002

Homburg, V. M. F. (2008). *Understanding e-government: Information systems in public administration.* London, UK: Routledge.

Homburg, V. M. F., & Georgiadou, Y. (2009). A tale of two trajectories: How spatial data infrastructures travel in time and space. *The Information Society, 25*(5), 303–314. doi:10.1080/01972240903212524

Horst, M., Kuttschreuter, M., & Gutteling, J. M. (2007). Perceived usefulness, personal experiences, risk perception and trust as determinants of adoption of e-government services in the Netherlands. *Computers in Human Behavior, 23*(4), 1838–1852. doi:10.1016/j.chb.2005.11.003

Hu, Q., Saunders, C., & Gebelt, M. (1997). Research report: Diffusion of information systems outsourcing: A re-evaluation of influence sources. *Information Systems Research, 8*(3), 288. doi:10.1287/isre.8.3.288

Imhoff, C., Loftis, L., & Geiger, J. (2001). *Building the customer-centric enterprise, data warehousing techniques for supporting customer relationship management.* New York, NY: John Wiley & Sons.

Janssen, D., & Rotthier, S. (2005). Trends and consolidations in e-government implementation. In Bekkers, V. J. J. M., & Homburg, V. M. F. (Eds.), *The information ecology of e-government (e-government as institutional and technological innovation in public administration)* (2nd ed., pp. 37–52). Amsterdam, The Netherlands: IOS Press.

Karat, C. M., Blom, J. O., & Karat, J. (Eds.). (2004). *Designing personalized user experiences in eCommerce.* Dordrecht, The Netherlands: Kluwer Academic. doi:10.1007/1-4020-2148-8

Layne, K., & Lee, J. (2001). Developing fully functional e-government: A four stage model. *Government Information Quarterly, 18*(2), 122–136. doi:10.1016/S0740-624X(01)00066-1

Leadbeater, C. (2004). *Personalisation through participation: A new script for public services.* London, UK: Demos.

Lips, A. M. B., & Hof, d. S., Prins, J. E. J., & Schudelaro, A. A. P. (2004). *Issues of online personalisation in commercial and public service delivery.* Nijmegen, The Netherlands: Wolf Legal.

McClure, C. R., & Sprehe, J. T. (2000). *Performance measures for federal agencies: Final report.* Washington, DC: Defense Technical Information Center.

Miceli, G., Ricotta, F., & Costabile, M. (2007). Customizing customization: A conceptual framework for interactive personalization. *Journal of Interactive Marketing, 21*(2), 6–25. doi:10.1002/dir.20076

Montgomery, A. L., & Smith, M. D. (2009). Prospects for personalization on the internet. *Journal of Interactive Marketing, 23*(2), 130–137. doi:10.1016/j.intmar.2009.02.001

Moon, M. J. (2002). The evolution of e-government among municipalities: Rhetoric or reality? *Public Administration Review*, 62(4), 424–433. doi:10.1111/0033-3352.00196

Moon, M. J., & deLeon, P. (2001). Municipal reinvention: Managerial values and diffusion among municipalities. *Journal of Public Administration: Research and Theory*, 11(3), 327–352.

Moon, M. J., & Norris, D. F. (2005). Does managerial orientation matter? The adoption of reinventing government and e-government at the municipal level. *Information Systems Journal*, 15(1), 43–60. doi:10.1111/j.1365-2575.2005.00185.x

Norris, D. F., & Moon, M. J. (2005). Advancing e-government at the grassroots: Tortoise or hare? *Public Administration Review*, 65(1), 64–75. doi:10.1111/j.1540-6210.2005.00431.x

OECD. (2009). *Rethinking e-government services (user-centred approaches)*. Paris, France: OECD.

Oulasvirta, A., & Blom, J. (2008). Motivations in personalisation behaviour. *Interacting with Computers*, 20(1), 1–16. doi:10.1016/j.intcom.2007.06.002

Pampel, F. (2000). *Logistic regression: A primer*. Thousand Oaks, CA: Sage.

Paskaleva, K. (2008). Assessing local readiness for city e-governance in Europe. *International Journal of E-Government Research*, 4(4), 17–20. doi:10.4018/jegr.2008100102

Peppers, D., Rogers, M., & Dorf, B. (1999). *The one to one fieldbook: The complete toolkit for implementing a 1 to 1 marketing program*. New York, NY: Double Day.

Pieterson, W., Ebbers, W., & van Dijk, J. (2007). Personalization in the public sector: An inventory of organizational and user obstacles towards personalization of electronic services in the public sector. *Government Information Quarterly*, 24(1), 148–164. doi:10.1016/j.giq.2005.12.001

Pollitt, C., van Thiel, S., & Homburg, V. M. F. (Eds.). (2007). *New public management in Europe: Adaptation and alternatives*. Basingstoke, UK: Palgrave Macmillan.

Preston, D. S., & Karahanna, E. (2009). Antecedents of IS strategic alignment: A nomological network. *Information Systems Research*, 20(2), 159–179.

Reddick, C. G. (2004). Empirical models of e-government growth in local governments. *E-Service Journal*, 3(2), 59-84.

Reddick, C. G. (2009). Factors that explain the perceived effectiveness of e-government: A survey of United States city government information technology directors. *International Journal of E-Government Research*, 5(2), 1–15. doi:10.4018/jegr.2009040101

Reich, B. H., & Benbasat, I. (2000). Factors that influence the social dimension of alignment between business and information technology objectives. *Management Information Systems Quarterly*, 24(1), 81–113. doi:10.2307/3250980

Roberts, M. (2007). *Internet marketing: Integrating online and offline strategies*. New York, NY: McGraw-Hill.

Rogers, E. (1995). *Diffusion of innovations* (4th ed.). New York, NY: Free Press.

Schuppan, T. (2009). E-government in developing countries: Experiences from sub-Saharan Africa. *Government Information Quarterly*, 26(1), 118–127. doi:10.1016/j.giq.2008.01.006

Searby, S. (2003). Personalisation - an overview of its use and potential. *BT Technology Journal*, 21(1), 13–19. doi:10.1023/A:1022439824138

Strauss, A., & Corbin, J. (1998). *Basics of qualitative research: Grounded theory procedures and techniques*. Thousand Oaks, CA: Sage.

Vankalo, M. (2004). *Internet-enabled techniques for personalizing the marketing program*. Helsinki, Finland: Swedish School of Economics and Business Administration.

Venkatesh, V., Morris, M. G., Davis, G. B., & Davis, F. D. (2003). User acceptance of information technology: Toward a unified view. *Management Information Systems Quarterly, 27*(3), 425–478.

Vesanen, J. (2007). What is personalization? A conceptual framework. *European Journal of Marketing, 41*(5-6), 409–418. doi:10.1108/03090560710737534

Vesanen, J., & Raulas, M. (2006). Building bridges for personalization: A process model for marketing. *Journal of Interactive Marketing, 20*(1), 5–20. doi:10.1002/dir.20052

Wang, H., Lee, M., & Wang, C. (1998). Consumer privacy concerns about internet marketing. *Communications of the ACM, 41*(3), 63–70. doi:10.1145/272287.272299

Watson, R. T., & Mundy, B. (2001). A strategic perspective of electronic democracy. *Communications of the ACM, 44*(1), 27–30. doi:10.1145/357489.357499

West, D. M. (2004). E-government and the transformation of service delivery and citizen attitudes. *Public Administration Review, 64*(1), 15–27. doi:10.1111/j.1540-6210.2004.00343.x

Wind, J., & Rangaswamy, A. (2001). Customerization: The next revolution in mass customization. *Journal of Interactive Marketing, 15*(1), 13–32. doi:10.1002/1520-6653(200124)15:1<13::AID-DIR1001>3.0.CO;2-#

ENDNOTES

[1]   Note that population size has dropped throughout the time frame covered due to ongoing reorganizations and mergers, particularly of smaller municipalities. This process of upscaling continues on in 2010 (there are currently 431 municipalities).

[2]   Throughout the time interval covered, some items of the questionnaires were added, reformulated and/or dropped. This has resulted in N/A scores in Table 1. The wording of the most important item of the questionnaire for the research goal of this paper (personalized counters) has not changed throughout the time interval covered.

[3]   Using the 0 – 50k inhabitants city category as reference category.

APPENDIX

Correlation Matrix with Independent Variables

Table 5. Coefficients[a]

Model		Unstandardized Coefficients		Standardized Coefficients	t	Sig.	Collinearity Statistics	
		B	Std. Error	Beta			Tolerance	VIF
1	(Constant)	0.219	0.035		6.343	0.000		
	SizeCateg	0.201	0.036	0.358	5.591	0.000	0.728	1.373
	EGovernment	0.000	0.050	0.000	0.003	0.998	0.978	1.022
	Innovation	-0.098	0.124	-0.049	-0.788	0.432	0.769	1.301
	Responsibility	-0.020	0.062	-0.018	-0.323	0.747	0.916	1.091

a. Dependent variable: PersCounter2008

Table 6. Collinearity diagnostics[a]

Model	Dimension	Eigenvalue	Condition Index	Variance Proportions				
				(Constant)	SizeCateg	PolProgramICT	Innovation	Responsibility
1	1	2.542	1.000	0.05	0.05	0.05	0.04	0.06
	2	1.049	1.556	0.07	0.12	0.10	0.31	0.01
	3	0.632	2.006	0.04	0.00	0.14	0.08	0.82
	4	0.449	2.381	0.00	0.83	0.00	0.57	0.09
	5	0.328	2.785	0.84	0.00	0.71	0.00	0.03

a. Dependent variable: PersCounter2008

This work was previously published in the International Journal of Electronic Government Research, Volume 7, Issue 3, edited by Vishanth Weerakkody, pp. 21-37, copyright 2011 by IGI Publishing (an imprint of IGI Global).

Chapter 14
Evaluating and Designing Electronic Government for the Future:
Observations and Insights from Australia

Nigel Martin
The Australian National University, Australia

John Rice
University of Adelaide, Australia

ABSTRACT

This paper uses data from a program of customer interviews and focus group research conducted by the Australian government to develop an electronic services evaluation and design framework. A proven theory building approach has been used to develop and confirm the various components of electronic government (e-government) use and satisfaction from original government studies conducted in Australia and to create the new evaluation framework. Building on the extant e-government literature, the reintroduction of the original data into the framework yielded some emergent observations and insights for future e-government design, including the somewhat paradoxical importance of human contacts and interactions in electronic channels, service efficiency and process factors that impinge on customer satisfaction and dissatisfaction, and a potential growth trajectory for telephony based e-government for older segments of the community.

INTRODUCTION

In 2004, the Australian Government commissioned an exploratory study into Australians' use and satisfaction with e-government services over 2004-2005 (Commonwealth of Australia, 2005).

This single use study was repeated in 2006, 2007 and 2008 to sample services use and customer satisfaction over time (Commonwealth of Australia, 2006, 2007, 2008). The intent of the study was to explore the following: (1) how people use the electronic and physical service delivery channels

DOI: 10.4018/978-1-4666-2458-0.ch014

to contact government (i.e. the study concentrated on the electronic and physical service domains); (2) satisfaction with these service channels, and the reasoning for the levels of satisfaction and dissatisfaction; (3) motivating factors and barriers to using online and telephony service channels; and (iv) preferences for future services delivery. Importantly, the study was also directed at assessing what potential changes in the Australian community (e.g. demographic, socio-economic, technological) might impact future e-government offerings. However, while the methodology used telephone interviews combined with community focus groups to explore specific service delivery issues, no contextual or evaluative model was developed for the study.

Over the past twenty years, researchers and analysts have asserted that the development of a logical or contextual evaluation model is an important cornerstone of social science investigations, commercial assessments and research inquiries (Bernard, 2000; Bickman 1987, 1990; Bryman, 2004; Chen, 1990; Cooper & Schindler, 2007; Weiss, 1998; Wholey et al., 1994). Experts suggest that the model forms a useful frame of guidance for the description of constructs and their inter-relationships, including contextual factors, enabling objects, outcomes and outputs, integrated behaviours, and future intentions and preferences (Wholey, 1983). Accordingly, our study was motivated by the requirement to identify and model e-government constructs and more fully comprehend their relationships. In doing this, we are able to contribute to a broader understanding of electronic public services mechanisms and what directions future e-government designs might take in the light of changing human and technological contexts (e.g. ageing populations, growing work commitments, varying technology skill levels). This study combined theory building practices with the original federal government studies on

electronic services use and satisfaction to create an evaluation model. Some of the original data has been reanalysed in the context of this new model in order to recursively inform future service design directions and options for government.

The theory building approach is suited to this study as it calls for a detailed examination and analysis of the component parts (i.e. the original research data and initial results) and the mapping of the components or constructs into a higher level representation of the phenomenon under analysis (i.e. the evaluation model) (Berkley & Gupta, 1994; Glaser, 1992; Glaser & Strauss, 1967; Strauss, 1987; Strauss & Corbin, 1990). Indeed by using theory building, the abstraction and specification of the evaluation model has offered additional insights on e-government design not previously exposed during the initial analysis. Accordingly, the approach adds to our overall understanding, and highlights the importance, of technical e-government services and process design (Chen et al., 2006; Goldstein et al., 2002; Hill et al., 2002; Karwan & Markland, 2006; Tax & Stuart, 1997), particularly in the light of such a substantial consumer research program. The results of this study are considered to be internationally applicable and comparable.

The balance of the article is developed as follows. We discuss the background to the original study and data collection by the Australian government. Next, we develop a discussion of the extant e-government literature that relates primarily to electronic services design, implementation and delivery into the community. This is followed by a description of the research method, including the theory building, and compilation of the proposed evaluation model. Important trends and results, including alternative insights on electronic services design, from the reintroduction of the data into the model are discussed. The paper concludes with a summary of key remarks.

BACKGROUND: THE ORIGINAL STUDIES

The original commercially based studies were commissioned by the Australian federal government (through the Department of Finance and Deregulation) in order to determine what e-government services were 'actually wanted' by citizens, having regard to current services preferences and future e-government demands. In taking this stance, the federal government took a national leadership position on e-government services, stating that all levels of government (i.e. national, state and municipal) needed to ensure 'citizen founded service delivery' going forward, thereby meeting the needs of individuals, businesses and the community (Commonwealth of Australia, 2005, 2006, 2007, 2008). In essence, the studies were intended to inform multiple levels of government on the emerging citizen and governmental requirements for future e-government design and development. This approach is consistent with the future directions for e-government strategy enunciated in Jaeger and Thompson (2003).

During these inquiries, over 16,000 members of the community were telephone interviewed, coupled with seventeen regional focus groups conducted around Australia. Table 1 shows a summary of the program participants. Given the maturity of this multi-year e-government evalua-

tion program, the 2008 study and user responses formed the basis for developing our evaluation model. In the 2008 study, the interview and focus group participants were persons aged 18 years and older, and were sourced using random digit dialing of telephone numbers (previous studies used the electronic Australian White Pages directory and a Roy Morgan Research Single Source database of electronic services users). Gender and age quotas were applied to ensure representative sampling of the Australian population, with the interview sample stratified by area and over-sampled in regional areas to ensure valid regional analyses. Focus group participants were online home users with varying levels of experience (i.e. experienced users had accessed/used a government website within the previous 12 months). The collected data was weighted in accordance with the Australian Bureau of Statistics estimates for national population distributions, including gender and age factors.

FOUNDATIONS OF ELECTRONIC GOVERNMENT DEVELOPMENT AND DESIGN

The foundations of e-government development and design are a rich tapestry of studies that examine and explicate a diverse range of systemic

Table 1. Studies sample summaries

Year	Telephone Interview Sample Size (n)	Focus Group Sample Size	Focus Group Locations
2005	3,839	33	Metropolitan Victoria and South Australia, and regional Victoria and Western Australia
2006	5,040	33	Metropolitan New South Wales and Queensland, and regional New South Wales and South Australia
2007	4,016	34	Metropolitan Tasmania and Victoria, and regional New South Wales/Victoria and Queensland
2008	3,650	47	Metropolitan New South Wales, Queensland and Western Australia, and regional Victoria and South Australia

Source: Commonwealth of Australia (2005, 2006, 2007, 2008)

constructs, relationships and behaviours. A separation of the literature into the supply (services designed and delivered by public authorities) and demand (services evaluated and consumed by citizens) sides of e-government shows a broad range of issues covered through the discipline's cumulative tradition. In supplying e-government services, researchers assert that public agencies must look closely at the opportunities to integrate and market multiple customer services (i.e. create a desirable one stop services hub); fund, create and incentivize scalable technological infrastructures; provide secure information repositories and privacy protections; and, assure quality information sets for clients (Lee et al., 2005; Trimi & Sheng, 2008; Weiling & Kwok, 2004; West, 2004; Wimmer, 2002). Other studies have shown that executive leadership and visionary support, and the innovative spirit of service implementation managers are critical for e-government delivery and adoption (Moon & Norris, 2005; Schedler & Summermatter, 2007); while further investigations suggest that smaller and more nimble local and regional government structures are enablers of successful e-government initiatives (Holden et al., 2003; Moon, 2002; Moon & Norris, 2005; Norris & Moon, 2005). Additionally, an examination of e-government adoption literature using a designer's lens suggests that interface structure and useability, systems security features, personal privacy sealing and protection, and, the velocity, quality and convenience of the service interaction are key design determinants in the systems adoption space (Belanger & Carter, 2008; Carter & Belanger, 2005a; Ebrahim & Irani, 2005; Kumar et al., 2007; Tung & Rieck, 2005).

In contrast, inquiries that focused on the evaluation of e-government services by individuals and organizations argued that interaction complexity; information intake loads; systems content, navigation and reliability; transactional security and privacy; and the relative advantages of e-government channels (compared with other service modes) are important design issues (Bertot et al., 2008; Carter & Belanger, 2005b; Gupta & Jana, 2003; Irani et al., 2008; Peters et al., 2004; Wang et al., 2005). Also, a further group of studies concentrated on services consumption by citizens, highlighting the importance of understanding service access and convenience behaviours; meeting customer satisfaction levels, systemic personalization demands, and individual needs; and, meeting the various clients' value propositions (Jaeger & Thompson, 2003; Milward & Snyder, 1996; Pieterson et al., 2007; Pieterson & Ebbers, 2008; Wimmer et al., 2001). Importantly, we also noted some crossover aspects of the literature that touched on the e-government services supply and demand conditions. As an example, some studies found positive (e.g. lower cost of services delivery) and negative (e.g. low take up rates by customers) impacts from e-government delivery and citizen adoption, while also confirming that technological (e.g. lack of infrastructure, poor legacy system design) and human (e.g. insufficient customer skills and training, low socio-economic position) barriers to e-government adoption continue to persist (Moon & Norris, 2005; Norris & Moon, 2005). Hence, this type of combinative literature, that more directly informs our study, poses that multiple government service channels (i.e. human and technology based) must be retained in the light of attempting to overcome digital divide barriers, merging the government and citizen perspectives of e-government, and addressing the personal, situation and task based characteristics of government business contacts (Ebbers et al., 2008; Grönlund, 2002; Pieterson, 2010; Reddick, 2005, 2010; Teerling & Pieterson, 2010). In a positive sense, the depth of the discipline's literature will allow us to draw on all of these seminal works in e-government as we discuss the results and observations from our study.

METHODOLOGY

The research methodology adopted in this study is based on the combination of theory building and the secondary analysis of government-collected data for evaluation model development and retesting (Glaser, 1992; Glaser & Strauss, 1967; Strauss, 1987; Strauss & Corbin, 1990). In this study, the secondary data analysis was used to identify the major model components or constructs which were then combined with the relevant theory (from the extant literature) to form the evaluation model (Berkley & Gupta, 1994). Importantly, this allowed the evaluation model to be based on actual e-government user comments and behaviours rather than strictly theoretical constructs and components. We would offer that this enables the results of the study to be applied to future e-government design in a practical and informative way.

In the first part of the study, the 2008 government report and the collected data are reviewed and analysed in order to identify and confirm the major model constructs. As an example, the User Satisfaction component of the proposed model can be directly linked to the interview questions (e.g. Q9D: How satisfied were you with the ease

of finding the specific information or service you were after?; Q9E: How satisfied were you with the ease of using the service?), interview responses, and the consolidated chapter of the study report (e.g. Chapter 6: Satisfaction with Service Delivery) (Commonwealth of Australia, 2008). This provides the traceable linkage between the data and the proposed evaluation model construct. Table 2 shows examples of these linkages.

In the second part of the study, established theories are applied to the constructs in order to further develop the model, including the key relationships, sequences, and behaviours. As an example, decision-making theories might be used to support and validate the evaluation model component related to service channel selection and reasoning. Similarly, end user satisfaction theories could be used to substantiate and reinforce the user satisfaction component of the model. Importantly, the integrated theories assist in validation and provide support for the proposed model.

In the final part of the study, the summarized model is also retested for key insights and additional observations by reusing or reintroducing the collected data. This specific activity allows the model to release new and emergent insights related

Table 2. Example evaluation model components and interview linkages

Evaluation Model Component	Gov. Report Reference	Interview Questions
Factors impacting the selection of the electronic channel	Chapter 7: Why people choose a particular service delivery channel to contact government	Q6: Thinking of your most recent contact, why did you do it by the Internet? Q13: What, if anything, would encourage you to use the Internet more often for accessing government services?
Online Channel	Chapter 2: Introduction Chapter 4: Use of electronic services through the Internet	Q1: Do you use the Internet? Q12: Thinking of ALL the contacts that you had with government agencies and services over the past 12 months, about what proportion of these took place over the Internet?
User Satisfaction and Dissatisfaction	Chapter 6: Satisfaction with service delivery	Q9(a): How satisfied were you with the outcome of the services received? Q9(b): How satisfied were you with the ease of finding specific information?
Future Use Preferences	Chapter 10: Future service delivery preferences	Q11: If you could access government services by telephone, over the Internet, by mail, in-person, or by some other method, what would be your preferred way of doing it?

Source: Commonwealth of Australia (2008)

to future services design that may not have been visible during the original data collection (where no model was present). In this sense, while the data was collected to meet a particular governmental requirement, the new evaluation model enables secondary use of the source datasets.

DEVELOPING THE EVALUATION MODEL

The following sections of the article present a discussion on each of the components of the evaluation model, including the explanatory theory that assists in validating and supporting each component. The components are examined in sequential order starting with the context of the e-government service delivery and culminating with a broader discussion of future service preferences and options. Readers might note that the model construction draws on more well-established technology adoption theory, and so for the purposes of temporal analysis has been separated into the current customer behaviours and outcomes, and future intended behaviours and e-government preferences that may emerge over time (Davis, 1989; Fishbein & Ajzen, 1975; Salam et al., 2005). Although based on actual user behaviours and responses, the linearity of the model should not be interpreted to suggest that all users are fixed in their views or actions within any of the vertical layered constructs. The model allows for users to modify and adopt different personal positions within any layer and hence represents the highly changeable nature of human behaviours, particularly in relation to engaging with e-government systems and processes.

Services Delivery Context

Complex systems theory suggests that human economies can form organized complex and adaptive systems (Johnson, 2001, 2007; Weaver, 1948). The parts of these systems can be largely

interactive, and with a differentiated structure are capable of dynamic interaction with other systems. The systems are also considered to emerge due to their inherent organized and adaptive behaviours. In relation to the first part of the proposed evaluation model, the collected data is directed towards the broader level of government structures and contacts, service delivery channels, types of interactions, different technologies, and available services as important contextual components of the research (Commonwealth of Australia, 2008; Moon, 2002; Moon & Norris, 2005; Pieterson, 2010; Weiling & Kwok, 2004). Accordingly, these aspects of the broader economy form the systemic context for e-government services usage (or non-usage).

Service Channel Selection and Reasoning

In selecting a government service channel, it is likely that citizens would consider the various benefits and drawbacks as part of a decision-making process (Teale et al., 2003). While various high level decision-making models exist, normative and incremental models may provide some direction for the analysis of citizens' channel or domain choices. In applying normative decision-making schemes, a citizen may establish a clear business objective, understand their problem or issue, and evaluate the various options prior to making that choice (Baron, 1994, 1996, 2000; Blau, 1964). Comparatively, citizens' that apply an incremental approach to decisions may look towards progressing their current business activities in different ways (i.e. build on current experience and actions, avoid risk) (Lindblom, 1959; Lindblom & Cohen, 1979; Lindblom & Dahl, 1976; Lindblom & Woodhouse, 1993). These two decision frames show that citizens can opt for newer electronic service channels or retain the use of proven physical channels.

In addition, other studies have shown that citizens and electronic service users may apply varying reasons for selecting a specific service channel or domain (Adams et al., 1992; Belanger et al., 2002; Davis, 1989; Moon & Welch, 2004; Pieterson, 2010; Rogers, 1995). Some typical reasoning constructs, including ease of use or convenience; trust, security and privacy; service access and usefulness; or, awareness of service availability, have consistently appeared in past e-government studies (Milward & Snyder, 1996; Pieterson et al., 2007; Teerling & Pieterson, 2010; West 2004; Wimmer, 2002). The second part of the proposed model, consistent with the user data (i.e. channel convenience, availability, usability, and features; personal awareness and access), identifies factors that shape channel choices (Commonwealth of Australia, 2008).

Service Channel Usage

The definition of usable electronic public services encompasses the deployment of information and communications technologies (ICT) for government operations, citizen engagement, communication of public information, and public service provision (Sharma, 2004, 2006; Sharma & Gupta, 2003). The major service channel in this study is the Government to Citizen (G2C) conduit where government provides online access to public information and services to citizens. In the Australian context, typical G2C applications enfold the capacity to place calls to contact centres and engage in question-answer exchanges, file income tax returns, pay rates and taxes, renew boat, car, trailer and caravan licenses, pay traffic infringement notices, book vehicular inspections and tests, acquire government information, complete and transmit online forms and documents, and receive government payments and benefits. These typical e-government services are mirrored in other countries and jurisdictions (Ebbers et al., 2008; Moon, 2002; Pieterson & Ebbers, 2008; Reddick, 2005, 2010). The initial studies collected information on the use of electronic (Internet and telephone) and physical (postal mail services and physical

in-person) channels, including users' willingness or ability to provide personal information using online channels (Commonwealth of Australia, 2008). This user data supports the channel usage part of the proposed model.

User Satisfaction and Dissatisfaction

The measurement of user satisfaction dates back to the multi-factor test instruments developed by Bailey and Pearson (1983) and Ives et al. (1983). These studies offered respondents a number of factors (e.g. accuracy, timeliness, confidence in the system, volume of output, feelings of control, vendor support) for their selection and ranking, given the factors relative importance to each respondent. Other following studies introduced the temporal dimension of evolving and changing ICT and variations in user behaviours (Cheung & Lee, 2005; Doll & Torkzadeh, 1988; McKinney et al., 2002). As examples, Cheung and Lee (2005) and McKinney et al. (2002) developed instruments to measure the satisfaction of users with electronic portals and the broader online environment (information viewing), respectively. In the Doll and Torkzadeh (1988) study, the researchers developed and tested an instrument that was focused on end user satisfaction. The definition of an end user was characterized by those users that exclusively interacted with the computer interface (other types of users also interrelated with web developers and operations and helpdesk staff).

In terms of how user satisfaction might be defined in the proposed evaluation model, some of the noted studies provide suitable options. For instance, Ives et al. (1983) define user information satisfaction as the perceived extent to which the available information system meets user information requirements. Doll and Torkzadeh (1988) offer a much broader definition of user satisfaction seeking to examine the user's overall satisfaction with a specific computer system. In this study, the user satisfaction definition has to be expanded to enfold all the service channels, and might be stated as 'the user's overall satisfaction with a government service'. This approach is consistent with other e-government research that examines the issues of customer services usage and satisfaction (Ebbers et al., 2008; Milward & Snyder, 1996; Pieterson & Ebbers, 2008; Wimmer et al., 2001) The data collected during the interviews and focus groups rated user satisfaction in terms of the outcome achieved by the user, time taken to obtain a reply to an enquiry, the ease of finding the required information or service, and, the ease of using the government service (Commonwealth of Australia, 2008). The initial study also collected data on user satisfaction in relation to the types of transaction executed, and the level of government from which the service was obtained. The collected data suitably augments the satisfaction related parts of the proposed model.

Contingent Intended Behaviours

The customers' intentions to use or access electronic services (information or transactions) have generally been considered to include some preconditions or contingent factors. Several electronic government and business studies have shown that the perceived ease of use and/or usefulness of the service; trust, privacy and security related to the online environment; infrastructural enhancement and improvements; computer and online service accessibility; and, an awareness of what might be achieved using electronic service channels can shape and mediate the intentions of current and potential users (Jaeger & Thompson, 2003; Lee et al., 2005; Lee-Kelley & James, 2003; Salam et al., 2005; Sohail & Shanmugham, 2003; Tan & Teo, 2000; Titah & Barki, 2006; Warkentin et al., 2002; Weiling & Kwok, 2004). Accordingly, the clients' intentions to use or increase their use of online public services may be influenced by one or several of these contingent factors. In a relevant example related to online financial transactions adoption, Sohail and Shanmugham (2003) found that on-

line service accessibility, awareness, attitudes to change, ease of use, and general convenience can impact and shape customer adoption behaviours. In a specific government services context, Warkentin et al. (2002) devised a model that included ease of use, systems usefulness, trust, risk and behavioural control (including self-confidence) constructs as precursors to clients' intention to engage with electronic service channels.

The initial study collected information on the factors that may precipitate increased or first-time use of the online channel by citizens (Commonwealth of Australia, 2008). In particular, the participants were asked to consider website usability, website content, online infrastructure improvements, better online access, increased awareness of online capabilities, computer and online skills development, customer convenience, personal privacy and data security, and transactional costs as factors that may impact online usage behaviours. Also, the study examined the selected contingent factors within the various channel preferences (i.e. online, telephony, postal mail, and physically in-person) in order to observe any potential service channel adoption trends (e.g. improved customer access may enable first time online channel selection). This data supports the user intentions portion of the proposed model.

Future Channel Preferences

The customers' future interaction preferences might be considered to be fundamentally grounded in consumer behaviours. Customer preference research suggests that potential users of public and private online services may exhibit varying behaviours related to interpersonal experiences and the associated willingness to change (Durkin, 2006; Zeithaml & Gilly, 1987); the capacity to learn, understand and engage in new and innovative service offerings, especially in the growing area of mobile government (Carpenter & Nakamoto, 1989; Kahneman & Snell, 1990; Lee et al., 2005;

Trimi & Sheng, 2008; Tversky & Kahneman, 1974); the lack of trust in non face-to-face transactions and relationships (Durkin, 2006; Durkin et al., 2003; Holden et al., 2003; Lockett & Littler, 1997); the need for human contact and personal interaction (Durkin et al., 2003; Dwyer et al., 1987; Pieterson & Ebbers, 2008; Reddick, 2010); the establishment of an intimate relationship with a website or online service (Li et al., 2006); and, the differences in the types of personal business tasks being undertaken (Ebbers et al., 2008; Pieterson & Ebbers, 2008; Smart et al., 2001). Specifically, some of these studies found that the non-adoption of technologies was based on the strong preference for personal human interaction (Pieterson & Ebbers, 2008; Zeithaml & Gilly, 1987), while others found that consumers can continuously learn about innovative products and service offerings with their preferences changing and evolving over time (Carpenter & Nakamoto, 1989; Lee et al., 2005; Trimi & Sheng, 2008).

The data collected during the initial study focused on identifying the actual business interaction channel used, and the stated customer preference (Commonwealth of Australia, 2008). The interview and focus group participants were allocated to their major business channel usage segment (i.e. online, telephony, postal mail, and physically in-person) and were requested to identify their future channel preference under ideal conditions (i.e. all services access methods available and affordable). The initial study also examined the stated business channel preferences by age profile, and investigated the customer preferences for government website structure. The three website structures available for selection were milestone events in the consumers' life (e.g. having a baby, purchasing a home, retiring from work), topic areas (e.g. transport, driving licenses, arts and entertainment, recreation), and government department name (e.g. Department of Transport). This data supports the future service preferences segment of the proposed model.

Proposed Evaluation Model

The proposed evaluation model is depicted in Figure 1 and is a linear, six part representation of public services usage by customers in varying socio-economic groups. The model commences with the broader service delivery context that feeds into the various factors that impact the selection of physical or electronic channels. The customers' selection of the service method is the important decision precursor to the use of the channel (next part of the model). Following the customer service interactions and experiences, the users' feelings of satisfaction or dissatisfaction form the next sequential element of the model. The first four elements of the service usage model represent the clients' current behaviours and outcomes. Having undertaken the government service and attained a level of satisfaction (or dissatisfaction), users are probed for views on what typical factors, if any, may stimulate first time or the expanded use of the electronic channels. The final part of the proposed model asks users to identify future government service channel preferences (physical or electronic). The final two parts of the model embody the clients' future behaviours, intentions and e-government preferences.

DISCUSSION OF OBSERVATIONS AND INSIGHTS

A discussion of the complementary observations and insights following reconsideration of the collected data in the context of the proposed model is presented in the following sections. The outcomes of the secondary analysis are focused in the area of qualitative customer behaviours. Specifically, we discuss why some customers make certain decisions and use specific service channels or domains; what issues or processes may drive customer satisfaction and/or dissatisfaction; what types of issues or factors may stimulate increased use of a specific service channel or domain; and,

Figure 1. Proposed evaluation model

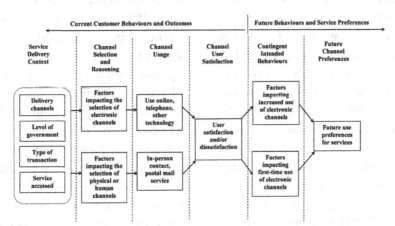

what services some sections of the community may prefer in the future. In looking to these insights, there are important issues that should be kept in mind.

First, we should remember that Australia is fast reaching a critical juncture in its history. Similar to the economies of Canada and United States, the Australian population is undergoing a substantial shift in age profile. Approximately 14 per cent of the Australian population is aged over 65 years (nominal retirement age) with future population ageing projected to have significant impacts on reduced workforce participation, health services growth, technology skills shortages and enlarged housing demand (Australian Bureau of Statistics, 2009). What this means is that the socio-economic well-being of the nation will become increasingly dependent on a smaller number of labour force participants paying taxes and providing financial inputs to governments' revenues. This may place financial and funding pressures on governments in the area of public infrastructure development and services delivery, including e-government (Lee et al., 2005; Moon, 2002; Weiling & Kwok, 2004). Hence, the smaller revenue pool leaves the potential for future generations of Australians to be subjected to comparatively lower average living standards.

Second, it could be argued that some workers in the future will be time poor with potentially longer working hours coupled to shorter periods of discretionary rest and personal activities. Any future shortfall in technically skilled labour threatens to make this situation significantly worse. Hence, as workers get busier and skill levels move into deficit, the need for efficient and effective public service delivery systems and processes will grow (Milward & Snyder, 1996; Pieterson & Ebbers, 2008; Pieterson et al., 2007; Wimmer et al., 2001). These changes in the demography of working Australia are not insignificant. A key argument flowing from the following observations and insights is that any future e-government designs will need to be consistent with movements in local community and regional profiles.

Factors Impacting Channel Selection: Keeping It Real for Customers

Using the 2008 study data, one of the important results is that, despite the emergence and expanded use of online technologies, government customers continue to rely on 'real' person contacts as a means of transacting government business (Commonwealth of Australia, 2008). The study shows that 34% of all participants' most recent government contact took place in-person, with this behaviour underpinned by the preference to speak with a real person (14% of in-person customers) and the ability to question, explain and clarify issues (11% of in-person customers). Other channel utilization results also show trends towards this personal interaction. For example, 29% of the interviewed regular web users (e.g. bloggers, surfers) who were queried as to why they chose not to contact the government using the online channel stated a definite need or preference for speaking or meeting with a 'real' person (Pieterson & Ebbers, 2008). Similarly, 22% of the interviewed telephone users who were queried as to why they chose to contact the government using the voice channel stated a clear preference for speaking with a 'real' person, being able to ask questions and get information, and/or explaining and clarifying important issues (i.e. informational e-citizen preference) (Lee et al., 2005; Reddick, 2005). Therefore, when we look at the channel selection and reasoning segment of our evaluation model, despite any underlying predilections for pure online customer interactions, the results suggest to us that the ability to contact a 'real' person in government service delivery is a key factor in channel selection (Ebbers et al., 2008; Lee et al., 2005; Pieterson & Ebbers, 2008). Accordingly, the presence of human contacts appears to be a consistent and ongoing system design requirement for e-government (Cook et al., 2002; Hill et al., 2006; Reddick, 2010; Tax & Stuart, 1997).

Factors Impacting Channel Selection: Customer Convenience and Time-Saving

In selecting electronic public services, clients in the 2008 study suggested that convenience (i.e. accessing the service at a time that suits them) and time-saving (i.e. using the service took less time compared with other channels) were key determinants for channel selection. In the study, 56% of respondents who had used the Internet for government service contact had done so on the contributory basis of overall personal convenience, while 19% of online users had used the channel as a time-saving measure. In the telephony channel, 44% of the user group stated that convenience was a principal reason for service selection, while 14% of users considered the voice channel to require less time (Commonwealth of Australia, 2008). The concept of 'convenience' typically connotes a measure of personal and task management and discretion as to when business might be conducted, while the 'time-saving' construct might normatively represent individual productivity in the e-government contact (Bertot et al., 2008; Carter & Belanger, 2005a, 2005b; Ebbers et al., 2008; Pieterson & Ebbers, 2008). The matters of personal convenience and productivity have been consistent and discrete customer-centric issues in earlier e-government studies (Milward & Snyder, 1996; Wimmer, 2002; Wimmer et al., 2001). However, a different view of these two determinants suggests a close corresponding relationship, where customers who use e-government services can determine the sequence and timing of their business interactions, while also creating 'time and space' to improve personal efficiency and productivity. Consequently, based on this observation, we would propose that system designers may ultimately need to ensure that user convenience and time-efficiency are intrinsic co-characteristics of future electronic service delivery systems and designs (Bertot et al., 2008; Karwan & Markland, 2006; Lee & Perry, 2002; Pieterson, 2010; Schedler & Summermatter, 2007; Wimmer, 2002; Wimmer et al., 2001). Put simply, in the future busy members of the community will need convenient and efficient e-government system options.

User Satisfaction or Dissatisfaction: Understanding Customer Service and Processes

The results from the 2008 focus groups provided a useful, if not a somewhat confounding, view of client satisfaction (Commonwealth of Australia, 2008). The participants alluded to a number of customer service concept factors that contributed towards a satisfactory experience, including courteous and responsive staff members, knowledgeable staff members, timely and efficient services delivery, meeting commitments, and fulfilling promises. Unsurprisingly, this part of the study suggests that client satisfaction is closely aligned with the customer service concept. However, in comparison, client dissatisfaction is not considered to represent a diametrically opposite condition. Focus group members stated that, while treatment from staff can have a material impact on the service experience, a number of complex process issues can converge to deliver a less satisfied client. Some of the mentioned process issues include difficulty in accessing the organization and/or the correct or best service contact (person), inappropriate or no information available, no assistance or help available, inefficient or overly complex processes and/or systems, non-response to communications, and poor corporate-level communications (Ebrahim & Irani, 2005; Milward & Snyder, 1996; Peters et al., 2004; Pieterson et al., 2007; Wang et al., 2005; Wimmer et al., 2001).

These results do not in any way diminish the requirement for sound customer service in avoiding client dissatisfaction. Indeed, the interview results show that suboptimal levels of customer service were experienced by 62% of those 355 participants who noted dissatisfaction with their latest government service outcome (i.e. approximately 221 customers received some form of poor customer service). However, when we look at these results in the light of the user satisfaction component of our model, some important results for service designers emerged. First, the customer service concept might be considered to possess a primary relationship with the satisfaction construct. That is, good quality customer service from government employees and a sense of personal satisfaction are synonymous in the eyes of e-government users (Lee et al., 2005). Second, several complex process-driven dimensions (some non-customer service or staff-client

interaction related) can shape and determine the dissatisfaction of a customer interaction. Hence, we would offer that future e-government design schemas must take account of efficiency issues such as high visibility and well marketed service access points (West, 2004), information quality and search precision, and elimination of service non-response (Goldstein et al., 2002; Hill et al., 2002; Kumar et al., 2007).

Factors Impacting Increased Channel Use: Taking a Human View of Service Delivery

A comparison of interview participants' most recent government contact for the 2004-2005 and 2008 periods shows a substantial shift or reverse trend in contact behaviours (Commonwealth of Australia, 2005, 2008). In the 2004-2005 study, 47% of participants used electronic domain channels compared with 59% of respondents using physical domain contacts (note, the interviews allowed participants to report using more than one channel for the same public service). In the 2008 study, the trend is reversed with 68% of participants using electronic channels compared with 43% of respondents using mail or in-person contacts. While this appears to be a positive electronic services growth trend, a further interpretation is also possible. A re-aggregation of the data into telephone and in-person (personal), and online and mail (impersonal) contacts shows an important complementary outcome. In 2004-2005, 74% of participants opted for real person contacts compared with 32% of users using impersonal channels. In 2008, 64% of those interviewed took the real person contact option compared to the 37% impersonal channel users. Although in decline, the results show that a substantial number of customers have a continued reliance on personal contact with government employees (i.e. a human view) during the interaction. This result demonstrates the ongoing importance of human interactions and is consistent with other contemporary e-government studies (Ebbers et al., 2008; Pieterson & Ebbers, 2008; Pieterson et al., 2007). Therefore, while electronic services might exhibit an inclined usage trajectory, it could be argued that 'real' person contacts play a very important role in the delivery and management of public services as depicted in Figure 2. We would argue that this viewpoint model describes an important and highly complementary 'human' dimension in future government systems design and implementation, while reinforcing the message: "don't forget the person in public services design and delivery" (Cook et al., 2002; Hill et al., 2006; Reddick, 2010; Tax & Stuart, 1997).

Future Channel Preferences: A Growing Role for Public Telephony Services

One of the more instructive trends that emerged from the 2008 study is the potential for expanded future use of telephony for older customer groupings (Commonwealth of Australia, 2008). The interviews found that 79% of people who accessed a public service in the previous 12 months are also online users. Importantly, while 94% of respon-

dents aged in the 18-24 year group were general online users, the percentages decrease markedly in the older age group segments (i.e. 81% for 45-54 years, 74% for 55-64 years, and 44% for 65 years and over). While there has been some growth in casual Internet use by older members of the community since 2004-2005 (i.e. +18% in the 55-64 years, and +16% in the 65 years and over groups), general online use is favoured by the younger age groups. However, when the service preference data is introduced, as outlined in Table 3, the potential for expanded telephony based services is evident.

The trends show a future growth preference for government service telephony with increasing customer age. These results suggest that public agencies should consider the development of complementary and higher quality telephony based services (e.g. more customer call and contact centres, less complex interactive voice response systems, mobile telephony friendly voice and text services) that caters specifically for the needs of older customers who may not readily engage with the government in online environments (Berkley & Gupta, 1997; Danziger & Andersen, 2002; Reddick, 2010). We also note

Figure 2. Complementary views of multi-domain e-government services

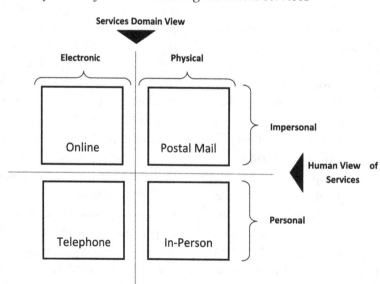

Table 3. Telephone and Online service channel preferences

Age Group	18-24 Yrs	25-34 Yrs	35-44 Yrs	45-54 Yrs	55-64 Yrs	65+ Yrs	Use Trend with Increasing Age
Online	58%	61%	52%	43%	39%	14%	Decrease ↓
Telephone	22%	26%	32%	34%	37%	50%	Increase ↑

Source: Commonwealth of Australia (2008)

that the large growth in mobile telephony services in Australia (i.e. 18.4 million in 2004-05 to 24.2 million in 2008-09) will support the future development of more innovative e-government systems (ACMA, 2005, 2009; Lee et al., 2005; Trimi & Sheng, 2008).

CONCLUSION

In concluding this article, we duly acknowledge that this study represents a conventional piece of research based on theory building techniques and the secondary use of interview response and focus group data drawn from e-government users in the Australian community. However, equally we argue that the application of actual user data in the development of the evaluation model provides for a practical and informative set of observations and insights that can assist future e-government system and process designs. As we noted earlier, this is very important given Australia's ageing population and potential demographic changes in the future (Australian Bureau of Statistics, 2009).

Specifically, this study identified several important issues for future e-government design. First, the model assisted in clarifying and highlighting the importance of 'real' person contacts and human issues in services delivery. The observations from user behaviour shows that, irrespective of user technology savvy or any push from governments to conduct more business online, users have needs (e.g. questioning, exploration, clarification, informational) that can only be met by interacting with humans (Pieterson & Ebbers,

2008; Reddick, 2005, 2010; Teerling & Pieterson, 2010). Hence, pure non-mediated online channels are unlikely to work in all government service delivery scenarios. Second, customer convenience and time savings are complementary and important characteristics in the design of e-government services. The evaluation suggests that a significant number of users in the community will take the decision to engage with e-government platforms on the basis of personal convenience and/or task productivity. Hence, future designs require these personal and task characteristics to be co-resident in e-government systems or processes if user take-up rates are to be enhanced (Ebbers et al., 2008; Pieterson & Ebbers, 2008; Pieterson et al., 2007). Third, while customer service quality and user satisfaction with e-government services are closely related, customer dissatisfaction can be driven by public agency process factors or issues. Recasting of the focus group data suggests that overly complex and disjointed processes can be inefficient, time wasting and damaging to busy customer interactions which, in turn, lead to user dissatisfaction. Designers of e-government would do well to remember that these process issues are critical for system users, and must be considered in the holistic construction of future technology systems (Grönlund, 2002; Milward & Snyder, 1996; Pieterson et al., 2007). Fourth, a simple reanalysis shows the true value of telephony based e-government to older clients and customers in the community. While younger users may easily adopt online service channels, older sections of the community prefer the use of telephony systems for transacting their business. In essence, we think that future designs will need to creatively embrace the use of voice and telephonic systems, in fixed and mobile formats, as part of the ongoing development of e-government infrastructure (Lee et al., 2005; Trimi & Sheng, 2008; Weiling & Kwok, 2004). In summarizing these insights, future projections of age and socio-economic profiles for Australia point to the need to cater for busier, older, and possibly less technically skilled users of e-government (Australian Bureau of Statistics, 2009).

In summary, past government studies show that Australia is moving forward with e-government developments at all tiers of public sector operations (Commonwealth of Australia, 2005, 2006, 2007, 2008). That said, e-government designers must continue to be mindful that, while the online environment continues to grow and thrive in terms of consumer usage, in an ageing Australian population (increased by 5 years in the last 2 decades to a median age of 38 years due to low fertility rates and longer life expectancy) (Australian Bureau of Statistics, 2009), human contact is still valued and needed by growing sectors of the community. Given some of our reanalysis, it appears unlikely that pure unmediated online systems will meet all users' service requirements in the future. We also think it is important that governments of all persuasions remember that consumers are driven by various factors, including convenience, personal productivity, technological skills (i.e. the ability to use the technology infrastructure and systems), and possibly socio-economic standing (i.e. the ability to afford the technology infrastructure and systems). Therefore, while a dazzling array of high value digital communication technologies continues to emerge (e.g. 3-dimensional high definition audio visual systems), there is a hope that our observations and insights, based on past users' behaviour, are not lost in future e-government designs.

ACKNOWLEDGMENT

The authors acknowledge the support and assistance of Australian Government Information Management Office within the federal Department of Finance and Deregulation.

REFERENCES

Adams, D., Nelson, R., & Todd, P. (1992). Perceived usefulness, ease of use and usage of information technology: A replication. *Management Information Systems Quarterly*, 227–247. doi:10.2307/249577

Australian Bureau of Statistics. (2009). Cat No. 3201.0 -. *Population by Age and Sex, Australian States and Territories*, (June): 2009. Retrieved from http://abs.gov.au/AUSSTATS.

Australian Communications and Media Authority (ACMA). (2005). *ACMA telecommunications performance report, December 2005*. Retrieved from http://www.acma.gov.au/WEB/STANDARD/pc=PC_100376

Australian Communications and Media Authority (ACMA). (2009). *ACMA communications report, November 2009*. Retrieved from http://www.acma.gov.au/WEB/STANDARD/pc=PC_311972#

Bailey, J. E., & Pearson, S. W. (1983). Development of a tool for measuring and analyzing computer user satisfaction. *Management Science*, *29*(5), 530–545. doi:10.1287/mnsc.29.5.530

Baron, J. (1994). Nonconsequentialist decisions. *The Behavioral and Brain Sciences*, *17*, 1–42. doi:10.1017/S0140525X0003301X

Baron, J. (1996). Norm-endorsement utilitarianism and the nature of utility. *Economics and Philosophy*, *12*, 165–182. doi:10.1017/S0266267100004144

Baron, J. (2000). *Thinking and deciding*. Cambridge, UK: Cambridge University Press.

Bélanger, A., & Carter, L. (2008). Trust and risk in e-government adoption. *The Journal of Strategic Information Systems, 17*, 165–176. doi:10.1016/j.jsis.2007.12.002

Bélanger, F., Hiller, J., & Smith, W. (2002). Trustworthiness in electronic commerce: The role of privacy, security, and site attributes. *The Journal of Strategic Information Systems, 11*, 245–270. doi:10.1016/S0963-8687(02)00018-5

Berkley, B. J., & Gupta, A. (1994). Improving service quality with information technology. *International Journal of Information Management, 14*, 109–121. doi:10.1016/0268-4012(94)90030-2

Bernard, H. R. (2000). *Social research methods: Qualitative and quantitative approaches*. Newbury Park, CA: Sage.

Bertot, J. C., Jaeger, P. T., & McClure, P. M. (2008, May 18-21). Citizen centered e-government services: Benefits, costs and research needs. In *Proceedings of the 9th Annual International Digital Government Research Conference*, Montreal, QC, Canada (pp. 137-142).

Bickman, L. (1987). The functions of program theory. In Bickman, L. (Ed.), *New directions for program evaluation* (pp. 5–17). San Francisco, CA: Jossey-Bass.

Bickman, L. (1990). Study designs. In Yuan, Y. T., & Rivest, M. (Eds.), *Preserving families: Evaluating resources for practitioners and policymakers* (pp. 132–166). Newbury Park, CA: Sage.

Blau, P. M. (1964). *Exchange and power in social life*. New York, NY: John Wiley & Sons.

Bryman, A. (2004). *Social research methods*. Oxford, UK: Oxford University Press.

Carpenter, G. S., & Nakamoto, K. (1989). Consumer preference formation and pioneering advantage. *JMR, Journal of Marketing Research, 26*(3), 285–298. doi:10.2307/3172901

Carter, L., & Belanger, F. (2005a). The influence of perceived characteristics of innovating on e-government adoption. *Electronic. Journal of E-Government, 2*(3), 11–20.

Carter, L., & Belanger, F. (2005b). The utilization of e-government services: Citizen trust, innovation and acceptance factors. *Information Systems Journal, 15*(1), 5–25. doi:10.1111/j.1365-2575.2005.00183.x

Chen, C. C., Wu, C. S., & Wu, R. C. F. (2006). e-Service enhancement priority matrix: The case of an IC foundry company. *Information & Management, 43*, 572–586. doi:10.1016/j.im.2006.01.002

Chen, H. T. (1990). *Theory-driven evaluations*. Thousand Oaks, CA: Sage.

Cheung, C. M. K., & Lee, M. K. O. (2005, January 3-6). The asymmetric effect of website attribute performance on satisfaction: An empirical study. In *Proceedings of the 38th Hawaii International Conference on System Sciences*, Honolulu, HI.

Commonwealth of Australia. (2002). *Centrelink annual report 2001-2002 – Short message service trial* (p. 119). Canberra, Australia: AGPS.

Commonwealth of Australia. (2005). *Australians' use of and satisfaction with e-government services*. Canberra, Australia: AGPS.

Commonwealth of Australia. (2006). *Australians' use of and satisfaction with e-government services*. Canberra, Australia: AGPS.

Commonwealth of Australia. (2007). *Australians' use of and satisfaction with e-government services*. Canberra, Australia: AGPS.

Commonwealth of Australia. (2008). *Australians' use of and satisfaction with e-government services*. Canberra, Australia: AGPS.

Cook, L. S., Bowen, D. E., Chase, R. B., Dasu, S., Stewart, D. M., & Tansik, D. A. (2002). Human issues in service design. *Journal of Operations Management, 20*, 159–174. doi:10.1016/S0272-6963(01)00094-8

Cooper, D. R., & Schindler, P. S. (2007). *Business research methods* (10th ed.). New York, NY: McGraw-Hill.

Danziger, J. N., & Andersen, K. V. (2002). The impacts of information technology on public administration: An analysis of empirical research from the 'Golden Age' of transformation. *International Journal of Public Administration, 25*(5), 591–627. doi:10.1081/PAD-120003292

Davis, F. (1989). Perceived usefulness, perceived ease of use and user acceptance of information technology. *Management Information Systems Quarterly, 13*(3), 319–340. doi:10.2307/249008

Doll, W. J., & Torkzadeh, G. (1988). The measurement of end user computing satisfaction. *Management Information Systems Quarterly, 12*(2), 258–274. doi:10.2307/248851

Durkin, M. (2006). Neglecting the remote relationship: Lessons from internet banking. *Monash Business Review, 2*(1), 1–8.

Durkin, M., McCartan-Quinn, D., O'Donnell, A., & Howcroft, B. (2003). Retail bank customer preferences: Personal and remote interactions. *International Journal of Retail and Distribution Management, 31*(4), 177–189. doi:10.1108/09590550310469176

Dwyer, F., Schurr, P., & Oh, S. (1987). Developing buyer-seller relationships. *Journal of Marketing, 51*, 11–27. doi:10.2307/1251126

Ebbers, W., Pieterson, W., & Noordman, H. (2008). Electronic government: Rethinking channel management strategies. *Government Information Quarterly, 25*, 181–201. doi:10.1016/j.giq.2006.11.003

Ebrahim, Z., & Irani, Z. (2005). E-government adoption: Architecture and barriers. *Business Process Management Journal, 11*(5), 589–611. doi:10.1108/14637150510619902

Fishbein, M., & Ajzen, I. (1975). *Belief, attitude, intention, and behavior: An introduction to theory and research*. Reading, MA: Addison-Wesley.

Glaser, B. G. (1992). *Basics of grounded theory analysis: Emergence versus forcing*. Mill Valley, CA: Sociology Press.

Glaser, B. G., & Strauss, A. L. (1967). *Discovery of grounded theory: Strategies for qualitative research*. Mill Valley, CA: Sociology Press.

Goldstein, S. M., Johnston, R., Duffy, J. A., & Rao, J. (2002). The service concept: The missing link in service design research? *Journal of Operations Management, 20*, 121–134. doi:10.1016/S0272-6963(01)00090-0

Grönlund, Å. (2002). *Electronic government: Design, applications and management*. London, UK: IGI Global.

Gupta, M. P., & Jana, D. (2003). E-Government evaluation: A framework and case study. *Government Information Quarterly, 20*, 365–387. doi:10.1016/j.giq.2003.08.002

Hill, A. V., Collier, D. A., Froehle, C. M., Goodale, J. C., Metters, R. D., & Verma, R. (2002). Research opportunities in service process design. *Journal of Operations Management, 20*, 189–202. doi:10.1016/S0272-6963(01)00092-4

Holden, S. H., Norris, D. F., & Fletcher, P. D. (2003). Electronic government at the local level: Progress to date and future issues. *Public Performance & Management Review, 26*(4), 325–344. doi:10.1177/1530957603026004002

Irani, Z., Love, P. E. D., & Jones, S. (2008). Learning lessons from evaluating e-government: Reflective case experiences that support transformational government. *The Journal of Strategic Information Systems, 17*(2), 155–164. doi:10.1016/j.jsis.2007.12.005

Ives, B., Olson, M. H., & Baroudi, J. J. (1983). The measurement of user information satisfaction. *Communications of the ACM, 26*(10), 785–793. doi:10.1145/358413.358430

Jaeger, P. T., & Thompson, K. M. (2003). E-government around the world: Lessons, challenges, and future directions. *Government Information Quarterly, 20*, 389–394. doi:10.1016/j.giq.2003.08.001

Johnson, N. F. (2007). *Two's company, three is complexity: A simple guide to the science of all sciences.* Oxford, UK: Oneworld.

Johnson, S. (2001). *Emergence: The connected lives of ants, brains, cities, and software.* New York, NY: Scribner.

Kahneman, D., & Snell, J. (1990). Predicting utility. In Hogarth, R. (Ed.), *Insights in decision-making: A tribute to Hillel J. Einhorn* (pp. 295–310). Chicago, IL: University of Chicago Press.

Karwan, K. R., & Markland, R. E. (2006). Integrating service design principles and information technology to improve delivery and productivity in public sector operations: The case of the South Carolina DMV. *Journal of Operations Management, 24*, 347–362. doi:10.1016/j.jom.2005.06.003

Kumar, V., Mukerji, B., Butt, I., & Persaud, A. (2007). Factors for successful e-government adoption: A conceptual framework. *Electronic. Journal of E-Government, 5*(1), 63–76.

Lee, G., & Perry, J. L. (2002). Are computers boosting productivity? A test of the paradox in state governments. *Journal of Public Administration: Research and Theory, 12*(1), 77–102.

Lee, S. M., Tan, X., & Trimi, S. (2005). Current practices of leading e-government countries. *Communications of the ACM, 48*(10), 99–104. doi:10.1145/1089107.1089112

Lee-Kelley, L., & James, T. (2003). E-government and social exclusion: An empirical study. *Journal of Electronic Commerce in Organizations, 1*(4), 1–15. doi:10.4018/jeco.2003100101

Li, D., Browne, G., & Wetherbe, J. (2006). Why do internet users stick with a specific web site? A relationship perspective. *International Journal of Electronic Commerce, 10*(4), 105–141. doi:10.2753/JEC1086-4415100404

Lindblom, C. E. (1959). The science of muddling through. *Public Administration Review, 19*, 79–88. doi:10.2307/973677

Lindblom, C. E., & Cohen, D. K. (1979). *Usable knowledge: Social science and social problem solving.* New Haven, CT: Yale University Press.

Lindblom, C. E., & Dahl, R. A. (1976). *Politics, economics, and welfare: Planning and politico-economic systems resolved into basic social processes.* Chicago, IL: University of Chicago Press.

Lindblom, C. E., & Woodhouse, E. J. (1993). *The policy-making process* (3rd ed.). Upper Saddle River, NJ: Prentice Hall.

Lockett, A., & Littler, D. (1997). The adoption of direct banking services. *Journal of Marketing Management, 13*, 791–811. doi:10.1080/0267257X.1997.9964512

McKinney, V., Yoon, K., & Zahedi, F. M. (2002). The measurement of web-customer satisfaction: An expectation and disconfirmation approach. *Information Systems Research, 13*(3), 296–315. doi:10.1287/isre.13.3.296.76

Milward, H. B., & Snyder, L. O. (1996). Electronic government: Linking citizens to public organizations through technology. *Journal of Public Administration: Research and Theory, 6*(2), 261–275.

Moon, M. J. (2002). The evolution of e-government among municipalities: Rhetoric or reality. *Public Administration Review, 62*(4), 424–433. doi:10.1111/0033-3352.00196

Moon, M. J., & Norris, D. F. (2005). Does managerial orientation matter? The adoption of reinventing government and e-government at the municipal level. *Information Systems Journal, 15*(1), 43–60. doi:10.1111/j.1365-2575.2005.00185.x

Moon, M. J., & Welch, E. W. (2004, January 5-8). Same bed, different dreams? A comparative analysis of citizen and bureaucrat perspectives on e-Government. In *Proceedings of the 37th Hawaii International Conference on System Sciences*, Honolulu, HI.

Norris, D. F., & Jae Moon, M. (2005). Advancing e-government at the grassroots: Tortoise or hare? *Public Administration Review, 65*(1), 64–75. doi:10.1111/j.1540-6210.2005.00431.x

Peters, R., Janssen, M., & Engers, T. (2004, October 25-27). Measuring e-government impact: Existing practices and shortcomings. In *Proceedings of the Sixth International Conference on Electronic Commerce*, Delft, The Netherlands.

Pieterson, W. (2010). Citizens and service channels: Channel choice and channel management implications. *International Journal of Electronic Government Research, 6*(2), 37–53. doi:10.4018/jegr.2010040103

Pieterson, W., & Ebbers, W. (2008). The use of service channels by citizens in the Netherlands: Implications for multi-channel management. *International Review of Administrative Sciences, 74*(1), 95–110. doi:10.1177/0020852307085736

Pieterson, W., Ebbers, W., & van Dijk, J. (2007). Personalization in the public sector: An inventory of organizational and user obstacles towards personalization of electronic services in the public sector. *Government Information Quarterly, 24*(1), 148–164. doi:10.1016/j.giq.2005.12.001

Reddick, C. G. (2005). Citizen interaction with e-government: From the streets to servers. *Government Information Quarterly, 22*, 38–57. doi:10.1016/j.giq.2004.10.003

Reddick, C. G. (2010). Comparing citizens' use of e-government to alternative service channels. *International Journal of Electronic Government Research, 6*(2), 54–67. doi:10.4018/jegr.2010040104

Rogers, E. M. (1995). *Diffusion of innovations.* New York, NY: Free Press.

Salam, A. F., Iyer, L., Palvia, P., & Singh, R. (2005). Trust in e-commerce. *Communications of the ACM, 48*(2), 73–77. doi:10.1145/1042091.1042093

Schedler, K., & Summermatter, L. (2007). Customer orientation in electronic government: Motives and effects. *Government Information Quarterly, 24*, 291–311. doi:10.1016/j.giq.2006.05.005

Sharma, S. K. (2004). Assessing e-government implementation. *Electronic Government Journal, 1*(2), 198–212. doi:10.1504/EG.2004.005178

Sharma, S. K. (2006). An e-government services framework. In Khosrow-Pour, M. (Ed.), *Encyclopedia of Commerce, E-Government and Mobile Commerce, Information Resources Management Association* (pp. 373–378). Hershey, PA: IGI Global. doi:10.4018/978-1-59140-799-7.ch061

Sharma, S. K., & Gupta, J. N. D. (2003). Building blocks of an e-government – a framework. *Journal of Electronic Commerce in Organizations*, *1*(4), 34–48. doi:10.4018/jeco.2003100103

Smart, K. L., Whiting, M. E., & Bell DeTienne, K. (2001). Assessing the need for printed and online documentation: A study of customer preference and use. *Journal of Business Communication*, *38*(3), 285–314. doi:10.1177/002194360103800306

Sohail, M. S., & Shanmugham, B. (2003). E-banking and customer preferences in Malaysia: An empirical investigation. *Information Sciences*, *150*, 207–217. doi:10.1016/S0020-0255(02)00378-X

Strauss, A. L. (1987). *Qualitative analysis for social scientists*. Cambridge, UK: Cambridge University Press. doi:10.1017/CBO9780511557842

Strauss, A. L., & Corbin, J. (1990). *Basics of qualitative research: Grounded theory procedures and techniques*. Thousand Oaks, CA: Sage.

Tan, M., & Teo, T. S. H. (2000). Factors influencing the adoption of internet banking. *Journal of the AIS*, *1*(5), 1–42.

Tax, S. S., & Stuart, I. (1997). Designing and implementing new services: The challenges of integrating service systems. *Journal of Retailing*, *73*(1), 105–134. doi:10.1016/S0022-4359(97)90017-8

Teale, M., Dispenza, V., Flynn, J., & Currie, D. (2003). *Management decision-making: Towards an integrative approach*. Essex, UK: Pearson Education.

Teerling, M. L., & Pieterson, W. (2010). Multi-channel marketing: An experiment on guiding citizens to the electronic channels. *Government Information Quarterly*, *27*(1), 98–107. doi:10.1016/j.giq.2009.08.003

Titah, R., & Barki, H. (2006). E-government adoption and acceptance: A literature review. *International Journal of Electronic Government Research*, *2*(3), 23–57. doi:10.4018/jegr.2006070102

Trimi, S., & Sheng, H. (2008). Emerging trends in M-government. *Communications of the ACM*, *51*(5), 53–58. doi:10.1145/1342327.1342338

Tung, L. L., & Rieck, O. (2005). Adoption of electronic government services among business organizations in Singapore. *The Journal of Strategic Information Systems*, *14*, 417–440. doi:10.1016/j.jsis.2005.06.001

Tversky, A., & Kahneman, D. (1974). Judgment under uncertainty: Heuristics and biases. *Science*, *185*, 1124–1131. doi:10.1126/science.185.4157.1124

Wang, L., Bretschneider, S., & Gant, J. (2005, January 3-6). Evaluating web-based e-government services with a citizen-centric approach. In *Proceedings of the 38ᵗʰ Hawaii International Conference on System Sciences*, Honolulu, HI.

Warkentin, M., Gefen, D., Pavlou, P. A., & Rose, G. M. (2002). Encouraging citizen adoption of e-government by building trust. *Electronic Markets*, *12*(3), 157–162. doi:10.1080/101967802320245929

Weaver, W. (1948). Science and complexity. *American Scientist*, *36*, 536–544.

Weiling, K., & Kwok, K. W. (2004). Successful e-government in Singapore. *Communications of the ACM*, *47*(6), 95–99. doi:10.1145/990680.990687

Weiss, C. H. (1998). *Evaluation: Methods for studying programs and policies* (2nd ed.). Upper Saddle River, NJ: Prentice Hall.

West, D. M. (2004). E-government and the transformation of service delivery and citizen attitudes. *Public Administration Review*, *64*(1), 15–27. doi:10.1111/j.1540-6210.2004.00343.x

Wholey, J. S. (1983). *Evaluation and effective public management*. Boston, MA: Little, Brown.

Wholey, J. S., Hatry, H. P., & Newcomer, K. E. (1994). *Handbook of practical program evaluation*. San Francisco, CA: Jossey-Bass.

Wimmer, M., Traunmüller, R., & Lenk, K. (2001, January 3-6). Electronic business invading the public sector: Considerations on change and design. In *Proceedings of the 34ᵗʰ Hawaii International Conference on System Sciences*, Maui, HI.

Wimmer, M. A. (2002). Integrated service modelling for online one-stop government. *Electronic Markets*, *12*(3), 149–156. doi:10.1080/101967802320245910

Zeithaml, V. A., & Gilly, M. C. (1987). Characteristics affecting the acceptance of retailing technologies: A comparison of elderly and non-elderly consumers. *Journal of Retail Banking*, *63*(1), 49–68.

This work was previously published in the International Journal of Electronic Government Research, Volume 7, Issue 3, edited by Vishanth Weerakkody, pp. 38-56, copyright 2011 by IGI Publishing (an imprint of IGI Global).

Chapter 15
Evaluating Citizen Adoption and Satisfaction of E-Government

Craig P. Orgeron
Mississippi Department of Information Technology Services, USA

Doug Goodman
University of Texas at Dallas, USA

ABSTRACT

Governments at all levels are faced with the challenge of transformation and the need to reinvent government systems in order to deliver efficient and cost effective services. E-government presents a tremendous impetus to move forward in the 21st century with higher quality, cost-effective, government services, and a better relationship between citizens and government. This research considers theoretical foundations from the Technology Acceptance Model (TAM), the Web Trust Model (WTM), and SERVQUAL to form a parsimonious model of citizen adoption and satisfaction for e-government services. The authors find that usefulness, or end-user convenience, to be the principal determinant of e-government adoption and satisfaction, unaffected even when controlling demographic variables such as race, income, and education are introduced.

INTRODUCTION

Electronic government (e-government) has in recent years attracted much attention as scholars have suggested that by leveraging cutting-edge information technology, government may reap benefits of increased efficiency, effectiveness, and citizen communication with public sector agencies

(Chadwick & May, 2003; Ho, 2002; Melitski, 2001; West, 2004). E-government is defined as the application of information technology to make available Internet-based services between public sector agencies and citizens, private sector organizations, employees, and other nongovernmental agencies (Carter & Belanger, 2004, 2005). E-government offers potential impact on the business of government in two fundamental, yet crucial,

DOI: 10.4018/978-1-4666-2458-0.ch015

ways: by improving service delivery, including costs; and by improving communication between citizens and government (Fountain, 2001).

The primary objective of this research is to analyze theoretical foundations from well-known models in e-commerce scholarship—the Technology Acceptance Model (TAM) (Gefen, Elena, & Straub, 2003; Gefen & Straub, 2000; Moon & Kim, 2001), the Web Trust Model (WTM) (Gefen et al., 2003; Belanger, Hiller, & Smith, 2002; McKnight, Choudhury, & Kacmar, 2002), and SERVQUAL (Devaraj, Ming, & Kohli, 2002; Parasuraman, Berry, & Zeithaml, 1988, 1991)—to form a model of the essential components that inform citizen adoption and satisfaction of e-government services. SERVQUAL, perhaps the most frequently used service quality measurement scale, is comprised of five service quality dimensions (tangibles, reliability, responsiveness, assurance, and empathy) that apply across traditional, i.e. not online, industries (Zeithaml et al., 1996). Specifically, the work of Carter and Belanger (2004, 2005) linking the Technology Acceptance Model and the Web Trust Model is uniquely leveraged to form a heuristic model which theoretically associates antecedents of e-government adoption with a citizen-based assessment of on-line service quality – a connection heretofore not advanced in the scholarly literature. Though this research is newly conceived, the desire is for public administrators to have a reliable model from which government agencies can more fully understand what impels citizens to adopt a specific e-government application or service, as well as understand what constitutes service quality.

This study links the three research areas in order to investigate the impact of Web-based tools on e-government adoption and satisfaction. We propose an integrated framework of e-government satisfaction and adoption. This framework suggests that a combination of factors – technology adoption, trust, and service quality – influence an individual's adoption propensity and service quality perception (Figure 1). While researchers

have continued to document differences between e-commerce and e-government (Jorgensen & Cable, 2002; Warkentin, Gefen, Pavlou, & Rose, 2002), e-commerce models continue to be utilized to examine adoption of on-line services in the public sector (Carter & Belanger, 2004, 2005). Indeed, certain scholars have specifically called for an interdisciplinary approach to more fully realize the impact of Internet technology on e-government participation (Tolbert & McNeal, 2003).

An extensive exploratory schedule can be developed from the proposed e-government adoption and satisfaction framework (Figure 1). Given the recent focus of research examining e-government program development (Cohen & Eimicke, 2001; Fountain, 2001; Ho, 2002; Moon, 2002; Thomas & Streib, 2003), as well as research probing user adoption of e-commerce (Gefen et al., 2003; McKnight et al., 2002; Carter & Belanger, 2004, 2005) in combination with the escalating push to develop innovative e-government services (Horrigan, 2004; Norris, Fletcher, & Holden, 2001), the question of interest is:

What technology adoption, trust, and service quality factors influence an individual's general proclivity to adopt e-government services and an individual's perceptions of e-government service quality?

Recent scholarship has been devoted to understanding the impact of e-government on the ability of public sector agencies to deliver services with increased efficiency and effectiveness (Chadwick & May, 2003; Fountain, 2001; Ho, 2002; Melitski, 2001; West, 2004, 2005). That e-government services, delivered via advanced information technology solutions, can provide benefits of enhanced efficiency, effectiveness, and citizen communication with public sector agencies is advantageous to elected officials, public managers, as well as to the citizenry. Indeed, as government agencies increase efficiency and ameliorate operating costs, citizens are increasingly able to access

Figure 1. Theoretical Research Framework

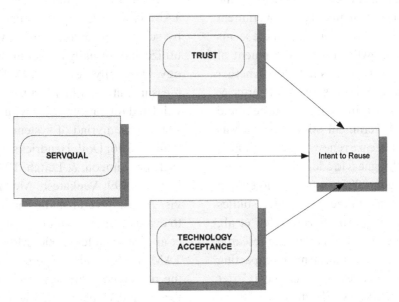

on-line services from an attentive, citizen-centric government (Kettl, 2000). Thus, while research has indicated that a vast majority of government agencies have an inadequate working knowledge of what drives citizen adoption of e-government services (Norris et al., 2001), the desire in this research is to offer insight into what impels e-government adoption, as well as to understand what constitutes acceptable service quality.

BACKGROUND

Participatory forms of e-government, such as on-line public hearings or e-voting, are less common than informational uses or on-line transactions, such as tax e-filing. Carter and Belanger (2004, 2005) note that public sector agencies at all levels of government have leveraged e-government applications to foster buying goods and services, the dissemination of information and forms, and the acceptance of bids and proposals (GAO, 2001). Arguably, both the public sector and the citizenry benefit from the implementation of e-government services. As public sector agencies reduce costs

and improve efficiency, citizens receive quicker, better aligned services from a more focused and streamlined government (Kettl, 2000).

Implementation and acceptance of e-government on-line services, such as renewing a driver's license, are dependent upon the readiness of citizens to adopt these web-based services. In recent years, various scholars have sought to understand how and why consumers continued to utilize electronic commerce (e-commerce) offerings (Gefen et al., 2003; McKnight et al., 2002). In a similar analytical vein, though to a much lesser degree, research designs are being proposed to study foundational elements directly influencing citizen adoption of e-government services (Warkentin et al., 2002). In 2001, an e-government survey dispensed to executive administrators at government agencies found that 74.2% of the public sector managers noted that their agencies had established a Web presence; however, an inordinate number, 90.5%, of these government agencies had not conducted a survey to better understand what impels citizens to adopt a specific e-government application or service (Norris et al., 2001).

Carter and Belanger (2004, 2005) call for the development of a prudent model of e-government adoption. The authors write that "while there seems to be substantial growth in the development of e-government initiatives, it is not clear whether citizens will embrace those services" (Carter & Belanger, 2005, p. 6). Indeed, the "success and acceptance of e-government initiatives, such as online voting and license renewal, are contingent upon citizens' willingness to adopt these services" (Carter & Belanger, 2005, p. 6). A burgeoning research stream has utilized academic studies of user adoption of e-commerce (Gefen et al., 2003; McKnight et al., 2002) to inform research focused on analyzing essential elements impacting citizen adoption of e-government services (Carter & Belanger, 2004, 2005; Warkentin et al., 2002).

Similarly, in recent years, research has focused on the relevance of trust as a decisive precursor to online activity, principally due to the consumer's confidence that the transaction will occur as expected (Gefen, 2000). As with technology adoption research, scholars have leveraged the import of the trust relationship in e-commerce transactions, and conducted trust-centric studies in the e-government context (Belanger et al., 2002; CEG, 2003; Chadwick, 2001; GAO, 2001; Hiller & Belanger, 2001; Hoffman, Novak, & Peralta, 1999). In addition to technology adoption and trust, scholars have centered attention on service quality in the e-commerce context, leveraging one of the most widely used service quality measurement scales, SERVQUAL (Parasuraman et al., 1988), to operationalize consumers' perceived service quality through reliability, responsiveness, empathy, and assurance of e-commerce applications (Carr, 2002).

Technology Acceptance Model

The Technology Acceptance Model (TAM) is derived from the theory of reasoned action, expectancy theory, and self-efficacy theory (Fishbein & Ajzen, 1975; Robey, 1979b; Bandura, 1977). TAM is an often-cited theoretical model used by scholars to predict an individual's intent to utilize and formally accept information technology. Originally developed by Davis (1989), the measures utilized in TAM have been tested and validated for various users with a range of understanding, a myriad of system types, and gender (Chua, 1996; Doll, Hendrickson, & Deng, 1998; Jackson, Simeon, & Leitch, 1997; Karahanna & Straub, 1999; Venkatesh, Morris, Davis, & Davis, 2003). Several studies have also used TAM to evaluate user adoption of e-commerce (Gefen et al., 2003; Gefen, 2000; Moon & Kim, 2001). TAM proposes that the perceived ease of use and the perceived usefulness are underlying causes for an individual's attitude toward a specific technology or information system. Davis defines perceived usefulness as, "the degree to which a person believes that using a particular system would enhance his or her job performance" (p. 320). Further, Davis defines perceived ease of use as, "the degree to which a person believes that using a particular system would be free of effort" (p. 320). The attitude toward a specific technology or information system consequently informs an individual's intent to adopt that technology or system, and is similarly a predictor of the individual's eventual acceptance of the technology (Bhattacherjee, 2001: Davis, Bagozzi, & Warshaw, 1989; Lucas & Spitler, 1999; Moon & Kim, 2001; Venkatesh & Davis, 2000).

Trust

In an economic exchange of goods and services, trust is the belief that the parties involved in the transaction will ethically meet expected commitments dependably and in a socially appropriate manner (Hosmer, 1995; Kumar, Sheer, & Steenkamp, 1995; Luhmann, 1979; Zucker, 1986). Belanger et al. (2002) define trustworthiness as "the perception of confidence in the electronic marketer's reliability and integrity" (p. 247). Specifically, trust is important in scenarios where the trusting party is dependent on this behavior, as is generally believed to be the case in e-commerce transactions (Gefen, 2000; Meyer & Goes, 1988; Rousseau, Sitkin, Burtand, & Camerer, 1998). Scholars researching relationships in e-commerce transactions note the significance of trust as a critical antecedent to online activity, primarily due to the consumer's belief that the transaction will occur as expected (Gefen, 2000). Specifically, due to the fact that online transactions are, at least to a certain degree impersonal, trust becomes an even greater predictor of behavior, as in the online environment retailers can engage in unethical behavior, particularly in the handling of an individual's personally identifiable information (Gefen, 2000; Kollock, 1999; Reichheld & Sasser, 1990). Given the importance of the trust relationship in e-commerce transactions, when this trust is broken, or simply not established, consumers will avoid doing initial or repeat business with a particular retailer (Gefen, 2000; Jarvenpaa & Tractinsky, 1999; Reichheld & Sasser). In the e-government context, while many Americans believe the e-government potentially can improve government service delivery, trust is stunted due to privacy and security issues, both revolving around the sharing and potential misuse of personal information (Belanger et al., 2002; CEG, 2003; Chadwick, 2001; GAO, 2001; Hiller & Belanger, 2001; Hoffman et al., 1999).

Various scholars have focused research toward the understanding of the institutional view of trust within the e-commerce context (McKnight et al., 2002; Tan & Thoen, 2001). Within this context institutional trust is specifically referred to as the institutional structures which enable the transacting to interact successfully. Scholars have suggested that since organizations are comprised of individuals, institutional trust has a direct influence on organizational trust (Zaheer, McEvily, & Perrone, 1998). Zucker (1986) argued that

institutional trust is the most essential means by which trust is produced in an impersonal economic setting lacking familiarity and similarity. Taking into consideration the scholarship produced by various scholars (Mayer, Davis, & Schoorman, 1995; McKnight & Cummings, 1998; McKnight et al., 2002; Zucker), particular measures have been constructed with the goal of developing a model of multi-dimensional trust in e-commerce, with specific attention given to users' initial trust in a Web vendor (McKnight et al., 2002). McKnight et al. identify one of the four major constructs as institution-based trust, and classify it as a significant part of Internet-based transactions (McKnight & Chervany, 2002). Structural assurance and situational normality are the two dimensions which comprise this construct. First, structural assurance asserts that, "one believes structures like guarantees, regulations, promises, legal recourse, or other procedures are in place to promote success" (McKnight et al., p. 339). Second, situational normality refers to beliefs that success is probable, specifically due to a normal environment – an environment whereby the interacting parties have the attributes of competence, benevolence, and integrity (McKnight et al., 2002). Typically, in the e-commerce context, situational normality will presume security safeguards such as confidentiality, integrity, authentication, non-repudiation, availability, and access control mechanisms (Ratnasingam & Pavlou, 2002).

SERVQUAL

Varying scholars have noted that quality service is a personal appraisal by an individual customer that the service received is the service that was expected (Parasuraman, Zeithaml, & Berry, 1985; Watson, Pitt, & Kavan, 1998). In the traditional retail market, service quality is concerned with the appearance of the store, as well as the quality of the relationship between the service providers and the customer. In this context, one of the most widely used service quality measurement scales, SERVQUAL (Parasuraman, et al., 1988), was developed. SERVQUAL is comprised of five service quality dimensions that apply across traditional, i.e. not online, industries (Zeithaml, Berry, & Parasuraman, 1996). These five service quality dimensions constructs are listed in Table 1.

Until more definitive studies were conducted, researchers remained split regarding the applicability of the SERVQUAL scale to an e-commerce, on-line transaction, though a small group of scholars sought to leverage the dimensions of SERVQUAL within the information technology context (Kettinger & Lee, 1994; Pitt, Watson, & Kavan, 1995). Though criticized by many scholars, the work of these early studies focused on the use of SERVQUAL to measure the service quality of the information technology function within organizations (Kettinger & Lee, 1997; Pitt, Watson, & Kavan, 1997; Carr, 2002; Van Dyke, Prybutok, & Kappelman, 1999). As e-commerce research surged in the late 1990s, researchers have since applied service quality measures in order to assess the quality of search engines (Xie, Wang, & Goh, 1998) and specific features associated with Web site success (Liu & Arnett, 2000). SERVQUAL, as originally developed, was designed to measure the difference between expected service and perceived service in order to assess what was termed the "service gap." While this "gap appraisal" is a distinctive feature of the

SERVQUAL scale, its precision and value within the information technology, and specifically e-commerce context, has been disputed (Van Dyke, Kappelman, & Prybutok, 1997). Due to the fact that perception is the consequence of the assessment process of the service and expectation, the dual-survey approach may not be necessary in the e-commerce realm (Kettinger & Lee, 1997; Van Dyke et al., 1997). Recent research has specifically utilized the SERVQUAL dimensions in a single survey to operationalize consumers' perceived service quality through reliability, responsiveness, empathy, and assurance of e-commerce applications.

MODEL AND HYPOTHESES

According to Brown and Brudney (1998), researchers have documented that "attitudinal and perceptual measures" (p. 338) have been found to be preferred measures for determining benefits realized from the implementation of information technology systems and applications. Robey (1979a) and Rivard (1987) cited a shift from quantitative measures toward perceptual measures for assessing information technology and system benefits. Components previously identified in the Technology Acceptance Model (TAM) (Gefen et al., 2003; Gefen & Straub, 2000; Moon & Kim, 2001), the Web Trust Model (WTM) (Gefen et al.; Belanger et al., 2002; McKnight et al., 2002), and SERVQUAL (Devaraj et al., 2002; Parasuraman et al., 1988; Parasuraman et al., 1991) were operationalized for this research study.

The dependent variable (Reuse Intent), the intermediate variables (Trust in Internet, Trust in Government, Ease of Use, and Usefulness) and independent variables (Reliability, Responsiveness, Empathy, and Assurance Reuse Intent) were operationalized in a technique utilized by Cats-Baril and Thompson (1998) through standardizing and summing the responses to survey responses. Table 2 depicts the operational variables.

Table 1. SERVQUAL Constructs

Construct	Definition
Tangibles	Facilities, equipment, personnel, and communication materials
Reliability	Ability to perform service dependably and accurately
Responsiveness	Willingness to help and respond to customer need
Assurance	Ability of staff to inspire confidence and trust
Empathy	Extent to which caring individualized service is given

Consideration is now given to the specific formulation of testable hypotheses and the operationalization of variables relevant to this research study. The following hypotheses will be tested in this study briefly outlined above and described in Table 3.

To form the basis for analysis, and thus create a model of the essential components that inform citizen adoption of e-government services, nine total variables were utilized. A graphical depiction of the model is presented in Figure 2.

METHODS

An online e-government adoption and satisfaction survey was administered to identify a consistent model from which public sector managers can more completely understand what impels citizens to adopt a specific e-government application or service, as well as understand e-government service quality. The population for this survey consisted of approximately 200,000 people who have completed an on-line transaction via the Mississippi.gov portal from July 2005 through July 2007. This population was selected due to three primary considerations. First, the two-year window was utilized due to the decay of reliable email addresses as time increases from the transaction (Wren, Grissom, & Conway, 2006). As explained below about 12% of the sample contained bad email addresses. Second, nine of eleven on-line transactions offered via the Mississippi.gov portal are payment-based, thus the

Table 2. Operational Variables

Name	Description	Scale	Theoretical Construct
Reliability (Independent)	Assesses service quality reliability of MISSISSIPPI.GOV e-government applications. Variable operationalized by standardizing and summing the responses.	7-Point Likert	**SERVQUAL**
Responsiveness (Independent)	Assesses service quality responsiveness of MISSISSIPPI.GOV e-government applications. Variable operationalized by standardizing and summing the responses.	7-Point Likert	**SERVQUAL**
Empathy (Independent)	Assesses service quality empathy of MISSISSIPPI.GOV e-government applications. Variable operationalized by standardizing and summing the responses.	7-Point Likert	**SERVQUAL**
Assurance (Independent)	Assesses service quality assurance of MISSISSIPPI.GOV e-government applications. Variable operationalized by standardizing and summing the responses.	7-Point Likert	**SERVQUAL**
Reuse Intent (Dependent)	Assesses reuse intent of the citizen utilizing MISSISSIPPI.GOV e-government applications. Variable operationalized by standardizing and summing the responses.	7-Point Likert	**TAM**
Trust in Internet (Independent)	Assesses internet trust of the citizen utilizing MISSISSIPPI.GOV e-government applications. Variable operationalized by standardizing and summing the responses.	7-Point Likert	**Web Trust**
Trust in Government (Independent)	Assesses government trust of the citizen utilizing MISSISSIPPI.GOV e-government applications. Variable operationalized by standardizing and summing the responses.	7-Point Likert	**Web Trust**
Ease of Use (Independent)	Assesses ease of use of MISSISSIPPI.GOV e-government applications. Variable operationalized by standardizing and summing the responses.	7-Point Likert	**TAM**
Usefulness (Independent)	Assesses usefulness of MISSISSIPPI.GOV e-government applications. Variable operationalized by standardizing and summing the responses.	7-Point Likert	**TAM**

Table 3. Proposed Hypotheses

H₁	An increase in Internet Trust will increase the Reuse Intent of an individual to utilize MISSISSIPPI.GOV e-government applications.
H₂	An increase in Government Trust will increase the Reuse Intent of an individual to utilize MISSISSIPPI.GOV e-government applications.
H₃	An increase in the Ease of Use of MISSISSIPPI.GOV e-government applications will increase the Reuse Intent of an individual to utilize the applications.
H₄	An increase in the Usefulness of MISSISSIPPI.GOV e-government applications will increase the Reuse Intent of an individual to utilize the applications.
H₅	An increase in the Service Quality Reliability of MISSISSIPPI.GOV e-government applications will result in an increase of the Reuse Intent of an individual.
H₆	An increase in the Service Quality Responsiveness of MISSISSIPPI.GOV e-government applications will result in an increase of the Reuse Intent of an individual.
H₇	An increase in the Service Quality Empathy of MISSISSIPPI.GOV e-government applications will result in an increase of the Reuse Intent of an individual.
H₈	An increase in the Service Quality Assurance of MISSISSIPPI.GOV e-government applications will result in an increase of the Reuse Intent of an individual.

majority of citizens interacting with government on-line are submitting a payment. Finally, if a citizen does not utilize a payment-based on-line transaction, that interaction is not recorded in a transaction log, thus the record of interaction is not maintained beyond the point of transaction – simply put, the data does not exist. A list of interactive, real-time applications was provided by the Mississippi Department of Information Technology Services (ITS, 2006). On-line government transactions that did not have a payment component were not included in the population. Thus, the sampling frame consisted of all citizens who have utilized on-line government monetary transactions via the Mississippi.gov portal.

Between July 2005 and July 2007 approximately 200,000 people completed a monetary transaction through one of MS state government's Websites. A table of recommended sample sizes (n) for populations (N) with finite sizes, developed by Krejcie and Morgan and adapted by Patten (2004),

was utilized to determine estimated sample size. According to Patten's adapted methods, a sample size of 384 is needed to reach a 95% confidence interval. For this study, a web-based survey was utilized to gather data relevant to citizen acceptance of e-government applications. In order to encourage a high response rate, Dillman (2000) suggests multiple contacts. For this study, up to five contacts were made per potential participant.

The data for this research study were collected via on-line survey administered to a random sample of 10,000 prior users of the Mississippi.gov e-government Web portal for a two-year period spanning from 2005 through 2007. Early in the survey process, it was discovered that nearly 12 percent of the email address utilized were unsound, thus nearly 1,200 of the originally delivered surveys were returned undeliverable. Overall, 795 surveys were received via the Web-based survey tool. Of this response set, 147 incomplete surveys were eliminated due to invalid or predominantly incomplete responses, leaving a response of 648 surveys.

Males accounted for 55% of the survey respondents. A plurality of respondents (30.2%) are in their 40s closely followed by respondents in their 50s (28.4%). The survey responders are well-educated with 68.3% indicating that they possess a college degree with a fourth of all respondents holding a post-graduate degree. A majority of respondents (56.7) reported income over $70,000. As significant, while the sample is nearly evenly divided on gender, an overwhelming majority of the respondents were Caucasian (91.7%). Only 5.3% of the respondents were African-American. Similar affluence was noted in the 93.4 percent of respondents reporting use of a computer at home to access the Internet or World Wide Web.

Figure 2. Model of the Essential Components that Inform Citizen Adoption of e-Government Services

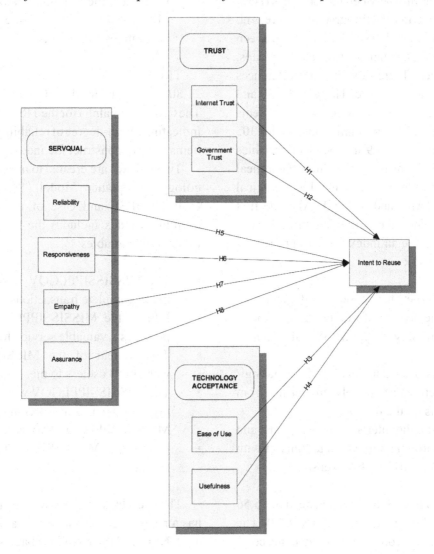

ANALYSIS

The dependent variable, Reuse Intentions (RE-USE), was created by summing together the following Likert-scaled variables (1=Strongly Disagree to 7=Strongly Agree):

- I will continue to use the Web for gathering information from the MISSISSIPPI.GOV website.
- I will continue to use MISSISSIPPI.GOV services provided over the Web.

- Interacting with MISSISSIPPI.GOV over the Web is something that I will continue to do.
- I will not hesitate to provide information to the MISSISSIPPI.GOV website.
- I will continue to use the Web to inquire about MISSISSIPPI.GOV online services.

REUSE ranges from 5 to 35 with a mean of 28.47 and a standard deviation of 4.62 (N=611). The Cronbach's alpha score for the survey items in comprising the dependent variable is .922 indicating a high reliability between the variables (Hair, et al, 2006). In terms of demographics, there is no difference in means on the REUSE index between males and females, racial groups, income groups, and Internet users. There are significant differences in the index in terms of age. Those under 30 and over 60 are least likely to agree with the items in the REUSE index, especially those under 30.

The model includes 9 independent variables that are used to measure the three theoretical constructs discussed above: Trust, Technological Acceptance (TAM) and SERVQUAL. The first variable combines the following three survey questions to create an index measuring Trust of the Internet (TRI):

- The Internet has enough safeguards to make me feel comfortable using it to interact online with the MISSISSIPPI.GOV website.
- I feel assured that legal and technological structures adequately protect me from problems on the Internet.
- In general, the Internet is now a robust and safe environment in which to transact with the MISSISSIPPI.GOV website.

TRI ranges from 3 to 21 with a mean of 15.56 and a standard deviation of 3.29 (N=640). The Cronbach's alpha score of the survey items comprising the TRI is .896 indicating a high reliability between the variables.

The next independent variable is an index measuring trust of state government, TRG. The index is created by summing together the following four, Likert-type survey items:

- I think I can trust the administrators of the MISSISSIPPI.GOV website.
- The MISSISSIPPI.GOV website can be trusted to carry out online transactions faithfully.
- In my opinion, the MISSISSIPPI.GOV website is worthy of my trust.

- I trust the administrators of the MISSISSIPPI.GOV website to keep my best interests in mind.

TRG ranges from 4 to 28, and it has a mean of 21.80 and a standard deviation of 3.85 (N=631). The Cronbach's alpha for the TRG variable is .936 indicating a high-degree of reliability between the items used to construct the index.

Two indexes are created to measure the Technology Acceptance Model (TAM) construct: USEFULNESS and ease of use (EOU.) The usefulness index includes the following scaled Likert-type variables:

- The MISSISSIPPI.GOV web site enables me to complete transactions more quickly.
- I think the MISSISSIPPI.GOV web site provides a valuable service for me.
- The content of the MISSISSIPPI.GOV web site is useless to me. (recoded)
- The MISSISSIPPI.GOV web site enhances my effectiveness in searching for and using MISSISSIPPI.GOV services.
- I find the MISSISSIPPI.GOV web site useful.

The usefulness index ranges from 5 to 35 and has a mean of 28.58 and a standard deviation of 4.82 (N=617). USE has a Cronbach's alpha of .883 indicating a high-degree of reliability between the survey items used to measure the usefulness of the Internet.

The ease of use (EOU) index was created by summing together the following survey items:

- Learning to interact with the MISSISSIPPI.GOV web site has been easy for me.
- I believe interacting with the MISSISSIPPI.GOV web site is a clear and understandable process.
- Interaction with the MISSISSIPPI.GOV web site provides user-friendly navigation.

- It has been easy for me to become skillful at using the MISSISSIPPI.GOV web site.
- I find the MISSISSIPPI.GOV web site difficult to use. (recoded)

EOU ranges 5 to 35 and has a mean of 27.44 and a standard deviation of 5.21. The ease of use index has a Cronbach's alpha of .927 indicating a high-degree of reliability between the index items.

Finally, four variables are created to measure different facets of the quality of service: Reliability (REL), Responsive (RES), Empathy (EMP), and Assurance (ASR). The following survey items are combined to form the respective indexes.

Reliability (REL):
- I believe that the MISSISSIPPI.GOV website is reliable.
- I believe that what I ask for is what I get when using the MISSISSIPPI.GOV website.
- I think that the MISSISSIPPI.GOV website performs online services accurately.
- I rely on the MISSISSIPPI.GOV website to deliver online services promptly.

Responsiveness (RES):
- I believe the MISSISSIPPI.GOV website is responsive to my needs.
- In the case of any problem, I think the MISSISSIPPI.GOV website offers prompt service.
- The help desk functions available through the MISSISSIPPI.GOV website will address any concerns that I have.

Empathy (EMP):
- I can access the MISSISSIPPI.GOV website at my convenience in order to transact business.
- The MISSISSIPPI.GOV website can address the specific needs of each user.
- I am satisfied with the payment options (e.g., different credit cards) offered through the MISSISSIPPI.GOV website.

Assurance (ASR):
- My decision to use the MISSISSIPPI.GOV website was a good one.
- I feel safe in my transactions with the MISSISSIPPI.GOV website.
- The MISSISSIPPI.GOV website had answers to many of my questions about online services.

The indexes have the following characteristics. REL ranges from 4 to 28 and a mean of 22.41 and a standard deviation of 3.93. The reliability index has a Cronbach's alpha of .893 again indicating a high-degree of reliability. RES ranges from 3 to 21 and a mean of 14.92 and a standard deviation of 2.83. The responsiveness index has a Cronbach's alpha of .770. The empathy index ranges from 2 to 21 and a mean of 16.50 and a standard deviation 2.73. The EMP index has a Cronbach's alpha of .754. Finally, ASP ranges from 3 to 21 and a mean of 16.67 and a standard deviation 2.69. The assurance index has a Cronbach's alpha of .775. All of the Cronbach's alpha scores indicate a high-degree of reliability.

Ordinary-least squares multiple regression was employed in order to examine the influence of specific variables drawn from Technology Acceptance Model, Trust, and SERVQUAL constructs, upon e-government adoption and satisfaction perceptions (Table 4). With the development of the regression models, the amount of variance explained equals about 80 percent, thus attaining a noteworthy level of predictive capability.

Model 1 includes the eight independent variables tested. Model 2 is presented with the inclusion of the five demographic control variables (Gender, Race, Age, Education, and Income) in addition to the eight independent variables; the overall model fit remains virtually unchanged. The Adjusted R^2 changed from .797 to .809. The inclusion of the three demographic control variables was negligible. None of these demographic characteristics are statistically significant in affecting Reuse Intent.

Table 4. OLS regression intent to reuse

Independent Variable	Model 1 B (Std. Error)	Model 2 B (Std. Error)
Constant	1.697 (.650)**	.937 (.817)
Trust		
TRI	.083 (.050)*	.074 (.050)
TRG	.142 (.050)**	.190 (.052)***
TAM		
USE	.634 (.040)***	.646 (.041)***
EOU	.027 (.033)	.004 (.035)
SERVQUAL		
REL	-.048 (.060)	-.055 (.063)
RES	.053 (.057)	.045 (.058)
EMP	.027 (.073)	.018 (.075)
ASR	.202 (.082)**	.239 (.083)***
Characteristics		
Male	--	.025 (.202)
African-American	--	.441 (.433)
Age	--	.047 (.044)
Income	--	-.049 (.081)
Education	--	-.028 (058)
Adj. R²	.797	.809
F	249.593***	154.682***

*p<10; **p<.05; ***p<.01

These results suggest that the regression models are high in predictive value and accurateness as a foundation for understanding e-government adoption and satisfaction (Hair et al., 2006). Both Model 1 and the Model 2, portray similar analytical frameworks in finding three principal influences:

X_{USE}, Usefulness; X_{TRI} Trust in the Internet (Model 1), X_{TRG}, Government Trust; and X_{ASR}, Assurance. Although the impact of X_{USE} (Usefulness) is the strongest of the three significant independent variables, an increase in any of these variables results in an increase in e-government adoption and satisfaction. In particular, an increase of one point in the user's perception of Usefulness (X_{USE}) will produce an average increase of nearly (.634) of a point on the e-government Reuse Intent scale (Y_{REUSE}). Analogous outcomes are observed for the remaining significant independent variables. However, concerning the three other significant independent variables (X_{TRI} Trust in the Internet, X_{TRG}, Government Trust and X_{ASR}, Assurance), Reuse Intent (Y_{REUSE}) is not as definite. While these three variables were statistically significant inclusions in both models, their collective explained variance was only .03 out of an overall model R^2 of .797 (Model 1).

It is noteworthy to point out that the four chief influences (X_{USE}, Usefulness; X_{TRI} Trust in the Internet; X_{TRG}, Government Trust; and X_{ASR}, Assurance) are primary components of the perceptual constructs acknowledged at the inception of this study – the Technology Acceptance Model, Trust, and SERVQUAL, respectively. These analytical constructs, which are theorized to characterize measures of citizen opinions of e-government adoption and satisfaction, ought to be well thought-out in any conclusions. To argue that these three independent variables are exclusive influences on citizen adoption and satisfaction of e-government would be to understate the multifaceted patterns of collinearity between variables. To that end, these influential variables have greater interpretive power when considered as part of perceptual constructs recognized at the initiation of this research, in conjunction with the remaining variables from the constructs in any conclusions reached via this research. Public sector administrators charged with the management of information technology now have research results which measure precise influences of essential variables, as well as the theoretical constructs which should be the basis for strategic planning with respect to policy and program development targeted at positively impacting user adoption and satisfaction of e-government.

Table 5 depicts results of hypotheses testing based on the multiple regression analysis. As depicted in Figure 2, the research framework and proposed research model were proposed based on a distinct prospect for the establishment of a wide-ranging view of e-government adoption and satisfaction that conflates fundamental theoretical constructs from known models in e-commerce scholarship, specifically the Technology Acceptance Model (TAM) (Gefen et al., 2003; Gefen & Straub, 2000; Moon & Kim, 2001), the Web Trust Model (WTM) (Gefen et al.; Belanger et al., 2002; McKnight et al., 2002), and SERVQUAL (Devaraj et al., 2002; Parasuraman et al., 1988; Parasuraman et al., 1991). The scholarly research of Carter and Belanger (2004, 2005) linking the Technology Acceptance Model and the Web Trust Model is further developed via the inclusion of SERVQUAL to form a model which hypothetically associates antecedents of e-government adoption with a citizen-based appraisal of on-line service quality – a connection as yet not examined in the scholarly literature (Figure 1 and Figure 2). The reconstituted research model, as represented in Figure 3, depicts the findings contained in this study.

The central assertion of this research was that e-government adoption and satisfaction would be dependent upon the collective effects of three factors: technology acceptance, trust, and service quality. This inclusive viewpoint can provide a basis for ongoing research on e-government adoption and satisfaction. The research hypotheses suggested that eight variables would predict intention to reuse an e-government application offered via the Mississippi.gov Web portal. After analyzing the research model documented in the opening chapter of this study, three variables were established as significant, as is depicted in Figure

Table 5. Multivariate Hypotheses Testing (Model 1)

Hypothesis	Variable	B	T-Value	Support
H1	Internet Trust	.083	1.666*	YES
H2	Government Trust	.142	2.837***	YES
H3	Ease of Use	.027	.821	NO
H4	Usefulness	.634	16.008***	YES
H5	Reliability	-.048	-.793	NO
H6	Responsive-ness	.053	.936	NO
H7	Empathy	.027	.366	NO
H8	Assurance	.202	2.479**	YES
*p<.10; **p<.05; ***p<.01				

3. A sole technology adoption factor, Usefulness, had a significant impact on e-government adoption and satisfaction. Only one trust factor, Government Trust, was found to be a significant predictor of e-government adoption and satisfaction.

DISCUSSION

The movement to e-government, at its heart, is changing the way citizens and businesses interact with government. E-government offers a huge potential in seeking innovative ways to reach the ideal of government of people, by people and for people. This study strove to unite the three theory-centric research areas in order to investigate the impact of Web-based tools on e-government adoption and satisfaction. Based on the aforementioned literature, this study proposed an integrated framework of e-government satisfaction and adoption. This theoretical framework suggested that a combination of factors – technology adoption, trust, and service quality – influence an individual's adoption propensity and service quality perception. In assessing the theoretical impacts of this research, and despite the continued use of e-commerce models to examine adoption of on-line services

*Figure 3. Reconstituted model of e-government adoption and satisfaction (Note: * indicates statistically significant unstandardized regression coefficient.)*

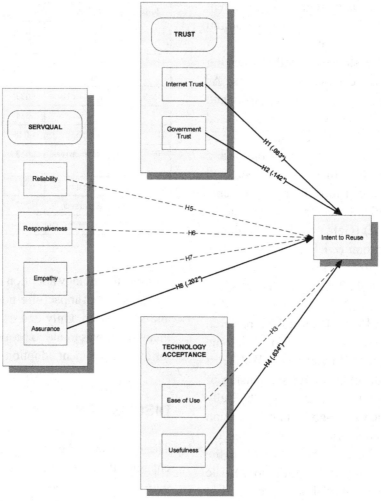

in the public sector (Carter & Belanger, 2004, 2005), the specific call by scholars for an interdisciplinary approach to more fully realize the impact of Internet technology on e-government participation (Tolbert & McNeal, 2003) has been achieved. Indeed, a great deal of recent scholarship has concentrated on understanding the impact of e-government on the capacity of government agencies to offer services with enhanced efficiency and effectiveness (Chadwick & May, 2003; Fountain, 2001; Ho, 2002; Melitski, 2001; West, 2004, 2005). Specifically, while academic research has documented that a majority of government agen-

cies have a derisory working knowledge of what drives citizen adoption of e-government services (Norris et al., 2001), the aspiration for this research was to offer theoretical insight into what impels e-government adoption, as well as to understand what constitutes acceptable service quality.

Implications for Practice and Policy

This study was executed in part by utilizing existing empirically validated measures from the technology adoption literature (Davis, 1989; Gefen, 2000; Gefen et al., 2003; Moon & Kim,

2001) and applying these measures specifically to the e-government realm. These measures were applied to a broad sample of e-government users from across the state of Mississippi. The results indicate that of the existing technology adoption measures (Ease of Use and Usefulness), Usefulness is significant and a reliable indicator in the research model, which sought to understand both adoption and satisfaction with service quality. From an implications perspective, the overwhelming impact of Usefulness in addressing both willingness to adopt and service quality satisfaction, addresses the fact that fiscal resources are one of the primary limiting aspects in information technology innovation within the public sector. As noted by West (2005), "[n]ew technology costs money, and it takes jurisdictions with substantial revenues to develop electronic government" (p. 58). Thus, citizens increasingly willing to pay for enhanced usefulness of e-government systems may offset the fiscal shortfalls experienced by many governments. Indeed, funding e-government through "commercial ads on government websites, charging user fees (or convenience fees) to access specific services, or levying premium charges to enter particular website sections where business data are available" (West, 2005, p. 58) may warrant greater attention.

Contributions to Theory

This study was accomplished in part by leveraging existing empirically validated measures from trust literature (Gefen, 2000; Meyer & Goes, 1988; McKnight et al., 2002; Rousseau et al., 1998; Tan & Thoen, 2001) and applying these measures specifically to the e-government realm. An institutional focus was noted as a principal construct contained in the multifaceted trust model, as institution-based trust has evolved into the leading gauge of on-line transactions (McKnight & Chervany, 2002; McKnight et al., 2002). In recent research, scholars have utilized the institutional component of trust to examine adoption of e-

government transactions offered by government agencies (Carter & Belanger, 2004, 2005). The results of the study indicate that of the existing trust measures (Trust in Government and Trust in Internet), Trust in Government is significant and a reliable indicator in the research model, which sought to understand both adoption and satisfaction with service quality. From an implications perspective, the impact of Trust in Government in addressing both the willingness to adopt and service quality satisfaction is a theoretical finding which opposes recent research. Research, comprehensive research by West (2005) reported no statistically significant relationship between the use of government websites and views about trust, confidence, or government effectiveness. Indeed, West (2005) reported that "[e]-government users are no more likely than nonusers to be trusting or confident about government or to believe the government is effective in solving problems" (p. 134). From the policy implication perspective, as well as from a theory-based standpoint, while West (2005) suggests that e-government has not altered citizen attitudes of government, the research presented in this study suggests that e-government is associated with enhancing levels of trust and beliefs about the effectiveness of government problem solving.

Furthermore, this study was accomplished in part by leveraging one of the most cited models for studying service quality, SERVQUAL, a validated measurement scale comprised of five service quality dimensions (Parasuraman et al., 1988). Specific to the focus of this study, more recent research has been undertaken to leverage the SERVQUAL dimensions to operationalize consumers' perceived service quality of e-commerce (Carr, 2002). With no identified research utilizing SERVQUAL in an e-government environment, the inclusion of this construct in the research model represented an exploratory feature of the study. The results of the study indicate that of the existing SERVQUAL measures (Reliability, Responsiveness, Empathy, and Assurance), Assurance is significant and a reliable indicator in the research model, which sought to understand both adoption and satisfaction with service quality. However, the challenge in documenting policy implications is "the absence of an agreed-upon consensus as to what constitutes successful performance" (West, 2005, p. 44). Rather, what is clear is that while Assurance is a significant predictor of e-government adoption and service quality satisfaction, it is an insipid predictor, and the remaining SERVQUAL measures (Reliability, Responsiveness, and Empathy) are of no significant predictive value. Indeed, from a theoretical implications perspective, this study furthers the work of Carter and Belanger (2004, 2005) connecting the technology acceptance measures and trust measures via the introduction of SERVQUAL to form a model which links antecedents of e-government adoption with a citizen-based assessment of on-line service quality – an association as yet not examined in the scholarly literature. However weak the remaining SERVQUAL measures (Reliability, Responsiveness, and Empathy) perform in the model, it is notable that the three chief influences (Usefulness, Government Trust, and Assurance) are primary components of the perceptual constructs acknowledged at the inception of this study – the Technology Acceptance Model, Trust, and SERVQUAL, respectively.

Limitations and Recommendations for Future Research

As the data collected and analyzed will be relevant only to users of the Mississippi.gov Internet portal, it is noted that interpretations of results should be cautious with respect to generalizability. The varied dimensions of the independent variables in the model represent a distinct strength; that is, the model presents a diverse means of interpreting the effect of perceived service quality on adoption antecedents of e-government applications. Conversely, it could be argued that any one of the conceptualizations of the variables could be

handled differently. Garnering behaviors from attitudinal surveys can be difficult, and the creation of a theoretically solid scale designed to measure a latent construct takes a great deal of effort and expertise. Thus, that this model is built upon established research is a plus.

At a time in history when many Americans possess a distinct lack of interest in politics generally and the administration of government specifically, many committed public sector managers are seeking innovative means for citizens to access government services in a manner complimentary of a modern, technologically-savvy society. E-government is representative of an ongoing initiative that may provide the citizenry more efficient and effective access to government services offered via the Internet. Given the vast, untapped potential of e-government services, future research should explore specific factors which enhance adoption and drive service quality. This study sought to shed light on only a sliver of this latent potential, though via the analysis conducted, additional research subjects of interest were created. This concluding section offers several ideas for ongoing research leveraging additional data collected in this study and data to come from future research projects.

At the outset of this study, the overall research framework was presented and discussed. In the context of this research agenda three primary frameworks were noted: technology acceptance, trust, and service quality. With respect to this model, with a focus on institution-based trust, it is plausible for future research to focus instead on characteristic-based trust and disposition to trust. Both of these constructs have been the focus of recent research into e-government adoption (Carter & Belanger, 2005; Pavlou, 2003; Warkentin et al., 2002). While the core focus of institution-based trust is related to an individual's attitudes toward technology, characteristic-based trust, on the other hand, is related to an individual's attitudes toward the service provider. However, as Trust in Government was found to be significant in assessing e-government adoption and satisfaction, it is suggested that this element be explored further.

CONCLUSION

Notwithstanding the limitations of this research, this study strove to leverage to make theoretical foundations from well-known models in e-commerce scholarship to fashion a model of the necessary elements that inform citizen adoption of and satisfaction with of e-government services. To that end, this research endeavors to make contributions to the fields of public administration and information systems. Expressly, this research suggests that a blend of technology acceptance, trust, and service quality factors unite to impact e-government adoption and satisfaction. The findings encapsulated in this study can provide impetus for future research on e-government adoption and satisfaction. Given that the provisioning of e-government services is evolving at a rapid pace, scholars should take a more comprehensive approach to evaluating e-government applications by including both political and technical factors in e-government adoption and satisfaction models. Additionally, public sector agencies should mull over the societal impacts of e-government on how citizens interact with both elected officials and the bureaucratic structures of government. While the potential exists for e-government to enhance interaction among certain segments of the population, the potential also exists for it to disenfranchise other population segments. Research into e-government will, no doubt, continue to unsheathe challenges in public management; these challenges offer the opportunity for both scholars and practitioners of public administration to continue to discover, analyze, and respond to the striking changes wrought by the persistent march of information technology.

ACKNOWLEDGMENT

The research for this study was completed by Craig Orgeron, under the supervision of Dr. Doug Goodman, as part of a dissertation submitted to the faculty of Mississippi State University in partial fulfillment of the requirements for the degree of Doctor of Philosophy in Public Policy and Administration in the Department of Political Science and Public Administration.

REFERENCES

Bandura, A. (1977). Self-efficacy: Toward a unifying theory of behavioral change. *Psychological Review*, *84*, 191–215. doi:10.1037/0033-295X.84.2.191

Belanger, F., Hiller, J., & Smith, W. (2002). Trustworthiness in electronic commerce: The role of privacy, security, and site attributes. *The Journal of Strategic Information Systems*, *11*, 245–270. doi:10.1016/S0963-8687(02)00018-5

Bhattacherjee, A. (2001). Understanding information systems continuance: An expectation-confirmation model. *Management Information Systems Quarterly*, *25*, 351–370. doi:10.2307/3250921

Brown, M. M., & Brudney, J. L. (1998). A 'smarter, better, faster, and cheaper' government? Contracting for geographic information systems. *Public Administration Review*, *58*, 335–345. doi:10.2307/977563

Carr, C. (2002). A psychometric evaluation of the expectations, perceptions, and difference-scores generated by the IS-adapted SERVQUAL instrument. *Decision Sciences*, *33*, 281–296. doi:10.1111/j.1540-5915.2002.tb01645.x

Carter, L., & Belanger, F. (2004, January). Citizen adoption of electronic government initiatives. In *Proceedings of the 37th Annual Hawaii International Conference on System Sciences*, Big Island, HI (pp. 119-128).

Carter, L., & Belanger, F. (2005). The utilization of e-government services: Citizen trust, innovation, and acceptance factors. *Information Systems Journal*, *15*, 5–25. doi:10.1111/j.1365-2575.2005.00183.x

Cats-Baril, W. L., & Thompson, R. L. (1998). *Information technology and management*. Burr Ridge, IL: Irwin.

Chadwick, C., & May, C. (2003). Interaction between states and citizens in the age of the Internet: E-government in the United States, Britain, and the European Union. *Governance: An International Journal of Policy, Administration, and Institutions*, *16*, 271–300.

Chadwick, S. (2001). Communicating trust in e-commerce interactions. *Management Communication Quarterly*, *14*, 653–658. doi:10.1177/0893318901144009

Chua, P. (1996). An empirical assessment of a modified technology acceptance model. *Journal of Management Information Systems*, *13*, 185–204.

Cohen, S., & Eimicke, W. (2001). *The use of the Internet in government service delivery*. Washington, DC: Pricewaterhouse Coopers Endowment for the Business of Government, E-government Series.

Council for Excellence in Government (CEG). (2003). *The new e-government equation: Ease, engagement, privacy, and protection*. Retrieved from http://www.cio.gov/documents/egovpoll2003.pdf

Davis, F. (1989). Perceived usefulness, perceived ease of use, and user acceptance of information technology. *Management Information Systems Quarterly*, *13*, 319–340. doi:10.2307/249008

Davis, F., Bagozzi, R., & Warshaw, P. (1989). User acceptance of computer technology: A comparison of two theoretical models. *Management Science*, *35*, 982–1003. doi:10.1287/mnsc.35.8.982

Devaraj, S., Ming, F., & Kohli, R. (2002). Antecedents of B2C channel satisfaction and preference: Validating e-commerce metrics. *Information Systems Research*, *13*, 316–333. doi:10.1287/isre.13.3.316.77

Dillman, D. (2000). *Mail and Internet surveys: The tailored design method* (2nd ed.). New York, NY: John Wiley & Sons.

Doll, W., Hendrickson, A., & Deng, X. (1998). Using Davis's perceived usefulness and ease-of-use instrument for decision making: A confirmatory and multigroup invariance analysis. *Decision Sciences*, *29*, 839–869. doi:10.1111/j.1540-5915.1998.tb00879.x

Fishbein, M., & Ajzen, I. (1975). *Belief, attitude, intentions, and behavior: An introduction to theory and research*. Reading, MA: Addison-Wesley.

Fountain, J. E. (2001). *Building the virtual state: Information technology and institutional change*. Washington, DC: Brookings Institution.

Gefen, D. (2000). E-commerce: The role of familiarity and trust. *Omega: The International Journal of Management Science*, *28*, 725–737. doi:10.1016/S0305-0483(00)00021-9

Gefen, D., Elena, K., & Straub, D. (2003). Trust and TAM in on-line shopping: An integrated model. *Management Information Systems Quarterly*, *27*, 51–90.

Gefen, D., & Straub, D. (2000). The relative importance of perceived ease-of-use in IS adoption. *Journal of the Association for Information Systems*, *8*, 1–28.

General Accounting Office (GAO). (2001). *Electronic government: Challenges must be addressed with effective leadership and management* (Tech. Rep. No. GAO-01-959T). Washington, DC: Government Printing Office.

Hair, J., Black, W., Babin, B., Anderson, R., & Tatham, R. (2006). *Multivariate data analysis* (6th ed.). Upper Saddle River, NJ: Pearson/Prentice Hall.

Hiller, J., & Belanger, F. (2001). *Privacy strategies for electronic government*. Washington, DC: PricewaterhouseCoopers Endowment for the Business of Government, E-Government Series.

Ho, A. (2002). Reinventing local governments and the e-government initiative. *Public Administration Review, 62*, 434–445. doi:10.1111/0033-3352.00197

Hoffman, D., Novak, T., & Peralta, M. (1999). Building consumer trust on-line. *Communications of the ACM, 42*, 80–85. doi:10.1145/299157.299175

Horrigan, J. B. (2004). *How Americans get in touch with government*. Washington, DC: Pew Internet & American Life.

Hosmer, L. (1995). Trust: The connecting link between organizational theory and philosophical ethics. *Academy of Management Review, 20*, 379–403.

Jackson, C., Simeon, C., & Leitch, R. (1997). Toward an understanding of the behavioral intention to use an information system. *Decision Sciences, 28*, 357–389. doi:10.1111/j.1540-5915.1997.tb01315.x

Jarvenpaa, S., & Tractinsky, N. (1999). Consumer trust in an Internet store: A cross-cultural validation. *Journal of Computer-Mediated Communication, 5*, 1–35.

Jorgensen, D. J., & Cable, S. (2002). Facing the challenges of e-government: A case study of the city of Corpus Christi, Texas. *S.A.M. Advanced Management Journal, 67*, 15–23.

Karahanna, E., & Straub, D. (1999). The psychological origins of perceived usefulness and perceived ease of use. *Information & Management, 35*, 237–250. doi:10.1016/S0378-7206(98)00096-2

Kettinger, W., & Lee, C. (1994). Perceived service quality and user satisfaction with the information-services function. *Decision Sciences, 25*, 737–766. doi:10.1111/j.1540-5915.1994.tb01868.x

Kettinger, W., & Lee, C. (1997). Pragmatic perspectives on the measurement of information systems service quality. *Management Information Systems Quarterly, 21*, 223–240. doi:10.2307/249421

Kettl, D. (2000). *The global public management revolution: A report on the transformation of governance*. Washington, DC: The Brookings Institution.

Kollock, P. (1999). The production of trust in online markets. *Advances in Group Processes, 16*, 99–123.

Kumar, N., Scheer, L., & Steenkamp, J. (1995). The effects of supplier fairness on vulnerable resellers. *JMR, Journal of Marketing Research, 32*, 54–65. doi:10.2307/3152110

Liu, C., & Arnett, K. (2000). Exploring the factors associated with web site success in the context of electronic commerce. *Information & Management, 38*, 23–33. doi:10.1016/S0378-7206(00)00049-5

Lucas, H., & Spitler, V. (1999). Technology use and performance: A field study of broker workstations. *Decision Sciences Journal, 30*, 291–311. doi:10.1111/j.1540-5915.1999.tb01611.x

Luhmann, N. (1979). *Trust and power*. Chichester, UK: John Wiley & Sons.

Mayer, R., Davis, J., & Schoorman, D. (1995). An integrative model of organization trust. *Academy of Management Review, 20*, 709–734.

McKnight, H., & Chervany, N. (2002). What trust means in e-commerce customer relationships: An interdisciplinary conceptual typology. *International Journal of Electronic Commerce, 6*, 35–53.

McKnight, H., Choudhury, V., & Kacmar, C. (2002). Developing and validating trust measures for e-commerce: An integrative typology. *Information Systems Research, 13*, 334–359. doi:10.1287/isre.13.3.334.81

McKnight, H., & Cummings, L. (1998). Initial trust formation in new organizational relationships. *Academy of Management Review, 23*, 473–490.

Melitski, J. (2001). *The world of e-government and e-governance*. Retrieved from http://www.aspanet.org

Meyer, A., & Goes, J. (1988). Organizational assimilation of innovations: A multilevel contextual analysis. *Academy of Management Journal, 31*, 897–923. doi:10.2307/256344

Mississippi Department of Information Technology Services (ITS). (2006). *Annual report*. Jackson, MS: ITS.

Moon, M. J. (2002). The evolution of e-government among municipalities: Rhetoric or reality? *Public Administration Review, 62*, 424–434. doi:10.1111/0033-3352.00196

Moon, M. J., & Kim, Y. (2001). Extending the TAM for a world-wide-web context. *Information & Management, 28*, 217–230. doi:10.1016/S0378-7206(00)00061-6

Mossenburg, K., Tolbert, C., & Stansbury, M. (2003). *Virtual inequality: Beyond the digital divide*. Washington, DC: Georgetown University Press.

Norris, D., Fletcher, P., & Holden, S. (2001). Is your local government plugged in? *Public Management, 83*, 4–11.

Norris, P. (2001). *Digital divide: Civic engagement, information poverty, and the Internet worldwide*. Cambridge, UK: Cambridge University Press.

Parasuraman, A., Berry, L., & Zeithaml, V. (1988). A multiple-item scale for measuring consumer perceptions of service quality. *Journal of Retailing, 64*, 12–40.

Parasuraman, A., Berry, L., & Zeithaml, V. (1991). Refinement and reassessment of the SERVQUAL scale. *Journal of Retailing, 67*, 420–450.

Parasuraman, A., Zeithaml, V., & Berry, L. (1985). A conceptual model of service quality and its implications for future research. *Journal of Marketing, 49*, 41–50. doi:10.2307/1251430

Patten, M. L. (2004). *Understanding research methods* (4th ed.). Glendale, CA: Pyrczak Publishing.

Pavlou, P. (2003). Consumer acceptance of electronic commerce: Integrating trust and risk with the technology acceptance model. *International Journal of Electronic Commerce, 7*, 69–103.

Pitt, L., Watson, R., & Kavan, B. (1995). Service quality – A measure of information systems effectiveness. *Management Information Systems Quarterly, 19*, 173–187. doi:10.2307/249687

Pitt, L., Watson, R., & Kavan, B. (1997). Measuring information systems service quality: Concerns for a complete canvas. *Management Information Systems Quarterly, 21*, 209–221. doi:10.2307/249420

Ratnasingam, P., & Pavlou, P. (2002, May). Technology trust: The next value creator in B2B electronic commerce. In *Proceedings of the Information Resources Management Association International Conference*, Seattle, WA (pp. 889-894).

Reichheld, F., & Sasser, W. (1990). Zero defections: Quality comes to services. *Harvard Business Review, 68*, 2–9.

Rivard, S. (1987). Successful implementation of end-user computing. *Interfaces, 17*, 25–53. doi:10.1287/inte.17.3.25

Robey, D. (1979a). Implementation and the organizational impacts of information systems. *Interfaces, 17*, 72–84. doi:10.1287/inte.17.3.72

Robey, D. (1979b). User attitudes and management information system use. *Academy of Management Journal, 22*, 527–538. doi:10.2307/255742

Rousseau, D., Sitkin, S., Burtand, R., & Camerer, C. (1998). Not so different after all: A cross-discipline view of trust. *Academy of Management Review, 23*, 393–404. doi:10.5465/AMR.1998.926617

Tan, Y., & Thoen, W. (2001). Toward a generic model of trust for electronic commerce. *International Journal of Electronic Commerce, 5*, 61–74.

Thomas, J., & Streib, G. (2003). The new face of government: Citizen-initiated contacts in the era of e-government. *Journal of Public Administration: Research and Theory, 13*, 83–102. doi:10.1093/jpart/mug010

Tolbert, C. J., & McNeal, R. S. (2003). Unraveling the effects of the Internet on political participation. *Political Research Quarterly, 56*, 175–185.

Van Dyke, T., Kappelman, L., & Prybutok, V. (1997). Measuring information systems service quality: Concerns on the use of the SERVQUAL questionnaire. *Management Information Systems Quarterly, 21*, 195–208. doi:10.2307/249419

Van Dyke, T., Prybutok, V., & Kappelman, L. (1999). Cautions on the use of the SERVQUAL measure to assess the quality of information systems services. *Decision Sciences, 30*, 877–891. doi:10.1111/j.1540-5915.1999.tb00911.x

Venkatesh, V., & Davis, F. (2000). A theoretical extension of the technology acceptance model: Four longitudinal field studies. *Management Science, 46*, 186–204. doi:10.1287/mnsc.46.2.186.11926

Venkatesh, V., Morris, M., Davis, G., & Davis, F. (2003). User acceptance of information technology: Toward a unified view. *Management Information Systems Quarterly, 27*, 425–478.

Warkentin, M., Gefen, D., Pavlou, P., & Rose, G. (2002). Encouraging citizen adoption of e-government by building trust. *Electronic Markets, 12*, 157–163. doi:10.1080/101967802320245929

Watson, R., Pitt, L., & Kavan, C. (1998). Measuring information systems service quality: Lessons from two longitudinal case studies. *Management Information Systems Quarterly, 22*, 61–79. doi:10.2307/249678

West, D. (2004). E-government and the transformation of service delivery and citizen attitudes. *Public Administration Review, 64*, 15–28. doi:10.1111/j.1540-6210.2004.00343.x

West, D. (2005). *Digital government: Technology and public sector performance*. Princeton, NJ: Princeton University Press.

Wren, J. D., Grissom, J. E., & Conway, T. (2006). E-mail decay rates among corresponding authors in MEDLINE. *EMBO Reports, 7*, 122–127. doi:10.1038/sj.embor.7400631

Xie, M., Wang, H., & Goh, T. (1998). Quality dimensions of Internet search engines. *Journal of Information Science, 24*, 365–372. doi:10.1177/016555159802400509

Zaheer, A., McEvily, B., & Perrone, V. (1998). Does trust matter? Exploring the effects of interorganizational and interpersonal trust on performance. *Organization Science, 9*, 141–159. doi:10.1287/orsc.9.2.141

Zeithaml, V., Berry, L., & Parasuraman, A. (1996). The behavioral consequences of service quality. *Journal of Marketing, 60*, 31–46. doi:10.2307/1251929

Zucker, L. (1986). Production of trust: Institutional sources of economic structure . In Staw, B., & Cummings, L. (Eds.), *Research in organizational behavior* (pp. 53–111). Greenwich, CT: JAI Press.

This work was previously published in the International Journal of Electronic Government Research, Volume 7, Issue 3, edited by Vishanth Weerakkody, pp. 57-78, copyright 2011 by IGI Publishing (an imprint of IGI Global).

Chapter 16
Identifying Barriers to E–Government Services for Citizens in Developing Countries:
An Exploratory Study

Subhajyoti Ray
Xavier Institute of Management, Bhubaneswar, India

ABSTRACT

Although the use of ICT by government has demonstrated its potential in improving government services, worldwide there are more failures than successes of e-Government projects. In the context of developing countries, including India, authors have observed equally high failure rates. Therefore, it is important to understand the barriers to implementation of e-Government, especially in developing countries. This paper develops a comprehensive understanding of barriers to e-Government services for citizens in developing countries. This study was carried out in India, a developing country with a massive commitment to e-Government at policy and implementation levels. Based on variables identified from research, a survey of the key practitioners in e-Government was conducted to generate evidence on perceptions of barriers to e-Government. Even though a relatively small number of responses were received, the responses could be evaluated using principal component analysis to understand the latent structure of the barriers. Finally, 7 critical factors with 30 items are extracted that describe the latent structure of barriers to e-Government in development.

DOI: 10.4018/978-1-4666-2458-0.ch016

INTRODUCTION

Although e-Government has demonstrated its potential in improving public services, worldwide there are more failures than successes (Heeks, 2003). It is not uncommon to observe in the broader area of information systems (IS) that one person's failure is another's success (Lyytinen & Hirschheim, 1987; Sauer, 1993). Yet the fact that a high percentage of (IS) projects fail is well established. For example, Hochstrasser and Griffiths (1991), conclude that up to 70% of all information systems projects do not deliver their objectives.

A rich body of knowledge on factors that cause failure of IS projects in private sector organizations is available (Wallace et al., 2004). On the other hand there is no single list of challenges to e-government initiatives as information systems in public organizations especially in developing countries (Garcia & Pardo, 2005). Also most of the studies on barriers to e-Government are based in developed countries, though some authors have suggested that lessons from developed countries can be useful in developing countries if they are applied proficiently (Weerakkody & Dwivedi, 2007). Even within the developed countries there are differences in barriers to ICT adoption on dimension like e.g. skill and access (Carter & Weerakkody, 2008). Furthermore, developing country contexts are expected to experience different barriers that do not exist in a developed country for a variety of reasons. For example the difference in connectivity infrastructure, across developed and developing (Chen et al., 2007) are expected to bring up new kinds of barriers in developing countries especially for citizen services. Introducing E-Government in developing countries is expected to require more far reaching efforts than those in developed countries (Schuppan, 2009).

Therefore the purpose of this paper is to comprehensively identify the barriers to e-Government services to citizens in developing countries. This research is also timely as many develop-

ing countries have committed significantly to e-Government (Gupta & Jana, 2003) and have at the same time experienced widespread failures of projects (Heeks, 2003). For example in the past decade there has been a significant surge in E-Government related activity in India. This is most noticeable in the way E-Government has been conceptualized in India in terms of its expected outcomes and delivery model; and also the way the government has gone about implementing E-Government at national and sub-national levels (Ray, 2010). Howver, barriers to implementation e.g. poor project management, remain that affect the project success rates (Ray, 2010). The transition from policy formulation to implementation still eludes many developing nations (Lau et al., 2008).

A clearer understanding of barriers to e-Government implementation in this context can help in improving the successes rate of projects.

REVIEW OF LITERATURE

The inability to identify, understand and then manage causes of failure is cited as a major cause of IS project problems such as cost and schedule overruns, unmet user requirements and ineffective system implementation (Alter & Ginzberg, 1978; Barki, Rivard, & Talbot, 2001; Boehm, 1991; Charette, 1991; McFarlan, 1981). Like most information technology based projects, e-Government projects too have been known to exhibit high failure rates (Heeks, 2003), indicating the need to understand and identify causes of failure. However there are significant differences between private and public sector organizations in terms of environmental factors e.g. market exposure, organizational environment transaction e.g. public scrutiny and expectation, and internal structure and process factors e.g. complexity of objectives and decision criteria (Rainey et al., 1976) that necessitates examining the barriers to e-Government afresh. At a conceptual level Heeks and Bhatnagar (1999) identified the main reason for failure of e-Government projects as the concept-reality. The concept-reality gaps pertain to the mismatch or gap between conception of a change brought about by IS and the current reality. These gaps can occur on Information, Technology, Processes, Objectives, Staff, Management and Other (ITPOSMO) dimensions. An example of qualitative analysis of the ITPOSMO framework applied to e-Government projects in Africa can be found in Heeks (2002). Few other studies have looked at very specific reasons of failure of e-Government projects. For example, Jaeger and Thompson (2003) assert that an e-Government system would fail if the government did not take an active role in educating citizens about the value of e-Government. Compounding this is the difference between developed and developing countries that bring in additional barriers (Chen, 2007).

Odedra-Straub (2003) states that developing countries have severe limitations in terms of connectivity and user access to online government. This often leads to a low user base, as the system would not be equally accessible by all citizens. Linked to this is the lack of skills and training which are required to effectively use an e-Government system that is available to government officials and citizens. This problem has been referred to by numerous academics (Heeks, 1999; Moon, 2002; Ho, 2002) and also particularly for developing countries (Ndou, 2004). In a study on ICT adoption in the public sector in Bangladesh, authors find that lack of knowledge and attitude as key stumbling blocks (Imran, 2009). The same study also concluded that ICT skill could be a key driver for attitude change. Another study based on the Brazilian Central Bank found high risk for managers, hidden costs and lack of coordination as some of the obstacles for e-Government (Joia, 2007). Lam (2005) found four categories of barriers: strategy, technology, policy and organization that cater deter e-Government integration projects. Zaed (2007) finds inadequate levels of e-readiness for e-Government in Arab countries as a barrier to e-Government. They conclude the

lack of coordination between agencies, poor skills and quality of network connectivity speeds as impediments to e-Government. Salman (2004) in his study of impediments to implementing information technology in general and e-commerce in particular in the context of developing countries finds that human condition, political aspects and environmental issues are critical to any progress. Specifically, the lack of political and leadership support was found to be barriers for e-Government implementation in developing countries (Molla & Licker, 2005). Bwalya (2009) is his study of e-Government implementation in Zambia concludes that there is need to inculcate culture awareness (local language content, cultural incorporation), and build inexpensive IT infrastructure before meaningful progress can happen. A cross country analysis by Shin et al. (2008) find 6 success factors: changes in work process, technical/human resources, organizational culture/values, vision/strategy/internal leadership, external/financial support, and laws/regulations/policies for e-Government in developing countries.

The need to reengineer government processes to adapt to the new technology and the culture of an e-Government system are other potential risks to the project as these might be perceived as a reduction of their authority by some stakeholders (Ebrahim & Irani, 2005; Peterson, 1998). For example process reengineering was seen to be a significant challenge in moving to transformational government (Weerakkody & Dhillon, 2008). Also resistance in various other forms reduces the chance of deriving benefits from use of ICT in government especially in developing countries (Ndou, 2004). Dawes and Pardo (2002) identified the existence of multiple, and sometimes conflicting, goals in the public sector as an additional challenge faced by information systems in the public sector. In another study on broadband adoption in India, costs and speed of connection were seen to be important considerations (Dwivedi et al., 2008) thus suggesting that with low income levels broadband adoption is likely to be slow.

The review suggests that a variety of methods have been adopted to understand impediments and success factors for e-Government in developing countries. At the same time these studies have focused at different levels e.g. national level or sub-national level while a few have also focused at project level. In the Indian context the literature is of great use in highlighting some key barriers in general but do not help in understanding the project level barriers in much depth. For example there is both political and financial support for e-Government with monitoring from the top most political office of the country and yet there are project failures. Clearly there is a need to understand in some detail the barriers to e-government project implementation for India in particular and for developing countries in general.

METHODOLOGY

The research uses a qualitative approach to generate a list of items that are barriers to e-Government in developing countries context. The research relies on semi-structured interviews, case and document reviews, literature reviews and observation (Myers, 1997; Silverman, 2000; Walsham, 1995) Open ended interviews were conducted with key people involved in two e-Government projects in different settings. First was a large urban municipal authority in the Western part of India that had implemented e-Services projects. The second was a project on land records computerization in Eastern part of the India. In both cases the interviews were taken of staff operating the system, project IT vendors, and project managers from within the government. Besides theses interviews, documents of several case studies on e-Government failure and literature on information systems and e-Government failure were analyzed to understand the key barriers to e-Government in developing countries. A set of 39 items were generated that were included in a questionnaire. The questionnaire was discussed with two differ-

ent experts in e-Government research to ascertain face validity (Fink, 1995). This led to combining a few items to reflect the barrier better and resulted in a questionnaire which had 32 items.

A survey of practitioners of the National Informatics Centre of India, who are closely associated with implementing e-Government, was undertaken thereafter. The national informatics centre (NIC) is the main organization that has been implementing e-Government projects in country and providing support to the government agencies at all levels. The staff of NIC have ground level knowledge of individual projects that are being implemented as they are the once who face day to day challenges in implementing and maintaining e-Government projects throughout the country. The details of the survey are given next.

Survey

Questionnaires were emailed to the officers of NIC. The respondents (officers of the NIC) were asked to rate each item on a 5 point scale, based on her perception of its importance. A rating of 5 meant that the variable was a strong barrier and 1 meant the variable was weak barrier. Of 312 officers contacted for the survey, only 59 responded. Even though the response rate was low the chance of response bias was ruled out primarily because of the following reasons. The questions required the respondent to rate the importance of an item based on her perception. The questions were short and clear with no ambiguity. There was no socially desirable response; rating one item more than other had no consequence for the respondent. Also the questionnaire had no leading questions that would hint the reader that responding in a certain way was desirable.

The mean rating for the 32 items in descending order of means rounded to two decimals is presented in Table 1.

The items were also examined for their reliability. The tendency toward consistency found in repeated measurements is referred to as reli-

Table 1. Mean rating of risk items (n=59)

S. No.	Risk item	Mean Score
1	Artificial/unrealistic deadlines for project completion	3.66
2	Lack of effective project management	3.53
3	Lack of information technology infrastructure needed to support the project e.g. networking, email, computers etc.	3.42
4	Lack of funding	3.41
5	Inadequately identified system requirements	3.31
6	Inexperienced project manager	3.29
7	Citizens do not have adequate access to the service centers/kiosks	3.17
8	Stale or inadequate data for sustaining the project	3.12
9	Lack of attention to access of e-services by poor/women/underprivileged	3.07
10	Senior management not being aware of the true potential of information technology	3.07
11	Incompetent project development team members	3.03
12	Change in project leadership	3.03
13	Employees are unwilling to share information in the organization	3.03
14	Inadequate estimation of required resources to complete project	3.03
15	Information is not given due importance in decision making	3.02
16	Project development vendor not being selected in an objective manner	2.98
17	Citizens not being aware of the e-Government project	2.97
18	Citizen not being aware of the services delivered under the project	2.95
19	Corruption related income will reduce if e-Government project is implemented	2.95
20	Inadequate users' training	2.93
21	Information Technology illiteracy among users	2.93
22	The e-Government project generates information that can create discomfort for the political powers	2.90
23	Irregular energy/power supply	2.85
24	Project Vendor/developer suggesting too many design/scope changes in the project	2.64
25	Initial data entry needed to support the project	2.63
26	Information exchange happens informally in the organization	2.50
27	Project uses new/untested technology	2.49
28	The e-Government changes the roles and duties of staff	2.44
29	Middle men are involved in the provision of government services	2.39
30	The e-Government project diminishes the powers of the bureaucracy	2.36
31	The e-Government project reduces the privileges of the bureaucracy	2.34
32	The project is promoted/closely associated with a particular political group	2.29

ability (Carmines & Zeller, 1979). One of the popular tests for reliability is testing for the internal consistency for a given administration of the instrument. Cronbach's alpha as a measure of internal consistency ascertains how well a set of items measures a latent construct. Cronbach's alpha (Cronbach, 1951) can be written as a function of the number of test items and the average inter-correlation as follows.

$$\alpha = \frac{N \cdot \bar{r}}{1 + (N-1) \cdot \bar{r}}$$

Here N is equal to the number of items, i.e. 32, and r-bar is the average inter-item correlation among the items. Nunnally (1978, p. 245) recommends that instruments used in basic research should have reliability of about .70 or better, while trying to increase reliabilities much beyond .80 is a waste of time. Cronbach alpha computed from the sample of 59 respondents was found to be 0.89, thus indicating very high internal reliability of the 32 item instrument to assess risk in e-Government projects.

While these items do inform the practitioner the nature and sources of risk in an e-Government project, it does not help in the understanding of the underlying structure of risk. In order understand the latent structure of risk, exploratory factor analysis of the survey data was done. This is discussed in the next section.

ANALYSIS

Exploratory factor analysis is widely employed technique to discover the basic structure of a domain. Factor analysis requires large samples, mainly because correlations, the key input to factor analysis, stabilize only if samples are large. Therefore a sample of size 59 by traditional standards is quite small for factor analysis of 32 variables. However, it is also not uncommon to see research studies with similar items to sample size ratio. In examination of best practices of factor analysis, Costello and Osborne (2005) find that 25.8% of research studies had a sample size to item ratio of 2:1. Hence factor analysis may still be a useful technique to examine the nature of risk in e-Government project despite the relatively low sample size to item ratio. In the following sections we discuss the details of statistical analysis and findings.

Sample Adequacy Check

Sample adequacy check (Table 2) is used to determine if a set of variables will factor well or not and accordingly decision of dropping variables can be taken. KMO (Kaiser-Meyer-Olkin) statistic is used to check for sample adequacy, based on examination of correlation and partial correlation. The overall KMO statistic for a set of variables can take a value between 0 and 1, with 0.6 being accepted as the bare minimum, before any meaningful factor analysis can be done (Hutcheson and Sofroniou, 1999). To increase overall KMO, variables can be dropped that have a low individual KMO values.

The KMO statistic for the 32 variables based on 59 observations was 0.627 indicating acceptable levels but also the scope of improving the overall factorability of the variables. At this the factor structure based on 32 variables was also found hard to interpret. Therefore, two variables namely, "*stale or inadequate data to sustain the project*", and "*IT illiteracy among users*" that had the lowest individual KMO with the values being 0.377 and 0.444 respectively, were dropped from factor analysis.

The overall KMO statistic for the remaining 30 variables was found to be 0.697, indicating improved factorability of the variables. The findings from the factor analysis of the 30 variables are discussed next.

Factor Extraction and Loading

Principal component method was employed for factor extraction, as it is the most common method employed for data reduction and factor structuring. The number of factor to extract was based on the criterion that Eigen value of the factor be greater than 1. In all, 7 factors with Eigen value of more than 1 emerged, explaining 74.71% of the total variance in the 30 variables. Also all variables had high communality, the minimum being 0.586 for the variable "*Artificial/unrealistic*

Table 2. Sample adequacy check

Total number of variables	Over all KMO	Variable considered for dropping (lowest KMO)	Factor structure
32	0.627	*stale or inadequate data to sustain the project (0.377)*	Not interpretable
31	0.643	*IT illiteracy among users (0.430)*	Not interpretable
30	0.697	*None*	Interpretable

deadlines for project completion", thus indicating good explanation by the factors. In the social sciences, communalities are low to moderate varying between .40 and .70 (Costello & Osborne, 2005). As the initial factor structures were not clean, varimax rotation was used to obtain a clearer factor structure. The rotated component matrix is given in Table 3.

Although several criteria exist to decide significant factor loadings and cross loadings, a thumb rule often followed is that any loading of less that 0.32 is not significant (Tabachnick & Fidell, 2001; Costello & Osborne, 2005). As none of the loading scores were less than 0.32, it was decided to choose that factor for a variable for which it had the highest loading. The seven factors with labels, the percentage of variance explained, and the loading variables are presented in Table 4.

Though all the variables were included in the factor on which they had the highest loading, three variables namely; *The e-Government project reduces the privileges of the bureaucracy, The e-Government project diminishes the powers of the bureaucracy* and *Project leadership changes* loaded 0.4 or higher on two factors. A loading of 0.4 is bare minimum loading recommended for small samples (Hair et al., 1998; Stevens, 2002).

DISCUSSION

A large number of reasons for failure of e-Government projects in developing countries are proposed in literature. E-Government project implementers and planners are faced with innumerable challenges that are interdependent making it hard for them to interpret and efficiently manage the challenges. A few basic concepts that are central to the understanding of barriers to e-Government in developing countries are the key to uncovering the challenges faced by e-Government projects. We attempted to address the question: what are the key barriers that practitioners should be aware of during implementation of e-Government projects. Factor analysis was done to identify seven key barriers that explain the hitherto unexplained phenomenon of barriers to e-Government in developing countries.

The interpretation of seven factors are discussed below

1. **General Project Issues:** The general label was given to the first factor as a high number of items loaded on to this factor making any specific labeling of the factor difficult. This is also the recommended procedure for naming factors if they cannot be clearly defined in terms of the original variables (Malhotra, 2002). As the name suggests general factor identifies well know and common sources of failure in information technology projects. Thus general barriers to implementation arise from project complexity, project environment and poor project management.

2. **Inadequate Citizen Awareness and Access to Project Services:** One of the major benefits of e-Government projects, is the near and convenient access to government services. Therefore barrier to citizen identifies all those hurdles that prevent a smooth access to e-Government services, including few and far located service centers and poor awareness among citizens about the services.

Table 3. Rotated Component Matrix

Item	1	2	3	4	5	6	7
Senior management not being aware of the true potential of information technology	0.104	0.143	0.231	0.006	0.864	0.011	0.034
Information is not given due importance in decision making	0.254	0.125	0.261	-0.064	0.734	0.125	-0.054
Employees are unwilling to share information in the organization	0.102	-0.053	0.738	0.278	0.181	0.125	0.039
The e-Government project generates information that can create discomfort for the political powers	-0.148	0.179	0.742	0.159	0.190	0.253	0.105
Information exchange happens informally in the organization	0.358	0.280	0.728	-0.133	0.120	-0.190	0.133
The e-Government project reduces the privileges of the bureaucracy	-0.085	0.512	0.367	0.080	0.020	0.627	0.047
The e-Government project diminishes the powers of the bureaucracy	-0.007	0.508	0.331	0.066	-0.037	0.684	0.165
Middle men are involved in the provision of government services	-0.155	0.293	0.755	0.153	0.084	-0.010	-0.112
Initial data entry needed to support the project	0.192	0.467	0.145	0.553	0.228	-0.162	0.251
Inadequate users' training	0.229	0.210	0.338	0.758	-0.078	0.034	-0.037
Irregular energy/power supply	0.193	-0.003	0.221	0.868	0.071	0.048	0.076
Citizens not being aware of the e-Government project	0.101	0.781	0.211	0.267	0.261	0.108	-0.116
Citizens do not have adequate access to the service centers/ kiosks	-0.022	0.833	0.276	0.226	0.032	0.019	0.113
Lack of attention to access of e-services by poor/women/underprivileged	-0.124	0.890	0.120	0.001	-0.006	0.191	0.132
Citizen not being aware of the services delivered under the project	-0.128	0.691	-0.118	-0.133	0.059	0.294	0.297
Corruption related income will reduce if e-Government project is implemented	-0.102	0.354	0.099	0.099	0.406	0.518	0.389
The e-Government changes the roles and duties of staff	-0.073	0.303	0.122	0.166	0.089	0.168	0.763
Project uses new/untested technology	0.614	-0.235	0.328	0.108	-0.299	-0.093	0.349
Incompetent project development team members	0.855	0.019	-0.026	0.163	-0.032	-0.131	-0.089
Inadequate estimation of required resources to complete project	0.683	0.224	0.143	0.319	0.141	-0.097	0.099
The project is promoted/closely associated with a particular political group	0.729	0.060	0.095	0.239	0.016	-0.043	-0.181
Project Vendor/developer suggesting too many design/scope changes in the project	0.488	-0.095	0.221	0.206	0.038	-0.631	0.089
Project development vendor not being selected in an objective manner	0.539	0.003	0.054	0.287	0.340	-0.360	0.100
Change in project leadership	0.318	-0.022	-0.095	0.407	0.615	-0.269	0.283
Lack of information technology infrastructure needed to support the project e.g. networking, email, computers etc.	0.329	0.175	-0.215	0.532	-0.134	-0.084	0.374
Inexperienced project manager	0.745	0.036	-0.232	-0.204	0.251	0.006	-0.073
Lack of funding	0.683	-0.193	-0.243	0.266	0.143	-0.020	-0.022
Artificial/unrealistic deadlines for project completion	0.701	-0.242	0.106	0.064	0.122	0.004	0.072
Lack of effective project management	0.609	-0.189	0.067	-0.092	0.475	-0.064	0.277
Inadequately identified system requirements	0.583	0.252	-0.054	0.140	0.271	-0.168	0.461

Table 4. Factor Loadings of 30 Variables

Factor Label (% of variance explained)	Variables included in the factor	Factor Loading
General Project Issues (18.39%)	Project uses new/untested technology	0.614
	Incompetent project development team members	0.855
	Inadequate estimation of required resources to complete project	0.683
	The project is promoted/closely associated with a particular political group	0.729
	Inexperienced project manager	0.745
	Lack of funding	0.683
	Artificial/unrealistic deadlines for project completion	0.701
	Lack of effective project management	0.609
	Inadequately identified system requirements	0.583
	Project development vendor not being selected in an objective manner	0.539
	Project Vendor/developer suggesting too many design/scope changes in the project	0.488
Inadequate citizen awareness and access to project services (13.83%)	Citizens not being aware of the e-Government project	0.781
	Citizens do not have adequate access to the service centers/kiosks	0.833
	Lack of attention to access of e-services by poor, women and underprivileged	0.890
	Citizen not being aware of the services delivered under the project	0.691
Non transparency in the organization (10.98%)	Employees are unwilling to share information in the organization	0.738
	The e-Government project generates information that can create discomfort for the political powers	0.742
	Information exchange happens informally in the organization	0.728
	Middle men are involved in the provision of government services	0.755
Operational failure (9.62%)	Initial data entry needed to support the project	0.553
	Inadequate users' training	0.758
	Irregular energy/power supply	0.868
	Lack of information technology infrastructure needed to support the project e.g. networking, email, computers etc.	0.532
Top management apathy (9.02%)	Senior management not being aware of the true potential of information technology	0.864
	Information is not given due importance in decision making	0.734
	Change in project leadership	0.615
Diminishing power of employees (7.103%)	The e-Government project reduces the privileges of the bureaucracy	0.627
	The e-Government project diminishes the powers of the bureaucracy	0.684
	Corruption related income will reduce if e-Government project is implemented	0.518
Maladapted staff (5.74%)	The e-Government changes the roles and duties of staff	0.763

3. **Non Transparency in the Organization:** The success of an e-Government project also depends on the how information is shared within and outside the organization. A culture of non transparency, informal information exchanges, information secrecy, and middle men being used to deliver services acts as a barrier to e-Government implementation.

4. **Operational Failure:** e-Government projects run the risk of failing because they may simply become very difficult to keep operational. For example, poor infrastructure, high

maintenance costs and heavy data entry load may force reverting to the manual system of functioning thus making the e-Government project ineffective.

5. **Top Management Apathy:** e-Government project can also fail if due importance by the topmost authority is not given to the project. Changing project leader midway, not being appreciative of information or information technology are symptoms of lack of importance senior management gives to e-Government project.

6. **Diminishing Power of Employees:** e-Government projects can also fail if they threaten some of the existing powers and privileges of the employees. Such power and privileges allow employee to enjoy tangible and intangible benefits which they do not wish to sacrifice. In the event that e-Government project reduces such powers, resistance to the project is a likely outcome, thus threatening the chances of project success.

7. **Maladapted Staff:** Any introduction of information technology alters the role of the people involved in the process, thereby creating confusion, fear or disinterest. Thus e-Government projects are at a risk because staff may not appreciate or like their new roles and would try to find ways and means to revert to old ways of working, thus reducing success chances of the e-Government project.

LIMITATIONS

This study suffered from the drawback of limited data collection. A 32 item risk scale was factor analysed using 59 observations. This is by traditional norms a small observation to item ratio (Costello & Osborne, 2005). It is quite possible that with a much larger sample an improved factor structure

in term of interpretability and reliability will be obtained. Also the survey and analysis was based on respondents from a single country and non probabilistic which can limit the generalizability of the results to other countries.

CONCLUSION

E-Government projects have experienced high failure rates and therefore it was necessary to revisit the causes of failure. This paper identifies 7 factors that describe reasons for failure in e-Government projects, they are: general project factor, inadequate citizen awareness of and access to project services, non transparency in the organization, operational risk, top management apathy, diminishing power of employees and maladapted staff. These factors describe more clearly the sources of risk in e-Government project. There are implications of the findings for the researcher and the practitioner. Researcher can use the factors to identify strategies that can best control these failure factors. Such understanding will help in proposing an overall success model for e-Government projects. Failure factors like diminishing power of employees has implications not only for IT based projects but also for other interventions that usher change in government organizations. For the researcher it would be useful to examine if one or more of this factors is more pervasive in affecting the success chances of any transformation initiatives in the public organization.

For the practitioner the research provides a more comprehensive understanding of failure factors especially in the context of an e-Government project designed for service delivery to citizens. This can help the practitioner to improve the success chances of the project by being alert to any manifestation of the failure factors and take early remedial action. The processes of monitoring the failure factors can become a key component of the overall project management effort.

REFERENCES

Aicholzer, G., & Schmutzer, R. (2000). Organizational challenges to the development of electronic government. In *Proceedings of the 11ᵗʰ International Workshop on Database and Expert Systems Applications*, New York, NY.

Alter, S., & Ginzberg, M. (1978). Managing uncertainty in MIS implementation. *Sloan Management Review, 20*(1), 23–31.

Arrow, K. (1970). *Essays in the theory of risk-bearing*. Amsterdam, The Netherlands: North-Holland.

Barki, H., Rivard, S., & Talbot, J. (1993). Toward an assessment of software development risk. *Journal of Management Information Systems, 10*(2), 203–236.

Boehm, B. W. (1991). Software risk management: Principles and practices. *IEEE Software, 8*(1), 32–41. doi:10.1109/52.62930

Bwalya, K. J. (2009). Factors affecting adoption of e-government in Zambia. *Electronic Journal of Information Systems in Developing Countries, 38*(4), 1–13.

Carmines, E. G., & Zeller, R. A. (1979). *Reliability and validity assessment*. Thousand Oaks, CA: Sage.

Carter, L., & Weerakkody, V. (2008). E-Government adoption: A cultural comparison. *Information Systems Frontiers, 10*(4), 473–482. doi:10.1007/s10796-008-9103-6

Charette, R. N. (1991). The risks with risk analysis. *Communications of the ACM, 34*(6), 106–106. doi:10.1145/103701.103705

Chen, Y., & Wayne, W. (2006). Electronic government implementation: A comparison between developed and developing countries. *International Journal of Electronic Government Research, 3*(2), 45–61. doi:10.4018/jegr.2007040103

Costello, A. B., & Osborne, J. W. (2005). Best practices in exploratory factor analysis: Four recommendations for getting the most from your analysis. *Practical Assessment. Research Evaluation, 10*(7), 1–9.

Cronbach, L. J. (1951). Coefficient alpha and the internal structure of tests. *Psychometrika, 16*(3), 297–334. doi:10.1007/BF02310555

Dada, D. (2006). Failure of e-government in developing countries: A literature review. *Electronic Journal of Information Systems in Developing Countries, 26*(7), 12–34.

Dawes, S. S., & Pardo, T. (2002). Building collaborative digital government systems. In McIver, W. J., & Elmagarmid, A. K. (Eds.), *Advances in digital government: Technology, human factors, and policy*. Boston, MA: Kluwer Academic. doi:10.1007/0-306-47374-7_16

Ebrahim, Z., & Irani, Z. (2005). E-Government adoption: Architecture and barriers. *Business Process Management Journal, 11*(5), 589–611. doi:10.1108/14637150510619902

Fink, A. (Ed.). (1995). *The survey handbook (Vol. 1)*. Thousand Oaks, CA: Sage.

Gil-García, J. R., & Pardo, T. A. (2005). E-government success factors: Mapping practical tools to theoretical foundations. *Government Information Quarterly, 22*(2), 187–216. doi:10.1016/j.giq.2005.02.001

Gupta, M. P., & Jana, D. (2003). E-government evaluation: A framework and case study. *Government Information Quarterly, 20*(1), 365–387. doi:10.1016/j.giq.2003.08.002

Hair, J. F., Anderson, R. E., Tatham, R. L., & Black, W. C. (1998). *Multivariate data analysis*. Upper Saddle River, NJ: Prentice Hall.

Heeks, R. (2003). e-Government in Africa: Promise and practice. *Information Polity, 7*(2), 97–114.

Heeks, R. (2003). *Most e-government-for-development projects fail: How can risks be reduced?* Manchester, UK: University of Manchester.

Heeks, R., & Bhatnagar, S. (1999). Understanding success and failure in information age reform. In Heeks, R. (Ed.), *Reinventing government in information age*. London, UK: Roultedge. doi:10.4324/9780203204962

Ho, A. (2002). Reinventing local government and the e-government initiative. *Public Administration Review, 62*(4), 434–444. doi:10.1111/0033-3352.00197

Hocstrasser, B., & Griffiths, C. (1991). *Controlling IT investments strategy and management*. London, UK: Chapman Hall.

Hutcheson, G., & Sofroniou, N. (1999). *The multivariate social scientist: Introductory statistics using generalized linear models*. Thousand Oaks, CA: Sage.

Imran, A. (2009, January 5-8). Knowledge and attitude, the two major barriers to ICT adoption in LDC are the opposite side of a coin: An empirical evidence from Bangladesh. In *Proceedings of the 42nd Hawaii International Conference on System Sciences*, Waikoloa, HI (pp. 1-10).

Jaeger, P. T., & Thomson, K. M. (2003). e-Government around the world, lessons, challenges and future directions. *Government Information Quarterly, 20*(4), 389–394. doi:10.1016/j.giq.2003.08.001

Joia, L. A. (2007). A heuristic model to implement government-to-government projects. *International Journal of Electronic Government Research, 3*(1), 1–18. doi:10.4018/jegr.2007010101

Lam, W. (2005). Barriers to e-government. *Journal of Enterprise Information Management, 18*(5), 511–530. doi:10.1108/17410390510623981

Lau, T. Y., Mira, A., Lin, C., & Atkin, D. J. (2008). Adoption of e-government in three Latin American countries: Argentina, Brazil and Mexico. *Telecommunications Policy, 32*(2), 88–100. doi:10.1016/j.telpol.2007.07.007

Lyytinen, K., & Hirschheim, R. (1987). Information systems failures: A survey and classification of empirical literature. In Zorkoczy, P. (Ed.), *Oxford surveys in information technology*. New York, NY: Oxford University Press.

Maccrimmon, K. R., & Wehrung, D. A. (1984). The risk in-basket. *The Journal of Business, 57*(3), 367–387. doi:10.1086/296269

Malhotra, K. N. (2002). *Marketing research: An applied orientation*. New Delhi, India: Pearson Education.

March, G. J., & Shapira, Z. (1987). Managerial perspectives on risk and risk taking. *Management Science, 33*(11), 1404–1418. doi:10.1287/mnsc.33.11.1404

McFarlan, F. W. (1981). Portfolio approach to information systems. *Harvard Business Review*.

Molla, A., & Licker, P. S. (2005). eCommerce adoption in developing countries: A model and instrument. *Information & Management, 42*(6), 877–899. doi:10.1016/j.im.2004.09.002

Moon, M. J. (2002). The evolution of e-government among municipalities: Rhetoric or reality? *Public Administration Review, 62*(4), 424–433. doi:10.1111/0033-3352.00196

Mursu, A., Soriyan, H. A., Olufokunbi, K., & Korpela, M. (2000). Information systems development in a developing country: Theoretical analysis of special requirements in Nigeria and Africa. In *Proceedings of the 33rd Hawaiian International Conference on System Sciences* (Vol. 2, pp. 1-10).

Myers, M. D. (1997). Qualitative research in information systems. *Management Information Systems Quarterly, 21*(2), 241–242. doi:10.2307/249422

Ndou, V. D. (2004). E-Government for developing countries: Opportunities and challenges. *Electronic Journal of Information Systems in Developing Countries, 18*(1), 1–24.

Nunnally, J. C. (1978). *Psychometric theory* (2nd ed.). New York, NY: McGraw-Hill.

Odedra-Straub, M. (2003). E-Commerce and development: Whose development? *Electronic Journal of Information Systems in Developing Countries, 11*(2), 1–5.

Ojo, S. O. (1996). Socio-cultural and organisational issues in IT application in Nigeria. In Odedra-Straub, M. (Ed.), *Global information technology and socio-economic development* (pp. 99–109). Marietta, GA: Ivy League Publishing.

Peterson, S. B. (1998). Saints, demons, wizards and systems: Why information technology reform fail or underperforms in public bureaucracies in Africa. *Public Administration and Development, 18*(1), 37–60. doi:10.1002/(SICI)1099-162X(199802)18:1<37::AID-PAD990>3.0.CO;2-V

Rainey, H. G., Backoof, R. W., & Levene, C. H. (1976). Comparing public and private organizations. *Public Administration Review, 36*(2), 233–234. doi:10.2307/975145

Ray, S. (2010). Conceptualization and implementation of e-government in India. In Reddick, C. G. (Ed.), *Comparitive e-government* (pp. 391–408). New York, NY: Springer. doi:10.1007/978-1-4419-6536-3_20

Salman, A. (2004). Elusive challenges of e-change management in developing countries. *Business Process Management, 10*(2), 140–157. doi:10.1108/14637150410530226

Sauer, C. (1993). *Why information systems fail: A case study approach*. Oxford, UK: Alfred Waller Ltd.

Schuppan, T. (2009). E-Government in developing countries: Experiences from sub-Saharan Africa. *Government Information Quarterly, 26*(1), 118–127. doi:10.1016/j.giq.2008.01.006

Shin, S., Song, H., & Kang, M. (2008). *Implementing e-government in developing countries: Its unique and common success factors.* Paper presented at the Annual Meeting of the APSA Annual Meeting, Boston, MA.

Silverman, D. (2000). *Doing qualitative research: A practical handbook*. London, UK: Sage.

Standish Group. (2001). *Extreme chaos*. Retrieved from http://www.standishgroup.com/chaos/introduction.pdf

Stevens, J. (2002). *Applied multivariate statistics for the social sciences* (4th ed.). Mahwah, NJ: Lawrence Erlbaum.

Wallace, L., Kiel, M., & Rai, A. (2004). How software risk affects project performance: An investigation of the dimensions of risk and an exploratory model. *Decision Sciences, 35*(2), 289–321. doi:10.1111/j.00117315.2004.02059.x

Walsham, G. (1995). The emergence of interpretivism in IS research. *Information Systems Research, 6*(4), 376–394. doi:10.1287/isre.6.4.376

Weerakkody, V., & Dhillon, G. (2008). Moving from e-government to t-government: A study of process reengineering challenges in a UK local authority context. *International Journal of Electronic Government Research, 4*(4), 1–16. doi:10.4018/jegr.2008100101

Zaied, A., Nasser, H., Khairalla, F. A., & Al-Rashed, W. (2007). e-Readiness in the Arab countries: Perceptions towards ICT environment in public organisations in the state of Kuwait. *Electronic. Journal of E-Government, 5*(1), 77–87.

This work was previously published in the International Journal of Electronic Government Research, Volume 7, Issue 3, edited by Vishanth Weerakkody, pp. 79-91, copyright 2011 by IGI Publishing (an imprint of IGI Global).

Chapter 17
Are You Being Served?
Transforming E-Government through Service Personalisation

Jeremy Millard
Danish Technological Institute, Denmark

ABSTRACT

In terms of public services, governments do not yet know how to treat users as different and unique individuals. At worst, users are still considered an undifferentiated mass, or at best as segments. However, the benefits of universal personalisation in public services are within reach technologically through e-government developments. Universal personalisation will involve achieving a balance between top-down government- and data-driven services, on the one hand, and bottom-up self-directed and user-driven services on the other. There are at least three main technological, organisational and societal drivers. First, top-down data-driven, often automatic, services based on the huge data resources available in the cloud and the technologies enabling the systematic exploitation of these by governments. Second, increasing opportunities for users themselves or their intermediaries to select or create their own service environments, bottom-up, through 'user-driven' services, drawing directly on the data cloud. Third, a move to 'everyday', location-driven e-government based largely on mobile smart phones using GPS and local data clouds, where public services are offered depending on where people are as well as who they are and what they are doing. This paper examines practitioners and researchers and describes model current trends based on secondary research and literature review.

1. THE MOVE TOWARDS UNIVERSAL PERSONALISATION

When it comes to public services, governments do not yet know how to treat users (citizens or businesses) as different and unique individuals.

At worst, users are still considered as an undifferentiated mass, or at best as templates (segments). However, the benefits of universal personalisation in public services are within reach technologically through e-government developments, although organisational inertia will always lag what could otherwise be accomplished. (There is of course an argument that such a lag is highly desirable.)

DOI: 10.4018/978-1-4666-2458-0.ch017

Moving towards universal personalisation will involve achieving a balance between top-down government- and data-driven services, on the one hand, and bottom-up self-directed and user-driven services on the other. Whether this balance will be complementary or contradictory is likely to characterise the landscape of public e-services in the medium term.

There are at least three main technological, organisational and societal drivers (Figure 1):

1. Top-down data-driven, often automatic, services based on the huge data resources available in the cloud and the technologies enabling the systematic exploitation of these by governments.
2. Increasing opportunities for users themselves, their intermediaries or non-public sector actors to select or create their own service environments, bottom-up, through 'user-driven' services, drawing directly on the data cloud.
3. A move to 'everyday', location-driven e-government based largely on mobile smart phones using GPS and local data clouds, where public services are offered depending on where you are as well as who you are and what you are doing.

How people understand public services and use them is likely to change dramatically over the next five to ten years, as society becomes more diverse and personal aspirations change. As users of services, people are becoming more reluctant to submit to standardised relationships with large, impersonal organisations. The more is learnt about the factors shaping well-being, life styles and quality of life in the 21st Century, the clearer it will be that current services do not always meet these requirements nor genuinely engage with the particular needs of individual users in providing the personal value they need (Leadbeater, Bartlett, & Gallagher 2008).

Demands for public services are increasingly diverse in their expression, whilst public budgets are being cut because of the financial crisis and other constraints (Osimo, 2010). Not only are there new demands but also existing demands require more sophisticated responses. And, new demands often feed off existing demands – the more access to knowledge and learning we have, for example, the more likely we are to seek more of it. To use resources effectively, therefore, services must be personalised. But for personalised public services to promote public value as well as personal value, they must also be genuinely universal and available for all.

Hence the importance of universal personalisation. This needs new types of standards that move away from those based on delivery processes and outputs, such as waiting time for the delivery of a service is one week for all, or that the level of service quality is homogeneous regardless of who uses it. Instead, standards need to be built around public value outcomes which directly reflect the personal values and needs of the individual (related, for example, to his or her socio-economic profile, specific situation, context of service request, role in the service, behaviour, etc.). The move will thus be from process and output-related standards to more open standards based upon impact and user value. This also means that in future public service audits need to be based on outcomes/impacts and not just (as now) on processes/outputs, which also implies that audits must be set in their operational context and incorporate non-public sector actors, especially users and their intermediaries, in service design and measurement.

Personalised services represent a step on from user segmentation, in which a user's membership of a group determines the service offered, given that an individual could be a member of many groups requiring services from many agencies simultaneously. Membership of a group does not capture the precise individual service need. Personalised services are also a more focused expression

Figure 1. Three approaches to service personalisation

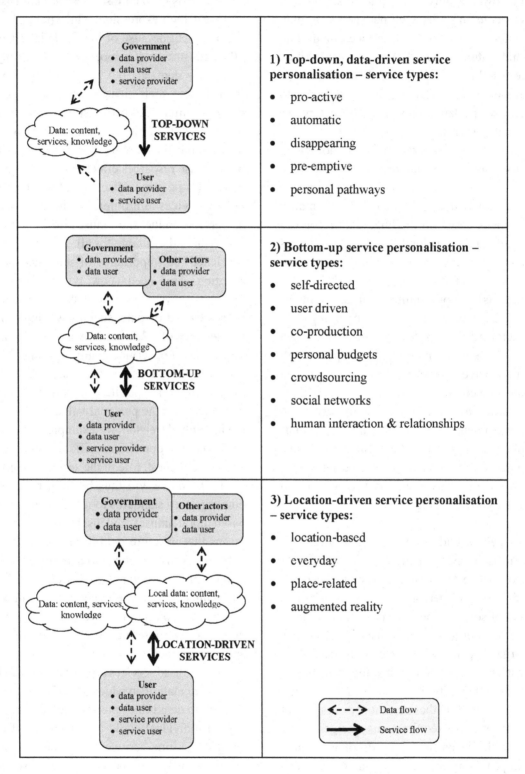

of user-centric services (cc:eGov, 2007) in which the end user's interests and needs are in principle the guiding criteria for designing and delivering services rather than those of the service provider.

User segmentation, user centricity and personalisation can be extremely costly for the public sector to develop as highly nuanced personal welfare systems. This may be mitigated, however, by increased personal and public value benefits, as well as closer adherence to statutory and other responsibilities placed on the public administration. Such strategies may also mean reducing the dis-benefits of the government-centric standardised approach which often waste or duplicate resources through inappropriate services which do not meet user needs, or in duplicating service offers by more than one disconnected agency. This standardised approach typically also results in shunting problems from one agency to another, and thereby even compounding future problems through increased social dysfunction and more anti-social behaviour.

2. RESEARCH METHODOLOGY

The methodological approach adopted in the preparation of this paper rests upon both secondary research and a thorough examination of relevant literature. The former draws on primary and secondary research, often involving case studies, interviews and workshops, undertaken on behalf of the European Commission, the OECD, and the United Nations over the last decade in the context of a number of e-government related studies. These provide the basis for exploring and modelling current and future e-government service developments across Europe as well as globally. This is supplemented by a review of relevant literature both directly related to e-government as well as complementary fields, as indicated in the bibliography.

The current paper is thus a think piece which attempts to describe and model current trends aimed both at practitioners as well as researchers.

3. TOP-DOWN, DATA-DRIVEN SERVICE PERSONALISATION

According to Tim Berners-Lee (the so-called father of the Internet), we are entering the age of the semantic web which exploits the internet of data rather than the internet of documents we now have. This is built on a new RDF (Resource Description Framework) standard for metadata in the same way as document standards currently use html or xml. This will enable intelligent uses of the internet like asking questions rather than simply searching for key words, as well as more automatic data exchanges between databases, data mining, etc. This enables machines as well as people to understand, share and reason during application execution time, and thus allows adding, changing and implementing new relationships or interconnecting programmes in new and different ways. It will make it much easier to link data about individuals across different sources in more intelligent ways.

When this is coupled with emerging Web 3.0 techniques (Web 3.0 technologies include widescale ubiquitous seamless networks [sometimes called grid computing], networked and distributed computing and the 'cloud', open ID, open semantic web, large scale distributed databases and artificial intelligence) and the huge data resources available, governments will be able to pro-actively target services down to the level of the individual, in many cases automatically by letting the data 'speak for itself'. It will also will possible for the government to initiate actions to deliver or enhance services, for example, when a user is warned that action could be required, the government can pre-fill data in an application form that it already possesses to the extent permitted by law. There may be personal privacy and trust issues arising from such services, of course. A recent car tax advertisement in the UK from the transport authorities included the statement "If you haven't paid, we know where you are." Balancing the power of information against other social and cultural values is becoming a critical issue (Catherine Fieschi, Demos Think Tank, personal communication, June 5, 2008).

Another possibility is complete *automatic service delivery* in which the agency takes full responsibility to initiate, deliver and terminate a service. In this case, the input and responsibility of the user is minimised and may even disappear altogether, such as the birth of a child automatically triggering regular child benefit payments, or the automatic allocation of a new tax code because of a tax-payer's new family dependent. Such services are therefore sometimes termed 'disappearing services' because the user does not need to act and may not even notice them, although they might notice if the service was not delivered (Millard, Kubieck, & Westholm, 2004; Capgemini, 2007).

Pro-active and automatic services are reflections of the increasing recognition that public services should get it right first time, which implies both that services should be joined-up and also that government needs to engage with users to learn what really matters to them and then act on what they have learnt (HM Treasury, 2007). However, proactive and automatic services are clearly not relevant for all types of service, but tend to be restricted to services for which most if not all necessary data already exist within the public sector, or to which the public sector has legal access, and often tend to be more routine though not necessarily simple, services. In such a task, the public sector will also face the challenge that some users do not wish to receive the service, or cannot use it, despite it being offered, so that intelligence should also be used to cater for this. The implication is also that the service must, in certain situations be capable of being invoked, opened-up or closed-down by the user,

as well as being moved from invisible to visible mode, or vice versa.

Another approach to personalised services, of which there are as yet few real life examples, is pre-emptive or early-intervention services.

In Colorado USA, data analysis to identify at-risk children is being used to provide anger management classes and behaviour modification programmes to prevent juvenile delinquency. In the United Kingdom there has been talk of targeting babies due to be born in at-risk families by providing parents-to-be with special ante-natal parenting classes, and additional child visitor and family support services once babies are born. Also, in the United Kingdom, some early intervention services have been provided over the last five years through the 'Sure-Start' programme, particularly aimed at deprived areas and families, with significant success. Both in Colorado and now in Nottingham UK, the public sector is collaborating with local companies and civil sector partners to cover some of the up-front costs, but also to exploit resources and expertise they cannot deliver on their own (Blueprints, 2008; http://www.kidsource.com/kidsource/content/early.intervention.html).

Similarly, in the health sector there is a longer tradition of preventive medicine, but now some of these ideas and approaches are being tailored to social and other public sector services. The downside of this approach is that it may be seen as an attempt at social engineering or manipulation, as well as be open to accusations of fostering a 'nanny-state'. Conversely, however, it could be seen as an attempt at intelligent intervention, which, overall, is a significant change in how we think of the welfare state and a considerable extension of the type of services and the role of the public sector not seen before and largely enabled by ICT.

Pre-emptive services are seen as long-term programmes, imposing up-front costs but eventually much larger savings, although this inevitably involves some risk as no immediate results are visible. This means they typically require political consensus in which the major political parties are in agreement (also given the typically short-term nature of politics). The aim is to circumvent future problems, which can be predicted using ICT-enabled simulation and decision-support tools through analysing longitudinal socio-economic data on social deprivation, anti-social behaviour, crime, health, educational needs, etc. The lessons are then applied to high risk individual community, family or personal situations before the problems themselves actually appear.

Other recent developments have built on this approach through the construction of *personalised pathways*, or individual 'story-lines'.

The For example, the United Kingdom is implementing 'customer journey mapping' (Perrin, 2008) as a tool of customer insight which can be applied to help organisations understand how users define and experience services from their own point of view. Journey mapping can be used to reduce duplication and shorten the length of processes, thereby both improving user experience and driving efficiency – it's not an either-or situation. It can help design a seamless, streamlined experience that cuts across silos by recognising when and where it makes sense to join things up for the user, thereby helping to drive change in government. It can also help to inform performance indicators and standards so that progress can be tracked and measured over time.

An earlier and similar approach from the Netherlands is the method of mapping service user journeys (Imke Vrijling of the Dutch Government, 8 November 2006) as part of the programme to reduce the administrative burden for citizens in the Netherlands, designed to eliminate unnecessary activities and better match the supply and demand sides.

Personalisation also requires services to be actively shaped in response to individual profiles. This does not mean separate, isolated pathways as many of the activities involved in being healthy, learning effectively or using any public service are collaborative and intensively social. But it does mean that provider organisations must be capable of adapting and reconfiguring what they offer to ensure that it fits the profile of individual needs. This in turn requires structures of governance, resourcing and accountability that reward improved outcomes and support the flexibility required to offer personalisation on a mass scale. The intelligent use of ICT is clearly essential here. Also implicit is that the system has to know things about the individual with whom it is interacting, and that immediately raises issues of privacy and security.

The need for flexibility and diversity in universal personalisation adds to the complexity of the system, which can make it more difficult for the agency to comprehend, much less govern, its services through hierarchical coordination. Yet this is still the basic method at the heart of most structures and concepts of government, and conditions the behaviour of politicians, regulators, managers and professionals. Instead, the public sector should treat public services as complex adaptive systems and not according to the mechanistic models that have traditionally dominated government thinking.

Seen from the perspective of the individual user, personalising services is equivalent to making them simple, as well as efficient and effective, in the sense that the user does not have to wade through the 99% of the regulations that are not germane, but sees only what is a precise fit to his or her needs or wishes.

For example, Portugal has focused strongly on administrative simplification in order to make life easy for citizens and businesses through its 'Simplex' Programme. This is based on driving forward cooperation across institutional barriers where there is a tradition for silo organisation, for example using the 'life-event' approach so that users can experience 'seamless' government (MENA Working Group, 2010).

A classic case of complexity is the 2008 announcement in the UK that poor families are missing out on council tax rebates worth £1.8bn a year because the rules for claiming relief are complex and poorly advertised, and this is one of the main reasons why the government was predicted to miss its target for halving child poverty by 2010 (*The Guardian*, 7 March 2008). What is probably needed is to make such services, especially to disadvantaged groups as here, pro-active entitlements which the back-office system itself should implement. However, this clearly requires highly robust data protection, as well as changing regulations about the data to which governments have legitimate access (for example to personal bank accounts). The latter is unlikely to happen in the UK, although it is standard practice in most Scandinavian countries where tax and benefits have been pro-active services for many years.

In summary, personalisation and individual service targeting means that ICT can help in performing two important tasks:

- Squeezing out data and information presented to a user that he or she does not need in order to benefit from the service – simplification for the user in the front-office.
- Squeezing out administrative procedures and processes as well as transaction costs that the agency does not need to employ when offering and delivering a service – burden reduction for the agency in the back-office.

4. BOTTOM-UP, USER-DRIVEN SERVICE PERSONALISATION

Some of the technological and organisational developments described above can also provide the basis for bottom-up services where users or their intermediaries are involved in creating a service for example either from standardised blocks or from scratch. This will make it possible for public agencies and other organisations, enterprises and users themselves to make their data (content and functionalities) available in the cloud. 'Self-directed' services mean that users will either select a highly specialised service somewhere in the cloud using advanced search engines, or select from modular reusable elements provided as 'apps' or widgets as content or functionality which can be combined as building blocks into highly personalised services. Combining apps normally requires programming skills and a technical background. However, if a user without a technical background is able simply to drag and connect app icons on a web page, this would revolutionise services. The necessary semantic-based service-oriented architectures are already in place or under development (Corral, 2010).

One step further is full 'user-driven' services when data as content, functionality or service elements from the cloud is combined with the user's own unique content in order to mash together services on their own platforms. For both self-directed and user-driven services, user avatars or automatic electronic agents will be employed, whilst going through the 'front door' of a portal or website to access fixed services will be seen by an increasing number of users as a clumsy or even unnecessary solution to their needs.

As Web 2.0 technologies like social software and social networking tools become more ubiquitous and are deployed on a larger scale, existing public value chains will change and can now also include users in new user-producer relationships, providing new definitions of personal as well as public value. The production and distribution of relevant content and information is now incorporating a move from formal organisations to decentralised networks, often with an ad hoc character. Consumers become 'prosumers' and users become 'pro-ams', and thus take up new roles in the value chain, leading to what has been called the 'democratisation of innovation' (Von Hippel, 2005).

Web 2.0 tools are starting to 'democratise' the means of production, of distribution and of supply, i.e., the whole value chain. Add to these the widespread availability of other tools, like cameras, recording equipment, sensors, etc. which used to be the preserve of professionals but can now be purchased in any shopping centre, and the portfolio of tools widely available becomes a potentially potent mix. If public services are seen from a purely supply and demand perspective (which is important, but by no means the main determinant), the technology can help to move production and use towards an almost 'perfect market', as is already starting to take place in the commercial sector in areas like news, media, music and publishing (Anderson, 2006). These technologies enable bottom-up and personalised communication and information sharing, and have immense potential for user-driven services, systems and innovation, where users or user groups are themselves involved in designing and delivering services, thus further blurring the roles and tasks of suppliers and users (Leadbeater, 2004).

Leadbeater, Bartlett, and Gallagher (2008) talk of self-directed services which can "mobilise the intelligence of thousands of people to get better outcomes for themselves and more value for public money...". Johnston and Stewart-Weeks (2007) describe the "changed relationship with citizens....in which citizens need to be given a much greater role in shaping public services. 'Black box' government, where dedicated civil servants try to work out which services will suit people best, need to give way to transparent government where citizens themselves can see and intervene in debates about how services can be made more citizen-centric."

This is the key to unlocking the potential of universal personalisation, i.e., the recognition that personal value (the value for the individual user) is created when a service is used, rather than when it is delivered. Thus the creation of value for the individual user of a service is, at least in part, dependent on the user him- or herself. The challenge is how to define more systematically the processes of 'co-production' through which personal and public value are created, and then to connect different co-production activities to generate economies of scale and wider systems of support.

Many, though of course not all, users (citizens, businesses and civil servants) are no longer prepared just to be passive recipients of government and e-government services, however personalised these may be, as this is still essentially top-down.

Some experiments in the United Kingdom have been applying a much more bottom-up approach to the public sector for several years (Leadbeater, 2006), especially in health, education and crime where few designers have traditionally worked. One example reveals how the UK government is dealing with diabetes which costs the UK National Health Service £5 million per day and is one of the main causes of premature death. The average diabetic spends just three hours a year with doctors, but thousands of hours a year managing their own condition themselves. The biggest gains will come from enabling diabetics to become more effective at self-diagnosis and self-management, for example by equipping them with appropriate ICT tools, techniques and peer support. Similarly, 90% of health care is delivered in the home. People want more home-based solutions that they feel they control. The health information available to patients on the internet is transforming their role – no longer passive, they can question and participate.

There can, however, also be challenges thrown up by detailed health information available on the internet.

Research in the United Kingdom in 2008 revealed that because parents were accessing information about food allergies in very young children, about 25% consulted their GPs about the issue which is much greater than the pre-internet average of less than 5%, as well as being much higher than the actual long-term historical incidence of the condition of about 7% (*The Guardian*, 28 February 2008). On the one hand, this put much greater strain on GP resources and time, yet on the other hand it undoubtedly saved some lives which would otherwise have probably been lost. This illustrates that, as people become more aware and knowledgeable, they are likely to increase their demand for public services as well as for different types of more sophisticated and costly services.

Google has recently moved into the health market, which makes less use of ICT than other sectors of comparable size, by offering secure repositories for all an individual's health related data: "health information should be easier to access and organise, especially in ways that make it as simple as possible to find the information that is most relevant to a specific patient's needs" (*The Guardian*, 28 February 2008). Microsoft is doing the same market as part of a concerted move to provide commercial services for patients to manage their own care. The idea is first to put the patient in control by choosing which professionals see your data, and second to enable better remote monitoring to cut down on the number of office visits and hospital emergencies. The two companies reckon that because of mobility and longer lives, people's medical records may be left behind when they move. It is entirely possible to discover, when in your 50s, that you have no accessible medical history and, for example, no idea when you were vaccinated or against what.

More recent thinking in the UK, Netherlands and elsewhere includes trials in the management of personal budgets for social services. As part of the 'Putting People First' programme, 2,000 disabled persons across the United Kingdom have been given a financial allocation, in cash form if they wish but in most cases this is held by the local authority to be spent in line with the person's own wishes once their care plan is approved. This can be spent on their own choice of care assistants, to join clubs rather than day centres, and go to hotels or on package breaks rather than to residential homes for respite care. Although the pilots have not yet been fully assessed, the emerging results are so positive that ministers have decided to push ahead and make the approach the basis of all adult social care services. The care services minister

said: "There is absolutely no doubt that people who use individual budgets say it has transformed their lives" (*The Guardian*, 10 December 2007). ICT has been the enabling tool in linking the six government departments whose efforts and resources needed to be integrated to implement these trials, and has also been used by some of the disabled people and their careers to access necessary information and make their choices. This is an example of the top-down initiation of bottom-up inputs and control (Le Grand, 2007):

Clearly, there are issues here to do with, first, can individuals and their families know what is needed and what they want, and, second, can they be relied upon to be truthful, or at least not exploit the system. Individual control and choice do not always work, of course. The limited experience already gained (such as the 'Putting People First' programme described) shows that there needs to be probably quite strict frameworks and guidelines, plus some vetting and approval by personal advisers. This could, if done badly, reintroduce bureaucracy, so it should be implemented through well-trained front-line staff who wields considerable discretion within flexible rules but ones designed not to permit obvious cheating. It is also a question of learning by doing, on both sides, so that the user will also need to demonstrate responsibility in return for being offered additional rights. This is, at base, what empowerment is all about, but this also implies the need for an empowerment contract. An important trend therefore is that of the 'responsible citizen', i.e., where the citizen has much more control and power over their own data and services but also needs to exercise this responsibly (Graham Colclough, CapGemini, personal communication, May 7, 2008).

New approaches to 'crowdsourcing services' are appearing in which content and inputs are sourced from a wide range of users and others actors who have particular knowledge and interests not possessed by the government itself.

The grassroots' initiative "Let's do it" in Estonia helped to clean up the whole country from illegal waste and garbage in just one day (http://www.teeme2008.ee/; http://www.letsdoitworld.org/news). This initiative virally disseminated to other countries, including, India, Portugal, Latvia, and Slovenia. Through their website (and other media) the initiators involved government, businesses and volunteers. Over 700 participants mapped approximately 10,000 tons of waste, including all the toxic dumps in the country left over from the Soviet era, (while using Internet-enabled phones) and more than 50,000 volunteers were mobilised to clean up the garbage.

Other examples include the self help networks using SMS, mobile phones and internet of citizens hit by natural disasters such as Hurricane Katrina in New Orleans and the Niigata earthquake in Japan, although the public authorities quickly channeled the real-time on-the-ground intelligence they were providing to improve their own handling of the disasters (2008 Anthony Williams and colleagues, nGenera, personal communication May 28-29, 2008!).

Many citizen groups, like mothers of young children or patients with heart disease, are increasingly forming both offline and online social networks, where they not only provide mutual social support but also exchange and build real knowledge and value about child rearing or heart disease. What is the role of government and the professional in this context? Perhaps facilitating, providing legal or other professional advice, some finance, etc.? For example, civil servants who are expert in a particular area could be mandated to service such groups, with the usual caveats which are already in place concerning the quality of that advice and who is accountable if something goes wrong. Such social networks could also themselves become a source of expertise, and government could assist in mediated this to other groups or

individuals who may need it. Clearly the role of the professional changes to include a more facilitating and advisory function for the purpose of enabling users to determine their own services, but also to ensure that the collective experience and opinions of the users can be acted upon and re-used (Catherine Fieschi, Demos Think Tank, personal communication, June 5, 2008). These approaches mix and strengthen both peer support and professional support. This approach thus has two benefits, i.e., citizen empowerment but also the creation and re-use of data and knowledge (2008 William Perrin and colleagues, Transformational Government Unit, personal communication, June 5, 2008!).

One of the recommendations of the Australian government's 2009 Report from the Government 2.0 Taskforce is to encourage public servants to engage online. Revised online engagement guidelines for public servants have been issued, including the declaration that Web 2.0 provides public servants with unprecedented opportunities to open up government decision making and implementation to contributions from the community. The lead agency is recommended to regularly review online engagement guidelines, using Government 2.0 approaches to ensure the process is open and transparent. The default position in agencies should be that employees are encouraged and enabled to engage online. Agencies should support employee enablement by providing access to tools and addressing internal technical and policy barriers. Innovative Government 2.0 tools should be used by employees to engage with their customers, citizens and/or communities of interest in different aspects of the agency's work. A culture needs to be created that gives their staff an opportunity to experiment and develop new opportunities for engagement from their own initiative, rewarding those especially who create new engagement/participation tools or methods that can quickly be absorbed into the mainstream practice that lifts the performance of the department or agency. In addition, the lead agency should establish an online forum on which agencies can record their initiatives and lessons learned (Australian Government Information Management Office, 2009).

Up until the 1990s the focus was on the physical provision of a service, whereas today, in the health service for instance, what is important is not only about being treated but also about how you are treated. For example, valuing human relationships and warmth with smiles, taking patients seriously and not talking down to them, courtesy, a cup of tea, etc., i.e., equivalent to Maslow's belongingness, love and esteem needs, as being one step on from more basic physiological needs (Maslow, 1954). It is noteworthy that, as the technology advances bringing with it increasing efficiency and effective delivery outcomes (a clinically successful operation, more home help for the elderly or better job placement for the unemployed), that these achievements become readily accepted and even taken for granted by users, so what really counts is high quality human interaction and relationships and being treated with respect and dignity. In fact, having such a customer service approach does seem to work out cheaper, quicker and more effective. Cost and cost effectiveness will continue to be highly important (2008 William Perrin and colleagues, Transformational Government Unit, June 5, 2008!).

5. EVERY DAY, LOCATION-DRIVEN SERVICE PERSONALISATION

Tremendous progress has been made over the last twenty years in rolling out e-government services. For example in Europe the latest benchmarking (Capgemini et al., 2010) show that full online availability of the basket of 20 e-government services across the 27 Member States increased from 20% in 2001 to over 80% in 2010, whilst online sophistication increased from 81% in 2007 to 90% in 2010. However there are also issues

of concern. There is something of a crisis in e-government as currently rolled out, for example the flat lining of citizen usage of e-government services between 2004 and 2010. In this timeframe although there was an increase from 23% to 30% use by citizens between 2005 and 2007, by 2010 this had only risen a further 2% by 2010 to 32%. Use of e-government services by enterprises has, in contrast, continued to rise steadily (Eurostat, 2010). Similar findings concerning both the supply and demand sides of e-government have been made by the OECD in its 2009 report on re-thinking e-government services, thus demonstrating that these challenges are widespread (OECD, 2009). The recent McKinsey report (Baumgarten & Chui, 2009) on e-government 2.0 also noted "However, despite the continued allocation of enormous resources, progress on the e-government front appears to have plateaued over the past few years." Most countries still seem to be in the Government 1.0 paradigm in which take-up is low and initiatives are expensive and often fail (Millard, 2010).

Evidence like this shows that the public sector is facing important challenges and needs to re-think how public services can be oriented towards the creation of public value and user empowerment. There needs to be a strong move towards ensuring that e-government serves the needs of society rather than government. Many user surveys show that, although citizens who use the internet also tend to use e-government services and find them useful, they typically do so only two or three times per year (Rambøll, 2006; Millard, 2006). Such services tend to deliver large scale administrative services designed to make existing government functions work more efficiently and effectively, such as tax and procurement systems, automation of registrations, permits and licenses, etc., rather than really thinking about what citizens need in their everyday lives. It is clear that most current e-government services are simply existing services put online which are still basically silo-centric, top-down, with little service innovation, expensive, and with just as many failures as successes.

In other words, their main focus remains first and foremost to serve the needs of government.

As shown, moves towards service personalisation through user-driven services is starting to happen but remains on a small scale. Often leading the way, however, is not the government or public administration but civil society organisations and social entrepreneurs. Such services start from asking the question what do citizens need from public services to make their lives better, i.e., how can the service improve the daily life of citizens where they live and work.

One archetypal example is the FixMyStreet service (built by mySociety using some clever code: http://www.fixmystreet.com/) in the United Kingdom designed and run by the mySociety (http://www.mysociety.org/) civil society organisation staffed by volunteers. This service allows any citizen to report any problems in their street or neighbourhood ranging from broken street lights or paving, abandoned vehicles or rubbish, graffiti, etc. The citizen does not need to know which authority is responsible as the site automatically passes the complaint to the correct department and then traces and tracks its progress on behalf of the citizen until the problem is solved. To do this, mySociety had to obtain relevant public sector information and data about authorities' roles and procedures, contact points, etc. Many of these data were already in the public domain, although not all, but were widely scattered and not easily accessible digitally. The value added which mySociety brought was to gather dispersed data, 'mash' them together in appropriate ways, and to visualise and map them in an easy to use format for citizens. They had to reach across administrative silos, something perhaps difficult for the public sector to do itself.

Many of the early innovative user-centred services, like FixMyStreet launched in 2007, have been designed as web portals for PCs connected to the Internet (note that FixMyStreet is also now available for mobile phones as an iPhone app written by MySociety from the App Store in iTunes. There is also an Android app written by a volunteer, Anna Powell-Smith, available from the Android Market). However, many citizens in OECD countries, and especially in the emerging economies where traditional fixed infrastructures are not as well developed as in the more advanced economies, still do not have easy or regular access to these technologies. And even if they do, they may not be available where and when needed, especially when moving around. People are instead turning to mobile phones, particularly smart and G3 enabled, for much of their communication to satisfy their everyday personal and commercial needs. Mobile is arguably best placed to meet this demand now that bandwidths are rapidly increasing and becoming widely available and affordable. This is a situation that is likely to accelerate in the future because of the release of spectrum as countries switch from analogue to digital broadcasting as part of the so-called 'digital dividend'. This switch over, and the vastly improved capacities it represents, is also likely to re-focus attention on the potential of digital TV as another universal everyday medium. There is thus an explosive growth of m-services directed at these new mobile devices, exploiting the fact that mobile is universal, from anywhere at any time in real time, highly flexible and highly personal.

Given this, it is highly likely that location-based services will become the norm. E-government using multiple channels, intermediaries and adapted value chains will empower communities and localities by promoting subsidiarity at local and neighbourhood level.

The 'Love Clean Streets' initiative in the London Borough of Lewisham, United Kingdom, enables residents to use mobile phones to upload photos of junk, graffiti, vandalism or any other problem on the streets (for examples see, http://www.lewisham.gov.uk/NewsAndEvents/News/LoveCleanStreetsCleansUp.htm?wbc_purpose=Basic&WBCMODE=Pr; http://lovelewisham.wordpress.com/; http://www.bbc.co.uk/programmes/p006h6qf). This provides both evidence and better information about the problems citizens wish to report to the local authority by using a smart phone which captures the GPS coordinates together with the image, and can directly route these to the municipality's street cleaning teams using their own mobile devices on the streets to adjust their work schedules. Once the problem is fixed, the street team takes and uploads photos of the completed work, which can also be emailed back to the original complainant, who can also be alerted by SMS or RSS feed. The new innovation in this example is that staff can directly integrate data and evidence from citizens into their work scheduling, which is one step on from simply enabling citizens to send in information on problems to a civil servant sitting in an office. Frontline staff are also encouraged to use the mobile devices for their own personal use, thereby providing an incentive for them to adopt the technology and the new way of working, and this starts to blur the boundary between the personal and professional use of such tools.

These developments are starting to show how local resources, know-how and skills can be leveraged for developing new types of 'everyday e-government' in which government and public sector services are all around us and used constantly. For example in health, education, care, transport, infrastructures, utilities, parking, accidents, clean and safe environments, congestion and pollution watch, culture, amenities, leisure, sports, security, crime watch, weather, participation, engagement, etc.

Many e-government services have become more locally oriented in recent years where they seem to be having their biggest impacts, often in cooperation with local civil society and private sector actors. The focus on geographical localisation and place-related services will expand even more over the next five years, particularly in the context of 'localised modularisation' which is already successfully used by commercial services in delivering big cost reductions and quality improvements.

The Stockholm eGovernment programme in Sweden is implementing more than 50 eServices:

- Online application for parking permits (reducing the administrative process time from 10 minutes to 1 minute and customer waiting time from one week to an immediate response), booking and payment of swimming lessons, booking for marriage ceremonies (100% increase in processed booking with a 50% reduction in total processing time)
- Complaints and comments
- eInvoicing
- An online care diary, online applications for choice of daycare and school, etc.

In addition to these more administrative services, everyday e-government services are also being rolled out in Stockholm related directly to local circumstances and needs, such as personalised pedestrian navigation and travel information. From a user-centric perspective, the Stockholm Compare Services website allows the user to identify, compare and locate public services within a specific neighbourhood. The website incorporates contact information for the city's various agencies and covers approximately 4,000 municipality services from child and senior citizen care to waste recycling centres. Two thirds of Stockholm's inhabitants find the compare services website helpful, allowing them an increased degree of choice. The site is used by 100,000 to 150,000 citizens every month (Kelly & Meyerhof Nielsen, in press).

The impact of GPS will make it into a true 'peoples' technology' built into everyday mobile devices and providing precise locations and navigation support for all services and activities. This will include surfing government sites, accessing and creating information, sending and receiving messages from governments, mashing your own 'public' services, taking, sending and receiving pictures and video, as well as traditional voice services. Local services will also be developed in real-time to handle both routine and non-routine tasks, including emergencies, dependent on where the user is located. This will include location-based participation, for example helping to re-design the park you're walking in or the hospital organisation which kept you waiting and you think you have a solution, so that a location or an event creates the opportunity for services, content and dialogue.

Other possibilities are imaginable if governments also start to join up their activities and share data in appropriate ways through ubiquitous sensing and data collection in order to develop unobtrusive systems which support, assist and delight citizens in highly personalised ways. For example, hazard checking systems which analyse whether a given action (such as imposing a speeding fine) if taken straightaway in a specific context for a specific person would harm or inconvenience them (Witbrock, 2009). If so, the system may delay, omit or modify the action. Similarly, benefit checking applications would analyse whether a given action in a specific context for a specific person would help or delight them. For example displaying locality information about crime, air pollution, or congestion for citizens to select where, when, and how they move around. If so, the system may offer, implement or accelerate the action. In both cases, the system will learn from each action in each situation.

Thus, if we look at what people are using in their everyday lives, there is already massive growth in mobile, smart and 'augmented reality' 'apps' for personal and commercial purposes often offered for highly specific uses on local scales. However, so-called m-government is still very much in its infancy. For example, only a small fraction of the iPhone's 185,000 apps are related to 'public services', although there is some small start to public service and democracy apps particularly in the USA. There is, as yet little focus in Europe on this huge potential. Mobile eGovernment services are starting to appear in Europe but do not yet feature in most authorities strategic plans. The

main exception appears to be in the UK, e.g., "Directgov on your mobile" (http://www.direct.gov.uk/en/Hl1/Help/YourQuestions/DG_069492). These developments are likely to be driven by the rapid transformation of the 'net' generation into responsible adults needing public services and demanding the same quality and flexibility they receive from other providers.

According to a CNN report in the United States (Sutter, 2009):

A host of larger U.S. cities from San Francisco to New York have quietly been releasing treasure troves of public data to web and mobile application developers. That may sound dull. But tech geeks transform banal local government spreadsheets about train schedules, complaint systems, potholes, street lamp repairs and city garbage into useful applications for mobile phones and the Web. "Instead of people saying, 'Well, it's the government's job to fix that'... people are taking ownership and saying, 'Hey, wait a minute. Government is us. We are government. So let's take a responsibility and start changing things ourselves.'

According to the report, these sorts of apps tend to be created only in places where the municipal government has released its data sets in a format that can be easily crunched. The public data is the fuel that makes these applications work. So far, local governments releasing their data sets are usually large and fairly tech savvy, such as San Francisco, Washington and New York. San Francisco is, however, also working with others to develop a national standard for municipal government data sets and the programs that make them useful. That way, an app that tracks rubbish in San Francisco could be used by people in any town or city, as long as the local authority's public data is posted online in the right format. This could enable cities without big tech communities to benefit from the trend. Brian Purchia, spokesman for the San Francisco mayor's office, said "For some cities and for some governments I could understand that transition can be a scary thing….but we feel like it makes governments more accountable, and it makes them function better…..what I really see is a monumental change for how government works. This is just really the starting point. *"*

An important premise in many, though not all, of these initiatives is that tech communities are better able to make government data useful than the governments themselves. For example, in the United States in 2009 the 'Apps for Democracy' competition in Washington DC awarded $20,000 in prizes for developers and yielded 47 web, iPhone and Facebook apps in 30 days with a value to the city of $2,300,000 (http://www.appsfordemoc-racy.org/). Peter Corbett, CEO for iStrategyLabs and organiser of the competition said *"*I think the government realises that they don't have all of the money to do things people want them to do……government forgot that the biggest asset that they have are actual citizens… [and] many developers work free..*"* Also in 2009, the United Kingdom's Power of Information Taskforce ran competitions entitled 'Show us a better way – what would you create with public information?' and offered a £20,000 prize fund to develop the best ideas. More recently in 2010, Victoria in Australia has launched an apps contest for government, and the United Kingdom announced a new online government apps store.

Denmark is also starting to consider releasing public data to encourage new types of services as well as boosting the economy. According to Kelly and Meyerhof Nielsen (in press), the value of releasing government data to developers is somewhere between DKK 100 and 1,000 million (€ 13.42 and 134.23 million). Based on an analysis by Gartner and the Danish IT and Telecom Agency, the potential in Denmark is around DKK 3.3 billion (€ 0.45 billion). In November 2010, this agency together with the Copenhagen IT University organised a 'Data Camp' attracting twelve public authorities and 40 developers, data analysts and IT experts. Together they created 18 digital products plus various ideas in a single day. According to

the Danish Minister for Science, Innovation and Technology: "The idea is to create growth and new digital solutions for citizens and public authorities. Denmark is a country without many of the traditional raw materials, but we can find the raw materials in the data and building application on this..." (Danish National IT & Telecom Agency, 2010; Computerworld, 2010a) (translated by the author from the original Danish quote).

There are a number of studies which point to substantial social and economic gains from releasing public sector data in machine readable format. A UK study (Newbery et al., 2008) showed that releasing data stimulates business innovation, growth and jobs through value added services and new products, and that the benefits outweigh the loss of income from license fees from the then current practice of 'loss recovery' by more than €200 million per year for just six data sources alone. In May 2009, the European Commission reported that the commercial impact of common EU rules on the re-use of public sector information would be about €27 billion (European Commission, 2003). Although there are barriers such as discriminatory practices, monopoly markets, lack of transparency, discrimination between potential users, high charges for public sector information and complex licensing policies, as well as practical problems like lack of awareness on what public sector information is available, commercial re-use by the European private sector is estimated to have a value of €27 billion. The 2010 "Open data study" (Hogge, 2010) provides evidence that "there are substantial social and economic gains to be made from opening government data to the public" (Hogge, 2010).

6. CONCLUSION

This article has looked at some of the drivers of ICT-enabled public services over the next five to ten years all of which give increasing power and opportunities both on the supply and demand sides to personalise services so that they match quite precisely individual user requirements and desires.

On the one hand, government is enabled to observe and analyse societal developments right down to individual behaviour using the vast amount of data available to it in conjunction with new ICT tools. In this way, a benign government can provide much higher quality and valuable services for users, especially those who may be disadvantaged in some way and unable themselves to get involved in selecting or creating their own services. There are also obvious threats in such developments. These include reductions in personal privacy as well as the possibility that government may not always be benign, and, even more likely, that government may not always be competent. However, we should not forget that third sector, private and commercial services, as well as the actors providing such services, are subject to the same caveats. Moreover, the latter are not subject to the same accountability frameworks which ensure that governments remain responsible, such as elections, transparency and oversight. This, in turn, relates to the extent to which users can trust government, particularly when it comes to using their data responsibly and wisely.

On the other hand, users either individually or in communities, groups and localities, as well as through intermediaries of various types, are empowered to select and create their own services. Users are likely to be expert in what their problems are as only they possess the fine grained knowledge about what they really need. The government- and data-driven approach, however well-meaning and intelligent, is likely to miss this latent, tacit knowledge possessed by users which is largely kept dormant and suppressed by the top-down delivery approach to services in which professionals are largely in control and assumed to have all the knowledge, thereby cajoling users to become largely passive.

The dangers in this bottom-up approach are, however, also manifold, including issues of exclusion related to the digital as well as wider societal divides and inequalities. This might mean that more personalised, higher quality and useful services could become the preserve of the better off and more competent segments of society, and not least the already more prosperous localities with more resources to draw on. Also, can governments (and thereby the tax-payer) trust users to behave responsibly when enabled through greater choice and empowerment to directly access public resources, and what should be the extent of restraint or monitoring in order to minimise this danger. This shows that trust is a double-edged sword – it is not only a question of can users trust their government, but also can government trust users. Further, there are important issues related to the role of government and the public sector more generally when data, tools and opportunities are given to other actors (not just users but also civil and commercial actors) to create public services. This starts to question what is meant by a 'public service', who owns it, who is responsible for it and who is accountable if something goes wrong. Of course, this is a very necessary and useful debate which, if properly conducted, will help transform public services using ICT to achieve universal personalisation.

The move to 'everyday' and location-driven e-government, based largely on mobile smart phones using GPS, where public services are offered depending on where users are, as well as who they are and what they are doing, represents a specific and rapidly growing type of bottom-up service. Such services are very much data-driven but largely in a local context where users are given a lot more choice and control. It is also much easier for users themselves or their intermediaries to participate in constructing and designing their own services at local level where knowledge and resources are closer to hand and more amenable.

There is a clear tension between purely top-down data-driven services, on the one hand, and bottom-up user-driven services on the other. Both derive from the same technological advances and both offer big benefits as well as lurking dangers whilst serving different purposes and types of need. The challenge is to ensure they are complementary and that transformational government using ICT really does deliver universal personalisation and thereby better services for all.

REFERENCES

Anderson, C. (2006). *The long tail -- why the future of business is selling less of more: The new economics of culture and commerce.* New York, NY: Hyperion.

Australian Government Information Management Office. (2009). *Engage: Getting on with Government 2.0.* Retrieved from http://www.finance.gov.au/publications/gov20taskforcereport/

Baumgarten, J., & Chui, M. (2009). E-government 2.0. *The McKinsey Quarterly, 2009*(4).

Blueprints. (2008). *Promising program descriptions.* Retrieved from http://www.cde.state.co.us/artemis/ucb1210/ucb610919bp032008internet.pdf

Capgemini, I. D. C. Rand Europe, Sogeti, & DTi. (2010). *Digitizing public services in Europe: Putting ambition into action – 9th benchmark measurement.* Brussels, Belgium: European Commission.

Capgemini. (2007). *The user challenge: Benchmarking The supply of online public services.* Brussels, Belgium: European Commission.

Citizen-Centric eGovernment (cc:eGov). (2007). *A handbook for citizen-centric eGovernment.* Brussels, Belgium: European Commission.

Computerworld. (2010a). *Danmark sidder på milliardpotentiale i offentlige data.* Retrieved from http://www.computerworld.dk/art/111997?page=2

Corral, M. (2010). *Put user in the centre for services: A reference model.* Brussels, Belgium: European Commission.

Danish National IT & Telecom Agency. (2010). *Data camp: Offentlige data blev forvandlet til digitale produkter.* Retrieved from http://www.itst.dk/nyheder/nyhedsarkiv/2010/data-camp-offentlige-data-blev-forvandlet-til-digitale-produkter

European Commission. (2003). *Commission calls for action to unlock public sector information re-use.* Retrieved from http://ec.europa.eu/information_society/newsroom/cf/itemdetail.cfm?item_id=4891

Eurostat. (2010). *Information society statistics: e-Government usage by individuals.* Retrieved from http://epp.eurostat.ec.europa.eu/tgm/table.do?tab=table&init=1&language=en&pcode=tsiir130&plugin=1

Frissen, V., Millard, J., Hujiboom, N., Svava Iversen, J., Kool, L., & Kotterink, B. (2007). *The future of eGovernment: An exploration of ICT-driven models of eGovernment for the EU in 2020.* Retrieved from http://ipts.jrc.ec.europa.eu/publications/pub.cfm?id=1481

Hogge, B. (2010). *Open data study.* Retrieved from http://www.soros.org/initiatives/information/focus/communication/articles_publications/publications/open-data-study-20100519/open-data-study-100519.pdf

Johnston, P., & Stewart-Weeks, M. (2007). *The Connected Republic 2.0 -- New possibilities & new value for the public sector.* Retrieved from http://www.cisco.com/web/about/ac79/docs/wp/TCR_WP_0821FINAL.pdf

Kelly, A., & Meyerhoff Nielsen, M. (in press). Scandinavia 2.0: The response to the economic crisis. *European Journal of ePractice.*

Le Grand, J. (2007). *The other invisible hand: Delivering public services through choice and competition.* Princeton, NJ: Princeton University Press.

Leadbeater, C. (2004). *Personalisation through participation*. London, UK: Demos Think Tank.

Leadbeater, C. (2006). *The user innovation revolution – How business can unlock the value of customers' ideas*. London, UK: National Consumer Council.

Leadbeater, C., Bartlett, J., & Gallagher, N. (2008). *Making it personal*. London, UK: Demos Think Tank.

Maslow, A. H. (1943). A theory of human motivation. *Psychological Review, 50,* 370–396. doi:10.1037/h0054346

MENA Working Group. (2010, April 27-28). *Making life easy for citizens and businesses in Portugal – e-government and administrative simplification.* Paper presented at the Meeting of the MENA Working Group, Dubai, UAE.

Millard, J. (2006). The business and economic implications of ICT use: Europe's transition to the knowledge economy. In Compañó, R., Pascu, C., Bianchi, A., Burgelman, J.-C., Barrios, S., Ulbrich, M., & Maghiros, I. (Eds.), *The future of the information society in Europe: Contributions to the debate*. Seville, Spain: Institute of Prospective Technological Studies.

Millard, J. (Ed.). (2007). *European eGovernment 2005-2007: Taking stock of good practice and progress towards implementation of the i2010 eGovernment action plan.* Retrieved from http://www.epractice.eu/files/download/awards/ResearchReport2007.pdf

Millard, J. (2008). 21st century eGovernance -- turning the world upside down. *European Review of Political Technologies, 5.*

Millard, J. (2008). *Report on the FP7 consultation workshop on ICT for governance and policy modelling.* Brussels, Belgium: European Commission.

Millard, J. (2010). Government 1.5 – is the bottle half full or half empty? *European Journal of ePractice, 2010*(9).

Millard, J., & Horlings, E. (2008). *Research report on value for citizens: A vision of public governance in 2020.* Retrieved from http://ec.europa.eu/information_society/activities/egovernment/studies/docs/research_report_on_value_for_citizens.pdf

Millard, J., Kubieck, H., & Westholm, H. (2004). *Reorganisation of government back-offices for better ePS – European good practices (back-office reorganisation) prepared for the European Commission eGovernment unit. Brussels.* Belgium: European Commission.

Millard, J., Meyerhoff Nielsen, M., Warren, R., Smith, S., Macintosh, A., Tarabanis, K., et al. (2009). *European eParticipation summary report.* Retrieved from http://islab.uom.gr/eP/index.php?option=com_docman&task=cat_view&gid=36&&Itemid=82

Millard, J., Shahin, J., Pedersen, K., Huijboom, N., & van den Broek, T. (2009). *I2010 eGovernment action plan progress study: Final report.* Retrieved from http://www.dti.dk/27666

Millard, J., Warren, R., Leitner, C., & Shahin, J. (2007). *Towards the eGovernment vision for EU in 2010: Research policy challenges.* Seville, Spain: Institute of Prospective Technological Studies.

Newbery, D., Bently, L., & Pollock, R. (2008). *Models of public sector information provision via trading funds.* Cambridge, UK: Cambridge University Press.

OECD. (2009). *Rethinking e-Government services: User-centred approaches.* Paris, France: OECD.

Osimo, D. (2010). Government 2.0 - Hype, hope, or reality? *European Journal of ePractice, 2010*(9).

Perrin, W. (2008, March 6-7). *Making government work better.* Paper presented at the OECD eGovernment Leaders Conference, The Hague, The Netherlands.

Sutter, J. D. (2009). *Cities embrace mobile apps, 'Gov 2.0'.* Retrieved from http://www.cnn.com/2009/TECH/12/28/government.web.apps/index.html

Treasury, H. M. (2007). *Service transformation agreement.* Retrieved from http://www.hm-treasury.gov.uk

Von Hippel, E. (2005). *Democratizing innovation.* Cambridge, MA: MIT Press.

Witbrock, M. (2009). *ICT for governance and policy modeling* (Tech. Rep. No. FP7-ICT-2009-4). Brussels, Belgium: European Commission.

This work was previously published in the International Journal of Electronic Government Research, Volume 7, Issue 4, edited by Vishanth Weerakkody, pp. 1-18, copyright 2011 by IGI Publishing (an imprint of IGI Global).

Chapter 18
Evaluating Local Partnership Incentive Policies:
A Realist Approach

Maddalena Sorrentino
Università degli Studi di Milano, Italy

Alessandro Spano
Università degli Studi di Cagliari, Italy

Benedetta Bellò
Università degli Studi di Cagliari, Italy

ABSTRACT

Current research tells little about how to assess the public incentive policies designed to persuade local governments to set up partnerships. This first paper of ongoing research illustrates an evaluation method based on the 'realist approach', the tenets of which assign a key role to the context in which the mechanisms of a public programme work (or not). The evaluation framework is intended to be a tool to assist and inform future policymaking and practice. The paper provides a picture of the current scientific debate by exploring the relevant literature; outlines a research path aimed at building an empirically-based model for assessing public policies to promote and support local partnerships in the Italian Region of Sardinia; and indicates a possible context of use for the theory through an illustrative example.

INTRODUCTION

The emergence (indeed dominance) of joint initiatives to address multifaceted social problems is a widespread phenomenon (Hulst & van Montfort, 2007a, 2007b; Isett et al., 2011; O'Toole, 1993) that has received considerable attention in the debate on Transformational government or T-Government (Irani et al., 2007; King & Cotterill, 2007; Klievink & Janssen, 2009; Brown & Parker, 2011; Weerakkody, Dwivedi, Dhillon, & Williams, 2007). At the local level, collaboration initiatives bring together two or more distinct public authorities to cooperate in achieving a common

DOI: 10.4018/978-1-4666-2458-0.ch018

goal (e.g., to provide services) and as an alternative to traditional hierarchical governance (Kenis & Provan, 2009). When the area of collaboration is not only operational (e.g., limited to the delivery of services) but also encompasses policy formulation and planning, the joint action has more ambitious aims and objectives (i.e., "co-design", in the words of Ranade & Hudson, 2003).

Most European countries have at some point put considerable political support behind the development of inter-municipal cooperation through the use of statutory obligations and financial incentives (Hulst & van Montfort, 2007b). The key advantages commonly attributed to collaboration initiatives include enhanced efficiency, the fostering of innovation and flexibility, and better service outcomes (Dawes & Préfontaine, 2003; May & Winter, 2007; Provan & Kenis, 2008). Finally, as part of a wider T-Government strategy, collaborative arrangements can more effectively meet the future challenges of reducing waste and inefficiency by reorganising or reusing back-end information systems, processes, facilities, maintenance contracts, and sharing investments (Becker, Niehaves, & Krause, 2009; Cabinet Office, 2009; Janssen, Joha, & Weerakkody, 2007; Kamal, Weerakkody, & Jones, 2009; Luna-Reyes, Gil-Garcia, & Cruz, 2007; Oliver, 1990; Weerakkody, Dhillon, Dwivedi, & Currie, 2008).

The presumed performance benefits of collaborative arrangements have attracted increased attention from policymakers and practitioners alike (Kenis & Provan, 2009). In tandem, the growing demand for public spending accountability raises questions as to whether and under what conditions these arrangements 'are actually performing at a level that justifies the costs of collaboration' (Kenis & Provan, 2009). Although many studies have assessed joint working in terms of efficiency and effectiveness, there has been far less interest in how incentive policies actually affect partnership performance, which is fairly surprising, given that the new managerial strategies tout performance evaluation as a guiding principle and that

in countries (like the UK) 'partnership working has a long history in the public sector' (Lamie & Ball, 2010, p. 109; ODPM, 2006). Moreover, the research has tended 'to focus primarily on the outcome of an evaluation to the detriment of the mechanism and context aspects' (Gill & Turbin, 1999, p. 180) and, thus, provides the rationale and motivations for this study.

This paper argues that the success of an evaluation effort largely depends on the evaluation design and, in particular, on the assumptions that underpin the design itself. In order to better understand why some collaborative arrangements perform well and others do not, or in what specific circumstances some publicly-funded partnerships develop or stagnate, it is necessary to find an approach that recognises the crucial role of the context. 'Collaboration takes place in a specific context' (Luna-Reyes et al., 2007, p. 810) and is shaped and reshaped in the course of everyday life according to the personal preferences or motivations of the public officials, the politicians and the local authority managers. In turn, personal preference 'is mediated by organisational conditions' (Brodkin, 2011, p. i260). The paper suggests that the so-called 'realist approach' (Pawson & Tilley, 1997) with its emphasis on the context is useful to address the policy evaluation puzzle in multi-organisational settings.

The purpose of this paper is to highlight the potential of the realist approach in the evaluation of incentive-based policies. To accomplish that, the paper illustrates a concrete experience of what is still a fledgling evaluation research project, in which the authors are directly involved. Specifically, the research team has been asked to develop an evidence-based framework for assessing public policies to promote and support inter-municipal partnerships in the Italian Region of Sardinia.

Thus, the main contribution of this paper is to extend our understanding of policy evaluation by applying the realist approach to the assessment of local government partnerships. As far as we are aware, this is the first attempt to apply such an approach to inter-municipal collaboration. The paper also aims to provide valuable information about partnership implementation and working that the policy leaders responsible for shaping and funding collaborations will find of use in the redesign of public intervention in this field. The paper begins with a review of the selected literature that deals with the government influence exerted on public authorities and their decisions to set up and develop collaborations. The key tenets of the realist evaluation, seen as a means to address the evaluation puzzle of policies that promote inter-municipal cooperation, are then presented. Subsequently, the paper charts the roadmap of an ongoing evaluation project in which the incentive-based policies launched by the Italian Region of Sardinia will be analysed through the lens of the realist approach and compared with those of the Lombardy Region. A fragment of the most distinctive phase of the realist evaluation is provided and commented to demonstrate the capability of the realist research design.

RELATED LITERATURE

Providing evaluative feedback about comprehensive reform challenges evaluators (Yin & Davis, 2006). When talking about the depth of performance, Bouckaert and Halligan (2008), make a distinction between the "micro", "meso" and "macro" levels. The micro level refers to an individual public-sector organization, the meso level to a plurality of public organizations in a specific policy field, while the macro level is government-wide or even country-wide. This paper focuses primarily on the "meso" level, in that it will deal with municipalities that join together to form a special purpose vehicle to deliver services on behalf of all the partners. This section reviews the international literature that addresses the government influence exerted on the local authorities and their decisions to set up and develop collaborations. The studies selected here discuss

different collaborative forms that pursue a variety of service objectives and functions.

A characteristic of research into inter-organisational collaboration (other common terms used interchangeably include: collaborations, partnerships, inter-organisational relations and networks) is the wide variety of disciplines, paradigms, theoretical perspectives and sectorial focuses from which the subject is tackled (Brinkerhoff, 2002; Huxham, 2003; Mandell & Steelman, 2003). Another peculiar aspect is that, until now, researchers have made no significant effort to develop, integrate and test systematically the insights generated in previous works (Hulst & van Montfort, 2007b; Kenis & Provan, 2009; O'Toole, 1986). The general understanding is that there is still much to learn about partnership assessment (Jacobs, 2010; O'Leary & Bingham, 2009; Oliver, 1990). This is especially so in those cases where external pressure, e.g., laws and policy programmes, directly or indirectly influence the local authorities' decision on the partnership's governance typology and the services it is asked to deliver.

The research of Hulst and van Montfort (2007b) and Hulst, van Montfort, Haveri, Airaksinen, and Kelly (2009), who comparatively analysed collaborative arrangements across eight European countries (Belgium, Finland, France, Germany, Italy, Spain, the Netherlands and the United Kingdom) provides a springboard for our discussion. The authors adopted a new-institutionalist perspective according to a line of reasoning that can be summed up in four points (Hulst et al., 2009). First, collaborative behaviour and decisions are the result of interaction between institutional values, norms, informal rules and beliefs and actor rationality. Second, institutions provide meaning and influence the way actors define their interests and preferences. Third, the institutional context shapes the opportunities and constraints actors face and sets the game rules for actors pursuing their goals. While existing institutions shape the strategies and conduct of actors, in turn, action and actors can materialise in new institutions. Fourth, path dependency plays a crucial role: strategic choices made at one point in history limit the range of possibilities for later strategic options as much as existing institutions leave their tracks in new institutions.

Research into the strategies that promote local collaborations (Hulst et al., 2009) suggests that statutory obligations and conditions to drive cooperation frequently face resistance from local governments, leading the individual municipalities to devise avoidance strategies. However, policies that use financial incentives to promote cooperation seem more effective, although there are cases in which the cooperation is more symbolic than real.

Statutory obligations and financial incentives to promote inter-municipal cooperation are normative and coercive pressures brought by governments to persuade potential partners to adopt collaboration initiatives. Significant variations can be observed between one country and another and, while there is some of evidence of good practices in the field of incentivisation, the overall picture is anything but stable (Hulst et al., 2009). In fact, the past few decades have witnessed numerous *shifts*: from single-purpose to multi-purpose arrangements, from horizontal to vertical forms of cooperation, and from standing bureaucratic organisations to contractual agreements. How can these shifts be explained? What determines whether the local governments set up single-purpose or multi-purpose arrangements? The authors recognise the role played by national legislation and incentive structures, alongside that of local preferences and environmental factors, in shaping collaborative forms and their subsequent development over time.

T-Government cannot be achieved by individual organizations, but requires a whole-of-a-government view (Brown & Parker, 2011). Dawes and Préfontaine (2003) recognise the need to put digital government collaboration initiatives in a suitable institutional framework. More

often, legitimacy begins with a basis in law or regulation, but, in a study of the implementation of new inter-municipal structures to support the development of eGovernment in Italy's peripheral areas, Ferro and Sorrentino (2010) endorse the effectiveness of the incentive policies to reward voluntary collaborative behaviour. When the partner municipalities consider the funding allocated by the central or regional governments insufficient, the launch of new initiatives may become problematic. Moreover, the authors state that despite the enabling role of public funds in advancing the setting up of voluntary joint initiatives, once the funds expire the future of these latter is far from certain. Focusing exclusively on the analysis of mandates among public healthcare organisations, Rodriguez, Langley, Beland, and Denis (2007) demonstrated that an inappropriate use of the economic incentives by the mandating agency led to disappointing results in two joint initiatives out of three.

The model proposed by Ansell and Gash (2008) also assigns a crucial role to incentives, whereby these critically influence whether or not this form of governance will produce successful voluntary collaboration. Further "mandated forms of collaboration may be critical where incentives to participate are weak, but mandated cooperation can also disguise the lack of real commitment on the part of stakeholders" (Ansell & Gash, 2008, p. 560). Therefore, even when collaborative governance is mandated, achieving "buy-in is still an essential aspect of the collaborative process" (Ansell & Gash, 2008). "The incentives that stakeholders have to enter into collaboration will loom large as a factor in explaining whether collaborative governance can be successful. Incentives to participate are low when stakeholders can achieve their goals unilaterally or through alternative means" (Ansell & Gash, 2008, p. 552).

The form of network governance, the type of network – whether initially formed as voluntary or mandated – and its developmental stage are the three exogenous factors identified by Kenis and

Provan (2009) in an article that investigates public network performance. These authors argue that where a network stands on each of these factors will determine the appropriateness of specific criteria for assessing the overall performance of the collaborative arrangement.

The "potential robust effects" that external incentive-based programmes can have in precipitating collaboration among institutional entities in a highly-fragmented policy area, i.e., the healthcare sector, have been illustrated by Berry, Krutz, Langner, and Budetti (2008). The authors conclude that public funding is both the mechanism and the incentive that motivates partners to try to overcome collaboration challenges. The funding directly addresses the resource constraints, while even a modest level of external support and technical assistance can stimulate significant programmatic change and inter-organisational linkages within public agencies to optimize the provision of services.

To sum up, most of the abovementioned studies agree on the fact that the availability of funds and other incentive mechanisms is a necessary but insufficient condition for public agencies to launch and develop collaborative arrangements, even though there are plenty of studies that claim the opposite. For example, a survey on the motivation to co-operate at local level gave cost reduction (48.3%) and quality improvement (36.9%) as the main reasons cited by the public managers, while financial incentives were considered less important (8.7%) (Meneguzzo & Cepiku, 2008). The review also suggests that while public policies to promote cooperation can motivate joint efforts they are unable to provide much guidance on the conditions for their use or functioning, neither can they answer the question: in what contexts do the public actors embark on collaboration and why, in other similar contexts and *despite* the financial incentives, do they fail to launch collaborative initiatives? The paper seeks to answer that question by adopting an evaluation approach that expressly acknowledges the impact of the contextual conditions and the complexity of assessing policies (such as those to promote inter-municipal cooperation) that require multifaceted interventions and investments in resources that go beyond joint action.

REALIST EVALUATION IN A NUTSHELL

This section outlines the key tenets of the realist evaluation. We present the basic concepts of this multifaceted approach, identifying the aspects most useful to achieve the paper's aims in the available space and focusing on the need for clarity. The guidelines to this approach can be found in the original texts (Pawson, 2002, 2003; Pawson, Greenhalgh, Harvey, & Walshe, 2005; Pawson & Tilley, 1997, 2004).

The realist approach falls into the category of theory-oriented approaches (Stame, 2004), meant as evaluation approaches that require an understanding of the theoretical assumptions on which the policy or programme in question is based to verify its efficacy. More simply, the theoretical assumptions are the whole of the beliefs that underpin the action, i.e., the assumptions of causal relationship between the inputs and outputs of a policy.

The realist approach adopts a peculiar research design (Pawson et al., 2005; Pawson & Tilley, 1997). The first assumption is that the social conditions are indispensable prerequisites to determine the value of a public policy because these can significantly alter the effects observed. Therefore, instead of studying the cause-effect relationship between programme and results, it is more appropriate to investigate the interaction, or what is called the *mechanism* (M), between the implementation of the policy and the contingent conditions into which it is introduced and implemented. The meaning of *context* (C) is broad and varied according to the analysis level considered. It is not only the temporal space-place in which the programme is carried out, but also the whole of the rules, norms and values that it permeates, as well as its characterising limits and possibilities. If the various contexts regularly show a positive interaction with that programme then it means that it 'works'. The evaluative feedback to the policymakers will be positive or negative solely after regular successes have been observed in multiple contexts. The *outcome* (O), which consists of the intended and unintended consequences of programmes, is generated by the activation of different mechanisms in different contexts (Pawson & Tilley, 2004, p. 8), according to the formula: O = C+M.

Therefore "[realist] evaluation is based on the CMO configuration" (Stame, 2004, p. 62). This contingent view has two important consequences. First, no public policy can be considered a planned action that, almost mechanically, produces results. Neither is collaboration inevitable or automatic in programme and policy implementation (Berry et al., 2008). Rather, each policy with its relative intervention programmes is more of an opportunity that agents can choose to take, being, in their turn, conditioned by the context in which they act. In practice, public policies only rarely take into account that interaction; instead, each aspect is addressed separately. Second, given the complexity of the different contexts, it is always difficult to say whether a single input (e.g., additional funding) caused a given output: in complex social settings an input never works alone (Stame, 2004).

PROJECT BACKGROUND AND RESEARCH SETTING

Project Background

In order to better understand inter-municipal collaboration in the Italian context, it should be noted that the option to reduce the number of municipalities (roughly 8,100 in total, about 60% of which have fewer than 3,000 residents)

is a political non-starter, at least for the time being. Therefore, Italy is unlikely to champion the streamlining achieved by other countries, such as Japan, which cut the total number of municipalities from 3,300 in 1999 to the current 1,800 (Kudo, 2010). In Italy, municipal collaborative arrangements are considered essential to defend the historical role of the small municipalities. Therefore, incentivisation is seen as a necessary tool to build a municipal system that is generally more balanced and more capable of responding not only to the needs of the citizens, but also to those of the good functioning of an overall system that is structured across several territorial levels (Pizzetti, 2008).

Italy introduced an associative form of local government in 1990 called the *Unione dei Comuni* (Union of Municipalities or "UM"). The UM differs from the traditional collaborative forms (such as, Partnering Agreements, Consortia, and Mountain Communities) in three ways: *1)* it adds a new entity to those already in existence (the provincial and regional governments); *2)* it has full juridical and operational autonomy over all the functions delegated to it by the member municipalities; and *3)* is mandated with important territorial governance functions at a supra-municipal level.

The processes for establishing the 313 Italian UM (Testa, 2010) were voluntary up to now, with the UM qualifying for state and regional financial contributions for a period of 8-10 years from start-up. But that situation is about to become more stringent. The reduced flow of resources provided by the upper levels of government in 2010 and the introduction of partnership set-up obligations will drastically curtail the discretional power of the municipalities in their approach to inter-municipal collaboration strategies. One instance is Law 122/2010, a controversial law enacted by the Italian government that introduces new obligations for municipalities with less than 5,000 inhabitants and requires the UM to share important functions, from economic-financial management and control to local police and social services. Basically, the small municipalities are now obliged to adhere to Partnering Agreements or to a UM, while in the past, the choices of form and scope of collaboration depended solely on the strategies of the individual councils. In addition, as of 2010, only the UM will be able to apply for the financial support provided by the upper institutional levels; this corroborates the idea that Italy's central and regional governments intend to support exclusively the strongest and most formal forms of cooperation, i.e., those oriented to joint policy formulation and planning.

Research Setting

The research project is being carried out by the Public Investment Evaluation Unit of the Sardinian regional administration and has the objective of assessing the collaborative incentive policies to which the Region has dedicated substantial programmes and policy instruments. The UM are important landmarks in the institutional fabric of this region. Regional Law 12 of 2005 defines the scope, the functions, the governance mechanisms and the incentive-based programmes of the UM. Currently, Sardinia has 30 UM in operation (Testa, 2010) and, while 48.8% of Sardinian municipalities belong to a UM, more significantly 32.6% (versus a national average of 9.5%) of the region's population live in a UM partner municipality.

The research project has a dual goal. First, as a learning exercise, it aims to enlighten the regional policymakers as to the results of the actions undertaken, while showing them how experience can improve both decisions and practice. Second, it promotes accountability, the Regional Council requires hard facts to identify how successful the UM have been in meeting the needs and/or solving the problems that led to the regional administration's intervention.

The paper will provide a snapshot of how the research, which is still in its early stages, will proceed to highlight the added value of the proposed evaluation approach.

RESEARCH DESIGN

Case studies have a distinctive place in evaluation research (Yin, 1994). The main source of qualitative evidence on local strategic partnerships and the wider policy framework is provided by a multiple-case study methodology, in other words, "an empirical inquiry that investigates a contemporary phenomenon within its real-life context, especially when the boundaries within phenomenon and context are not clearly evident" (Yin, 1994, p. 13).

Two Italian regions (Sardinia and Lombardy) will be analysed from a comparative perspective. A sample of 10 Sardinian UM will be studied in-depth and compared with a similar sample of Lombard UM. The choice of two regions so different in economic, socio-demographic and institutional terms (Sardinia is a special charter region, while Lombardy, the country's most advanced region, has an ordinary charter) is due to the institutional reform (based on decentralisation and federalism) underway in Italy. The structural change to a state of more federalist matrix should translate, once up and running, into: *1*) the municipalities' adoption of public service production and management methods oriented to productivity and economic efficiency; and *2*) the progressive narrowing of the gaps between the different areas of the country. As a result of this latter, the most advanced regions will act as benchmarks for the others, by which, the state means that, going forward, it will use the standard costs of the best performers as the main criterion when allocating the Regions with the funds needed to operate and deliver local services.

The adoption of a comparative approach is meant to provide useful information on the effects produced by the policies under investigation and to help the understanding of the "patterns of winners and losers" (Pawson et al., 2005) in both the contexts analysed. The methodology includes data triangulation through interviews, focus groups, and documentation. Figure 1 provides an overview of the research design and its key phases;

Figure 1. The research design (adapted from Yin, 1994; Pawson & Tilley, 2004)

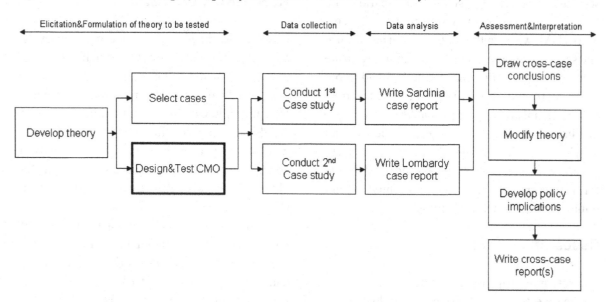

the specific object of this paper is shown in the box with the bold border.

The first phase (*eliciting and formalising the policy theories to be tested*) draws on multiple sources of evidence, including academic and professional literature, reports, and other documents. The formulation of the programme theory in terms of CMO (Context, Mechanisms, Outcomes) is based on the analysis of documentation and interviews with a small sample of policymakers, programme architects and UM representatives, each of whom will give an account of their personal experience and knowledge of collaboration initiatives. It will then be possible to formulate preliminary *embryonic* hypotheses as CMO configurations. In this phase the focus is on: *1*) the context in which the policy aims to introduce changes in areas related to the provision of local government services by promoting cooperative arrangements between municipalities; *2*) the mechanisms put in place to make the policy work; and *3*) the output pattern, including the intended and unintended consequences, generated by different mechanisms in different contexts (Pawson & Tilley, 2004). In fact, according to Sayer (1984), the relationship between a mechanism and its

effects is not a given, but depends on the specific conditions (context) in which it works.

The second phase *(data collection)* involves gathering information about how the incentive policy was implemented in each Region (i.e., Sardinia and Lombardy). Data (both qualitative and quantitative from multiple sources of evidence) will be gathered from a sample of UM in Sardinia and Lombardy, with the aim of matching information to those various leads. Interviews and focus groups (FG) with UM managers and UM chief administrative officers will enable us to develop new concepts and test the preliminary (and rival) hypotheses. The researchers' "constant comparison" and categorization (Glaser & Strauss, 1967; Strauss & Corbin, 1994) of the interviews and FGs will lead to a deeper conceptualization through a bottom-up approach (Cicognani, 2002). After the material has been coded, a structured questionnaire will be designed to put to a wider sample of UM managers and UM chief administrative officers. At the date of writing, four interviews with UM managers had been completed in Sardinia.

The third *(data analysis)* phase consists of recombining the evidence through explanation-building techniques (Yin, 1994). Our main expectation is that there will be a nuanced outcome pattern within and across the UM and relative interventions. The purpose of this phase is to verify whether or not the CMO configurations built in the first phase are capable of explaining the policy's outcomes in different contexts.

The fourth and final phase (*assessment and interpretation*) aims to verify whether or not the analysis supports or refutes the theories about how the policy worked. In this phase it is likely that some outcomes will remain contradictory and rather blurred, but we expect the analysis to provide the pillars on which to build an evaluation framework that can guide the regional policymakers to design programmes more in tune with the contexts in which they want to implement them. Figure 2 summarises the research path and the current status of each phase.

AN ILLUSTRATIVE EXAMPLE

Reflection on earlier research cases and the extant literature have convinced us of the usefulness of the realist evaluation's contribution to the Sardinian UM research project. This section will attempt to demonstrate that contribution "on paper" in the elicitation and formulation phase, the 'most distinctive phase' (Pawson & Tilley, 2004, p. 11) of the realist evaluation.

Given that, at the time of writing, the data-collection phase had only just kicked off, we will selectively use the findings of a recent research on the Lombard partnerships (Sorrentino & Simonetta, in press) and try to collect data according to those inputs. In particular, for the first research phase, we will select themes that appear to cut across the different cases.

After briefly illustrating the salient points of the Lombardy case, the regional policy to stimulate voluntary inter-municipal partnerships will be broken down into its component mechanisms and their surrounding contexts and outcomes. This will enable us to formulate a few (purposely limited for reasons of space) hypotheses of CMO configurations "in order to come up with some mechanisms through which [such a policy] might work, and to highlight some differing contexts which might shape which mechanisms are activated, and thus to suggest an outcome pattern of potential successes and failures" (Pawson & Tilley, 2004, p. 26). Nevertheless, we point out that these provisional configurations (outlined in Table 1) are neither exhaustive nor mutually exclusive.

The Lombardy Case

Over the past few years, each of Italy's 20 Regions has enacted its own legislation on inter-municipal incentive policies. To obtain the relative policy resources, Lombardy, for example, requires that applicants submit a project containing information on, among other things, the partners, the goals of the collaboration, the area of intervention and the expected results; the projects are then reviewed and selected by a regional commission. The financial

Figure 2. Research workplan

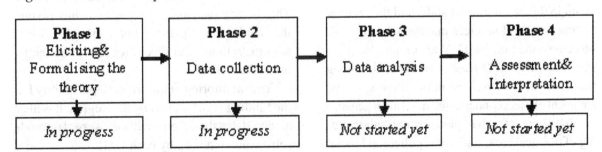

321

Table 1. Illustrative CMO configurations

#	Potential Contexts	Plausible Mechanisms	Possible Outcomes
1	Municipalities are keen to commit (C1)	Incentives encourage local collaboration and joint policy planning (M1)	The UM develops and grows (O1)
2	The municipalities have previous collaboration experience (C2)	Incentives encourage local collaboration and joint policy planning (M1)	The UM is likely to be successful (O2)
3	The political payoff of collaborative initiatives is low for the elected officials (C3)	Collaboration is a positive value (normative pressure) (M2)	"Paper" implementation (O3)
4	The Region lacks adequate evaluation capabilities (C4)	Collaboration is a positive value (normative pressure) (M2)	Average low quality of the collaboration projects presented by the municipalities (O4) Merely formal monitoring (O4.1)
5	There is no clear overview of the incentive policies launched by the Region (C5)	Collaboration is a positive value (normative pressure) (M2)	Dispersion/waste of public funds (O5) The gap between the local areas widens (O6)
6	The benefits fail to concretise within the political lifecycle of each partner municipality (C6)	The reorganisation of public services into a larger area aims to achieve economies of scale and a better use of resources (M3)	The UM is likely to end up stagnating (O7)
7	The scarce organisational and managerial skills of the smallest municipalities is a hurdle to UM implementation (C7	Collaboration enables the small municipalities to fill the gap between the larger municipalities (M4)	The UM manages only basic services (O8)
8	The smallest municipalities fear losing their autonomy (C8)	Union equates to stronger (M5)	Bilateral agreements (other than the UM) are dominant (O9)
9	Trust and commitment among partners (C9)	The UM makes it easier to negotiate with other entities and opens the door to state and EU funding categories (M6)	The UM spurs innovation at the local level (O10)
10	Collusive behaviour by the partner municipalities (C10)	Additional funds are always useful when resources are scarce (M7)	Stagnation/less critical services are transferred to the UM (O11)
11	Funding deemed inadequate (C11)	Additional funds are always useful when resources are scarce (M7)	No collaboration (O12)
12	Availability of other forms of funding from upper government levels (C12)	Additional funds are always useful when resources are scarce (M7)	Consortia or other standing organisations are set up (O13)
13	Substantial pressure on lead municipality (C13)	Collaboration requires an investment that goes beyond joint action (M8)	The UM stagnates (O14)

contributions disbursed to the UM of the Lombardy Region vary in line with the following criteria: population density; total number of participating municipalities; number of staff; and the number of functions and services managed by the UM. Moreover, the Lombard UM are required to manage in association at least three of the following functions and/or services: information systems; technical office; economic-financial management; tax management; urban planning and safeguarding of the local area; staff; local police; and social care services. The selected UM receive an initial

extraordinary contribution to cover the cost of the design and launch phase and then an annual contribution for a maximum period of 10 years. The subsidy system is designed to mainly favour the small municipalities but leaves the local administrations with much freedom of action to make their choices.

The monitoring of the projects that qualify for the funding is carried out by the Region, it is also assumed that the outputs will be assessed through self-evaluation (i.e., by each UM).

Designing CMO Configurations

A brief outline of the criteria on which the incentive policies are based is necessary to grasp the assumptions (the 'theory') that underpin these policies in order to understand the causal relationship between the inputs and outputs (Stame, 2004). The policy theory assumes that the financial incentives encourage municipalities to set up joint activities in which they would otherwise show little interest. The intention of the legislator is to spur the growth of inter-municipal collaborative processes through both the creation of new UM and the participation of municipalities in existing UM.

Semi-structured interviews with 'key' informants (i.e., 20 mayors and 18 UM managers) (Sorrentino & Simonetta, in press) enable us to start identifying some of the mechanisms (M) that seem to come into play in Lombard UM:

- Cooperation between municipalities translates, over time, into a better capacity for joint strategic and policy planning;
- The reorganisation of public services into a larger area aims to achieve economies of scale in the production and delivery phases;
- Cooperation is the means to induce a propositional attitude in the entities and their staff, which could then be extended to other environments and/or policy domains;
- The UM makes it easier to speak and negotiate with other entities and opens the door to state and European Union funding categories;
- Collaboration heightens the visibility of the public interventions to citizens;
- Collaboration requires an investment of resources that goes beyond joint action.

And the contexts (C):

- In terms of political consensus, the collaboration payoff is low because the citizens are used to dealing directly with their own municipality (or even the mayor in the case of the small municipalities). The elected officials do not rank the UM high on the vote-winning agenda;
- The expected benefits of the UM fail to concretise within the political lifecycle of each partner municipality;
- The small municipalities rarely have the organisational resources and skills needed to implement a dynamic UM;
- The Lombardy Region – like Italy's PA environment – has no advanced evaluation capabilities. Its monitoring of the UM mainly focuses on their administrative/formal aspects;
- The fairly unselective requirements to obtain funding means there is no competition over the quality of the aggregation projects;
- When the collaboration commitment is poor, the partner municipalities transfer to the UM only basic services (e.g., public lighting, billboard advertising, promotional tourism initiatives);
- The amount of the funding from the Region is deemed inadequate to offset the 'costs' of the collaboration. Joining or setting up a UM leads to a loss of autonomy and hits especially the lead municipality with a work overload (administrative, management and relational).

While the outcomes (O) show mixed success:

- Only 16% of local public services are delivered in associative form through different types of partnerships;
- Lombardy has about 500 collaborative initiatives governed by different contractual arrangements depending on the theme/service involved. Generally, the dominant trend is to create loose forms (e.g., bilateral agreements between two neighbouring

municipalities) as opposed to a consortium or a standing organisation;

- Lombardy is the Italian region with the highest number (60) of UM;
- 71% of the UM are made up of no more than three municipalities, most of which, once established, make no progress and so stagnate;
- The most dynamic UM are those found in areas that have already implemented collaborative forms (e.g., district healthcare plans);
- Only in rare cases do the partnerships implemented by the Lombard municipalities deal with "internal" functions, such as financial, administrative and personnel management;
- Most UM are created to manage public services and not to address local area planning and development in a concerted way;
- The average size of the UM is too small, making it hard to achieve economies of scale or improve service efficacy.

The 13 CMO configurations outlined in Table 1 are a reworking of the three earlier lists.

First and foremost, this simulation exercise underscores how the interaction between public incentives, UM stakeholders and UM performance deserves attention. Evaluators should begin breaking down the possible mechanisms (some of which have been identified here) into much greater detail. While it is acknowledged that this example is merely illustrative, the above CMO configurations indicate that the financial incentives are more of a tool that help the councils to consider the collaboration option rather than an all-encompassing solution. Incentive-based policies impact the actors' perceptions 'about the desirability of collaboration' (Fuller & Vu, 2011, p. 362) and help '[to create] an environment that enables collaboration to gain a higher reward' (Fuller & Vu, 2011).

Second, the above-proposed example not only suggests that the policy in question does not operate in the same way everywhere in Lombardy, and, therefore, that the variations in results are inevitable, but also that the same outcome (e.g., UM stagnation) can, in reality, be the result of highly diverse implementation paths (see: CMO numbers 6, 10 and 13). Further, this approach shows that the decision to establish relationship and the translation of collaboration strategies into concrete actions are "commonly based on multiple contingency" (Oliver, 1990, p. 242) that can change over time.

The grid should be considered purely as a simulated attempt to develop a "middle-range evaluation theory" (Pawson, 2002, p. 349). As indicated above, the CMO configurations are a preliminary hypothesis that has yet to be tested and fine-tuned. Pawson (2003) quoted in Blamey and Mackenzie (2007, p. 451) refers to this activity as 'concentrating your fire'. Nevertheless, the reader should not be misled by the relative ease with which it is possible to highlight plausible CMO configurations; the real problem inherent the application of the realist approach is to successfully validate the CMO configurations through consistent data, keeping to the research timetable. This could be a major aspect that requires the attention of both the academic evaluators and the practitioners.

Despite the limitations spoken of earlier, the example given enables us to see that the logic of the realist evaluation differs vastly to that advocating the use of 'best practices', which, conversely, seek to extend the same way of addressing and solving the problems ubiquitously. The difference between realist evaluation and new public management (NPM) is even sharper. NPM cares little about capturing significant dimensions of informal practice or understanding '*how* policy work is done' (Brodkin, 2011, p. i273 original emphasis). Paradoxically, new managerialism contributes "to a politics of opacity, while appearing to contribute to one of transparency" (Brodkin, 2011, p. i273).

CONCLUSION

Although the problem of assessing joint working in terms of efficiency and effectiveness is well understood by researchers, they have shown far less interest in how incentive policies actually affect partnership performance. Drawing on the realist approach, the paper suggests the need to assess these policies within their *context*, and to ask what *mechanisms* are acting to produce which *outcomes* (Gill & Turbin, 1999). As far as we are aware, this is the first attempt to adopt such an approach to evaluate the public policies that promote and support the setting up of inter-municipal partnerships.

As a pioneer of the realist approach, the purpose of the paper is twofold. First, it seeks to broaden our understanding of partnership implementation and working, and so be of practical use to the policy leaders. Second, it suggests the potential value of the realist approach to the evaluation of incentive-based policies. The review of the relevant literature that expressly addresses the role of public incentives confirms that the paper's first aim has been part accomplished, not least in highlighting the major issues that the policy leaders who shape and fund collaborations need to take into account. However, the same cannot be said of the second aim. We are aware that the ongoing research project briefly illustrated here allows only for tentative conclusions to be drawn on the evaluation challenges that it seeks to address, and that we are not yet able to establish whether and to what extent the policies we propose to evaluate can be captured within an overarching approach such as the realist evaluation. It might be possible to make further advances on completion of the research project commissioned by the Sardinia Region and, above all, when the findings of the in-depth studies that hopefully will be developed by other scholars come available. Clearly, the current situation is not satisfactory from either the scientific perspective or from the policy designers' and public managers' viewpoint. The conclusion is that to open the policy evaluation black box never more than in this case has it been so necessary for the scholarly community to draw on the knowledge and experience of those who work on a day-to-day basis in the local partnership landscape.

AKNOWLEDGMENT

The authors would like to thank the Editor and the anonymous reviewers for their insightful comments and suggestions. An earlier version of this article was presented at the tGov2011 Workshop held on 17-18 March 2011 at Brunel University, West London.

REFERENCES

Ansell, C., & Gash, A. (2008). Collaborative governance in theory and practice. *Journal of Public Administration: Research and Theory*, *18*(4), 543–571. doi:10.1093/jopart/mum032

Becker, J., Niehaves, B., & Krause, A. (2009, August 6-9). *Shared services strategies and their determinants: A multiple case study analysis in the public sector.* Paper presented at the Americas Conference on Information Systems, San Francisco, CA.

Berry, C., Krutz, G. S., Langner, B. E., & Budetti, P. (2008). Jump-starting collaboration: The ABCD initiative and the provision of child development services through Medicaid and collaborators. *Public Administration Review*, *68*(3), 480–490. doi:10.1111/j.1540-6210.2008.00884.x

Blamey, A., & Mackenzie, M. (2007). Theories of change and realistic evaluation. *Evaluation*, *13*(4), 439–455. doi:10.1177/1356389007082129

Bouckaert, G., & Halligan, J. (2008). *Managing performance. International comparisons*. New York, NY: Routledge.

Brinkerhoff, J. M. (2002). Assessing and improving partnership relationships and outcomes: A proposed framework. *Evaluation and Program Planning, 25*(3), 215–231. doi:10.1016/S0149-7189(02)00017-4

Brodkin, E. Z. (2011). Policy work: Street-level organizations under new managerialism. *Journal of Public Administration: Research and Theory, 21*(2), i253–i277. doi:10.1093/jopart/muq093

Brown, P. F., & Parker, C. (Eds.). (2011). *Transformational government framework primer version 1.0*. Retrieved from http://docs.oasis-open.org/tgf/TGF-Primer/v1.0/cnd01/TGF-Primer-v1.0-cnd01.pdf

CabinetOffice. (2009). *What do we mean by sharing services?* Retrieved from http://www.cabinetoffice.gov.uk/

Cicognani, E. (2002). *Psicologia sociale e ricerca qualitativa*. Rome, Italy: Carocci.

Dawes, S., & Préfontaine, L. (2003). Understanding new models of collaboration for delivering government services. *Communications of the ACM, 46*(1), 40–42. doi:10.1145/602421.602444

Ferro, E., & Sorrentino, M. (2010). Can inter-municipal collaboration help the diffusion of E-Government in peripheral areas? Evidence from Italy. *Government Information Quarterly, 27*(1), 17–25. doi:10.1016/j.giq.2009.07.005

Fuller, B. W., & Vu, K. M. (2011). Exploring the dynamics of policy interaction: Feedback among and impacts from multiple, concurrently applied policy approaches for promoting collaboration. *Journal of Policy Analysis and Management, 30*(2), 359–380. doi:10.1002/pam.20572

Gill, M., & Turbin, V. (1999). Evaluating 'realistic evaluation'. Evidence from a study of CCTV. *Crime Prevention Studies, 10*, 179–199.

Glaser, B. G., & Strauss, A. I. (1967). *The discovery of grounded theory: Strategies for qualitative research*. New York, NY: Aldine.

Hulst, R., & van Montfort, A. (2007a). Inter-municipal cooperation: A widespread phenomenon. In Hulst, R., & van Montfort, A. (Eds.), *Inter-municipal cooperation in Europe* (pp. 1–21). Dordrecht, The Netherlands: Springer-Verlag. doi:10.1007/1-4020-5379-7_1

Hulst, R., & van Montfort, A. (Eds.). (2007b). *Inter-municipal cooperation in Europe*. Dordrecht, The Netherlands: Springer-Verlag. doi:10.1007/1-4020-5379-7

Hulst, R., van Montfort, A., Haveri, A., Airaksinen, J., & Kelly, J. (2009). Institutional shifts in inter-municipal service delivery. *Public Organization Review, 9*(3), 263–285. doi:10.1007/s11115-009-0085-8

Huxham, C. (2003). Theorizing collaboration practice. *Public Management Review, 5*(3), 401–423. doi:10.1080/1471903032000146964

Irani, Z., Sahraoui, S., Ozkan, S., Ghoneim, A., & Elliman, T. (2007). *T-government for benefit realisation*. Paper presented at the European and Mediterranean Conference on Information Systems.

Isett, K. R., Mergel, I. A., LeRoux, K., Mischen, P. A., & Rethemeyer, R. K. (2011). Networks in public administration scholarship: Understanding where we are and where we need to go. *Journal of Public Administration: Research and Theory, 21*(1), 157–173. doi:10.1093/jopart/muq061

Jacobs, K. (2010). The politics of partnerships: A study of police and housing collaboration to tackle anti-social behaviour on Australian public housing estates. *Public Administration, 88*(4), 928–942. doi:10.1111/j.1467-9299.2010.01851.x

Janssen, M., Joha, A., & Weerakkody, V. (2007). Exploring relationships of shared service arrangements in local government. *Transforming Government: People. Process and Policy, 1*(3), 271–284.

Kamal, M., Weerakkody, V., & Jones, S. (2009). The case of EAI in facilitating e-Government services in a Welsh authority. *International Journal of Electronic Government Research, 29*(2), 161–165.

Kenis, P., & Provan, K. G. (2009). Towards an exogenous theory of public network performance. *Public Administration, 87*(3), 440–456. doi:10.1111/j.1467-9299.2009.01775.x

King, S., & Cotterill, S. (2007). Transformational government? The role of information technology in delivering citizen-centric local public services. *Local Government Studies, 33*(3), 333–354. doi:10.1080/03003930701289430

Klievink, B., & Janssen, M. (2009). Realizing joined-up government. Dynamic capabilities and stage models for transformation. *Government Information Quarterly, 26*(2), 275–284. doi:10.1016/j.giq.2008.12.007

Kudo, H. (2010). E-Governance as strategy of public sector reform: Peculiarity of Japanese IT policy and its institutional origin. *Financial Accountability & Management, 26*(1), 65–84. doi:10.1111/j.1468-0408.2009.00491.x

Lamie, J., & Ball, R. (2010). Evaluation of partnership working within a community planning context. *Local Government Studies, 36*(1), 109–127. doi:10.1080/03003930903435815

Luna-Reyes, L. F., Gil-Garcia, J. R., & Cruz, C. B. (2007). Collaborative digital government in Mexico: Some lessons from federal Web-based interorganizational information integration initiatives. *Government Information Quarterly, 24*(4), 808–826. doi:10.1016/j.giq.2007.04.003

Mandell, M. P., & Steelman, T. A. (2003). Understanding what can be accomplished through interorganizational innovations. *Public Management Review, 5*(2), 197–224. doi:10.1080/1461667032000066417

May, P. J., & Winter, S. C. (2007). Collaborative service arrangements. *Public Management Review, 9*(4), 479–502. doi:10.1080/14719030701726473

Meneguzzo, M., & Cepiku, D. (Eds.). (2008). *Network pubblici. Strategia, struttura e governance*. Milano, Italy: McGraw-Hill.

O'Leary, R., & Bingham, L. B. (Eds.). (2009). *The collaborative public manager*. Washington, DC: Georgetown University Press.

O'Toole, L. J. (1986). Policy recommendations for multi-actor implementation: An assessment of the field. *Journal of Public Policy, 6*(2), 181–210. doi:10.1017/S0143814X00006486

O'Toole, L. J. (1993). Interorganizational policy studies: Lessons drawn from implementation research. *Journal of Public Administration: Research and Theory, 3*(2), 232–251.

ODPM. (2006). *National evaluation of LSPs: Formative evaluation and action research programme 2002-2005: Final report*. Retrieved from http://www.communities.gov.uk/documents/localgovernment/pdf/143381.pdf

Oliver, C. (1990). Determinants of interorganizational relationships: Integration and future directions. *Academy of Management Review, 15*(2), 241–265.

Pawson, R. (2002). Evidence-based policy: The promise of `realist synthesis'. *Evaluation, 8*(3), 340–358. doi:10.1177/135638902401462448

Pawson, R. (2003). Nothing as practical as a good theory. *Evaluation, 9*(4), 471–490. doi:10.1177/1356389003094007

Pawson, R., Greenhalgh, T., Harvey, G., & Walshe, K. (2005). Realist review-a new method of systematic review designed for complex policy interventions. *Journal of Health Services Research & Policy, 10*(1), 21–34. doi:10.1258/1355819054308530

Pawson, R., & Tilley, N. (1997). *Realistic evaluation.* London, UK: Sage.

Pawson, R., & Tilley, N. (2004). *Realist evaluation.* Retrieved from http://www.communitymatters.com.au/RE_chapter.pdf

Pizzetti, F. (2008). Piccoli comuni e grandi compiti: La specificità italiana di fronte ai bisogni delle società mature. In Formiconi, D. (Ed.), *Comuni, insieme, più forti!* Torriana, Italy: EDK Editore.

Provan, K. G., & Kenis, P. (2008). Modes of network governance: Structure, management, and effectiveness. *Journal of Public Administration: Research and Theory, 18*(2), 229–252. doi:10.1093/jopart/mum015

Ranade, W., & Hudson, B. (2003). Conceptual issues in inter-agency collaboration. *Local Government Studies, 29*(3), 32–50. doi:10.1080/03003930308559378

Rodriguez, C., Langley, A., Beland, F., & Denis, J.-L. (2007). Governance, power, and mandated collaboration in an interorganizational network. *Administration & Society, 39*(2), 150–193. doi:10.1177/0095399706297212

Sayer, A. (1984). *Method in social science.* London, UK: Hutchinson. doi:10.4324/9780203310762

Sorrentino, M., & Simonetta, M. (in press). Analysing the implementation of local partnerships: An organisational perspective. *Transforming Government: People. Process and Policy.*

Stame, N. (2004). Theory-based evaluation and types of complexity. *Evaluation, 10*(1), 58–76. doi:10.1177/1356389004043135

Strauss, A. I., & Corbin, J. (1994). Grounded theory methodology: An overview. In Denzin, N. K., & Lincoln, Y. S. (Eds.), *Handbook of qualitative research* (pp. 273–285). Thousand Oaks, CA: Sage.

Testa, P. (Ed.). (2010). *Lo stato delle Unioni.* Roma, Italy: Cittalia.

Weerakkody, V., Dhillon, G., Dwivedi, Y., & Currie, W. (2008, August 14-17). *Realising transformational stage e-government: Challenges, issues and complexities.* Paper presented at the Americas Conference on Information Systems, Toronto, ON, Canada.

Weerakkody, V., Dwivedi, Y. K., Dhillon, G., & Williams, M. D. (2007, December 28-30). *Realising T-Government: A UK local authority perspective.* Paper presented at the Fifth International Conference on Electronic Government, Hyderabad, India.

Yin, R. K. (1994). *Case study research* (2nd ed.). Thousand Oaks, CA: Sage.

Yin, R. K., & Davis, D. (2006). Adding new dimensions to case study evaluations: The case of evaluating comprehensive reforms. *New Directions for Evaluation, 113*, 75.

This work was previously published in the International Journal of Electronic Government Research, Volume 7, Issue 4, edited by Vishanth Weerakkody, pp. 19-34, copyright 2011 by IGI Publishing (an imprint of IGI Global).

Chapter 19
Transforming Public–Private Networks:
An XBRL–Based Infrastructure for Transforming Business–to–Government Information Exchange

Niels de Winne
Delft University of Technology, The Netherlands

Nitesh Bharosa
Delft University of Technology, The Netherlands

Marijn Janssen
Delft University of Technology, The Netherlands

Remco van Wijk
Delft University of Technology, The Netherlands

Joris Hulstijn
Delft University of Technology, The Netherlands

ABSTRACT

Companies are required by law to report all kinds of information to various public agencies. Since most public agencies are autonomous and define their information demands independent of each other, companies have to report information to various agencies in different ways. Accordingly, governments are initiating programs that aim to transform business-to government information exchange to reduce the administrative burden for companies and improve the accountability at the same time. Yet little research is available on the type of transformations needed and the role of the infrastructure. Drawing on a case study, this paper investigates the interplay between technical infrastructure and transformation. In this case study an information brokerage infrastructure based on the Extensible Business Reporting Language (XBRL) was developed providing a one stop shop for companies and public agencies. The case study shows that the infrastructure should be flexible enough to accommodate changes over time but stable enough to attract a large user-base. The increase in efficiency and effectiveness of information exchange processes requires extensive transformation from both public and private parties.

DOI: 10.4018/978-1-4666-2458-0.ch019

INTRODUCTION

The exchange of information between private companies and public sector organizations becomes more and more important (Gil-Garcia, Chengalur-Smith, & Duchessi, 2007). Companies exchange a plethora of information with government agencies like the statistical agency, tax office, chambers of commerce and various inspection services. In many countries such as Australia, the United Kingdom and the Netherlands, politicians have agreed that business-to-government information exchange should take place electronically and should be standardized in order to reduce the administration burden. In addition the information quality can be improved by capturing information at the source resulting in an improved accountability of companies to governments.

It is a general belief that technology holds the capacity for strengthening efficiency, providing tools for security, and furthermore being an instrument for streamlining of e-Government procedures (Irani, Elliman, & Jackson, 2007). Technology has been put forward as "a catalyst for social, economic and political change" (Fountain, 2001, p. 45). Technologies are carriers of e-Government reform aims to change the government and how they interact with their constituents, in this case businesses and citizens. The introduction of public-private information exchange are often initiated as a technology project for developing an infrastructure and the need for transformation is only recognized after some time. Infrastructures support many users and are the shared responsibility of several organizational entities (Janssen, Chun, & Gil-Garcia, 2009). Infrastructures have no central authority, are governed by networks and contain both emerging and purposefully designed parts (Janssen, Chun, & Gil-Garcia, 2009). Infrastructure are not static entities, but dynamic and evolving as technological innovations are introduced or the social practice is changed (Ciborra, 2000). Hanseth et al. (1996) depict these infrastructures as information infrastructure to

emphasis a more holistic, socio-technical and evolutionary perspective to the growth in the combined social and technical complexity at the center of an empirical scrutiny. Key characteristics of such infrastructures are openness, the need for standards and facilitating a diversity of stakeholders. In a similar vein, Janssen et al. (2009) call these 'next generation of digital government structures' to emphasize the contribution to e-government and characteristics such as emerging, evolution, self-organizing, coordination and connectivity and use by many different users. Successful infrastructures are considered to hold considerable benefits for businesses and governments in that cross-organizational information sharing is enabled, reducing costs of already existing interactions and enabling new ones (Hanseth & Lyytinen, 2010). Opportunity costs and political and social problems influence the development of such infrastructures (Hanseth & Lyytinen, 2010). The complexity and dynamic relations between infrastructural components results that developments frequently do not have the anticipated effects which leads to unintended consequences when adopted by users (Hanseth et al., 1996).

Private organizations exchange information with public organizations to comply with legal requirements. Reporting may serve purposes such as tax, statistics and industry regulation. The amount of reporting has significantly grown over the recent years particularly as a result of more stringent industry regulations like Sarbanes-Oxley Act (Sarbanes-Oxley, 2002) and Basel II (BASEL_II, 2004). A typical company often ends up reporting the same information multiple times to different government agencies in different formats which results in significant administrative costs for companies. The Extensible Business Reporting Language (XBRL) is hailed as providing a foundation for the exchange of reports and data (Debreceny, Felden, Ochocki, Piechocki, & Piechocki, 2009). XBRL was originally developed as a XML-based standard for external financial reporting. Nowadays it can also be used for internal financial and non-financial reporting which makes it possible to use this for a broader range of reporting functions including statistical, taxes, and inspection data. XBRL enables interoperability among applications regardless of the differences in the internal systems. The broader use of XBRL provides the opportunity to create a one-stop-shop for reporting information by integrating the reporting functions.

Often new technology developments are used to reinforce existing organization structures (Fountain, 2001) and do not transform them. Transformation the information-exchange networks is far more difficult than changing the operational level, since the former kind of change can alter the distribution of resources and power (Ostrom, Gardner, & Walker, 1994). The adoption of e-government requires transformation of the public sector, i.e., meaning radical changes in core processes across organizational boundaries (Kim, Pan, & Pan, 2007; Murphy, 2005; Weerakkody & Dhillon, 2008). Transformational government can be defined as:

[T]he ICT-enabled and organisation-led transformation of government operations, internal and external processes and structures to enable the realisation of services that meet public-sector objectives such as efficiency, transparency, accountability and citizen centricity. (Weerakkody, Janssen, & Dwivedi, 2011, p. 321)

Although there is much research about information exchange, empirical research on the transformations needed for the realization of a standardized public-private information infrastructure is scarce. The *objective* of this research is to analyze and understand transformations driven by the introduction of the XBRL-infrastructure. This should help to understand the broader range of implications for both practice and theory. For this purpose, we employed the case study approach. We studied the development and (partial) use of a standardized public-private information exchange infrastructure for business-to-government reporting in the Netherlands. The next section discusses the details of the research approach, followed by a rich description of the case study. Typical issues are distilled and discussed. Finally, conclusions are drawn and avenues for further research are provided.

RESEARCH APPROACH

Due to the complex nature of infrastructures and the need to gain a deeper understanding of the phenomenon at hand, a qualitative approach based on case study research was adopted for this research (Yin, 2009). Case study research can provide deep insight in the transformation enabled by the XBRL-based infrastructure. Case study research is a commonly used qualitative method (see for example Orlikowski & Lacono, 2001). The financial domain is chosen as the case study context as this domain is a front-runner and has experienced the need for considerable transformations. Furthermore, the financial reporting domain has been used as a benchmark for reporting in other domains (e.g., education, health and immigration).

We examined the companies and public organizations involved by reading reports and interviewing fifteen representatives from the various organizations. We conducted semi-structured interviews which focused on identifying the main components of the XBRL-based infrastructure and the necessary adaptations to the current business-to-government reporting systems and actor roles when using the developed infrastructure. Publicly available and internal documents relating to the history and development were gathered and examined. In addition, magazine papers were analyzed to obtain an adequate understanding of the development in time and issues at hand. These documents provide a good overview of the history and development problems and stakeholders motives, while internal documents contained information concerning the design choices, business case and development methods used. The following sections proceeds with the case study background and findings.

CASE STUDY: STANDARDIZED BUSINESS REPORTING

Standard Business Reporting (SBR) is the international name for standardized reporting processes originating from accountants and auditors. SBR is commonly based on open technology standards and works from the perspective of inter-government accounting and compliance. SBR considers financial reporting as a process of successive links in the information exchange value chain in which data, processes and technology are applied as unambiguous as possible. Although SBR can be used for a broader range of reports and information exchange, the case study investigated in this paper is limited to the financial domain. The project is initiated in 2004 using a different name by joint efforts of the Ministries of Justice and Finance. The Ministry of Justice is the responsible ministry for checking whether businesses operate compliant to sector specific laws and regulations, whereas the Ministry of Finance the responsible is for the tax and financial issues. At a later stage the Ministry of Economics joined this project as being

responsibility for the collection and processing of statistical data. In May 2006 the first companies were able to submit their annual account using SBR. Figure 1 depicts the information exchange infrastructure for SBR.

Technical Infrastructure

The information flows between businesses and government agencies, depicted in Figure 1, is facilitated by a standardized infrastructure. This infrastructure consists of three basic elements: (1) a standardized information exchange format, (2) a national taxonomy and (3) and a gateway/information broker. We explain these components hereafter.

XBRL stands for the eXtensible Business Reporting Modeling Language and started in 1998 under the auspices of the American Institute of Certified Public Accountants (AICPA). XBRL is built on top of XML for the reporting arena. After a while the XBRL international was formed to coordinate efforts in the further development of this open standard. XBRL.org has more than 170 members and supports XBRL standards in the international arena. XBRL International has released XBRL specifications 2.1 in 2003 which is the newest specification, although there are various recommendations (http://xbrl.org/SpecRecom-

Figure 1. Overview of main actors in the financial case study

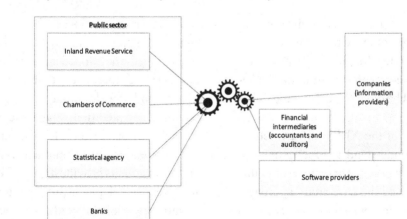

mendations/). In contrast to the use of XML in web services, XBRL is report oriented instead of being transaction oriented (Grey, 2005). This enables to drill down to information and transfer even complete databases (Grey, 2005). XBRL is aimed at facilitating the exchange of reports in information chains, including public-private information exchange. The fundamental idea of XBRL is to allow for a separation of reporting facts from reporting meta-data (Engel, Hamsher, Walis, vun Kannon, & Shuetrim, 2003; Spies, 2010). Facts are grouped and categorized by tags: labels which designate the beginning and end of data elements. The intended meaning of the tagged values is specified by means of so called meta-data: data about data. Taken together, all meta-data forms a taxonomy. A specific piece of XBRL which contains data is called an instance.

A taxonomy classifies data in such a way that it can be standardized, shared and re-used across the actors involved in SBR. The data model for information exchange is laid down in a national taxonomy. Here, a taxonomy refers to a hierarchical structure separating data into specific classes of data based on common characteristics. The taxonomy represents a generic way to classify data to prove it is unique and without redundancy. This includes both primary and generated data elements. XBRL documents or instances are based on a specific taxonomy. The situation is often more complicated as there are often a set of taxonomies. A taxonomy is a kind of dictionary of terms and concepts, but goes beyond the functionalities of a single dictionary, as rules can be included. The rules can depict relationships between concepts and can be used for validation purposes. Taxonomies accept financial reporting standards, and allows automatic exchange and extraction of financial statements across heterogeneous technologies (Grey, 2005).

Financial reporting includes annual reports, SEC filings, reports from companies to investors, regulators, investors, and financial analysts, general ledger information and audit schedules.

Taxonomies go beyond traditional financial reporting and can include tax filing, chambers of commerce reports and so on. Taxonomies cannot be modified because other organizations are also using them; however, it is possible to extend the existing taxonomies. In this way supplements can be created for other purposes. Using these supplement organization are free to use XBRL for other purposes. The many elements are highly interconnected, which makes it difficult to change them like in other infrastructure's. "The individual elements are very interdependent, and their size and complexity make them extremely difficult to control and manage" (Hanseth, 2000, p. 56). This is true for the taxonomies, but also for the relationship with the other stakeholders.

The main component of the infrastructure is the gateway, which serves as an interface between citizen or company and public agencies. The gateway is a secured electronic postal service for business-to-government reporting. Businesses can provide their information and the gateway ensures that the information is validated and then distributed to the right public parties. In this way information can be provided once and can be provided to the relevant parties. The gateway confirms acknowledge safe receipt, yet, the gateway cannot confirm if all aspects are fulfilled. Using technology checks and controls are possible, but only the responsible public organization can only confirm if the data provided is suitable for their purposes. This infrastructure provides functionalities for identification and authentication, to establish secure connections, to provide reports and store them in a dependable way, and to receive a response whether the report is acceptable and validated according to the XBRL syntax. The gateway ensures that all submitted data is checked if they are well-formed, e.g., XBRL compliant, and validated, e.g., match the taxonomies. The gateway for sending XBRL reports to Dutch government agencies, like tax office, bureau of statistics and filing the annual financial statements. The gateway is built using open standards, in particular SOAP and web services for interface definitions, and Business Process Management Notation (BPMN) for process definitions (both manual and technical). The gateway also provides database functionality for storing, querying and retrieving messages, and for archiving.

TRANSFORMATION OF THE NETWORK STRUCTURES

Transformations in the Information Flows

The redesigned information exchange infrastructure for business-to-government reporting and the need to reduce the administrative burden, result in changes in the roles and functions of the actors in the network. Public organizations collaboratively define their information needs and standardize their efforts. Hence, they need to collaborate to architect the information taxonomy. This requires new ways of governance in which architect frequently communicate with each other and do understand each other situations and problems. Furthermore, decisions are made together instead of in isolation.

For private organizations, especially the role of financial intermediaries is subject to scrutiny. In the traditional situations companies hand in their data to the financial intermediary, this can be manually or providing their reports from the accounting systems. The financial intermediary ensures that the data is entered in the system, creates the various accountancy reports, checks the data and, if necessary, ensures that an audit is conducted before submitting the data to the public agencies. Using the XBRL-based infrastructure the creation of financial reports is done using an open standard. Consequently, organizations are able to innovate and new applications emerged as well as new organizations entered the market by developing and providing new services. Some software vendors are developing plug-ins in their

software to automatically submit the required data to the public agencies without involving intermediaries. They also include the option for including delegates; reports are automatically generated and companies and financial intermediaries can be added as delegates to audit data, which can be submitted afterwards. As such, some roles of the financial intermediaries become superfluous. Especially the data entry role is not necessary anymore and often the creation of financial reports is automatically done and only needs to be verified.

Transformations in the Regulatory and Auditing Approaches

This type of information exchange goes beyond the simple exchange between a company and many government agencies. Whereas in the past the focus was on traditional ways of reporting, the online and real-time availability of information creates the opportunity for new ways of ensuring compliance and auditing. System-based audits and continuous auditing are important developments resulting in transformation. *System-based auditing* (SB) refers to the situation that the company systems and the information stored in the system is audited instead of the reports. *Continuous auditing* (CA) refers to the situation that when information becomes available, the auditor must be positioned in such a way to provide written assurance simultaneously or shortly after the occurrence of relevant events. A company's information system provides the necessary information when changes happens and will be the subject of the audit (Alles, Kogan, & Vasarhelyi, 2008). In essence auditing becomes part of the operational processes of the companies. Auditing is not limited to the financial process and done by private organizations, as many public enforcement organizations conduct types of audits to determine whether or not companies comply with regulations.

Both in SB and CA there is a shift away from the traditional annually auditing which looks backwards based on some collected financial information. Instead, the operational processes and their supporting systems are subject of the auditing. The issues are fundamentally different form standard reporting (Alles et al., 2008). Using SBR and CA requires considerable transformation of the information delivery chain is necessary. The information and type of information of businesses should be delivered online using XBRL. For public and private organizations information becomes available in real-time and inspection and auditing practices will be changed. This requires considerable change in thinking and their practices.

DISCUSSION

Complexity of the Infrastructure

Complexity is coming from the exponential increase in the number of stakeholders using this infrastructure and the heterogeneity of included components, relationship, and their dynamic and unexpected interactions. The case involves millions of possible companies (users) and thousands of financial intermediaries, and many software developers and governmental organizations. The infrastructure development is a socio-technical endeavor in which technology development influence the roles of the stakeholders and result in a shift of the network. A condition is that the technical infrastructure needs to evolve allowing more types of information to be exchanged and to adapt to the changing roles of public and private stakeholders. Hence, the initial infrastructure was found to be different from the infrastructure at a later stage. This corresponds with two typical design problems of infrastructure; "the bootstrap problem: information infrastructures need to directly meet early users' needs in order to be initiated; and (2) the adaptability problem: local designs need to recognize unbounded scale and functional uncertainty" (Hanseth & Lyytinen, 2010, p. 1).

The development and design of the technical infrastructure requires the creation of a comprehensive, robust, secure, scalable and flexible system. The latter requires dealing with changes over time, as it is hard to predict how the final infrastructure should look like. From a social point of view, it requires organizing and involving heterogeneous actors with diverging interests. Designers have to come up early on with solutions that should persuade users to adopt and ensure a growing base of users. The volatility of developments has the consequence that the business case changed over time due to a change in legislation, a shift in the roles of actors and increasing insight about the potential and limitations of the technical infrastructure. During the infrastructure development, various initiatives should be fostered to ensure that a diversity of solutions is experimented with, whilst at a certain time these initiatives should converge to a single standard. Users and software providers are hesitant to adopt when there are not standards set providing a long term perspective. Their investment might not result in any value and new investments might be needed due to the changes. On the other side, a user community is necessary to help in selecting the initiatives and to learn from the experiences.

In the future all kinds of changes can be expected. The infrastructure is influences by all kind of factors and evolves over time. Changes in the existing infrastructure are influenced by the following factors.

- Updates of the international XBRL standard (new recommendations and versions);
- Changes in the taxonomies (regular releases, updates and extensions);
- New functionality and changes in the infrastructure functions (identification, authentication, validations, distribution etc.);
- Change in legislation resulting in the need to change reporting structures to ensure compliancy with laws.

Apart from these factors influencing the existing infrastructure, also the scope of the use of the infrastructure can be extended. This includes long-term developments like:

- The extensions of the domains supported; extending beyond the financial domains which generates the involvement of new stakeholders which provides its own dynamics and needs;
- New forms of continues and system-based auditing. Development of continuous auditing and change in positions of controls changes influence the way reporting is conducted.

The many stakeholders that are evolved with have different aims and goals and follow different directions influences the development of the infrastructure.

Adoption, Scaling and Flexibility

Like generic infrastructure complexity originates from the vast number of stakeholders involved, its openness evolves over time (see for example Hanseth, 1996). The initial borders have changed as the role of private parties (financial intermediaries) is affected. Also the functionality provided by the broker is affected due to new development and the rise of parties that can provide functionality. In addition, the interplay between which data, processes and technology complicates the infrastructure development. Although the layered nature enables the independent development, changes might influence and pose new requirements on the other layers.

Organizations involved in the development of the initial infrastructure are the frontrunners that might not represent all the other organizations. Hence, the design and use phase are disconnected and in the use phase a broader range of stakeholders is involved. Even though extensive standardiza-

tion efforts have taken place, new stakeholders might enter the arena that do not agree or might have other requirements. There is reason to create flexibility rather than to standardize on a single uniform solution. In an open infrastructure there are typically multiple solutions to satisfy the diversity of demands. The infrastructure exhibits openness as old components can be replaced and new components can be added and integrated with them. The infrastructure is both enabled and constrained by the installed base of users and by the physical components.

An important element of the openness of the infrastructure is that organizations can extend taxonomies freely. The main advantage is that it enables parties to enjoy the benefits that standardization and integration of information systems offers by implementing XBRL. The downside is that the diversity poses a risk to the current users and to the degree of standardization, as different taxonomies may, use different definitions and might not be interoperable. This might result into 'forking' in which different taxonomies are not able to be used in parallel resulting in the need for having higher investments and blocking the adoption as companies might be reluctant to adopt to something which might provide limited benefits and is subject to changes. In short, allowing different taxonomies to emerge may amount to short-term flexibility, but it may also lead to long-term problems of interoperability.

Collaboration with Software Vendors and Banks

Providing reporting information to the government requires modification in the applications used by the companies. In the infrastructure development a collaborative approach is taken to work with private organizations, predominantly commercial accounting software developers, accountants, payroll tax professionals and bookkeepers. This allows not only gaining their input, but helps the company to anticipate for changes in the infrastructure. Especially the software vendors play an important role, as when the infrastructures changes, there might also be changes necessary in the software.

A number of software vendors are in the process of enabling its software to allow their clients (the companies and the financial intermediaries) to communicate directly with the public organizations receiving financial reports. Many software companies, however, were initially hesitant to step in. They were afraid that they had to make too many changes to their software as there was no standard. This would result in the need to change regularly and making continuous investment resulting in less profit or even a loss. Hence, a certain level of maturity and stability of the infrastructure is required before software vendors supported the information exchange infrastructure. Therefore, more research on these types of factors is necessary to develop further understanding.

The banks developed their own taxonomy and process infrastructure independent on the pubic and infrastructure. Despite resulting in variety this was strongly supported as the exception was that "the adoption of XBRL by banks could function as a catalyst for the use of the XBRL-infrastructure for information exchanges with public organisations". This again shows the open nature and the need for flexibility to support a broader range of functionality than might initially be anticipated. Nevertheless the open nature results in diversity and slowed down the adoption by software vendors. As such, finding the right balance is essential.

CONCLUSION AND RECOMMENDATIONS

Companies exchange a plethora of information with government agencies and a common infrastructure can ensure a correct and reliable information exchange at low costs. The financial reporting infrastructure presented in the case study poses a set of unique challenges regarding its design, use and management. The introduction of the infrastructure has implications on the organization and relationships among public and private organizations. The increase of efficiency and effectively of the information exchange processes requires extensive transformation of the information exchange among these parties. Not only should public organizations collaborate with each other and coordinate their interactions, also the roles of private companies involved in the information exchange are shifting. Even regulatory and auditing roles and approaches are changing. Anticipating all the transformations at the beginning of the infrastructure development project is difficult, therefore the infrastructure should be able to adapt to changes which are not anticipated on from the start. This requires flexibility of the infrastructure to support a variety of options. Hence, such a public-private infrastructure should be designed as a shared, open, heterogeneous and evolving socio-technical system that is able to adapt and support various ways of information exchange.

Transformation and the infrastructure development is intertwined and complex as many stakeholders are involved. There are many forces influencing the development. Over time the roles of the organizations in the network have changed and new practices have been developed to take advantage of the new potential provided by the infrastructure. The development of the infrastructure requires trade-off between keeping options open to ensure flexibility and standardizing enabling the involvement of a large user base. In such an open infrastructure the involvement of users, financial intermediaries, software vendors and public organizations is essential as they are all affected by the infrastructure.

The understanding of the transformation of the infrastructure for facilitating information exchange is in its formative stages and more research is necessary on the various aspects. Further, the enabling and constraining role of the infrastructure should be analyzed in more detail. Transformations and the factors influencing the transformation are still largely unknown. Especially the interplay between social and technical aspects needs to be researched to provide guidance for further development.

ACKNOWLEDGMENT

This research was supported by the Standard Business Reporting Knowledge Dissemination program which is funded by Logius and the Dutch Ministry of the Interior and Kingdom Relations.

REFERENCES

Alles, M. G., Kogan, A., & Vasarhelyi, M. A. (2008). Putting continuous auditing theory into practice: Lessons from two pilot implementations. *Journal of Information Systems*, *22*(2), 195–214. doi:10.2308/jis.2008.22.2.195

Ciborra, C. U. (2000). A critical review of the literature on the management of corporate information infrastructures. In Ciborra, C. U. (Ed.), *From control to drift: The dynamics of corporate information infrastructures*. Oxford, UK: Oxford University Press.

Debreceny, R., Felden, C., Ochocki, B., Piechocki, M., & Piechocki, M. (2009). *XBRL for interactive data: Engineering the information value chain*. Berlin, Germany: Springer-Verlag. doi:10.1007/978-3-642-01437-6

Engel, P., Hamsher, W., & Walis, H. vun Kannon, D., & Shuetrim, G. (2003). *Extensible business reporting language (XBRL) -- Recommendation*. Retrieved from http://www.xbrl.org

Fountain, J. (2001). *Building the virtual state. Information technology and institutional change*. Washington, DC: Brookings Institution.

Gil-Garcia, R., Chengalur-Smith, I., & Duchessi, P. (2007). Collaborative e-Government: Impediments and benefits of information-sharing projects in the public sector. *European Journal of Information Systems*, *16*(2), 121–133. doi:10.1057/palgrave.ejis.3000673

Grey, G. L. (2005). *XBRL: Potential opportunities and issues for Internal Auditors*. Altamone Springs, FL: Institute of Internal Auditors Research Foundations (IIARF).

Hanseth, O. (2000). The economics of standards. In Ciborra, C. U. (Ed.), *From control to drift: The dynamics of corporate information infrastructures*. Oxford, UK: Oxford University Press.

Hanseth, O., & Lyytinen, K. (2010). Design theory for adaptive complexity in information infrastructures. *Journal of Information Technology*, *25*(1), 1–19. doi:10.1057/jit.2009.19

Hanseth, O., Monteiro, E., & Hatling, M. (1996). Developing information infrastructure: The tension between standardization and flexibility. *Science, Technology & Human Values*, *21*(4), 407–442. doi:10.1177/016224399602100402

Irani, Z., Elliman, T., & Jackson, P. (2007). Electronic transformation of government in the UK: A research agenda. *European Journal of Information Systems*, *16*(4), 327–335. doi:10.1057/palgrave.ejis.3000698

Janssen, M., Chun, S. A., & Gil-Garcia, J. R. (2009). Building the next generation of digital government infrastructures. *Government Information Quarterly*, *26*(2), 233–237. doi:10.1016/j.giq.2008.12.006

Kim, H., Pan, G., & Pan, S. (2007). Managing IT-enabled transformation in the public sector: A case study on e-government in South Korea. *Government Information Quarterly*, *24*, 338–352. doi:10.1016/j.giq.2006.09.007

Murphy, J. (2005). *Beyond e-government the world's most successful technology-enabled transformations, executive summary*. New York, NY: INSEAD.

Orlikowski, W., & Lacono, S. (2001). Desperately seeking the "IT" in IT research-A call to theorizing the IT artifact. *Information Systems Research*, *12*(2), 121–134. doi:10.1287/isre.12.2.121.9700

Ostrom, E., Gardner, R., & Walker, J. (1994). *Rules, games and common-pool resources*. Ann Arbor, MI: University of Michigan Press.

Resnick, P., Zeckhauser, R., & Avery, C. (1995). *Roles for electronic broker*. Mahwah, NJ: Lawrence Erlbaum.

Sarbanes-Oxley. (2002). *Act of 2002*. Retrieved from http://www.soxlaw.com/index.htm

Sarkar, M. B., Butler, B., & Steinfield, C. (1995). Intermediaries and cybermediaries: A continuing role for mediating players in the electronic marketplace. *Journal of Computer-Mediated Communication*, *1*(3).

Spies, M. (2010). An ontology modelling perspective on business reporting. *Information Systems*, *35*, 404–416. doi:10.1016/j.is.2008.12.003

Weerakkody, V., & Dhillon, G. (2008). Moving from e-government to t-government: A study of process re-engineering challenges in a UK local authority perspective. *International Journal of Electronic Government Research*, *4*(4), 1–16. doi:10.4018/jegr.2008100101

Weerakkody, V., Janssen, M., & Dwivedi, Y. K. (2011). Transformational change and business process reengineering (BPR): Lessons from the British and Dutch public sector. *Government Information Quarterly*, *28*(3), 320–328. doi:10.1016/j.giq.2010.07.010

Yin, R. (2009). *Case study research: Design and methods* (4th ed.). Thousand Oaks, CA: Sage.

This work was previously published in the International Journal of Electronic Government Research, Volume 7, Issue 4, edited by Vishanth Weerakkody, pp. 35-45, copyright 2011 by IGI Publishing (an imprint of IGI Global).

Chapter 20

What Drives a Successful Technology Implementation?
Exploring Drivers and Challenges of RFID Systems Implementation in a Public Sector Organisation

Kawal Kapoor
Swansea University, UK

Michael D. Williams
Swansea University, UK

Yogesh K. Dwivedi
Swansea University, UK

Mohini Singh
RMIT University, Australia

Mark J. Hughes
Swansea University, UK

ABSTRACT

Radio Frequency Identification (RFID) is revolutionizing item identification and tracking. The technology demonstrates complexities in terms of (a) huge initial capital investment, (b) validating the need for RFID followed by its implementation decisions, (c) risks associated with consumer acceptance and consequences of incorrect implementation, and (d) capability to support enhancements and upgrades in cordial agreement with the individual implementer organizations. This paper explores the extent of RFID implementation at the Swansea University Library, examining the Social, Technological, Economic, and Managerial (STEM) aspects directly associated with implementation. A focused interview approach was resorted to, for data collection purposes. The core implementation team for RFID at Swansea University was interviewed to gain insights into the study's areas of interest. It was found that self service is the most sought after benefit. It simplifies stock management and enhances security at the libraries. Although the cost of the system remains a concern, varying on the basis of the scale of implementation, vandalism also continues to exist but to a reduced degree. University libraries are public sector organizations, consequently leading these findings to have an insinuation for RFID implementations in other public sector organizations as well.

DOI: 10.4018/978-1-4666-2458-0.ch020

INTRODUCTION

RFID sought introduction by Harry Stockman in 1948 in his milestone report "Communication by Means of Reflected Power" (Stockman, 1948). RFID refers to the technology of reading and writing data remotely using radio waves. RFID found its first ever application in the Royal British Air Force's *Identify Friend or Foe* system which now finds its use across a wide range of utilities (Hicks, 1999). Roberts (2006), describes RFID as one of the most pervasive computing technology acquiring momentum as an electromagnetic proximity identification and data transaction system. RFID is becoming a powerful technology enabling industries achieve total business visibility whilst optimizing business processes & minimizing operational costs (Fleisch & Tellkamp, 2005). Despite new entrants, RFID succeeds to be found almost everywhere, from automated toll taking for speeding vehicles to access cards that now have been made a norm to gain access into office buildings (Landt, 2005). Daily streams witness RFID assisting in preventing thievery of goods & automobiles, traffic control, automated management of parking areas & vehicle access control, business campuses and airports, ski lifting, supply chain management and more (Juban & Wyld, 2004; Reyes & Frazier, 2007). Farms use tags to keep a track of their animals & the warehouses tag their goods to better manage inventory (Want, 2004). The food Drug Administration is using RFID to identify drugs and thwart counterfeiting & DVD's also are carrying these tags to prevent movie piracy (O'Conner, 2005).

Although RFID proves to bring in numerous benefits, its implementation is not a simple task. The technology has its own complexities in terms of – (1) huge initial investment involved in the set-up and infrastructure, the economic aspect (2) ascertaining the need for RFID and validation of the implementation decisions by the implementation managers, the technical aspect (3) backfire effects both in the case of consumer acceptance and risks associated with the wrong implementation, the social aspect (4) ability to make most of the technology with enhancements and upgrades along with the steady organizational support, the managerial aspect. The library at Swansea University is a classic example of a *successful implementation* of RFID. It was thought of as a prospective opportunity to learn and better understand the importance of deploying such technologies in an academic set-up as vast as theirs. This paper is to explore the extent of implementation of RFID systems at the Swansea University Library to better understand the augmentation RFID is capable of providing at an academic library, whilst trying to examine the - Social, Technological, Economic, and Managerial, i.e. the *STEM* aspects directly associated with the implementation of RFID at the university library. This will be essentially aimed at an empirical examination of available literature & its subsequent comparison to real time findings at the Swansea University Library in implementing RFID within their library management system.

The paper is structured in a manner as exemplified; the structure will be articulated across diversified sections. The next section will concentrate on presenting a review of available literature on earlier implementations of RFID to explore its application areas along with the comprehensive analysis of the benefits and caveats associated with the technology. This will be followed by an account of the adopted research methodology. The quantitative findings will then be documented which will be followed by the discussion of the STEM aspects probed into, on the basis of literature review, personal interviews, informal discussions, and review sessions- all of which will be carried out with respect to the library at Swansea University. The study will near closure with the recommendations presented in direct relation with the collected data. Finally, the conclusions for the study will be effectively deduced.

LITERATURE REVIEW

The increasing accessibility of RFID technology offers many prospects to improve business processes (Lee & Ozer, 2007). It has the potential to be an enterprise wide technology with inter-organizational implications in the same vein as the internet and networked PCs (Roh *et al.*, 2009). Over the last years, RFID has been a topic frequently discussed in companies, academia, media, journals and conference proceedings (Irani *et al.*, 2010 & Ngai *et al.*, 2008). One reason for such interest is the possible strategic value of this technology (Pedroso *et al.*, 2009). Use of RFID in tracking and accessing applications first surfaced during the 1980s (Landt, 2005). RFID tags can be found almost everywhere, from books, goods, grocery items to automobiles and even underneath human skin (Chen *et al.*, 2010; Lee *et al.*, 2007 & Tu *et al.*, 2005). Singapore, a pioneer in RFID technology has been the first country in the world to implement RFID systems across all of its 21 public libraries (Ayre, 2004). The extensive application of RFID can result in significant savings in labor costs, enhance customer service, reduce vandalism and provide an updated track of media collections (Erwin *et al.*, 2003). According to Coyle 2005), RFID will allow libraries to upgrade their functions with increased efficiency. Firms may need to upgrade their existing applications and invest in new hardware and software, to aggregate & filter the data generated by RFID (Kohn *et al.*, 2005). The RFID technology has contributed for improvements in various competitive operational capabilities; quality assurance, improved customer service, speed, high read rates, flexibility and more (Kumar *et al.*, 2009; Lee *et al.*, 2009; Tesoriero *et al.*, 2010 & Wen, 2010). Most conveniently, the information stored on the tag can be updated on demand (Roberts, 2006).

Deploying RFID within the inventory systems facilitates efficient tracking of in-library use of materials, easy finding of reservation items, weeding the collection, checking the shelf order and

increase in savings (Boss, 2006). Inventory that previously took weeks/months to be completed can now been shortened to hours with RFID (Bansode & Desale, 2009). RFID also allows for automated material handling which leads to better administration of peak return volumes (Molnar and Wagner, 2004). The RFID tags are *durable* and last longer (Yu, 2007). The read ranges are also longer and reliability much higher while operating in harsh environments (Sorensen *et al.*, 2010). Roberts (2006) views cost of the tags as a major constraint in the widespread use of RFID. Cost, which over the last decade was a barrier, is now abating with a gradual fall in the prices of the technology's components attributed to an increase in the demand for the technology. Kumar *et al.* (2009) in their paper explain that the prying with metal and high liquid content affects reliable reads. Another common concern with RFID is a lack of standardization. Middleware design is yet another challenge that most RFID implementations face. Chen *et al.* (2010) while discussing the design issues for RFID systems show the need for a middleware design to integrate the RFID system with the other systems.

Exit gate sensors pose problems reading multiple items causing declining responsiveness and accuracy. As Smart and Schaper (2004) explain, this degradation will be apparent when there are five or more tags. Vandalism is an added problem. As mentioned by Coyle (2005), despite much care being taken in tagging the items, vandals succeed in identifying these tags to rip them off the item and disable the RFID transponders. RFID has remained entitled to much attention in recent years. As Atkinson (2004) states, an ever greater concern is that, should RFID tags become truly ubiquitous, embedded in virtually all consumer products. According to Edwards and Fortune (2008), RFID tags in the UK libraries are passive in nature and there is almost no problem with data privacy as the data protection laws are well understood and most RFID tags only contain information about the book. The recycling of paper, metal, plastic, glass and others may be hindered by the adhesives, metal pieces used in antennae, computer chips, and the conductive inks within RFID tags. As Kumar *et al.* (2009) mention, these can induce certain contaminations which can alter the properties of the materials being recycled. User resistance commonly surfaces by the apprehensions built by the users. The staff generally retaliates on the basis of the idea that RFID systems are deployed to basically replace human involvement. From the customer point of view, the resistance primarily comes from the idea that their privacy might be at stake. Creusen *et al.* (2009) insist that the consumer attitude towards the technology impacts its usage and adoption.

This section will focus on envisaging the benefits and challenges for RFID implementation, in the Swansea University Library context. This library houses and manages academic collections. RFID deployment at such an extensive academic house of collections can yield major benefits and ease out many day to day operations. Since this report revolves around the STEM aspects of the implementation, both the benefits and challenges will be conceived under these aspects for conceptualizing purposes.

The Social Facet

With RFID at the library, there will be a reduction in labor in terms of inventory management and issue/service desk operations. This in effect will contribute towards reduced staff injury and lesser human involvement. From the challenges point of view, a key concern is of privacy & security. This will remain valid in case of the student/staff cards being used in the library carrying any personal information or bank details which may be subject to the risk of misuse. Since libraries encourage cross borrowing and other collaborative services amongst libraries, standardization automatically becomes a critical requisite to be enforced. Lastly, customer acceptance can become an alarming subject. It is necessary to ensure that the users at

the library are well informed and effectively assisted to be gradually acquainted with the systems.

The Technological Facet

Owing to the continuous circulation at an academic library, such a deployment will visibly introduce simplicity in the check-in and check-out operations with self-issue/return terminals. By bringing in automation, the need of staff at desks will be eliminated making them available for other floor requirements, resulting in an increase in their overall efficiency. Inventory management will also see minimized efforts. Tracing of missing and lost items will become a lot easier. There will be increased inventory visibility helping in better management of stock-out conditions. The ability of the RFID readers to capture multiple tag information will improve the response time and lead to reducing cycle times. The fact that these systems do not require any line of sight makes them convenient, efficient, and very practical in a library context.

The Economical Facet

At a library as big as Swansea University Library, this implementation should earn cost effective benefits and outweigh the most critiqued economical aspects which are, the high equipment costs and investments involved with its implementation. These equipments come with a longer lifetime and will work out to be a feasible option with the library's functional requirements. These systems are low maintenance gadgets and should fit well with the library's management systems in the long run.

The Managerial Facet

The most frequently anticipated resistance from the staff may have to be carefully handled to fully appreciate the revenues from the implementation. Staff support is critical and only effectual management will be capable of winning their coordination. RFID can help the library better manage the available capacity and assist in its future plans for capacity expansion if desired. For a proficient system it will be deemed vital to lucratively incorporate the middleware design in a manner that will amplify the performance of these automated systems. The other challenges to be battled will be vandalism, theft and counterfeit. RFID, to an appreciable extent will shield against them but it is also important to bear in mind that although there is less scope for these to be completely eradicated.

All the benefits will come with a package of associated caveats. Despite the challenges in the implementation of a technology such as RFID in the Swansea University Library, it is highly anticipated that the benefits yielded will positively overshadow the caveats and prove to be an efficient and worthwhile arrangement implemented for an able and proficient library management system.

RESEARCH METHOD

According to Newman and Benz (1998), the *qualitative method* is a naturalistic approach which is used while examining and inferring actuality to develop a theory explaining what was experienced. The qualitative methods have advantage, in that they allow for data to be collected from a small group. This served best for the present scenario where only two members from the staff were available for interview purposes. Denzin and Lincoln (2005), describe qualitative research as a field of inquiry that runs across disciplines, fields and subject matters. From the study's perspective, an Interview approach was reckoned as the appropriate choice. Kvale (1983) describes Qualitative research interview as "an interview, whose purpose is to gather descriptions of the life-world of the interviewee with respect to interpretation of the meaning of the described phenomena" (p.

174). Britten (1995) explains that there are three major kinds of interviews – (1) *structured* (2) *semi-structured* (3) *in-depth*. A combination of *semi-structured & in-depth interviews* will be used for this report. *Face-to-Face Interviews* are characterized by synchronous communication in time and place. According to Opdenakker (2006), they have an advantage of social cues such as the interviewee's voice, tone and body language which provide the interviewer with added information that compounds the vocal answer of the interviewee for a question. These interviews upon permission can also be tape or video recorded for better interpretation post interview.

Data Collection

- **Scenario:** To learn the RFID implementation at an academic library whilst exploring the associated STEM aspects, it was obligatory to access information from reliable and authentic sources having a firsthand experience with the implementation of the technology at the university library.
- **Target Source:** The planning and implementation team was thought of as the most appropriate source of the information required for the study.
- **Method Formulation:** To successfully accumulate the required information, it was important to interact with the people involved in the implementation which allowed to ask questions, seek answers, and encourage discussion in an *information sharing* kind of environment for which the face-to-face interview was found best suited.
- **Brief:** When the core planning and implementation team at the Swansea University Library was contacted, it was intimated that two members, i.e., the project manager and the project officer of the implementation team would be available for discus-

sion purposes. It was decided that multiple interviews will be conducted. The progress of the report was considered as a base for designing the stages across which the interviews were to be scheduled. These progress points were marked as illustrated.

Phase I: Semi-Structured Interview

(Interview Duration – 60 Minutes)

This was a kick-off interview and being semi-structured in nature, it was expected to encourage an open ended discussion with the team to gain insight into what the library features in terms of RFID as a technology. In its initial stage, the interview was directed towards familiarizing the team with the purpose of the study and obtaining their inputs on the relevance of the topic of study. Having established the association, the interview progressed with a broad introduction to RFID integration with the library management system, which was consequently followed by questions to the team. Both, the questions asked during the interview and the information shared by the team were on a higher level.

Phase II: In-Depth Interview

(Interview Duration – 90 Minutes)

The second round of interview was planned after the completion of literature review for the study. It was critical from the study point of view to achieve a direct relation between the existing literature and the practical findings from the study. Having documented the relevant literature, the interview was conducted along the lines of the collected facts. This time the interview was more structured, with more direct questions from the researcher. It served as an access to the typical facts and figures which were aimed at.

Both the interviews were *manually recorded (note taking)* for future analysis purposes.

FINDINGS

Background to RFID Project at Swansea University Library

As a part of the South West Wales Higher Education Partnership (SWWHEP) Library Services - Swansea University, Swansea Metropolitan University and Trinity College Carmarthen collaborated to create a Virtual Academic Library. This project was funded by the Higher Education Funding Council for Wales (HEFCW) Reconfiguration and Collaboration Fund. The Virtual Academic Library project was initiated as a three-year long project with a budget of over £1 million. This project is considered to be one of the biggest projects in Wales and one of the biggest in the UK. The entire implementation process ran over a period of about 13 months, a brief calendar record of which is captured in Table 1.

This project was designed for the 17,000 higher education students and 1,200 academic staff in South West Wales. Table 2 has been constructed to provide an overview of the extensive tagging that took place under this project.

This paper will in specific detail concentrate on the RFID implementation at the library in Swansea University. The Swansea University library houses a stock of about 800,000 items, all of which are tagged. There are about 100,000-120,000 low circulated items which upon request

Table 1. Record of calendar time

Dates/Period	Events
September 2007	Funding Awarded
September 2007 - February 2008	Staff Recruitment
Late April 2008	Tender Issued
July 2008	Tender Awarded
Late August 2009	Go Live (RFID Implementation marked Completed)

Table 2. Record of tagged items

Library	Books / Journals	CD's / DVD's	Videos	Audio Cassettes
Swansea University	800,000	3000	2000	200
Swansea Metropolitan University	315,000	1500	1500	-
Trinity College Carmarthen	160,000	2500	2200	400

or call are tagged then and there before being issued at the issue desk.

The tags used in the library are passive in nature. The entire tagging effort was split over two groups across the day. The tagging staff was employed to work only part time each day to help maintain concentration levels and avoid errors from surfacing due to long tagging hours. Tagging time was uneven. It varied depending upon the type of stock, distance from shelves, time of tagging during the day, the people involved in tagging and so on. It took 12 months to complete tagging all items. It was a record when a team alone completed tagging 2560 in a day. An average of 1000 items per day, per team, was tagged. In total, 3000-5000 items a day were successfully tagged.

Why Radio Frequency Identification?

The team at Swansea University deployed RFID systems seeking an explicit set of benefits and outcomes. It was divulged in the interviews that, in return for the initial capital investment, the project with RFID aspired to; revolutionize services, ensure effective collaboration and produce significant long term cost savings and bring about enhancements in the following areas:

- **Cross Borrowing:** To facilitate a common method of borrowing for across all three educational institutions.
- **Circulation:** Self-issue/return would become a much simpler and faster task with RFID. Up to 10 items can be issued concurrently, without the need to scan individual barcodes. Also RFID does not require *line of sight*, which would mean that the

books need not be opened or positioned in any specific manner.

- **Free Staff Time:** To relieve staff time away from the issue desk duties (Items Issue and Return) for engagement in other tasks and responsibilities. This will also save staff costs at the desk and release library staff from routine tasks to provide more direct help to the patrons.
- **Stock Management and Control:** To better manage collections, easily track misshelved/lost/hidden items, simplify stock checks and the process of moving items across locations while facilitating collaborative efforts.

With RFID in service, the library gained much more. While interviewing, a list of benefits were proposed to be weighed in correlation to the RFID implementation at the Swansea University Library. All the benefits accumulated via literature were then justified for a real-time successfully implemented project in a brief manner which will be showcased in the following sections.

Model of Implementation

The implementation team followed no specific model of implementation. The basis of this implementation process lies within the many *Best Practices Visits* to the libraries that already have successfully implemented RFID systems, coupled with experience & extensive communication with the relevant experts in the RFID industry. There was no formal cost-benefit analysis conducted either. A convincing rationale was initially introduced in the bid to justify the need for and benefits that could be yielded with the integration of RFID with the library management systems.

RFID Machinery in House

The Swansea University Library at present houses the listed set of RFID specific machinery,

1. **Automated Sorter:** Sorters (Figure 1) introduce automatic material handling by allowing for automatic shifting and sorting of items in the correct bins for re-shelving.
2. **Self-Service Units:** These automated units (Figure 2) allow patrons to issue and return books themselves without any need for physical staff
3. **Security Gates:** Security gates (Figure 3) incorporate sensors meant for detecting if the items being moved out of the library have been appropriately checked out or not.
4. **Stock Wand:** Stock wand (Figure 4) is used to read the books sitting on the shelves dur-

ing stock management without having to remove or orient them at specific angles.

In the near future they plan to install promotional wall displays, popularly called '*Wonder-Wall*' and also bring in the self fine payment machines.

Costs

Attributing to confidentiality, the costs that the team revealed are not the precise figures but an approximate estimate (Table 3). (Some of the figures may not reflect the current price trends but would be in relation to the prices in 2007, when the university began the RFID implementation process.)

According to the team, the book tags were priced at about 12-15p per tag while the AV tags get slightly more expensive. The self service terminals massively vary depending on the scale of requirement and specification of the unit. These prices also fluctuate from supplier to supplier.

Figure 1. Automated sorter

Figure 2. Self service units

Figure 3. Security gates

Figure 4. Stock wand

The maintenance costs are more or less similar to the previously deployed electromagnetic systems. The team sees this cost to be very reasonable and reveal that maintenance costs are expected to work out at five percent of the purchase cost each year. Additional costs were incurred for technical training in managing the systems which was nominal, and also while engaging temporary staff for tagging purposes.

Open RFID in Libraries Specification, ORILS

The main staff behind RFID implementation at university library sees the most critical reason for flaws in RFID implementation efforts across libraries as, a simple case of *misunderstanding* in *what the libraries aim to achieve* and *what technology they end up purchasing* which effectively occurs at the specification point during the procurement process. He goes on to explain that such issues in general have been addressed by the recommended checklist of standard specifications like the *UK Core Specification* (UKCS). However the *Virtual Academic Library Project* (VALP) team had a functional specification for RFID in place used for their procurement process in 2008, which

a handful of suppliers and industry analysts saw as the most comprehensive until date. Following which, in February 2009 ORILS came into existence from the work undertaken by *VALP* for the South West Wales Higher Education Partnership (SWWHEP).

ORILS was released under a Creative Commons 'Share A Like' license, with a website / google group. Feedback from both the group and RFID suppliers indicate that ORILS standard has formed either part or all of a specification in almost 12 procurements across the UK since its release. To date the ORILS spec is due a set of revisions

Table 3. Record of involved costs

ARTICLE	COST (Per Article)
Book Tag	12p-15p
AV Tag	£1.50
Security Gate	£4500-£5000
Staff Station	£1000-£2000
Self Service Terminal	£9000-£15000
Stock Wand	£4000
Automated Sorter	3 way- £35000-£40000 5 way- £70000+
Maintenance	Discussed Below
Tagging	Discussed Below

for 2011 as a part of its possible adoption by the National Acquisitions Group (NAG) as the official library recommended standard for the UK.

Actualizing Benefits

Automation/Reduces Labor/ Eliminates Human Errors

The most evident feature of RFID is automation. With the deployment of Self-Issue/Return terminals, the library savored the benefits of automation. This service reduces the staff work at the issue desks as most of their work is now shifted to the patrons. Human involvement always carries a scope of introducing errors, which were seen to be considerably reduced with the launch of RFID systems.

Capacity Expansion

The installed RFID systems have contributed to capacity expansion by easing out congestion and making management and location of lost, misplaced and requested items effortless and much quicker. Swansea university library is the longest opening academic library in Wales.

Cost Effectiveness/Inexpensive

The implementation team definitely does not consider the RFID implementation and its components cheap to buy. However they see it to be extremely cost effective. The staff release at the library desks, added staff time available to be expended in other work demanding areas, efficient inventory management, automation and more lead to effectual cost. This effectiveness is definitely not evident in the first year of implementation but over a period of time, i.e. 3-5 years the entire RFID system almost becomes self financing.

Easy and Low Maintenance

There were very few instances of downtime at the library. The self sorters experienced a minor breakdown. There were only two occasions when the engineer had to be brought in to fix the interruption. In both cases, the recorded lost time was not more than 30 minutes. Hence these systems are deemed low maintenance systems.

Enhanced Customer Satisfaction

The customer here will be the students and staff using the RFID enabled services. The students find it convenient to use the self service terminals in comparison to tolerating waiting times for service at library desks. Staff on the other hand will be relieved of attending increased number of students, rigorous desk services and extensive effort with inventory and item management.

Inventory Tracking and Visibility

Inventory management has become a lot more efficient and less time consuming. The library saw a drastic reduction in the time taken to effortlessly locate the misplaced and lost items which can also be easily recognized and new items for replacement can be ordered and restocked well in time. The team shared that there has been no inventory done in the last 15 years. When asked to provide an approximate estimate for doing a full inventory for the library, with RFID it was reported that the entire library could be done within 2 weeks and with a single staff member.

Reduces Theft and Counterfeiting

The team agrees on this capability of the RFID systems to aid reduction in theft. The library enjoys the secure system of keeping a check on the items moving in and out of the library. Since there never had been a count of what was lost before and neither has there been a check on the rate of lost items at present, there are no figures to substantially justify this benefit on papers.

Reduction of Staff Injury

Staff injury was never a problem in the Swansea University Library. Thus reduction in staff injury cannot be appreciated much as an RFID instilled benefit within this library. Although, the library evaluates this factor more in terms of reducing the risk if repetitive staff injury at the library with the aid of RFID systems.

Enables Self Service

Self service is one of the most prominent features of the Swansea University Library. There are three self-issue terminals and one self-return terminal installed shifting most work from library staff to patrons.

No Line Of Sight Required

The readers capture data from the tagged items without the need of any line of read.

Longer Lifetime

The team expects the life span of tags to be around 15-20 years. The other equipments on the other hand, given regular maintenance are expected to operate over a period of 7-10 years.

Facilitates Communication with Multiple Tags Simultaneously

The readers capture up to ten items in one issue transaction justifying the ability of the RFID readers to read multiple tags simultaneously.

Cycle Time Reduction

The 'multiple-tag read' ability results in cycle time reduction.

Substantiating Challenges

Cost

According to the team, cost although reducing by the day, is not cheap in terms of capital investment and continues to be a challenge.

Middleware Design

One of staff interviewed explains that "The RFID software communicates data about borrower and item to the LMS via SIP2, and the transactions are actually processed by the LMS before passing back confirmation information which the RFID system then displays on screen for the borrower." These systems have to be SIP2 protocol compliant which provides the standard for communications between the RFID and library systems. SIP2, Standard Interchange Protocol – Version 2 is a recognized international standard, incorporation and management of which can be viewed as a challenge.

Perpendicular Orientation of the Tag / Large Number of Tagged Objects Randomly Placed

The orientation factor does not pose much of a challenge. To safeguard items from vandals, the university library places multiple tags within its items. In case of a vandal succeeding in tampering a tag in the item, the other tags placed elsewhere will trick the tampering and the security systems upon exit will detect if the item is being exited without being properly checked out. The problem of the tag orientation arises when two tags are placed or situated over one another which in effect can lead to faulty detection and thus care is taken to avoid such placements.

Standardization

This challenge affects the 'Interlibrary Loans' amongst the various library systems and the 'Interoperability' between supplier and hardware. This essentially asks for the software/hardware vendors of the library RFID systems to deliver standardized products. The specific areas of concentration were of, communication standards (ISO 15693 & ISO 18000-3) for tags and that of the data to be written on these tags. While the challenge remained, ISO 28560 was brought in frame to enhance the quintessence of RFID in libraries. Since Swansea University, Swansea Metropolitan University and Trinity College Carmarthen together allow their patrons to enjoy cross borrowing, standardization was dealt with as a challenge during the implementation process.

Managerial Issues/Staff and User Resistance/Customer Acceptance

The University handled these issues well and escaped hindrances from the managerial aspect. There was no need for change in any policy and hence no changes were introduced. Staff resistance could have been a problem but the implementation team took measures well ahead in the planning stage by encouraging staff involvement in the implementation process. Replacement of staff with this technology was never an agenda for the core team at the Swansea University. The staff accompanied the core team at demonstrations of already installed RFID systems where they had all their queries answered. These visits helped the staff capture the real idea behind bringing in the RFID systems at the Swansea University Library. The library observed that there are always a percentage of people who are either not comfortable or by choice do not prefer to use the self service terminals. To serve this particular population of

users a certain proportion of staff will be retained at the circulation points.

Vandalism

There were a couple of incidents where the staff located meddled tags disposed inside the library. In any case, it is impossible for these tags to go out of the library as the security gates will have the alarms go on upon detection. Such disposed tags can then at least be used to read which item was manhandled and the replacements can within no time be ordered. However care is taken to cautiously place the tags in a manner unidentifiable to patrons and as already mentioned sometimes by multi tagging a single item, the vandals are tricked.

Privacy and Security

The team shared that privacy and security are a big issue in the United States. However, this has not yet affected the UK with the same intensity. As far as the library is concerned, the tags here do not carry any personal information or any information whatsoever which can be directly identifiable without reference to another highly secure system.

Recycling

The team does not fully consider this as a challenge.

Liability and Effectiveness

While the library awards the liability of RFID systems a 10 on 10, effectiveness scores an 8 on 10, the reason being that, the library sees improvement – in contributing towards increasing the effectiveness with the self service terminals. The plan is to make staff more readily available around the self terminals to assist users in case of problems encountered, in either using them or to help new users to familiarize with these systems.

The idea is to have staff accessible for both support and to encourage patrons to use these terminals.

The annual Library & Information Services Survey, 2010 disclosed that, the RFID enabled *Self-Issue & Self-Return* was the highly ranked service with 68.6% of respondents in favor of it as the most satisfactory service, making it the most popular library service for 2010.

Recommendations from the Project Team

Project manager who led RFID at the Virtual Academic Library Project, when asked provided a list of recommendations for libraries considering RFID implementation

- Do the much essential pre-project research. Do not rely on just any report available in the market. Research is crucial – No skimping affordable here.
- Management and staffing issues need to be well managed and taken care of to avoid any undesirable holds.
- It is equally important to have your end users well informed about the technology.
- RFID in most libraries see implementation by the professional techies while it might be of much worth to involve your own people and staff in the implementation process. "It's about people management & library processes much more than technology basically."
- RFID definitely is a 'Value for Money' investment.
- RFID allows for operations which were not in place earlier.
- It is critical that the idea behind doing it, which is implementing RFID, is absolutely clear before doing it i.e. "to know why you are implementing RFID is the critical bit of planning as without that guiding principle error will occur."

DISCUSSION AND RECOMMENDATIONS

This piece of discussion will concentrate on a direct comparison of literature review with the compilation of results from both qualitative and quantitative research instruments. The application in focus for the study being libraries, finds enormous amount of literary work available. The unanimously mentioned benefit in almost all research papers is that of *Self Service* (Ayre, 2005; Engel, 2006 & Hicks, 1999) which also finds relevance as one of the chief motives at our study source i.e., the library at Swansea University which has self-issue/return terminals installed to enable self service and free staff time from the issue desks for engagement in other tasks. Another benefit which most libraries seek with RFID is the *Stock Management* (Boss, 2006 & Erwin *et al.*, 2003). The interviews revealed that the library aimed at superior stock management and control with RFID for easily tracing lost/ mis-shelved items, stock checks and moving items across facilities. Literature shows that *Cost* continues to remain an issue of concern for most implementers (Kumar *et al.*, 2009 & Roberts, 2006). As scripted previously, the implementation team agrees with the fact and presents a strong consent on the view that the RFID technology along with its components is not a cheap buy. It cannot be denied that the market today is seeing reducing prices pertinent to the technology, yet the decline in prices is not to an extent that can be affordable by all aspirants of the technology (Abad *et al.*, 2009). However both literature and interviews have a like opinion that the investment works out feasible in the long run over the years. The other most challenged caveats according to the literature are *Privacy & Security* (Roberts, 2006 & Erwin *et al.*, 2003). However, this controversial issue was deemed irrelevant from the Swansea University perspective for now as the library cards do not carry patron specific personal information that can be subject to any malice whatsoever. Where literature shows that

Managerial Issues in terms of *Staff Resistance* surfaces in nearly every RFID implementation case (Pramatari & Theotokis, 2009), the case of resistance was very well handled at the university library. The management took measures ahead in time with as much staff involvement in the implementation process to arrest the possibilities of resistance. Escaping *Vandalism* is universally most sought after by the libraries. The literature provides no strong evidence of succeeding in complete removal of this attribute with RFID (Coyle, 2005; Engel, 2006 & Kern, 2004). Likewise, the Swansea Library divulges a diminution in vandalized cases but at the same time there are no figures recorded by the library to provide an exact estimate of the decrease in the theft rate.

Given the benefits that RFID has to offer and importantly the associated costs, it becomes important to streamline the *upgrades* that are being aimed at, to ensure successful implementation of the desired equipments suited for the upgrade. In summary, the management should have an unambiguous implementation plan with a complete assessment of the specific set of benefits being aimed at with this integration.

A *cost-benefit analysis* will have to be carried out to make certain if the integration plan is worthwhile. Not necessarily will all implementation platforms find the RFID costs affordable. The tag costs and related equipment expenditure still are issues of concern (Abad *et al.*, 2009; Kumar *et al.*, 2009). However, the benefits yielded in a couple of years from the implementation apparently prove be noteworthy and add value to the system.

Staff resistance is an expected phenomenon with almost every RFID implementation process (Coyle, 2005; Kern, 2004; Hildner, 2006; Pramatari & Theotokis, 2009). To effectively manage the staff apprehension is a critical managerial task. As suggested in the interview with the core implementation team at Swansea University Library, the best way to avoid staff resistance would be to actively involve the staff in the implementation process and communicate to them through different possible ways that RFID is a service enhancement strategy and not a staff replacement strategy.

CONCLUSION

Acknowledged literary records were picked and compiled together in a sequential manner under exclusive sections as a representative of established mark that RFID has achieved with its numerous applications. Along with the bestowed benefits that the technology renders, its challenges were also addressed. Some of the key conclusions can be listed as follows:

- RFID is the most sought after modern day implementation for libraries.
- Although the initial equipment costs are high, the benefits yielded by the technology in the longer run bring in higher returns making it a worthwhile investment.
- Issue/Return of books and Stock Management in libraries has been made a lot easier with the introduction of RFID.
- Staff management, security and privacy continue to remain issues of concern but to a reduced degree than without RFID.

Every research study bears limitations and so does this study in terms of the reach of this study. The study could have borne more generalized results, had it widened its scope over more libraries than just one academic library. From a futuristic perspective, an enhancement would mean spreading the research even wider taking into account an increased number of libraries within a single study. This would aid in comparing and contrasting the findings from different institutional implementations to arrive at more clear and valid set of possibilities that may occur in future implementation cases with an aim to prepare the implementers of those possible occurrences.

The face-to-face interviews conducted involved only two members from the core implementation team. An increased number of participants in the interviews may have revealed a wider range of perspectives and could have led to a broad information collection source. It would also have been a good idea to involve the staff members in the interview to accumulate data from the managerial perspective. Other target interviewees whose contribution could have enhanced the qualitative data quality would have been the members involved in tagging, the maintenance team and the stock management team.

This paper can prove to be a *handy reference for future academic work* in the RFID arena as well as, serve as a *knowledge transferable document* for introducing this technology for a population new to RFID or for those at a beginner level.

REFERENCES

Abad, E., Palacio, F., Nuin, M., de Zarate, A. G., Juarros, A., & Gomez, J. M. (2009). RFID smart tag for traceability and cold chain monitoring of foods: Demonstration in an intercontinental fresh fish logistic chain. *Journal of Food Engineering, 93*(4), 394–399. doi:10.1016/j.jfoodeng.2009.02.004

Atkinson, W. (2004). Tagged: The risks and rewards of RFID technology. *Risk Management, 14*(1).

Ayre, L. B. (2005). RFID and libraries. In Garfinkel, S., & Rosenberg, B. (Eds.), *Wireless privacy: RFID, Bluetooth and 802.11* (pp. 228–241). Reading, MA: Addison-Wesley.

Bansode, S. Y., & Desale, S. K. (2009). Implementation of RFID technology in University of Pune Library. *Program-Electronic Library and Information Systems, 43*(2), 202–214. doi:10.1108/00330330910954406

Boss, R. W. (2004). RFID technology for libraries. *Library Technology Reports, 39*(6).

Britten, N. (1995). Qualitative research: Qualitative interviews in medical research. [PubMed]. *British Medical Journal, 311,* 251–253. doi:10.1136/bmj.311.6999.251

Chen, M., Gonzalez, S., Leung, V., Zhang, Q., & Li, M. (2010). A 2g-Rfid-based e- healthcare system. *IEEE Wireless Communications, 17*(1), 37–43. doi:10.1109/MWC.2010.5416348

Coyle, K. (2005). Management of RFID in libraries. *Journal of Academic Librarianship, 31*(5), 486–489. doi:10.1016/j.acalib.2005.06.001

Denzin, N. K., & Lincoln, Y. S. (2005). Introduction: The discipline and practice of qualitative research. In Denzin, N. K., & Lincoln, Y. S. (Eds.), *The Sage handbook of qualitative research* (3rd ed., pp. 1–33). Thousand Oaks, CA: Sage.

Edwards, S., & Fortune, M. (2008). *BIC e4libraries project: A guide to RFID in libraries.* Retrieved from http://www.bic.org.uk/files/pdfs/090109%20library%20guide%20final%20rev.pdf

Engel, E. (2006). *RFID implementations in California libraries: Costs and benefits, report.* Washington, DC: U.S. Institute of Museum and Library Services.

Erwin, E., & Kern, C. (2003). Radio-frequency-identification for security and media circulation in libraries. *Library & Archival Security, 18*(2), 23–38. doi:10.1300/J114v18n02_04

Fleisch, E., & Tellkamp, C. (2005). Inventory inaccuracy and supply chain performance: A simulation study of a retail supply chain. *International Journal of Production Economics, 95*(3), 373–385. doi:10.1016/j.ijpe.2004.02.003

Hicks, P. (1999). RFID and the book trade. *Publishing Research Quarterly, 15*(2), 21–23. doi:10.1007/s12109-999-0025-z

Hildner, L. (2006). Defusing the threat of RFID: Protecting consumer privacy through technology-specific legislation at the state level. *Harvard Civil Rights-Civil Liberties Law Review, 41*(1), 133–176.

Irani, Z., Gunasekaran, A., & Dwivedi, Y. K. (2010). Radio Frequency Identification (RFID): Research trends and framework. *International Journal of Production Research, 49*(9), 1–27.

Juban, R., & Wyld, D. (2004). Would you like chips with that? Consumer perspectives of RFID. *Management Research News, 11*(12), 29–44. doi:10.1108/01409170410784653

Kern, C. (2004). Radio-frequency-identification for security and media circulation in libraries. *The Electronic Library, 22*(4), 317–324. doi:10.1108/02640470410552947

Kohn, W., Brayman, V., & Littleton, J. (2005). Repair-control of enterprise systems using RFID sensory data. *IIE Transactions, 37*(4), 281–290. doi:10.1080/07408170590516953doi:10.1080/07408170590516953

Kumar, P., Reinitz, H. W., Simunovic, J., Sandeep, K. P., & Franzon, P. D. (2009). Overview of RFID technology and its applications in the food industry. *Journal of Food Science, 74*(8), 101–106. PubMed doi:10.1111/j.1750-3841.2009.01323.x

Kvale, S. (1983). The qualitative research interview: A phenomenological and a hermeneutical mode of understanding. *Journal of Phenomenological Psychology, 14*, 171–196. doi:10.1163/156916283X00090

Landt, J. (2005). The history of RFID. *IEEE Potentials, 24*(4), 8–11. doi:10.1109/MP.2005.1549751

Lee, H., & Ozer, O. (2007). Unlocking the value of RFID. *Production and Operations Management, 16*(1), 40–64. doi:10.1111/j.1937-5956.2007.tb00165.x

Lee, L. S., Fiedler, K. D., & Smith, J. S. (2008). Radio frequency identification (RFID) implementation in the service sector: A customer-facing diffusion model. *International Journal of Production Economics, 112*(2), 587–600. doi:10.1016/j.ijpe.2007.05.008

Lee, S. H., Ngai, A. W., & Zhang, K. (2007). The quest to improve Chinese healthcare: Some fundamental issues. *International Journal of Health Care Quality Assurance, 20*(1), 416–428. doi:10.1108/09526860710763334

Lee, Y. M., Cheng, F., & Leung, Y. T. (2009). A quantitative view on how RFID can improve inventory management in a supply chain. *International Journal of Logistics- Research and Applications, 12*(1), 23-43.

Molnar, D., & Wagner, D. (2004). Privacy and security in library RFID: Issues, practices, and architectures. In *Proceedings of the 11th ACM Conference on Computer and Communications Security* (pp. 25-29).

Myung, J., Lee, W., & Shih, T. K. (2006). An adaptive memoryless protocol for RFID tag collision arbitration multimedia. *IEEE Transactions, 8*(5), 1096–1101.

Newman, I., & Benz, C. R. (1998). *Qualitative-quantitative research methodology: Exploring the interactive continuum.* Edwardsville, IL: Southern Illinois University Press.

Ngai, E. W. T., Moon, K. K. L., Riggins, F. J., & Yi, C. Y. (2008). RFID research: An academic literature review (1995-2005) and future research directions. *International Journal of Production Economics, 112*(2), 510–520. doi:10.1016/j.ijpe.2007.05.004

O'Conner, M. C. (2005). *Group studies RFID to stop digital piracy.* RFID Journal.

Opdenakker, R. (2006). Advantages and disadvantages of four interview techniques in qualitative research. *Forum Qualitative Sozial Forschung, 7*(4), 11.

Pedroso, M. C., Zwicker, R., & De Souza, C. A. (2009). RFID adoption: Framework and survey in large Brazilian companies. *Industrial Management & Data Systems, 109*(7), 877–897. doi:10.1108/02635570910982256

Pramatari, K., & Theotokis, A. (2009). Consumer acceptance of RFID-enabled services: A model of multiple attitudes, perceived system characteristics and individual traits. *European Journal of Information Systems, 18*(6), 541–552. doi:10.1057/ejis.2009.40

Reyes, P. M., Frazier, G. V., Prater, E. L., & Cannon, A. R. (2007). RFID: The state of the union between promise and practice. *International Journal of Integrated Supply Management, 3*(2), 125–134. doi:10.1504/IJISM.2007.011972

Roberts, C. M. (2006). Radio frequency identification (RFID). *Computers & Security, 25*(1), 18–26. doi:10.1016/j.cose.2005.12.003

Roh, J. J., Kunnathur, A., & Tarafdar, M. (2009). Classification of RFID adoption: An expected benefits approach. *Information & Management, 46*(6), 357–363. doi:10.1016/j.im.2009.07.001

Smart, L., & Schaper, L. (2004). Making sense of RFID. *Library Journal, 4*.

Sorensen, K. B., Christiansson, P., & Svidt, K. (2010). Ontologies to support RFID-based link between virtual models and construction components. *Computer-Aided Civil and Infrastructure Engineering, 25*(4), 285–302. doi:10.1111/j.1467-8667.2009.00638.x

Stockman, H. (1948). Communication by means of reflected power. *Proceedings of the IRE, 36*(10), 1196–1204. doi:10.1109/JRPROC.1948.226245

Tesoriero, R., Tebar, R., Gallud, J. A., Lozano, M. D., & Penichet, V. M. R. (2010). Improving location awareness in indoor spaces using RFID technology. *Expert Systems with Applications, 37*(1), 894–898. doi:10.1016/j.eswa.2009.05.062

Tu, Y. J., Zhou, W., & Piramuthu, S. (2009). Identifying RFID-embedded objects in pervasive healthcare applications. *Decision Support Systems, 46*(1), 586–593. doi:10.1016/j.dss.2008.10.001

Want, R. (2004). The magic of RFID. *ACM Queue; Tomorrow's Computing Today, 2*(7), 41–48. doi:10.1145/1035594.1035619

Want, R. (2006). An introduction to RFID Technology. *IEEE Pervasive Computing / IEEE Computer Society* [and]. *IEEE Communications Society, 5*(1), 25. doi:doi:10.1109/MPRV.2006.2

Wen, W. (2010). An intelligent traffic management expert system with RFID technology. *Expert Systems with Applications, 37*(4), 3024–3035. doi:10.1016/j.eswa.2009.09.030

Yu, S. C. (2007). RFID implementation and benefits in libraries. *The Electronic Library, 25*(1), 54–64. doi:10.1108/02640470710729119

This work was previously published in the International Journal of Electronic Government Research, Volume 7, Issue 4, edited by Vishanth Weerakkody, pp. 46-63, copyright 2011 by IGI Publishing (an imprint of IGI Global).

Chapter 21
Reflecting on E–Government Research:
Toward a Taxonomy of Theories and Theoretical Constructs

Nripendra P. Rana
Swansea University, UK

Yogesh K. Dwivedi
Swansea University, UK

Michael D. Williams
Swansea University, UK

Janet Williams
University of Glamorgan, UK

ABSTRACT

After more than a decade of research in the field of e-government, it is now timely and appropriate to reflect upon the overall developmental directions in the area. This paper explores research progress to date by systematically analyzing the existing body of knowledge on e-government related issues, and reveal if there is lack of theoretical development and rigor in the area. Usable data relating to e-government research currently available were collected from 779 research articles identified from the ISI Web of Knowledge database, and by manually identifying relevant articles from dedicated journals on electronic government such as Transforming Government: People, Process, and Policy (TGPPP), Electronic Government, an International Journal (EGIJ), and International Journal of Electronic Government Research (IJEGR). Based on the investigation of the various studies, findings reveal that generic e-government applications were explored more than any specific applications, and the technology acceptance model (TAM) was the most utilized theory to explain research models. Although a large number of theories and theoretical constructs were borrowed from the reference disciplines, their utilization by e-government researchers appears largely random in approach. The paper also presents limitations and further research directions for future researchers.

DOI: 10.4018/978-1-4666-2458-0.ch021

INTRODUCTION

Electronic government refers to the use of information technology to enhance the efficiency, effectiveness, transparency, and accountability of the public governments (Kraemer & King, 2003; World Bank, 2000). Viewed as essential, yet inevitable transformation projects (Jaeger, 2003), the implementation of e-government systems has been attracting growing research interest, and is believed to represent one of the most significant information technology (IT) implementation and organizational transformation challenges of the next decades (Marche & McNiven, 2003; Warkentin et al., 2002).

Within the last twelve years, governments across the world have attempted adopting electronic government as a means of delivering information and services to citizens 24 hours a day, seven days a week. Nearly all national governments, most sub-national or state governments, and large numbers of local governments have established websites through which they provide e-government (Norris & Lloyd, 2006) services to the citizens, employees of the private and public sectors, and various organizations at different levels.

After a few years of rapid growth in this field, it is now time to pause and reflect on the state of e-government research—what is it all about? The e-government field emerged in the late 1990s as a context within which to share experiences among experts. As the field has grown to considerable size, a substantial intellectual wealth has also been generated; hence, questions about both austerity and relevance should be asked (Gronlund, 2005). One of the major criticisms of existing e-government research is lack of theoretical and methodological rigour. However, such criticisms are largely based on views and opinion and no attempt yet made to explore theoretical diversity and rigour in existing e-government research. Therefore, the aim of this paper is to present retrospections of the existing e-government research by exploring the diversity of theories and theoretical constructs utilized to examine the various issues within e-government context. The main focus is to identify different theories, theoretical models, constructs and variables being used for such research studies. It also explores the various e-government applications that are implemented in various countries and subsequently examined and published by e-government researchers.

The remaining paper is organized as follows: The next section will provide an overview of the research method utilized. The findings will then be presented and discussed in subsequent sections. The last section of this paper will outline conclusions, limitations and future research directions.

METHODOLOGY

This study employed a bibliometric and systematic review approach to identify, collect and analyze relevant e-government publications in order to achieve specified aim. Firstly, we collected the list of all the articles from the comprehensive online database *ISI Web of Knowledge* by using some of the keywords such as "electronic government", "online government", "digital democracy", "adoption", "acceptance", "usage", "diffusion", "implementation" and "impact" with certain permutation and combination to obtain the appropriate articles in our field of research. A more restricted search process was used by the combination of *logical OR* and *logical AND* to filter out those articles which are mainly in the area of IT adoption, diffusion, usage, application and implementation. We obtained a list of 823 articles on electronic government from the keywords. Our main intention was to find out all the possible articles on electronic government acceptance, adoption, implementation, usage, and diffusion from different conferences and journals. These 823 articles were then looked for their full availability through *Google Scholar®*. Out of total 823 articles, we got an access of 433 journal and conference articles.

In addition to these articles, we also explored articles from dedicated journals like *TGPPP*, *EGIJ*, and *IJEGR*. *TGPPP* had total of 85 articles on electronic government in all its editions from the year 2007 till year 2010 and 26 of them were found to be relevant for our purpose. Similarly, 91 out of 171 articles from *EGIJ* and 83 out of 90 articles from *IJEGR* were found appropriate for this study. For analysis of the constructs used and their significance, the different electronic government applications explored, and the various theories or models applied while conducting the studies, all 779 available articles were analyzed. It was found that total 434 articles were appropriate consisting of the articles from *ISI Web of Knowledge* and the dedicated journal articles. These 434 usable articles were again scanned for their use of constructs and variables, and the use of existing theories, models, or frameworks to base their studies. It was found that 112 articles used the various constructs and variables whereas 70 of them used the different existing models and theories either in their original structure or in the altered form. From the proper examination of theories and models, it was also found that a total 30 different types of theories, models, or frameworks were used to analyze those studies. From the investigation of 112 articles which used constructs and variables were collected in their independent and dependent states of relationships. The significance of their relationship was then identified and established between the constructs and their applicability and contexts were also looked for. The applications of all these e-government articles were identified and similar applications were organized together to visualize the frequency of studies using a specific applications. Then, these applications were broadly categorized into 31 similar applications.

FINDINGS

Table 1 shows all those e-government articles which have partially or fully utilized the models

or theories. It was found that 70 articles used such theories and models. The analyses of the theories and models of these studies indicate that TAM is the widely utilised model (23 studies) in the electronic government research till date. This is followed by information system (IS) success model and updated success model (11 studies) (DeLone & McLean, 1992, 2003), diffusion of innovation, and unified theory of acceptance and use of technology (UTAUT) (9 studies each), theory of planned behavior (TPB) (8 studies), extended TAM (TAM2) (5 studies), theory of reasoned action, structuration theory, and trust model (3 studies each) were seen as the most frequently used theories and models in the various electronic government research studies. Whereas only one occurrence of theories or models such as resident decision model, IS planning and investment model, social cognitive theory, leadership theory, stakeholder theory, actor network theory, Schutzian theory of human agency, dynamic info-inclusion model, theory of connection, grounded theory, governance theory, structuration model of technology, transaction cost analysis, coordination theory, institutional theory, complexity theory, and intermediation theory was used as a basis of establishing the models for different electronic government studies.

In addition, out of 70 studies which made some existing theory as a basis for explaining their models or frameworks, 20 of them used more than one model or theory for explaining their e-government models. Five studies (Fu et al., 2006; Gumussoy & Calisir, 2009; Horst et al., 2007; Lu et al., 2010; Ojha et al., 2009) have used TAM and TPB together. Four studies (Carter & Belanger, 2005; Gumussoy & Calisir, 2009; Lean et al., 2009; Shareef et al., 2009) used even three models or theories to propose and test an integrated research model. Three studies (Hu et al., 2007; Sambasivan et al., 2010; Segovia et al., 2009) used TAM and DeLone and McLean's (2003) IS success model together for presenting their research

Table 1. Use of theories and models in various studies

Theory/Model/Framework	Source(s)
Theory of Reasoned Action (TRA)	Belanger & Carter (2008), Ojha et al. (2009), Tang et al. (2009)
Theory of Planned Behavior (TPB)	Chu et al. (2004), Fu et al. (2006), Gumussoy & Calisir (2009), Horst et al. (2007), Hung et al. (2006), Hung et al. (2009), Lu et al. (2010), Kanat & Ozkan (2009)
Decomposed Theory of Planned Behavior (DTPB)	Lau (2004), Lau & Kwok (2007)
Technology Acceptance Model (TAM)	Carter (2008), Carter & Belanger (2005), Chiang (2009), Colesca & Dobrica (2008), Dimitrova & Chen (2006), Fu et al. (2006), Gumussoy & Calisir (2009), Horst et al. (2007), Hsu (2005), Hu et al. (2007), Lean et al. (2009), Lee & Rao (2009), Lu et al. (2010), Ojha et al. (2009), Phang et al. (2006), Sahu & Gupta (2007), Sambasivan et al. (2010), Segovia et al. (2009), Shareef et al. (2009), Sang et al. (2009), Tang et al. (2009), Vathanophas et al. (2008), Vonk et al. (2007)
Extended Technology Acceptance Model (TAM2)	Al-Shafi & Weerakkody (2009), Sang et al. (2009), Sang et al. (2010), Seyal & Pijpers (2004), Wang (2002)
Diffusion of Innovation (DOI)/Diffusion Theory/ Innovation Diffusion Theory (IDT)	Carter & Belanger (2005), Choudrie et al. (2007), Dimitrova & Chen (2006), Dwivedi & Williams (2008), Gumussoy & Calisir (2009), Lean et al. (2009), Sang et al. (2009), Shareef et al. (2009), Tung & Rieck (2005)
IS Success Model (DeLone & McLean, 1992, 2003)	Floropoulos et al. (2010), Gotoh (2009), Hsu & Chen (2007), Hu et al. (2007), Mirchandani et al. (2008), Ozkan et al. (2009), Prybutok et al. (2008), Sambasivan et al. (2010), Segovia et al. (2009), Teo et al. (2008), Wang & Liao (2008)
IS Success Model (Myers et al., 1997)	Sun et al. (2006)
Trust Model/Trustworthiness/Initial Trust Model	Carter & Belanger (2005), Lean et al. (2009), Li et al. (2008)
Unified Theory of Acceptance and Use of Technology (UTAUT)	Belanger & Carter (2005), Carter & Schaupp (2009), Hung et al. (2007), Loo et al. (2009), Sahu & Gupta (2007), Schaupp et al. (2010), van Dijk et al. (2008), Wang & Shih (2009), Yeow & Loo (2009)
Resident Decision Model	Hamner & Al-Qahtani (2009)
IS Planning and Investment Model	Krell & Matook (2009)
Social Cognitive Theory	Loo et al. (2009)
Leadership Theory	Luk (2009)
Stakeholder theory	Luk (2009)
Actor Network Theory	Ajad & Faraj (2009)
Active Agent Framework based on Structuration Theory/ Giddens Structuration Theory	Senyucel (2007), Parvez (2008)
Schutzian Theory of Human Agency	Fu-Lai & Yu (2008)
Dynamic Info-Inclusion model (D2I)	Joia (2004)
Theory of Connection	Davidrajuh (2004)
Grounded Theory	Hsu (2005)
Governance Theory	Kolsaker (2006)
Giddens Structuration Theory	Parvez (2006)
Owanda Orlikowski's Structurational Model of Technology (SMT)	Parvez (2006)
Transaction Cost Analysis (TCA)	Shareef et al. (2009)
Coordination Theory	Janssen & Kuk (2007)
Institutional Theory	Luna-Reyes et al. (2008)
Complexity Theory	Falivene & Silva (2008)
Seddon's (1997) IS Success Sub-Model	Floropoulos et al. (2010)
Intermediation Theory	Janssen & Klievink (2009)

model. One study (Tang et al., 2009) used TAM and TRA together whereas the other few studies have used two similar models to explain the resulting research frameworks for e-government such as Sang et al. (2009) used TAM and TAM2, Floropoulos et al. (2010) used two success models: DeLone and McLean's (2003) updated IS success model, and Seddon's (1997) IS success sub-model, and Parvez (2006) based his model on Giddens structuration theory, and Orlikowski's structurational model of technology (SMT).

Table 2 shows the list of 29 broader applications along with the countries of their implementation from 112 those studies which have used their constructs in their e-government articles. The analyses of the various applications being used by the studies indicate that e-government in general (with minor variations) was the most widely utilised application (35 studies). This is followed by e-government services (19 studies). As far as specific electronic government applications are concerned, online tax filing system was researched maximum number (7 studies) of times. This is followed by information systems and technology (6 studies), and electronic filing, and broadband (5 studies each). Electronic or internet voting application and website applications were analysed three times each while each of the applications such as internet services, information kiosks, electronic procurement, wireless technology and smartcard applications were examined in two studies each. However, many specific applications such as electronic learning, telephone channel integration, channel perception, electronic stamping, centralized customer service systems, enterprise application, electronic commerce, electronic tendering system, electronic complaint system, electronic reverse auction; online innovation, telecommunication, electronic channels, and virtual community were used in only one study each.

Table 3 contains the list of some such independent variables which were most frequently used by the electronic government research studies. The analysis of the independent and dependent constructs from 112 studies signify that the construct "perceived ease of use" or "ease of use" was used maximum number of times (24 studies) followed by "perceived usefulness" or "usefulness" (23 studies), "trust" (20 studies) in its different forms. Whereas the control variables "age" and "education" or "educational level" that were used in 16 studies each for establishing relationship with other dependent constructs in the context of citizen as well as employee. The use of control variables such as "gender" (12 studies), and "years of internet experience" (4 studies) have been used only for citizens" context. The other most frequently used constructs in the context of citizen as well as employee were "trust" (20 studies), "service quality" (8 studies), "compatibility" (12 studies), "subjective norm" (11 studies), "self-efficacy" (10 studies), "relative advantage" (10 studies), "facilitating conditions" (10 studies), "behavioral intention" (8 studies), "perceived behavioral control" (7 studies), "system quality" (7 studies), "performance expectancy" (8 studies), "effort expectancy" (7 studies), "social influence" (7 studies), "information quality" (6 studies), "perceived risk" (6 studies), "image" (6 studies), "attitude" (6 studies), and "satisfaction" (4 studies). It was also visualized that relatively a very few constructs have been used in the organizational context, for example "perceived benefits" was used for citizen as well as organization whereas leadership triad was used purely for organizational purposes. There are more than 300 independent constructs which were used very less frequently and have not been included here due to words and space constraints. Out of these constructs, although 76 independent constructs have been used in the context of organization, their frequency of use in e-government research is very low.

Table 2. E-Government applications in various countries

Application(s)	Country	Study
E-Government/Digital Government/E-Government and E-Democracy/Digital Democracy/E-Government and Online Engagement/Central Excise E-Government	USA	Belanger & Carter (2008), Carter (2008), Chen & Dimitrova (2006), McNeal et al. (2003), McNeal et al. (2007), Moon & Norris (2005), Prybutok et al. (2008), Reddick (2006), Reddick (2009), Tolbert et al. (2008), West (2004)
	UK	Dwivedi & Williams (2008), Kolsaker & Lee-Kelley (2006)
	Canada	Parent et al. (2005), Reddick (2005)
	Cambodia	Sang et al. (2009)
		Sang et al. (2010)
	South Korea	Kim & Holzer (2006), Lim & Tang (2007)
	India	Chhabra & Jaiswal (2008), Mitra & Gupta (2008), Sahu & Gupta (2007)
	Various Countries	Das et al. (2009), Srivastava & Teo (2006), Srivastava & Teo (2007a), Srivastava & Teo (2007b)
	Taiwan	Sun et al. (2006)
		Hsu & Chen (2007)
	Thailand, Indonesia	Mirchandani et al. (2008)
	Spain	Serrano-Cinca et al. (2008)
	Belgium	Verdegem & Verleye (2009)
	Romania	Colesca (2009)
	European Union	Pina et al. (2009)
	Slovenia	Kunstelj et al. (2007)
	Singapore	Teo et al. (2008)
E-Government Services/Online Service Delivery/ Online Government Service /Government Internet Services /Online Services /E-Government Information and Services /Electronic Government Services /Online Public Information and Services /Online Government-to-Citizen Services/ Intergovernmental services	USA	Belanger & Carter (2008), Carter & Belanger (2005), Dimitrova & Chen (2006), Lee & Rao (2009)
	Netherlands	Horst et al. (2007), van Deursen & van Dijk (2009), Veenstra & Zuurmond (2009)
	Taiwan	Hung et al. (2009), Wang & Liao (2008)
	China	Tang et al. (2009)
	Malaysia	Lean et al. (2009)
	Japan	Gotoh (2009)
	Various Countries	Boyer-Wright & Kottermann (2008)
	Romania	Colesca & Dobrica (2008)
	Hong Kong	Lau (2004)
	Singapore	Tung & Rieck (2005)
	Turkey	Kanat & Ozkan (2009)
	UK	Barnes & Vidgen (2004)
E-Learning	Turkey	Ozkan et al. (2009)
I-Voting/E-Voting System	USA	Belanger & Carter (2010), Moynihan & Silva (2008)
	Taiwan	Chiang (2009)
Information and Communication Technology (ICT)/ Information Systems/ Organizational Information Systems/ Information Technology	India, South Africa	Bussell (2007)
	Australia	Krell & Matook (2009)
	USA	Li et al. (2008), Shelley II et al. (2006)
	South Korea	Kim & Lee (2006)

continued on following page

Table 2. Continued

Application(s)	Country	Study
	China	Phang et al. (2006)
Telephone Channel Integration/Channel Perception	Netherlands	Pieterson & Teerling (2009), Pieterson et al. (2008)
Internet/Government Internet Services	Brunei	Seyal & Pijpers (2004)
	Netherlands	van Dijk et al. (2008)
	USA	Norris (2005)
	UK	Norris & Curtice (2006)
Information Kiosks	Taiwan	Hung et al. (2007), Wang & Shih (2009)
E-Stamping	Hong Kong	Luk (2009)
E-Procurement System	Malaysia	Kaliannan & Awang (2010), Sambasivan et al. (2010)
Enacted Technology/ E-Government Technology	Mexico	Luna-Reyes et al. (2008)
	Thailand	Vathanophas et al. (2008)
E-Filing	USA	Carter & Schaupp (2009), Schaupp & Carter (2010), Schaupp et al. (2010)
	Taiwan	Fu et al. (2004), Wang (2002)
Centralized Customer Service Systems	USA	Reddick (2009)
Enterprise Application	Pakistan	Khoumbati & Themistocleous (2007)
Broadband	Pakistan	Dwivedi et al. (2007), Khoumbati et al. (2007)
	Bangladesh	Dwivedi et al. (2007), Shareef et al. (2009)
	Saudi Arabia	Dwivedi & Weerakkody (2007)
E-Commerce	Hong Kong	Lau & Kwok (2007)
ATM and Smartcard Application	Malaysia	Loo et al. (2009), Yeow & Loo (2009)
E-Tendering System	Taiwan	Chu et al. (2004)
Online Tax filing and Payment/ Taxation Information System/ E-Tax/ Paperless Income Tax Filing/ Electronic Tax Filing/ Tax Filing Websites/ Taxation Services	Taiwan	Fu et al. (2006), Hung et al. (2006), Lu et al. (2010)
	Greece	Floropoulos et al. (2010)
	Hong Kong	Hu et al. (2007)
	India	Ojha et al. (2009)
	Turkey, South Korea	Lee et al. (2008)
	Portugal	Pinho & Macedo (2008)
Electronic Complaint System	Taiwan	Chu et al. (2008)
E-Reverse Auction	Various Countries	Gumussoy & Calisir (2009)
Online Innovation	USA	Hinnant & O'Looney (2002)
Telecommunication	Africa	Mbarika & Byrd (2009)
Wireless Location Technology/ Wi-Fi	USA, EU	Seeman et al. (2007)
	Qatar	Al-Shafi & Weerakkody (2009)
Electronic Channels	Netherlands	Teerling & Pieterson (2010)
Virtual Community	Spain	Casalo et al. (2008)
Website/ E-Government Websites	USA	Chai et al. (2006), Esterling (2005)
	Thailand	Wangpipatwong et al. (2009)

Table 3. Independent and dependent constructs and their significance of relationship

Independent Constructs	Dependent Constructs	Studies with Significant Relation	Studies with Non-Significant Relation
Age +#	Intention to Use	Belanger & Carter (2010), van Dijk et al. (2008)	Phang et al. (2006), van Dijk et al. (2008)
	Trust on e-Government	Colesca (2009)	
	Perceived Ease of Use	Colesca & Dobrica (2008)	
	Perceived Usefulness	Colesca & Dobrica (2008), Al-Shafi & Weerakkody (2009)	
	Frequency of Use of e-Government Information	Dimitrova & Chen (2006)	
	Frequency of Use of e-Government Services	Dimitrova & Chen (2006)	
	Trusting Beliefs	Li et al. (2008)	
	Improved Administration	Moynihan & Silva (2008)	Moynihan & Silva (2008)
	Operational Skill Assignment	van Deursen & van Dijk (2009)	
	Formal Skill Assignment		
	Information Skill Assignment		van Deursen & van Dijk (2009)
	Government Gateway Adoption	Dwivedi & Williams (2008)	
	Attitude	Dwivedi & Weerakkody (2007)	
	Advantages of IT	Shelley II et al. (2006)	
	Disadvantages of IT		
	Public IT Access		
	E-Participation		
	Education		Shelley II et al. (2006)
	Public Information Search	Chen & Dimitrova (2006)	
	Online Transaction		Chen & Dimitrova (2006)
	Public Policy Input		
	Overall Political Activism	Norris & Curtice (2006)	
Education/ Educational Level +#	Intention to Use	Phang et al. (2006), van Dijk et al. (2008)	Belanger & Carter (2010), van Dijk et al. (2008)
	Trust on e-Government		Colesca (2009)
	Perceived Ease of Use	Colesca & Dobrica (2008)	
	Perceived Usefulness	Colesca & Dobrica (2008), Al-Shafi & Weerakkody (2009)	
	Frequency of Use of e-Government Information		Dimitrova & Chen (2006)
	Frequency of Use of e-Government Services	Dimitrova & Chen (2006)	
	Employee Knowledge-Sharing Capabilities		Kim & Lee (2006)
	Improved Administration	Moynihan & Silva (2008)	Moynihan & Silva (2008)
	Operational Skill Assignment	van Deursen & van Dijk (2009)	
	Formal Skill Assignment		
	Information Skill Assignment		
	Government Gateway Adoption	Dwivedi & Williams (2008)	

continued on following page

Table 3. Continued

Independent Constructs	Dependent Constructs	Studies with Significant Relation	Studies with Non-Significant Relation
	Attitude		Dwivedi & Weerakkody (2007)
	Prior Experience		Vathanophas et al. (2008)
	Advantages of IT	Shelley II et al. (2006)	
	Public IT Access		
	E-Participation		
	Public Information Search		
	Online Transaction	Chen & Dimitrova (2006)	Chen & Dimitrova (2006)
	Public Policy Input		
	Political Activism	Norris & Curtice (2006)	
Gender/Sex+	Trust on e-Government		Colesca (2009)
	Perceived Ease of Use		Colesca & Dobrica (2008)
	Perceived Usefulness		Colesca & Dobrica (2008), Al-Shafi & Weerakkody (2009)
	Frequency of Use of e-Government Information		Dimitrova & Chen (2006)
	Trusting Beliefs	Li et al. (2008)	
	Operational Skill Assignment		van Deursen & van Dijk (2009)
	Formal Skill Assignment		
	Information Skill Assignment		
	Intention to Use		Phang et al. (2006), van Dijk et al. (2008)
	Government Gateway Adoption	Dwivedi & Williams (2008)	
	Attitude towards Adoption of Broadband		Dwivedi & Weerakkody (2007)
	Public Information Search	Chen & Dimitrova (2006)	
	Online Transaction		Chen & Dimitrova (2006)
	Public Policy Input		
	Political Activism		Norris & Curtice (2006)
Trust* +#/ Trust of the E-Filer/ Trust in E-Government Agent/ Trust in Government/ Trust in E-Government Website*/ Trust in Technology/ Trust of the Internet	Attitude	Hung et al. (2006)	Hung et al. (2009)
	Employee Knowledge-Sharing Capabilities		Kim & Lee (2006)
	Future Development	Kunstelj et al. (2007)	
	Future Use		
	Motivators		
	Intention to Use	Belanger & Carter (2008), Carter (2008), Carter & Schaupp (2009), Lean et al. (2009), Sang et al. (2009), Sang et al. (2010), Schaupp & Carter (2010), Tang et al. (2009)	Sambasivan et al. (2010)
	Commitment	Vathanophas et al. (2008)	
	Perceived Ease of Use		
	Perceived Risk	Schaupp & Carter (2010)	Belanger & Carter (2008), Fu et al. (2006), Schaupp et al. (2010)
	Internet Competence	Lee & Rao (2009)	

continued on following page

Table 3. Continued

Independent Constructs	Dependent Constructs	Studies with Significant Relation	Studies with Non-Significant Relation
	Information Quality	Teo et al. (2008)	
	System Quality		
	Service Quality		
	Trust in e-Government Website		Teo et al. (2008)
	Trust on e-Government	Colesca (2009)	
Perceived Ease of Use*/ Ease of Use +#	Attitude	Al-Shafi & Weerakkody (2009), Hung et al. (2006), Hung et al. (2009), Lau (2004), Lau & Kwok (2007), Seyal & Pijpers (2004)	Chu et al. (2004)
	Perceived Usefulness	Al-Shafi & Weerakkody (2009), Chiang (2009), Chu et al. (2004), Colesca & Dobrica (2008), Fu et al. (2006), Kim & Holzer (2006), Lu et al. (2010), Phang et al. (2006), Sang et al. (2010), Seyal & Pijpers (2004), Wang (2002)	Gumussoy & Calisir (2009)
	Perceived Behavioral Control	Chu et al. (2004)	
	Intention to Use/BI	Carter (2008), Carter & Belanger (2005), Dwivedi et al. (2007b), Fu et al. (2006), Khoumbati et al. (2007), Ojha et al. (2009), Phang et al. (2006), Sambasivan et al. (2010), Sang et al. (2009), Vathanophas et al. (2008), Wang (2002)	Fu et al. (2006), Gumussoy & Calisir (2009), Sang et al. (2010), Tang et al. (2009)
	Satisfaction	Colesca & Dobrica (2008)	Teerling & Pieterson (2010)
	Perceived Credibility	Wang (2002)	
	EG System Adoption	Shareef et al. (2009)	
Perceived Usefulness*/ Usefulness +#	Attitude	Al-Shafi & Weerakkody (2009), Chiang (2009), Chu et al. (2004), Hung et al. (2006), Hung et al. (2009), Lau (2004), Lau & Kwok (2007), Lu et al. (2010)	Seyal & Pijpers (2004)
	Trust on e-Government	Colesca (2009)	
	Satisfaction	Colesca & Dobrica (2008)	
	Intention to Use/BI	Al-Shafi & Weerakkody (2009), Carter (2008), Dwivedi & Weerakkody (2007), Fu et al. (2006), Gumussoy & Calisir (2009), Lean et al. (2009), Phang et al. (2006), Sambasivan et al. (2010), Sang et al. (2009), Sang et al. (2010), Tang et al. (2009), Vathanophas et al. (2008), Wang (2002)	
	Perceived Behavioral Control	Lu et al. (2010)	
	EG System Adoption		Shareef et al. (2009)
Service Quality* +#	Perceived Usefulness	Floropoulos et al. (2010)	
	User Satisfaction	Floropoulos et al. (2010), Sun et al. (2006), Teo et al. (2008), Wang & Liao (2008)	Pinho & Macedo (2008)
	Trust	Parent et al. (2005)	
	External Political Efficacy		Parent et al. (2005)

continued on following page

Table 3. Continued

Independent Constructs	Dependent Constructs	Studies with Significant Relation	Studies with Non-Significant Relation
	Intention to Use	Pinho & Macedo (2008)	Teo et al. (2008)
	Attitude		Dwivedi & Weerakkody (2007)
	Use/Continued Use	Wang & Liao (2008), Wangpipatwong et al. (2009)	
Compatibility +#	Intention to Use/BI	Carter & Belanger (2005), Ojha et al. (2009)	Sang et al. (2009), Sang et al. (2010)
	Perceived Ease of Use	Fu et al. (2006), Gumussoy & Calisir (2009)	Fu et al. (2006)
	Perceived Usefulness	Fu et al. (2006), Gumussoy & Calisir (2009)	
	Attitude	Hung et al. (2006), Hung et al. (2009), Lau (2004), Lau & Kwok (2007)	Dwivedi & Weerakkody (2007)
	EG System Adoption		Shareef et al. (2009)
Subjective Norm* +#	Behavioral Intention	Chu et al. (2004), Fu et al. (2006), Gumussoy & Calisir (2009), Hung et al. (2006), Hung et al. (2009), Lau (2004), Lau & Kwok (2007), Lu et al. (2010)	
	Perceived Usefulness	Sang et al. (2010)	Gumussoy & Calisir (2009), Vathanophas et al. (2008)
	Trusting Beliefs		
	Trusting Attitude	Li et al. (2008)	
	Trusting Intention		
Satisfaction* +#	E-government Adoption	Colesca & Dobrica (2008)	
	Trust	Kunstelj et al. (2007)	
	Future Development		
	Future Use		Kunstelj et al. (2007)
	Motivators		
	Intention	Chai et al. (2006), Pinho & Macedo (2008)	
Behavioral Intention*/ Online Tax Filing Intention +#	Use/Adoption Behavior	Chu et al. (2004), Dwivedi et al. (2007), Gumussoy & Calisir (2009), Hung et al. (2007), Lau (2004), Lau & Kwok (2007), Wang & Shih (2009)	
	On-line Tax Filing Behavior	Lu et al. (2010)	
Perceived Behavioral Control* +#	Behavioral Intention	Chu et al. (2004), Gumussoy & Calisir (2009), Hung et al. (2006), Hung et al. (2009), Lau (2004), Lau & Kwok (2007), Lu et al. (2010)	
	Behavior/Actual Use	Chu et al. (2004), Gumussoy & Calisir (2009)	
	Perceived Ease of Use	Gumussoy & Calisir (2009)	
Self-Efficacy/ PC Self-Efficacy/ Computer Self-Efficacy +#	Perceived Behavioral Control	Hung et al. (2006), Hung et al. (2009)	Carter (2008), Chu et al. (2004)
	Intention to Use/BI	Fu et al. (2006), Sahu & Gupta (2007)	Khoumbati et al. (2007)
	Perceived Usefulness	Seyal & Pijpers (2004), Wang (2002)	
	Perceived Ease of Use		
	Perceived Credibility	Wang (2002)	

continued on following page

Table 3. Continued

Independent Constructs	Dependent Constructs	Studies with Significant Relation	Studies with Non-Significant Relation
Years of Internet Experience/ Prior Internet Experience +	Trust on e-Government	Colesca (2009)	
	Perceived Ease of Use	Colesca & Dobrica (2008)	
	Perceived Usefulness		
	Intention to Use		Phang et al. (2006)
	Operational Skill Assignment	van Deursen & van Dijk (2009)	
	Formal Skill Assignment		van Deursen & van Dijk (2009)
	Information Skill Assignment		
System Quality* +#	Perceived Usefulness	Floropoulos et al. (2010)	
	User Satisfaction	Teo et al. (2008), Wang & Liao (2008), Sun et al. (2006)	Floropoulos et al. (2010), Gotoh (2009)
	Intention to Continue Using		Teo et al. (2008)
	Use/Continued Use	Wangpipatwong et al. (2009)	Wang & Liao (2008)
	Result Quality	Gotoh (2009)	
Relative Advantage +#	Intention to Use/BI	Lean et al. (2009), Ojha et al. (2009), Sang et al. (2009), Sang et al. (2010)	Carter & Belanger (2005), Khoumbati et al. (2007)
	EG System Adoption	Shareef et al. (2009)	
	Attitude	Dwivedi et al. (2007), Lau (2004), Lau & Kwok (2007)	
Information Quality* +#	Perceived Usefulness	Floropoulos et al. (2010), Kim & Holzer (2006)	
	User Satisfaction	Floropoulos et al. (2010), Sun et al. (2006)	Teo et al. (2008)
	Intention to Continue Using	Teo et al. (2008)	
	Use/Continued Use	Wang & Liao (2008), Wangpipatwong et al. (2009)	
Perceived Risk* +#	Intention to Use/BI	Belanger & Carter (2008), Fu et al. (2006), Schaupp & Carter (2010), Schaupp et al. (2010)	Fu et al. (2006), Sambasivan et al. (2010)
	Attitude	Hung et al. (2006)	
Image +#	Intention to Use/BI		Carter & Belanger (2005), Ojha et al. (2009)
	Perceived Usefulness	Sang et al. (2009), Sang et al. (2010)	Vathanophas et al. (2008)
	EG System Adoption		Shareef et al. (2009)
Facilitating Conditions +#	Perceived Behavioral Control	Chu et al. (2004), Hung et al. (2006), Hung et al. (2009)	
	Use Behavior	Hung et al. (2007), Wang & Shih (2009)	
	Intention to Use	Sambasivan et al. (2010), Schaupp et al. (2010), Yeow & Loo (2009), Sahu & Gupta (2007)	Yeow & Loo (2009)
Attitude* +#	Intention/BI	Dwivedi et al. (2007), Hung et al. (2006), Hung et al. (2009), Lau (2004), Lu et al. (2010)	Al-Shafi & Weerakkody (2009)
Performance Expectancy +#	Intention to Use/BI	Carter & Schaupp (2009), Hung et al. (2007), Wang & Shih (2009), Sahu & Gupta (2007), Schaupp et al. (2010), van Dijk et al. (2008), Yeow & Loo (2009)	van Dijk et al. (2008)
	Attitude	Sahu & Gupta (2007)	

continued on following page

Table 3. Continued

Independent Constructs	Dependent Constructs	Studies with Significant Relation	Studies with Non-Significant Relation
Effort Expectancy +#	Behavioral Intention	Hung et al. (2007), Sahu & Gupta (2007), van Dijk et al. (2008), Wang & Shih (2009), Yeow & Loo (2009)	Carter & Schaupp (2009), Schaupp et al. (2010)
	Self-Efficacy	Sahu & Gupta (2007)	
Social Influence +#@	Behavioral Intention	Hung et al. (2007), Wang & Shih (2009), Carter & Schaupp (2009), Sahu & Gupta (2007), Schaupp et al. (2010), Yeow & Loo (2009)	
	Adoption Decision	Tung & Rieck (2005)	

[**Legend**: *: Constructs used as both independent and dependent; +: Constructs used for citizen; #: Constructs used for employee; @: Constructs used for organization; +#: Constructs used for citizen as well as employee; +#@: Constructs used for citizen, employee as well as organization]

DISCUSSION

Considering a large number of studies using constructs, theories, and applications to perform the electronic government research, this section will provide the discussion on the various findings on electronic government research studies.

Looking at the theories or models used by the studies to include different constructs, it was seen that few studies used even three theories and models to present the proposed model. For example, a study by Carter and Belanger (2005) shows the combination of three models to present their research model. The theoretical models, in particular TAM and DOI, have overlapping constructs. The complexities construct from DOI is similar to the perceived ease of use (PEOU) construct from TAM. Similarly, some researchers have suggested that perceived usefulness and relative advantage are the same constructs (Carter & Belanger, 2005). Carter and Belanger (2005) argue that they included both DOI and TAM in the e-government adoption because DOI adds up significant contribution to the prophecy of adoption intent (Plouffe et al., 2001). But, combining similar constructs together definitely raises the issues of repeating the similar constructs and would make the resulting model less interesting and repetitive in nature which likely to add

minimal contribution to the existing knowledge. The studies by Dimitrova and Chen (2006), Gumussoy and Calisir (2009), and Lean et al. (2009) also explained their research models based on the models of TAM and DOI. Similarly, Floropoulos et al. (2010) adapted both Seddon's (1997) IS success sub-model, and DeLone and McLean (2003) updated IS success model saying that both these models revised DeLone and McLean are used to guide the identification and development of the resulting research model (Floropoulos et al., 2010). However, as long as DeLone and McLean represents all the constructs defined by Seddon's success sub-model, there is no need for adding up the additional model to represent the resulting framework. The study by Loo et al. (2009) has used constructs from UTAUT and SCT in their research model saying that UTAUT model does not include anxiety as a direct determinant whereas it is proposed as a direct determinant in this study (Loo et al., 2009). However, this raises a question of the credibility of the formation of unified theory when it is said that it is a combination of eight different models consisting of SCT as one of the theories. If UTAUT is being used with any of the eight models it is constituted with, why certain context of constructs of eight individual models was not taken into consideration. The study by Sang et al. (2009) used both TAM and TAM2 together with DOI model to frame the research model. As we know that TAM2 is the extension of TAM and all the constructs of TAM are also available in TAM2, there is no need to take TAM explicitly when TAM2 is being considered in the model.

The findings on various electronic government applications revealed that generic applications on e-government or e-government services in their various forms were used the most. This may provide the overall trend of the e-government status in the various countries but it may not be able to provide the specific area of development in the same context. The initial studies in general can provide the overall trend of e-government growth in different countries, but there is a need to know more specific areas of development in e-government at wider level. The larger number of research in the generic field of e-government may be due to the ease of collecting data from citizen and employee about the digital nature of government as well. More studies are being conducted in developed countries such as USA, UK; and some European countries indicate more number of e-government availability of more number of such services and hence creates a wider opportunities for research there.

However, developing countries' e-government status also creates a huge possibility to explore the trends of e-government to suggest the government of the countries to apply it in a relevant manner. Such efforts of research is growing rapidly even in some developing countries like India, Malaysia, Taiwan, Thailand, Portugal, and South Korea like countries. The findings also revealed that there are few studies which were conducted more than once in the context of similar applications in the same country. For example, 11 studies (Belanger & Carter, 2008; Carter, 2008; Chen & Dimitrova, 2006; McNeal et al., 2003, 2007; Moon & Norris, 2005; Prybutok et al., 2008; Reddick, 2006, 2009; Tolbert et al., 2008; West, 2004) which were conducted in general on e-government in the USA. There is a growing need of looking into

specific applications in different contexts rather than to perform research on similar topics in the context of same country.

Moreover, there are some specific applications which were repetitively conducted in the context of the same country with few of them using some common author(s) such as Information Kiosks application (Hung et al., 2007; Wang & Shih, 2009) was investigated twice in Taiwan, e-procurement system (Kaliannan & Awang, 2010; Sambasivan, 2010) was examined twice in context of Malaysia, e-filing system was explored thrice in the context of the USA with Schaupp and Carter as the common authors in all the three studies and used almost similar constructs in each of their research papers whereas the same application was observed two times (Fu et al., 2004; Wang, 2002) in the context of Taiwan, e-tax filing applications (Fu et al., 2006; Hung et al., 2006; Lu et al., 2010) was researched thrice in the context of Taiwan, and telephone channel integration (Pieterson & Teerling, 2009; Pieterson et al., 2008) was investigated twice in the context of Netherlands with Pieterson and Teerling (2009) as the common authors at both these occasions. All these studies based on the specific applications indicate that such repetitive research were conducted just for the sake of publishing papers in different journals rather than for the need of uncovering some new facts. The further research must take these existing studies into consideration to contribute something new to the society rather than publishing the similar work with a little change.

The observation of independent and dependent constructs and their significance divulged that majority of constructs were used for individual purpose whereas a very few of them were used in the context of organization. The main reason for exploring e-government in individual context might be largely because of the fact that the adoption and diffusion of e-government can most likely to benefit the people first who get directly impacted with the online government facilities and services available to them. Moreover, there is a need of e-government research which can uncover more organizational concerns. In addition, there are studies (Chen & Dimitrova, 2006; Fu et al., 2006; Moynihan & Silva, 2008; Teo et al., 2009; van Dijk et al., 2008) where the relationship between same set of independent and dependent constructs was found to be both significant as well as non-significant under different models and circumstances. The requirement is to investigate all such studies which produce conflicting significance for their different models between same set of constructs to dig out the appropriate reasons for this gap. The majority of constructs is under-represented and has been used mostly in only one study hence; there is a need for more representations of such constructs in contexts of similar instances. The analysis of the control variable "gender" points out that almost 90% of its dependent constructs have non-significant relationship with it. It raises a serious question about considering such variables whose impact on the other variables is always non-significant.

CONCLUSION

The purpose of this study is to examine the research advancement by systematically analyzing the existing body of knowledge on e-government related issues, and reveal if there is lack of theoretical development and rigor in the area. This purpose was achieved by examining the use of IS/IT acceptance theories and models in the e-government research, identifying the various e-government applications related research in the perspective of different countries to see the status of overall development of research in the concerned area, and verifying a range of independent and dependent constructs to judge the trends of the variables used in such research. The following prominent points extracted from the findings and discussions presented in this study are:

- 63% (N=70) of the total studies (N=112) using some constructs have employed some existing theories and models to explain their research models.

- TAM (N=23) is the widely utilized theory to explain the e-government research. This is followed by DeLone and McLean's IS success model (N=11), DOI (N=9), UTAUT (N=9), and TPB (N=8) as some of the most frequently utilized models in e-government research.

- Although UTAUT is a unified model consisting of eight models (Venkatesh et al., 2003) including SCT, both have been used together to represent an e-government research model.

- TAM2 and TAM, and DeLone and McLean (1997, 2003) IS success model, and Seddon's (1997) IS success sub-model have been used together in studies even though TAM2, and DeLone and McLean's (1997, 2003) model contain almost all the variables of TAM and Seddon's (1997) models respectively.

- Compared to specific applications, generic e-government applications and services have been explored in majority (N=52) of the total cases (N=112).

- Online tax filing application was seen as the most explored specific e-government research application followed by information and communication technology, e-filing system, and broadband technology as some of the more frequently researched technologies.

- Majority (N=70) of the overall e-government research studies (N=112) were conducted in the developed countries like USA, UK, Australia, and Canada like countries.

- There are few studies (N=10) which have repeatedly used the same e-government application in the context of the same country more than once in different journal papers.

- The majority of constructs explored for the e-government research were for individuals. The constructs in the organizational contexts are still under-represented.
- Almost 90% of the relationships of 'gender' with the dependent constructs were found to be non-significant.

LIMITATIONS AND FUTURE RESEARCH DIRECTIONS

The first limitation is in the terms of some more studies which could have been carried out on some research papers which were not accessible through researchers' library. There are more than 100 papers which are still inaccessible and would have helped in performing some more accurate analysis and conclusion. Secondly, this study does not take into consideration about the moderating variables and their significance on the constructs. Thirdly, this study does not consider the quantitative method to measure the overall performance of the constructs and the ongoing trends of the e-government research. Fourthly, this study has not considered the diagrammatic representations among various constructs where the overall relations can be easily visualized in a pictorial form and would have clearly represented the general scenario of all the constructs being investigated under different applications, and studies. Lastly, the information regarding keywords, source of publications, methodology, and sample size would have provided some more useful trends of the e-government research till now.

These limitations of the existing study can be proved to be a step forward toward the future research directions. More papers which could not be accessed because of their privileged access rights might be taken into consideration in the future research to explore more about the ongoing e-government research. The significance of the impact of moderators on the relationship of the constructs can be elaborately analyzed in the

future research. Moreover, performing the meta-analysis on the collective quantitative data to see the combined effect of the relationship between the constructs will be a further future research direction. The future researcher can provide combined diagrammatic representation that may provide to see the impact of the constructs and their relationships to get enabled with more explicit illustration of the variables. The future researchers may separately study the significance of relationship between the constructs for individuals and organizations. It can also uncover more about the e-government researches by collecting some information of the previous studies such as the source of publications, and keywords to know the area which is being more focused and under represented.

REFERENCES

Al-Shafi, S., & Weerakkody, V. (2009). Implementing free Wi-Fi in public parks: An empirical study in Qatar. *International Journal of Electronic Government Research*, 5(3), 21–35. doi:10.4018/jegr.2009070102

Azad, B., & Faraj, S. (2009). E-Government institutionalizing practices of a land registration mapping system. *Government Information Quarterly*, 26(1), 5–14. doi:10.1016/j.giq.2008.08.005

Barnes, S. J., & Vidgen, R. (2004). Interactive e-government services: Modelling user perceptions with eQual. *Electronic Government, an International Journal*, 1(2), 213-228.

Belanger, F., & Carter, L. (2008). Trust and risk in e-government adoption. *The Journal of Strategic Information Systems*, 17(2), 165–176. doi:10.1016/j.jsis.2007.12.002

Belanger, F., & Carter, L. (2010). The digital divide and internet voting acceptance. In *Proceedings of the Fourth International Conference on Digital Society* (pp. 307-310).

Belanger, F., & Carter, L. D. (2005). U-Government: A framework for the evolution of e-government. *Electronic Government, an International Journal, 2*(4), 426-445.

Boyer-Wright, K. F., & Kottemann J. E. (2008). High-level factors affecting availability of online government services worldwide. *Electronic Government, an International Journal, 5*(4), 375-389.

Bussell, J. (2007). Electoral competition and digital development in India and South Africa. In *Proceedings of the IEEE Conference on Information and Communication Technologies and Development* (pp. 1-9).

Carter, L. (2008). E-Government diffusion: A comparison of adoption constructs. *Transforming Government: People, Process, and Policy, 2*(3), 147–161. doi:10.1108/17506160810902167

Carter, L., & Belanger, F. (2005). The utilization of e-government services: Citizen trust, innovation and acceptance factors. *Information Systems Journal, 15*(1), 5–25. doi:10.1111/j.1365-2575.2005.00183.x

Carter, L., & Schaupp, L. C. (2009). Relating acceptance and optimism to e-file adoption. *International Journal of Electronic Government Research, 5*(3), 62–74. doi:10.4018/jegr.2009070105

Casalo, L. V., Cisneros, J., Guinaliu, M., & Orus, C. (2008). Effects of a virtual citizen community: The case of Expo Zaragoza. *Electronic Government, an International Journal, 5*(2), 131-145.

Chai, S., Herath, T. C., Park, I., & Rao, H. R. (2006). Repeated use of e-gov web sites: A satisfaction and confidentiality perspective. *International Journal of Electronic Government Research, 2*(3), 1–22. doi:10.4018/jegr.2006070101

Chen, Y., & Dimitrova, D. V. (2006). Electronic government and online engagement: Citizen interaction with government via web portals. *International Journal of Electronic Government Research, 2*(1), 54–76. doi:10.4018/jegr.2006010104

Chhabra, S., & Jaiswal, M. (2008). E-government organizational performance framework: Case study of Haryana State in India - A log linear regression analysis. *International Journal of Electronic Government Research, 4*(3), 57–80. doi:10.4018/jegr.2008070104

Chiang, L. (2009). Trust and security in the e-voting system. *Electronic Government, an International Journal, 6*(4), 343-360.

Choudrie, J., Brinkman, W., & Pathania, R. (2007). Using diffusion theory to determine the digital divide in e-services: Two UK local-area perspectives. *Electronic Government, an International Journal, 4*(3), 345-359.

Chu, P. Y., Hsiao, N., Lee, F. W., & Chen, C. W. (2004). Exploring success factors for Taiwan's government electronic tendering system: Behavioral perspectives from end users. *Government Information Quarterly, 21*(2), 219–234. doi:10.1016/j.giq.2004.01.005

Chu, P. Y., Yeh, S., & Chuang, M. (2008). Reengineering municipality citizen electronic complaint system through citizen relationship management. *Electronic Government, an International Journal, 5*(3), 288-309.

Colesca, S. E. (2009). Understanding trust in e-government. *The Engineering Economist, 3*(3), 7–15.

Colesca, S. E., & Dobrica, L. (2008). Adoption and use of e-government services: The case of Romania. *Journal of Applied Research and Technology, 6*(3), 204–217.

Das, J., DiRienzo, C., & Burbridge, J. Jr. (2008). Global e-government and the role of trust: A cross country analysis. *International Journal of Electronic Government Research, 5*(1), 1–18. doi:10.4018/jegr.2009010101

Davidrajuh, R. (2004). Planning e-government start-up: A case study on e-Sri Lanka. *Electronic Government, an International Journal, 1*(1), 92-106.

DeLone, W. H., & McLean, E. R. (1992). Information systems success: The quest for the dependent variable. *Information Systems Research, 3*(1), 60–95. doi:10.1287/isre.3.1.60

DeLone, W. H., & McLean, E. R. (2003). The DeLone and McLean model of information systems success: A ten year update. *Journal of Management Information Systems, 19*(4), 9–30.

Dimitrova, D. V., & Chen, Y. C. (2006). Profiling the adopters of e-government information and services - The influence of psychological characteristics, civic mindedness, and information channels. *Social Science Computer Review, 24*(2), 172–188. doi:10.1177/0894439305281517

Dwivedi, Y. K., Khan, N., & Papazafeiropoulou, A. (2007). Consumer adoption and usage of broadband in Bangladesh. *Electronic Government, an International Journal, 4*(3), 299-313.

Dwivedi, Y. K., Khoumbati, K., Williams, M. D., & Lal, B. (2007). Factors affecting consumers' behavioural intention to adopt broadband in Pakistan. *Transforming Government: People. Process and Policy, 1*(3), 285–297.

Dwivedi, Y. K., & Weerakkody, V. (2007). Examining the factors affecting the adoption of broadband in the Kingdom of Saudi Arabia. *Electronic Government, an International Journal, 4*(1), 43-58.

Dwivedi, Y. K., & Williams, M. D. (2008). Demographic Influence on UK citizens e-government adoption. *Electronic Government, an International Journal, 5*(3), 261-274.

Esterling, K., Lazer, D. M. J., & Neblo, M. A. (2005). Home (Page) style: Determinates of the quality of the house members' web sites. *International Journal of Electronic Government Research, 1*(2), 50–63. doi:10.4018/jegr.2005040103

Falivene, G. M., & Silva, G. M. (2008). Reflections and proposals on public officials training and promotion of e-government. *International Journal of Electronic Government Research, 4*(2), 43–58. doi:10.4018/jegr.2008040104

Floropoulos, J., Spathis, C., Halvatzis, D., & Tsipouridou, M. (2010). Measuring the success of the Greek Taxation Information System. *International Journal of Information Management, 30*(1), 47–56. doi:10.1016/j.ijinfomgt.2009.03.013

Fu, J. R., Chao, W. P., & Farn, C. K. (2004). Determinants of taxpayers' adoption of electronic filing methods in Taiwan: An exploratory study. *Journal of Government Information, 30*(5-6), 658–683. doi:10.1016/j.jgi.2004.11.002

Fu, J. R., Farn, C. K., & Chao, W. P. (2006). Acceptance of electronic tax filing: A study of taxpayer intentions. *Information & Management, 43*(1), 109–126. doi:10.1016/j.im.2005.04.001

Fu-Lai, T. Y., & Yu, T. (2008). Uncertainty, human agency and e-government. *Transforming Government: People, Process, and Policy, 2*(4), 283–296. doi:10.1108/17506160810917963

Gotoh, R. (2009). Critical factors increasing user satisfaction with e-government services. *Electronic Government, an International Journal, 6*(3), 252-264.

Gronlund, A. (2005). State of the art in e-gov research: Surveying conference publications. *International Journal of Electronic Government Research, 1*(4), 1–25. doi:10.4018/jegr.2005100101

Gumussoy, C. A., & Calisir, F. (2009). Understanding factors affecting e-reverse auction use: An integrative approach. *Computers in Human Behavior, 25*(4), 975–988. doi:10.1016/j.chb.2009.04.006

Hamner, M., & Al-Qahtani, F. (2009). Enhancing the case for electronic government in developing nations: A people-centric study focused in Saudi Arabia. *Government Information Quarterly*, *26*(1), 137–143. doi:10.1016/j.giq.2007.08.008

Hinnant, C. C., & O'Looney, J. A. (2003). Examining pre-adoption interest in online innovations: An exploratory study of e-service personalization in the public sector. *IEEE Transactions on Engineering Management*, *50*(4), 436–447. doi:10.1109/TEM.2003.820133

Horst, M., Kuttschreuter, M., & Gutteling, J. M. (2007). Perceived usefulness, personal experiences, risk perception and trust as determinants of adoption of e-government services in The Netherlands. *Computers in Human Behavior*, *23*(4), 1838–1852. doi:10.1016/j.chb.2005.11.003

Hsu, F. M., & Chen, T. Y. (2007). Understanding information systems usage behavior in e-government: The role of context and perceived value. In *Proceedings of the Pacific Asia Conference on Information Systems*.

Hsu, L. (2005). The adoption and implementation of projects-ABCDE (MOEA) – Based on Grounded and TAM theory. *Electronic Government, an International Journal*, *2*(2), 144-159.

Hung, S. Y., Chang, C. M., & Yu, T. J. (2006). Determinants of user acceptance of the e-Government services: The case of online tax filing and payment system. *Government Information Quarterly*, *23*(1), 97–122. doi:10.1016/j.giq.2005.11.005

Hung, S. Y., Tang, K. Z., Chang, C. M., & Ke, C. D. (2009). User acceptance of intergovernmental services: An example of electronic document management system. *Government Information Quarterly*, *26*(2), 387–397. doi:10.1016/j.giq.2008.07.003

Hung, Y. H., Wang, Y. S., & Chou, S. C. T. (2007). User acceptance of e-government services. In *Proceedings of the Pacific Asia Conference on Information Systems*.

Jaeger, P. T. (2003). The endless wire: E-government as global phenomenon. *Government Information Quarterly*, *20*, 323–331. doi:10.1016/j.giq.2003.08.003

Janssen, M., & Klievink, B. (2009). The role of intermediaries in multi-channel service delivery strategies. *International Journal of Electronic Government Research*, *5*(3), 36–46. doi:10.4018/jegr.2009070103

Janssen, M., & Kuk, G. (2007). E-Government business models for public service networks. *International Journal of Electronic Government Research*, *3*(3), 54–71. doi:10.4018/jegr.2007070104

Joia, L. A. (2004). Bridging the digital divide: Some initiatives in Brazil. *Electronic Government, an International Journal*, *1*(3), 300-315.

Kaliannan, M., & Awang, H. (2009). Adoption and use of e-government services: A case study on e-procurement in Malaysia. In Bulucea, C. A., Mladenov, V., Pop, E., Leba, M., & Mastorakis, N. (Eds.), *Recent advances in e-activities, information security and privacy* (pp. 88–93). Stevens Point, WI: WSEAS Press.

Kanat, I. E., & Ozkan, S. (2009). Exploring citizens' perception of government to citizen services: A model based on theory of planned behaviour (TPB). *Transforming Government: People, Process, and Policy*, *3*(4), 406–419. doi:10.1108/17506160910997900

Khoumbati, K., Dwivedi, Y. K., Lal, B., & Chen H. (2007). Broadband adoption in Pakistan. *Electronic Government, an International Journal*, *4*(4), 451-465.

Khoumbati, K., & Themistocleous, M. (2007). Application of fuzzy simulation for the evaluation of enterprise application integration in healthcare organisations. *Transforming Government: People. Process and Policy*, *1*(3), 230–241.

Kim, C., & Holzer, M. (2006). Public administrators' acceptance of the practice of digital democracy: A model explaining the utilization of online policy forums in South Korea. *International Journal of Electronic Government Research, 2*(2), 22–48. doi:10.4018/jegr.2006040102

Kim, S., & Lee, H. (2006). The impact of organizational context and information technology on employee knowledge-sharing capabilities. *Public Administration Review, 66*(3), 370–385. doi:10.1111/j.1540-6210.2006.00595.x

Kolsaker, A. (2006). Reconceptualising e-government as a tool of governance: The UK case. *Electronic Government, an International Journal, 3*(4), 347-355.

Kolsaker, A., & Lee-Kelley, L. (2006). 'Mind the Gap': E-government and e-democracy. In M. A. Wimmer, H. J. Scholl, A. Gronlund, & K. V. Andersen (Eds.), *Proceedings of the 5th International Conference on Electronic Government* (LNCS 4084, pp. 96-106).

Kraemer, K. L., & King, J. L. (2003). *Information technology and administrative reform: Will the time after e-government be different?* Retrieved from http://www.crito.uci.edu

Krell, K., & Matook, S. (2009). Competitive advantage from mandatory investments: An empirical study of Australian firms. *The Journal of Strategic Information Systems, 18*(1), 31–45. doi:10.1016/j.jsis.2008.12.001

Kunstelj, M., Jukic, T., & Vintar, M. (2007). Analysing the demand side of e-government: What can we learn from slovenian users? In M. A. Wimmer, J. Scholl, & A. Gronlund (Eds.), *Proceedings of the 6th International Conference on Electronic Government* (LNCS 4656, pp. 305-317).

Lau, A. S. M. (2004). Strategies to encourage the adoption of G2C e-government services in Hong Kong. *Electronic Government, an International Journal, 1*(3), 273-292.

Lau, A. S. M., & Kwok, V. W. S. (2007). How e-government strategies influence e-commerce adoption by SMEs. *Electronic Government, an International Journal, 4*(1), 20-42.

Lean, O. K., Zailani, S., Ramayah, T., & Fernando, Y. (2009). Factors influencing intention to use e-government services among citizens in Malaysia. *International Journal of Information Management, 29*(6), 458–475. doi:10.1016/j.ijinfomgt.2009.03.012

Lee, J., & Rao, H. R. (2009). Task complexity and different decision criteria for online service acceptance: A comparison of two e-government compliance service domains. *Decision Support Systems, 47*(4), 424–435. doi:10.1016/j.dss.2009.04.009

Lee, K. C., Kirlidog, M., Lee, S., & Lim, G. G. (2008). User evaluations of tax filing web sites: A comparative study of South Korea and Turkey. *Online Information Review, 32*(6), 842–859. doi:10.1108/14684520810923962

Li, X., Hess, T. J., & Valacich, J. S. (2008). Why do we trust new technology? A study of initial trust formation with organizational information systems. *The Journal of Strategic Information Systems, 17*(1), 39–71. doi:10.1016/j.jsis.2008.01.001

Lim, J. H., & Tang, S. Y. (2008). Urban e-government initiatives and environmental decision performance in Korea. *Journal of Public Administration: Research and Theory, 18*(1), 109–138. doi:10.1093/jopart/mum005

Loo, W. H., Yeow, P. H. P., & Chong, S. C. (2009). User acceptance of Malaysian government multipurpose smartcard applications. *Government Information Quarterly, 26*(2), 358–367. doi:10.1016/j.giq.2008.07.004

Lu, C. T., Huang, S. Y., & Lo, P. Y. (2010). An empirical study of on-line tax filing acceptance model: Integrating TAM and TPB. *African Journal of Business Management, 4*(5), 800–810.

Luk, S. C. Y. (2009). The impact of leadership and stakeholders on the success/failure of e-government service: Using the case study of e-stamping service in Hong Kong. *Government Information Quarterly, 26*(4), 594–604. doi:10.1016/j.giq.2009.02.009

Luna-Reyes, L. F., Gil-Garcia, J. R., & Estrada-Marroquin, M. (2008). The impact of institutions on interorganizational IT projects in the Mexican federal government. *International Journal of Electronic Government Research, 4*(2), 27–42. doi:10.4018/jegr.2008040103

Marche, S., & McNiven, J. D. (2003). E-government and e-governance: The future isn't what it used to be. *Canadian Journal of Administrative Sciences, 20*(1), 74–86. doi:10.1111/j.1936-4490.2003.tb00306.x

Mbarika, V. W., & Byrd, T. A. (2009). An exploratory study of strategies to improve Africa's least developed economies' telecommunications infrastructure: The stakeholders speak. *IEEE Transactions on Engineering Management, 56*(2), 312–328. doi:10.1109/TEM.2009.2013826

McNeal, R. S., Schmeida, M., & Hale, K. (2007). E-disclosure laws and electronic campaign finance reform: Lessons from the diffusion of e-government policies in the States. *Government Information Quarterly, 24*(2), 312–325. doi:10.1016/j.giq.2006.06.006

McNeal, R. S., Tolbert, C. J., Mossberger, K., & Dotterweich, L. J. (2003). Innovating in digital government in the American states. *Social Science Quarterly, 84*(1), 52–70. doi:10.1111/1540-6237.00140

Mirchandani, D. A., Johnson, J. H., & Joshi, K. (2008). Perspectives of citizens towards e-government in Thailand and Indonesia: A multigroup analysis. *Information Systems Frontiers, 10*(4), 483–497. doi:10.1007/s10796-008-9102-7

Mitra, R. K., & Gupta, M. P. (2008). A contextual perspective of performance assessment in eGovernment: A study of Indian Police Administration. *Government Information Quarterly, 25*(2), 278–302. doi:10.1016/j.giq.2006.03.008

Moon, M. J., & Norris, D. F. (2005). Does managerial orientation matter? The adoption of reinventing government and e-government at the municipal level. *Information Systems Journal, 15*(1), 43–60. doi:10.1111/j.1365-2575.2005.00185.x

Moynihan, D. P., & Silva, C. L. (2008). The administrators of democracy: A research note on local election officials. *Public Administration Review, 68*(5), 816–827. doi:10.1111/j.1540-6210.2008.00923.x

Myers, B. L., Kappelman, L. A., & Prybutok, V. R. (1997). A comprehensive model for assessing quality and productivity of the information systems function: Toward a theory for information systems assessment. *Information Resources Management Journal*, 6–25.

Norris, F. D., & Lloyd, B. A. (2006). The scholarly literature on e-government: Characterizing a nascent field. *International Journal of Electronic Government Research, 2*(4), 40–56. doi:10.4018/jegr.2006100103

Norris, P. (2005). The impact of the internet on political activism: Evidence from Europe. *International Journal of Electronic Government Research, 1*(1), 20–39. doi:10.4018/jegr.2005010102

Norris, P., & Curtice, J. (2006). If you build a political web site, will they come? The Internet and political activism in Britain. *International Journal of Electronic Government Research, 2*(2), 1–21. doi:10.4018/jegr.2006040101

Ojha, A., Sahu, G. P., & Gupta, M. P. (2009). Antecedents of paperless income tax filing by young professionals in India: An exploratory study. *Transforming Government: People, Process, and Policy, 3*(1), 65–90. doi:10.1108/17506160910940740

Ozkan, S., Koseler, R., & Baykal, N. (2009). Evaluating learning management systems: Adoption of hexagonal e-learning assessment model in higher education. *Transforming Government: People, Process, and Policy, 3*(2), 111–130. doi:10.1108/17506160910960522

Parent, M., Vandebeek, C. A., & Gemino, A. C. (2005). Building citizen trust through e-government. *Government Information Quarterly, 22*(4), 720–736. doi:10.1016/j.giq.2005.10.001

Parvez, Z. (2006). Examining e-democracy through a double structuration loop. *Electronic Government, an International Journal, 3*(3), 329-346.

Parvez, Z. (2008). E-Democracy from the perspective of local elected members. *International Journal of Electronic Government Research, 4*(3), 20–35. doi:10.4018/jegr.2008070102

Phang, C. W., Sutanto, J., Kankanhalli, A., Li, Y., Tan, B. C. Y., & Teo, H. H. (2006). Senior citizens' acceptance of information systems: A study in the context of e-government services. *IEEE Transactions on Engineering Management, 53*(4), 555–569. doi:10.1109/TEM.2006.883710

Pieterson, W., & Teerling, M. (2009). Channel integration in governmental service delivery: The effects on citizen behavior and perceptions. In M. A. Wimmer, H. J. Scholl, M. Janssen, & R. Traunmuller (Eds.), *Proceedings of the International Conference on Electronic Government* (LNCS 5693, pp. 222-233).

Pieterson, W., Teerling, M., & Ebbers, W. (2008). Channel perceptions and usage: Beyond media richness factors. In M. A. Wimmer, H. J. Scholl, & E. Ferro (Eds.), *Proceedings of the International Conference on Electronic Government* (LNCS 5184, pp. 219-230).

Pina, V., Torres, L., & Royo, S. (2009). E-government evolution in EU local governments: A comparative perspective. *Online Information Review, 33*(6), 1137–1168. doi:10.1108/14684520911011052

Pinho, J. C., & Macedo, I. M. (2008). Examining the antecedents and consequences of online satisfaction within the public sector: The case of taxation services. *Transforming Government: People. Process and Policy, 2*(3), 177–193.

Plouffe, C., Hulland, J., & Vandenbosch, M. (2001). Research report: Richness versus parsimony in modeling technology adoption decisions – understanding merchant adoption of a smart card-based payment system. *Information Systems Research, 12*, 208–222. doi:10.1287/isre.12.2.208.9697

Prybutok, V. R., Zhang, X. N., & Ryan, S. D. (2008). Evaluating leadership, IT quality, and net benefits in an e-government environment. *Information & Management, 45*(3), 143–152. doi:10.1016/j.im.2007.12.004

Reddick, C. G. (2005). Citizen-initiated contacts with Ontario local e-government: Administrators' responses to contacts. *International Journal of Electronic Government Research, 1*(4), 45–62. doi:10.4018/jegr.2005100103

Reddick, C. G. (2006). Information resource managers and e-government effectiveness: A survey of Texas state agencies. *Government Information Quarterly, 23*(2), 249–266. doi:10.1016/j.giq.2005.11.006

Reddick, C. G. (2009). The adoption of centralized customer service systems: A survey of local governments. *Government Information Quarterly, 26*(1), 219–226. doi:10.1016/j.giq.2008.03.005

Sahu, G. P., & Gupta, M. P. (2007). Users' acceptance of e-government: A study of Indian central excise. *International Journal of Electronic Government Research, 3*(3), 1–21. doi:10.4018/jegr.2007070101

Sambasivan, M., Wemyss, G. P., & Rose, R. C. (2010). User acceptance of a G2B system: A case of electronic procurement system in Malaysia. *Internet Research, 20*(2), 169–187. doi:10.1108/10662241011032236

Sang, S., Lee, J. D., & Lee, J. (2009). E-government adoption in ASEAN: The case of Cambodia. *Internet Research, 19*(5), 517–534. doi:10.1108/10662240910998869

Sang, S., Lee, J. D., & Lee, J. (2010). E-government adoption in Cambodia: A partial least squares approach. *Transforming Government: People, Process, and Policy, 4*(2), 138–157. doi:10.1108/17506161011047370

Schaupp, L. C., & Carter, L. (2010). The impact of trust, risk and optimism bias on e-file adoption. *Information Systems Frontiers, 12*(3), 299–309. doi:10.1007/s10796-008-9138-8

Schaupp, L. C., Carter, L., & McBride, M. E. (2010). E-file adoption: A study of US taxpayers' intentions. *Computers in Human Behavior, 26*(4), 636–644. doi:10.1016/j.chb.2009.12.017

Seddon, P. B. (1997). A respecification and extension of the DeLone and McLean model of IS success. *Information Systems Research, 8*(3), 240–253. doi:10.1287/isre.8.3.240

Seeman, E. D., O'Hara, M. T., Holloway, J., & Forst, A. (2007). The impact of government intervention on technology adoption and diffusion: The example of wireless location technology, *Electronic Government, an International Journal, 4*(1), 1-19.

Segovia, R. H., Jennex, M. E., & Beatty, J. (2009). Paralingual web design and trust in e-government. *International Journal of Electronic Government Research, 5*(1), 36–49. doi:10.4018/jegr.2009091803

Senyucel, Z. (2007). Assessing the impact of e-government on providers and users of the IS function: A structuration perspective. *Transforming Government: People, Process, and Policy, 1*(2), 131–144. doi:10.1108/17506160710751968

Serrano-Cinca, C., Rueda-Tomas, M., & Poitillo-Tarragona, P. (2009). Determinants of e-government extension. *Online Information Review, 33*(3), 476–498. doi:10.1108/14684520910969916

Seyal, A. H., & Pijpers, G. G. M. (2004). Senior government executives' use of the internet: A Bruneian scenario. *Behaviour & Information Technology, 23*(3), 197–210. doi:10.1080/0144929041000166 9978

Shareef, M. A., Kumar, U., Kumar, V., & Dwivedi, Y. K. (2009). Identifying critical factors for adoption of e-government. *Electronic Government, an International Journal, 6*(1), 70-96.

Shelley, M. C. II, Thrane, L. E., & Shulman, S. W. (2006). Generational differences in information technology use and political involvement. *International Journal of Electronic Government Research, 2*(1), 36–53. doi:10.4018/jegr.2006010103

Srivastava, S. C., & Teo, T. S. H. (2006). Performance impacts of e-government: An international perspective. In *Proceedings of the Pacific Asia Conference on Information Systems.*

Srivastava, S. C., & Teo, T. S. H. (2007a). E-government payoffs: Evidence from cross-country data. *Journal of Global Information Management, 15*(4), 20–40. doi:10.4018/jgim.2007100102

Srivastava, S. C., & Teo, T. S. H. (2007b). What facilitates e-government development? A cross-country analysis. *Electronic Government, an International Journal, 4*(4), 365-378.

Sun, S., Ju, T. L., & Chen, P. (2006). E-government impacts on effectiveness: A survey study of an e-official-document system. *Electronic Government, an International Journal, 3*(2), 174-189.

Tang, H., Chung, S. H., & Se, C. W. (2009). Examining the impact of possible antecedents on service usage: An empirical study on Macao e-government. *Electronic Government, an International Journal, 6*(1), 97-109.

Teerling, M. L., & Pieterson, W. (2010). Multi-channel marketing: An experiment on guiding citizens to the electronic channels. *Government Information Quarterly, 27*(1), 98–107. doi:10.1016/j.giq.2009.08.003

Teo, T. S. H., Srivastava, S. C., & Jiang, L. (2008). Trust and electronic government success: An empirical study. *Journal of Management Information Systems, 25*(3), 99–131. doi:10.2753/MIS0742-1222250303

Tolbert, C. J., Mossberger, K., & McNeal, R. (2008). Institutions, policy innovation, and e-government in the American states. *Public Administration Review, 68*(3), 549–563. doi:10.1111/j.1540-6210.2008.00890.x

Tung, L. L., & Rieck, O. (2005). Adoption of electronic government services among business organizations in Singapore. *The Journal of Strategic Information Systems, 14*(4), 417–440. doi:10.1016/j.jsis.2005.06.001

van Deursen, A. J. A. M., & van Dijk, J. A. G. M. (2009). Improving digital skills for the use of online public information and services. *Government Information Quarterly, 26*(2), 333–340. doi:10.1016/j.giq.2008.11.002

van Dijk, J. A. G. M., Peters, O., & Ebbers, W. (2008). Explaining the acceptance and use of government Internet services: A multivariate analysis of 2006 survey data in The Netherlands. *Government Information Quarterly, 25*, 379–399. doi:10.1016/j.giq.2007.09.006

van Veenstra, A. F., & Zuurmond, A. (2009). Opening the black box: Exploring the effect of transformation on online service delivery in local governments. In M. A. Wimmer, H. J. Scholl, M. Janssen, & R. Traunmuller (Eds.), *Proceedings of the International Conference on Electronic Government* (LNCS 5693, pp. 234-244).

Vathanophas, V., Krittayaphongphun, N., & Klomsiri, C. (2008). Technology acceptance toward e-government initiative in Royal Thai Navy. *Transforming Government: People, Process, and Policy, 2*(4), 256–282. doi:10.1108/17506160810917954

Venkatesh, V., Morris, M. G., Davis, G. B., & Davis, F. D. (2003). User acceptance of information technology: Toward a unified view. *Management Information Systems Quarterly, 27*(3), 425–478.

Verdegem, P., & Verleye, G. (2009). User-centered e-government in practice: A comprehensive model for measuring user satisfaction. *Government Information Quarterly, 26*(3), 487–497. doi:10.1016/j.giq.2009.03.005

Vonk, G., Geertman, S., & Schot, P. (2007). New technologies stuck in old hierarchies: The diffusion of geo-information technologies in Dutch public organizations. *Public Administration Review, 67*(4), 745–756. doi:10.1111/j.1540-6210.2007.00757.x

Wang, Y. S. (2002). The adoption of electronic tax filing systems: An empirical study. *Government Information Quarterly, 20*(4), 333–352. doi:10.1016/j.giq.2003.08.005

Wang, Y. S., & Liao, Y. W. (2008). Assessing eGovernment systems success: A validation of the DeLone and McLean model of information systems success. *Government Information Quarterly, 25*(4), 717–733. doi:10.1016/j.giq.2007.06.002

Wang, Y. S., & Shih, Y. W. (2009). Why do people use information kiosks? A validation of the unified theory of acceptance and use of technology. *Government Information Quarterly, 26*(1), 158–165. doi:10.1016/j.giq.2008.07.001

Wangpipatwong, S., Chutimaskul, W., & Papasratorn, B. (2009). Quality enhancing the continued use of e-government web sites: Evidence from e-citizens of Thailand. *International Journal of Electronic Government Research*, 5(1), 19–35. doi:10.4018/jegr.2009092202

Warkentin, M., Gefen, D., Pavlou, P. A., & Rose, G. M. (2002). Encouraging citizen adoption of e-government by building trust. *Electronic Markets*, *12*(3), 157–162. doi:10.1080/101967802320245929

West, D. M. (2004). E-government and the transformation of service delivery and citizen attitudes. *Public Administration Review*, *64*(1), 15–27. doi:10.1111/j.1540-6210.2004.00343.x

Yeow, P. H. P., & Loo, W. H. (2009). Acceptability of ATM and transit applications embedded in multipurpose smart identity card: An exploratory study in Malaysia. *International Journal of Electronic Government Research*, 5(2), 37–56. doi:10.4018/jegr.2009040103

This work was previously published in the International Journal of Electronic Government Research, Volume 7, Issue 4, edited by Vishanth Weerakkody, pp. 64-88, copyright 2011 by IGI Publishing (an imprint of IGI Global).

Compilation of References

Abad, E., Palacio, F., Nuin, M., de Zarate, A. G., Juarros, A., & Gomez, J. M. (2009). RFID smart tag for traceability and cold chain monitoring of foods: Demonstration in an intercontinental fresh fish logistic chain. *Journal of Food Engineering, 93*(4), 394–399. doi:10.1016/j.jfoodeng.2009.02.004

Aberbach, J. D., & Christensen, T. (2005). Citizens and consumers: an NPM dilemma. *Public Management Review, 7*(2), 225–245. doi:10.1080/14719030500091319

Accenture. (2005). *Governments Must Move Beyond e-Government Initiatives to Enhance Customer Service for Citizens, Accenture Study Finds.* Retrieved from http://accenture.tekgroup.com/article_display.cfm? article_id=4205.

Ackoff, R. (1967). Management misinformation systems. *Management Science,* 147–156.

Adams, N. J., Macintosh, A., & Johnston, J. (2005). e-Petitioning: Enabling Ground-up Participation. In M. Funabashi & A. Grzech (Eds.), *Challenges of Expanding Internet: E-Commerce, E-Business and E-Government: Proceedings of the 5th IFIP Conference on e-Commerce, E-Business and E-Government,* Poznan, Poland.

Adams, N., Haston, S., Gillespie, N., & Macintosh, A. (2003, September). *Conventional and Electronic Service Delivery Within Public Authorities: The Issues And Lessons From The Private Sector.* Paper presented at the 2nd International Conference on Electronic Government, Prague, Czech Republic.

Adams, D., Nelson, R., & Todd, P. (1992). Perceived usefulness, ease of use and usage of information technology: A replication. *Management Information Systems Quarterly,* 227–247. doi:10.2307/249577

Addison, T. (2003). E-commerce project development risks: Evidence from a Delphi survey. *International Journal of Information Management, 23,* 25–40. doi:10.1016/S0268-4012(02)00066-X

Agarwal, R., & Prasad, J. (1998). The antecedents and consequents of user perceptions in information technology adoption. *Decision Support Systems, 22*(1), 15–29. doi:10.1016/S0167-9236(97)00006-7

Ahmed, N. (2006). *An overview of e-participation models.* Retrieved February 6, 2010, from http://unpan1.un.org/intradoc/groups/public/documents/UN/UNPAN023622.pdf

Aichholzer, G. (2004). Scenarios of e-Government in 2010 and implications for strategy design. *Electronic. Journal of E-Government, 2*(1), 1–10.

Aicholzer, G., & Schmutzer, R. (2000). Organizational challenges to the development of electronic government. In *Proceedings of the 11th International Workshop on Database and Expert Systems Applications,* New York, NY.

Ajzen, I. (1991). The theory of planned behavior. *Organizational Behavior and Human Decision Processes, 50*(2), 179–211. doi:10.1016/0749-5978(91)90020-T

Ajzen, I., & Fishbein, M. (1972). Attitudes and normative beliefs as factors influencing intentions'. *Journal of Personality and Social Psychology, 21,* 1–9. doi:10.1037/h0031930

Ajzen, I., & Fishbein, M. (1980). *Understanding Attitudes and Predicting Social Behavior.* Englewood Cliffs, NJ: Prentice Hall.

Alavi, M., Kayworth, T. R., & Leidner, D. E. (2005). An empirical examination of the influence of organizational culture on knowledge management practices. *Journal of Management Information Systems, 22*(3), 191–224. doi:10.2753/MIS0742-1222220307

Alcock, R., & Lenihan, D. G. (2001). *Opening the e-government file: governing in the 21st century; results of the crossing boundaries cross-country tour*. Ottawa, ON, Canada: Centre for Collaborative Government.

Allen, B. A., Juillet, L., Paquet, G., & Roy, J. (2001). E-Governance & government on-line in Canada: Partnerships, people & prospects. *Government Information Quarterly*, *18*(2), 93–104. doi:10.1016/S0740-624X(01)00063-6

Allen, C., Kania, D., & Yaeckel, B. (2001). *One-to-one web marketing: Build a relationship marketing strategy one customer at a time*. New York, NY: John Wiley & Sons.

Alles, M. G., Kogan, A., & Vasarhelyi, M. A. (2008). Putting continuous auditing theory into practice: Lessons from two pilot implementations. *Journal of Information Systems*, *22*(2), 195–214. doi:10.2308/jis.2008.22.2.195

Al-Nuaim, H. (2009). How "E" are Arab municipalities? An evaluation of Arab capital municipal web sites. *International Journal of E-Government Research*, *5*(1), 50–63. doi:10.4018/jegr.2009010104

Al-Sebie, M., Irani, Z., & Eldabi, T. (2005). Issues relating to the transaction stage of the e-government system. *Electronic Government, an International Journal*, *2*(4), 446-459.

Al-Shafi, S., & Weerakkody, V. (2009). Implementing free Wi-Fi in public parks: An empirical study in Qatar. *International Journal of Electronic Government Research*, *5*(3), 21–35. doi:10.4018/jegr.2009070102

Alter, S., & Ginzberg, M. (1978). Managing uncertainty in MIS implementation. *Sloan Management Review*, *20*(1), 23–31.

Amoako-Gyampah, K., & Salam, A. F. (2004). An Extension of the Technology Acceptance Model in an ERP Implementation Environment. *Information & Management*, *41*, 731–745. doi:10.1016/j.im.2003.08.010

Andersen, D. F., & Dawes, S. S. (1991). *Government Information Management. A Primer and Casebook*. Eaglewood Cliffs, NJ: Prentice Hall.

Andersen, K. V., & Henriksen, H. Z. (2006). E-government maturity models: Extension of the Layne and Lee model. *Government Information Quarterly*, *23*(2), 236–248. doi:10.1016/j.giq.2005.11.008

Anderson, C. (2006). *The long tail -- why the future of business is selling less of more: The new economics of culture and commerce*. New York, NY: Hyperion.

Anderson, K. V., & Henriksen, H. Z. (2005). The first leg of e-government research: Domains and application areas 1998-2003. *International Journal of Electronic Government Research*, *1*(4), 26–44. doi:10.4018/jegr.2005100102

Anonymous. (2007). *Malaysia broadband market*. Retrieved from http://www.budde.com.au/Research/Malaysia-Broadband-Market.html

Ansell, C., & Gash, A. (2008). Collaborative governance in theory and practice. *Journal of Public Administration: Research and Theory*, *18*(4), 543–571. doi:10.1093/jopart/mum032

Archer, N. P. (2005). An overview of the change management process in e-government. *International Journal of Electronic Business*, *3*(1), 68–87. doi:10.1504/IJEB.2005.006389

Ardagna, D., & Pernici, B. (2006). Dynamic web service composition with QoS constraints. *International Journal of Business Process Integration and Management*, *1*(4), 233–243. doi:10.1504/IJBPIM.2006.012622

Arellano, J. (2008). Human RFID Chip Implants. *Rural Telecommunications*, *27*(1), 8.

Arrow, K. (1970). *Essays in the theory of risk-bearing*. Amsterdam, The Netherlands: North-Holland.

Asif, Z., & Mandviwalla, M. (2005). Integrating the supply chain with RFID. *Communications of the Association for Information Systems*, *15*, 393–427.

Atkinson, R. D., & Castro, D. (2008). *Digital Quality of Life: Understanding the Personal and Social Benefits of the Information Technology Revolution*. Retrieved from http://archive.itif.org/index.php?id=179

Atkinson, W. (2004). Tagged: The risks and rewards of RFID technology. *Risk Management*, *14*(1).

Australian Bureau of Statistics. (2009). Cat No. 3201.0 -. *Population by Age and Sex, Australian States and Territories*, (June): 2009. Retrieved from http://abs.gov.au/AUSSTATS.

Australian Communications and Media Authority (ACMA). (2005). *ACMA telecommunications performance report, December 2005.* Retrieved from http://www.acma.gov.au/WEB/STANDARD/pc=PC_100376

Australian Communications and Media Authority (ACMA). (2009). *ACMA communications report, November 2009.* Retrieved from http://www.acma.gov.au/WEB/STANDARD/pc=PC_311972#

Australian Government Information Management Office. (2009). *Engage: Getting on with Government 2.0.* Retrieved from http://www.finance.gov.au/publications/gov20taskforcereport/

Ayre, L. B. (2005). RFID and libraries. In Garfinkel, S., & Rosenberg, B. (Eds.), *Wireless privacy: RFID, Bluetooth and 802.11* (pp. 228–241). Reading, MA: Addison-Wesley.

Azad, B., & Faraj, S. (2009). E-Government institutionalizing practices of a land registration mapping system. *Government Information Quarterly, 26*(1), 5–14. doi:10.1016/j.giq.2008.08.005

Baggaley, A. R. (1981). Multivariate analysis: An introduction for consumers of behavioral research. *Evaluation Review, 5,* 123–131. doi:10.1177/0193841X8100500106

Bailey, J. E., & Pearson, S. W. (1983). Development of a tool for measuring and analyzing computer user satisfaction. *Management Science, 29*(5), 530–545. doi:10.1287/mnsc.29.5.530

Ballmer, S. (2002). The promise of e-government. *Outlook Journal, 1.* Retrieved from http://www.accenture.com/NR/rdonlyres/E4DDAA5B-566F-4CD6-ADA0-E48AD0E1DA1D/0/Ballmer.pdf

Bandura, A. (1977). Self-efficacy: Toward a unifying theory of behavioral change. *Psychological Review, 84,* 191–215. doi:10.1037/0033-295X.84.2.191

Banker, R. D., Chang, H., & Pizzini, M. J. (2004). The Balanced Scorecard: judgmental effects of performance measures linked to strategy. *Accounting Review, 79*(1), 1–23. doi:10.2308/accr.2004.79.1.1

Bansode, S. Y., & Desale, S. K. (2009). Implementation of RFID technology in University of Pune Library. *Program-Electronic Library and Information Systems, 43*(2), 202–214. doi:10.1108/00330330910954406

Baranauskas, M. C. C. (2009). Socially aware computing. In *Proceedings of the 6th International Conference on Engineering and Computer Education*, Buenos Aires, Argentina.

Baranauskas, M. C. C., Hornung, H., & Martins, M. C. (2008). Design Socialmente Responsável: Desafios de Interface de Usuário no Contexto Brasileiro. In *Proceedings of the 35th Seminário Integrado de Software e Hardware*, Porto Alegre, Brazil (pp. 91-105).

Baringhorst, S. (2009). Political Campaigning in Changing Media Cultures – Typological and Historical Approaches. In Baringhorst, S., Kneip, V., & Niesyto, J. (Eds.), *Political Campaigning on the Web.* London: Transaction Publishers.

Barki, H., Rivard, S., & Talbot, J. (1993). Toward an assessment of software development risk. *Journal of Management Information Systems, 10*(2), 203–236.

Barki, H., Rivard, S., & Talbot, J. (2001). An integrative contingency model of software project risk management. *Journal of Management Information Systems, 17*(4), 37–69.

Barnes, S. J., & Vidgen, R. (2004). Interactive e-government services: Modelling user perceptions with eQual. *Electronic Government, an International Journal, 1*(2), 213-228.

Barnickel, N., Fluegge, M., & Schmidt, K. (2006). Interoperability in eGovernment through Cross-Ontology Semantic Web Service Composition. In *Proceedings of the 3rd European Semantic Web Conference*, Budva, Montenegro.

Baron, J. (1994). Nonconsequentialist decisions. *The Behavioral and Brain Sciences, 17,* 1–42. doi:10.1017/S0140525X0003301X

Baron, J. (1996). Norm-endorsement utilitarianism and the nature of utility. *Economics and Philosophy, 12,* 165–182. doi:10.1017/S0266267100004144

Baron, J. (2000). *Thinking and deciding.* Cambridge, UK: Cambridge University Press.

Barua, A., Kriebel, C. H., & Mukhopadhyay, T. (1995). Information Technologies and Business Value: An Analytic and Empirical Investigation. *Information Systems Research, 6*(1), 3–23. doi:10.1287/isre.6.1.3

Baumgarten, J., & Chui, M. (2009). E-government 2.0. *The McKinsey Quarterly, 2009*(4).

Beaudin, D. (2001). *A Content Analysis of Disability Access on Government Websites in Australia, the United Kingdom, and the United States.* Retrieved from http://ils.unc.edu/MSpapers/2722.pdf

Beaumaster, S. (2002). Local government IT implementation issues: A challenge for public administration. In *Proceedings of the 35th Hawaii International Conference on System Sciences* (Vol. 5, p. 128).

Becker, J., Niehaves, B., & Krause, A. (2009, August 6-9). *Shared services strategies and their determinants: A multiple case study analysis in the public sector.* Paper presented at the Americas Conference on Information Systems, San Francisco, CA.

Beddie, L., Macintosh, L., & Malina, A. (2001). E-democracy and the Scottish Parliament. In Schmid, B., Stanoevska-Slabeva, K., & Tschammer, V. (Eds.), *Towards the e-society: E-commerce, e-business, and e-government* (pp. 695–706). Dordrecht, The Netherlands: IFIP, Kluwer Academic Publishers.

Bekkers, V., & Moody, R. (2009). Visual Culture and Electronic Government: Exploring a New Generation of E-Government. In M.A. Wimmer et al. (Eds.), *EGOV 2009* (LNCS 5693, pp. 257-269).

Bekkers, V. J. J. M., & Homburg, V. M. F. (2007). The myths of e-government: Looking beyond the assumptions of a new and better government. *The Information Society, 23*(5), 373–382. doi:10.1080/01972240701572913

Bekkers, V. J. J. M., & Homburg, V. M. F. (Eds.). (2005). *The information ecology of e-government (E-government as institutional and technological innovation in public administration)* (2nd ed.). Amsterdam, The Netherlands: IOS Press.

Bekkers, V., & Homburg, V. (2007). The myths of e-government: Looking beyond the assumptions of a new and better government. *The Information Society, 23*(5), 373–382. doi:10.1080/01972240701572913

Belanger, F., & Carter, L. (2010). The digital divide and internet voting acceptance. In *Proceedings of the Fourth International Conference on Digital Society* (pp. 307-310).

Belanger, F., & Carter, L. D. (2005). U-Government: A framework for the evolution of e-government. *Electronic Government, an International Journal, 2*(4), 426-445.

Belanger, F., & Carter, L. (2008). Trust and risk in e-government adoption. *The Journal of Strategic Information Systems, 17*, 165–176. doi:10.1016/j.jsis.2007.12.002

Bélanger, F., Hiller, J., & Smith, W. (2002). Trustworthiness in electronic commerce: The role of privacy, security, and site attributes. *The Journal of Strategic Information Systems, 11*, 245–270. doi:10.1016/S0963-8687(02)00018-5

Benbasat, I., & Barki, H. (2007). Quo Vadis, TAM? *Journal of the Association for Information Systems, 8*(4), 211–218.

Benbasat, I., Dexter, A. S., & Mantha, R. W. (1980). Impact of Organizational Maturity on Information System Skill Needs. *Management Information Systems Quarterly, 4*(1), 21–34. doi:10.2307/248865

Bendavid, Y., Lefebvre, E., Lefebvre, E., & Wamba, S. (2008). Exploring the impact of RFID technology and the EPC network on mobile B2B eCommerce: A case study in the retail industry. *International Journal of Production Economics, 112*, 614–629. doi:10.1016/j.ijpe.2007.05.010

Berce, J., Lanfranco, S., & Vehovar, V. (2008). eGovernance: Information and communication technology, knowledge management and learning culture. *Informatica, 32*, 189–205.

Berkley, B. J., & Gupta, A. (1994). Improving service quality with information technology. *International Journal of Information Management, 14*, 109–121. doi:10.1016/0268-4012(94)90030-2

Berman, J., & Mulligan, D. K. (2003). Digital Grass Roots. Issue Advocacy in the Age of the Internet. In Anderson, D. M., & Cornfield, M. (Eds.), *The Civic Web, Online Politics and Democratic Value* (pp. 77–93). Lanham, MD: Rowman & Littlefield.

Bernard, H. R. (2000). *Social research methods: Qualitative and quantitative approaches.* Newbury Park, CA: Sage.

Berry, C., Krutz, G. S., Langner, B. E., & Budetti, P. (2008). Jump-starting collaboration: The ABCD initiative and the provision of child development services through Medicaid and collaborators. *Public Administration Review, 68*(3), 480–490. doi:10.1111/j.1540-6210.2008.00884.x

Bertot, J. C., Jaeger, P. T., & McClure, P. M. (2008, May 18-21). Citizen centered e-government services: Benefits, costs and research needs. In *Proceedings of the 9th Annual International Digital Government Research Conference*, Montreal, QC, Canada (pp. 137-142).

Bertot, J. C. (2003). The multiple dimensions of the digital divide: More than the technology 'haves' and 'have nots'. *Government Information Quarterly, 20*(2), 185–191. doi:10.1016/S0740-624X(03)00036-4

Bertot, J. C., & Jaeger, P. T. (2006). User-centred e-government: Challenges and benefits for government Web sites. *Government Information Quarterly, 23*(2), 163–169. doi:10.1016/j.giq.2006.02.001

Bertot, J. C., & Jaeger, P. T. (2008). The e-Government paradox: Better customer service doesn't necessarily cost less. *Government Information Quarterly, 25*(2), 149–154. doi:10.1016/j.giq.2007.10.002

Beynon-Davies, D., Owens, I., Williams, M. D., & Hill, R. (2003). *Electronic consultation in the national assembly for Wales*. Paper presented at ECIS, Naples, Italy.

Bhattacherjee, A. (2001). Understanding information systems continuance: An expectation-confirmation model. *Management Information Systems Quarterly, 25*, 351–370. doi:10.2307/3250921

Bhuptani, M., & Moradpour, S. (2005). *RFID Field Guide: Deploying Radio Frequency Identifications Systems.*

Bickman, L. (1987). The functions of program theory. In Bickman, L. (Ed.), *New directions for program evaluation* (pp. 5–17). San Francisco, CA: Jossey-Bass.

Bickman, L. (1990). Study designs. In Yuan, Y. T., & Rivest, M. (Eds.), *Preserving families: Evaluating resources for practitioners and policymakers* (pp. 132–166). Newbury Park, CA: Sage.

Biever, C. (2007). Uproar flares over alzheimer's tags. *New Scientist, 14.* doi:10.1016/S0262-4079(07)61223-8

Bingham, L. B., Nabatchi, T., & O'Leary, R. (2005). The New Governance: Practices and Processes for Stakeholder and Citizen Participation in the Work of Government. *Public Administration Review, 65*(5), 547–558. doi:10.1111/j.1540-6210.2005.00482.x

Blamey, A., & Mackenzie, M. (2007). Theories of change and realistic evaluation. *Evaluation, 13*(4), 439–455. doi:10.1177/1356389007082129

Blau, P. M. (1964). *Exchange and power in social life*. New York, NY: John Wiley & Sons.

Blueprints. (2008). *Promising program descriptions*. Retrieved from http://www.cde.state.co.us/artemis/ucb1210/ucb610919bp032008internet.pdf

Bødker, S. (2006). When second wave HCI meets third wave challenges. In *Proceedings of the 4th Nordic Conference on Human-Computer Interaction* (pp. 1-8). New York, NY: ACM Press.

Boeck, H., & Wamba, S. (2007). RFID and buyer-seller relationships in the retail supply chain. *International Journal of Retail & Distribution Management, 36*(6), 433–460. doi:10.1108/09590550810873929

Boehm, B. W. (1991). Software risk management: Principles and practices. *IEEE Software, 8*(1), 32–41. doi:10.1109/52.62930

Bonacin, R., Melo, A. M., Simoni, C. A. C., & Baranauskas, M. C. C. (2009). Accessibility and interoperability in e-gov systems: Outlining an inclusive development process. *Universal Access in the Information Society, 9*(1), 17–33. doi:10.1007/s10209-009-0157-0

Bonett, M. (2001). Personalization of web services: Opportunities and challenges. *Ariadne, 28*.

Boss, R. W. (2004). RFID technology for libraries. *Library Technology Reports, 39*(6).

Botta-Genoulaz, V., Millet, P. A., & Grabot, B. (2005). A survey of the recent literature on ERP systems. *Computers in Industry, 56*, 510–522. doi:10.1016/j.compind.2005.02.004

Bouckaert, G., & Halligan, J. (2008). *Managing performance. International comparisons*. New York, NY: Routledge.

Boyer-Wright, K. F., & Kottemann J. E. (2008). High-level factors affecting availability of online government services worldwide. *Electronic Government, an International Journal, 5*(4), 375-389.

Boyne, G. A. (2002). Public and private management: What's the difference. *Journal of Management Studies, 39*(1), 97–122. doi:10.1111/1467-6486.00284

Braak, S. W., Oostendorp, H., Prakken, H., & Vreeswijk, G. A. W. (2006, September). *A critical review of argument visualization tools: do users become better reasoners?* Paper presented at the European Conference on Artificial Intelligence, Trento, Italy.

Bradley, R. V., Pridmore, J. L., & Byrd, T. A. (2006). Information systems success in the context of different corporate cultural types: An empirical investigation. *Journal of Management Information Systems, 23*(2), 267–294. doi:10.2753/MIS0742-1222230211

Brady, M. K., & Robertson, C. J. (1999). An exploratory study of service value in the USA and Ecuador. *International Journal of Service Industry Management, 10*(5), 469–486. doi:10.1108/09564239910289003

Bresnahan, T., Brynjolfsson, E., & Hitt, L. M. (2002). Information technology, workplace organization, and the demand for skilled labor: Firm-level evidence. *The Quarterly Journal of Economics, 117*(1), 339–376. doi:10.1162/003355302753399526

Breu, R., Hafner, M., Weber, B., & Novak, A. (2005). Model Driven Security for Inter-organizational Workflows in e-Government. In M. Böhlen et al. (Eds.), *E-Government: Towards Electronic Democracy* (LNCS 3416, pp. 122-133).

Brewster, S. A. (1998). Using non-speech sounds to provide navigation cues. *ACM Transactions on Computer-Human Interaction, 5*(3), 224–259. doi:10.1145/292834.292839

Brinkerhoff, J. M. (2002). Assessing and improving partnership relationships and outcomes: A proposed framework. *Evaluation and Program Planning, 25*(3), 215–231. doi:10.1016/S0149-7189(02)00017-4

Brinkhoff, T. (2010). *City Population.* Retrieved January 1, 2010, from http://www.citypopulation.de

Britten, N. (1995). Qualitative research: Qualitative interviews in medical research. [PubMed]. *British Medical Journal, 311*, 251–253. doi:10.1136/bmj.311.6999.251

Broache, A. (2006). *RFID passports arrive for Americans.* Retrieved March 2010 from http://news.cnet.com/RFiD-passports-arrive-for-Americans/2100-1028_3-6105534.html

Brodkin, E. Z. (2011). Policy work: Street-level organizations under new managerialism. *Journal of Public Administration: Research and Theory, 21*(2), i253–i277. doi:10.1093/jopart/muq093

Broekhuizen, T. (2006). *Understanding channel purchase intentions: Measuring online and offline shopping value perceptions.* Ridderkerk, The Netherlands: Labyrinth Publications.

Brown, P. F., & Parker, C. (Eds.). (2011). *Transformational government framework primer version 1.0.* Retrieved from http://docs.oasis-open.org/tgf/TGF-Primer/v1.0/cnd01/TGF-Primer-v1.0-cnd01.pdf

Brown, M. M., & Brudney, J. L. (1998). A 'smarter, better, faster, and cheaper' government? Contracting for geographic information systems. *Public Administration Review, 58*, 335–345. doi:10.2307/977563

Brown, M. M., & Brudney, J. L. (2003). Learning organizations in the public sector: A study of piece agencies employing information and technology to advance knowledge to advance knowledge. *Public Administration Review, 63*(1), 30–43. doi:10.1111/1540-6210.00262

Brown, T. A. (2006). *Confirmatory factor analysis for applied research.* New York, NY: Guilford Press.

Bruschi, D., Fovino, I. N., & Lanzi, A. (2005). *A Protocol for Anonymous and Accurate E-Polling, Proceedings of E-Government: Towards Electronic Democracy.* Paper presented at the International Conference TCGOV 2005, Bolzano, Italy.

Bryman, A. (2004). *Social research methods.* Oxford, UK: Oxford University Press.

Brynjolfsson, E., & Hitt, L. (1996). Paradox lost? Firm-level evidence on the returns to information systems. *Management Science, 42*(4), 541–558. doi:10.1287/mnsc.42.4.541

Brynjolfsson, E., & Hitt, L. (2000). Beyond computation: Information technology, organizational transformation and business performance. *The Journal of Economic Perspectives, 14*(4), 23–48. doi:10.1257/jep.14.4.23

Brynjolfsson, E., & Yang, S. (1996). Information technology and productivity: A review of the literature. *Advances in Computers, 43*, 179–214. doi:10.1016/S0065-2458(08)60644-0

Bussell, J. (2007). Electoral competition and digital development in India and South Africa. In *Proceedings of the IEEE Conference on Information and Communication Technologies and Development* (pp. 1-9).

Butt, I., & Persuad, A. (2005). Towards a citizen centric model of e-government adoption. In *Proceedings of the 3rd International Conference of E-Governance* (pp. 6-15).

Bwalya, K. J. (2009). Factors affecting adoption of e-government in Zambia. *Electronic Journal of Information Systems in Developing Countries, 38*(4), 1–13.

Cabinet Office of UK. (2000). *Review of major government IT projects – successful IT: Modernizing government in action.* Retrieved from http://www.ogc.gov.uk

CabinetOffice. (2009). *What do we mean by sharing services?* Retrieved from http://www.cabinetoffice.gov.uk/

Campbell, D. (2003). Intra-and intersectoral effects in environmental disclosures: Evidence for legitimacy theory? *Business Strategy and the Environment, 12*(6), 357–371. doi:10.1002/bse.375

Cantwell, D. (2006). *RFID R&D opportunities and the supply chain.* Paper presented at the RFID Academic Convocation, Cambridge, MA.

Capgemini, I. D. C. Rand Europe, Sogeti, & DTi. (2010). *Digitizing public services in Europe: Putting ambition into action – 9th benchmark measurement.* Brussels, Belgium: European Commission.

Capgemini. (2007). *The user challenge: Benchmarking The supply of online public services.* Brussels, Belgium: European Commission.

Carmines, E. G., & Zeller, R. A. (1979). *Reliability and validity assessment.* Thousand Oaks, CA: Sage.

Carpenter, G. S., & Nakamoto, K. (1989). Consumer preference formation and pioneering advantage. *JMR, Journal of Marketing Research, 26*(3), 285–298. doi:10.2307/3172901

Carr, C. (2002). A psychometric evaluation of the expectations, perceptions, and difference-scores generated by the IS-adapted SERVQUAL instrument. *Decision Sciences, 33*, 281–296. doi:10.1111/j.1540-5915.2002.tb01645.x

Carrol, J. M., & Rosson, M. B. (2003). Design rationale as theory. In Carrol, J. M. (Ed.), *HCI models, theories and frameworks: Toward a multidisciplinary science* (pp. 431–461). San Francisco, CA: Morgan Kaufmann. doi:10.1016/B978-155860808-5/50015-0

Carroll, J., Dawson, L. L., & Swatman, P. A. (1998). Using Case Studies to Build Theory: Structure and Rigour. In *Proceedings of the 9th Australasian Conference on Information Systems,* Sydney, NSW, Australia.

Carroll, J., & Swatman, P. (2000). Structured-case: a methodological framework for building theory in information systems research. *European Journal of Information Systems, 9*, 235–242. doi:10.1057/palgrave/ejis/3000374

Carson, R. T. (2000). Contingent valuation: A user's guide. *Environmental Science & Technology, 34*(8), 1413–1418. doi:10.1021/es990728j

Carter, L., & Belanger, F. (2004, January). Citizen adoption of electronic government initiatives. In *Proceedings of the 37th Annual Hawaii International Conference on System Sciences,* Big Island, HI (pp. 119-128).

Carter, L. (2008). E-Government diffusion: A comparison of adoption constructs. *Transforming Government: People, Process, and Policy, 2*(3), 147–161. doi:10.1108/17506160810902167

Carter, L., & Belanger, F. (2005). The utilization of e-government services: Citizen trust, innovation and acceptance factors. *Information Systems Journal, 15*(1), 5–25. doi:10.1111/j.1365-2575.2005.00183.x

Carter, L., & Belanger, F. (2005a). The influence of perceived characteristics of innovating on e-government adoption. *Electronic. Journal of E-Government, 2*(3), 11–20.

Carter, L., & Schaupp, L. C. (2009). Relating acceptance and optimism to e-file adoption. *International Journal of Electronic Government Research, 5*(3), 62–74. doi:10.4018/jegr.2009070105

Carter, L., & Weerakkody, V. (2008). E-Government adoption: A cultural comparison. *Information Systems Frontiers, 10*(4), 473–482. doi:10.1007/s10796-008-9103-6

Carver, S. (2001, December). *The Future of Participatory Approaches Using Geographic Information: developing a research agenda for the 21st Century*. Paper presented at ESF-NSF Meeting on Access and Participatory Approaches in Using Geographical Information, Spoleto, Italy.

Casalo, L. V., Cisneros, J., Guinaliu, M., & Orus, C. (2008). Effects of a virtual citizen community: The case of Expo Zaragoza. *Electronic Government, an International Journal, 5*(2), 131-145.

Cash, J. I., McFarlan, F. W., McKenney, J. L., & Applegate, L. M. (1992). *Corporate Information Systems Management: Text and Cases* (3rd ed.). Homewood, IL: Irwin.

Cassel, C., Hackl, P., & Westlund, A. H. (1999). Robustness of partial least-squares method for estimating latent variable quality structures. *Journal of Applied Statistics, 26*(4), 435–446. doi:10.1080/02664769922322

Cats-Baril, W. L., & Thompson, R. L. (1998). *Information technology and management*. Burr Ridge, IL: Irwin.

Caudle, S., Gorr, W., & Newcomer, K. (1991). Key information systems management issues for the public sector. *Management Information Systems Quarterly, 15*(2), 170–188. doi:10.2307/249378

Ceravolo, P., Corallo, P., & Elia, G. (2008). Semantic web-based profiled knowledge discovery in community of practice. *International Journal of Business Process Integration and Management, 3*(4), 256–270. doi:10.1504/IJBPIM.2008.024983

CETIC. (2008). *Centro de Estudos sobre as tecnologias da informação e da comunicação: TIC Domicílios e Usuários 2008*. Retrieved from http://www.cetic.br/usuarios/tic/2008-total-brasil/index.htm

Chadwick, C., & May, C. (2003). Interaction between states and citizens in the age of the Internet: E-government in the United States, Britain, and the European Union. *Governance: An International Journal of Policy, Administration, and Institutions, 16*, 271–300.

Chadwick, S. (2001). Communicating trust in e-commerce interactions. *Management Communication Quarterly, 14*, 653–658. doi:10.1177/0893318901144009

Chai, S., Herath, T. C., Park, I., & Rao, H. R. (2006). Repeated use of e-gov web sites: A satisfaction and confidentiality perspective. *International Journal of Electronic Government Research, 2*(3), 1–22. doi:10.4018/jegr.2006070101

Chang, I. C., Li, Y. C., Hung, W. F., & Hwang, H. G. (2005). An empirical study on the impact of quality antecedents on taxpayer's acceptance of internet tax-filing systems. *Government Information Quarterly, 32*(4), 389–410. doi:10.1016/j.giq.2005.05.002

Chan, J. B. L. (2001). The technological game: How information technology is transforming police practice. *Criminology & Criminal Justice, 1*(2), 139–159. doi:10.1177/1466802501001002001

Charabaldis, Y., Askaounis, D., Gionis, G., Lampathaki, F., & Metaxiotis, K. (2006) Organising Municipal e-Government Systems: A Multi-facet Taxonomy of e-Services for Citizens and Businesses. In M. A. Wimmer (Ed.), *Electronic Government: Proceedings of the 5th International Conference, EGOV 2006*, Krakow, Poland. Berlin: Springer-Verlag.

Charette, R. N. (1991). The risks with risk analysis. *Communications of the ACM, 34*(6), 106–106. doi:10.1145/103701.103705

Charih, M., & Robert, J. (2004). Government on-line in the federal government of Canada: The organizational issues. *International Review of Administrative Sciences, 70*(2), 373–384. doi:10.1177/0020852304044262

Chatfield, A., Hirokazu, T., & Wamba, S. (2009). *E-Government Challenge in Disaster Evacuation Response: The Role of RFID Technology in Building Safe and Secure Local Communities*. Wollongong, NSW, Australia: University of Wollongong.

Chatman, J. A., & Jehn, K. A. (1994). Assessing the relationship between industry characteristics and organizational culture: How different can you be? *Academy of Management Journal, 37*(3), 522–553. doi:10.2307/256699

Chau, P. Y. K. (1996). An empirical assessment of a modified technology acceptance model. *Journal of Management Information Systems, 13*(2), 185–204.

Checkland, P., & Scholes, J. (1999). *Soft Systems Methodology in Action*. West Sussex, UK: John Wiley & Sons.

Chellappa, R. (2005). Personalization versus privacy: An empirical examination of the online consumer's dilemma. *Information Technology Management, 6*(2-3), 181. doi:10.1007/s10799-005-5879-y

Chen, A. N. K., Sen, S., & Shao, B. B. M. (2005). Strategies for effective Web services adoption for dynamic e-businesses. *Decision Support Systems, 42*(2), 789–809. doi:10.1016/j.dss.2005.05.011

Chen, A., Labrie, R., & Shao, B. (2003). An XML adoption framework for electronic business. *Journal of Electronic Commerce Research, 4*(1), 1–14.

Chen, C. C., Wu, C. S., & Wu, R. C. F. (2006). e-Service enhancement priority matrix: The case of an IC foundry company. *Information & Management, 43*, 572–586. doi:10.1016/j.im.2006.01.002

Cheney, P. H., & Dickson, G. W. (1982). Organizational characteristics and information systems: an exploratory investigation. *Academy of Management Journal, 25*(1), 170–182. doi:10.2307/256032

Chen, H. T. (1990). *Theory-driven evaluations.* Thousand Oaks, CA: Sage.

Chen, M. (2003). Factors affecting the adoption and diffusion of XML and Web services standards for e-business systems. *International Journal of Human-Computer Studies, 58*, 259–279. doi:10.1016/S1071-5819(02)00140-4

Chen, M., Chen, A., & Shao, B. (2003). The implications and impacts of Web services to electronic commerce research and practices. *Journal of Electronic Commerce Research, 4*(4), 128–139.

Chen, M., Gonzalez, S., Leung, V., Zhang, Q., & Li, M. (2010). A 2g-Rfid-based e- healthcare system. *IEEE Wireless Communications, 17*(1), 37–43. doi:10.1109/MWC.2010.5416348

Chen, Y. C., Chen, H. M., Ching, R. K. H., & Huang, W. W. (2007). Electronic government implementation: A comparison between develop and developing countries. *International Journal of Electronic Government Research, 3*(2), 45–61. doi:10.4018/jegr.2007040103

Chen, Y. C., & Dimitrova, D. V. (2006). Electronic government and online engagement: Citizen interaction with government via web portals. *International Journal of Electronic Government Research, 2*(1), 54–76. doi:10.4018/jegr.2006010104

Chen, Y.-C., & Thurmaier, K. (2008). Advancing e-government: Financing challenges and opportunities. *Public Administration Review, 68*(3), 537–548. doi:10.1111/j.1540-6210.2008.00889.x

Chen, Y., Chen, H. M., Ching, R. K. H., & Huang, W. W. (2007). Electronic Government Implementation: A Comparison between Developed and Developing Countries. *International Journal of Electronic Government Research, 3*(2), 45–61. doi:10.4018/jegr.2007040103

Chen, Y., & Wayne, W. (2006). Electronic government implementation: A comparison between developed and developing countries. *International Journal of Electronic Government Research, 3*(2), 45–61. doi:10.4018/jegr.2007040103

Chen, Z., & Dubinsky, A. J. (2003). A conceptual model of perceived customer value in e-commerce: A preliminary investigation. *Psychology and Marketing, 20*(4), 323–347. doi:10.1002/mar.10076

Cheong, J. H., & Park, M.-C. (2005). Mobile internet acceptance in Korea. *Internet Research, 15*(2), 125–140. doi:10.1108/10662240510590324

Chetty, J., & Coetzee, M. (2009). *Considering Contracts for Governance in Service-Oriented Architectures. Information and Computer Security Architecture (ICSA).* Retrieved from http://icsa.cs.up.ac.za/issa/2008/Proceedings/Research/6.pdf

Cheung, C. M. K., & Lee, M. K. O. (2005, January 3-6). The asymmetric effect of website attribute performance on satisfaction: An empirical study. In *Proceedings of the 38th Hawaii International Conference on System Sciences*, Honolulu, HI.

Cheung, C. M. K., Chan, G. W. W., & Limayem, M. (2005). A critical review of online consumer behavior: Empirical research. *Journal of Electronic Commerce in Organizations, 3*(4), 1–19. doi:10.4018/jeco.2005100101

Chhabra, S., & Jaiswal, M. (2008). E-government organizational performance framework: Case study of Haryana State in India - A log linear regression analysis. *International Journal of Electronic Government Research, 4*(3), 57–80. doi:10.4018/jegr.2008070104

Chiang, L. (2009). Trust and security in the e-voting system. *Electronic Government, an International Journal, 6*(4), 343-360.

Chin, W. W. (1998). Commentary: Issues and opinion on structural equation modeling. *Management Information Systems Quarterly*, *22*(1), vii–xvi.

Chiou, J.-S. (2004). The antecedents of consumers' loyalty toward internet service providers. *Information & Management*, *41*(6), 685–695. doi:10.1016/j.im.2003.08.006

Chircu, A. M., & Lee, D. H. (2003). Understanding IT investments in the public sector: The case of e-government. In *Proceedings of the Ninth Americas Conference on Information Systems* (p. 99).

Choudrie, J., Brinkman, W., & Pathania, R. (2007). Using diffusion theory to determine the digital divide in e-services: Two UK local-area perspectives. *Electronic Government, an International Journal, 4*(3), 345-359.

Choudrie, J., & Dwivedi, Y. K. (2005a). Investigating the research approaches for examining the technology adoption in the household. *Journal of Research Practice*, *1*(1), 1–12.

Choudrie, J., & Dwivedi, Y. K. (2005b). The demographics of broadband residential consumers of a British local community: The London Borough of Hillingdon. *Journal of Computer Information Systems*, *45*(4), 93–101.

Choudrie, J., & Dwivedi, Y. K. (2006a). A comparative study to examine the socio-economic characteristics of broadband adopters and non-adopters. *Electronic Government: An International Journal, 3*(3), 272–288.

Choudrie, J., & Dwivedi, Y. K. (2006b). Investigating factors influencing adoption of broadband in the household. *Journal of Computer Information Systems, 46*(4), 25–34.

Choudrie, J., Ghinea, G., & Weerakkody, V. (2004). Evaluating global e-government sites: A view using web diagnostic tools. *Electronic Journal of E-Government*, *2*(2), 105–114.

Choudrie, J., & Weerrakody, V. (2007). Horizontal Process Integration in E-Government: the Perspective of a UK Local Authority. *International Journal of Electronic Government Research*, *3*(3), 22–39. doi:10.4018/jegr.2007070102

Chu, P. Y., Yeh, S., & Chuang, M. (2008). Reengineering municipality citizen electronic complaint system through citizen relationship management. *Electronic Government, an International Journal, 5*(3), 288-309.

Chua, P. (1996). An empirical assessment of a modified technology acceptance model. *Journal of Management Information Systems, 13*, 185–204.

Chu, C.-W., & Lu, H.-P. (2007). Factors influencing online music purchase intention in Taiwan. *Internet Research*, *17*(2), 139–155. doi:10.1108/10662240710737004

Chu, P. Y., Hsiao, N., Lee, F. W., & Chen, C. W. (2004). Exploring success factors for Taiwan's government electronic tendering system: Behavioral perspectives from end users. *Government Information Quarterly, 21*(2), 219–234. doi:10.1016/j.giq.2004.01.005

Ciborra, C. (1997). De profundis? Deconstructing the concept of strategic alignment. *Scandinavian Journal of Information Systems, 9*(1), 67–82.

Ciborra, C. (2002). *The labyrinths of information*. Oxford, UK: Oxford University Press.

Ciborra, C. U. (2000). A critical review of the literature on the management of corporate information infrastructures. In Ciborra, C. U. (Ed.), *From control to drift: The dynamics of corporate information infrastructures*. Oxford, UK: Oxford University Press.

Cicognani, E. (2002). *Psicologia sociale e ricerca qualitativa*. Rome, Italy: Carocci.

CISCO. (2006). *Quality of Service*. Retrieved from http://www.cisco.com/en/US/products/ps6558/products_ios_technology_home.html

Citizen-Centric eGovernment (cc:eGov). (2007). *A handbook for citizen-centric eGovernment*. Brussels, Belgium: European Commission.

Citrin, A. V., Sprott, D. E., Sliverman, S. N., & Stem, D. E. Jr. (2000). Adoption of Internet Shopping: the role of consumer innovativeness. *Industrial Management & Data Systems, 100*(7), 29–300. doi:10.1108/02635570010304806

City, A. (2010). *Auckland city business and economy report 2007*. Retrieved January 1, 2010, from http://www.aucklandcity.govt.nz/auckland/economy/business/2007/population.asp

Clarkson, M. B. E. (1995). A Stakeholder Framework for Analyzing and Evaluating Corporate Social Performance. *Academy of Management Review, 20*(1), 92–117. doi:10.2307/258888

Claver, E., Llopis, J., Gonzalez, M. R., & Gasco, J. L. (2006). The performance of information systems through organizational culture. *Information Technology & People*, *14*(3), 247–260. doi:10.1108/09593840110402149

Cohen, S., & Eimicke, W. (2001). *The use of the Internet in government service delivery*. Washington, DC: Pricewaterhouse Coopers Endowment for the Business of Government, E-government Series.

Cohen, S., & Eimicke, W. (2003). The Future of E-Government: A Project of Potential Trends and Issues. In *Proceedings of the 36th Hawaii International Conference on System Sciences*.

Coleman, S., & Grøtze, J. (2001). *Online public engagement in policy deliberation*. Edinburgh, UK: Hansard Society and BT.

Colesca, S. E. (2009). Understanding trust in e-government. *The Engineering Economist*, *3*(3), 7–15.

Colesca, S. E., & Dobrica, L. (2008). Adoption and use of e-government services: The case of Romania. *Journal of Applied Research and Technology*, *6*(3), 204–217.

Coltman, T., Gadh, R., & Michael, K. (2008). RFID and Supply Chain Management. Introduction to the Special Issue. *Journal of Theoretical and Applied Electronic Commerce Research*, *3*(1), 3–6.

Commission of the European Communities. (2005). *i2010 – a European information society for growth and employment*. Retrieved from http://www.eluxembourg.public.lu/eLuxembourg/i2010.pdf

Commission of the European Communities. (2006). *i2010-eGovernment Action Plan: accelerating egovernment in Europe for the benefit of all*. Retrieved from http://ec.europa.eu/information_society/activities/egovernment/docs/action_plan/comm_pdf_com_2006_0173_f_en_acte.pdf

Commonwealth of Australia. (2002). *Centrelink annual report 2001-2002 – Short message service trial* (p. 119). Canberra, Australia: AGPS.

Commonwealth of Australia. (2005). *Australians' use of and satisfaction with e-government services*. Canberra, Australia: AGPS.

Commonwealth of Australia. (2006). *Australians' use of and satisfaction with e-government services*. Canberra, Australia: AGPS.

Commonwealth of Australia. (2007). *Australians' use of and satisfaction with e-government services*. Canberra, Australia: AGPS.

Commonwealth of Australia. (2008). *Australians' use of and satisfaction with e-government services*. Canberra, Australia: AGPS.

Computerworld. (2010a). *Danmark sidder på milliardpotentiale i offentlige data*. Retrieved from http://www.computerworld.dk/art/111997?page=2

Conklin, J., & Begeman, M. L. (1988). gIBIS: A hypertext tool for exploratory policy discussion. *ACM Transactions on Information Systems*, *6*(4), 303–331. doi:10.1145/58566.59297

Cooke, R., & Lafferty, J. (1987). *Organizational culture inventory (OCI)*. Plymouth, MI: Human Synergistics.

Cook, L. S., Bowen, D. E., Chase, R. B., Dasu, S., Stewart, D. M., & Tansik, D. A. (2002). Human issues in service design. *Journal of Operations Management*, *20*, 159–174. doi:10.1016/S0272-6963(01)00094-8

Cooper, D. R., & Schindler, P. S. (2007). *Business research methods* (10th ed.). New York, NY: McGraw-Hill.

Corral, M. (2010). *Put user in the centre for services: A reference model*. Brussels, Belgium: European Commission.

Costello, A. B., & Osborne, J. W. (2005). Best practices in exploratory factor analysis: Four recommendations for getting the most from your analysis. *Practical Assessment. Research Evaluation*, *10*(7), 1–9.

Cotterill, S., & King, S. (2007). Public sector partnerships to deliver local E-government: A social network study. In M. A. Wimmer, H. J. Scholl, & A. Grölund (Eds.), *Proceedings of the 6th International Conference on Electronic Government* (LNCS 4656, pp. 240-251).

Council for Excellence in Government (CEG). (2003). *The new e-government equation: Ease, engagement, privacy, and protection*. Retrieved from http://www.cio.gov/documents/egovpoll2003.pdf

Coyle, K. (2002). Open source, open standards. *Information Technology and Libraries*, *21*(1), 33–36.

Coyle, K. (2005). Management of RFID in libraries. *Journal of Academic Librarianship*, *31*(5), 486–489. doi:10.1016/j.acalib.2005.06.001

Criado, J. I., Hughes, O., & Teicher, J. (2002, April 8-10). e-Government and managerialism: a second revolution in public management. In *Proceedings of the 6th International Research Symposium on Public Management.*

Criado, J. I., & Ramilo, M. C. (2003). E-government in practice: An analysis of Web site orientation to the citizens in Spanish municipalities. *International Journal of Public Sector Management*, *16*(3), 191–218. doi:10.1108/09513550310472320

Cronbach, L. J. (1951). Coefficient alpha and the internal structure of tests. *Psychometrika*, *16*(3), 297–334. doi:10.1007/BF02310555

Curtin, J., Kauffman, R., & Riggins, R. (2007). Making the most out of RFID technology: a research agenda for the study of the adoption, usage and impact of RFID. *Information Technology Management*, *8*(2), 87–110. doi:10.1007/s10799-007-0010-1

Czarniawska, B., & Sevon, B. (2005). *Global ideas: How ideas, objects and practices travel in the global economy*. Copenhagen, Denmark: Copenhagen Business School Press.

Dabholkar, P. A., & Bagozzi, R. P. (2002). An attitudinal model of technology-based self-service: Moderating effects of consumer traits and situational factors. *Journal of the Academy of Marketing Science*, *30*(3), 184–201.

Dada, D. (2006). Failure of e-government in developing countries: A literature review. *Electronic Journal of Information Systems in Developing Countries*, *26*(7), 12–34.

Dahlberg, L., & Siapera, S. (2006). *Radical Democracy and the Internet: Interrogating Theory and Practice*. New York: Palgrave Macmillan.

Dalcher, D., & Genus, A. (2003). Avoiding IS/IT implementation failure. *Technology Analysis and Strategic Management*, *15*(4), 403–407. doi:10.1080/095373203000136006

Danish National IT & Telecom Agency. (2010). *Data camp: Offentlige data blev forvandlet til digitale produkter*. Retrieved from.http://www.itst.dk/nyheder/nyhedsarkiv/2010/data-camp-offentlige-data-blev-forvandlet-til-digitale-produkter

Danziger, J. N., & Andersen, K. V. (2002). The impacts of information technology on public administration: An analysis of empirical research from the 'Golden Age' of transformation. *International Journal of Public Administration*, *25*(5), 591–627. doi:10.1081/PAD-120003292

Das, R. (2005). *RFID tag sales in 2005 - how many and where?* Retrieved from http://www.idtechex.com/products/en/articles/00000398.asp

Das, J., DiRienzo, C., & Burbridge, J. Jr. (2008). Global e-government and the role of trust: A cross country analysis. *International Journal of Electronic Government Research*, *5*(1), 1–18. doi:10.4018/jegr.2009010101

David, L., & Henderson-Sellers, B. (2001). Characteristics of web development processes. In *Proceedings of the International Conference on Advances in Infrastructure for Electronic Business, Science and Education on the Internet* (p. 21). e-Cidadania. (2007). *Systems and methods for the constitution of a culture mediated by information and communication technology*. Retrieved from http://www.nied.unicamp.br/ecidadania

Davidrajuh, R. (2004). Planning e-government start-up: A case study on e-Sri Lanka. *Electronic Government, an International Journal*, *1*(1), 92-106.

Davies, C. (1997). Organizational influences on the university electronic library. *Information Processing & Management*, *33*(3), 377–392. doi:10.1016/S0306-4573(96)00070-2

Davis, F. D. (1986). *A Technology Acceptance Model for Empirically Testing New End-User Information Systems: Theory and Results*. Unpublished doctoral dissertation, Massachusetts Institute of Technology.

Davis, F. (1989). Perceived usefulness, perceived ease of use, and user acceptance of information technology. *Management Information Systems Quarterly*, *13*, 319–340. doi:10.2307/249008

Davis, F. D. (1989). Perceived usefulness, perceived ease of use, and user acceptance of information technology. *Management Information Systems Quarterly*, *13*(3), 319–340. doi:10.2307/249008

Davis, F. D. (1993). User acceptance of information technology: System characteristics, user perceptions, and behavior impacts. *International Journal of Man-Machine Studies*, *39*, 475–487. doi:10.1006/imms.1993.1022

Davis, F. D., Bagozzi, R. P., & Warshaw, P. R. (1989). User acceptance of computer technology: A comparison of two theoretical models. *Management Science*, *35*(8), 982–1003. doi:10.1287/mnsc.35.8.982

Davis, F., Bagozzi, R., & Warshaw, P. (1989). User acceptance of computer technology: A comparison of two theoretical models. *Management Science*, *35*, 982–1003. doi:10.1287/mnsc.35.8.982

Dawes, S. S. (2008). The evolution and continuing challenges of e-government. *Public Administration Review*, *68*, 86–102. doi:10.1111/j.1540-6210.2008.00981.x

Dawes, S. S., & Pardo, T. (2002). Building collaborative digital government systems. In McIver, W. J., & Elmagarmid, A. K. (Eds.), *Advances in digital government: Technology, human factors, and policy*. Boston, MA: Kluwer Academic. doi:10.1007/0-306-47374-7_16

Dawes, S., Bloniarz, P., Connelly, D., Kelly, K., & Pardo, T. (1999). Four realities of IT innovation in government. *Public Management*, *28*(1), 1–5.

Dawes, S., & Préfontaine, L. (2003). Understanding new models of collaboration for delivering government services. *Communications of the ACM*, *46*(1), 40–42. doi:10.1145/602421.602444

Deakins, E., & Dillon, R. (2002). E-government in New Zealand: The local authority perspective. *International Journal of Public Sector Management*, *15*(4), 375–399. doi:10.1108/09513550210435728

Deal, T. E., & Kennedy, A. A. (1982). *Corporate culture: The rites and rituals of corporate lives*. Reading, MA: Addison-Wesley.

Debreceny, R., Felden, C., Ochocki, B., Piechocki, M., & Piechocki, M. (2009). *XBRL for interactive data: Engineering the information value chain*. Berlin, Germany: Springer-Verlag. doi:10.1007/978-3-642-01437-6

Deegan, C., & Gordon, B. (1996). A study of the environmental disclosure policies of Australian corporations. *Accounting and Business Review*, *26*(3), 187–199. doi:10.1080/00014788.1996.9729510

Dehning, B., Richardson, V. J., & Zmud, R. W. (2003). The value relevance of announcements of transformational information technology investments. *Management Information Systems Quarterly*, *27*, 637–656.

Delen, D., Hardgrave, B., & Sharda, R. (2007). RFID for Better Supply-Chain Management through Enhanced Information Visibility. *Production and Operations Management*, *16*(5), 613–624. doi:10.1111/j.1937-5956.2007.tb00284.x

Delone, W. H., & McLean, E. R. (1992). Information systems success; the quest for the dependent variable. *Information Systems Research*, *3*(1), 60–95. doi:10.1287/isre.3.1.60

Delone, W. H., & McLean, E. R. (2003). The DeLone and McLean Model of Information Systems Success: A Ten-Year Update. *Journal of Management Information Systems*, *19*(4), 9–30.

DeLone, W., & Mclean, E. (2003). The DeLone and Mclean model for information systems success: A ten year update. *Journal of Management Information Systems*, *19*(4), 9–30.

DeLong, D. W., & Fahey, L. (2000). Diagnosing cultural barriers to knowledge management. *The Academy of Management Executive*, *14*(4), 113–127.

Denzin, N. K., & Lincoln, Y. S. (1998). *Collecting and interpreting qualitative materials*. Thousand Oaks, CA: Sage.

Denzin, N. K., & Lincoln, Y. S. (2005). Introduction: The discipline and practice of qualitative research. In Denzin, N. K., & Lincoln, Y. S. (Eds.), *The Sage handbook of qualitative research* (3rd ed., pp. 1–33). Thousand Oaks, CA: Sage.

Department of Defense. (1996). *Software Reuse Executive Primer*. Retrieved from http://sw-eng.falls-church.va.us/ReuseIC/policy/primer/primer.htm

Department of Interior. (2003). e-Government strategy. Retrieved from http://www.doi.gov/e-government/

Devadoss, P. R., Pan, S. L., & Huang, J. C. (2002). Structurational analysis of e-government initiatives: a case study of SCO. *Decision Support Systems, 34*(3), 253–269. doi:10.1016/S0167-9236(02)00120-3

Devaraj, S., Ming, F., & Kohli, R. (2002). Antecedents of B2C channel satisfaction and preference: Validating e-commerce metrics. *Information Systems Research, 13,* 316–333. doi:10.1287/isre.13.3.316.77

Diego, D. N., & Cornford, T. (2005, May 26-28). ICT, Innovation and Public Management: Governance, Models & Alternatives for e-Government Infrastructures. In *Proceedings of the 13th European Conference on Information Systems, Information Systems in a Rapidly Changing Economy, ECIS 2005,* Regensburg, Germany.

Dillman, D. (2000). *Mail and Internet surveys: The tailored design method* (2nd ed.). New York, NY: John Wiley & Sons.

DiMaggio, P. J., & Powell, W. W. (1983). The iron cage revisited: Institutional isomorphism and collective rationality in organizational fields. *American Sociological Review, 48*(2), 147–160. doi:10.2307/2095101

Dimitrova, D. V., & Chen, Y. (2006). Profiling the Adopters of E-Government Information and Services: The Influence of Psychological Characteristics, Civic Mindedness, and Information Channels. *Social Science Computer Review, 24*(2), 172. doi:10.1177/0894439305281517

Dimitrova, D. V., & Chen, Y. C. (2006). Profiling the adopters of e-government information and services - The influence of psychological characteristics, civic mindedness, and information channels. *Social Science Computer Review, 24*(2), 172–188. doi:10.1177/0894439305281517

Ding, Y., Fensel, D., Klein, M., & Omelayenko, B. (2002). The semantic web: yet another hip? *Data & Knowledge Engineering, 41,* 205–227. doi:10.1016/S0169-023X(02)00041-1

Dishaw, M. T., & Strong, D. M. (1999). Extending the technology acceptance model with task-technology fit constructs. *Information & Management, 36*(1), 9–21. doi:10.1016/S0378-7206(98)00101-3

Doll, W. J., & Torkzadeh, G. (1988). The measurement of end user computing satisfaction. *Management Information Systems Quarterly, 12*(2), 258–274. doi:10.2307/248851

Doll, W., Hendrickson, A., & Deng, X. (1998). Using Davis's perceived usefulness and ease-of-use instrument for decision making: A confirmatory and multigroup invariance analysis. *Decision Sciences, 29,* 839–869. doi:10.1111/j.1540-5915.1998.tb00879.x

Donaldson, T., & Preston, L. E. (1995). The Stakeholder Theory of the Corporation: Concepts, Evidence, and Implications. *Academy of Management Review, 20*(1), 65–91. doi:10.2307/258887

Dos Santos, B. L., Peffers, K., & Mauer, D. C. (1993). The impact of information technology investment announcements on the market value of the firm. *Information Systems Research, 4*(1), 1–23. doi:10.1287/isre.4.1.1

Downing, J. D., & Brooten, L. (2007). ICTs and political movements. In Mansell, R., Avgerou, C., Quah, D., & Silverstone, R. (Eds.), *The Oxford handbook of information and communication technologies* (pp. 537–560). Oxford, UK: Oxford University Press.

Dunleavy, P., Margetts, H., Bastow, S., & Tinkler, J. (2005). *New public management is dead – long live digital-era governance.* Oxford, UK: Oxford University Press.

Durkin, M. (2006). Neglecting the remote relationship: Lessons from internet banking. *Monash Business Review, 2*(1), 1–8.

Durkin, M., McCartan-Quinn, D., O'Donnell, A., & Howcroft, B. (2003). Retail bank customer preferences: Personal and remote interactions. *International Journal of Retail and Distribution Management, 31*(4), 177–189. doi:10.1108/09590550310469176

Dutton, W. H., Cheong, P. H., & Park, N. (2004). An ecology of constraints on e-learning in higher education: The case of virtual learning environment. *Prometheus, 22*(2), 131–149. doi:10.1080/0810902042000218337

Dwivedi, Y. K. (2005). *Investigating adoption, usage, and impact of broadband: UK households.* Unpublished doctoral dissertation, Brunel University, London, UK.

Dwivedi, Y. K., & Weerakkody, V. (2007). Examining the factors affecting the adoption of broadband in the Kingdom of Saudi Arabia. *Electronic Government, an International Journal, 4*(1), 43-58.

Dwivedi, Y. K., & Williams, M. D. (2008). Demographic Influence on UK citizens e-government adoption. *Electronic Government, an International Journal, 5*(3), 261-274.

Dwivedi, Y. K., Khan, N., & Papazafeiropoulou, A. (2007). Consumer adoption and usage of broadband in Bangladesh. *Electronic Government, an International Journal, 4*(3), 299-313.

Dwivedi, Y. K., Williams, M. D., Lal, B., Weerakkody, V., & Bhatt, S. (2007, December 28-30). Understanding factors affecting consumer adoption of broadband in India: A pilot study. In *Proceedings of the 5th International Conference on E-Governance*, Hyderabad, India.

Dwivedi, Y. K., Choudrie, J., & Brinkman, W. P. (2006). Development of a survey instrument to examine consumer adoption of broadband. *Industrial Management & Data Systems, 106*(5), 700–718. doi:10.1108/02635570610666458

Dwivedi, Y. K., & Irani, Z. (2009). Understanding the adopters and non-adopters of broadband. *Communications of the ACM, 52*(1), 122–125. doi:10.1145/1435417.1435445

Dwivedi, Y. K., Khan, N., & Papazafeiropoulou, A. (2007). Consumer adoption and usage of broadband in Bangladesh. *Electronic Government: An International Journal, 4*(3), 299–313. doi:10.1504/EG.2007.014164

Dwivedi, Y. K., Khoumbati, K., Williams, M. D., & Lal, B. (2007). Factors affecting consumers' behavioural intention to adopt broadband in Pakistan. *Transforming Government: People. Process and Policy, 1*(3), 285–297.

Dwivedi, Y. K., Papazafeiropoulou, A., Gharavi, H., & Khoumbati, K. (2006). Examining the socio-economic determinants of adoption of an e-government initiative 'Government Gateway.'. *The Electronic Government: An International Journal, 3*(4), 404–419. doi:10.1504/EG.2006.010801

Dwivedi, Y. K., & Weerakkody, V. (2007). Examining the factors affecting the adoption of broadband in the Kingdom of Saudi Arabia. *Electronic Government: An International Journal, 4*(1), 43–58. doi:10.1504/EG.2007.012178

Dwivedi, Y. K., Weerakkody, V., & Williams, M. D. (2009). Guest editorial: From implementation to adoption: Challenges to successful E-Government diffusion. *Government Information Quarterly, 26*(1), 3–4. doi:10.1016/j.giq.2008.09.001

Dwyer, F., Schurr, P., & Oh, S. (1987). Developing buyer-seller relationships. *Journal of Marketing, 51*, 11–27. doi:10.2307/1251126

Earl, M. J. (1993). Experiences in strategic information systems planning. *Management Information Systems Quarterly, 17*(1), 1–24. doi:10.2307/249507

Eastin, M. S. (2002). Diffusion of e-commerce: An analysis of the adoption of four e-commerce activities. *Telematics and Informatics, 19*(3), 251–267. doi:10.1016/S0736-5853(01)00005-3

Ebbers, W. E., Pieterson, W. J., & Noordman, H. N. (2008). Electronic government: Rethinking channel management strategies. *Government Information Quarterly, 25*(2), 181–201. doi:10.1016/j.giq.2006.11.003

Ebbers, W., Pieterson, W., & Noordman, H. (2008). Electronic government: Rethinking channel management strategies. *Government Information Quarterly, 25*, 181–201. doi:10.1016/j.giq.2006.11.003

Ebrahim, Z., & Irani, Z. (2005). E-government adoption: Architecture and barriers. *Business Process Management Journal, 11*(5), 589–611. doi:10.1108/14637150510619902

EC. Commission of the European Communities. (2003). *European Interoperability Framework*. Retrieved from http://ec.europa.eu/idabc/servlets/Doc?id=18060

EC. Commission of the European Communities. (2003). *Linking-up Europe: The importance of interoperability for e-government services.* Brussels, Belgium: Author.

Eckerson, W. (1999). 15 rules for enterprise portals. *Oracle Magazine.* Retrieved from http://www.oracle.com/oramag/oracle/99-Jul/49ind.html

Eder, L. B., & Igbaria, M. (2001). Determinants of intranet diffusion and infusion. *Omega, 29*(3), 233–242. doi:10.1016/S0305-0483(00)00044-X

Edmiston, K. D. (2003). State and local e-government: Prospects and challenges. *American Review of Public Administration, 33*(1), 20–45. doi:10.1177/0275074002250255

Edwards, S., & Fortune, M. (2008). *BIC e4libraries project: A guide to RFID in libraries.* Retrieved from http://www.bic.org.uk/files/pdfs/090109%20library%20guide%20final%20rev.pdf

E-Governance Standards. (n.d.). *IFEG Version 2.4 Report, NIC.* Retrieved from http://egovstandards.gov.in/

Ellis, A. (2004). Using the New Institutional Economics in e-Government to deliver transformational change. *Electronic. Journal of E-Government, 2*(2), 126–138.

Elpez, I., & Fink, D. (2006, June 25-28). Information systems success in the public sector: Stakeholders' perspectives and emerging alignment model. In *Proceedings of Informing Science + Information Technology Education Joint Conference*, Greater Manchester, UK.

Engel, P., Hamsher, W., & Walis, H. vun Kannon, D., & Shuetrim, G. (2003). *Extensible business reporting language (XBRL) -- Recommendation.* Retrieved from http://www.xbrl.org

Engel, E. (2006). *RFID implementations in California libraries: Costs and benefits, report.* Washington, DC: U.S. Institute of Museum and Library Services.

Erwin, E., & Kern, C. (2003). Radio-frequency-identification for security and media circulation in libraries. *Library & Archival Security, 18*(2), 23–38. doi:10.1300/J114v18n02_04

Esrock, S. L., & Leichty, G. (1998). Social responsibility and corporate Web pages: Self-presentation or agenda-setting? *Public Relations Review, 24*(3). doi:10.1016/S0363-8111(99)80142-8

Esterling, K., Lazer, D. M. J., & Neblo, M. A. (2005). Home (Page) style: Determinates of the quality of the house members' web sites. *International Journal of Electronic Government Research, 1*(2), 50–63. doi:10.4018/jegr.2005040103

EURIM. (2002). *Interoperability - Joined Up Government Needs Joined Up Systems* (EURIM No. 36). Retrieved from http://www.eurim.org.uk/resources/briefings/br36.pdf

European Commission. (2002). *List of Basic Public Services.* Retrieve from http://ec.europa.eu/information_society/eeurope/2002/ action_plan/pdf/basicpublicservices.pdf

European Commission. (2003). *Commission calls for action to unlock public sector information re-use.* Retrieved from http://ec.europa.eu/information_society/newsroom/cf/itemdetail.cfm?item_id=4891

European Commission. (2006). *i2010 eGovernment action plan: Accelerating eGovernment in Europe for the benefit of all.* Retrieved from http://ec.europa.eu/information_society/ newsroom/cf/itemshortdetail.cfm?item_id=3140

European Commission. (2008). *Progress on EU sustainable development strategy: Final report.* Retrieved from http://ec.europa.eu/sustainable/docs/sds_progress_report.pdf

Eurostat. (2010). *Information society statistics: e-Government usage by individuals.* Retrieved from http://epp.eurostat.ec.europa.eu/tgm/table.do?tab=table&init=1&language=en&pcode=tsiir130&plugin=1

Evans, D., & Yen, D. C. (2006). E-Government: Evolving relationship of citizens and government, domestic and international development. *Government Information Quarterly, 23*(2), 207–235. doi:10.1016/j.giq.2005.11.004

Falivene, G. M., & Silva, G. M. (2008). Reflections and proposals on public officials training and promotion of e-government. *International Journal of Electronic Government Research, 4*(2), 43–58. doi:10.4018/jegr.2008040104

Fang, Z. (2002). E-government in digital era: concept, practice and development. *International Journal of the Computer, the Internet and Management, 10*(2), 1-22.

Ferro, E., & Sorrentino, M. (2010). Can intermunicipal collaboration help the diffusion of E-Government in peripheral areas? Evidence from Italy. *Government Information Quarterly, 27*(1), 17–25. doi:10.1016/j.giq.2009.07.005

Field, A. (2009). *Discovering statistics using SPSS* (3rd ed.). London, UK: Sage.

Finger, M., & Pecoud, G. (2003). *From e-Government to e-Governance? Towards a model of e-governance.* Paper presented at the 3rd European Conference on e-Government, Dublin, Ireland.

Finger, M., & Pécoud, G. (2003). From e-Government to e-Governance? Towards a model of e-Governance. *Electronic. Journal of E-Government, 1*(1), 1–10.

Fink, A. (Ed.). (1995). *The survey handbook (Vol. 1)*. Thousand Oaks, CA: Sage.

Finnimore, S. (2008). *E-Petitions – the Queensland Experience*. Paper presented at the Anzacatt Seminar.

Fishbein, M., & Ajzen, I. (1975). *Belief, attitude, intentions, and behavior: An introduction to theory and research*. Reading, MA: Addison-Wesley.

Fleisch, E., & Tellkamp, C. (2005). Inventory inaccuracy and supply chain performance: A simulation study of a retail supply chain. *International Journal of Production Economics, 95*(3), 373–385. doi:10.1016/j.ijpe.2004.02.003

Floropoulos, J., Spathis, C., Halvatzis, D., & Tsipouridou, M. (2010). Measuring the success of the Greek Taxation Information System. *International Journal of Information Management, 30*(1), 47–56. doi:10.1016/j.ijinfomgt.2009.03.013

Flynn, N. (2002). *Public sector management* (4th ed.). London, UK: Pearson Education.

Fontana, J. (2006). Here come RFID-enabled passports. *New World (New Orleans, La.), 23*, 18.

Fornell, C., & Larcker, D. (1981). Evaluating structural equation models with unobservable variables and measurement error. *JMR, Journal of Marketing Research, 18*(1), 39–50. doi:10.2307/3151312

Foster, K. R., & Jaeger, J. (2007). RFID inside: The murky ethics of implanted chips. *IEEE Spectrum*, 24–29. doi:10.1109/MSPEC.2007.323430

Fountain, J. E. (2007). *Bureaucratic reform and e-government in the United States: An institutional perspective*. Retrieved from http://www.inst-informatica.pt/servicos/informacao-e-documentacao/biblioteca-digital/gestao-e-organizacao/EUA_07_006FountainBureauReform.pdf

Fountain, J. (2001). *Building the virtual state. Information technology and institutional change*. Washington, DC: Brookings Institution.

Fountain, J. E. (2001). Paradoxes of public sector customer service. *Governance: An International Journal of Policy and Administration, 14*(1), 55–73.

Fowler, F. J. Jr. (2002). *Survey research methods*. London, UK: Sage.

Fraser, J., Adams, N., Macintosh, A., McKay-Hubbard, A., Lobo, T. P., Pardo, P. F., et al. (2003, May). *Knowledge Management Applied to e-Government Services: the Use of an Ontology*. Paper presented at the 4th Working Conference on Knowledge Management in Electronic Government, Rhodes, Greece.

Frey, K. N., & Holden, S. H. (2005). Distribution channel management in e-government: Addressing federal information policy issues. *Government Information Quarterly, 22*(4), 685–701. doi:10.1016/j.giq.2006.01.001

Frissen, V., Millard, J., Hujiboom, N., Svava Iversen, J., Kool, L., & Kotterink, B. (2007). *The future of eGovernment: An exploration of ICT-driven models of eGovernment for the EU in 2020*. Retrieved from http://ipts.jrc.ec.europa.eu/publications/pub.cfm?id=1481

Fu, J. R., Chao, W. P., & Farn, C. K. (2004). Determinants of taxpayers' adoption of electronic filing methods in Taiwan: An exploratory study. *Journal of Government Information, 30*(5-6), 658–683. doi:10.1016/j.jgi.2004.11.002

Fu, J. R., Farn, C. K., & Chao, W. P. (2006). Acceptance of electronic tax filing: A study of taxpayer intentions. *Information & Management, 43*(1), 109–126. doi:10.1016/j.im.2005.04.001

Fu-Lai, T. Y., & Yu, T. (2008). Uncertainty, human agency and e-government. *Transforming Government: People, Process, and Policy, 2*(4), 283–296. doi:10.1108/17506160810917963

Fulk, J. (1993). Social construction of communication technology. *Academy of Management Journal, 36*, 921–950. doi:10.2307/256641

Fulk, J., Schmitz, J., & Steinfield, C. W. (1990). A social influence model of technology use. In Fulk, J., & Steinfield, C. W. (Eds.), *Organizations and Communication Technology*. Newbury Park, CA: Sage.

Fuller, B. W., & Vu, K. M. (2011). Exploring the dynamics of policy interaction: Feedback among and impacts from multiple, concurrently applied policy approaches for promoting collaboration. *Journal of Policy Analysis and Management, 30*(2), 359–380. doi:10.1002/pam.20572

Furlong, S. (2008). Applicability of autonomic computing to e-government problems. *Transforming Government: People. Process and Policy, 2*(1), 8–18.

Galliers, R. D. (1997). Reflection on Information Systems: Twelve Points to Debate. In Mingers, J., & Stowell, F. (Eds.), *Information Systems: An Emerging Discipline.* Berkshire, UK: McGraw-Hill.

Gallivan, M., & Srite, M. (2005). Information technology and culture: Identifying fragmentary and holistic perspectives of culture. *Information and Organization, 15*(4), 295–338. doi:10.1016/j.infoandorg.2005.02.005

Garcia, A. C. B., Maciel, C., & Pinto, F. B. (2005). A quality inspection method to evaluate e-government sites. In M. A. Wimmer, R. Traunmüller, A. Grönlund, & K. V. Andersen (Eds.), *Proceedings of the 4th International Conference on Electronic Government* (LNCS 3591, pp. 198-209).

Garfinkel, S., & Rosenberg, B. (2006). *RFID: Applications, Security, and Privacy.* Upper Saddle River, NJ: Addison- Wesley.

Garson, D. (2009). *Quantitative research in public administration.* Retrieved from http://faculty.chass.ncsu.edu/garson/PA765/pa765syl.htm

Garson, G. D. (2003). *Toward an information technology research agenda for public administration.* Hershey, PA: Idea Group Publishing. doi:10.4018/978-1-59140-060-8.ch014

Gauld, R. (2007). Public sector information systems failures: Lessons from a New Zealand hospital organization. *Government Information Quarterly, 24*, 102–114. doi:10.1016/j.giq.2006.02.010

Gefen, D. (2000). E-commerce: The role of familiarity and trust. *Omega: The International Journal of Management Science, 28*, 725–737. doi:10.1016/S0305-0483(00)00021-9

Gefen, D., Elena, K., & Straub, D. (2003). Trust and TAM in on-line shopping: An integrated model. *Management Information Systems Quarterly, 27*, 51–90.

Gefen, D., & Straub, D. (2000). The relative importance of perceived ease-of-use in IS adoption. *Journal of the Association for Information Systems, 8*, 1–28.

Gefen, D., & Straub, D. (2005). A practical guide to factorial validity using PLS-Graph: Tutorial and annotated example. *Communications of the Association for Information Systems, 16*, 91–109.

General Accounting Office (GAO). (2001). *Electronic government: Challenges must be addressed with effective leadership and management* (Tech. Rep. No. GAO-01-959T). Washington, DC: Government Printing Office.

Ghattas, J., & Soffer, P. (2008). Facilitating flexibility in inter-organisational processes: a conceptual model. *International Journal of Business Process Integration and Management, 3*(1), 5–14. doi:10.1504/IJBPIM.2008.019343

Gilbert, D., Balestrini, P., & Littleboy, D. (2004). Barriers and benefits in the adoption of e-government. *International Journal of Public Sector Management, 17*(4), 286–301. doi:10.1108/09513550410539794

Gil-Garcia, J. R., Chengalur-Smith, I., & Duchessi, P. (2007). Collaborative e-Government; impediments and benefits of information-sharing projects in the publc sector. *European Journal of Information Systems, 16*, 121–133. doi:10.1057/palgrave.ejis.3000673

Gil-Garcia, J. R., & Theresa, A. P. (2005). E-government success factors: Mapping practical tools to theoretical foundations. *Government Information Quarterly, 22*(2), 187–216. doi:10.1016/j.giq.2005.02.001

Gil-Garcia, R., Chengalur-Smith, I., & Duchessi, P. (2007). Collaborative e-Government: Impediments and benefits of information-sharing projects in the public sector. *European Journal of Information Systems, 16*(2), 121–133. doi:10.1057/palgrave.ejis.3000673

Gill, M., & Turbin, V. (1999). Evaluating 'realistic evaluation'. Evidence from a study of CCTV. *Crime Prevention Studies, 10*, 179–199.

Gitlin, T. (1980). *The whole world is watching: Mass media in the making and unmaking of the new left.* Berkeley, CA: University of California Press.

Glaser, B. G. (1992). *Basics of grounded theory analysis: Emergence versus forcing.* Mill Valley, CA: Sociology Press.

Glaser, B. G., & Strauss, A. I. (1967). *The discovery of grounded theory: Strategies for qualitative research.* New York, NY: Aldine.

Goldkuhl, G. (2007). What does it mean to serve the citizen in e-services? – Towards a practical theory founded in socio-instrumental pragmatism. *International Journal of Public Information Systems, 3*(3), 135–159.

Goldstein, S. M., Johnston, R., Duffy, J. A., & Rao, J. (2002). The service concept: The missing link in service design research? *Journal of Operations Management, 20,* 121–134. doi:10.1016/S0272-6963(01)00090-0

Gomez, R., & Ospina, A. (2001). The Lamp without a Genie: Using Telecentres for Development without expecting Miracles. *The Journal of Development Communication, 12*(2), 26–31.

Gomond, G., & Picavet, M. (1999). Framework for Managing Intranet-based Applications. In *Proceedings of the 7th International Conference on Emerging Technologies and Factory Automation* (Vol. 2, pp. 1011-1019).

Gotoh, R. (2009). Critical factors increasing user satisfaction with e-government services. *Electronic Government, an International Journal, 6*(3), 252-264.

Gottschalk, P. (2009). Maturity levels for interoperability in digital government. *Government Information Quarterly, 26,* 75–81. doi:10.1016/j.giq.2008.03.003

Gouscos, D., Kalikakis, M., Legal, M., & Papadopoulou, S. (2007). A general model of performance and quality for one-stop e-government service offerings. *Government Information Quarterly, 24,* 860–885. doi:10.1016/j.giq.2006.07.016

Government, C. I. O. (2007). *The HKSARG Interoperability Framework, Office of the Government Chief Information Officer, The Government of the Hong Kong Special Administrative Region.* Retrieved from http://www.ogcio.gov.hk

Graber, D. A. (2002). The Internet and Politics. Emerging Perspectives. In Price, M. E., & Nissenbaum, H. F. (Eds.), *Academy and the Internet. Digital Formations* (*Vol. 12,* pp. 90–119). New York: Peter Lang.

Grant, G., & Chau, D. (2005). Developing a Generic Framework for E-Government. *Journal of Global Information Management, 13*(1), 1–31. doi:10.4018/jgim.2005010101

Green, K. R. (1982). Municipal administrators' receptivity to citizens' and elected officials' contacts. *Public Administration Review, 42*(4), 346–353. doi:10.2307/975978

Gremler, D. D. (2004). The critical incident technique in service research. *Journal of Service Research, 7*(1), 65–89. doi:10.1177/1094670504266138

Grey, G. L. (2005). *XBRL: Potential opportunities and issues for Internal Auditors.* Altamone Springs, FL: Institute of Internal Auditors Research Foundations (IIARF).

Grönlund, Å. (2002). *Electronic government: Design, applications and management.* London, UK: IGI Global.

Gronlund, A. (2005). State of the art in e-gov research: Surveying conference publications. *International Journal of Electronic Government Research, 1*(4), 1–25. doi:10.4018/jegr.2005100101

Grundén, K. (2009). A Social Perspective on Implementation of e-Government - a Longitudinal Study at the County Administration of Sweden. *Electronic. Journal of E-Government, 7*(1), 65–76.

Gugliotta, A., Cabral, L., Domingue, J., & Roberto, V. Rowlatt, & M., Davies, R. (2005). *A Semantic Web Service-based Architecture for the Interoperability of E-government Services.* Paper presented at the International Conference on E-Government (ICEG2005), Ottawa, ON, Canada.

Guijarro, L. (2004, August 30-September 3). Analysis of the interoperability frameworks in e-government initiatives. In *Proceedings of the Third International Conference EGOV,* Zaragoza, Spain.

Guijarro, L. (2006). Interoperability frameworks and enterprise architectures in e-government initiatives in Europe and the United States. *Government Information Quarterly, 24,* 89–101. doi:10.1016/j.giq.2006.05.003

Guijarro, L. (2009). Semantic interoperability in eGovernment initiatives. *Computer Standards & Interfaces, 31*(1), 174–180. doi:10.1016/j.csi.2007.11.011

Gulati, R., & Gargiulo, M. (1999). Where do interorganizational networks come from? *American Journal of Sociology*, *104*(5), 1439–1493. doi:10.1086/210179

Gummerson, E. (1998). *Qualitative Methods in Management Research*. Newbury Park, CA: Sage.

Gumussoy, C. A., & Calisir, F. (2009). Understanding factors affecting e-reverse auction use: An integrative approach. *Computers in Human Behavior*, *25*(4), 975–988. doi:10.1016/j.chb.2009.04.006

Guo, X., & Lu, J. (2007). Intelligent e-government services with personalized recommendation techniques. *International Journal of Intelligent Systems*, *22*, 401–417. doi:10.1002/int.20206

Gupta, M. P., & Jana, D. (2003). E-government evaluation: A framework and case study. *Government Information Quarterly*, *20*(4), 365–387. doi:10.1016/j.giq.2003.08.002

Gupta, M. P., Kumar, P., & Bhattacharya, J. (2005). *Government Online: Opportunities and Challenges*. New York: Tata McGraw-Hill.

Hacker, K. L., & van Dijk, J. (2000). *Digital Democracy: Issues of Theory and Practice*. Thousand Oaks, CA: Sage.

Hackney, R. A., & McBride, N. K. (1995). The efficacy of information systems in the public sector: Issues of context and culture. *International Journal of Public Sector Management*, *8*(6), 17–29. doi:10.1108/09513559510099991

Hair, J., Anderson, R., Tatham, R., & Black, W. (1998). *Multivariate data analysis* (5th ed.). Upper Saddle River, NJ: Prentice Hall.

Hair, J., Black, W., Babin, B., Anderson, R., & Tatham, R. (2006). *Multivariate data analysis* (6th ed.). Upper Saddle River, NJ: Pearson/Prentice Hall.

Halevy, A. Y. (2001). Answering queries using views: A survey. *Very Large Database Journal*, *10*(4), 270–294. doi:10.1007/s007780100054

Hamner, M., & Al-Qahtani, F. (2009). Enhancing the case for electronic government in developing nations: A people-centric study focused in Saudi Arabia. *Government Information Quarterly*, *26*(1), 137–143. doi:10.1016/j.giq.2007.08.008

Hancke, G. P. (2008, July). *Eavesdropping Attacks on High-Frequency RFID Tokens. Proceedings of the 4th Workshop on RFID Security (RFIDsec '08)*. Retrieved from http://www.rfidblog.org.uk/Hancke-RFIDsec08-Eavesdropping.pdf

Hanseth, O. (2000). The economics of standards. In Ciborra, C. U. (Ed.), *From control to drift: The dynamics of corporate information infrastructures*. Oxford, UK: Oxford University Press.

Hanseth, O., & Lyytinen, K. (2010). Design theory for adaptive complexity in information infrastructures. *Journal of Information Technology*, *25*(1), 1–19. doi:10.1057/jit.2009.19

Hanseth, O., Monteiro, E., & Hatling, M. (1996). Developing information infrastructure: The tension between standardization and flexibility. *Science, Technology & Human Values*, *21*(4), 407–442. doi:10.1177/016224399602100402

Hanson, W. (2009). *Trees talk with Technology*. Retrieved March 2010 from http://www.govtech.com/dc/689715.

Hanson, W. (1999). *Principals of internet marketing*. Cincinnati, OH: South Western.

Han, W., & Huang, S. (2007). An empirical analysis of risk components and performance on software projects. *Journal of Systems and Software*, *80*, 42–50. doi:10.1016/j.jss.2006.04.030

Harvard Business Press. (2009). *SWOT Analysis II: Looking Inside for Strengths and Weaknesses*. Boston: Author.

Havermans, D., & Woudenberg, B. M. (2007). *Vermenigvuldigen door delen (11 stappen om te komen tot intergemeentelijke ICT samenwerking)*. Den Haag, The Netherlands: ZENC.

Hayashi, E. C. S., & Baranauskas, M. C. C. (2008). Facing the digital divide in a participatory way – an exploratory study. In *Proceedings of the 20th IFIP World Computer Congress on Human-Computer Interaction Symposium* (Vol. 272, pp. 143-154).

Hayashi, E. C. S., Neris, V. P. A., Rodriguez, C., Miranda, L. C., Hornung, H., Santana, V. F., et al. (2009). *Preliminary evaluation of VilanaRede - An inclusive social network system* (Tech. Rep. No. IC-09-40). Campinas, Brazil: University of Campinas.

Heath, W. (2000). *Europe's readiness for e-Government.* Retrieved from http://www.egov.vic.gov.au/pdfs/e-readiness.pdf

Heeks, R. (2002). *E-Government for Development.* Manchester, UK: Institute for Development Policy and Management (IIPM), University of Manchester.

Heeks, R. (2003). *Success and failure rates of egovernment in developing/transitional countries: Overview.* Retrieved from http://www.egov4dev.org/success/sfrates.shtml

Heeks, R. (2009). Success and Failure in E-Government Projects. In *EGovernment for Development* (pp. 1-3).

Heeks, R. (1998). *Information systems for public sector management.* Manchester, UK: Institute for Development Policy and Management.

Heeks, R. (1999). *Reinventing Government in the Information Age.* New York: Routledge. doi:10.4324/9780203204962

Heeks, R. (2003). e-Government in Africa: Promise and practice. *Information Polity, 7*(2), 97–114.

Heeks, R. (2003). *Most e-government-for-development projects fail: How can risks be reduced?* Manchester, UK: University of Manchester.

Heeks, R., & Bailur, S. (2007). Analyzing e-government research: Perspectives, philosophies, theories, methods, and practice. *Government Information Quarterly, 24,* 243–265. doi:10.1016/j.giq.2006.06.005

Heeks, R., & Bhatnagar, S. (1999). Understanding success and failure in information age reform. In Heeks, R. (Ed.), *Reinventing government in information age.* London, UK: Roultedge. doi:10.4324/9780203204962

Hefetz, A., & Warner, M. (2004). Privatization and its reverse: Explaining the dynamics of the government contracting process. *Journal of Public Administration: Research and Theory, 14*(2), 171–190. doi:10.1093/jopart/muh012

Heintze, T., & Bretschneider, S. (2000). Information technology and restructuring in public organizations: Does adoption of information technology affect organizational structures, communications and decision making? *Journal of Public Administration: Research and Theory, 10*(4), 801–830. doi:10.1093/oxfordjournals.jpart.a024292

Hellstrom, D. (2009). The cost and process of implementing RFID technology to manage and control returnable transport items. *International Journal of Logistics Research and Applications, 12*(1), 1–21. doi:10.1080/13675560802168526

Henderson, J. C., & Venkatraman, N. (1999). Strategic alignment: Leveraging information technology for transforming organizations. *IBM Systems Journal, 38*(2), 472. doi:10.1147/SJ.1999.5387096

Hernes, T. (2005). Four ideal-type organizational responses to New Public Management reforms and some consequences. *International Review of Administrative Sciences, 71*(1), 5–17. doi:10.1177/0020852305051680

Herring, S., Scheidt, L. A., Bonus, S., & Wright, E. (2004, January). *Bridging the Gap: A Genre Analysis of Weblogs.* Paper presented at the Hawaii International Conference on Systems Science HICSS-37.

Hicks, P. (1999). RFID and the book trade. *Publishing Research Quarterly, 15*(2), 21–23. doi:10.1007/s12109-999-0025-z

Hildner, L. (2006). Defusing the threat of RFID: Protecting consumer privacy through technology-specific legislation at the state level. *Harvard Civil Rights-Civil Liberties Law Review, 41*(1), 133–176.

Hill, A. V., Collier, D. A., Froehle, C. M., Goodale, J. C., Metters, R. D., & Verma, R. (2002). Research opportunities in service process design. *Journal of Operations Management, 20,* 189–202. doi:10.1016/S0272-6963(01)00092-4

Hiller, J. S., & Bélanger, F. (2001). Privacy strategies for electronic government. In Abramson, M. A., & Means, G. E. (Eds.), *E-Government 2001* (pp. 162–198). Lanham, MD: Rowman & Littlefield.

Hinnant, C. C., & O'Looney, J. A. (2003). Examining pre-adoption interest in online innovations: An exploratory study of e-service personalization in the public sector. *IEEE Transactions on Engineering Management, 50*(4), 436–447. doi:10.1109/TEM.2003.820133

Hinton, P. R., Brownlow, C., McMurray, I., & Cozens, B. (2004). *SPSS explained.* London, UK: Routledge.

Hirlinger, M. W. (1992). Citizen-initiated contacting of local government officials: A multivariate explanation. *The Journal of Politics, 54*(2), 553–564. doi:10.2307/2132039

Hitt, L. M., & Brynjolfsson, E. (1996). Productivity, Business Profitability, and Consumer Surplus: Three Different Measures of Information Technology Value. *Management Information Systems Quarterly*, 121–142. doi:10.2307/249475

Hitz, M., Leitner, G., & Melcher, R. (2006). Usability of web applications. In Kappel, G., Pröll, B., Reich, S., & Retschitzegger, W. (Eds.), *Web engineering: The discipline of systematic development of web applications* (pp. 219–246). Chichester, UK: John Wiley & Sons.

Ho, A. (2002). Reinventing local governments and the e-government initiative. *Public Administration Review*, *62*, 434–445. doi:10.1111/0033-3352.00197

Ho, A. T. (2002). Reinventing local governments and the e-government initiative. *Public Administration Review*, *62*(4), 434–444. doi:10.1111/0033-3352.00197

Ho, A. T. K., & Ni, A. Y. (2004). Explaining the adoption of e-government features: A case study of Iowa County treasurer's offices. *American Review of Public Administration*, *34*(2), 164–180. doi:10.1177/0275074004264355

Hocstrasser, B., & Griffiths, C. (1991). *Controlling IT investments strategy and management*. London, UK: Chapman Hall.

Hoffman, D., Novak, T., & Peralta, M. (1999). Building consumer trust on-line. *Communications of the ACM*, *42*, 80–85. doi:10.1145/299157.299175

Hogge, B. (2010). *Open data study*. Retrieved from http://www.soros.org/initiatives/information/focus/communication/articles_publications/publications/open-data-study-20100519/open-data-study-100519.pdf

Holden, S. H., Norris, D. F., & Fletcher, P. D. (2003). Electronic government at the local level. *Public Performance & Management Review*, *26*(4), 325–344. doi:10.1177/1530957603026004002

Holden, S. H., Norris, D. F., & Fletcher, P. D. (2003). Electronic government at the local level: Progress to date and future issues. *Public Performance and Management Review*, *26*(4), 325–344. doi:10.1177/1530957603026004002

Holzinger, A., Searle, G., Kleinberger, T., Seffah, A., & Javahery, H. (2008). Investigating usability metrics for the design and development of applications for the elderly. In K. Miesenberger, J. Klaus, W. Zagler, & A. Karshmer (Eds.), *Proceedings of the 11th International Conference on Computers Helping People with Special Needs* (LNCS 5105, pp. 98-105).

Homburg, V. M. F. (2008). *Understanding e-government: Information systems in public administration*. London, UK: Routledge.

Homburg, V. M. F., & Georgiadou, Y. (2009). A tale of two trajectories: How spatial data infrastructures travel in time and space. *The Information Society*, *25*(5), 303–314. doi:10.1080/01972240903212524

Hong, W., Thong, J. Y. L., Wong, W.-M., & Tam, K.-Y. (2002). Determinants of user acceptance of digital libraries: An empirical examination of individual differences and system characteristics. *Journal of Management Information Systems*, *18*(3), 97–124.

Horan, T., & Abhichandani, T. (2006). Evaluating user satisfaction in an e-government initiative: Results of structural equation modeling and focus group discussions. *Journal of Information Technology Management*, *16*, 33–44.

Hornung, H., & Baranauskas, M. C. C. (2007), Interaction design in eGov systems: Challenges for a developing country. In *Proceedings of the 34th Seminário Integrado de Software e Hardware*, Porto Alegre, Brazil (pp. 2217-2231).

Hornung, H., Baranauskas, M. C. C., & de Andrade Tambascia, C. (2008). Assistive technologies and techniques for web based eGov in developing countries. In *Proceedings of the 10th International Conference on Enterprise Information Systems*, Setúbal, Portugal (pp. 248-255).

Horrigan, J. B. (2004). *How Americans get in touch with government*. Washington, DC: Pew Internet & American Life.

Horst, M., Kuttschreuter, M., & Gutteling, J. M. (2007). Perceived usefulness, personal experiences, risk perception and trust as determinants of adoption of e-government services in The Netherlands. *Computers in Human Behavior*, *23*(4), 1838–1852. doi:10.1016/j.chb.2005.11.003

Hosmer, L. (1995). Trust: The connecting link between organizational theory and philosophical ethics. *Academy of Management Review, 20*, 379–403.

Hsu, F. M., & Chen, T. Y. (2007). Understanding information systems usage behavior in e-government: The role of context and perceived value. In *Proceedings of the Pacific Asia Conference on Information Systems.*

Hsu, L. (2005). The adoption and implementation of projects-ABCDE (MOEA) – Based on Grounded and TAM theory. *Electronic Government, an International Journal, 2*(2), 144-159.

Huang, C., Lo, C., Chao, K., & Younas, M. (2006). Reaching consensus: A moderated fuzzy web services discovery method. *Information and Software Technology, 48*(6), 410–423. doi:10.1016/j.infsof.2005.12.011

Huenerfauth, M. P. (2002). *Developing design recommendations for computer interfaces accessible to illiterate users.* Unpublished master's thesis, University College Dublin, Dublin City, Ireland.

Hulst, R., & van Montfort, A. (2007a). Inter-municipal cooperation: A widespread phenomenon. In Hulst, R., & van Montfort, A. (Eds.), *Inter-municipal cooperation in Europe* (pp. 1–21). Dordrecht, The Netherlands: Springer-Verlag. doi:10.1007/1-4020-5379-7_1

Hulst, R., & van Montfort, A. (Eds.). (2007b). *Inter-municipal cooperation in Europe.* Dordrecht, The Netherlands: Springer-Verlag. doi:10.1007/1-4020-5379-7

Hulst, R., van Montfort, A., Haveri, A., Airaksinen, J., & Kelly, J. (2009). Institutional shifts in inter-municipal service delivery. *Public Organization Review, 9*(3), 263–285. doi:10.1007/s11115-009-0085-8

Hung, Y. H., Wang, Y. S., & Chou, S. C. T. (2007). User acceptance of e-government services. In *Proceedings of the Pacific Asia Conference on Information Systems.*

Hung, S. Y., Chang, C. M., & Yu, T. J. (2006). Determinants of user acceptance of the e-Government services: The case of online tax filing and payment system. *Government Information Quarterly, 23*(1), 97–122. doi:10.1016/j.giq.2005.11.005

Hung, S. Y., Tang, K. Z., Chang, C. M., & Ke, C. D. (2009). User acceptance of intergovernmental services: An example of electronic document management system. *Government Information Quarterly, 26*(2), 387–397. doi:10.1016/j.giq.2008.07.003

Hung, S.-Y., Ku, C.-Y., & Chang, C.-M. (2003). Critical factors of WAP services adoption: An empirical study. *Electronic Commerce Research and Applications, 2*(1), 42–60. doi:10.1016/S1567-4223(03)00008-5

Hu, P. J., Chau, P. Y. K., Sheng, O. R. L., & Tam, K. Y. (1999). Examining the technology acceptance model using physician acceptance of telemedicine technology. *Journal of Management Information Systems, 16*, 91–112.

Hu, Q., Saunders, C., & Gebelt, M. (1997). Research report: Diffusion of information systems outsourcing: A re-evaluation of influence sources. *Information Systems Research, 8*(3), 288. doi:10.1287/isre.8.3.288

Hussey, J., & Hussey, R. (1997). *Business research: a practical guide for undergraduate and postgraduate students.* Basingstoke, UK: Macmillan Business.

Hutcheson, G., & Sofroniou, N. (1999). *The multivariate social scientist: Introductory statistics using generalized linear models.* Thousand Oaks, CA: Sage.

Huxham, C. (2003). Theorizing collaboration practice. *Public Management Review, 5*(3), 401–423. doi:10.1080/1471903032000146964

Iacopini, G. (2007). *21st Century Democracy: ePetitioning and local government.* London: New Local Government Network (NLGN).

Iacouvou, C. L., Benbasat, I., & Dexter, A. S. (1995). Electronic data interchange and small organizations: adoption and impact of technology. *Management Information Systems Quarterly, 19*(4), 465–485. doi:10.2307/249629

IBGE. (2000). *Instituto Brasileiro de Geografia e Estatística: Demographic censuses.* Retrieved from http://www.ibge.gov.br/english/estatistica/ populacao/default_censo_2000.shtm

IBM. (2008). *Introduction to DB2 for z/OS, version 9.1.* Retrieved from http://publib.boulder.ibm.com/infocenter/dzichelp/v2r2/topic/com.ibm.db29.doc.intro/dsnitk12.pdf?noframes=true

IEEE. (2006). *IEEE Standard Computer Dictionary: A Compilation of IEEE Standard Computer Glossaries.* Retrieved from http://www.sei.cmu.edu/str/indexes/glossary/interoperability.html

ILSMH European Association. (1998). *Make it simple - European easy-to-read guidelines.* Retrieved from http://www.inclusion-europe.org/publications.htm

Imhoff, C., Loftis, L., & Geiger, J. (2001). *Building the customer-centric enterprise, data warehousing techniques for supporting customer relationship management.* New York, NY: John Wiley & Sons.

Imran, A. (2009, January 5-8). Knowledge and attitude, the two major barriers to ICT adoption in LDC are the opposite side of a coin: An empirical evidence from Bangladesh. In *Proceedings of the 42nd Hawaii International Conference on System Sciences*, Waikoloa, HI (pp. 1-10).

Information Society Commission. (2003). *eGovernment: More than an automation of government services.* Retrieved from http://www.isc.ie/downloads/egovernment.pdf

Intelcities project. (2004). *Intelligent Cities, 6th Framework Programme.* Retrieved from http://intelcities.iti.gr/intelcities

International Monetary Fund. (2009). *World economic outlook database.* Retrieved from http://www.imf.org/external/pubs/ft/weo/2009/01/weodata/index.aspx

IPM. (2005). *Instituto Paulo Montenegro: Indicador de Alfabetismo Funcional.* Retrieved from http://www.ipm.org.br/ipmb_pagina.php? mpg=4.02.00.00.00&ver=por

Irani, Z., Sahraoui, S., Ozkan, S., Ghoneim, A., & Elliman, T. (2007). *T-government for benefit realisation.* Paper presented at the European and Mediterranean Conference on Information Systems.

Irani, Z., & Elliman, T. (2008). Creating social entrepreneurship in local government. *European Journal of Information Systems*, *17*(4), 336–342. doi:10.1057/ejis.2008.35

Irani, Z., Elliman, T., & Jackson, P. (2007). Electronic transformation of government in the UK: A research agenda. *European Journal of Information Systems*, *16*(4), 327–335. doi:10.1057/palgrave.ejis.3000698

Irani, Z., Gunasekaran, A., & Dwivedi, Y. K. (2010). Radio Frequency Identification (RFID): Research trends and framework. *International Journal of Production Research*, *49*(9), 1–27.

Irani, Z., & Love, P. E. D. (2001). The Propagation of Technology Management Taxonomies for Evaluating Investments in Manufacturing Resource Planning (MRPII). *Journal of Management Information Systems*, *17*(3), 161–177.

Irani, Z., Love, P. E. D., Elliman, T., Jones, S., & Themistocleous, M. (2005). Evaluationg e-government: learning from the experiences of two UK local authorities. *Information Systems Journal*, *15*, 61–82. doi:10.1111/j.1365-2575.2005.00186.x

Irani, Z., Love, P. E. D., & Jones, S. (2008). Learning lessons from evaluating e-government: Reflective case experiences that support transformational government. *The Journal of Strategic Information Systems*, *17*(2), 155–164. doi:10.1016/j.jsis.2007.12.005

Isett, K. R., Mergel, I. A., LeRoux, K., Mischen, P. A., & Rethemeyer, R. K. (2011). Networks in public administration scholarship: Understanding where we are and where we need to go. *Journal of Public Administration: Research and Theory*, *21*(1), 157–173. doi:10.1093/jopart/muq061

Ives, B., Olson, M. H., & Baroudi, J. J. (1983). The measurement of user information satisfaction. *Communications of the ACM*, *26*(10), 785–793. doi:10.1145/358413.358430

Jackson, C. M., Chow, S., & Leitch, R. A. (1997). Toward an understanding of the behavioural intentions to use an information system. *Decision Sciences*, *28*, 357–389. doi:10.1111/j.1540-5915.1997.tb01315.x

Jackson, C., Simeon, C., & Leitch, R. (1997). Toward an understanding of the behavioral intention to use an information system. *Decision Sciences*, *28*, 357–389. doi:10.1111/j.1540-5915.1997.tb01315.x

Jacobs, K. (2010). The politics of partnerships: A study of police and housing collaboration to tackle anti-social behaviour on Australian public housing estates. *Public Administration*, *88*(4), 928–942. doi:10.1111/j.1467-9299.2010.01851.x

Jaeger, P. T. (2003). The endless wire: E-government as global phenomenon. *Government Information Quarterly*, *20*, 323–331. doi:10.1016/j.giq.2003.08.003

Jaeger, P. T., & Thompson, K. M. (2003). E-government around the world: Lessons, challenges, and future directions. *Government Information Quarterly, 20,* 389–394. doi:10.1016/j.giq.2003.08.001

Janssen, D., & Rotthier, S. (2005). Trends and consolidations in e-government implementation. In Bekkers, V. J. J. M., & Homburg, V. M. F. (Eds.), *The information ecology of e-government (e-government as institutional and technological innovation in public administration)* (2nd ed., pp. 37–52). Amsterdam, The Netherlands: IOS Press.

Janssen, M., Chun, S. A., & Gil-Garcia, J. R. (2009). Building the next generation of digital government infrastructures. *Government Information Quarterly, 26*(2), 233–237. doi:10.1016/j.giq.2008.12.006

Janssen, M., Joha, A., & Weerakkody, V. (2007). Exploring relationships of shared service arrangements in local government. *Transforming Government: People. Process and Policy, 1*(3), 271–284.

Janssen, M., Joha, A., & Zuurmond, A. (2009). Simulation and animation for adopting shared services: Evaluating and comparing alternative arrangements. *Government Information Quarterly, 26*(1), 15–24. doi:10.1016/j.giq.2008.08.004

Janssen, M., & Klievink, B. (2009). The role of intermediaries in multi-channel service delivery strategies. *International Journal of Electronic Government Research, 5*(3), 36–46. doi:10.4018/jegr.2009070103

Janssen, M., & Kuk, G. (2007). E-Government business models for public service networks. *International Journal of Electronic Government Research, 3*(3), 54–71. doi:10.4018/jegr.2007070104

Jarvenpaa, S., & Tractinsky, N. (1999). Consumer trust in an Internet store: A cross-cultural validation. *Journal of Computer-Mediated Communication, 5,* 1–35.

Jayaramanan, V., Rossb, A. D., & Agarwal, A. (2008). Role of information technology and collaboration in reverse logistics supply chains. *International Journal of Logistics: Research and Applications, 11*(6), 409–425. doi:10.1080/13675560701694499

Jeyaraj, A., Rottman, J. W., & Lacity, M. C. (2006). A review of the predictors, linkages, and biases in IT innovation adoption research. *Journal of Information Technology, 21*(1), 1–23. doi:10.1057/palgrave.jit.2000056

Jiang, J. J., Hsu, M., & Klein, G. (2000). E-commerce user behavior model: An empirical study. *Human Systems Management, 19,* 265–276.

Jiang, J., & Klein, G. (1999). Risks to different access of system success. *Information & Management, 36,* 263–272. doi:10.1016/S0378-7206(99)00024-5

Johnson, C. L. (2007). A framework for pricing government e-services. *Electronic Commerce Research and Applications, 6*(4), 484–489. doi:10.1016/j.elerap.2007.02.005

Johnson, K. L., & Misic, M. M. (1999). Benchmarking: a tool for Web site evaluation and improvement. *Electronic Networking Applications and Policy, 9,* 383–392. doi:10.1108/10662249910297787

Johnson, N. F. (2007). *Two's company, three is complexity: A simple guide to the science of all sciences.* Oxford, UK: Oneworld.

Johnson, S. (2001). *Emergence: The connected lives of ants, brains, cities, and software.* New York, NY: Scribner.

Johnston, P., & Stewart-Weeks, M. (2007). *The Connected Republic 2.0 -- New possibilities & new value for the public sector.* Retrieved from http://www.cisco.com/web/about/ac79/docs/wp/TCR_WP_0821FINAL.pdf

Johnston, H. R., & Carrico, S. R. (1988). Developing capabilities to use information strategically. *Management Information Systems Quarterly, 12*(1), 36–48. doi:10.2307/248801

Joia, L. A. (2004). Bridging the digital divide: Some initiatives in Brazil. *Electronic Government, an International Journal, 1*(3), 300-315.

Joia, L. A. (2007). A heuristic model to implement government-to-government projects. *International Journal of Electronic Government Research, 3*(1), 1–18. doi:10.4018/jegr.2007010101

Jorgensen, D. J., & Cable, S. (2002). Facing the challenges of e-government: A case study of the city of Corpus Christi, Texas. *S.A.M. Advanced Management Journal, 67,* 15–23.

Juban, R., & Wyld, D. (2004). Would you like chips with that? Consumer perspectives of RFID. *Management Research News, 11*(12), 29–44. doi:10.1108/01409170410784653

Juthla, D. N., Bodorik, P., Weatherbee, T., & Hudson, B. (2002). e-Government in execution: Building organizational infrastructure. In *Proceedings of the European Conference on Information Systems*, Gdansk, Poland.

Kahneman, D., & Snell, J. (1990). Predicting utility. In Hogarth, R. (Ed.), *Insights in decision-making: A tribute to Hillel J. Einhorn* (pp. 295–310). Chicago, IL: University of Chicago Press.

Kaliannan, M., & Awang, H. (2009). Adoption and use of e-government services: A case study on e-procurement in Malaysia. In Bulucea, C. A., Mladenov, V., Pop, E., Leba, M., & Mastorakis, N. (Eds.), *Recent advances in e-activities, information security and privacy* (pp. 88–93). Stevens Point, WI: WSEAS Press.

Kamal, M., Weerakkody, V., & Jones, S. (2009). The case of EAI in facilitating e-Government services in a Welsh authority. *International Journal of Electronic Government Research*, *29*(2), 161–165.

Kambil, A., Kalis, A., Koufaris, M., & Lucas, H. C. (2000). Influences on the corporate adoption of Web technology. *Communications of the ACM*, *43*(11), 264–271. doi:10.1145/352515.352528

Kampitaki, D., Tambouris, E., & Tarabanis, K. (2008). e-Electioneering: Current Research Trends. In *Electronic Government* (LNCS 5184, pp. 184-194).

Kanat, I. E., & Ozkan, S. (2009). Exploring citizens' perception of government to citizen services: A model based on theory of planned behaviour (TPB). *Transforming Government: People, Process, and Policy*, *3*(4), 406–419. doi:10.1108/17506160910997900

Kannabiran, G., & Banumathi, T. (2008). E-Governance and ICT Enabled Rural Development in Developing Countries: Critical Lessons from RASI Project in India. *International Journal of Electronic Government Research*, *4*(3), 1–19. doi:10.4018/jegr.2008070101

Kanungo, S. (1998). An empirical study of organizational culture and network-based computer use. *Computers in Human Behavior*, *14*(1), 79–91. doi:10.1016/S0747-5632(97)00033-2

Kanungo, S., Sadavarti, S., & Srinivas, Y. (2001). Relating IT strategy and organizational culture: An empirical study of public sector units in India. *The Journal of Strategic Information Systems*, *10*(1), 29–57. doi:10.1016/S0963-8687(01)00038-5

Karahanna, E., & Straub, D. (1999). The psychological origins of perceived usefulness and perceived ease of use. *Information & Management*, *35*, 237–250. doi:10.1016/S0378-7206(98)00096-2

Karantjias, A., Polemi, N., Stamati, T., & Martakos, D. (2010a). Advanced e-Government enterprise Strategies & Solutions. *International Journal of Electronic Governance*.

Karantjias, A., Polemi, N., Stamati, T., & Martakos, D. (2010b). *A user-centric & federated Single-Sign-On IAM system for SOA e/m-frameworks*. International Journal of Electronic Government. doi:10.1504/EG.2010.033589

Karat, C. M., Blom, J. O., & Karat, J. (Eds.). (2004). *Designing personalized user experiences in eCommerce*. Dordrecht, The Netherlands: Kluwer Academic. doi:10.1007/1-4020-2148-8

Karkkainen, M., & Holmstrom, J. (2002). Wireless product identification: enabler for handling efficiency, customisation and information sharing. *Supply Chain Management: An International Journal*, *7*(4), 242–252. doi:10.1108/13598540210438971

Karwan, K. R., & Markland, R. E. (2006). Integrating service design principles and information technology to improve delivery and productivity in public sector operations: The case of the South Carolina DMV. *Journal of Operations Management*, *24*, 347–362. doi:10.1016/j.jom.2005.06.003

Kaylor, C., Deshazo, R., & Van Eck, D. (2001). Gauging e-government: A report on implementing services among American cities. *Government Information Quarterly*, *18*(4), 293–307. doi:10.1016/S0740-624X(01)00089-2

Keen, P. G. W. (1997). *The process edge: Creating value where it counts*. Boston, MA: Harvard Business School Press.

Keil, M., Cule, P., Lyytinen, K., & Schmidt, R. (1998). A framework for identifying software project risks. *Communications of the ACM, 41*, 76–83. doi:10.1145/287831.287843

Kelly, A., & Meyerhoff Nielsen, M. (in press). Scandinavia 2.0: The response to the economic crisis. *European Journal of ePractice.*

Kelly, K. L. (1995). *A framework for evaluating public sector geographic information systems (Tech. Rep. No. CTG.GIS-005).* Albany, NY: University at Albany SUNY.

Kenis, P., & Provan, K. G. (2009). Towards an exogenous theory of public network performance. *Public Administration, 87*(3), 440–456. doi:10.1111/j.1467-9299.2009.01775.x

Kennaway, J. R., Glauert, J. R. W., & Zwitserlood, I. (2007). Providing signed content on the Internet by synthesized animation. *ACM Transactions on Computer-Human Interaction, 14*(3), 15. doi:10.1145/1279700.1279705

Keong, L. M. (2007). *Malaysia lowers broadband target.* Retrieved from http://www.zdnetasia.com/malaysia-lowers-broadband-targets-62032069.htm

Kernaghan, K. (2005). Moving towards the virtual stage: Integrating services and service channels for citizen centered delivery. *International Review of Administrative Sciences, 71*(1), 119–131. doi:10.1177/0020852305051688

Kern, C. (2004). Radio-frequency-identification for security and media circulation in libraries. *The Electronic Library, 22*(4), 317–324. doi:10.1108/02640470410552947

Kettinger, W., & Lee, C. (1994). Perceived service quality and user satisfaction with the information-services function. *Decision Sciences, 25*, 737–766. doi:10.1111/j.1540-5915.1994.tb01868.x

Kettinger, W., & Lee, C. (1997). Pragmatic perspectives on the measurement of information systems service quality. *Management Information Systems Quarterly, 21*, 223–240. doi:10.2307/249421

Kettl, D. (2000). *The global public management revolution: A report on the transformation of governance.* Washington, DC: The Brookings Institution.

Ke, W., & Wei, K. K. (2004). Successful e-government in Singapore. *Communications of the ACM, 47*(6), 95–99. doi:10.1145/990680.990687

Khor, A. K. H. (2009). *Social contract theory, legitimacy theory and corporate social and environmental disclosure policies: Constructing and theoretical framework.* Retrieved from http://www.docstoc.com/docs/3446392/Social-Contract-Theory-Legitimacy-Theory-and-Corporate-Social-and-Environmental

Khoumbati, K., Dwivedi, Y. K., Lal, B., & Chen H. (2007). Broadband adoption in Pakistan. *Electronic Government, an International Journal, 4*(4), 451-465.

Khoumbati, K., & Themistocleous, M. (2007). Application of fuzzy simulation for the evaluation of enterprise application integration in healthcare organisations. *Transforming Government: People. Process and Policy, 1*(3), 230–241.

Kim, S. (2008). *A management capacity framework for local governments to strengthen transparency in local governance in Asia.* Retrieved from from http://www.ungc.org/pds/UNPOG_Local_Governance_Project_Report_SoonheeKim.pdf

Kim, S., & Lee, H. (2004). Organizational factors affecting knowledge sharing capabilities in e-government: An empirical study. In *Proceedings of the Annual National Conference on Digital Government Research*, Seattle, WA (pp. 1-11).

Kim, C., & Holzer, M. (2006). Public administrators' acceptance of the practice of digital democracy: A model explaining the utilization of online policy forums in South Korea. *International Journal of Electronic Government Research, 2*(2), 22–48. doi:10.4018/jegr.2006040102

Kim, H., Pan, G., & Pan, S. (2007). Managing IT-enabled transformation in the public sector: A case study on e-government in South Korea. *Government Information Quarterly, 24*, 338–352. doi:10.1016/j.giq.2006.09.007

Kim, H.-W., Chan, H. C., & Gupta, S. (2007). Value-based adoption of mobile internet: An empirical investigation. *Decision Support Systems, 43*(1), 111–126. doi:10.1016/j.dss.2005.05.009

Kim, S., Kim, H. J., & Lee, H. (2009). An institutional analysis of an e-government system for anti-corruption: The case of OPEN. *Government Information Quarterly*, *26*(1), 42–50. doi:10.1016/j.giq.2008.09.002

Kim, S., & Lee, H. (2006). The impact of organizational context and information technology on employee knowledge-sharing capabilities. *Public Administration Review*, *66*(3), 370–385. doi:10.1111/j.1540-6210.2006.00595.x

King, S., & Cotterill, S. (2007). Transformational government? The role of information technology in delivering citizen-centric local public services. *Local Government Studies*, *33*(3), 333–354. doi:10.1080/03003930701289430

King, W. R., & He, J. (2006). A meta-analysis of the technology acceptance model. *Information & Management*, *43*(6), 740–755. doi:10.1016/j.im.2006.05.003

Kleijnen, M., de Ruyter, K., & Wetzels, M. (2007). An assessment of value creation in mobile service delivery and the moderating role of time consciousness. *Journal of Retailing*, *83*(1), 33–46. doi:10.1016/j.jretai.2006.10.004

Klievink, B., & Janssen, M. (2009). Realizing joined-up government. Dynamic capabilities and stage models for transformation. *Government Information Quarterly*, *26*(2), 275–284. doi:10.1016/j.giq.2008.12.007

Kline, R. B. (2005). *Principles and practice of structural equation modeling*. New York, NY: Guilford Press.

Kling, R. (2000). Learning about information technologies and social change: The contribution of social informatics. *The Information Society*, *16*(3), 217–232. doi:10.1080/01972240050133661

Klischewski, R. (2004). Information Integration or Process Integration? How to Achieve Interoperability in Administration. In R. Traunmüller (Ed.), *EGOV 2004* (LNCS 3183, pp. 57-65).

Klischewski, R., & Scholl, H. J. (2006). Information quality as a common ground for key players in e-government integration and interoperability. In *Proceedings of the Hawaii International Conference on System Sciences (HICSS)*.

Kohn, W., Brayman, V., & Littleton, J. (2005). Repair-control of enterprise systems using RFID sensory data. *IIE Transactions*, *37*(4), 281–290. doi:10.1080/0740817 0590516953doi:10.1080/07408170590516953

Kollock, P. (1999). The production of trust in online markets. *Advances in Group Processes*, *16*, 99–123.

Kolsaker, A. (2006). Reconceptualising e-government as a tool of governance: The UK case. *Electronic Government, an International Journal*, *3*(4), 347-355.

Kolsaker, A., & Lee-Kelley, L. (2006). 'Mind the Gap': E-government and e-democracy. In M. A. Wimmer, H. J. Scholl, A. Gronlund, & K. V. Andersen (Eds.), *Proceedings of the 5th International Conference on Electronic Government* (LNCS 4084, pp. 96-106).

Koussouris, S., Tsitsanis, A., Gionis, G., & Psarras, J. (2008). Designing Generic Municipal Services Process Models towards eGovernment Interoperability Infrastructures. *Electronic Journal for E-Commerce Tools and Applications*. Retrieved from http://www.ejeta.org/specialMay08-issue.php

Kovadid, Z. J. (2005). The impact of national culture on worldwide egovernment readiness. *Informing Science: International Journal of an Emerging Transdiscipline*, *8*, 143–158.

Kraemer, K. L., & King, J. L. (2003). *Information technology and administrative reform: Will the time after e-government be different?* Retrieved from http://www.crito.uci.edu

Kraemer, K., & King, J. L. (2006). Information technology and administrative reform: Will e-government be different? *International Journal of Electronic Government Research*, *2*(1), 1–20. doi:10.4018/jegr.2006010101

Krell, K., & Matook, S. (2009). Competitive advantage from mandatory investments: An empirical study of Australian firms. *The Journal of Strategic Information Systems*, *18*(1), 31–45. doi:10.1016/j.jsis.2008.12.001

Kudo, H. (2010). E-Governance as strategy of public sector reform: Peculiarity of Japanese IT policy and its institutional origin. *Financial Accountability & Management*, *26*(1), 65–84. doi:10.1111/j.1468-0408.2009.00491.x

Kumar, P., Reinitz, H. W., Simunovic, J., Sandeep, K. P., & Franzon, P. D. (2009). Overview of RFID technology and its applications in the food industry. *Journal of Food Science*, *74*(8), 101–106. PubMed doi:10.1111/j.1750-3841.2009.01323.x

Kumar, N., Scheer, L., & Steenkamp, J. (1995). The effects of supplier fairness on vulnerable resellers. *JMR, Journal of Marketing Research*, *32*, 54–65. doi:10.2307/3152110

Kumar, V., Mukerji, B., Butt, I., & Persaud, A. (2007). Factors for successful e-government adoption: A conceptual framework. *Electronic. Journal of E-Government*, *5*(1), 63–76.

Kunstelj, M., Jukic, T., & Vintar, M. (2007). Analysing the demand side of e-government: What can we learn from slovenian users? In M. A. Wimmer, J. Scholl, & A. Gronlund (Eds.), *Proceedings of the 6ʰ International Conference on Electronic Government* (LNCS 4656, pp. 305-317).

Kvale, S. (1983). The qualitative research interview: A phenomenological and a hermeneutical mode of understanding. *Journal of Phenomenological Psychology*, *14*, 171–196. doi:10.1163/156916283X00090

Kwon, D., Watts-Sussman, S., & Collopy, F. (2002). Value frame, paradox and change: The constructive nature of information technology business value. *Systems and Organizations*, *2*(4), 196–220.

Lai, V., & Mahapatra, R. (1997). Exploring the research in information technology implementation. *Information & Management*, *32*, 187–201. doi:10.1016/S0378-7206(97)00022-0

Lakhani, H., Guerriero, L., Hatton, L., & Lau, C. (2009). Transforming organizational culture through decision support at Bloorview Kids Rehab. *Electronic Healthcare*, *7*(3), 1–8.

Lamie, J., & Ball, R. (2010). Evaluation of partnership working within a community planning context. *Local Government Studies*, *36*(1), 109–127. doi:10.1080/03003930903435815

Lam, W. (2005). Barriers to e-government. *Journal of Enterprise Information Management*, *18*(5), 511–530. doi:10.1108/17410390510623981

Landsbergen, D. J., & Wolken, G. Jr. (2001). Realizing the promise: Government information systems and the fourth generation of information technology. *Public Administration Review*, *61*(2), 206–220. doi:10.1111/0033-3352.00023

Landt, J. (2005). The history of RFID. *IEEE Potentials*, *24*(4), 8–11. doi:10.1109/MP.2005.1549751

Lane, J. E. (1995). *The public sector: Concepts, models and approaches*. London, UK: Sage.

LaPorte, T. M., & Demchak, C. C., & AnddeJong, M. (2002). Democracy and bureaucracy in the age of the Web: Empirical findings and theoretical speculations. *Administration & Society*, *34*(4), 411–446. doi:10.1177/0095399702034004004

Lau, A. S. M. (2004). Strategies to encourage the adoption of G2C e-government services in Hong Kong. *Electronic Government, an International Journal*, *1*(3), 273-292.

Lau, A. S. M., & Kwok, V. W. S. (2007). How e-government strategies influence e-commerce adoption by SMEs. *Electronic Government, an International Journal*, *4*(1), 20-42.

Lau, T. Y., Mira, A., Lin, C., & Atkin, D. J. (2008). Adoption of e-government in three Latin American countries: Argentina, Brazil and Mexico. *Telecommunications Policy*, *32*(2), 88–100. doi:10.1016/j.telpol.2007.07.007

Lau, T., Aboulhoson, M., Lin, C., & Atkin, D. (2008). Adoption of E-government in three Latin American countries: Argentina, Brazil and Mexico. *Telecommunications Policy*, *32*(2), 88–100. doi:10.1016/j.telpol.2007.07.007

Layne, K., & Lee, J. (2001). Developing fully functional e-government: A four stage model. *Government Information Quarterly*, *18*(2), 122–136. doi:10.1016/S0740-624X(01)00066-1

Le Grand, J. (2007). *The other invisible hand: Delivering public services through choice and competition*. Princeton, NJ: Princeton University Press.

Leadbeater, C. (2004). *Personalisation through participation: A new script for public services*. London, UK: Demos.

Leadbeater, C. (2006). *The user innovation revolution – How business can unlock the value of customers' ideas*. London, UK: National Consumer Council.

Leadbeater, C., Bartlett, J., & Gallagher, N. (2008). *Making it personal*. London, UK: Demos Think Tank.

Leahy, W., Chandler, P., & Sweller, J. (2003). When auditory presentations should and should not be a component of multimedia instruction. *Applied Cognitive Psychology*, *17*(4), 401–418. doi:10.1002/acp.877

Lean, O. K., Zailani, S., Ramayah, T., & Fernando, Y. (2009). Factors influencing intention to use e-government services among citizens in Malaysia. *International Journal of Information Management, 29*(6), 458–475. doi:10.1016/j.ijinfomgt.2009.03.012

Lederer, A. L., & Mendelow, A. L. (1987). Information resource planning: information systems managers' difficulty in determining top management's objectives. *Management Information Systems Quarterly, 13*(3), 388–399.

Lee, Y. M., Cheng, F., & Leung, Y. T. (2009). A quantitative view on how RFID can improve inventory management in a supply chain. *International Journal of Logistics-Research and Applications, 12*(1), 23-43.

Lee, A., & Baskerville, R. (2003). Generalizing in information systems research. *Information Systems Research, 14*(3), 221–243. doi:10.1287/isre.14.3.221.16560

Lee, B., & Menon, N. M. (2000). Information technology value through different normative lenses. *Journal of Management Information Systems, 16*(4), 99–119.

Lee, G., & Perry, J. L. (2002). Are computers boosting productivity? A test of the paradox in state governments. *Journal of Public Administration: Research and Theory, 12*(1), 77–102.

Lee, H., Irani, Z., Osman, I. H., Balci, A., Ozkan, S., & Medeni, T. D. (2008). Toward a reference process model for citizen-oriented evaluation of e-Government services. *Transforming Government: People Process and Policy, 2*(4), 297–310. doi:10.1108/17506160810917972

Lee, H., & Ozer, O. (2007). Unlocking the value of RFID. *Production and Operations Management, 16*(1), 40–64. doi:10.1111/j.1937-5956.2007.tb00165.x

Lee, J., & Rao, H. R. (2009). Task complexity and different decision criteria for online service acceptance: A comparison of two e-government compliance service domains. *Decision Support Systems, 47*(4), 424–435. doi:10.1016/j.dss.2009.04.009

Lee, K. C., Kirlidog, M., Lee, S., & Lim, G. G. (2008). User evaluations of tax filing web sites: A comparative study of South Korea and Turkey. *Online Information Review, 32*(6), 842–859. doi:10.1108/14684520810923962

Lee-Kelley, L., & James, T. (2003). E-government and social exclusion: An empirical study. *Journal of Electronic Commerce in Organizations, 1*(4), 1–15. doi:10.4018/jeco.2003100101

Lee, L. S., Fiedler, K. D., & Smith, J. S. (2008). Radio frequency identification (RFID) implementation in the service sector: A customer-facing diffusion model. *International Journal of Production Economics, 112*(2), 587–600. doi:10.1016/j.ijpe.2007.05.008

Lee, M., & Turban, E. (2001). A trust model for internet shopping. *International Journal of Electronic Commerce, 6*, 75–91.

Lee, S. H., Ngai, A. W., & Zhang, K. (2007). The quest to improve Chinese healthcare: Some fundamental issues. *International Journal of Health Care Quality Assurance, 20*(1), 416–428. doi:10.1108/09526860710763334

Lee, S. M., Tan, X., & Trimi, S. (2005). Current practices of leading e-government countries. *Communications of the ACM, 48*(10), 99–104. doi:10.1145/1089107.1089112

Lee, Y., Kozar, K. A., & Larsen, K. R. T. (2003). The technology acceptance model: Past, present, and future. *Communications of the Association for Information Systems, 12*, 752–780.

Lefebvre, L. A., Lefebvre, E., Bendavid, Y., Wamba, S. F., & Boeck, H. (2006). *RFID as an enabler of b-to-b e-commerce and its impact on business processes: a pilot study of a supply chain in the retail industry exploiting RFID digital information in enterprise collaboration.* Paper presented at the 39th Annual Hawaii International Conference on System Sciences (HICSS'06).

Legris, P., Ingham, J., & Collerette, P. (2003). Why do people use information technology? A critical review of the technology acceptance model. *Information & Management, 40*(3), 191–204. doi:10.1016/S0378-7206(01)00143-4

Leidner, D. E., & Kayworth, T. (2006). A review of culture in information systems research: Toward a theory of information technology culture conflict. *Management Information Systems Quarterly, 30*(2), 357–399.

Lekakos, G. (2007). Exploiting RFID digital information in enterprise collaboration. *Industrial Management & Data Systems*, *107*(8), 110–122. doi:10.1108/02635570710822778

LGAF project. (2007). *Local Government Access Framework*. Retrieved from http://wiki.kedke.org/wiki/

Li, D., Browne, G., & Wetherbe, J. (2006). Why do internet users stick with a specific web site? A relationship perspective. *International Journal of Electronic Commerce*, *10*(4), 105–141. doi:10.2753/JEC1086-4415100404

Light, P. (1997). *The tides of reform: Making government work 1945-1995*. New Haven, CT: Yale University Press.

Lim, J. H., & Tang, S. Y. (2008). Urban e-government initiatives and environmental decision performance in Korea. *Journal of Public Administration: Research and Theory*, *18*(1), 109–138. doi:10.1093/jopart/mum005

Lim, J. H., & Tang, S.-Y. (2007). Urban e-government initiatives and environmental decision performance in Korea. *Journal of Public Administration: Research and Theory*, *18*(1), 109–138. doi:10.1093/jopart/mum005

Lindblom, C. E. (1959). The science of muddling through. *Public Administration Review*, *19*, 79–88. doi:10.2307/973677

Lindblom, C. E., & Cohen, D. K. (1979). *Usable knowledge: Social science and social problem solving*. New Haven, CT: Yale University Press.

Lindblom, C. E., & Dahl, R. A. (1976). *Politics, economics, and welfare: Planning and politico-economic systems resolved into basic social processes*. Chicago, IL: University of Chicago Press.

Lindblom, C. E., & Woodhouse, E. J. (1993). *The policy-making process* (3rd ed.). Upper Saddle River, NJ: Prentice Hall.

Lin, H., & Lin, S. (2008). Determinants of e-business diffusion: A test of the technology diffusion perspective. *Technovation*, *28*(3), 135–145. doi:10.1016/j.technovation.2007.10.003

Lips, A. M. B., & Hof, d. S., Prins, J. E. J., & Schudelaro, A. A. P. (2004). *Issues of online personalisation in commercial and public service delivery*. Nijmegen, The Netherlands: Wolf Legal.

Li, S., Visich, J. K., Khumawala, B. M., & Zhang, C. (2006). Radio Frequency Identification Technology: Applications, Technical Challenges and Strategies. *Sensor Review*, *26*(3), 193–202. doi:10.1108/02602280610675474

Liu, C., & Arnett, K. (2000). Exploring the factors associated with web site success in the context of electronic commerce. *Information & Management*, *38*, 23–33. doi:10.1016/S0378-7206(00)00049-5

Liu, K. (2000). *Semiotics in information systems engineering*. Cambridge, UK: Cambridge University Press. doi:10.1017/CBO9780511543364

Liu, T., Dimpsey, R., Behroozi, A., & Kumaran, S. (2005). Performance modelling of a business process integration middleware. *International Journal of Business Process Integration and Management*, *1*(1), 43–52. doi:10.1504/IJBPIM.2005.006964

Li, X., Hess, T. J., & Valacich, J. S. (2008). Why do we trust new technology? A study of initial trust formation with organizational information systems. *The Journal of Strategic Information Systems*, *17*(1), 39–71. doi:10.1016/j.jsis.2008.01.001

Lloyd, R. M. (2002). Electronic Government. *Business and Economic Review*, *48*(4), 15–17.

Lockett, A., & Littler, D. (1997). The adoption of direct banking services. *Journal of Marketing Management*, *13*, 791–811. doi:10.1080/0267257X.1997.9964512

Loo, W. H., Yeow, P. H. P., & Chong, S. C. (2009). User acceptance of Malaysian government multipurpose smart-card applications. *Government Information Quarterly*, *26*(2), 358–367. doi:10.1016/j.giq.2008.07.004

Lu, C. T., Huang, S. Y., & Lo, P. Y. (2010). An empirical study of on-line tax filing acceptance model: Integrating TAM and TPB. *African Journal of Business Management*, *4*(5), 800–810.

Lucas, H. (1981). *Implementation: The key to successful information systems*. New York, NY: Columbia University Press.

Lucas, H., & Spitler, V. (1999). Technology use and performance: A field study of broker workstations. *Decision Sciences Journal*, *30*, 291–311. doi:10.1111/j.1540-5915.1999.tb01611.x

Luhmann, N. (1979). *Trust and power*. Chichester, UK: John Wiley & Sons.

Luk, S. C. Y. (2009). The impact of leadership and stakeholders on the success/failure of e-government service: Using the case study of e-stamping service in Hong Kong. *Government Information Quarterly*, *26*(4), 594–604. doi:10.1016/j.giq.2009.02.009

Luna-Reyes, L. F., Gil-Garcia, J. R., & Cruz, C. B. (2007). Collaborative digital government in Mexico: Some lessons from federal Web-based interorganizational information integration initiatives. *Government Information Quarterly*, *24*(4), 808–826. doi:10.1016/j.giq.2007.04.003

Luna-Reyes, L. F., Gil-Garcia, J. R., & Estrada-Marroquin, M. (2008). The impact of institutions on interorganizational IT projects in the Mexican federal government. *International Journal of Electronic Government Research*, *4*(2), 27–42. doi:10.4018/jegr.2008040103

Lusoli, W. (2005). The Internet and the European Parliament Elections: Theoretical perspectives, empirical investigations and proposals for research. *Information Polity*, *10*(3-4), 153–163.

Lyytinen, K., & Hirschheim, R. (1987). Information systems failures: A survey and classification of empirical literature. In Zorkoczy, P. (Ed.), *Oxford surveys in information technology*. New York, NY: Oxford University Press.

Maad, S., & Coghlan, B. (2008). Assessment of the potential use of grid portal features in e-government. *Transforming Government: People. Process and Policy*, *2*(2), 128.

Maccrimmon, K. R., & Wehrung, D. A. (1984). The risk in-basket. *The Journal of Business*, *57*(3), 367–387. doi:10.1086/296269

Mach, M., Sabol, T., & Paralic, J. (2006). Integration of eGov services: back-office versus front-office integration. In *Proceeding of the Workshop on Semantic Web for e-Government 2006, Workshop at the 3rd European Semantic Web Conference.*

Macintosh, A. (2004, January). *Characterizing E-Participation in Policy-Making*. Paper presented at the Thirty-Seventh Annual Hawaii International Conference on System Sciences (HICSS-37), Big Island, Hawaii.

Macintosh, A. (2006). e-Participation in Policy-making: the research and the challenges. In P. Cunningham & M. Cunningham (Eds.) E*xploiting the Knowledge Economy: Issues, Applications and Case Studies* (pp. 364-369). Amsterdam, The Netherlands: IOS Press.

Macintosh, A., & Whyte, A. (2006). Evaluating how e-Participation changes local democracy. In Z. Irani & A. Ghoneim (Eds.), *Proceedings of the e-Government Workshop 2006*. London: Brunel University.

Macintosh, A., Coleman, S., & Lalljee, M. (2005). *e-Methods for public engagement*. Bristol, UK: Bristol City Council.

Macintosh, A. (2007). E-democracy and e-participation research in Europe. *Integrated Series in Information Systems*, *17*, 85–102. doi:10.1007/978-0-387-71611-4_5

Mahrer, H. (2005). Politicians as patrons for e-democracy? Closing the gap between ideals and realities. *International Journal of Electronic Government Research*, *1*(3), 51–68. doi:10.4018/jegr.2005070104

Malaysia broadband market. (2007). Retrieved from http://www.budde.com.au/Research/Malaysia-Broadband-Market.html

Malaysian Institute of Accountants. (2007). *Malaysian Institute of Accountants Directory*. Retrieved from http://www.mia.org.my/new/members_memberfirms_directory.asp

Malhotra, K. N. (2002). *Marketing research: An applied orientation*. New Delhi, India: Pearson Education.

Malina, A., & Macintosh, A. (2002). e-Democracy: Citizen Engagement and Evaluation. In S. Friedrichs, T. Hart, & O. Schmidt (Eds.), *Balanced E-Government: Von der elektronischen Verwaltung zur digitalen Burgergesellschaft*. Gütersloh, Germany: Bertlesmann Foundation.

Mandell, M. P., & Steelman, T. A. (2003). Understanding what can be accomplished through interorganizational innovations. *Public Management Review*, *5*(2), 197–224. doi:10.1080/1461667032000066417

Maniatopoulos, G. (2005, July 4-6). e-Government movements of organizational change: A social shaping approach. In *Proceedings of the 4th International Critical Management Studies Conference*, Cambridge, UK.

Mann, I. J. S., Kumar, V., Mann, H., & Kumar, U. (2008). Scope of City E-Government Initiative. In Amitabh, O. (Ed.), *E-Governance in Practice* (pp. 173–184). New Delhi, India: G.I.F.T. Publishing.

Ma, Q., & Liu, L. (2004). The technology acceptance model: A meta-analysis of empirical findings. *Journal of Organizational and End User Computing, 16*(1), 59–72. doi:10.4018/joeuc.2004010104

Marche, S., & McNiven, J. D. (2003). E-government and e-governance: The future isn't what it used to be. *Canadian Journal of Administrative Sciences, 20*(1), 74–86. doi:10.1111/j.1936-4490.2003.tb00306.x

March, G. J., & Shapira, Z. (1987). Managerial perspectives on risk and risk taking. *Management Science, 33*(11), 1404–1418. doi:10.1287/mnsc.33.11.1404

Maslow, A. H. (1943). A theory of human motivation. *Psychological Review, 50*, 370–396. doi:10.1037/h0054346

Masters, Z., Macintosh, A., & Smith, E. (2004, September). *Young People and E-Democracy: Creating a Culture of Participation*. Paper presented at Third International Conference in E-Government, Zaragoza, Spain.

Mathieson, K. (1991). Predicting user intentions: Comparing the technology acceptance model with the theory of planned behavior. *Information Systems Research, 2*, 173–191. doi:10.1287/isre.2.3.173

Mayer, R., Davis, J., & Schoorman, D. (1995). An integrative model of organization trust. *Academy of Management Review, 20*, 709–734.

Maylor, H., & Blackmon, K. (2005). *Researching business and management*. New York, NY: Macmillan.

May, P. J., & Winter, S. C. (2007). Collaborative service arrangements. *Public Management Review, 9*(4), 479–502. doi:10.1080/14719030701726473

Mbarika, V. W., & Byrd, T. A. (2009). An exploratory study of strategies to improve Africa's least developed economies' telecommunications infrastructure: The stakeholders speak. *IEEE Transactions on Engineering Management, 56*(2), 312–328. doi:10.1109/TEM.2009.2013826

McClure, C. R., & Sprehe, J. T. (2000). *Performance measures for federal agencies: Final report*. Washington, DC: Defense Technical Information Center.

McCombs, M., & Ghanem, S. I. (2001). The convergence of agenda setting and framing. In Reese, S. D., Gandy, O. H. Jr, & Grant, A. E. (Eds.), *Framing public life: Perspectives on media and our understanding of the social world* (pp. 67–81). Mahwah, NJ: Lawrence Erlbaum.

McDermott, C. M., & Stock, G. N. (1999). Organizational culture and advanced manufacturing technology implementation. *Journal of Operations Management, 17*, 521–533. doi:10.1016/S0272-6963(99)00008-X

McFarlan, F. W. (1981). Portfolio approach to information systems. *Harvard Business Review, 59*, 142–150.

McGuire, M. (2006). Collaborative Public Management: Assessing What We Know and How We Know It. *Public Administration Review, 66*(1), 33–43. doi:10.1111/j.1540-6210.2006.00664.x

McKeen, J. D., & Smith, H. A. (2002). New developments in practice II: enterprise application integration. *Communications of the Association for Information Systems, 8*, 451–466.

McKinney, V., Yoon, K., & Zahedi, F. M. (2002). The measurement of web-customer satisfaction: An expectation and disconfirmation approach. *Information Systems Research, 13*(3), 296–315. doi:10.1287/isre.13.3.296.76

McKnight, H., & Chervany, N. (2002). What trust means in e-commerce customer relationships: An interdisciplinary conceptual typology. *International Journal of Electronic Commerce, 6*, 35–53.

McKnight, H., Choudhury, V., & Kacmar, C. (2002). Developing and validating trust measures for e-commerce: An integrative typology. *Information Systems Research, 13*, 334–359. doi:10.1287/isre.13.3.334.81

McKnight, H., & Cummings, L. (1998). Initial trust formation in new organizational relationships. *Academy of Management Review, 23*, 473–490.

McNeal, R. S., Schmeida, M., & Hale, K. (2007). E-disclosure laws and electronic campaign finance reform: Lessons from the diffusion of e-government policies in the States. *Government Information Quarterly, 24*(2), 312–325. doi:10.1016/j.giq.2006.06.006

McNeal, R. S., Tolbert, C. J., Mossberger, K., & Dotterweich, L. J. (2003). Innovating in digital government in the American states. *Social Science Quarterly, 84*(1), 52–70. doi:10.1111/1540-6237.00140

Mebus, A., Wiener, S., Buckheit, K., & Symmonds, J. (2008). *Corporate social responsibility and the fortune 100: Evidence for environmental themes.* Paper presented at the 2009 Conference of the National Communication Association, Chicago, IL.

Medhi, I., Prasad, A., & Toyama, K. (2007). Optimal audio-visual representations for illiterate users of computers. In *Proceedings of the 16th International Conference on World Wide Web* (pp. 873-882). New York, NY: ACM Press.

Meingast, M., King, J., & Mulligan, D. (2007). *Embedded RFID and Everyday Things: A Case Study of the Security and Privacy Risks of the U.S. e-Passport.* Paper presented at the EEE International Conference on RFID.

Melao, N., & Pidd, M. (2000). A Conceptual Framework for Understanding Business Process and Business Process Modeling. *Information Systems Journal, 10,* 105–129. doi:10.1046/j.1365-2575.2000.00075.x

Melitski, J. (2001). *The world of e-government and e-governance.* Retrieved from http://www.aspanet.org

Melville, N., Kraemer, K., & Gurbaxani, V. (2004). Review: Information Technology and Organizational Performance: An Integrative Model of IT Business Value. *Management Information Systems Quarterly, 28*(2), 283–322.

MENA Working Group. (2010, April 27-28). *Making life easy for citizens and businesses in Portugal – e-government and administrative simplification.* Paper presented at the Meeting of the MENA Working Group, Dubai, UAE.

Meneguzzo, M., & Cepiku, D. (Eds.). (2008). *Network pubblici. Strategia, struttura e governance.* Milano, Italy: McGraw-Hill.

Meyer, A., & Goes, J. (1988). Organizational assimilation of innovations: A multilevel contextual analysis. *Academy of Management Journal, 31,* 897–923. doi:10.2307/256344

Miceli, G., Ricotta, F., & Costabile, M. (2007). Customizing customization: A conceptual framework for interactive personalization. *Journal of Interactive Marketing, 21*(2), 6–25. doi:10.1002/dir.20076

Millard, J. (2008). 21st century eGovernance -- turning the world upside down. *European Review of Political Technologies, 5.*

Millard, J. (2010). Government 1.5 – is the bottle half full or half empty? *European Journal of ePractice, 2010*(9).

Millard, J. (Ed.). (2007). *European eGovernment 2005-2007: Taking stock of good practice and progress towards implementation of the i2010 eGovernment action plan.* Retrieved from http://www.epractice.eu/files/download/awards/ResearchReport2007.pdf

Millard, J., & Horlings, E. (2008). *Research report on value for citizens: A vision of public governance in 2020.* Retrieved from http://ec.europa.eu/information_society/activities/egovernment/studies/docs/research_report_on_value_for_citizens.pdf

Millard, J., Meyerhoff Nielsen, M., Warren, R., Smith, S., Macintosh, A., Tarabanis, K., et al. (2009). *European eP-articipation summary report.* Retrieved from http://islab.uom.gr/eP/index.php?option=com_docman&task=cat_view&gid=36&&Itemid=82

Millard, J., Shahin, J., Pedersen, K., Huijboom, N., & van den Broek, T. (2009). *I2010 eGovernment action plan progress study: Final report.* Retrieved from http://www.dti.dk/27666

Millard, J. (2006). The business and economic implications of ICT use: Europe's transition to the knowledge economy. In Compañó, R., Pascu, C., Bianchi, A., Burgelman, J.-C., Barrios, S., Ulbrich, M., & Maghiros, I. (Eds.), *The future of the information society in Europe: Contributions to the debate.* Seville, Spain: Institute of Prospective Technological Studies.

Millard, J. (2008). *Report on the FP7 consultation workshop on ICT for governance and policy modelling.* Brussels, Belgium: European Commission.

Millard, J., Kubieck, H., & Westholm, H. (2004). *Reorganisation of government back-offices for better ePS – European good practices (back-office reorganisation) prepared for the European Commission eGovernment unit. Brussels.* Belgium: European Commission.

Millard, J., Warren, R., Leitner, C., & Shahin, J. (2007). *Towards the eGovernment vision for EU in 2010: Research policy challenges.* Seville, Spain: Institute of Prospective Technological Studies.

Miller, M. M., & Riechert, B. P. (2001). The spiral of opportunity and frame resonance: Mapping the issue cycle in news and public discourse. In S. D. Reese O. H. Gandy Jr., & A. E. Grant, (Eds.), *Framing public life: Perspectives on media and our understanding of the social world* (pp. 107-122). Mahwah, NJ: Lawrence Erlbaum.

Milner, H. V. (2006). The Digital Divide: The Role of Political Institutions in Technology Diffusion. *Comparative Political Studies*, *39*(2), 176–199. doi:10.1177/0010414005282983

Milward, H. B., & Snyder, L. O. (1996). Electronic government: Linking citizens to public organizations through technology. *Journal of Public Administration: Research and Theory*, *6*(2), 261–275.

Ministry of National Economy. (1994). *Final report of integrated Mediterranean programs on information technology.*

Ministry of National Economy. (2001). *Operational programme 'information society': European union support framework III.*

Ministry to the Presidency of the Government. (1993). *Programme of administrative modernization 1993-1995.*

Ministry to the Presidency of the Government. (1994). *Operational programme 'Klisthenis' for the modernization of the Greek public administration: European community support framework II.*

Mirchandani, D. A., Johnson, J. H., & Joshi, K. (2008). Perspectives of citizens towards e-government in Thailand and Indonesia: A multigroup analysis. *Information Systems Frontiers*, *10*(4), 483–497. doi:10.1007/s10796-008-9102-7

Mississippi Department of Information Technology Services (ITS). (2006). *Annual report.* Jackson, MS: ITS.

Mitra, R. K., & Gupta, M. P. (2008). A contextual perspective of performance assessment in eGovernment: A study of Indian Police Administration. *Government Information Quarterly*, *25*(2), 278–302. doi:10.1016/j.giq.2006.03.008

Molla, A., & Licker, P. S. (2005). eCommerce adoption in developing countries: A model and instrument. *Information & Management*, *42*(6), 877–899. doi:10.1016/j.im.2004.09.002

Molnar, D., & Wagner, D. (2004). Privacy and security in library RFID: Issues, practices, and architectures. In *Proceedings of the 11th ACM Conference on Computer and Communications Security* (pp. 25-29).

Monnoyer-Smith, L. (2006). Citizen's deliberation on the Internet: An exploratory study. *International Journal of Electronic Government Research*, *2*(3), 58–74. doi:10.4018/jegr.2006070103

Monsuwé, T. P., Dellaert, B. G. C., & de Ruyter, K. (2004). What drives consumers to shop online? A literature review. *International Journal of Service Industry Management*, *15*(1), 102–121. doi:10.1108/09564230410523358

Montgomery, A. L., & Smith, M. D. (2009). Prospects for personalization on the internet. *Journal of Interactive Marketing*, *23*(2), 130–137. doi:10.1016/j.intmar.2009.02.001

Montoya-Weiss, M. M., Voss, G. B., & Grewal, D. (2003). Determinants of online channel use and overall satisfaction with a relational, multichannel service provider. *Journal of the Academy of Marketing Science*, *31*(4), 448–458. doi:10.1177/0092070303254408

Moon, M. J., & Welch, E. W. (2004, January 5-8). Same bed, different dreams? A comparative analysis of citizen and bureaucrat perspectives on e-Government. In *Proceedings of the 37th Hawaii International Conference on System Sciences*, Honolulu, HI.

Moon, D., Serra, G., & West, J. P. (1993). Citizens' contacts with bureaucratic and legislative officials. *Political Research Quarterly*, *46*(4), 931–941.

Moon, M. J. (2002). The evolution of e-government among municipalities: Rhetoric or reality. *Public Administration Review*, *62*(4), 424–433. doi:10.1111/0033-3352.00196

Moon, M. J., & deLeon, P. (2001). Municipal reinvention: Managerial values and diffusion among municipalities. *Journal of Public Administration: Research and Theory*, *11*(3), 327–352.

Moon, M. J., & Kim, Y. (2001). Extending the TAM for a world-wide-web context. *Information & Management*, *28*, 217–230. doi:10.1016/S0378-7206(00)00061-6

Moon, M. J., & Norris, D. F. (2005). Does managerial orientation matter? The adoption of reinventing government and e-government at the municipal level. *Information Systems Journal*, *15*(1), 43–60. doi:10.1111/j.1365-2575.2005.00185.x

Moon, Y. B. (2007). Enterprise resource planning: A review of the literature. *International Journal of Management and Enterprise Development, 4*(3), 235–264. doi:10.1504/IJMED.2007.012679

Moore, G. C., & Benbasat, I. (1991). Development of an instrument to measure the perceptions of adopting an information technology innovation. *Information Systems Research, 2*(3), 192–222. doi:10.1287/isre.2.3.192

Moreno-Jimenez, J. M., & Polasek, W. (2003). e-Democracy and Knowledge: A Multi-criteria Framework for the New Democratic Era. *Jouranl of Multi-Criteria Decision Analysis, 12*, 163–176. doi:10.1002/mcda.354

Mosca, L., & Santucci, D. (2009). Petitioning online. The Role of e-Petitions in Web Campaining. In Baringhorst, S., Kneip, V., & Niesyto, J. (Eds.), *Political Campaigning on the Web*. London: Transaction Publishers.

Mossenburg, K., Tolbert, C., & Stansbury, M. (2003). *Virtual inequality: Beyond the digital divide*. Washington, DC: Georgetown University Press.

Mowbray, T. J., & Zahavi, R. (1995). *The Essential CORBA: Systems Integration Using Distributed Objects*. New York: John Wiley & Sons.

Moynihan, D. P., & Silva, C. L. (2008). The administrators of democracy: A research note on local election officials. *Public Administration Review, 68*(5), 816–827. doi:10.1111/j.1540-6210.2008.00923.x

Muller, M. J., Hallewell Haslwanter, J. D., & Dayton, T. (1997). Participatory practices in the software lifecycle. In Helander, M., Landauer, T., & Prabhu, P. (Eds.), *Handbook of human-computer interaction* (pp. 255–297). Amsterdam, The Netherlands: Elsevier.

Murphy, J. (2005). *Beyond e-government the world's most successful technology-enabled transformations, executive summary*. New York, NY: INSEAD.

Mursu, A., Soriyan, H. A., Olufokunbi, K., & Korpela, M. (2000). Information systems development in a developing country: Theoretical analysis of special requirements in Nigeria and Africa. In *Proceedings of the 33rd Hawaiian International Conference on System Sciences* (Vol. 2, pp. 1-10).

Musolf, L. D., & Seidman, H. (1980). The blurred boundaries of public administration. *Public Administration Review, 40*(2), 124–130. doi:10.2307/975622

Myers, B. L., Kappelman, L. A., & Prybutok, V. R. (1997). A comprehensive model for assessing quality and productivity of the information systems function: Toward a theory for information systems assessment. *Information Resources Management Journal*, 6–25.

Myers, M. D. (1997). Qualitative research in information systems. *Management Information Systems Quarterly, 21*(2), 241–242. doi:10.2307/249422

Myung, J., Lee, W., & Shih, T. K. (2006). An adaptive memoryless protocol for RFID tag collision arbitration multimedia. *IEEE Transactions, 8*(5), 1096–1101.

Naiman, C. E., & Ouksel, A. M. (1995). A classification of semantic conflicts in heterogeneous database systems. *Journal of Organizational Computing, 5*(2), 167–193. doi:10.1080/10919399509540248

Navarra, D., & Cornford, T. (2003). A policy making view of e-government innovations in public government. In *Proceedings of the Americas Conference on Information Systems*.

Navarra, D. D., & Cornford, T. (2009). Globalization, networks, and governance: Researching global ICT programs. *Government Information Quarterly, 26*(1), 35–41. doi:10.1016/j.giq.2008.08.003

Ndou, V. D. (2004). E-Government for developing countries: Opportunities and challenges. *Electronic Journal of Information Systems in Developing Countries, 18*(1), 1–24.

Nelson, T. E., Clawson, R. A., & Oxley, Z. M. (1997). Toward a psychology of framing effects. *Political Behavior, 19*(3), 221–246. doi:10.1023/A:1024834831093

Neris, V. P. A., Martins, M. C., Prado, M. E. B. B., Hayashi, E. C. S., & Baranauskas, M. C. C. (2008). Design de interfaces para todos – Demandas da diversidade cultural e social. In *Proceedings of the 35th Seminário Integrado de Software e Hardware*, Porto Alegre, Brazil (pp. 76-90).

Neuman, W. L. (1991). *Social Research Methods: Qualitative and Quantitative Approaches*. Boston: Allyn and Bacon.

New York City. (2010). *The "Current" Population of New York City: Release of Population Estimates by the Census Bureau for July 1, 2008.* Retrieved January 1, 2010, from http://www.nyc.gov/html/dcp/html/census/popcur.shtml

Newbery, D., Bently, L., & Pollock, R. (2008). *Models of public sector information provision via trading funds.* Cambridge, UK: Cambridge University Press.

Newman, I., & Benz, C. R. (1998). *Qualitative-quantitative research methodology: Exploring the interactive continuum.* Edwardsville, IL: Southern Illinois University Press.

Ngai, E. W. T., Moon, K. K. L., Riggins, F. J., & Yi, C. Y. (2008). RFID research: An academic literature review (1995-2005) and future research directions. *International Journal of Production Economics, 112*(2), 510–520. doi:10.1016/j.ijpe.2007.05.004

Nielsen, J. (1993). *Usability engineering.* San Francisco, CA: Morgan Kauffman.

Noordhoek, P., & Saner, R. (2005). Beyond New Public Management: Answering the Claims of Both Politics and Society. *Public Organization Review: A Global Journal, 5*(1), 35-53.

Norris, D. F., Fletcher, P. D., & Holden, S. H. (2001). *Is your local government plugged in? Highlights of the 2000 electronic government survey.* Retrieved from http://www.umbc.edu/mipar/PDFs/e-gov.icma.final-4-25-01.pdf

Norris, D. F., & Jae Moon, M. (2005). Advancing e-government at the grassroots: Tortoise or hare? *Public Administration Review, 65*(1), 64–75. doi:10.1111/j.1540-6210.2005.00431.x

Norris, D., Fletcher, P., & Holden, S. (2001). Is your local government plugged in? *Public Management, 83,* 4–11.

Norris, F. D., & Lloyd, B. A. (2006). The scholarly literature on e-government: Characterizing a nascent field. *International Journal of Electronic Government Research, 2*(4), 40–56. doi:10.4018/jegr.2006100103

Norris, P. (2001). *Digital divide: Civic engagement, information poverty, and the Internet worldwide.* Cambridge, UK: Cambridge University Press.

Norris, P. (2005). The impact of the internet on political activism: Evidence from Europe. *International Journal of Electronic Government Research, 1*(1), 20–39. doi:10.4018/jegr.2005010102

Norris, P., & Curtice, J. (2006). If you build a political web site, will they come? The Internet and political activism in Britain. *International Journal of Electronic Government Research, 2*(2), 1–21. doi:10.4018/jegr.2006040101

Nunnally, J. C. (1978). *Psychometric theory* (2nd ed.). New York, NY: McGraw-Hill.

Oates, B. J. (2006). *Researching information systems and computing.* Thousand Oaks, CA: Sage.

O'Conner, M. C. (2005). *Group studies RFID to stop digital piracy.* RFID Journal.

Odedra-Straub, M. (2003). E-Commerce and development: Whose development? *Electronic Journal of Information Systems in Developing Countries, 11*(2), 1–5.

Odom, R. Y., Boxx, W. R., & Dunn, M. G. (1990). Organizational cultures, commitment, satisfaction, and cohesion. *Public Productivity & Management Review, 14*(2), 157–169. doi:10.2307/3380963

ODPM. (2006). *National evaluation of LSPs: Formative evaluation and action research programme 2002-2005: Final report.* Retrieved from http://www.communities.gov.uk/documents/localgovernment/pdf/143381.pdf

OECD. (2001). *Citizens as Partners: Information, Consultation and Public Participation in Policy-Making.* Paris: Author.

OECD. (2003). *Engaging Citizens Online for Better Policy-making.* Paris: Author.

OECD. (2009). *Rethinking e-Government services: User-centred approaches.* Paris, France: OECD.

Office of the E-Envoy. (2004). *E-Government Interoperability Framework, Version 6.0.* Retrieved from http://edina.ac.uk/projects/interoperability/e-gif-v6-0_.pdf

Ojha, A., Sahu, G. P., & Gupta, M. P. (2009). Antecedents of paperless income tax filing by young professionals in India: An exploratory study. *Transforming Government: People. Process and Policy, 3*(1), 65–90.

Ojo, S. O. (1996). Socio-cultural and organisational issues in IT application in Nigeria. In Odedra-Straub, M. (Ed.), *Global information technology and socio-economic development* (pp. 99–109). Marietta, GA: Ivy League Publishing.

Okot-Uma, R. W. (n.d.). *Electronic Governance: Reinventing Good Governance*. Retrieved from http://www.electronicgov.net/index.shtml

O'Leary, R., & Bingham, L. B. (Eds.). (2009). *The collaborative public manager*. Washington, DC: Georgetown University Press.

Oliver, C. (1990). Determinants of interorganizational relationships: Integration and future directions. *Academy of Management Review*, *15*(2), 241–265.

Olson, M. H. (1982). New information technology and organizational culture. *Management Information Systems Quarterly*, *6*(5), 71–92. doi:10.2307/248992

Opdenakker, R. (2006). Advantages and disadvantages of four interview techniques in qualitative research. *Forum Qualitative Sozial Forschung*, *7*(4), 11.

Organization for Economic Cooperation & Development (OECD). (2001). *The hidden threat to e-government - avoiding large government it failures*. Paris, France: OECD.

Organization for Economic Cooperation & Development (OECD). (2003). *The e-government imperative*. Paris, France: OECD.

Orlikowksi, W. J., & Baroudi, J. (1991). Studying information technology in organizations: research approaches and assumptions. *Information Systems Research*, *2*(1), 1–28. doi:10.1287/isre.2.1.1

Orlikowski, W., & Lacono, S. (2001). Desperately seeking the "IT" in IT research-A call to theorizing the IT artifact. *Information Systems Research*, *12*(2), 121–134. doi:10.1287/isre.12.2.121.9700

Osimo, D. (2010). Government 2.0 - Hype, hope, or reality? *European Journal of ePractice*, *2010*(9).

Ostrom, E., Gardner, R., & Walker, J. (1994). *Rules, games and common-pool resources*. Ann Arbor, MI: University of Michigan Press.

O'Toole, L. J. (1986). Policy recommendations for multi-actor implementation: An assessment of the field. *Journal of Public Policy*, *6*(2), 181–210. doi:10.1017/S0143814X00006486

O'Toole, L. J. (1993). Interorganizational policy studies: Lessons drawn from implementation research. *Journal of Public Administration: Research and Theory*, *3*(2), 232–251.

Oulasvirta, A., & Blom, J. (2008). Motivations in personalisation behaviour. *Interacting with Computers*, *20*(1), 1–16. doi:10.1016/j.intcom.2007.06.002

Overby, J. W., & Lee, E.-J. (2006). The effects of utilitarian and hedonic online shopping value on consumer preference and intentions. *Journal of Business Research*, *59*(10-11), 1160–1166. doi:10.1016/j.jbusres.2006.03.008

Ozkan, S., Koseler, R., & Baykal, N. (2009). Evaluating learning management systems: Adoption of hexagonal e-learning assessment model in higher education. *Transforming Government: People, Process, and Policy*, *3*(2), 111–130. doi:10.1108/17506160910960522

Pampel, F. (2000). *Logistic regression: A primer*. Thousand Oaks, CA: Sage.

Pandey, S., Welch, E., & Wong, W. (2006, December 7-10). Beyond pure efficiency and technological features: Developing a model of measuring e-governance and exploring its performance. In *Proceedings of the Conference on the Determinants of Performance in Public Organizations*, Pok Fu Lam, Hong Kong.

Parasuraman, A., Berry, L., & Zeithaml, V. (1988). A multiple-item scale for measuring consumer perceptions of service quality. *Journal of Retailing*, *64*, 12–40.

Parasuraman, A., Berry, L., & Zeithaml, V. (1991). Refinement and reassessment of the SERVQUAL scale. *Journal of Retailing*, *67*, 420–450.

Parasuraman, A., Zeithaml, V. A., & Malhotra, A. (2005). E-S-QUAL - a multiple-item scale for assessing electronic service quality. *Journal of Service Research*, *7*(3), 213–233. doi:10.1177/1094670504271156

Parasuraman, A., Zeithaml, V., & Berry, L. (1985). A conceptual model of service quality and its implications for future research. *Journal of Marketing*, *49*, 41–50. doi:10.2307/1251430

Parent, M., Vandebeek, C. A., & Gemino, A. C. (2005). Building citizen trust through e-government. *Government Information Quarterly, 22*(4), 720–736. doi:10.1016/j.giq.2005.10.001

Parker, R., & Bradley, L. (2000). Organizational culture in the public sector: Evidence from six organizations. *International Journal of Public Sector Management, 13*(2), 125–141. doi:10.1108/09513550010338773

Park, J., & Ram, S. (2004). Information systems interoperability: what lies beneath? *ACM Transactions on Information Systems, 22*(4), 595–632. doi:10.1145/1028099.1028103

Parvez, Z. (2006). Examining e-democracy through a double structuration loop. *Electronic Government, an International Journal, 3*(3), 329-346.

Parvez, Z. (2008). E-Democracy from the perspective of local elected members. *International Journal of Electronic Government Research, 4*(3), 20–35. doi:10.4018/jegr.2008070102

Paskaleva, K. (2008). Assessing local readiness for city e-governance in Europe. *International Journal of E-Government Research, 4*(4), 17–20. doi:10.4018/jegr.2008100102

Patel, N. V. (2007). Deferred Action: Theoretical model of process architecture design for emergent business processes. *International Journal of Business Science and Applied Management, 2*(3), 4–21.

Patten, D. (1991). Exposure, legitimacy and social disclosure. *Accounting, Organizations and Society, 10*(4), 297–308.

Patten, D. (1992). Intra-industry environmental disclosures in response to the Alaskan oil spill: a note on legitimacy theory. *Accounting, Organizations and Society, 17*(5), 471–475. doi:10.1016/0361-3682(92)90042-Q

Patten, M. L. (2004). *Understanding research methods* (4th ed.). Glendale, CA: Pyrczak Publishing.

Pavlou, P. (2003). Consumer acceptance of electronic commerce: Integrating trust and risk with the technology acceptance model. *International Journal of Electronic Commerce, 7*, 69–103.

Pawson, R., & Tilley, N. (2004). *Realist evaluation.* Retrieved from http://www.communitymatters.com.au/RE_chapter.pdf

Pawson, R. (2002). Evidence-based policy: The promise of `realist synthesis'. *Evaluation, 8*(3), 340–358. doi:10.1177/135638902401462448

Pawson, R. (2003). Nothing as practical as a good theory. *Evaluation, 9*(4), 471–490. doi:10.1177/1356389003094007

Pawson, R., Greenhalgh, T., Harvey, G., & Walshe, K. (2005). Realist review-a new method of systematic review designed for complex policy interventions. *Journal of Health Services Research & Policy, 10*(1), 21–34. doi:10.1258/1355819054308530

Pawson, R., & Tilley, N. (1997). *Realistic evaluation.* London, UK: Sage.

Pedroso, M. C., Zwicker, R., & De Souza, C. A. (2009). RFID adoption: Framework and survey in large Brazilian companies. *Industrial Management & Data Systems, 109*(7), 877–897. doi:10.1108/02635570910982256

Peppers, D., Rogers, M., & Dorf, B. (1999). *The one to one fieldbook: The complete toolkit for implementing a 1 to 1 marketing program.* New York, NY: Double Day.

Peristeras, V., Loutas, N., Goudos, S. K., & Tarabanis, K. (2007). Semantic interoperability conflicts in pan-European public services. In *Proceedings of the 15th European Conference on Information Systems (ECIS 2007),* St. Galen, Switzerland (pp. 2173-2184).

Perrin, W. (2008, March 6-7). *Making government work better.* Paper presented at the OECD eGovernment Leaders Conference, The Hague, The Netherlands.

Peters, R. M., Janssen, M., & van Engers, T. (2004). Measuring e-government impact: Existing practices and shortcomings. In *Proceedings of the 6th International Conference on Electronic Commerce*, Delft, The Netherlands (pp. 480-489).

Peters, R., Janssen, M., & Engers, T. (2004, October 25-27). Measuring e-government impact: Existing practices and shortcomings. In *Proceedings of the Sixth International Conference on Electronic Commerce*, Delft, The Netherlands.

Peterson, S. B. (1998). Saints, demons, wizards and systems: Why information technology reform fail or underperforms in public bureaucracies in Africa. *Public Administration and Development*, *18*(1), 37–60. doi:10.1002/(SICI)1099-162X(199802)18:1<37::AID-PAD990>3.0.CO;2-V

Peters, T. J., & Waterman, R. H. (1982). *In search of excellence*. New York, NY: Harper & Row.

Petrie, H., & Edwards, A. (2006). *Inclusive design and assistive technology as part of the HCI curriculum*. Paper presented at the First Joint BCS/IFIP WG13.1/ICS/EU CONVIVIO HCI Educators' Workshop, Limerick, Ireland.

Petrovic, O. (2004). New focus in e-government: From security to trust. In Gupta, M. P. (Ed.), *Towards E-government*. New Delhi, India: Tata McGraw-Hill.

Phang, C. W., Sutanto, J., Li, Y., & Kankanhalli, A. (2005). Senior Citizens' Adoption of E-Government: In Quest of the Antecedents of Perceived Usefulness. In *Proceedings of the 38th Hawaii International Conference on System Sciences*.

Phang, C. W., Sutanto, J., Kankanhalli, A., Li, Y., Tan, B. C. Y., & Teo, H. H. (2006). Senior citizens' acceptance of information systems: A study in the context of e-government services. *IEEE Transactions on Engineering Management*, *53*(4), 555–569. doi:10.1109/TEM.2006.883710

Pieterson, W., & Teerling, M. (2009). Channel integration in governmental service delivery: The effects on citizen behavior and perceptions. In M. A. Wimmer, H. J. Scholl, M. Janssen, & R. Traunmuller (Eds.), *Proceedings of the International Conference on Electronic Government* (LNCS 5693, pp. 222-233).

Pieterson, W., Teerling, M., & Ebbers, W. (2008). Channel perceptions and usage: Beyond media richness factors. In M. A. Wimmer, H. J. Scholl, & E. Ferro (Eds.), *Proceedings of the International Conference on Electronic Government* (LNCS 5184, pp. 219-230).

Pieterson, W. (2010). Citizens and service channels: Channel choice and channel management implications. *International Journal of Electronic Government Research*, *6*(2), 37–53. doi:10.4018/jegr.2010040103

Pieterson, W., & Ebbers, W. (2008). The use of service channels by citizens in the Netherlands: Implications for multi-channel management. *International Review of Administrative Sciences*, *74*(1), 95–110. doi:10.1177/0020852307085736

Pieterson, W., Ebbers, W., & van Dijk, J. (2007). Personalization in the public sector: An inventory of organizational and user obstacles towards personalization of electronic services in the public sector. *Government Information Quarterly*, *24*(1), 148–164. doi:10.1016/j.giq.2005.12.001

Pina, V., Torres, L., & Royo, S. (2007). Are ICTs improving transparency and accountability in the EU regional and local governments? An empirical study. *Public Administration*, *85*(2), 449–472. doi:10.1111/j.1467-9299.2007.00654.x

Pina, V., Torres, L., & Royo, S. (2009). E-government evolution in EU local governments: A comparative perspective. *Online Information Review*, *33*(6), 1137–1168. doi:10.1108/14684520911011052

Pinho, J. C., & Macedo, I. M. (2008). Examining the antecedents and consequences of online satisfaction within the public sector: The case of taxation services. *Transforming Government: People. Process and Policy*, *2*(3), 177–193.

Pitt, L., Watson, R., & Kavan, B. (1995). Service quality – A measure of information systems effectiveness. *Management Information Systems Quarterly*, *19*, 173–187. doi:10.2307/249687

Pitt, L., Watson, R., & Kavan, B. (1997). Measuring information systems service quality: Concerns for a complete canvas. *Management Information Systems Quarterly*, *21*, 209–221. doi:10.2307/249420

Pizzetti, F. (2008). Piccoli comuni e grandi compiti: La specificità italiana di fronte ai bisogni delle società mature. In Formiconi, D. (Ed.), *Comuni, insieme, più forti!* Torriana, Italy: EDK Editore.

Pliskin, N., Romm, T., & Lee, A. S. (1993). Presumed versus actual organizational culture. *The Computer Journal*, *36*(3), 143–152. doi:10.1093/comjnl/36.2.143

Plouffe, C., Hulland, J., & Vandenbosch, M. (2001). Research report: Richness versus parsimony in modeling technology adoption decisions – understanding merchant adoption of a smart card-based payment system. *Information Systems Research*, *12*, 208–222. doi:10.1287/isre.12.2.208.9697

Pollitt, C., van Thiel, S., & Homburg, V. M. F. (Eds.). (2007). *New public management in Europe: Adaptation and alternatives*. Basingstoke, UK: Palgrave Macmillan.

Poulymenakou, A., & Holmes, A. (1996). A contingency framework for the investigation of information systems failure. *European Journal of Information Systems*, *5*, 34–46. doi:10.1057/ejis.1996.10

Prager, J. (1994). Contracting out government services: Lessons from the private sector. *Public Administration Review*, *54*(2), 176–184. doi:10.2307/976527

Pramatari, K., & Theotokis, A. (2009). Consumer acceptance of RFID-enabled services: A model of multiple attitudes, perceived system characteristics and individual traits. *European Journal of Information Systems*, *18*(6), 541–552. doi:10.1057/ejis.2009.40

Prattipati, S. N. (2003). Adoption of e-Governance: Differences between countries in the use of online. *Journal of American Academy of Business*, *3*, 386–391.

Provan, K. G., & Kenis, P. (2008). Modes of network governance: Structure, management, and effectiveness. *Journal of Public Administration: Research and Theory*, *18*(2), 229–252. doi:10.1093/jopart/mum015

Prybutok, V. R., Zhang, X. N., & Ryan, S. D. (2008). Evaluating leadership, IT quality, and net benefits in an e-government environment. *Information & Management*, *45*(3), 143–152. doi:10.1016/j.im.2007.12.004

Puffenbarger, E., Teer, F., & Kruck, S. (2008). RFID: New Technology on the Horizon for IT Majors. *International Journal of Business Data Communications and Networking*, *4*(1), 64–79.

Quinn, R. E., & Rohrbaugh, J. (1981). A competing values approach to organizational effectiveness. *Public Productivity Review*, *5*(2), 122–140. doi:10.2307/3380029

Qureshi, S. (2005). e-Government and IT policy: Choices for government outreach and policy making. *Information Technology for Development*, *11*(2), 101–103. doi:10.1002/itdj.20006

Ragin, C. (1994). *Constructing social research*. Thousand Oaks, CA: Sage.

Rainer, R. K., Snyder, C. A., & Carr, H. H. (1991). Risk analysis for information technology. *Journal of Management Information Systems*, *8*(1), 192–197.

Rainey, H. G., Backoof, R. W., & Levene, C. H. (1976). Comparing public and private organizations. *Public Administration Review*, *36*(2), 233–234. doi:10.2307/975145

Rainey, H. G., & Steinbauer, P. (1999). Galloping elephants: Developing elements of a theory of effective government organizations. *Journal of Public Administration: Research and Theory*, *9*(1), 1–32. doi:10.1093/oxfordjournals.jpart.a024401

Ramos, A., Scott, W., Lloyd, D., O'leary, K., & Waldo, J. (2009). A Threat Analysis of RFID Passports. *Communications of the ACM*, *52*(12), 38–42. doi:10.1145/1610252.1610268

Ram, S., & Park, J. (2004). Semantic Conflict Resolution Ontology (SCROL): an ontology for detecting and resolving data and schema-level semantic conflicts. *IEEE Transactions on Knowledge and Data Engineering*, *16*(2), 189–202. doi:10.1109/TKDE.2004.1269597

Ranade, W., & Hudson, B. (2003). Conceptual issues in inter-agency collaboration. *Local Government Studies*, *29*(3), 32–50. doi:10.1080/03003930308559378

Rao, R., Tripathi, R., & Gupta, M. P. (2008). Key Issues of Personal Information Integration in Government-Employee E-government. In *Proceedings of the International Conference on E-governance 2008*.

Ratnasingam, P., & Pavlou, P. (2002, May). Technology trust: The next value creator in B2B electronic commerce. In *Proceedings of the Information Resources Management Association International Conference*, Seattle, WA (pp. 889-894).

Ray, S. (2010). Conceptualization and implementation of e-government in India. In Reddick, C. G. (Ed.), *Comparitive e-government* (pp. 391–408). New York, NY: Springer. doi:10.1007/978-1-4419-6536-3_20

Reddick, C. G. (2004). Empirical models of e-government growth in local governments. *E - Service Journal, 3*(2), 59-84.

Reddick, C. G. (2004a). A two-stage model of e-government growth: Theories and empirical evidence for U.S. cities. *Government Information Quarterly, 21*(1), 51–64. doi:10.1016/j.giq.2003.11.004

Reddick, C. G. (2005). Citizen interaction with e-government: From the streets to servers. *Government Information Quarterly, 22*, 38–57. doi:10.1016/j.giq.2004.10.003

Reddick, C. G. (2005). Citizen-initiated contacts with Ontario local e-government: Administrators' responses to contacts. *International Journal of Electronic Government Research, 1*(4), 45–62. doi:10.4018/jegr.2005100103

Reddick, C. G. (2006). Information resource managers and e-government effectiveness: A survey of Texas state agencies. *Government Information Quarterly, 23*(2), 249–266. doi:10.1016/j.giq.2005.11.006

Reddick, C. G. (2007). E-Government Adoption in Canadian Municipal Governments: A Survey of Ontario Chief Administrative Officers. In Norris, D. F. (Ed.), *Current Issues and Trends in E-Government Research*. Hershey, PA: Cybertech Publishing. doi:10.4018/978-1-59904-283-1.ch014

Reddick, C. G. (2009). Factors that explain the perceived effectiveness of e-government: A survey of United States city government information technology directors. *International Journal of E-Government Research, 5*(2), 1–15. doi:10.4018/jegr.2009040101

Reddick, C. G. (2009). The adoption of centralized customer service systems: A survey of local governments. *Government Information Quarterly, 26*(1), 219–226. doi:10.1016/j.giq.2008.03.005

Reddick, C. G. (2010). Comparing citizens' use of e-government to alternative service channels. *International Journal of Electronic Government Research, 6*(2), 54–67. doi:10.4018/jegr.2010040104

Reese, S. D. (2003). Framing public life: A bridging model for media research. In Reese, S. D., Gandy, O. H. Jr., & Grant, A. E. (Eds.), *Framing public life: Perspectives on media and our understanding of the social world* (pp. 7–32). Mahwah, NJ: Lawrence Erlbaum.

Reich, B. H., & Benbasat, I. (2000). Factors that influence the social dimension of alignment between business and information technology objectives. *Management Information Systems Quarterly, 24*(1), 81–113. doi:10.2307/3250980

Reichert, A. K., Webb, M. S., & Thomas, E. G. (2000). Corporate support for ethical and environmental policies: a financial management perspective. *Journal of Business Ethics, 25*(1), 53–65. doi:10.1023/A:1006078827535

Reichheld, F., & Sasser, W. (1990). Zero defections: Quality comes to services. *Harvard Business Review, 68*, 2–9.

Reid, D. (2006). *E-Passports at Risk from Cloning*. Retrieved from http://news.bbc.co.uk/2/hi/programmes/click_online/6182207.stm

Remenyi, D. (1998). *Doing research in business and management: an introduction to process and method*. Thousand Oaks, CA: Sage.

Resnick, P., Zeckhauser, R., & Avery, C. (1995). *Roles for electronic broker*. Mahwah, NJ: Lawrence Erlbaum.

Reyes, P. M., Frazier, G. V., Prater, E. L., & Cannon, A. R. (2007). RFID: The state of the union between promise and practice. *International Journal of Integrated Supply Management, 3*(2), 125–134. doi:10.1504/IJISM.2007.011972

Rivard, S. (1987). Successful implementation of end-user computing. *Interfaces, 17*, 25–53. doi:10.1287/inte.17.3.25

Roberti, M. (2009). Saluting the RFID Pioneers in the DOD. *RFID Journal*, 1-2.

Roberts, C. M. (2006). Radio frequency identification (RFID). *Computers & Security, 25*(1), 18–26. doi:10.1016/j.cose.2005.12.003

Roberts, M. (2007). *Internet marketing: Integrating online and offline strategies*. New York, NY: McGraw-Hill.

Roberts, R. W. (1992). Determinants of corporate social responsibility disclosures: An application of stakeholder theory. *Accounting, Organizations and Society, 17*(6), 595–612. doi:10.1016/0361-3682(92)90015-K

Robey, D. (1979a). Implementation and the organizational impacts of information systems. *Interfaces, 17*, 72–84. doi:10.1287/inte.17.3.72

Robey, D. (1979b). User attitudes and management information system use. *Academy of Management Journal*, *22*, 527–538. doi:10.2307/255742

Robey, D., & Azervedo, A. (1994). Culture analysis of organizational consequences of information technology. *Accounting, Management, and Information Technology*, *4*(1), 23–34. doi:10.1016/0959-8022(94)90011-6

Rodriguez, C., Langley, A., Beland, F., & Denis, J.-L. (2007). Governance, power, and mandated collaboration in an interorganizational network. *Administration & Society*, *39*(2), 150–193. doi:10.1177/0095399706297212

Rogers, E. (1995). *Diffusion of innovations* (4th ed.). New York, NY: Free Press.

Roh, J. J., Kunnathur, A., & Tarafdar, M. (2009). Classification of RFID adoption: An expected benefits approach. *Information & Management*, *46*(6), 357–363. doi:10.1016/j.im.2009.07.001

Romm, T., Pliskin, N., & Weber, Y. (1995). The relevance of organizational culture to the implementation of human resources information systems. *Asia Pacific Journal of Human Resources*, *33*(2), 51–63. doi:10.1177/103841119503300206

Rousseau, D., Sitkin, S., Burtand, R., & Camerer, C. (1998). Not so different after all: A cross-discipline view of trust. *Academy of Management Review*, *23*, 393–404. doi:10.5465/AMR.1998.926617

Royal Academy of Engineering and British Computer Society. (2004). *The challenges of complex IT projects*. London, UK: The Royal Academy of Engineering.

Roy, J. (2003). The relational dynamics of e-governance: A case study of the city of Ottawa. *Public Performance & Management Review*, *26*(4), 391–403. doi:10.1177/1530957603026004006

Rubin, A. M. (2002). The uses-and-gratifications perspective of media effects. In *Media Effects: Advances in Theory and Research* (2nd ed.). Mahwah, NJ: Lawrence Erlbaum Associates.

Ryan, N. (2001). Reconstructing citizens as consumers: Implications for new modes of governance. *Australian Journal of Public Administration*, *60*(3), 104–109. doi:10.1111/1467-8500.00229

Saarinen, T., & Vepsalainen, A. (1993). Managing the risks of information systems implementation. *European Journal of Information Systems*, *4*, 283–295. doi:10.1057/ejis.1993.39

Sabherwal, R., & King, W. R. (1992). Decision processes for developing strategic applications of information systems: a contingency approach. *Decision Sciences*, *23*(4), 917–943. doi:10.1111/j.1540-5915.1992.tb00426.x

Sabherwal, R., & Kirs, P. (1994). The alignment between organizational critical success factors and information technology capability in academic institutions. *Decision Sciences*, *25*(2), 301–330. doi:10.1111/j.1540-5915.1994.tb01844.x

Sahu, G. P., & Gupta, M. P. (2007). Users' acceptance of e-government: A study of Indian central excise. *International Journal of Electronic Government Research*, *3*(3), 1–21. doi:10.4018/jegr.2007070101

Salam, A. F., Iyer, L., Palvia, P., & Singh, R. (2005). Trust in e-commerce. *Communications of the ACM*, *48*(2), 73–77. doi:10.1145/1042091.1042093

Salman, A. (2004). Elusive challenges of e-change management in developing countries. *Business Process Management*, *10*(2), 140–157. doi:10.1108/14637150410530226

Sambasivan, M., Wemyss, G. P., & Rose, R. C. (2010). User acceptance of a G2B system: A case of electronic procurement system in Malaysia. *Internet Research*, *20*(2), 169–187. doi:10.1108/10662241011032236

Sang, S., Lee, J. D., & Lee, J. (2009). E-government adoption in ASEAN: The case of Cambodia. *Internet Research*, *19*(5), 517–534. doi:10.1108/10662240910998869

Sang, S., Lee, J. D., & Lee, J. (2010). E-government adoption in Cambodia: A partial least squares approach. *Transforming Government: People, Process, and Policy*, *4*(2), 138–157. doi:10.1108/17506161011047370

Santos, E. M. D. (2008). Implementing Interoperability Standards for Electronic Government: An Exploratory Case Study of the E-PING Brazilian Framework. *International Journal of Electronic Government Research*, *4*(3), 103–112. doi:10.4018/jegr.2008070106

Santos, E. M. D., & Reinhard, N. (2007). Setting interoperability standards for egovernment: An exploratory case study. *Electronic Government. International Journal (Toronto, Ont.)*, *4*(4), 379–394.

Sarbanes-Oxley. (2002). *Act of 2002.* Retrieved from http://www.soxlaw.com/index.htm

Sarkar, M. B., Butler, B., & Steinfield, C. (1995). Intermediaries and cybermediaries: A continuing role for mediating players in the electronic marketplace. *Journal of Computer-Mediated Communication, 1*(3).

Sauer, C. (1993). *Why information systems fail: A case study approach.* Oxford, UK: Alfred Waller Ltd.

Sayer, A. (1984). *Method in social science.* London, UK: Hutchinson. doi:10.4324/9780203310762

SBC. (2006). *Grand challenges in computer science research in Brazil – 2006 – 2016.* Retrieved from http://www.sbc.org.br/

Schaupp, L. C., & Carter, L. (2010). The impact of trust, risk and optimism bias on e-file adoption. *Information Systems Frontiers, 12*(3), 299–309. doi:10.1007/s10796-008-9138-8

Schaupp, L. C., Carter, L., & McBride, M. E. (2010). E-file adoption: A study of US taxpayers' intentions. *Computers in Human Behavior, 26*(4), 636–644. doi:10.1016/j.chb.2009.12.017

Schedler, K., & Scharf, M. C. (2001, October 3-5). *Exploring the interrelations between e-government and the new public management.* Paper presented at the First IFIP Conference on E-Commerce, E-Business, and E-Government, Zurich, Switzerland.

Schedler, K., & Summermatter, L. (2007). Customer orientation in electronic government: Motives and effects. *Government Information Quarterly, 24,* 291–311. doi:10.1016/j.giq.2006.05.005

Schein, E. H. (1985). *Organizational culture and leadership.* San Francisco, CA: Jossey- Bass.

Schein, E. H. (1986). What you need to know about organizational culture. *Training and Development Journal, 8*(1), 30–33.

Schmidt, R., Lyytinen, K., Keil, M., & Cule, P. (2001). Identifying software project risks: An international Delphi study. *Journal of Management Information Systems, 17,* 5–36.

Scholl, H. J., & Klischewski, R. (2007). E-Government Integration and Interoperability: Framing the Research Agenda. *International Journal of Public Administration, 30*(8), 889–920. doi:10.1080/01900690701402668

Schön, D., & Rein, M. (1994). *Frame reflection: Toward the resolution of intractable policy controversies.* New York, NY: BasicBooks.

Schuler, D., & Namioka, A. (Eds.). (1993). *Participatory design: Principles and practices.* Mahwah, NJ: Lawrence Erlbaum.

Schuppan, T. (2009). E-government in developing countries: Experiences from sub-Saharan Africa. *Government Information Quarterly, 26*(1), 118–127. doi:10.1016/j.giq.2008.01.006

Searby, S. (2003). Personalisation - an overview of its use and potential. *BT Technology Journal, 21*(1), 13–19. doi:10.1023/A:1022439824138

Seddon, P. B. (1997). A respecification and extension of the DeLone and McLean model of IS success. *Information Systems Research, 8*(3), 240–253. doi:10.1287/isre.8.3.240

Seeman, E. D., O'Hara, M. T., Holloway, J., & Forst, A. (2007). The impact of government intervention on technology adoption and diffusion: The example of wireless location technology, *Electronic Government, an International Journal, 4*(1), 1-19.

Segovia, R. H., Jennex, M. E., & Beatty, J. (2009). Paralingual web design and trust in e-government. *International Journal of Electronic Government Research, 5*(1), 36–49. doi:10.4018/jegr.2009091803

Seifert, J., & McLoughlin, G. (2007). *State e-government strategies: Identifying best practices and applications.* Retrieved from http://www.fas.org/sgp/crs/secrecy/RL34104.pdf

Seifert, J. W., & Chung, J. (2009). Using E-Government to Reinforce Government–Citizen Relationships: Comparing Government Reform in the United States and China. *Social Science Computer Review, 27*(1), 3–23. doi:10.1177/0894439308316404

Seifert, J. W., & Relyea, H. C. (2004). Do you know where your information is in the homeland security era? *Government Information Quarterly*, *21*(4), 399–405. doi:10.1016/j.giq.2004.08.001

Sellers, M. P. (2003). Privatization morphs into 'publicization': Businesses look a lot like government. *Public Administration*, *81*(3), 607–620. doi:10.1111/1467-9299.00363

Senyucel, Z. (2007). Assessing the impact of e-government on providers and users of the IS function: A structuration perspective. *Transforming Government: People, Process, and Policy*, *1*(2), 131–144. doi:10.1108/17506160710751968

Serra, G. (1995). Citizen-initiated contact and satisfaction with bureaucracy: A multivariate analysis. *Journal of Public Administration: Research and Theory*, *5*(2), 175–188.

Serrano-Cinca, C., Rueda-Tomas, M., & Poitillo-Tarragona, P. (2009). Determinants of e-government extension. *Online Information Review*, *33*(3), 476–498. doi:10.1108/14684520910969916

Sevilla, J., Herrera, G., Martínez, B., & Alcantud, F. (2007). Web accessibility for individuals with cognitive deficits: A comparative study between an existing commercial Web and its cognitively accessible equivalent. *ACM Transactions on Computer-Human Interaction*, *14*(3), 12. doi:10.1145/1279700.1279702

Seyal, A. H., & Pijpers, G. G. M. (2004). Senior government executives' use of the internet: A Bruneian scenario. *Behaviour & Information Technology*, *23*(3), 197–210. doi:10.1080/01449290410001669978

Shareef, M. A., Kumar, U., Kumar, V., & Dwivedi, Y. K. (2009). Identifying critical factors for adoption of e-government. *Electronic Government, an International Journal*, *6*(1), 70-96.

Sharma, S. K. (2004). Assessing e-government implementation. *Electronic Government Journal*, *1*(2), 198–212. doi:10.1504/EG.2004.005178

Sharma, S. K. (2006). An e-government services framework. In Khosrow-Pour, M. (Ed.), *Encyclopedia of Commerce, E-Government and Mobile Commerce, Information Resources Management Association* (pp. 373–378). Hershey, PA: IGI Global. doi:10.4018/978-1-59140-799-7.ch061

Sharma, S. K., & Gupta, J. N. D. (2003). Building blocks of an e-government – a framework. *Journal of Electronic Commerce in Organizations*, *1*(4), 34–48. doi:10.4018/jeco.2003100103

Shaughnessy, J. J., & Zechmeister, E. B. (1994). *Research Methods in Psychology* (3rd ed.). New York: McGraw Hill.

Shelley, M. C. II, Thrane, L. E., & Shulman, S. W. (2006). Generational differences in information technology use and political involvement. *International Journal of Electronic Government Research*, *2*(1), 36–53. doi:10.4018/jegr.2006010103

Sheth, J. N., Newman, B. I., & Gross, B. L. (1991). Why we buy what we buy: A theory of consumption values. *Journal of Business Research*, *22*(2), 159–170. doi:10.1016/0148-2963(91)90050-8

Shin, S., Song, H., & Kang, M. (2008). *Implementing e-government in developing countries: Its unique and common success factors*. Paper presented at the Annual Meeting of the APSA Annual Meeting, Boston, MA.

Shleifer, A. (1998). State versus private ownership. *The Journal of Economic Perspectives*, *12*(4), 133–150.

Shun, C., & Yunjie, X. (2006). Effects of outcome, process and shopping enjoyment on online consumer behaviour. *Electronic Commerce Research and Applications*, *5*(4), 272–281. doi:10.1016/j.elerap.2006.04.004

Silverman, D. (2000). *Doing qualitative research: A practical handbook*. London, UK: Sage.

Simon, H. A. (1998). Why public administration? *Journal of Public Administration: Research and Theory*, *8*(1), 1–11.

Sinrod, E. J. (2004). A look at the pros and cons of e-government. *USA Today*.

Sirgy, M. J. (1982). Self-concept in consumer behavior: A critical review. *The Journal of Consumer Research*, *9*(3), 287–300. doi:10.1086/208924

Sirohi, N., McLaughlin, E. W., & Wittink, D. R. (1998). A model of consumer perceptions and store loyalty intentions for a supermarket retailer. *Journal of Retailing*, *74*(2), 223–245. doi:10.1016/S0022-4359(99)80094-3

Smart, K. L., Whiting, M. E., & Bell DeTienne, K. (2001). Assessing the need for printed and online documentation: A study of customer preference and use. *Journal of Business Communication, 38*(3), 285–314. doi:10.1177/002194360103800306

Smart, L., & Schaper, L. (2004). Making sense of RFID. *Library Journal, 4*.

Smith, E., & Macintosh, A. (2007). *Existing E-Participation Practices with Relevance to WEB.DEP*. Retrieved from http://itc.napier.ac.uk/itc/documents/webdep_e-participation_practices.pdf

Smith, E., Macintosh, A., & Whyte, A. (2006, September). *Organized use of e-democracy tools for young people*. Paper presented at Electronic Government: Communications of the Fifth International EGOV Conference, Krakow, Poland.

Smith, A. (2006). Evolution and Acceptability of Medical Applications of RFID Implants Among Early Users of Technology. *Health Marketing Quarterly, 24*, 121–155. doi:10.1080/07359680802125980

Smith, J., Fishkin, K., Bing, J., Mamishev, A., Hilipose, M., & Rea, A. (2005). RFID-based techniques for human-activity detection. *Communications of the ACM, 48*(9), 39–44. doi:10.1145/1081992.1082018

Snider, J., Hill, P. H., & Martin, D. (2003). Corporate social responsibility in the 21st century: A view from the world's most successful firms. *Journal of Business Ethics, 48*(2), 175–187. doi:10.1023/B:BUSI.0000004606.29523.db

Soh, C., & Markus, M. L. (1995). *How IT Creates Business Value: A Process Theory Synthesis*. Paper presented at the Sixteenth International Conference on Information System, Amsterdam, The Netherlands.

Sohail, M. S., & Shanmugham, B. (2003). E-banking and customer preferences in Malaysia: An empirical investigation. *Information Sciences, 150*, 207–217. doi:10.1016/S0020-0255(02)00378-X

Songini, M. (2007). Washington State, DHS May Use RFID in Licenses. *Computerworld, 41*, 6.

Soon, C., & Gutiérrez, A. (2008). Effects of the RFID Mandate on Supply Chain Management. *Journal of Theoretical and Applied Electronic Commerce Research, 3*(1), 81–91.

Sorensen, K. B., Christiansson, P., & Svidt, K. (2010). Ontologies to support RFID-based link between virtual models and construction components. *Computer-Aided Civil and Infrastructure Engineering, 25*(4), 285–302. doi:10.1111/j.1467-8667.2009.00638.x

Sorrentino, M., & Simonetta, M. (in press). Analysing the implementation of local partnerships: An organisational perspective. *Transforming Government: People. Process and Policy.*

Spearman, W., & Associates. Inc. (2000). *Use of the Internet for electronic commerce in US cities with populations greater than 500,000*. Retrieved from http://www.prismonline.com

Spies, M. (2010). An ontology modelling perspective on business reporting. *Information Systems, 35*, 404–416. doi:10.1016/j.is.2008.12.003

Srivastava, D., Dar, S., Jagadish, H. V., & Levy, A. (1996). Answering queries with aggregation using views. In *Proceedings of the 22nd International Conference on Very Large Data Bases (VLDB'96)* (pp. 318-329).

Srivastava, S. C., & Teo, T. S. H. (2006). Performance impacts of e-government: An international perspective. In *Proceedings of the Pacific Asia Conference on Information Systems.*

Srivastava, S. C., & Teo, T. S. H. (2007b). What facilitates e-government development? A cross-country analysis. *Electronic Government, an International Journal, 4*(4), 365-378.

Srivastava, S. C., & Teo, T. S. H. (2007a). E-government payoffs: Evidence from cross-country data. *Journal of Global Information Management, 15*(4), 20–40. doi:10.4018/jgim.2007100102

Stafford, M. R., & Stern, B. (2002). Consumer bidding behavior on Internet auction sites. *International Journal of Electronic Commerce, 7*(1), 135–150.

Stame, N. (2004). Theory-based evaluation and types of complexity. *Evaluation, 10*(1), 58–76. doi:10.1177/1356389004043135

Standish Group. (1995). *The CHAOS report*. Retrieved from http://www.standishgroup.com

Standish Group. (2001). *Extreme chaos*. Retrieved from http://www.standishgroup.com

Standish Group. (2004). *Third quarter research report*. Retrieved from http://www.standishgroup.com

State Services Commission. (2007). *New Zealand E-government Interoperability Framework*. Retrieved from http://www.e.govt.nz

Statistics New Zealand. (2010). *Subnational Population Estimates: At 30 June 2009*. Retrieved January 1, 2010, from http://www.stats.govt.nz/browse_for_stats/population/estimates_and_projections/subnationalpopulationestimates_hotp30jun09.aspx

Stephanidis, C., Akoumianakis, D., Sfyrakis, M., & Paramythis, A. (1998). Universal accessibility in HCI: Process-oriented design guidelines and tool requirements. In *Proceedings of the 4th ERCIM Workshop on User Interfaces for All*.

Sterman, J. D. (2000). *Business dynamics: Systems thinking and modeling for a complex world*. New York, NY: McGraw-Hill.

Stevens, J. (2002). *Applied multivariate statistics for the social sciences* (4th ed.). Mahwah, NJ: Lawrence Erlbaum.

Stockman, H. (1948). Communication by means of reflected power. *Proceedings of the IRE*, *36*(10), 1196–1204. doi:10.1109/JRPROC.1948.226245

Stowers, G. N. L. (2004). Measuring the performance of e-government. *E-Government Series*, 1-52.

Stowers, G. N. L. (1999). Becoming cyberactive: state and local governments on the World Wide Web. *Government Information Quarterly*, *16*(2), 111–127. doi:10.1016/S0740-624X(99)80003-3

Straub, D. W., & Nance, W. D. (1990). Discovering and disciplining computer abuse in organization: a field study. *Management Information Systems Quarterly*, *14*(1), 45–55. doi:10.2307/249307

Strauss, A. I., & Corbin, J. (1994). Grounded theory methodology: An overview. In Denzin, N. K., & Lincoln, Y. S. (Eds.), *Handbook of qualitative research* (pp. 273–285). Thousand Oaks, CA: Sage.

Strauss, A. L. (1987). *Qualitative analysis for social scientists*. Cambridge, UK: Cambridge University Press. doi:10.1017/CBO9780511557842

Strauss, A. L., & Corbin, J. (1990). *Basics of qualitative research: Grounded theory procedures and techniques*. Thousand Oaks, CA: Sage.

Strover, S. (2001). Rural internet connectivity. *Telecommunications Policy*, *25*(5), 331–347. doi:10.1016/S0308-5961(01)00008-8

Suh, B., & Han, I. (2003). The Impact of Customer Trust and Perception of Security Control on the Acceptance of Electronic Commerce. *International Journal of Electronic Commerce*, *7*(3), 135–161.

Sumner, M. (2000). Risk factors in enterprise-wide ERP projects. *Journal of Information Technology*, *15*, 317–327. doi:10.1080/02683960010009079

Sun, S., Ju, T. L., & Chen, P. (2006). E-government impacts on effectiveness: A survey study of an e-official-document system. *Electronic Government, an International Journal*, *3*(2), 174-189.

Sunny, M., & McNiven, J. D. (2003). E-Government and E-Governance: The Future Isn't What It Used To Be. *Canadian Journal of Administrative Sciences*, *20*(1), 74–86.

Sutter, J. D. (2009). *Cities embrace mobile apps, 'Gov 2.0'*. Retrieved from http://www.cnn.com/2009/TECH/12/28/government.web.apps/index.html

Swanson, E. B. (1988). *Information System Implementation: Bridging the Gap Between Design and Utilization*. Homewood, IL: Irwin.

Sweeney, J. C., & Soutar, G. N. (2001). Consumer perceived value: The development of a multiple item scale. *Journal of Retailing*, *77*(2), 203–220. doi:10.1016/S0022-4359(01)00041-0

Tabachnick, B. G., & Fidell, L. S. (2001). *Using Multivariate Statistics* (4th ed.). Boston, MA: Allyn and Bacon.

Tambouris, E. (2008). *Survey of e-Participation Good Practice Cases*. Paper presented at the European e-Participation Workshop, eDem Conference 2008.

Tambouris, E., Gorilas, S., Kavadias, G., Apostolou, D., Abecker, A., Stojanovic, L., et al. (2004). Ontology-enabled E-goverment service configuration: an overview of the OntoGov project. In *Knowledge Management in Electronic Government* (LNAI 3035, pp. 106-111).

Tambouris, E., Manouselis, N., & Costopoulou, C. (2007). Metadata for digital collections of e-government resources. *The Electronic Library, 25*(2), 176–192. doi:10.1108/02640470710741313

Tang, H., Chung, S. H., & Se, C. W. (2009). Examining the impact of possible antecedents on service usage: An empirical study on Macao e-government. *Electronic Government, an International Journal, 6*(1), 97-109.

Tankard, J. W., Hendrickson, L., Jr., Silberman, J., Bliss, K. A., & Ghanem, S. (1991, August). *Media frames: Approaches to conceptualization and measurement.* Paper presented at the Annual Conference of the Association for Education in Journalism and Mass Communication, Boston, MA.

Tan, M., & Teo, T. S. H. (2000). Factors influencing the adoption of internet banking. *Journal of the AIS, 1*(5), 1–42.

Tan, Y., & Thoen, W. (2001). Toward a generic model of trust for electronic commerce. *International Journal of Electronic Commerce, 5*, 61–74.

Tapscott, D., & Agnew, D. (1999). Governance in the digital economy. *Finance & Development, 36*(4), 34–37.

Tax, S. S., & Stuart, I. (1997). Designing and implementing new services: The challenges of integrating service systems. *Journal of Retailing, 73*(1), 105–134. doi:10.1016/S0022-4359(97)90017-8

Teale, M., Dispenza, V., Flynn, J., & Currie, D. (2003). *Management decision-making: Towards an integrative approach.* Essex, UK: Pearson Education.

Teerling, M. L., & Pieterson, W. (2010). Multichannel marketing: An experiment on guiding citizens to the electronic channels. *Government Information Quarterly, 27*(1), 98–107. doi:10.1016/j.giq.2009.08.003

Teo, T. S. H., Srivastava, S. C., & Jiang, L. (2008). Trust and electronic government success: An empirical study. *Journal of Management Information Systems, 25*(3), 99–131. doi:10.2753/MIS0742-1222250303

Terwel, B. W., Harinck, F., Ellemers, N., & Daamen, D. D. L. (2009). How organizational motives and communications affect public trust in organizations: The case of carbon dioxide capture and storage. *Journal of Environmental Psychology, 29*(2), 290–299. doi:10.1016/j.jenvp.2008.11.004

Tesoriero, R., Tebar, R., Gallud, J. A., Lozano, M. D., & Penichet, V. M. R. (2010). Improving location awareness in indoor spaces using RFID technology. *Expert Systems with Applications, 37*(1), 894–898. doi:10.1016/j.eswa.2009.05.062

Testa, P. (Ed.). (2010). *Lo stato delle Unioni*. Roma, Italy: Cittalia.

Thatcher, J., Burkes, M., Heilmann, C., Henry, S., Kirkpatrick, A., & Lauke, P. (2006). *Web accessibility: Web standards and regulatory compliance.* Berkeley, CA: Friends of ED.

The Open Group. (2005). *Developer Declaration of Independence.* Retrieved from http://www.opengroup.org/declaration/declaration.htm.

Thomas, J. C., & Melkers, J. (1999). Explaining citizen-initiated contacts with municipal bureaucrats: Lessons from the Atlanta experience. *Urban Affairs Review, 34*(5), 667–690. doi:10.1177/10780879922184130

Thomas, J. C., & Melkers, J. (2000). Citizen contacting of municipal officials: Choosing between appointed administrators and elected leaders. *Journal of Public Administration: Research and Theory, 11*(1), 51–71. doi:10.1093/oxfordjournals.jpart.a003494

Thomas, J. C., & Streib, G. (2003). The new face of government: Citizen-initiated contacts in the era of e-government. *Journal of Public Administration: Research and Theory, 13*(1), 83–102. doi:10.1093/jpart/mug010

Tirschwell, P. (2009). Track and trace, the Army way. *Journal of Commerce, 10*(25), 1.

Titah, R., & Barki, H. (2006). e-Government adoption and acceptance: A literature review. *International Journal of Electronic Government Research, 2*(3), 23–57. doi:10.4018/jegr.2006070102

Tolbert, C. J., & McNeal, R. S. (2003). Unraveling the effects of the Internet on political participation. *Political Research Quarterly, 56*, 175–185.

Tolbert, C. J., Mossberger, K., & McNeal, R. (2008). Institutions, policy innovation, and e-government in the American states. *Public Administration Review, 68*(3), 549–563. doi:10.1111/j.1540-6210.2008.00890.x

Tolsby, J. (1998). Effects of organizational culture on a large scale IT introduction effort: A case study of the Norwegian army's EDBLF project. *European Journal of Information Systems, 7*(2), 108–114. doi:10.1057/palgrave.ejis.3000295

To, P.-L., Liao, C., & Lin, T.-H. (2007). Shopping motivations on Internet: A study based on utilitarian and hedonic value. *Technovation, 27*(12), 774–787. doi:10.1016/j.technovation.2007.01.001

Toregas, C. (2001). The politics of e-gov: The upcoming struggle for redefining civic engagement. *National Civic Review, 90*(3), 235–240. doi:10.1002/ncr.90304

Torres, L., Pina, V., & Acerete, B. (2005). E-government developments on delivering public services among EU cities. *Government Information Quarterly, 22*(4), 217–238. doi:10.1016/j.giq.2005.02.004

Traunmüller, R. (2005). *Cross-border and Pan-European Services: The Challenges Ahead, Institute for Informatics in Business and Government.* Retrieved from http://www.eisco2005.org/fileadmin/files/eisco2005/

Traunmuller, R., & Wimmer, M. (2004, August 30-September 3). e-Government: The challenges ahead. In *Proceedings of the Third International Conference EGOV*, Zaragoza, Spain.

Treasury, H. M. (2007). *Service transformation agreement.* Retrieved from http://www.hm-treasury.gov.uk

Trimi, S., & Sheng, H. (2008). Emerging trends in M-government. *Communications of the ACM, 51*(5), 53–58. doi:10.1145/1342327.1342338

Tripathi, R., Gupta, M. P., & Bhattacharya, J. (2007). Selected Aspects of Interoperability in One-stop Government Portal of India. In *Proceedings of the International Conference on E-Governance (ICEG) 2007.*

Trivellas, P., Reklitis, P., & Santouridis, I. (2006). Culture and MIS effectiveness patterns in a quality context: A case study in Greece. *International Journal of Knowledge. Culture and Change Management, 6*(3), 129–144.

Tung, L. L., & Rieck, O. (2005). Adoption of electronic government services among business organizations in Singapore. *The Journal of Strategic Information Systems, 14*(4), 417–440. doi:10.1016/j.jsis.2005.06.001

Turel, O., Serenko, A., & Bontis, N. (2007). User acceptance of wireless short messaging services: Deconstructing perceived value. *Information & Management, 44*(1), 63–73. doi:10.1016/j.im.2006.10.005

Tu, Y. J., Zhou, W., & Piramuthu, S. (2009). Identifying RFID-embedded objects in pervasive healthcare applications. *Decision Support Systems, 46*(1), 586–593. doi:10.1016/j.dss.2008.10.001

Tversky, A., & Kahneman, D. (1974). Judgment under uncertainty: Heuristics and biases. *Science, 185*, 1124–1131. doi:10.1126/science.185.4157.1124

UK Government. (2000). *e-Government Interoperability Framework (e-GIF).* Retrieved from http://xml.coverpages.org/egif-UK.html

UN & ASPA. (2002). *Benchmarking E-government: A Global Perspective.* New York: Author.

United Nations Department for Economic and Social Affairs (UN-DESA). (2009). *Member states participating in the 17th session of the commission for sustainable development.* Retrieved from http://www.un.org/esa/dsd/csd/csd_csd17_membstat.shtml

United Nations Development Programme. (2007). *Human development report 2007/2008. Fighting climate change: Human solidarity in a divided world.* Retrieved from http://hdr.undp.org/en/media/HDR_20072008_EN_Complete.pdf

United Nations Development Programme. (2008). *Human development indices.* Retrieved from http://hdr.undp.org/en/media/HDI_2008_EN_Tables.pdf

United Nations Environment Program (UNEP). (2007). *Annual report.* Retrieved from http://unpan1.un.org/intradoc/groups/public/documents/un/unpan028607.pdf

United Nations. (2008). *UN e-government survey 2008: From e-government to connected governance.* Retrieved from http://unpan1.un.org/intradoc/groups/public/documents/un/unpan028607.pdf

United Nations. (n.d.). *Millennium development goals indicators (Countries' Contribution to CO$_2$ Global Emissions, in Metric Tons).* Retrieved from http://millenniumindicators.un.org/unsd/mdg/Data.aspx

Universal Design. (2009). *The Center for Universal Design: Environments and products for all people.* Retrieved from http://www.design.ncsu.edu/cud/

van Deursen, A. J. A. M., & van Dijk, J. A. G. M. (2009). Improving digital skills for the use of online public information and services. *Government Information Quarterly, 26*(2), 333–340. doi:10.1016/j.giq.2008.11.002

van Dijk, J. A. G. M., Peters, O., & Ebbers, W. (2008). Explaining the acceptance and use of government Internet services: A multivariate analysis of 2006 survey data in The Netherlands. *Government Information Quarterly, 25*, 379–399. doi:10.1016/j.giq.2007.09.006

Van Dyke, T., Kappelman, L., & Prybutok, V. (1997). Measuring information systems service quality: Concerns on the use of the SERVQUAL questionnaire. *Management Information Systems Quarterly, 21*, 195–208. doi:10.2307/249419

Van Dyke, T., Prybutok, V., & Kappelman, L. (1999). Cautions on the use of the SERVQUAL measure to assess the quality of information systems services. *Decision Sciences, 30*, 877–891. doi:10.1111/j.1540-5915.1999.tb00911.x

van Veenstra, A. F., & Zuurmond, A. (2009). Opening the black box: Exploring the effect of transformation on online service delivery in local governments. In M. A. Wimmer, H. J. Scholl, M. Janssen, & R. Traunmuller (Eds.), *Proceedings of the International Conference on Electronic Government* (LNCS 5693, pp. 234-244).

Vankalo, M. (2004). *Internet-enabled techniques for personalizing the marketing program.* Helsinki, Finland: Swedish School of Economics and Business Administration.

Vathanophas, V., Krittayaphongphun, N., & Klomsiri, C. (2008). Technology acceptance toward e-government initiative in Royal Thai Navy. *Transforming Government: People, Process, and Policy, 2*(4), 256–282. doi:10.1108/17506160810917954

Vedlitz, A., Dyer, J. A., & Durand, R. (1980). Citizen contacts with local governments: A comparative view. *American Journal of Political Science, 24*(1), 50–67. doi:10.2307/2110924

Venkatesh, V. (1999). Creation of favourable user perceptions: Exploring the role of intrinsic motivation. *Management Information Systems Quarterly, 23*(2), 239–260. doi:10.2307/249753

Venkatesh, V., & Brown, S. (2001). A longitudinal investigation of personal computers in homes: Adoption determinants and emerging challenges. *Management Information Systems Quarterly, 25*(1), 71–102. doi:10.2307/3250959

Venkatesh, V., & Davis, F. (2000). A theoretical extension of the technology acceptance model: Four longitudinal field studies. *Management Science, 46*, 186–204. doi:10.1287/mnsc.46.2.186.11926

Venkatesh, V., & Davis, F. D. (2000). A theoretical extension of the technology acceptance model: Four longitudinal field studies. *Management Science, 46*(2), 186–204. doi:10.1287/mnsc.46.2.186.11926

Venkatesh, V., Morris, M. G., Davis, G. B., & Davis, F. D. (2003). User acceptance of information technology: Toward a unified view. *Management Information Systems Quarterly, 27*(3), 425–478.

Venkatesh, V., Morris, M., Davis, G., & Davis, F. (2003). User acceptance of information technology: Toward a unified view. *Management Information Systems Quarterly, 27*, 425–478.

Verdegem, P., & Verleye, G. (2009). User-centered e-government in practice: A comprehensive model for measuring user satisfaction. *Government Information Quarterly, 26*(3), 487–497. doi:10.1016/j.giq.2009.03.005

VeriChip. (n.d.). *Home.* Retrived from http://74.125.113.132/search?q=cache:kfVTExaNxxMJ:www.verichipcorp.com/+VeriChip.com&cd=8&hl=en&ct=clnk&gl=ca

Vernadat, F. B. (1996). *Enterprise Modelling and Integration: Principles and Applications.* London: Chapman & Hall.

Vesanen, J. (2007). What is personalization? A conceptual framework. *European Journal of Marketing, 41*(5-6), 409–418. doi:10.1108/03090560710737534

Vesanen, J., & Raulas, M. (2006). Building bridges for personalization: A process model for marketing. *Journal of Interactive Marketing, 20*(1), 5–20. doi:10.1002/dir.20052

Vlosky, R. P., & Wilson, D. T. (1994). *Interorganizational information system technology adoption effects on buyer-seller relationships in the retailer-supplier channel: an exploratory analysis.* Paper presented at the 10th IMP Annual Conference, Groningen, The Netherlands.

Von Hippel, E. (2005). *Democratizing innovation.* Cambridge, MA: MIT Press.

Vonk, G., Geertman, S., & Schot, P. (2007). New technologies stuck in old hierarchies: The diffusion of geo-information technologies in Dutch public organizations. *Public Administration Review, 67*(4), 745–756. doi:10.1111/j.1540-6210.2007.00757.x

W3C. (2009). *Web accessibility initiative (WAI).* Retrieved from http://www.w3.org/WAI/

Waisanen, B. (2002). The future of e-government: Technology-fueled management tools. *Public Management, 84*(5), 6–9.

Wallace, L., Keil, M., & Arun, R. (2004a). How software project risk affects project performance: An investigation of the dimensions of risk and an exploratory model. *Decision Sciences, 35*(2), 289–321. doi:10.1111/j.00117315.2004.02059.x

Wallace, L., Keil, M., & Arun, R. (2004b). Understanding software project risk: A cluster analysis. *Information & Management, 42*, 115–125. doi:10.1016/j.im.2003.12.007

Wallace, L., Kiel, M., & Rai, A. (2004). How software risk affects project performance: An investigation of the dimensions of risk and an exploratory model. *Decision Sciences, 35*(2), 289–321. doi:10.1111/j.00117315.2004.02059.x

Wallach, E. J. (1983). Individuals and organizations: The cultural match. *Training and Development Journal, 37*, 29–36.

Walser, K., Kuhn, A., & Reidl, R. (2009). Risk management in e-government from the perspective of IT governance. In *Proceedings of the 10th Annual International Conference on Digital Government Research: Social Networks: Making Connections between Citizens, Data and Government* (pp. 315-316).

Walsham, G. (1995). The emergence of interpretivism in IS research. *Information Systems Research, 6*(4), 376–394. doi:10.1287/isre.6.4.376

Wang, L., Bretschneider, S., & Gant, J. (2005, January 3-6). Evaluating web-based e-government services with a citizen-centric approach. In *Proceedings of the 38th Hawaii International Conference on System Sciences*, Honolulu, HI.

Wang, H., Lee, M., & Wang, C. (1998). Consumer privacy concerns about internet marketing. *Communications of the ACM, 41*(3), 63–70. doi:10.1145/272287.272299

Wangpipatwong, S., Chutimaskul, W., & Papasratorn, B. (2009). Quality enhancing the continued use of e-government web sites: Evidence from e-citizens of Thailand. *International Journal of Electronic Government Research, 5*(1), 19–35. doi:10.4018/jegr.2009092202

Wang, Y. S. (2003). The adoption of electronic tax filing systems: an empirical study. *Government Information Quarterly, 20*(4), 333–352. doi:10.1016/j.giq.2003.08.005

Wang, Y. S., & Liao, Y. W. (2008). Assessing eGovernment systems success: A validation of the DeLone and McLean model of information systems success. *Government Information Quarterly, 25*(4), 717–733. doi:10.1016/j.giq.2007.06.002

Wang, Y. S., & Shih, Y. W. (2009). Why do people use information kiosks? A validation of the unified theory of acceptance and use of technology. *Government Information Quarterly, 26*(1), 158–165. doi:10.1016/j.giq.2008.07.001

Wang, Y., Lo, H.-P., & Yang, Y. (2004). An integrated framework for service quality, customer value, satisfaction: Evidence from China's telecommunication industry. *Information Systems Frontiers, 6*(4), 325–340. doi:10.1023/B:ISFI.0000046375.72726.67

Want, R. (2004). The magic of RFID. *ACM Queue; Tomorrow's Computing Today, 2*(7), 41–48. doi:10.1145/1035594.1035619

Want, R. (2006). An introduction to RFID Technology. *IEEE Pervasive Computing / IEEE Computer Society* [and]. *IEEE Communications Society, 5*(1), 25. doi:doi:10.1109/MPRV.2006.2

Warkentin, M., Gefen, D., Pavlou, P. A., & Rose, G. M. (2002). Encouraging citizen adoption of e-government by building trust. *Electronic Markets, 12*(3), 157–162. doi:10.1080/101967802320245929

Warkentin, M., Gefen, D., Pavlou, P., & Rose, G. (2002). Encouraging citizen adoption of e-government by building trust. *Electronic Markets, 12,* 157–163. doi:10.1080/101967802320245929

Watson, R. T., & Mundy, B. (2001). A strategic perspective of electronic democracy. *Communications of the ACM, 44*(1), 27–30. doi:10.1145/357489.357499

Watson, R., Pitt, L., & Kavan, C. (1998). Measuring information systems service quality: Lessons from two longitudinal case studies. *Management Information Systems Quarterly, 22,* 61–79. doi:10.2307/249678

Weaver, W. (1948). Science and complexity. *American Scientist, 36,* 536–544.

Weerakkody, V., Dhillon, G., Dwivedi, Y., & Currie, W. (2008, August 14-17). *Realising transformational stage e-government: Challenges, issues and complexities.* Paper presented at the Americas Conference on Information Systems, Toronto, ON, Canada.

Weerakkody, V., Dwivedi, Y. K., Dhillon, G., & Williams, M. D. (2007, December 28-30). *Realising T-Government: A UK local authority perspective.* Paper presented at the Fifth International Conference on Electronic Government, Hyderabad, India.

Weerakkody, V., & Dhillon, G. (2008). Moving from e-government to t-government: A study of process re-engineering challenges in a UK local authority perspective. *International Journal of Electronic Government Research, 4*(4), 1–16. doi:10.4018/jegr.2008100101

Weerakkody, V., Janssen, M., & Dwivedi, Y. K. (2011). Transformational change and business process reengineering (BPR): Lessons from the British and Dutch public sector. *Government Information Quarterly, 28*(3), 320–328. doi:10.1016/j.giq.2010.07.010

Weiling, K., & Kwok, K. W. (2004). Successful e-government in Singapore. *Communications of the ACM, 47*(6), 95–99. doi:10.1145/990680.990687

Weiss, C. H. (1998). *Evaluation: Methods for studying programs and policies* (2nd ed.). Upper Saddle River, NJ: Prentice Hall.

Weng, S., Tsai, H., Liu, S., & Hsu, C. (2006). Ontology construction for information classification. *Expert Systems with Applications, 31,* 1–12. doi:10.1016/j.eswa.2005.09.007

Wen, W. (2010). An intelligent traffic management expert system with RFID technology. *Expert Systems with Applications, 37*(4), 3024–3035. doi:10.1016/j.eswa.2009.09.030

West, D. M. (2000). *Assessing e-government: the Internet democracy, and service delivery.* Retrieved from http://www.insidepolitics.org/egovtreport00.html

West, D. M. (2001). *State and Federal E-Government in the United States, 2001 Brown University.* Retrieved from http://www.brown.edu/Departments/Taubman_Center/polreports/egovt01us.html

West, D. M. (2001). *Urban E-Government: An Assessment of City Government Websites.* Retrieved from http://www.insidepolitics.org/egovt01city.html

West, D. M. (2008). *Improving technology utilization in electronic government around the world.* Retrieved from http://www.brookings.edu/~/media/Files/rc/reports/2008/0817_egovernment_west/0817_egovernment_west.pdf

West, D. (2004). E-government and the transformation of service delivery and citizen attitudes. *Public Administration Review, 64,* 15–28. doi:10.1111/j.1540-6210.2004.00343.x

West, D. (2005). *Digital government: Technology and public sector performance.* Princeton, NJ: Princeton University Press.

West, D. M. (2001). *State and Federal E-Government in the United States*. Providence, RI: Brown University.

West, D. M. (2004). E-government and the transformation of service delivery and citizen attitudes. *Public Administration Review, 64*(1), 15–27. doi:10.1111/j.1540-6210.2004.00343.x

West, D. M. (2005). *Digital Government: Technology and Public Sector Performance*. Princeton, NJ: Princeton University Press.

Wholey, J. S. (1983). *Evaluation and effective public management*. Boston, MA: Little, Brown.

Wholey, J. S., Hatry, H. P., & Newcomer, K. E. (1994). *Handbook of practical program evaluation*. San Francisco, CA: Jossey-Bass.

Whyte, A., & Macintosh, A. (2002). Analysis and Evaluation of e-Consultations. *e-Service Journal, 2*(1), 9-34.

Whyte, A., & Macintosh, A. (2003, November). *Evaluating EDEN's Impact on Participation in Local e-Government*. Paper presented at the International Conference on Public Participation and Information Technologies.

Whyte, A., Renton, A., & Macintosh, A. (2005). *e-Petitioning in Kingston and Bristol*. Edinburgh, UK: International Teledemocracy Centre, Napier University.

Wilkins, A. L., & Ouchi, W. G. (1983). Efficient cultures: Exploring the relationship between culture and organizational performance. *Administrative Science Quarterly, 28*, 468–481. doi:10.2307/2392253

Willcocks, L., & Margetts, H. (1994). Risk assessment and information systems. *European Journal of Information Systems, 3*(2), 127–138. doi:10.1057/ejis.1994.13

Williams, M. D., & Dwivedi, Y. K., Middleton, C., Wilson, D., Falch, M., Schultz, A. et al. (2007). Global diffusion of broadband: Current state and future directions for investigations. In T. McMaster, D. Wastell, E. Ferneley, & J. DeGross (Eds.), *Organizational dynamics of technology-based innovation: Diversifying the research agenda: IFIP TC8 WG 8.6 International Working Conference in Information and Communication Technology* (Vol. 235, pp. 529-532). New York, NY: Springer.

Williams, R., & Edge, D. (1996). The social shaping of technology. In *Information and Communication Technologies: Visions and Realities*. New York: Oxford University Press.

Wilmshurtst, D. W., & Frost, G. R. (2000). Corporate environmental reporting: A test of legitimacy theory. *Accounting, Auditing & Accountability Journal, 13*(5), 667–681.

Wimmer, M., Traunmüller, R., & Lenk, K. (2001, January 3-6). Electronic business invading the public sector: Considerations on change and design. In *Proceedings of the 34th Hawaii International Conference on System Sciences*, Maui, HI.

Wimmer, M. (2002). A European perspective towards online one-stop government. *Electronic Commerce Research and Applications, 1*, 92–103. doi:10.1016/S1567-4223(02)00008-X

Wimmer, M. A. (2002). Integrated service modelling for online one-stop government. *Electronic Markets, 12*(3), 149–156. doi:10.1080/101967802320245910

Wind, J., & Rangaswamy, A. (2001). Customerization: The next revolution in mass customization. *Journal of Interactive Marketing, 15*(1), 13–32. doi:10.1002/1520-6653(200124)15:1<13::AID-DIR1001>3.0.CO;2-#

Winter, S., & Mouritzen, P. E. (2001). Why people want something for nothing: The role of asymmetrical illusions. *European Journal of Political Research, 39*(1), 109–143. doi:10.1111/1475-6765.00572

Witbrock, M. (2009). *ICT for governance and policy modeling* (Tech. Rep. No. FP7-ICT-2009-4). Brussels, Belgium: European Commission.

Wittenburg, A., Matthes, F., Fischer, F., & Hallermeier, T. (2007). Building an integrated IT governance platform at the BMW Group. *International Journal of Business Process Integration and Management, 2*(4), 327–337. doi:10.1504/IJBPIM.2007.017757

Wolfinbarger, M., & Gilly, M. C. (2003). eTailQ: Dimensionalizing, measuring and predicting etail quality. *Journal of Retailing, 79*(3), 183–198. doi:10.1016/S0022-4359(03)00034-4

Wollschlaeger, M. (1998). Planning, Configuration and Management of Industrial Communication Networks Using Internet Technology. In. *Proceedings of the Global Telecommunications Conference, 2*, 1184–1189.

Woodall, T. (2003). Conceptualising 'value for the customer': An attributional, structural and dispositional perspective. *Academy of Marketing Science Review*, (12): 1–42.

World Bank. (2006). *Where is the wealth of nations? Measuring capital for the 21st century*. Retrieved from http://siteresources.worldbank.org/IN-TEEI/214578-1110886258964/20748034/All.pdf

World Bank. (n.d.). *Definition of e-government*. Retrieved from http://web.worldbank.org/wbsite/external/topics/extinformationandcommunicationandtechnologies/extegovernment/0,contentMDK:20507153~menuPK:702592~pagePK:148956~piPK:216618~theSitePK:702586,00.html

World Bank. (n.d.). *Data & statistics – country classification*. Retrieved from http://web.worldbank.org/wbsite/external/datastatistics/0,contentMDK:20420458~menuPK:64133156~pagePK:64133150~piPK:64133175~theSitePK:239419,00.html

World Travel & Tourism Council. (n.d.). *Tourism research – country reports*. Retrieved from http://www.wttc.org/eng/Tourism_Research/Tourism_Economic_Research/Country_Reports/

Wren, J. D., Grissom, J. E., & Conway, T. (2006). E-mail decay rates among corresponding authors in MEDLINE. *EMBO Reports, 7*, 122–127. doi:10.1038/sj.embor.7400631

Wu, J.-H., & Wang, S.-C. (2005). What drives mobile commerce? An empirical evaluation of the revised technology acceptance model. *Information & Management, 42*(5), 719–729. doi:10.1016/j.im.2004.07.001

Wu, N. C., Nystrom, M. A., Lin, T. R., & Yu, H. C. (2006). Challenges to global RFID adoption. *Technovation, 26*(12), 1317–1323. doi:10.1016/j.technovation.2005.08.012

Wyld, D. C. (2005). *RFID: The Right Frequency for Government*. Retrieved from http://www.businessofgovernment.org/pdfs/WyldReport4.pdf

Xenakis, A., & Macintosh, A. (2004c, September). *Trust in public administration e-transactions: e-voting in the UK*. Paper presented at DEXA 2004, Zaragoza, Spain.

Xenakis, A., & Macintosh, A. (2004d, September). *Levels of difficulty in introducing e-voting*. Paper presented at the International Conference in E-Government, EGOV 2004, Zaragoza, Spain.

Xenakis, A., & Macintosh, A. (2004a). Major Issues in Electronic Voting in the context of the UK pilots. *Journal of E-Government, 1*(1), 53–74. doi:10.1300/J399v01n01_06

Xenakis, A., & Macintosh, A. (2004b). E-voting: Who controls the e-electoral process? In Cunningham, P., & Cunningham, M. (Eds.), *E-Adoption and the Knowledge Economy, Issues, Applications, Case Studies* (pp. 739–744). Amsterdam, The Netherlands: IOS Press.

Xie, M., Wang, H., & Goh, T. (1998). Quality dimensions of Internet search engines. *Journal of Information Science, 24*, 365–372. doi:10.1177/016555159802400509

Yale and Columbia Universities. (2008). *Environmental performance index – country scores*. Retrieved from http://epi.yale.edu/CountryScores

Yang, Z., & Peterson, R. T. (2004). Customer perceived value, satisfaction, and loyalty: The role of switching costs. *Psychology and Marketing, 21*(10), 799–822. doi:10.1002/mar.20030

Yeow, P. H. P., & Loo, W. H. (2009). Acceptability of ATM and transit applications embedded in multipurpose smart identity card: An exploratory study in Malaysia. *International Journal of Electronic Government Research, 5*(2), 37–56. doi:10.4018/jegr.2009040103

Yildiz, M. (2007). E-government research: Reviewing the literature, limitations and ways forward. *Government Information Quarterly, 24*(3), 43–665. doi:10.1016/j.giq.2007.01.002

Yin, R. (2009). *Case study research: Design and methods* (4th ed.). Thousand Oaks, CA: Sage.

Yin, R. K. (1994). *Case study research* (2nd ed.). Thousand Oaks, CA: Sage.

Yin, R. K. (2003). *Case study research: design and methods* (3rd ed.). Thousand Oaks, CA: Sage.

Yin, R. K., & Davis, D. (2006). Adding new dimensions to case study evaluations: The case of evaluating comprehensive reforms. *New Directions for Evaluation, 113,* 75.

Yoon, J., & Chae, M. (2009). Varying criticality of key success factors of national e-Strategy along the status of economic development of nations. *Government Information Quarterly, 26*(1), 25–34. doi:10.1016/j.giq.2008.08.006

Yu, S. C. (2007). RFID implementation and benefits in libraries. *The Electronic Library, 25*(1), 54–64. doi:10.1108/02640470710729119

Zaheer, A., McEvily, B., & Perrone, V. (1998). Does trust matter? Exploring the effects of interorganizational and interpersonal trust on performance. *Organization Science, 9,* 141–159. doi:10.1287/orsc.9.2.141

Zaied, A., Nasser, H., Khairalla, F. A., & Al-Rashed, W. (2007). e-Readiness in the Arab countries: Perceptions towards ICT environment in public organisations in the state of Kuwait. *Electronic. Journal of E-Government, 5*(1), 77–87.

Zakareya, E., & Irani, Z. (2005). E-government adoption: Architecture and barrier. *Business Process Management Journal, 11*(5), 589–611. doi:10.1108/14637150510619902

Zambrano, R. (2008). E-governance and development: Service delivery to empower the poor. *International Journal of Electronic Government Research, 4*(2), 1–11. doi:10.4018/jegr.2008040101

Zammuto, R. F., & Krakower, J. Y. (1991). Quantitative and qualitative studies of organizational culture. In Woodman, R. W., & Pasmore, W. A. (Eds.), *Research in organizational change and development (Vol. 5).* Greenwich, CT: JAI Press.

Zarei, B., Ghapanchi, A., & Sattary, B. (2008). Toward national e-government development models for developing countries: A nine-stage model. *The International Information & Library Review, 40,* 199–207. doi:10.1016/j.iilr.2008.04.001

Zavetoski, S., & Shulman, S. W. (2002). The Internet and environmental decision-making: An introduction. *Organization & Environment, 15*(3), 323–327. doi:10.1177/1086026602153009

Zeithaml, V. A. (1988). Consumer perceptions of price, quality, and value: A means-end model and synthesis of evidence. *Journal of Marketing, 52*(3), 2–22. doi:10.2307/1251446

Zeithaml, V. A., & Gilly, M. C. (1987). Characteristics affecting the acceptance of retailing technologies: A comparison of elderly and non-elderly consumers. *Journal of Retail Banking, 63*(1), 49–68.

Zeithaml, V., Berry, L., & Parasuraman, A. (1996). The behavioral consequences of service quality. *Journal of Marketing, 60,* 31–46. doi:10.2307/1251929

Zetter, K. (2006). Clone E-Passports. *Wired,* 1-3.

Zmud, R. (1979). Individual differences and MIS success: A review of the empirical literature. *Management Science, 25*(10), 966–979. doi:10.1287/mnsc.25.10.966

Zucker, L. (1986). Production of trust: Institutional sources of economic structure. In Staw, B., & Cummings, L. (Eds.), *Research in organizational behavior* (pp. 53–111). Greenwich, CT: JAI Press.

About the Contributors

Vishanth Weerakkody is a Senior Lecturer in the Business School at Brunel University, UK and the Editor-in-Chief of the International Journal of Electronic Government Research. Prior to his academic career, Dr Weerakkody worked in a number of Multinational organisations, including IBM UK, in the area of software engineering, business systems design and process analysis. His current research interests include public sector process transformation and change, innovation and knowledge management in the public sector, citizen centric e-government and social inclusion. He has published over 100 peer reviewed articles, guest-edited special issues of leading journals and edited several books on ICT enabled transformational government and digital services adoption in the public sector. Dr Weerakkody has many years of R&D experience in the field of e-government in Europe and is currently a co-investigator in five European Commission funded e-government and public sector transformation projects.

* * *

M. Cecilia C. Baranauskas is Professor at the Institute of Computing, UNICAMP, Brazil. She received a BSc and MSc in Computer Science and a PhD in Electrical Engineering at UNICAMP, Brazil. She spent a sabbatical year as Honorary Research Fellow at the Staffordshire University and as a Visiting Fellow at the University of Reading, UK, working in the Applied Informatics with Semiotics Lab. She also received a *Cátedra Ibero-Americana Unicamp-Santander Banespa* to study accessibility issues on software engineering at Universidad Politécnica de Madrid, Spain. Her research interests have focused on human-computer interaction, particularly investigating different formalisms (including Organizational Semiotics and Participatory Design) in the analysis, design and evaluation of societal systems. She is leading several projects investigating the use of these formalisms in design contexts of e-Citizenship and e-Inclusion. Former IFIP TC13 representative, currently she is member of the BR-CHI (an ACM SIGCHI local chapter) Executive Council and member of the Special Committee for HCI at SBC (Brazilian Computing Society). Publications and the complete *curriculum vitae* can be accessed at http://lattes.cnpq.br/1750385790843118.

Benedetta Bellò earned a PhD in psychology of organizations. She currently has a temporary research contract with the department of economic and business science at the University of Cagliari, Italy, financed by Sardinia Region. Her research interests include mentoring in the workplace, organizational socialization process, organizational and individual performance evaluation.

Nitesh Bharosa received his PhD from the Delft University of Technology where he currently works as a research associate. His research interests include standard business reporting and information quality assurance in networks. His work has appeared in several journals including Decision Support Systems, Information Systems Frontiers and the Journal of Cognition, Technology and Work.

Jaijit Bhattacharya is an Adjunct Faculty at Department of Management Studies, Indian Institute of Technology (IIT) Delhi. He heads the Oracle-HP E-Governance Centre of Excellence at Oracle Corporation, which is a joint initiative of Oracle India and HP India in partnership with PricewaterHouseCoopers, Red Hat, NIC, CMC, Sify and IIIT Bangalore. The center focuses on E-Governance issues of South Asia and South-East Asia. He also advises governments on E-Governance strategies and has conducted workshops to enable government departments create their own E-Governance roadmap. Prior to this he has been the Country Director (Government Strategy) at Sun Microsystems, India. He did his Ph.D. in Computer Science from India Institute of Technology, Delhi prior to which he obtained his MBA from Indian Institute of Management, Calcutta and B. Tech in Electrical Engineering from Indian Institute of Technology, Kanpur. Jaijit is co-author of the book 'Government On-line - Opportunities and Challenges', published by Tata McGraw Hill. The book focuses on providing E-Government decision makers the information they need to architect a roadmap for the implementation of E-Governance projects. He has authored numerous papers and books on e-Governance and is an e-Governance Advisor to Government of Sri Lanka and to Government of Karnataka.

Andres Dijkshoorn is trainee Research Assistant and Ph.D. candidate in the Faculty of Social Sciences (Comparative Public Service Innovation research group) at Erasmus University Rotterdam. His research focuses on the diffusion of personalization in Dutch municipal e-government initiatives. Dijkshoorn has contributed to various books and research reports and has published various papers in national and international conference proceedings.

Yogesh K. Dwivedi is a senior lecturer in information systems and e-business at the school of business and economics, Swansea University, Wales, UK. He obtained his PhD and MSc in Information Systems from Brunel University, UK. He has co-authored several papers which have appeared in international referred journals such as CACM, DATA BASE, EJIS, ISJ, ISF, JCIS, JIT, JORS, and IMDS. He is Senior Editor of DATA BASE, Assistant Editor of TGPPP, Managing Editor of JECR and member of the editorial board/review board of several journals. He is a member of the AIS and IFIP WG8.6. He can be reached at ykdwivedi@gmail.com.

Ramzi El-Haddadeh is a full time faculty in the Business School at Brunel University, UK. He holds a PhD in data communication and information technology and has a multi-disciplinary research background in this field. His current research interests include electronic-government implementation, adoption and diffusion and information-security management. He currently serves as the Managing Editor for the International Journal of Electronic Government Research. He is currently an investigator in several European Commission-funded research projects on technology usability and adoption.

Kostas Ergazakis is a Senior Researcher at the School of Electrical and Computer Engineering, National Technical University of Athens, Greece.

Gisela Gil-Egui is an Associate Professor of Communication at Fairfield University (Connecticut, U.S.A.), where she teaches courses on mass media, new information technologies, and international communication. She obtained her Master's (1999) and Ph.D. (2005) degrees from Temple University in Philadelphia, PA. She also holds a Bachelor's degree in Journalism from Central University of Venezuela (1992). Her research focuses on telecommunications policy, e-government, international media, and institutional regimes for the governance of information and communication technologies, with an emphasis on issues related to universal access and the boundaries between private and public domains. Her scholarly work includes a number of book chapters and articles in prestigious communication journals, including New Media & Society, International Communication Gazette, and Information, Communication & Society.

Doug Goodman, PhD is an associate professor of public affairs in the School of Economic, Political, and Policy Sciences at the University of Texas at Dallas. Prior to relocating to the University of Texas at Dallas he was an associate professor and the graduate coordinator for the Department of Political Science & Public Administration at Mississippi State University. His articles appear in such journals as: *American Review of Public Administration, Review of Public Personnel Administration, Human Resource Development Quarterly, Political Research Quarterly*, and *Public Budgeting & Finance*.

M. P. Gupta is Professor and Chair-Information Systems Group & also Coordinator-Centre for Excellence in E-gov at the Department of Management Studies, Indian Institute of Technology Delhi (IIT Delhi), India. His research interests lie in the areas of IS/ IT planning and E-government. Prof. Gupta has authored the acclaimed book 'Government Online' and edited two others entitled 'Towards E-Government' and 'Promise of E-Government', published by McGraw Hill, 2005. His research papers have appeared in National and International Journals/Conference Proceedings. He was the recipient of the prestigious Humanities & Social Sciences (HSS) fellowship of Shastri Indo Canadian Institute, Calgary (Canada) and a Visiting Fellow at the University of Manitoba. He supervised e-government portal 'Gram Prabhat' which won the IBM Great Mind Challenge Award for the year 2003. He has steered several seminars and also founded the International Conference on E-governance (ICEG) in 2003 which is running into its seventh year. Under the umbrella of ICEG, more than 11 edited volumes have been released which are now available freely at www.iceg.net/2009/. He has guided several policy making committees on ICT in the Centre and State Governments in India. He is on the jury of Computer Society of India (CSI) E-gov Awards and also a member of Program Committee of several International Conferences. He is life member of Global Institute of Flexible Systems Management (GIFT), Systems Society of India (SSI) and Computer Society of India (CSI).

Vincent Homburg is Associate Professor in the Faculty of Social Sciences (Comparative Public Service Innovation research group) at Erasmus University Rotterdam, the Netherlands. Homburg edited *The Information Ecology of E-Government* (IOS Press, 2005, together with Victor Bekkers) and *The New Public Management in Europe* (Palgrave MacMillan, 2007, together with Christopher Pollitt and Sandra van Thiel) and published *Understanding E-Government* (Routledge, 2008). He has furthermore published over forty book chapters and articles in national and international journals (among others The Information Society, International Journal of Public Administration, Information Polity) focusing on electronic government and public management.

Heiko Hornung is currently a PhD candidate at the Institute of Computing in the University of Campinas, UNICAMP, Brazil. He holds a diploma in business informatics from Darmstadt University of Technology, Germany, and a master's degree in computer science from UNICAMP. His research interests span topics such as e-government, e-inclusion, interaction design, electronically-mediated human-human interaction, and universal access to information and knowledge. Publications and the complete *curriculum vitae* can be accessed at http://lattes.cnpq.br/ 5675803251363596.

Mark J. Hughes is head of collections at Swansea University's 'information services and systems' department. He has significant experience of implementing RFID projects in libraries, and is co-author of the 'Tendering for RFID Systems: A Core Specification for Libraries' paper jointly published by BIC and the NAG. He has also authored numerous journal articles on both RFID and Open Source systems for libraries. He can be reached at m.j.hughes@swansea.ac.uk.

Joris Hulstijn received his PhD from the University of Twente. He has published about natural language processing, multi-agent systems, artificial intelligence and law, and e-government. He is coordinating the Compliance Management master's programme at Delft University of Technology. His current research is concerned with the development of information systems to support compliance management.

Vikas Jain completed his Ph.D. from The George Washington University and is a graduate from Indian Institute of Technology, New Delhi, India. Vikas currently serves as Assistant Professor at the ITM department of The University of Tampa. His research interests include business value of information systems, post-adoptive information systems use, enterprise systems, and electronic government. He has worked for nearly 12 years in IT industry in different areas ranging from software development, IT market research and consulting, and e-learning. He has served as a special issue guest editor for Electronic Government: An International Journal, Journal of Global Information Technology Management (JGITM), and Journal of Organization and End User Computing. He also serves as an editorial review board member for International Journal of Electronic Government Research.

Marijn Janssen is an associate professor within the information and communication technology section and director of the interdisciplinary SEPAM master programme of the faculty of technology, policy and management (TPM) at Delft University of Technology. He serves on several editorial boards (including International Journal of E-Government Research, International Journal of E-Business Research, Government Information Quarterly and Information Systems Frontiers), has conducted and managed several research projects and is involved in the organization of a number of conferences. His research interests are in the field of e-government, business process management infrastructures, design, orchestration and shared services. He was ranked as one of the leading e-government researchers in 2009 and published over 200 refereed publications.

Shivraj Kanungo is currently Associate Professor in the Decision Sciences department at George Washington University's School of Business. His research interests include evaluating Information System value, IT for social development, decision support systems, software engineering and process improvement, and organizational culture. Prof. Kanungo holds a Ph.D. from The George Washington University and his masters and bachelors degree are from Southern Illinois University and Birla Institute of Technology and Science respectively. Dr. Kanungo is a successful consultant and has published four books. His latest book, CMMI Implementation: Embarking on High Maturity Practices, was co-authored with Asha Goyal from IBM.

Kawal Kapoor is a PhD candidate in the school of business and economics at Swansea University, Wales. She has her bachelor's in industrial engineering and management from JSSATE, India. She is a master of business administration and has her MBA degree awarded from Swansea University, Wales. Her ongoing PhD research is on the Diffusion of Innovations. She carries three years of work experience in the IT industry, as a software engineer with Accenture Services Private Limited, India. She can be reached at kawalkap@gmail.com.

Banita Lal is a lecturer in the Nottingham Business School, Nottingham Trent University, UK. She obtained her Ph.D. and M.Sc. in Information Systems from the School of Information Systems, Computing and Mathematics, Brunel University. Her research interests involve examining the individual and organizational adoption and usage of ICTs and technology-enabled alternative forms of working. She has published several research papers in internationally refereed journals such as Industrial Management and Data Systems, Information Systems Frontiers, Electronic Government, International Journal of Mobile Communications, and Transforming Government: People, Process and Policy, and has presented several papers at several international conferences. She can be reached at banita.lal@ntu.ac.uk.

Drakoulis Martakos is an Associate Professor at the Department of Informatics and Telecommunications at the National and Kapodistrian University of Athens. He received his B.Sc. in Physics, MSc in Electronics and Radio Communications, and Ph.D. in Real-Time Computing from the same university. Professor Martakos is a consultant to public and private organizations and a project leader in numerous national and international projects. He is author or co-author of more than 100 scientific publications and a number of technical reports and studies.

Alissa M. Mebus is a Marketing and Communications Associate at Symmetry Partners, LLC, a turn-key asset management program provider located in Glastonbury, Connecticut. She has also conducted research surrounding the relationship between the natural environment and big business. As an undergraduate student, her submission "Corporate Social Responsibility and the Fortune 100: Evidence for Environmental Themes" was accepted to the National Communication Association (NCA). Alissa graduated Magna Cum Laude from Fairfield University in 2009 with a Bachelor of Arts in Communication and English.

Nigel Martin is a Senior Lecturer in the School of Accounting and Business Information Systems within the College of Business and Economics at the Australian National University, and specialises in the theory and practice of corporate strategy, e-Government, IT innovation, enterprise systems architecture, and operational business management. He obtained his PhD in the area of enterprise architectures from the Australian National University in 2005.

Kostas Metaxiotis is Assistant Professor at the Department of Informatics, University of Piraeus.

Jeremy Millard is senior consultant with the Danish Technological Institute and associate research fellow at Brunel University, UK. He consults and teaches on technology and society in Europe and globally, and has worked with governments, regional agencies, and private and civil sectors worldwide. His clients also include the European Commission, the UN, the OECD and the WB. In addition to Europe, he works in Asia, the Middle East and Africa. Recent assignments for the European Commission include the European eGovernment annual benchmark, leading an impact assessment of the European eGovernment 2010 Action Plan, leading a large scale Europe-wide survey and analysis of eParticipation, and developing the eGovernment 2020 Vision Study on Future Directions of Public Service Delivery. He is currently working as an expert for the UN on the global eGovernment development survey, and for the OECD on back-office developments in support of user-centred eGovernment strategies.

Andreea Molnar is a Research Fellow at Brunel Business School. Prior to joining Brunel University, she has been a Research Associate at City University London, School of Health Sciences. She holds a PhD from National College of Ireland and MSc. in Modelling and Simulation from Babes-Bolyai University, Cluj-Napoca, Romania.

Amitabh Ojha is a senior civil servant with Government of India and currently on study leave to Indian Institute of Technology Delhi for his doctoral studies. He has held various important positions on Indian Railways, in the areas of electrical engineering, information systems, and general administration. In addition, he has had tenures as a Second Secretary at High Commission of India, London and as a Director with Ministry of Development of North Eastern Region, New Delhi. Mr Ojha holds a bachelors in electrical engineering (with gold medal) and a masters in software engineering from National Institute of Technology, Allahabad, India. His current research interest is in the areas of e-government adoption, effect of e-government on citizens' trust in government agencies, and administrative reforms through e-government. His research has appeared or is forthcoming in *Transforming Government*: *People, Process and Policy* and in edited volumes of *International Conference on E-Governance*.

Craig P. Orgeron, PhD currently serves as the Director of Strategic Services for the Mississippi Department of Information Technology Services (ITS). He has participated in numerous government information technology task forces and committees, such as the Digital Signature Committee, the Electronic Government Task Force, and the Governor's Commission on Digital Government, which led to the implementation of the enterprise electronic government in Mississippi. Dr. Orgeron holds a Ph.D. in public policy and administration from Mississippi State University. Dr. Orgeron is a certified public manager and a graduate of the Senator John C. Stennis State Executive Development Institute, as well as the Institute on International Digital Government Research, and the Harvard University, John F. Kennedy School of Government Executive Education Series, Leadership for a Networked World.

Nripendra P. Rana is a PhD candidate at school of business and economics, Swansea University, UK. He holds a BSc in Mathematics (Hons.), an MCA, an MTech, and an MPhil degree from Indian universities. He also holds an MBA with distinction from Swansea University, UK. He is currently working in the field of e-Government adoption and diffusion as a part of his PhD research. He has varied work experience of teaching in the area of computer engineering and applications at undergraduate and postgraduate levels. He also possesses a good experience in the field of software development. He can be reached at nrananp@gmail.com.

Subhajyoti Ray is an Associate Professor at the Xavier Institute of Management, Bhubaneswar, India. Dr. Subhajyoti Ray has done his master in Statistics at the Indian Statistical Institute and obtained PhD from Indian Institute of Management, Ahmedabad. His main area of research is eGovernment in developing countries. Prior to joining the academic profession he has worked for nearly 10 years in the central bank of the country.

John Rice is the Chief Researcher at the National Centre for Vocational Education Research in Australia. Dr Rice is a recognised expert and academic in the field of management, and specialises in the theory and practice of corporate strategy, innovation, and telecommunications services development. Dr Rice has a Bachelors degree in Business from QUT, Masters degrees from QUT and Griffith University in Brisbane and a PhD from Curtin University in Perth. His PhD investigated the emergence of alliance strategies by the multinational high technology firms Nokia and Ericsson.

G. P. Sahu is working as an Assistant Professor at the School of Management Studies, National Institute of Technology, Allahabad, India and has more than ten years of teaching and research experience. He obtained his PhD degree from Indian Institute of Technology (IIT) Delhi. His research interests are in the areas of MIS and E-Government. His research has appeared or is forthcoming in *International Journal of Electronic Governance, International Journal* of e-*Government Research (IJEGR), Transforming Government: People, Process and Policy*, and in edited volumes of various conference proceedings. He has coordinated several international conferences such as "5th International Conference on E-governance (ICEG 2007) at Hyderabad Central University, Hyderabad", 'ICEG 2006 at IIT Delhi", an International Conference on "Integrating World Market-Living Excellence through Technology and Beyond...." (January 5-6, 2002). He has also edited books on *"Integrating World Market"* in 2002, *"Delivering E-Government"* in 2006, and *"Adopting E-Governance"* in 2008. He was the Program Chair of the 6th International Conference on E-Governance, ICEG 2008 (18-20 December, 2008) at New Delhi, India. Dr. Sahu is a member of the Editorial Review Board of IJEGR and has guest edited international journals. He is also on the jury of CSI – Nihilent E-Governance Award. Email: gsahu@mnnit.ac.in.

Mohamad Hisyam Selamat is a lecturer in the College of Business, Universiti Utara Malaysia. He obtained his doctorate degree (PhD) on 'Developing Individuals for Developing Learning Based Systems' from Brunel University. He is the principal of student residential hall and a member in the university's research, postgraduate, publication, and administration committees. His current research encompasses the diffusion and adoption of broadband technology, the usability of electronic government web sites, the social aspects of information systems, knowledge management, organisational learning, outsourcing and electronic commerce. He has more than 30 papers in academic journals and international conferences on these topics. He can be reached at hisyam@uum.edu.my.

Sarah C. Sherrier graduated Cum Laude from Fairfield University in May 2009. She majored in Communication: Media Studies with a Minor in Mathematics. She is a member of the Communication Honors Society, Lambda Pi Eta, and Mathematics Honors Society, Pi Mu Epsilon. Sarah used her skills from both areas of her studies to research and compile organizational charts needed for this project. She began her professional career at a media agency in Manhattan, OMD, as an Assistant Print Analyst managing the media plans for various clients. Sarah is now working as an Account Executive for the OMD marketing agency, Green Room Entertainment.

Mohini Singh is professor of information systems at the school of business information technology at RMIT University in Australia. She earned her PhD from Monash University and has published widely in the areas of E-Business and New Technology and Innovation Management. Her publications comprise books, book chapters, journal and conference papers. She serves as a member on the editorial boards of a number of journals and co-chairs tracks on e-government and IT diffusion at a number of international conferences. The focus of her current research is on the diffusion of Web 2.0 technologies in business organisations, mobile technologies and e-government. She can be contacted at mohini.singh@rmit.edu.au.

Maddalena Sorrentino researches in organization theory and eGovernment at the department of economics, business and statistics at the University of Milan, Italy. She has written and edited several books and her articles have been published in a number of international journals and conference proceedings. She is also advisor to public institutions on themes related to organizational development.

Alessandro Spano is associate professor of public sector accounting and management at the department of economic and business science at the University of Cagliari, Italy. His research interests include management control systems, information systems, and performance measurement and evaluation.

T. Stamati has obtained a Degree in Computer Science from National and Kapodistrian University of Athens (Greece) in 1998. She also holds an MPhil Degree in Enterprise Modelling Techniques from University of Manchester Institute of Science and Technology (UMIST) (UK) and an MBA Degree from Lancaster University Business School (UK). She has extensive experience in top management positions in leading IT companies of the Greek and European private sector. She is currently Research Fellow at the Department of Informatics and Telecommunications of National and Kapodistrian University of Athens. Her current research interests include information systems, electronic government, systems migration, design and evaluation of methodological approaches for electronic services evolution and IT security.

Rakhi Tripathi is currently a Doctoral student at School of Information Technology, Indian Institute of Technology Delhi (IIT Delhi). Her specific area of research is 'Achieving Interoperability for a One-stop Government Portal in India'. She has previously worked as a Project Scientist for two years under the project 'Establishment of Nation-wide QoS Test-bed' at Department of Computer Science, Indian Institute of Technology Delhi. Prior to that, she obtained MS (Computer Science) in 2003 from Bowie State University, (University of Maryland, USA).

Tassos Tsitsanis is a PhD Student at the School of Electrical and Computer Engineering, National Technical University of Athens, Greece.

William F. Vásquez is an Assistant Professor of Economics at Fairfield University (Connecticut, U.S.A.), and specializes in development and environmental economics. He holds M.A. and Ph.D. degrees in Economics from the University of New Mexico. He has worked as a consultant for the International Food and Policy Research Institute (IFPRI), the United Nations Development Program (UNDP), the United Nations Economic Commission for Latin America and the Caribbean (ECLAC), and the Central American Institute of Fiscal Studies (ICEFI). His research interests include provision of public services (e.g. education, drinking water, e-government, and agricultural services), and their connection with environmentally sound policies. His research has been published in several economic and policy journals.

Remco van Wijk, Msc, graduated from the University of Greenwich. He is research and innovation coordinator at Thauris and is conducting a PhD research on quality assurance in lawmaking processes. He published a book research on the lawmaking process of the Dutch government. He published papers in the proceedings of several international conferences including AMCIS, ICEGOV, DGO and EGOV.

Janet Williams is a senior lecturer at the University of Glamorgan Business School. She holds BSc (Econ) and MSc (Econ) from Cardiff University. Her research interests are focused upon the social, economic and organisational implications of technological change, and utilisation of the internet.

Michael D. Williams is a professor in the school of business and economics at Swansea University in the UK. He holds a BSc from the CNAA, an MEd from the University of Cambridge, and a PhD from the University of Sheffield. He is a member of the British Computer Society and is registered as a chartered engineer. Prior to entering academia Professor Williams spent twelve years developing and implementing ICT systems in both public and private sectors in a variety of domains including finance, telecommunications, manufacturing, and local government, and since entering academia, has acted as consultant for both public and private organizations. He is the author of numerous fully refereed and invited papers within the ICT domain, has editorial board membership of a number of academic journals, and has obtained external research funding from sources including the European Union, the Nuffield Foundation, and the Welsh Assembly Government. He can be reached at m.d.williams@swansea.ac.uk.

Niels de Winne, Msc, graduated from the faculty of technology, policy and management (TPM) at Delft University of Technology. He also holds an EMITA (IT-auditing) degree. He is conducting his PhD research on public-private information exchange on the edge of technology, organization and governance. He has published papers in the proceedings of several international conferences including ICEGOV, DGO and EGOV.

Index